Professional Java Servlets 2.3

Subrahmanyam Allamaraju
John T. Bell
Simon Brown
Sam Dalton
Andrew Harbourne-Thomas
Bjarki Holm
Meeraj Moidoo Kunnumpurath
Sing Li
Tony Loton

Wrox Press Ltd. ®

Professional Java Servlets 2.3

First published January 2002

Published by Wrox Press Ltd,
Arden House, 1102 Warwick Road, Acocks Green,
Birmingham, B27 6BH, UK
Printed in the United States
ISBN 1-861005-61-X

Trademark Acknowledgements

Credits

Authors
Subrahmanyam Allamaraju
John T. Bell
Simon Brown
Sam Dalton
Andrew Harbourne-Thomas
Bjarki Holm
Meeraj Moidoo Kunnumpurath
Sing Li
Tony Loton

Technical Architect
Craig A. Berry

Technical Editors
Tabasam Haseen
Christian Peak
Daniel Richardson
Steve Rycroft

Category Manager
Emma Batch

Author Agent
Velimir Ilic

Project Administrators
Laura Hall
Claire Robinson
Christianne Bailey

Index
John Collin

Technical Reviewers
Kapil Apshankar
Steve Baker
Richard Bonneau
Jeff Cunningham
Sam Dalton
Cosmo Di Fazio
Justin Foley
Phil Hanna
Anne Horton
Graham Innocent
Dan Jepp
Tony Loton
Vinay Menon
Rick Moore
Navaneeth Krishnan
Stéphane Osmont
Sumit Pal
Phil Powers-DeGeorge
Trent Rosenbaum
Keyur Shah

Production Coordinator
Tom Bartlett

Illustrations
Tom Bartlett

Cover
Chris Morris

Proof Reader
Chris Smith

About the Authors

Subrahmanyam Allamaraju

Subrahmanyam is a Senior Engineer with BEA Systems. His interest in modeling lead him from his Ph.D. in Electrical Engineering to object-oriented programming, and then to distributed computing and software architecture. In this process, he drifted from his one-time home – the Indian Institute of Technology, to Computervision, and Wipro Infotech, and later to BEA Systems. You can find more about his current activities at his home page http://www.Subrahmanyam.com.

Subrahmanyam would like to thank Varaa for her hand in code samples (in the face of tight deadlines), and sharing his frustration as well as exhilaration.

Subrahmanyam contributed Chapter 5 to this book.

John T. Bell

John Bell is a Principal Engineer at Latitude360, a subsidiary of RWD Technologies. He has been providing technology solutions for over 20 years and has been developing Java-based web systems for the past several years. His primary areas of expertise are in object-oriented development and distributed processing systems. Recently he has been supporting DaimlerChrysler as lead architect for a number of Java-based web platform initiatives. He is now supporting Latitde360's own eLearning product development efforts. He has a Bachelor's degree in Electrical Engineering and a Masters degree in Computer Systems Management, both from the University of Maryland. In his spare time he plays with his kids, maintains computers for local charities, and writes strategy-based computer games. He is also active in the Christian and Missionary Alliance Church.

Many thanks to Latitude360 and RWD Technologies for providing me with the time, equipment, and software needed to work on this book.

Dedicated to my parents, my mother who gave me the gift of writing and my father who introduced me to electronics, computers, and engineering.

John contributed Chapter 14 to this book.

Simon Brown

Simon is a Technical Architect working in London and has been using Java since 1996. During this time he has been involved with many Java developments, acting as technical lead, mentor, and trainer. Outside of work he has spoken at several Java events, including JavaOne, has been published on *JavaWorld* and co-authored the 2nd Edition of *Professional JSP* from Wrox Press.

Simon graduated from the University of Reading in 1996 with a First Class BSc (Hons) degree in Computer Science. He has also attained many Sun certifications, including the Sun Certified Enterprise Architect for J2EE, Web Component Developer for J2EE, and Developer for the Java 2 Platform. Feel free to e-mail any questions or comments to projavaservlets@simongbrown.com.

I would once again like to thank my fiancée Kirstie for her encouragement, and also for putting up with me being tucked away in the spare room for hours at a time.

Simon contributed Chapter 12 to this book.

Sam Dalton

Sam is a Technical Architect, and is based in London. He has worked with Java and related technologies for a number of years, in various industries, including investment banking, insurance, and retail e-commerce.

Sam was fortunate enough to present and co-present several very popular sessions at JavaOne in 2001, and hopes to make many more appearances in the future.

Sam graduated from the University of Reading, with an honors degree in Computer Science, and is now a Sun Certified Programmer, Developer, and Web Component Developer for the Java 2 platform.

Many heartfelt thanks go to my wife Anne, who is always very supportive of my efforts, and always there with a nice cup of tea!

Sam contributed Chapter 4 to this book.

Andrew Harbourne-Thomas

Andrew Harbourne-Thomas is an independent consultant focusing on J2EE application design and development and project management. He started working life as an economist, worked as Economic Advisor to the Irish Trade Board (now Enterprise Ireland), followed by several years working as an independent consultant to top companies including Microsoft, focusing on technology, strategy, and project management.

He was always interested in evolving technologies and has been working with Java technologies since 1997, including some time with Bear Stearns IT division. His main interests include J2EE application architecture, web service design, extreme programming, and emerging technologies.

Andrew lives in Dublin, Ireland, and while escaping from Java his main pursuits include scuba diving and photography.

Thank you Miriam for your love, patience, and support.

Andrew contributed Chapters 1-3 and Appendix B to this book.

Bjarki Holm

For the past five years, Bjarki has been working at software engineering at VYRE Corporation in Reykjavík, developing on-line design and content management systems using servlets with an Oracle backend. Currently, he is taking time off from work to pursue his studies of electrical engineering and occasional writing opportunities at Wrox.

Bjarki contributed Chapter 6 to this book.

Meeraj Moidoo Kunnumpurath

Meeraj works as a Senior Information Specialist with EDS. He designs enterprise helpdesk and billing systems using J2EE and XML.

I dedicate my work for this book to the three most wonderful women in my life: my mother, my wife and my sister. May Allah bless the entire humankind.

Meeraj contributed Chapters 8 and 13 to this book.

Sing Li

First bitten by the computer bug in 1978, Sing has grown up with the microprocessor and the Internet revolution. His first PC was a $99 do-it-yourself COSMIC ELF computer with 256 bytes of memory and a 1 bit LED display. For two decades, Sing has been an active author, consultant, instructor, entrepreneur, and speaker. His wide-ranging experience spans distributed architectures, web services, multi-tiered server systems, computer telephony, universal messaging, and embedded systems. Sing has been credited with writing the very first article on the Internet Global Phone, delivering voice over IP long before it becomes a common reality. Sing has participated in several Wrox projects in the past, and has been working with (and writing about) Java, Jini, and JXTA since their very first available releases, and is an active evangelist for the unlimited potential of P2P system technology.

Sing contributed Chapters 7 and 9 to this book.

Tony Loton

Tony Loton is Principal Consultant/Director of LOTONtech Limited (http://www.lotontech.com).

He works through his company as an independent consultant, training instructor, and freelance author, and the current areas of interest at LOTONtech include Java-based speech synthesis and the automated extraction of information from the World Wide Web.

Tony holds a bachelors degree in Computer Science and Management and has over ten years IT experience, five or more working with Java, UML, and related technologies. His work has been published by Wrox Press, John Wiley & Sons, and a number of IT journals.

I dedicate my contribution to my children, Becky and Matt, the lights of my life.

Tony contributed Chapters 10 and 11 to this book.

Table of Contents

Table of Contents

Table of Contents

Table of Contents

Table of Contents

Table of Contents

Table of Contents

Table of Contents

Introduction

Welcome to *Professional Java Servlets 2.3*. This book is designed to show you how we can use **Java Servlet** technology to create powerful and portable enterprise components for use in web applications.

The web tier has emerged as the point of interaction between distributed business services, and so in this book we concentrate on using servlets as the engine behind web applications and component frameworks. We'll see how we can use servlets to control the flow of execution of applications, keep track of users of an application, intercept and modify requests and responses, and interact with web services.

With the development of the 2.3 version of the Servlet specification (finalized in September 2001), the expert group has made a number of changes including:

- ❏ Addition of Filtering
- ❏ Inclusion of listening or lifecycle events
- ❏ J2SE 1.2 required as underlying platform for web containers
- ❏ Incorporation of the Javadoc API definitions into the specifications
- ❏ Internationalization improvements
- ❏ Java Archive (JAR) dependencies
- ❏ Classloader improvements
- ❏ Various other changes such as new improved error attributes and new security attributes affecting HTTPS requests
- ❏ New classes and method changes and deprecation of the `javax.servlet.http.HttpUtils` class

The Servlets 2.3 API specification is also a key component in the Java 2 Patform, Enterprise Edition (J2EE) 1.3 specification, and as we will see in this book, plays a critical role as a controller in applications on the J2EE platform.

As we go along, we'll explain these concepts thouroughly, using plenty of complete, working examples to demonstrate their use.

Who is this Book For?

This book is aimed at developers who are familiar with the Java language and the core Java APIs. It is assumed that readers are familiar with some basic HTML and XML – although this isn't essential. We'll be using the latest specification of Java Servlet technology – version 2.3.

Servlets are rarely used in isolation but this book does not claim to be exhaustive in all areas, particularly in relation to other Java technologies and APIs such as JDBC, JNDI, and JavaServer Pages. *Professional Java Server Programming J2EE 1.3 Edition* from Wrox Press (ISBN 1-861005-37-7) provides an excellent introduction to the whole J2EE platform.

What's Covered in this Book

The book has the following structure:

- ❑ We start with an overview of how and where servlets fit into the enterprise.

- ❑ Chapters 2 and 3 cover the **Servlet 2.3 API**. We'll look at the lifecycle of servlets and understand how we can comsume and generate HTTP requests and responses.

- ❑ Although we'll have been running applications in earlier chapters, Chapter 4 explains the structure of web applications and how we should deploy them on a web server.

- ❑ Chapters 5-7 look at some of the powerful features of servlets – how we can maintain sessions, how we can persist servlets, and **filters**.

- ❑ In Chapter 8 we'll look at **JavaServer Pages (JSP)**, which is a technology that is complementary to Java Servlets.

- ❑ Chapters 9-11 will be spent looking at some of the issues that arise when web applications are deployed in production environments. We'll look at debugging techniques we can use to track down problems with our servlets and we'll understand the problems that can occur if we don't consider the effects of classloading and synchronization.

- ❑ In Chapters 12 and 13 we'll look at how the design of our web applications can affect the performance and maintainability. We'll look at the various patterns we can use to create better applications and we'll look at some techniques and tools we can apply to improve the performance and scalability of our web applications.

- ❑ Finally, in Chapter 14 we'll look at how we can use servlets as agents, to access information from **web services**.

What You Need to Use this Book

Most of the code in this book was tested with the Java 2 SDK version 1.3 (http://java.sun.com/j2se/1.3/) and Apache Tomcat 4 (http://jakarta.apache.org/tomcat/). However, running the examples in some chapters will require some additional software.

Several of the chapters require access to a database. For these chapters we have used MySQL (version 3.23) and the MM.MySQL JDBC driver (version 2.0.6). You can download both of these from http://www.mysql.com. The download includes full installation instructions.

There are several other pieces of software that a couple of chapters also require:

- ❑ Java 2 SDK version 1.4 – http://java.sun.com/j2se/1.4/
- ❑ The JavaBeans Activation Framework – http://java.sun.com/products/javabeans/glasgow/jaf.html
- ❑ XML Parsers: we have used Apache Xerces – http://xml.apache.org/xerces-j/index.html and the Apache Xalan XSLT processor – http://xml.apache.org/xalan-j/
- ❑ Apache SOAP 2.2 – from http://xml.apache.org/soap/index.html
- ❑ Apache AXIS – from http://xml.apache.org/axis/index.html

The code in the book will work on a single machine, provided it is networked (that is, it can see http://localhost/ through the local browser).

The complete sourcecode from the book is available for download from:

http://www.wrox.com/

Conventions

To help you get the most from the text and keep track of what's happening, we've used a number of conventions throughout the book.

For instance:

> **These boxes hold important, not-to-be forgotten information, which is directly relevant to the surrounding text.**

While the background style is used for asides to the current discussion.

As for styles in the text:

- ❑ When we introduce them, we **highlight** important words
- ❑ We show keyboard strokes like this: *Ctrl-A*
- ❑ We show filenames and code within the text like so: doGet()
- ❑ Text on user interfaces and URLs are shown as: Menu

We present code in three different ways. Definitions of methods and properties are shown as follows:

```
protected void doGet(HttpServletRequest req, HttpServletResponse resp)
                    throws ServletException, IOException
```

Example code is shown:

```
In our code examples, the code foreground style shows new, important,
    pertinent code
while code background shows code that's less important in the present context,
    or has been seen before.
```

Customer Support

We always value hearing from our readers, and we want to know what you think about this book: what you liked, what you didn't like, and what you think we can do better next time. You can send us your comments, either by returning the reply card in the back of the book, or by e-mail to feedback@wrox.com. Please be sure to mention the book title in your message.

How to Download the Sample Code for the Book

When you visit the Wrox site, http://www.wrox.com/, simply locate the title through our Search facility or by using one of the title lists. Click on Download in the Code column, or on Download Code on the book's detail page.

The files that are available for download from our site have been archived using WinZip. When you have saved the attachments to a folder on your hard-drive, you need to extract the files using a de-compression program such as WinZip or PKUnzip. When you extract the files, the code is usually extracted into chapter folders. When you start the extraction process, ensure your software (WinZip, PKUnzip, etc.) is set to use folder names.

Errata

We've made every effort to make sure that there are no errors in the text or in the code. However, no one is perfect and mistakes do occur. If you find an error in one of our books, like a spelling mistake or a faulty piece of code, we would be very grateful for feedback. By sending in errata you may save another reader hours of frustration, and of course, you will be helping us provide even higher quality information. Simply e-mail the information to support@wrox.com; your information will be checked and if correct, posted to the errata page for that title, or used in subsequent editions of the book.

To find errata on the web site, go to http://www.wrox.com/, and simply locate the title through our Advanced Search or title list. Click on the Book Errata link, which is below the cover graphic on the book's detail page.

E-mail Support

If you wish to directly query a problem in the book with an expert who knows the book in detail then e-mail support@wrox.com, with the title of the book and the last four numbers of the ISBN in the subject field of the e-mail. A typical e-mail should include the following things:

- ❏ The **title of the book, last four digits of the ISBN**, and **page number** of the problem in the Subject field.

- ❏ Your **name**, **contact information**, and the **problem** in the body of the message.

We *won't* send you junk mail. We need the details to save your time and ours. When you send an e-mail message, it will go through the following chain of support:

- ❏ Customer Support – Your message is delivered to our customer support staff, who are the first people to read it. They have files on most frequently asked questions and will answer anything general about the book or the web site immediately.

- ❏ Editorial – Deeper queries are forwarded to the technical editor responsible for that book. They have experience with the programming language or particular product, and are able to answer detailed technical questions on the subject.

- ❏ The Authors – Finally, in the unlikely event that the editor cannot answer your problem, they will forward the request to the author. We do try to protect the authors from any distractions to their writing; however, we are quite happy to forward specific requests to them. All Wrox authors help with the support on their books. They will e-mail the customer and the editor with their response, and again all readers should benefit.

The Wrox Support process can only offer support to issues that are directly pertinent to the content of our published title. Support for questions that fall outside the scope of normal book support is provided via the community lists of our http://p2p.wrox.com/ forum.

p2p.wrox.com

For author and peer discussion join the P2P mailing lists. Our unique system provides **programmer to programmer**™ contact on mailing lists, forums, and newsgroups, all in addition to our one-to-one e-mail support system. If you post a query to P2P, you can be confident that it is being examined by the many Wrox authors and other industry experts who are present on our mailing lists. At p2p.wrox.com you will find a number of different lists that will help you, not only while you read this book, but also as you develop your own applications. Particularly appropriate to this book are the **j2ee**, and **pro_java_server** lists.

To subscribe to a mailing list just follow these steps:

1. Go to http://p2p.wrox.com/

2. Choose the appropriate category from the left menu bar

3. Click on the mailing list you wish to join

4. Follow the instructions to subscribe and fill in your e-mail address and password

5. Reply to the confirmation e-mail you receive

6. Use the subscription manager to join more lists and set your e-mail preferences

Why this System Offers the Best Support

You can choose to join the mailing lists or you can receive them as a weekly digest. If you don't have the time, or facility, to receive the mailing list, then you can search our online archives. Junk and spam mails are deleted, and your own e-mail address is protected by the unique Lyris system. Queries about joining or leaving lists, and any other general queries about lists, should be sent to listsupport@p2p.wrox.com.

1

Servlets in the Enterprise

Java is a mature technology that can be broken down into separate platforms. You should already be familiar with the **Java 2 Platform, Standard Edition (J2SE)**. J2SE provides the core Java APIs and the Java Virtual Machine (JVM), as well as development tools such as the Java compiler. However, in this book we're going to concern ourselves with **Java 2 Platform, Enterprise Edition (J2EE)**. In fact we're going to concentrate on one part of J2EE – the **Java Servlet 2.3 API**.

J2EE builds upon J2SE, providing APIs and services for developing and deploying enterprise applications. Together the services and libraries of J2SE and J2EE enable the development of platform-independent, web-based Java applications. The J2EE platform also enables server vendors to provide environments in which the J2EE applications can be deployed and run.

- ❑ In this chapter we're going to begin by considering enterprise architecture with distributed applications, and the tiers involved in web application development.

- ❑ We will then examine how the J2EE architecture facilitates web development via web containers and Java servlets, and discuss the J2EE services and libraries that servlet developers may want to consider including in their applications.

- ❑ We will also discuss the advantages of using Java servlets that comply with the Servlet 2.3 specifications in our web applications.

- ❑ This will lead to a discussion of the roles that container vendors and developers have to play in implementing the Servlet specifications, and an introduction to the Tomcat web container/server, which is the reference implementation of the Servlet specifications.

- ❑ To round off the chapter, we will take a look the roles that servlets have to play in modern enterprise applications, which should hopefully illustrate their relevance and importance to enterprise application development.

However, before we begin to look at servlets in detail, let's take a high level view of enterprise architecture.

Enterprise Architecture

Today the architecture and infrastructure of an enterprise-scale application can be extremely diverse. An enterprise can consist of legacy mainframes from the 1960's coupled with modern systems. Over the past decade legacy and modern systems have been integrated using networks and the Internet.

Businesses retain their legacy systems because the economic cost of transferring their core business practices to a modern system is prohibitive. However, the consequence of maintaining legacy systems, introducing new systems, and merging them with systems from other organizations is that the architectural landscape of the enterprise is complicated.

Consider a financial services company that has existed for 30 years. Thirty years ago, it defined its core business processes on a mainframe system in COBOL. Over the years the company was involved in several acquisitions and mergers, and the business processes of these other companies were integrated with the system. These businesses developed applications using the best technology available at the time. The result is that today the company has a complex architecture that links many diverse hardware and software systems. Of course, these systems not only have to link up internally, but also externally via the Web.

The distributed environment of the Web allows employees working at a PC in their office to interact with any other connected system or resource, both within and outside the business. External systems (for example, those of suppliers) can be included in the network and hence communicate with the enterprise employees and systems through the Web. The problem is then to establish a common language or protocol to enable these systems to communicate.

Networks and Protocols

In developing for distributed computing systems, the underlying physical connections are the foundations upon which the system is built. Take away the network and your distributed applications will lose most of their usefulness. Often the basic network structure is transparent to the developer. Java's "write once, run anywhere" philosophy has led to the development of a strong arsenal of network-related APIs that makes development of distributed applications easier, making a basic understanding of the topology of the network over which we develop important. As we begin to work with servlets in a distributed environment, we start by looking briefly at the physical connections made between computers and how our systems are linked.

In a network, all linked systems are connected – whether by physical or wireless network. The network serves as a link for communication between computer systems and the software that runs on them. Three basic network topologies are shown in the following diagram:

❑ The **star** topology is used to connect computers to a central point, often known as a **hub**

❑ The **ring** topology connects computers in a closed loop where each computer connects to the next, until the loop is closed

❑ The **bus** topology connects to a single shared medium over which systems communicate

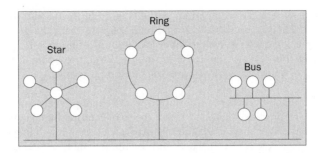

Of course these are not the only topologies used to implement a network. The topologies shown are used mainly in local area networks (LANs). They are the most common structures, with most of the alternative topologies being a derivative or combination of these. As new networking and communication technologies evolve, such as Bluetooth, the topology of the enterprise network tends to become more complex. The demands on the network (and network administrators) to support an ever-increasing range of technologies are a constant challenge.

Networks are designed to act as communication channels, allowing diverse and otherwise incompatible systems to connect to the same network and communicate. We are all aware of how our networks can include different operating systems and different devices in the same network. We can, using a browser communicate with a server that may run on a completely different operating system to that on which the browser is running. So, the question is, how do incompatible systems communicate?

> **Any resource can join the network, so long as it can communicate using the protocol(s) agreed for the network.**

A **protocol** is a set of rules agreed for communication. A number of protocols have been developed to specify common standards and message formats, so that different systems can exchange information and data. These protocols were designed to provide specific services and are layered to provide a (relatively) reliable networking service.

Layered Protocols	Server	Logical Connection	Client
5: Application	HTTP	- - - - - - - - - - - - - - -	HTTP
4: Transport	TCP	- - - - - - - - - - - - - - -	TCP
3: Internet	IP	- - - - - - - - - - - - - - -	IP
2: Network	Ethernet	- - - - - - - - - - - - - - -	Ethernet
1: Physical	Hardware	◄ - - - - - - - - - - - - ►	Hardware
		Physical Connection	

At the physical level, the hardware physical connection takes place between the communicating computers. This essentially comprises the network cards and the wired (or wireless) connection between the systems. This allows the computers to communicate by providing a medium over which messages can travel.

At the network layer, the network implements a protocol such as the Ethernet to facilitate communication between the computers. This deals with how data should be broken into frames and sent across the network. It also defines items like the size of data to be sent, the format for breaking up and reassembling large messages, and how to deal with network problems.

Messages sent from one system are wrapped up in the layered protocols and then sent across to another system via the network. The system that receives the message unwraps the message from within the layers of protocol. Logically, each equivalent layer is communicating with its corresponding level on the other computer. Each of these layers are, at the most basic level, providing a bridge between the systems, and the protocol layers above them provide additional services.

It is a little like a more reliable version of translation where the top levels communicate in the home language, but the message must be translated into a series of intermediate languages or codes before it can be exchanged. The receiver then sends the message back through a defined series of translators or decoders, until the message has been translated into the home language again.

TCP/IP

The **Transmission Control Protocol (TCP)** and the **Internet Protocol (IP)** layers are commonly grouped together because the two protocols provide complementary services. The TCP/IP protocols are by no means the only protocols that can be used for these layers, but they have, as the Web has developed, become the standard protocols for communication over the Web.

The Internet Protocol defines how pieces of data (known as **packets**) are formatted, as well as a mechanism for routing the packet to its destination. This protocol uses IP addresses of connected computers in the routing of data across the network. This is a relatively unreliable protocol, as data can be lost or arrive out of sequence. The Transmission Control Protocol provides the application layer with a connection-oriented communication service. This layer provides the reliability that the underlying IP layer lacks, by ensuring that all packets of data are received (and resent if necessary) and are reassembled in the correct order.

Together the TCP/IP protocols provide a reliable service, with the layers dividing the responsibilities between them to provide the reliable connections that the overlying application layer requires.

HTTP

The application layer of the communication is most frequently provided by the **HTTP** or **Hypertext Transfer Protocol**. Other protocols are in use also, such as the e-mail protocols POP3, SMTP, and IMAP, as well as the File Transfer Protocol (FTP), but HTTP is by far the most prevalent within web applications. Web containers and J2EE applications are required to support HTTP as a protocol for requests and responses. As this is the most common top-level protocol of the Web, by using this protocol applications can communicate with most servers with confidence that the message will be understood.

HTTP provides a defined format for sending and receiving requests, and acts as a common language that applications and systems developed on different systems and in different languages can all understand.

Why Not Use Remote Procedure Calls?

Remote Procedure Calls (RPC) is a mechanism by which a client can make specific requests to a program on a server (passing variables as required). The server then returns a result to the client that made the request. The client that makes a call must follow a predefined format.

In Java, RPC is implemented in **Remote Method Invocation (RMI),** by which Java applications can invoke methods of a class on a remote server according to the process defined for RMI method calls. This is done with the use of interfaces that define the remote object whose methods we want to call. The request is then made on the remote object, with the help of the interface, as if it was a local object. Java uses vendor-provided custom protocol implementations to convey the request. Sun uses the Java Remote Method Protocol over TCP/IP. Alternatively, RMI method invocation may be carried over the IIOP (Internet Inter-Orb Protocol) between Java applications (RMI-IIOP), which is language-independent, allowing interaction using a remote interface with any compliant object request broker (ORB).

CORBA (Common Object Broker Request Architecture) provides a language-independent mechanism for invoking methods or procedures on a remote application.

RMI and CORBA are more complex to implement than HTTP, making them inappropriate for many web applications. HTTP is the protocol of choice in the distributed environment, and for the majority of web-based applications (with all types of clients) is the pre-eminent choice, giving the best reliability and flexibility. It is therefore the most supported.

Both HTTP and RPC dictate that both client and server understand the common request-response process. However, if you update classes involved in RPC type requests, you frequently have to update both the client and server classes, even if the change only affected one side. With HTTP, so long as the format of requests is agreed, the server updates do not need any modification on the client (and vice versa).

> **HTTP is the standard language of the Web, used and understood by more servers and clients than other protocols. This makes it the ideal protocol to use for most web and servlet development.**

Tiered Architectures

The old model of two-tiered client-server development, where the client application connected directly with the data source, has been largely superceded. Enterprise applications are becoming more prevalently multi-tiered applications, spanning three or more tiers. The separation and consolidation of logical parts of the application into many different tiers has a couple of key benefits:

❑ By modularizing functions into specific tiers, we encapsulate related rules and functionality together, enabling easier maintenance and development

❑ Modularization also enhances the flexibility and reusability of business, presentation, or other logic in component-based development

❑ Developers with particular skills can focus on the logic specific to a particular tier (for instance database specialists can focus on the database tier), while the contract between tiers defines the relationships between tiers, and what services they can expect from the other tiers

Here's what a three-tiered architecture often looks like:

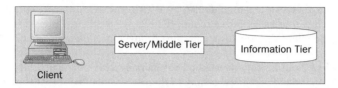

The **client tier** is where the data and information is described or displayed to the user.

The **server** or **middle tier** responds to client requests for data and/or actions. This is where the core application logic is usually held. However, the middle tier is frequently separated into two distinct tiers:

❑ The **business tier** is responsible for holding the business processing logic. It is concerned with implementing the business rules for the application faithfully.

❑ The **web tier** (or **presentation tier**) is reserved for presenting or wrapping the business data for the client. It responds to the client requests and forwards them to the business tier where the business logic is applied to the processing of the request.

The business tier will return the outcome of the request (data or other response) and the web tier will prepare the response for the client.

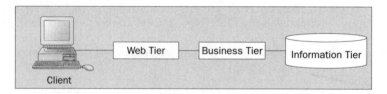

> **In this book we will focus on servlet development within web applications, which resides firmly in the web tier of the model.**

Finally, the **database/enterprise information tier** of the application is where the data or information resides. This is often described as the database layer, but equally can comprise a legacy information system, or indeed any other information system, including another server application. There may be many such systems in this layer providing data or services to the middle tier, either directly or indirectly.

The J2EE Platform

A number of services are often required by applications, specifically those in the middle tier. These services, such as security, database connections, and so on, are standard across many web applications, so providing them individually for each web application would significantly hinder development. We would like the server in the middle tier to make some (or all) of these services available to applications running on it, so that the application developer does not need to include code in each application to provide them. In this case server vendors provide the API libraries to support the services and the means for accessing them.

In Java terms, we have a developer-friendly situation where the provision of the services and APIs that support them have been standardized across compliant Java servers. This means that we can start application development on one standards-compliant server, and then deploy the application on another compliant server from a different vendor with little difficulty.

This is where the Java 2 Platform, Enterprise Edition comes into the picture. This is not a server, but a set of specifications for technologies, services, and architecture that a J2EE-compliant server must provide. From a programmer's point of view this allows us to focus on developing the application rather than having to learn about how it interacts with the server. Different vendors do provide additional services and tools on their servers, but having a standard framework allows the flexibility to deploy across different vendor's servers, assuming that we use the standard services and APIs provided for by the J2EE specifications.

Servlets are an integral part of J2EE. They sit on the web tier responding to, and processing, client requests. They provide the client tier with a standard gateway to the information available from the business or database/enterprise information tier. They can service many types of clients in a standard request-response cycle over any suitable protocol (such as HTTP).

Servlets are responsible in the J2EE model for providing dynamic content to the client. This means that they are the bridge between the client and the web application, and their main service is to exchange and transfer data with the client in the standard request response structure. As part of this process they receive client requests, usually with some additional information (for example request parameters). Then they process this information, communicating with other sources required to process the data, such as databases, or other information sources. Finally they return a response to the client.

The J2EE Container Architecture

The J2EE architecture views an application as a collection of related yet independent components, that interact with one another through the **container**. The container acts as an execution environment for the components and provides services for them. This relationship is illustrated below:

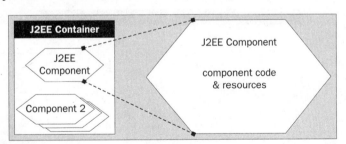

The above diagram illustrates the relationship where the container contains one, or more components. The components contain the Java code and resources (servlets, static files, property files, API, descriptors) required to perform their function. As part of the component deployment process we specify the container settings for each component, and for the J2EE application as a whole (using XML files as we'll see in Chapter 4). Once the application components are deployed, the range of J2EE services provided by the container are available to the components.

From the programmer's point of view, the J2EE platform vendor provides the container, subject to the J2EE specification. The programmer's responsibility is to develop the components, within the context of the container. The application developer does not need to understand specifically how the container receives requests (over socket connections) and maps them to a specific resource or any of the other responsibilities of the container. The J2EE container has this responsibility and the developer has only to worry about their specific components and application.

J2EE Container Types

The architecture of J2EE, which is component-based and platform-independent, allows us to develop enterprise applications that are much easier to write, build, and maintain due to the straightforward modularity of the design. The J2EE server provides specific containers for different component types. Business logic can be modularized and reused where possible, without having to directly manage any of the low level complexities such as resource pooling, transactions, and the management of state.

The diagram below shows the J2EE container architecture:

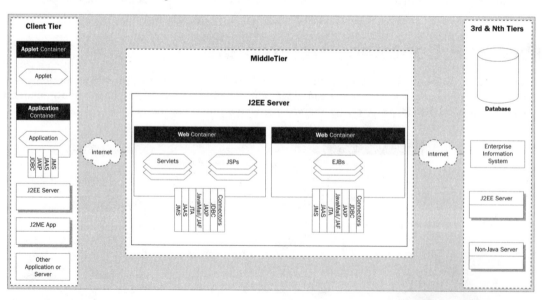

On the client side, two containers are specified by J2EE: the **applet container** and the **application container**. I have also included a J2EE server and an application server (covering J2EE and non-J2EE servers) as the client tier is not restricted to Java-based applets or applications, but may also include other servers or programs.

The middle tier is managed by a J2EE application server. This is a Java-based web server that provides a web container for our web application. To be J2EE platform-compliant it will also offer a J2EE EJB container and access to J2EE APIs such as JDBC, JNDI, and JAAS (more on these later). It may offer additional services or resources specific to the vendor, but at a minimum will comply with the J2EE specifications. BEA WebLogic Server, IBM WebSphere Application Server, and the iPlanet Application Server are examples of J2EE application servers.

This application server manages two containers. The **web container** contains and provides the services for the web components. The **EJB (Enterprise JavaBean) container** is the business tier of the J2EE platform. This is where the business logic resides.

Let's now take a closer look at all of these types of container.

Client Containers

When considering client containers it is important to remember that J2EE clients need not be J2EE-specified clients. The J2EE specifications do not mention Java 2 Platform, Micro Edition (J2ME) clients that may run on smaller hand-held devices (for instance cell phones or PDAs) and could be suitable clients for a J2EE server. There may be other non-Java applications or servers, or even J2EE servers, acting as clients.

For example, there may be an existing client-server-database three-tier application already running successfully in a company. As the business changes and develops, the business rules and logic governing this application may change and it may be better to rewrite part or all of the application. It may be simplest to rewrite the server side of the equation because this may be all that is affected, while the database and client (written in another language possibly) may be left unchanged. The client may be rewritten at a later stage, but users may be happy with the client as it stands and not want to change it.

Often, client components use HTTP to communicate with the server, but any other suitable protocol may be used as long as both client and server tiers support the protocol. Any number of communication methods can be used, from straight web-based (D/X)HTML for browsers, to WML for cell phones, to XML for applet/application or other clients, or serialized Java objects between Java-based applets or applications.

Java-based clients in J2EE applications will use a **thin client** structure, which means that a relatively lightweight client application communicates with the server. The server has the more complex and heavyweight responsibilities, such as connecting to one or more databases, connecting to other 'legacy' applications, providing other services (messaging, say), and any other processing of complex business logic. This is generally considered most efficient, as J2EE servers contain the wider range of services (which do not then have to be downloaded to the client) and are designed to be secure, fast, and reliable.

The specification also mentions that HTML pages may also be used to provide a more limited user interface for the J2EE application.

Application Container

The application container (provided by J2SE) runs the Java application from the client machine and normally uses the Swing (and/or Abstract Window Toolkit (AWT)) APIs to construct the graphical user interface. The diagram below shows the containers and a sample application:

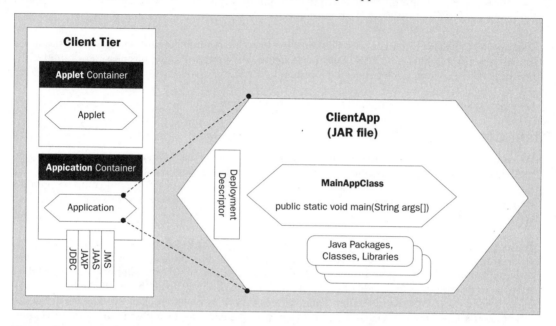

The application, as shown in the diagram above, is packaged in a JAR file. As expected, the application is executed from the main() method in the application class. The JAR file also includes any other classes or packages required by the application, and may also include (though not included in the J2EE specifications) any resource files, such as images, that may be required. The application container will provide access to the entire standard API included with J2SE and may provide additional services. The application may have access to all components that exist on the middle tier including servlets, JSP pages, and EJBs.

Generally though, the application will connect to the middle tier to send requests and receive responses. Normally the client is fully responsible for initiating requests, although the JMS (Java Message Service) API can be used to listen for event or message notification from the middle tier. The application container provides the client application with the run-time environment and access to the libraries of the Java 2 Platform, Standard Edition.

Applet Container

The J2EE specification also mentions the container in which the applet client will run, which may be in a browser or other application or device that supports the applet programming model. Applets are GUI-based, and are subject to more restrictions than other applications due to the Sandbox security model, which limits their access to the client machine. They are normally contained in a web page downloaded from the server and run within a sandboxed JVM within the browser; the applet clients are deployed from a J2EE server and then loaded by the client and executed. The applet is also limited to only contacting the server from which it was downloaded.

Middle Tier Containers

There are two containers that can be found on a J2EE application server, and these contain components from the middle tier: either web components or EJB components. Let's take a closer look at them.

The Web Container

A web container is a Java environment that manages the execution of all servlets and JavaServer Pages (JSP) (both of which are web components) for a web application. It is part of a web or application server that supplies the network services over which requests and responses are made. It must support HTTP, and optionally may support other protocols. It may be built into a web server or may be plugged in as a component to a web server. The container is responsible for the management of the lifecycle (initialization and destruction) and the invocation of the servlet and JSP instances.

For the programmer, the web container is where we place our web applications so that we can run them on the web server that provides the web container.

The EJB Container

Enterprise JavaBeans (EJB) are business components that contain the business rules or logic. There are two basic types of EJBs. Session beans are logic-oriented and deal with handling client requests (often from servlets) on one hand and the data processing logic on the other hand. Entity beans on the other hand are strongly coupled with the data itself and deal with data access and persistence.

EJBs are run in an EJB container. EJB components are reusable and are designed to be pooled and efficiently recycled for optimization. It is the EJB container's responsibility to manage the execution and pooling of EJBs for the application.

J2EE Web Components

So far we have looked at the J2EE's approach to modularization and development of J2EE applications. However, because we are focusing upon servlets in this book, to understand the roles they perform we need to examine the J2EE web tier in more detail. We have seen that J2EE containers provide services and an environment for application components, so we need to examine the web container and the components that can be deployed into, and managed by, the web container.

J2EE web components are usually JSP pages or servlets (they may also be filters, or lifecycle event listener classes, or tag libraries). The container has the responsibility of instantiating, initializing, calling, and destroying the web components deployed into it. It may create a pool of instances of a component, or it may execute methods on the instance in multiple threads corresponding to multiple requests.

Java Servlets

Servlets are Java classes that dynamically process requests and construct responses. In practice this often means that they dynamically generate HTML web pages in response to requests. However, they may also send data in other formats to clients, such as serialized Java objects (applets and Java applications), and XML. The servlets are run in a **servlet container**, and have access to the services provided by that container.

The client of the servlets can be a browser, applet, Java application, or any other client that can construct a request (normally an HTTP request that the servlet can recognize and respond to) and receive the response to it.

From the servlet's point of view the request must be properly formatted at the basic level (for example, if we are using an HTTP servlet it must be an HTTP request) and at the higher level where the servlet may expect certain data in a specific format from the client. Any client that correctly prepares the request will receive the appropriate response based on the processing logic in the servlet. Servlets should also be prepared to handle incorrectly configured requests, but it is the programmer's responsibility to decide how to handle this.

Servlet Lifecycle

Generally the lifecycle of a servlet is as follows:

1. The container is responsible for ensuring that the servlet is initialized before it processes requests.

2. Servlet components then receive requests from the client tier. The container actually receives the request, transparently maps the request to the appropriate component instance, and passes the component properly formatted request and response objects.

3. The servlet then processes the request, normally either with the help of the business-tier logic (EJB's) or by retrieving information directly from the database or enterprise information tier.

4. Once processing has been completed a response is returned to the client tier.

5. Finally, the container is responsible for destroying any servlet instances that it has created.

Steps 1 and 5 (initialization and destruction) execute once only, but steps 2, 3, and 4 will loop many times to process many requests.

Servlet Communication

Communication between a servlet and the outside world may occur at four points within a web application:

1. With the client, during a request/response cycle

2. With the servlet container, to access information about the container environment or to access JNDI resources

3. With other resources on the server, such as other servlets, EJBs, and so on

4. With external resources in order to fulfill the request, including databases, legacy systems, and EIS

Generally, a servlet's role is to communicate with the client. Communication with the container will be unlikely to produce data to return to the client, but instead access to resources that can provide a service. To be truly useful, a servlet is likely also to communicate with either other server components or external backend resources (often a database).

Servlet-Client Communication

Communication with the client can take many forms, with the most popular being **text-based** communication. In HTTP communication, some or all of the information parameters will be supplied as part of the request. In the server's response, there is a range of possible formats to return the data in, depending on the client.

The most obvious is the HTML page for display in the browser. This is the markup language of the Web and is ideal for business to consumer e-commerce sites. Alternately, if the client is a mobile phone, WML (Wireless Markup Language) is optimal. If you wish to send data back for editing in a spreadsheet type of package a CSV file (comma separated values) is a good option, and if you set the MIME type correctly your client browser may open up the client's spreadsheet program to process the file. For communication with systems written in other languages other than Java, XML is rapidly becoming the preferred option. It is also suitable for Java client applets or applications where data forms the substantive part of the communication.

Serialized Java objects can also be exchanged and may be the best option when data objects are already created on the server or client. They need no parsing (unlike XML or other text formats) and are ready to go. For an application with changing requirements, modifications to only client- or server-side code do not affect the other side – only changes to serialized object classes affect both. In this case it is usually good practice to separate such classes into a separate common package so that they can be clearly identified during early stages of testing and releases (and minor modifications).

Problems sometimes occur when server- (or client-)side modifications affect common classes, and the deployer might overlook this and update the server (or client) classes only. Then the application breaks because the client- and server-side versions of the common classes clash.

Servlets can also return files, either existing files or ones created specifically. By setting the appropriate MIME type we can dynamically serve many different files.

Implementing the Servlet Specification

The Servlet specification is just that, a specification. It outlines what a servlet container should do, what services it must provide, and a set of APIs (`javax.servlet` and `javax.servlet.http`) consisting of classes and interfaces that it must implement. It does not build or provide a servlet container per se, but defines the framework within which one may be built.

It also outlines what a servlet component deployed in a container can do and what services it should expect from the container in which it is deployed. This means that standard servlets or (servlet components if you like) can be deployed on any fully-compliant implementation of the Servlet specification.

This leads to two questions:

- **Who implements or builds the container?**
  Vendors that want to incorporate Servlet technologies into their product (usually some flavor of web server) implement the container. They provide the container as part of their product so that programmers can develop servlet-based web applications.

- **Who implements or builds the servlet components?**
  Programmers who want to develop web applications for the enterprise using Java/servlet technology build servlets and assemble them into web applications. Any servlets or web applications built within the standard Java and Servlet specification will run within any container that implements the servlet specifications. Of course this also assumes that the web application and container are matched to the same version of the specification.

However, the following questions then arise:

- Why define the container so that vendors must implement their own version of the container?

- Why do we need implementations other than the reference implementation?

To answer the second question first, the reference implementation is only that – a reference implementation. It may be freely used, adapted, enhanced and/or improved (subject to the license). Developers use the reference implementation to gain experience of the technologies. This experience is portable onto other servers that meet the same set of specifications. It is not necessarily the best implementation for a specific purpose, and vendors often implement their own version of the servlet container (or adapt/include the reference version) so that they can optimize its performance for some specific purpose.

This also answers the first question of why the definition is provided to allow different implementations. Vendors develop their own implementations based on adding some enhancement to their implementation that differentiates their version from competitors' versions. They may also implement the full J2EE specifications, or only the Servlet specification. In particular they may add additional web container management tools that enhance the administrator or developer's ability to deploy or redeploy components/web applications without having to restart the server.

In reality, this competition is generally a good thing for users, because it gives users a choice of containers that may have varying performance characteristics and possibly additional services. We, as programmers and users of these implementations (at least of Tomcat), have specific application requirements, including:

- Fast database performance

- Additional services or APIs

- Cost

- Reliability

The choice of implementations allows us the maximum flexibility (within a given budget) to choose the best implementation for our requirements. However, we need to be aware that using any additional non-standard services or APIs can tie the application to the specific server and reduce its portability. Application portability is important, as this allows us to move a web application if a particular implementation becomes more suitable.

Tomcat and Catalina

Tomcat, developed under the Jakarta Apache project (http://jakarta.apache.org/), supports the current version of the Servlet API 2.3. This current version of the Tomcat Servlet container, named **Catalina**, has been redeveloped from the ground up to meet the latest standards of flexibility and performance.

> **Tomcat 4 is the official Reference Implementation of the Servlet 2.3 and JavaServer Pages 1.2 API.**

The Apache project is a collection of open source projects related to web development. The Jakarta subproject is an umbrella for the Java open source projects. The sourcecode for the Sun Reference Implementation was released to the Apache subproject Tomcat, which is run by volunteers from the Java developer community.

The key advantages for developers (and users) of having the official Reference Implementation as a Jakarta Apache project is that the sourcecode is available to individuals (developers like us) and companies to use without needing to pay royalties. It should also provide the benefit of standardizing and improving the implementations of web containers and the deployment of web applications among competing products from different providers (in addition to bug fixes and future development being driven by the open source community). It is also likely to mean that Tomcat (or component parts of it like the Catalina servlet container) will become components in new servers/applications, which should be to the developers' advantage as well as being good for the product provider.

It is important to stress here that while we are going to be using Tomcat throughout this book, we could also use one of the many alternative implementations out there. These include Allaire's JRun, Iona's iPortal Application Server, BEA's WebLogic, IBM's WebSphere, and Oracle's Oracle9i Application Server.

However, by using Tomcat, we are learning about the standard implementation, about the API, and about how to develop web applications. When we develop a web application based on the Servlets 2.3 Specification on Tomcat, we know that we can move our application to another container that implements the same version of the Servlet specification, because all container implementators or vendors are implementing the same specification. Deploying and running the web application on another compliant container is a fairly standardized process across containers, so there is often little extra that needs to be learned to get up and running with a new container.

The Web Server-Web Container Relationship

A web server is the software that resides on a server computer. The purpose of the web server, as shown overleaf, is to receive client requests and return the relevant response of a static resource or a dynamically created response. Often the web server will receive requests over HTTP, but requests can be made over any suitable protocol that the web server supports.

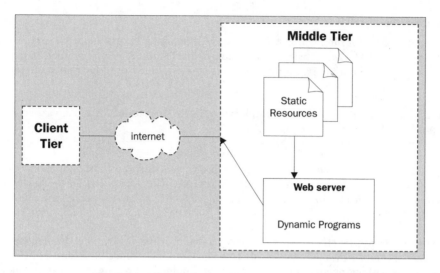

In Java enterprise server-side programming with servlets and J2EE technologies, the web server's purpose is similar to that described above. The web server receives requests from clients and maps the request to the appropriate resource. If the request is for a static resource (such as an HTML web page, or an image), it simply returns this resource to the client (or an error code if the resource could not be located).

The request could also be for a J2EE component, such as a servlet. In this case the J2EE server provides a web container and/or an EJB container to the web server. The web server then forwards requests for components within the containers to the specific container and then the container passes the request to the relevant component, which then processes the request and returns a response. This is shown below:

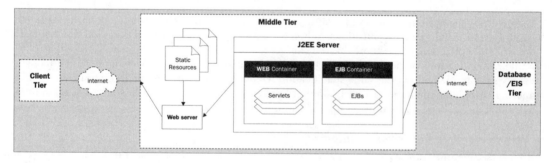

On a practical level the J2EE server may be integrated within the web server or may be "plugged" in. In the "plug in" process the web server is configured to recognize requests for components within the J2EE containers and to forward these requests to the appropriate container:

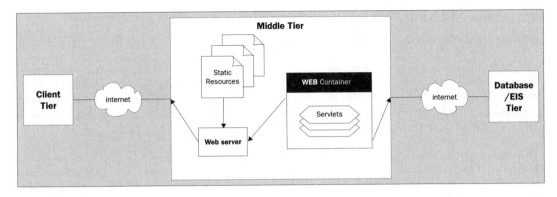

The web container does not receive requests directly from the client, but receives them from the web server. The web container can be configured as an add-on, or plugged into the web server, and receives the requests that map to components within the container. Examples of this configuration would include JRun-to-IIS, or Tomcat-to-Apache web server.

The case shown below is similar but slightly different. In this case the web container is an integral part of the web server. The web server functions similarly, providing static content as requested, but instead of forwarding requests to the plugged-in web container, the web container is internal to the web server and the request is passed internally to the web container:

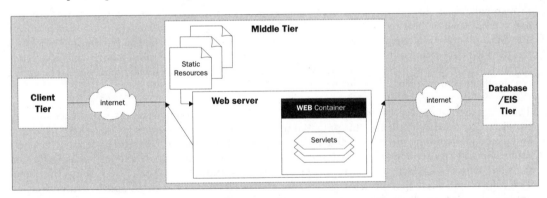

WebLogic, WebSphere, and Tomcat are examples of this scenario. As you have probably noticed, Tomcat (and others) can be configured with either setup as required.

Tomcat, run as a standalone server, provides web server functionality together with the web container for web applications. Like other such Java web servers it will run our web application, but does not provide the wider range of J2EE services that a full J2EE-compliant application server would. Examples developed in this book will work with Tomcat 4 in this setup.

Advantages of Using Servlets

So what are the benefits of using servlets?

Originally the Web consisted of static web pages. As the requirements for the Web evolved, static pages were not enough. Dynamically-created pages were required and the Common Gateway Interface (CGI) developed to fill this void. CGI works by passing the request to the CGI program which is spawned in a separate process. However, running the CGI script in a new process has obvious cost (in terms of time, and server processing resources) and scalability issues.

CGI scripts can be written in almost any language. Perl is the language most frequently used with CGI. However, it can cause problems with languages like C if poorly programmed, and CGI scripts suffer from the disadvantage of not being able to access the server's resources or information once started. Therefore CGI scripts cannot share or pool resources such as database connections where relevant, which impedes performance. Some improvements were made to the original concept, including FastCGI which made CGI processes persistent (eliminating some of the start-up costs), but still having the same scaling limitations. CGI is not as cross-platform as Java, but is still relatively cross-platform subject to support and testing.

Alternative options to CGI have been provided by server vendors including Netscape's (now iPlanet) server extension APIs (NSAPI). However, these APIs are server-specific and contain various security and reliability problems. Microsoft provides ASP that runs VBScript.

Probably the most obvious difference between CGI and Java is process execution. CGI scripts are executed in separate processes while Java servlets run within the server process, with obvious performance advantages. Servlet instances persist between calls so they do not have to be created on each call. Also servlets have access to the servlet container and information about the environment in which the servlet is running. This means that servlets can also share resources such as connections to databases. The end result is a significant improvement in performance and scalability over CGI applications.

The integration of servlets could pose risks for a server, but Java provides an error and exception handling process that eliminates this potential problem. Servlets and servers use the standard Java error and exception handling mechanism that means that servlet programmers should code their servlets robustly enough to cope with errors. In the event that they fail to anticipate every possible error, and the servlet does fail, the server catches the error gracefully and returns a standard error to the client. This informs the client that there was an error and protects the server against poorly written web applications. Servers also are protected against servlets that violate security through the security manager, which effectively sandboxes (restricts access for) the web application to the server's resources outside the web application's domain.

Servlets offer all of the services of CGI involved in request-response handling, and then add significantly by giving the servlet access to a full range of Java libraries including the J2SE API, the Servlets API, and often the full J2EE API (depending on the server). We can also include many other APIs from third-party vendors, such as JDBC drivers and XML parsers. These libraries and optional APIs are available cross-platform and cross-server.

Protocol Flexibility

The Servlet API provides two core packages:

- ❑ `javax.servlet`
- ❑ `javax.servlet.http`

Most applications tend to extend from `javax.servlet.http.HttpServlet` to create servlets, or from their own subclass of this, therefore implicitly choosing the HTTP protocol. This means that a common perception of servlets is that they are tied to HTTP.

However, there is no reason why we could not implement our own package extending from `javax.servlet` to develop our own protocol support, much as the `javax.servlet.http` supports HTTP-based servlets. It would be relatively simple to extend the Servlets API to support other protocols such as file transfer (FTP), and e-mail (POP3, SMTP, IMAP). It would also be relatively simple to develop and implement our own protocol appropriate for our application. We can also use the HTTP-based servlet to tunnel through firewalls that block other connections, as part of our application.

JSP Components

JavaServer Pages (JSPs) are an extension of servlet technology, because they simplify part of the process of creating web content. A JSP can contain directive tags, blocks of Java code (known as "scriptlets"), and HTML. The tags and scriptlets are used to generate dynamic content within the page. JSP pages are compiled into a servlet on first call, for execution.

The specifications tend to limit their identification of the uses of JSP pages to text-based documents, but, because JSP pages are an extension of servlets and servlet functionality, any use that a servlet may be put to may also be incorporated into a JSP. JSP pages are particularly useful components for generating page content, so they are normally used for presentation logic, and developers are discouraged from placing processing logic in them. We'll learn more about JavaServer Pages in Chapter 8.

Using Servlets with Other J2EE APIs

Servlets provide the web tier of the J2EE scenario, but servlets often need to use additional aspects and services of the J2EE platform to process client requests. We will now outline the J2EE services that servlet-based web applications may use. Some of these may only be available on servers that implement the full J2EE platform specifications; for example, web servers such as Tomcat, which provide a web container but no EJB container, implement only a subset of the J2EE specifications. Sun provides a complete J2EE Reference Implementation.

Connecting Servlets to Information Sources

At the heart of almost every servlet-based web application is the processing of data (at least one, if not two way). To do this the servlet needs access to information from EIS systems and databases. There are three main J2EE APIs that are associated with data access that may be used by servlets.

The J2EE Connector Architecture

The **Connector Architecture** gives developers a standard architecture for connecting J2EE and web applications to heterogeneous Enterprise Information Systems (EIS) (databases, legacy systems, enterprise resource planning systems, and so on). To you and I, these are pre-existing information systems that are available to the programmer through the Connector API.

This allows us to interact with a range of enterprise information systems and send data to and/or receive data from these systems. To use the Connector API to access such a system we need a **resource adapter** to support the EIS: this acts like a JDBC driver in database access.

The definition of and the inclusion of the Connector Architecture and API in J2EE is an important development, especially for companies with large pre-existing and possibly diverse systems that need to be accessed and interconnected. With this architecture we can begin to draw the resources of these diverse systems into our application in order to utilize existing services. This will become more significant as more companies get more involved in business-to-business electronic commerce.

Using this architecture, our web-based applications can access EIS's not normally available. Generally the preferred method to access such resources is to encapsulate the logic in an EJB, but where EJBs are not employed, our web applications can access them directly with the appropriate resource adapter.

Database Connectivity

JDBC provides a standard API to access a wide range of relational databases. It provides an application interface to access the database or build higher-level components on, and a service provider interface to attach the JDBC driver to the J2EE platform. We can use JDBC to connect to a database from servlets. JDBC is important in servlet development when we bypass the EJB/business tier and directly access the database tier.

Considering that many (if not most) enterprise applications are, in practice, servlet-based and do not use EJBs, access to the JDBC API is critical for most servlet-based web applications.

The Java Transaction Service

The **Java Transaction Service (JTS)** and API are potentially very valuable to many applications. Many J2EE and servlet-based applications rely heavily (at some level) on transactions and transaction processing, and the JTS provides an API for processing complex distributed (and non-distributed) transactions. The API allows a high level of control of the transactions, with control of committal and rollback.

This kind of transaction service allows transactions spanning multiple databases to be treated as a single transaction. If any part of the transaction fails, all parts of the transaction can be rolled back, or alternatively if no parts of the transaction fail, the service guarantees that the whole transaction (incorporating one or more transactions) will be successfully committed as if it were a single transaction.

JTS is most frequently used on the business EJB layer for processing transactions, but is available on J2EE servers for servlets as well. This will allow our applications to manage more complex transaction scenarios.

Messaging in J2EE

Servlets need to communicate beyond the client request-response cycle. They may only need to listen for special events that trigger messages sent over a message service, or they may need to send information to a user or administrator. In these cases servlets often make use of the JMS or JavaMail APIs to communicate outside the normal cycle.

The Java Message Service

The **Java Message Service (JMS)** provides a standard API for applications that need to incorporate messaging into their J2EE applications. It allows components to engage in reliable asynchronous communication (in other words, communication where the message does not have to be processed and acknowledged immediately after it has been received) by creating, sending, receiving, and reading messages.

We use JMS in web applications where our servlet may need to listen to JMS messages for updated information (stock prices and alerts etc.), or it may need to broadcast messages.

JavaMail

Where applications need to send messages/notifications of important errors or events, we can use the **JavaMail** API included in the J2EE platform. It is also used as an alternative to the asynchronous messaging of JMS, but can be slower and less dependable. The JavaMail API allows our applications to send or receive messages over some of the most widely-available Internet mail protocols such as SMTP, POP3, and IMAP, and also supports MIME. JavaMail relies on the JavaBeans Activation Framework (JAF) that is therefore included in the J2EE specifications.

The JavaMail API is useful in servlet-based web applications on many fronts. At the most basic level it can be used to send messages notifying relevant personnel of important events. This could include application-level events such as significant errors or warnings, or just alerts such as important news announcements, or messages direct from the client via a servlet.

Servlet Security and JAAS

Servlet applications often implement their own custom security architecture, but the **Java Authentication and Authorization Service (JAAS)** is often overlooked and not designed into the web application architecture.

The JAAS provides the ability to restrict the right to execute code based upon the privileges of the user attempting to call that code. This can be important for a client application where only certain types of users may use particular resources on the J2EE server (for instance we might want to restrict access to an administration servlet to administrators only).

There are two parts to the JAAS. The first is the reliable **authentication** of the client, regardless of the way that the client is connecting to the server. It specifies a pluggable authentication module for the J2EE platform so that modifications or upgrades to the authentication component can take place independently of any modifications to the J2EE application.

The second part is **authorization**, which allows programmers to specify the roles of the users that may have access to our application resources. Web components and EJB methods can be protected, requiring authorization of the caller. We can also restrict the use of specified classes and methods to certain types of users according to their roles.

The Java Naming and Directory Interface

The Java Naming and Directory Interface (JNDI) provides two distinct services on the J2EE platform. Firstly, a servlet can use JNDI to look up components such as EJBs, JDBC connections, and other servlets to get a reference to the selected resource. Secondly it makes available a standardized interface for accessing multiple naming and directory services such as the Lightweight Directory Access Protocol (LDAP).

The Java API for XML Processing

The **Java API for XML Processing (JAXP)** provides standardized support, through the API, for processing XML documents using different SAX parsers, DOM builders, and XSLT transformation engines. By configuring JAXP we can specify the particular implementations of SAX and DOM to use relevant to the requirements of the situation.

Servlets providing web services will definitely find use for this API, because XML documents are increasingly becoming both the source matter and the output of requests. XML has become ubiquitous and should be an integral part of the servlet programmers' technical arsenal.

Servlet Roles in Web Applications

We build web applications that consist of a number of servlets (and additional resources) that together function as an application.

Later in this section we will look at some example scenarios of how web applications use servlets in business today, and through the book we will see code examples of servlet use. In this section we will take a broad look at some of the roles that servlets can perform for us in our web applications.

Client requests may occur at irregular and unpredictable intervals, but the servlet will respond to the requests on demand. The servlet container provides the service of listening for requests and wrapping the client request and responses up in special Request and Response objects, but once it receives a request for the servlet, it invokes the servlet and passes it the Request and Response objects. Then the servlet processes the request and passes the client back a response.

However a servlet on its own is often of limited use, and a collection of related servlets form components of the web application. Alternatively we may have a single servlet that is the front door to the application, with this servlet delegating the request (based on the type of the request or other relevant criteria) to an appropriate handler that processes the request. In any case a good, object-oriented web application design is important for developing maintainable and extendable web applications.

Consider the following simple scenario. We want to build a simple, web-based reservations system for a hotel. Core functions of this system will be the ability to search the hotel bookings for availability and to pay for, and reserve rooms in advance. This is an ideal candidate for a servlet-based web application, as we would not consider exposing the reservations database directly on the web.

The reservations web application will consist of a number of servlets that process client requests through the database. Keeping it simple, we may use just three servlets in the application at first, together with a static HTML site (for information).

Our first servlet would be a search servlet that would be responsible for responding to client form-based searches. Information on room availability and rates for given search criteria, such as date and room type, are returned from the search. This servlet is an information servlet that searches for data, but does not change the data on the database. The servlet processes the request as follows:

1. It extracts the relevant request parameters and uses them to build a database query

2. Then it connects to the database and executes the query, receiving a result set from the database

3. Finally it presents the results returned in a manner agreeable to the client (often a well-formatted HTML table)

The second servlet would be a reservation servlet. The purpose of this is to allow the client to reserve an available room. This will update the database in the process of processing the request and reserving the room. The process would be as follows:

1. The servlet receives the request, and first checks that the information required is supplied (name, dates, and so on)

2. Then it would verify on the database that the room(s) requested are still available, and if so reserve them

3. Finally it would confirm to the client the provisional reservation of the room, pending payment

The final servlet in our reservations web application would be a payment servlet. This processes the client's payment details and updates the reservations database with the result. The steps involved here would be:

1. It receives the request from the client to pay for the room

2. It checks that the payment is for a valid reservation

3. If the reservation is still holding, it would process the payment by contacting the credit card company's system to process the payment details

4. Assuming that the payment was successful, this servlet would update the database and confirm the reservation

5. Finally it would inform the client that the payment was accepted and that the booking has been confirmed

The above scenario illustrates that a group of servlets can form the basis for a complete web application that fulfils the requirements of an enterprise application.

You should note that Java servlet-based web applications are naturally inclined to be at least three-tier applications. Since servlets operate on the request-response model, by definition there is a client and so we have two tiers at a minimum; servlet-based applications will usually need to exchange data with an additional tier too. This additional tier may be the EJB tier, or the database/enterprise information system tier.

Typical Servlet-Based Applications

To round off the chapter, we are going to discuss some typical application scenarios where servlets play an integral role within the application.

The range of potential business applications that can use servlets is immense. Almost any application could be written (or rewritten) to include servlets. Their strength, compared with alternative technologies, is their communication over the Internet (or intranet) using HTTP (or any other suitable protocol such as FTP or SMTP). Given security and firewall considerations, for many applications, HTTP is almost the only protocol available. Using HTTP also allows us to communicate with many other resources, such as web and database servers and other enterprise information systems and applications.

Servlets are ideal for client web browser (HTML over HTTP) based applications, and any other text-based communication is well supported. XML and WML communications are such examples. Emerging web services technologies will be well-placed to leverage servlets in the web tier of their applications.

However, traditional thinking about client-server programming and Internet or web development needs to broaden its perspective to look at the range of uses for servlet and J2EE technologies. Servlets are not just for HTML web applications. They are also useful for our deployed Java applications, perhaps deployed using Web Start type of technologies using JNLP (Java Network Launch Protocol).

Servlets can also be used in business applications to upload more data than just the request parameters. We can exchange the HTTP input parameters for a servlet input stream to read in serialized Java objects, files, text, or other relevant data from the client. Servlets are ideal for HTTP tunneling, which is client-server communication over HTTP due to firewall restrictions (often firewall protection restricts almost all communication except over HTTP). In tunneling we wrap an alternative protocol request in an HTTP request to bypass firewall limitations. While this may sound a little dubious, this does have many legitimate uses, such as streaming data and wrapping RMI requests.

Servlets are also ideal for connecting J2ME client devices and applications, and WAP/WML cell phones and such devices. Developments over the last few years in cell phone technology have seen the first text-based WML, and now Java applications are moving onto these devices. In Japan DoCoMo broke new ground by making Java widely available on the cell phone, and other markets, such as the US, are doing the same. Placing servlets on the web tier of mobile applications makes a strong match, as mobile devices require light clients, with processing pushed onto the server. Research in this area is strong with major investments, and forecasts indicate huge growth in cell and wireless devices over the next few years.

About two thirds of distributed enterprise applications being developed in Java within the broader spectrum of J2EE use only the web container with servlets on the middle tiers to process client requests, so servlets have an important role to play in distributed applications.

An E-Commerce Scenario

Consider a company that wants to get involved in an online supermarket. This could be a subsidiary of a distributor or wholesaler company. The company could have two enterprise critical web/J2EE applications:

❑ On the e-store front we see the **business-to-consumer** model in action to interact with customers

❑ In the backend we see a **business-to-business** model used to manage orders to suppliers and coordinate grocery deliveries to customers

On the business-to-consumer side, the customer uses a web browser to view the online store and make their order. The order process servlet application receives the client order and passes it on to the order manager J2EE application. The order manager application receives client orders from the order process servlet, or its own order servlet, and adds the details of the orders to the database. It also checks stock levels in the database and sends XML-based orders to suppliers for any items that will need restocking. It processes the delivery schedule as well for the manager client application. To do all this the order manager application has two servlets, one to process orders and one to deal with the manager application. This scheme is illustrated in the figure below:

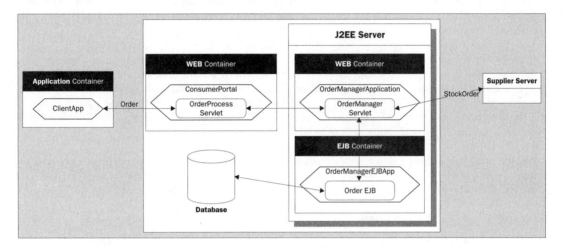

Consider the order process:

1. The client starts the process by placing the order

2. The web application's `OrderProcessServlet` receives it and checks the client credit, and then forwards it to the order manager application

3. The receiving servlet then stores the order in the database and orders any supplies required

4. The order is then acknowledged back to the client

5. If the supplier acknowledges the order, the order manager application sets and confirms the order delivery date to the client by e-mail

The servlets' role in this application is critical to the e-store's success. They are responsible for managing orders, getting the database stock levels checked (task delegated to an EJB) and, if necessary, ordering a restock of low supplies online from a supplier. The processing involved in this scenario is not excessively complex, but it is responsible for managing the stock levels, which is a critical task in itself. The rules for what levels are considered low and requiring a reorder would be encapsulated within the EJB, but the `OrderManagerServlet` is then responsible for sending the restock request if necessary.

The business-to-consumer aspect is dependent upon the `OrderProcessServlet` for receiving order requests and processing them. The business-to-business side of the company that predated the new e-store manages stock levels and orders, which are key components of this business' model.

The role of the servlet in this scenario is to act as the web interface to the consumer. This is very much a client-driven process and the servlets process their requests, manage (or delegate) the processing logic, and return to the client a web-based HTML response.

A Consumer-to-Business-to-Consumer Scenario

We can look at an e-business site that is set up to act as an intermediary between vendors and purchasers. It provides a place for members of the public to sell goods, either at a fixed price, or by auction to other members of the public. The site provides a sales notice board and can manage auctions by processing bids. It also provides a personalized service by displaying tailored pages, based on the customer's registration preferences.

It uses a HTML interface for the client side, and servlets on the server side to process requests, with a database to store user information, sales, and auction data. If we are involved in designing this, we need to consider the user base (total volume) and peak usage. We also need to design the application with a margin of error for these figures, which in reality means that we have to look at the upside to the figures if the web site is successful. We need to be most concerned about peak usage, as this is where any bottlenecks in code or scalability problems will be shown.

For the purposes of this example we will assume that this sales and auction e-business is going to plug into a online portal aimed at a specific local town, which will allow us to tailor the site for local preferences. The portal can provide us with some data in regards to the scale of usage and interest.

Given the scale and reliability required (we can't have the site falling over in the middle of all of our auctions), we need to consider running our web application on a clustered server setup. This should provide us with both scalability and reliability, by allowing us some fail-over protection.

From a security point of view, we will register participants with personal data and personal preferences, so passwords sent to a servlet over HTTPS may be considered sufficient for this portion. For the payments process we may use a more secure format of security for processing transactions, or alternatively we could place this section on a separate server (clustered for reliability), which may use higher security and encryption (possibly an applet interface communicating with a servlet over HTTPS, so that we can increase encryption). This will process credit card payments for auctions and other sales.

We may also have a separate database for payments processing, again more for security's sake since we can increase our protection around this database. Again, for the payments processing web application the role of servlets will be to receive and process the customer payment details. The main application will have details of sales made and dates processed, but does not need credit card and other payment details. This type of design will help improve security and improve consumer confidence in our systems.

Here's a diagram showing this scheme:

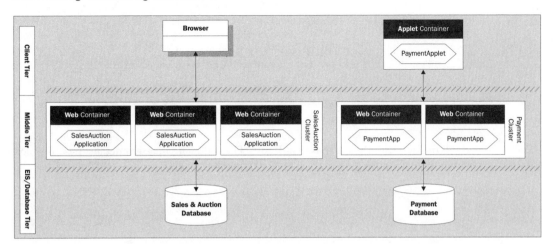

Remember that while diagrammatically the Payments and Sales Auction web applications are separately located, we may in practice cluster them across the same web containers. This is essentially a security decision.

We'll take a look at the servlets that could be involved in the process. It is important at this stage to understand that these servlets relate to specific processes between the client and our application, and in the final design may be implemented differently.

Firstly we have two applications – the payments processing application and the main application. The payments processing application will have one `PaymentServlet` to process payment details. The main application has a number of roles to fulfill:

❑ Registration to process user registrations

❑ Post Item to accept items for sale or auction

❑ Search to allow users to search the sales and auctions

❑ List to allow users to list and navigate categorized sales and auctions (this will have some similarities to the Search role as it will search on category, but may have a different presentation)

❑ Bid to process user bids on an action; this will inform the vendor by e-mail of bids if required

❑ Purchase to process item sales; this will also inform the vendor (and copy the purchaser) of the sale by e-mail

❑ Administration to allow a user to view their history (bids/purchases, sales etc.)

These roles will be allocated to a number of servlets (and a couple of JSP pages):

- ❑ `RegistrationServlet`

- ❑ `PostItemServlet`

- ❑ `SearchJSP` and `ListJSP` to present the output (in different ways) for the `SearchServlet`

- ❑ `BidJSP` and `PurchaseJSP` to present the result of a bid or purchase handled by the `OfferServlet`

- ❑ `AdministrationServlet`

Each of these will interact with the database via JDBC. The following diagram details the initial content for our applications, concentrating on the servlet web container layer:

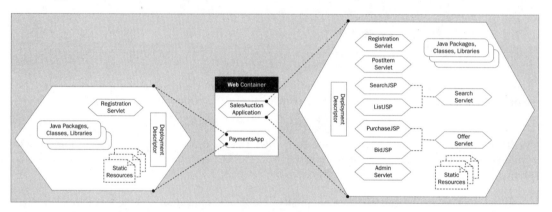

We may develop and use EJBs to encapsulate the business logic involved in the processing of the interactions and transaction, but as we are concentrating on the servlet side we have not detailed these on the diagram.

From the user's perspective the site has to be dynamic and constantly updated with information about auctions and sales of interest to the user. Within this web application, the servlets provide the flexibility and dynamism to allow the site to adapt to events (auctions and sales) created by the users.

The primary role of the servlets in the application is to interface with clients and process their requests. However, we also have a number of specific tasks or roles that the servlets perform, although they perform little processing of data. They act as a bridge between the client and the database. The servlets present the database data in a meaningful way, while updating the database as well when required.

A Modern Interface to a Legacy System Scenario

Lets take a look at a system that will provide an user interface application to a legacy system. Many firms still have a strong reliance on legacy systems for their core business processes. Therefore programmers are often asked to bridge the gap and create systems that can interface with them.

We can use servlets to do this, together with EJBs and the Connector API, as we described earlier in the chapter. The EJBs manage the business logic and access to the legacy system. The connector technology standardizes legacy and enterprise information system access through a standard API, in a similar way to how JDBC provides a standardized access API for databases. The servlet's role in this scenario is to act as a bridge between the client and the EJBs, transforming the requests from the client into a format that the EJBs can process, and translating the EJB's response into a format suitable for the client.

For example, consider a stock control system that runs on a legacy system. We need to create an application that can manage stock, allowing the user to change stock levels and other associated stock control functions. Additionally, users also want to be able to use a PDA type of device in the stock room to update the system when they connect back into the network. The advantage of using Java at the client end is that we can perform automated software updates, so once a new release is available, users immediately have access to it. We can also build a client for the PDA using J2ME, and we could build a workstation version for the J2SE client. The J2ME version downloads data and then allows the user to disconnect from the system and work on the stock floor updating the system. Once complete, the user can connect the PDA back into the network and update the system.

The clients will connect to the legacy system through a J2EE web application running servlets. The servlets receive requests and call on the EJBs to process the request. The EJBs use the Connector API to access and update data on the legacy application. The diagram below illustrates this:

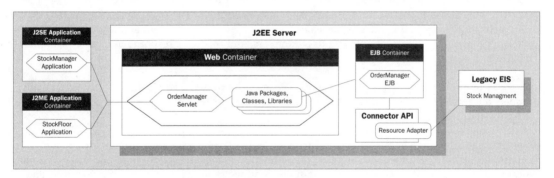

Obviously there would be other issues to sort out, such as locking/protecting the data that the stockroom staff are updating, and the application could incorporate this. Also caching of the data by the servlet for reuse rather than having to retrieve it for each request may be appropriate, depending on the response times.

In the Order Manager web application we will have one servlet to process all requests. We will use a `RequestHandlerFactory` class that will be responsible for mapping each request to the appropriate `RequestHandler` that will be able to process the request. The `RequestHandler` will interpret the request and wrap it appropriately for the EJB to process. The EJB then connects to the legacy Stock Management system and performs updates and access information as required. Using this system we can create accessible user interfaces to the legacy system that we can use on the stockroom computers and on PDA devices on the floor.

For the clients we can use XML over HTTP to enhance data, or we could serialize the data in Java objects. If we were going to be exchanging large files of information continuously we might consider using a different protocol like FTP, but data compression may be easier (using `java.util.zip.ZipOutputStream`). There would be other alternatives to XML or serialization (perhaps straight text or CSV), but these would probably be the frontrunners. If it was possible that other systems may want to connect to our web application it may be a better choice to use or include XML to ensure maximum flexibility.

XML also allows for XML-RPC or remote procedure calls over XML. We could incorporate a strong element of flexibility for client requests, by implementing the ability to allow clients to query the legacy EIS using XML-RPC calls to the servlet. This is moving towards implementing a web services scenario which we will look at next.

Thus we see that the servlet's role is limited in this scenario. It is really just the interlink between the client and the EJB-to-legacy system. In this case, most of the processing will probably occur on the legacy system. In fact there could already be a more limited legacy system application that this application is updating or replacing.

A Web Services Scenario

Distributed web applications have been around for a long time, but they have recently evolved into **web services** that expose functions (or methods) for remote execution across the Web. This means that, using web technologies and infrastructure (for example HTTP), we can set up an application to receive (or transmit) function requests, complete with parameters, and receive a response as a result. Chapter 14 looks a web services in more detail.

One way to implement a web service is to expose a servlet to XML-RPCs (remote procedure calls) that request the servlet to provide information in the response, corresponding to the procedure called and the parameters passed into the call.

Consider the scenario where we have a distributed Hotel Booking operation that stores data in geographic servers roughly corresponding to continents. It does this for optimal performance, since most requests for this data comes from within the continent where it is located. However for long distance requests, from a client of another continental server, our local server exposes the data by setting up a web application using servlets to process XML-RPC requests.

The web application that we develop looks like the following diagram:

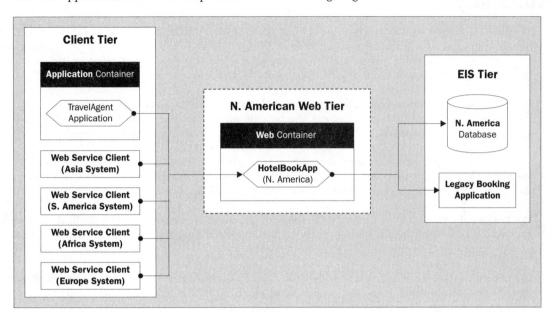

At the backend EIS tier we have a database, and also a Legacy Booking Application that is still in use for certain hotels.

On the web tier we place our HotelBookApp, which is a servlet-based web application. This application has servlets that are designed to receive XML-RPC requests. These XML-RPC requests allow other servers and/or clients to query the North American data using defined procedures.

The client tier of the application consists of North American travel agent users of the Java TravelAgentApplication, and our other servers that receive requests for information or bookings for North America.

Essentially this application setup is mirrored (but in reverse) on the other continental servers with the other servers providing access to their data through XML-based web services.

The servlet's role in this application is to receive and interpret the XML-RPC requests. They then have to map the request to the database or legacy booking application that performs the request, and once the servlet receives the response, it returns this as a response to the XML-RPC request. The servlet provides the web services to its own client application, and also to other servers. In turn, this application's servlet may make a similar XML-RPC request to the other continental web applications if it receives a request for information relevant to that region.

From the programmer's point of view, the servlets are standard servlets, probably running over HTTP (but not necessarily), perhaps using XML parsers a little more than many other web applications, but this is all part of the web service aspect.

Summary

We have considered servlets and how they fit into the multi-tiered J2EE infrastructure. J2EE and servlets offer a wide range of services through the range of APIs provided. Servlets have a range of advantages in enterprise web applications such as security, cross-platform and cross-server portability, protocol flexibility, as well as a wide range of J2EE APIs available for the servlet developer to make use of.

In the chapter we examined the J2EE container architecture and the web container architecture in particular. We saw that containers manage and provide services for the components they contain. Web applications and components, and their place in the web architecture were also discussed.

We noted that the Tomcat web server/container is the reference implementation of the Servlet 2.3 specifications, although there are many other implementations of the specifications too, which means that we can choose the one best suited to the needs of our web application.

We finished the chapter by considering the range of possibilities that business web applications could encompass, and examined the roles that servlets had to play in such applications. The variety of roles we saw illustrated the versatility of these components.

In the next chapter we will look at the Servlet 2.3 API in detail. We will see the recent developments in the API and start to develop and run servlets using the Tomcat reference implementation.

2

The Servlet 2.3 API

The current version of the Java Servlet API, 2.3, provides a mature technology for developing J2EE and J2SE-based web applications based around servlets.

The entire Servlet API is contained in two packages: `javax.servlet` and `javax.servlet.http`. The first package deals with generic servlets, and the second deals with specialized HTTP servlets.

The API contains 20 interfaces and 16 classes. The prevalence of interfaces in the API allows servlet implementations to be customized and optimized to the requirements of a specific servlet container. For example, the API specifies servlet request and response interfaces, but the container provides the underlying class implementations for them. From the container vendors' point of view, this allows them to determine the optimal implementation, given the characteristics and requirements of the container and the clients' requirements for the web application. These could include such objectives as optimization for HTTP access.

As developers, we don't need to know the details of how these classes have been implemented by the container. It is sufficient to be able to access methods within the classes according to the contract specified by the interface.

During the course of this chapter:

❑ We will examine the classes and interfaces of the Servlet API, focusing particularly on the `javax.servlet` package

❑ We will also be considering the classes and interfaces related to lifecycle of a servlet

❑ We'll look at the request-response cycle, and the interfaces and classes associated with it

❑ We will conclude the chapter by developing an application using the servlet classes and interfaces that we will discuss

The javax.servlet Package

The `javax.servlet` package provides the contract between the servlet/web application and the web container. It allows the servlet container vendor to focus on developing the container in the manner most suited to their requirements (or those of their customers), so long as they provide the specified implementations of the servlet interfaces for the web application. From the developer's perspective, the package provides a standard library to process client requests and develop servlet-based web applications.

Here is a class diagram of the classes and interfaces present in the `javax.servlet` package:

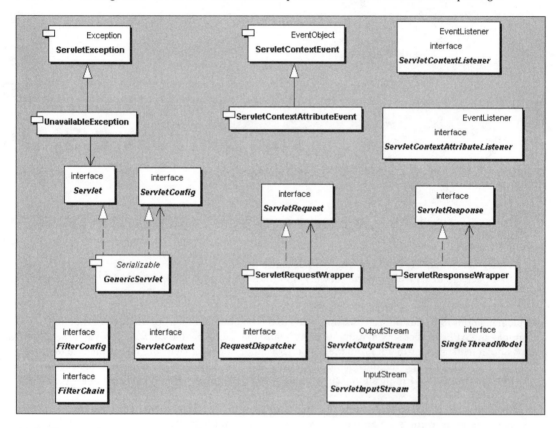

At the heart of the `javax.servlet` package is the `Servlet` interface that defines the core structure of a servlet. This is the basis for all servlet implementations, although for most servlet implementations, we subclass from a defined implementation of this interface that provides the basis for our web applications.

The additional interfaces and classes provide additional services to the developer. An example of such a service would be the servlet container providing the servlet with access to the client request through a standard interface. The `javax.servlet` package therefore provides the basis for developing a cross platform, cross servlet container web application, allowing the programmers to focus on the development of a web application.

Developers sometimes tend to focus on the `javax.servlet.http` package, but understanding the `javax.servlet` package will help you use both packages optimally. Additionally, should you need to, you can use this package to build your own servlet implementation that makes use of a different protocol from HTTP that is more suitable for your application. For example, we could extend from the `javax.servlet` package to implement an SMTP (Simple Mail Transfer Protocol) servlet that provides e-mail services to clients.

Let's now take a look at the interfaces, classes, and exception classes of the `javax.servlet` package.

The javax.servlet Interfaces

The `javax.servlet` package is composed of twelve interfaces. The servlet container provides the implementation of the seven interfaces below:

- ❑ `ServletConfig`
- ❑ `ServletContext`
- ❑ `ServletRequest`
- ❑ `ServletResponse`
- ❑ `RequestDispatcher`
- ❑ `FilterChain`
- ❑ `FilterConfig`

These are objects that the container must provide to the servlet to provide services to the web application. They are provided as interfaces so that the vendor can decide the most suitable implementation for their container.

The programmer building the web application implements the remaining five interfaces:

- ❑ `Servlet`
- ❑ `ServletContextListener`
- ❑ `ServletContextAttributeListener`
- ❑ `SingleThreadModel`
- ❑ `Filter`

The purpose behind defining these programmer interfaces is that the container may invoke the implementations using the methods defined in the interface. Hence, the servlet container only needs to know about the methods defined in the interface, while the details of the implementation are up to the developer.

The `Servlet` interface defines the lifecycle methods of the basic servlet: initialization, service, and destruction. The interface also includes the `getServletConfig()` method, which the servlet can use to access the `ServletConfig` object. The servlet container uses a `ServletConfig` object to pass initialization information to the servlet.

Probably the most important method of the ServletConfig interface is the getServletContext() method. This method returns the ServletContext object. The ServletContext object is used to communicate with the servlet container when we want to perform actions such as writing to a log file or dispatching requests. There is only one ServletContext object per web application (per JVM). This is initialized when the web application is started and destroyed only when the web application is being shut down.

The ServletContextListener interface is a lifecycle interface that programmers implement to listen for changes to the ServletContext. This means that lifecycle events such as the initialization and destruction of the ServletContext trigger a ServletContextListener implementation listening to this web application. A ServletContextAttributeListener object performs a similar function, but listens for changes to the attribute list on the ServletContext.

RequestDispatcher defines an object that manages client requests by directing them to the appropriate resource on the server.

The servlet container provides classes that implement the ServletRequest and ServletResponse interfaces. These classes provide the client request information to the servlet and the object used to send a response to the client.

The SingleThreadModel interface has no methods and is used to ensure that a servlet can only handle one request at a time.

Filter, FilterChain, and FilterConfig are new to version 2.3 of the API. They make up the filtering functionality now available to developers. A Filter can be used to filter both requests to and responses from from a servlet.

> *Filtering has a wide range of uses including authentication, logging, and localization. We will cover it in detail in Chapter 7.*

The javax.servlet Classes

There are seven classes contained in this package (plus two exception classes that we'll cover in a moment):

- ❑ GenericServlet
- ❑ ServletContextEvent
- ❑ ServletContextAttributeEvent
- ❑ ServletInputStream
- ❑ ServletOutputStream
- ❑ ServletRequestWrapper
- ❑ ServletResponseWrapper

The GenericServlet abstract class can be used to develop protocol-independent servlets, and requires only that we implement the service() method. Although it is more common to use the HttpServlet class (from the javax.servlet.http package) instead for use on the web over the HTTP protocol, it is relatively straightforward to extend from GenericServlet and implement our own protocol-based servlet. The biggest headache would be ensuring that the protocol was fully and accurately implemented.

The two classes `ServletContextEvent` and `ServletContextAttributeEvent` are the event classes used for notification about changes to the `ServletContext` and to its attributes respectively.

The `ServletInputStream` and the `ServletOutputStream` classes provide input and output streams for reading or sending binary data to and from the client.

Finally, the new wrapper classes (`ServletRequestWrapper` and `ServletResponseWrapper`) provide useful implementations of the `ServletRequest` and `ServletResponse` interfaces. These implementations can then be subclassed, to allow programmers to adapt or enhance the functionality of the wrapped object for their own web application. This might be done to implement a basic protocol agreed between the client and server, or to transparently adapt requests or responses to a specific format required by the web application.

The javax.servlet Exception Classes

There are two exceptions contained in the `javax.servlet` package:

- ❑ `ServletException`
- ❑ `UnavailableException`

`ServletException` is a general exception that a servlet can throw if it hits problems and has to give up. This might be thrown to indicate a problem with the user's request, processing the request, or sending the response.

This exception is thrown to the servlet container, and at this point the application loses control of the request being processed. The servlet container then has the responsibility of cleaning up the request and returning a response to the client. Depending upon the container's implementation and configuration, the container may return an error page to the user indicating a server problem.

Generally though, it is best only to throw `ServletExceptions` as a last resort. The preferred mechanism for dealing with an 'insurmountable problem' is to handle the problem, and then return an indication of the problem to the client.

The `UnavailableException` should be thrown when a filter or servlet is temporarily or permanently unavailable. This could apply to resources required by the servlet to process requests (such as a database, a Domain Name Server, or another servlet) not being available, or it may simply be that the servlet load factor is too high.

The Servlet Interface

All servlets must implement the `Servlet` interface, although most will extend from a class that has already implemented `Servlet`.

The API provides the abstract class `GenericServlet` that implements the `Servlet` interface. It provides concrete implementations of all but the `service()` method defined in the `Servlet` interface, so when we extend `GenericServlet` we must at least implement this method. However, it also means that when we are developing a servlet, much of the standard work can be left to the methods inherited from `GenericServlet`. We only need to override the other methods if we specifically want to alter the default implementation. We will be looking more closely at `GenericServlet` in the next section.

Lifecycle of a Servlet

The `Servlet` interface defines the following three lifecycle methods, called by the servlet container:

```
public void init(ServletConfig config) throws ServletException
public void service(ServletRequest req, ServletResponse res)
                                    throws ServletException, IOException
public void destroy()
```

When we talk about the servlet's **lifecycle** we are talking about the period of time that a servlet instance is created, 'lives', and dies. The servlet container will create instances of the servlet according to its design and how often the servlet is called. The container has a lot of freedom in managing the servlet's lifecycle, in that it can keep a single instance of a servlet around for a long time to process requests, pool a number of instances of the servlet to process requests, or instantiate a new servlet for each request. Obviously it makes sense for the container to manage servlet instances according to some optimal pattern of usage so as not to waste resources on the server.

The servlet lifecycle is clearly defined. A client makes a request to the web server, which redirects the request (as necessary) to the servlet container:

1. The loading and instantiation of the servlet is the responsibility of the servlet container. The container must locate the servlet classes, load the servlet using normal class loading procedures, and instantiate it so that it is ready for use.

2. The container initializes the servlet by calling the servlet's `init()` method. The container passes an object implementing the `ServletConfig` interface via the `init()` method. This object provides the servlet with access to the object that implements the `ServletContext` interface (which describes the servlet's run-time environment). The `init()` method is also responsible for performing any other initialization required by the servlet, which can include setting up resources that the servlet will require to process requests, such as database connections.

3. In the event that the servlet is unsuccessfully initialized, an `UnavailableException` or `ServletException` is thrown, the servlet is released, and attempts are made to instantiate and initialize a new servlet.

4. The servlet is now ready to handle client requests. The request and response information is wrapped in `ServletRequest` and `ServletResponse` objects respectively, which are then passed to the servlet's `service()` method. This method is then responsible for processing the request and returning the response.

5. Instances of both `ServletException` and `UnavailableException` can occur during request handling. If an exception is thrown the container is forced to clean up the request, possibly unloading the instance and calling the `destroy()` method of the servlet.

6. Once the servlet container decides to remove the servlet from service, the container must allow any `service()` method calls to terminate (or timeout). Then, it will call the servlet's `destroy()` method. Once the `destroy()` method has completed, the container will release the servlet instance for garbage collection. If it needs another instance of the servlet to process requests it must start the process again.

Obtaining Initialization Parameters

The `Servlet` interface defines another method that servlets must implement:

```
public ServletConfig getServletConfig()
```

The `getServletConfig()` method is designed to return a reference to the `ServletConfig` object, that contains initialization and startup parameters for the servlet. This object is passed to the servlet during initialization, and can be stored for future use by the servlet, although how the servlet will treat the `ServletConfig` object is not specified. Normally it is expected that a reference to it is stored in the servlet so that it can be accessed in the `getServletConfig()` method.

Servlet Threading Issues

It is important to understand that the container/server may receive many requests, and often these will occur simultaneously or virtually simultaneously so the container will be responsible for establishing separate threads to process each request. The `service()` method may be called simultaneously by the container in different threads to process many different requests.

While the container has the responsibility for handling the requests in separate threads, this can have implications for our servlets. We need to code our servlets to be thread-safe. For example, consider a class variable `count`. If this was accessed and updated from a `service()` method more than once, its value on the second and subsequent accesses could be altered by another thread servicing another request. Since the value can be altered in another thread, its value may become meaningless unless we manage or **synchronize** access to it. Servlets provide an alternative to this with the `SingleThreadModel` interface, which we will look at later in this chapter. Chapter 11 also looks in more detail at the synchronization issue.

Efficient Servlet Lifecycle Management

When the servlet instance is being unloaded from memory by the servlet container, the servlet container will call the `destroy()` method on the servlet. This is only called once all calls to the `service()` method underway have completed or timed out. Servlet instances may be unloaded at any time by the servlet container according to the container's policies. Obviously, the container has to have sensible policies regarding the loading and unloading of servlet instances, as there is a performance cost with inefficient or excessive object creation and destruction. For example, it would not usually make sense to instantiate a new servlet for every request, so containers usually reuse the instance to service more than one request.

The purpose of the `destroy()` method is to make sure that any finalization of data, releasing of resources, and so on, is carried out before the servlet instance is lost. This is one of the reasons why a server should always be shut down 'gracefully', using the appropriate shutdown command, rather than just closing the server window. Shutting down a server gracefully allows the server to complete any requests that are under way and to call the `destroy()` methods on any remaining servlet instances, ensuring no data is lost and resources are released properly.

Obtaining Information About a Servlet

There is one more method from the `Servlet` interface that must be implemented by servlets:

```
public String getServletInfo() throws ServletException, IOException
```

The `getServletInfo()` method is designed to return a `String` object containing information about the servlet. This is expected to contain information such as the servlet's author, the version, and copyright information. This method is designed to allow web server administration tools to display information about the servlet. What it actually returns is up to the programmer. The default implementations return an empty string.

The GenericServlet Class

The `GenericServlet` class is an abstract class implementation of the `Servlet` interface. It implements the methods as defined by the `Servlet` interface, and servlets normally extend from this class. In addition to those methods defined in the `Servlet` interface, `GenericServlet` defines several other methods. Let's now take a tour of the methods of this class. We'll group these methods by functionality.

Lifecycle Methods

`Servlet` initialization is carried out by an `init()` method:

```
public void init(ServletConfig config)
public void init()
```

You should recognize the first form of the `init(ServletConfig)` method; it is required by the `Servlet` interface. When called by the container, the `GenericServlet` implementation of the `init(ServletConfig)` method stores a reference to the `ServletConfig` object in the servlet, and then calls the second `init()` method above. This version of the `init()` method is provided as a convenience, to eliminate the need to call the superclass method (via `super.init(config)`) in your code.

> If you choose to override the **init(ServletConfig)** method, it is up to you to make sure that it calls the superclass method, otherwise the reference to the **ServletConfig** object will be lost:

As we saw in the previous section, the following method processes the client requests and is called by the servlet container:

```
public abstract void service(ServletRequest req, ServletResponse res)
```

It is declared abstract, because subclasses must implement a `service()` method to process their request (this is the purpose of the servlet!).

Called by the servlet container, the `destroy()` method is overridden if there is any persistence of data required, or if resources must be released:

```
public void destroy()
```

Servlet Environment Methods

Aside from getServletConfig() and getServletName(), the GenericServlet class provides a number of additional methods relating to the servlet and its environment.

With the ServletContext object that is contained in the ServletConfig object, we can access information about the servlet container in which the servlet is running. Calling the following method returns this ServletContext object:

```
public ServletContext getServletContext()
```

The getInitParameterNames() method returns an Enumeration of the names of the initialization parameters for the servlet:

```
public java.util.Enumeration getInitParameterNames()
```

This allows the servlet to access all initialization parameters without having to know their names in advance. When we have retrieved these names, we can use the following method to access their values:

```
public String getInitParameter(String name)
```

If the named parameter does not exist, null is returned.

Every servlet is known to the servlet container by a name. As we will learn in Chapter 4, this can be configured in the web application setup. Calling the following method will retrieve the name of this servlet's instance:

```
public String getServletName()
```

Utility Methods

Two logging methods are also provided by GenericServlet to allow the servlet to write to the web application's log file:

```
public void log(String msg)
public void log(String message, java.lang.Throwable t)
```

This is for debugging and development information mainly, but anything can be written to this file if required. It is also preferable to writing to the console. Frequently programmers are required to support production applications where they only have limited access to the server on which the application runs. Access may be limited to shared directories, such as log files, so it is good practice to use the log files rather than the console.

The location and name of the log file is normally specified on the application configuration, but the exact method is dependent on the container implementation.

A word of warning: while in test and pre-production environments verbose logging may be useful, in practice there can be performance implications for frequent logging for active, high-load applications. In production environments we should only be logging important information such as web application errors, security information, and other critical information.

If we use the log files excessively in busy production environments not only do we suffer the I/O costs of writing to the file excessively (with the overall implications for the server performance), but also we can lose sight of the important and useful information in the logs. Logging limited at most to the entry and exit of methods (and parameters/return values) is useful to identify the source of a problem, but this should be restricted only to important methods and points in the process.

Creating a Basic Servlet

So far we have learned the basic concepts behind the servlet API that allow us to create basic servlets. At this point we are ready to use what we have learned, by developing a `BasicServlet` that extends from the `GenericServlet` class to output a basic HTML web page. The servlet will output the following information:

- The name of the servlet (as known to the container)
- The number of times that the servlet has been executed
- The date and time that the servlet instance was initialized
- The current date and time on the server (for comparison)
- The servlet information available to the container

Once we have walked through the code, we will look at what we need to do to get this example running on the Catalina servlet container provided by the Tomcat web server.

```
package basicServlets;

import javax.servlet.GenericServlet;
import javax.servlet.ServletConfig;
import javax.servlet.ServletRequest;
import javax.servlet.ServletResponse;
import javax.servlet.ServletException;
import java.io.IOException;
import java.io.PrintWriter;
import java.util.Date;

public class BasicServlet extends GenericServlet {
```

The `BasicServlet` class extends from `GenericServlet` and implements the three `Servlet` lifecycle methods. The `service()` method is required, but overriding the initialization and destruction methods is optional. Additionally, we will also override the `getServletInfo()` method:

```
private static int count = 0;
private static final Date initialDate = new Date();
private Date thisDate;
```

We have three variables in this servlet. The first two are static. The integer count is used to monitor how many times the servlet has been run since the servlet was originally loaded (note that if the current servlet instance is unloaded it still maintains the count). Similarly, the initialDate object is designed to store the exact date and time the first instance was created. The thisDate object holds the exact date and time that the current instance was created. Realistically both the initialDate object and the thisDate object will be equal (or almost) as they are created on the first call. However, if this servlet instance was unloaded, or more than one instance was created, then these Date objects would differ.

In the init() method, we call the superclass init() method first to ensure this is processed and that the ServletConfig object reference is stored. We also initialize the thisDate variable here. Finally we also log the time the servlet instance was initialized. Also included is a (commented out) println() statement to the console so that you can see the initialization happening as you execute it:

```
public void init(ServletConfig config) throws ServletException {
    super.init(config);
    thisDate = new Date();
    //System.out.println("BasicServlet initialized at:" + thisDate);
    log("BasicServlet initialized at:" + thisDate);
}
```

The service() method will process the requests. In this case we output a simple HTML page using the PrintWriter object of the ServletResponse object:

```
public void service(ServletRequest request, ServletResponse response)
                            throws ServletException, IOException {
```

We first set the type of the data that we are going to send back to the client ("text/html") and then call the getWriter() method on the Response object. In the next section we will look at the ServletResponse interface in more detail:

```
response.setContentType("text/html");
PrintWriter out = response.getWriter();
```

The HTML page itself is simply output as text, sent to the PrintWriter object's println() method:

```
out.println("<html><head><title>BasicServlet</title></head>");
```

We include the getServletName() method so we can see what the servlet container knows this servlet instance as:

```
out.println("<body><h2>" + getServletName() + "</h2>");
out.println("This is a basic servlet.<br>");
out.println("<table><tr>");
```

We then output a small table with values that include the count of how many times the servlet has been executed since startup:

```
out.println("<tr><td><b>BasicServlet executed:</b></td><td>" +
            (++count) + " time(s)</td></tr>");
```

We also output the time the first instance of the servlet was initialized, the time the current instance was initialized, and the current time for comparison:

```
out.println("<tr><td><b>BasicServlet initialized at:</b></td><td>" +
            initialDate + "</td></tr>");
out.println("<tr><td><b>This instance initialized at:</b></td><td>" +
            thisDate + "</td></tr>");
out.println("<tr><td><b>Current Time:</b></td><td>" +
            new Date() + "</td></tr>");
```

Finally we call the getServletInfo() method to see what this information is, and close the page:

```
out.println("<tr><td><b>Servlet Information:</b></td><td>" +
            getServletInfo() + "</td></tr></body></html>");
out.close();
}
```

We have implemented the getServletInfo() method with information about the servlet version and date:

```
public String getServletInfo() {
    return "basicServlets.BasicServlet; Version: 1.0; (C) 2002.";
}
```

Finally we implement a destroy() method. It's not really necessary here (we haven't opened or created any resources that need to be explicitly released), but in this case, for illustrative purposes, it prints to the log when it is destroyed. Again there is a System.out.println() statement you can uncomment, in case you want to see this process on the console:

```
public void destroy() {
    //System.out.println("BasicServlet: destroy method called");
    log("destroy method called");
}
}
```

We have just created a basic servlet extending from the GenericServlet, which is our first step towards building full web applications. Throughout the chapter we will build on this to enhance our understanding of the Servlet API classes and interfaces. First we will have a look at how to compile this servlet and execute it on Tomcat.

Compiling and Running Servlets on Tomcat

In this section we will explain how to get your servlet running on Tomcat.

Appendix A contains instructions on how to acquire, install, and set up Tomcat on your computer. This section assumes that you have a basic installation of Tomcat running on your system.

To get the servlet running, we need to create a directory structure to house servlets. First locate your web applications directory in Tomcat, which will be located in the `%CATALINA_HOME%\webapps` directory (here `%CATALINA_HOME%` is the root directory of your Tomcat installation).

We need to create the application directory structure as shown below in the webapps directory:

```
servletAPI\
          WEB-INF
          classes\
                    basicServlets\
                    personalPortal\
          src\
              basicServlets\
              personalPortal\
```

Make sure the names of the folders are exactly as written above (including the same case). Place the `BasicServlet.java` file in the `basicServlets` subfolder of the sourcecode directory (`src`), ready for compilation. Then compile it from the `src` directory using the `javac` compiler, including `%CATALINA_HOME%\common\lib\servlet.jar` in your classpath. Finally, move the resulting class file into the `classes\basicServlets` directory, and restart Tomcat.

When the server is restarted, you can access the servlet on the following URL:

http://localhost:8080/servletAPI/servlet/basicServlets.BasicServlet

If you have successfully deployed your servlet, you should see the following page, which shows the information we wanted to know about the servlet:

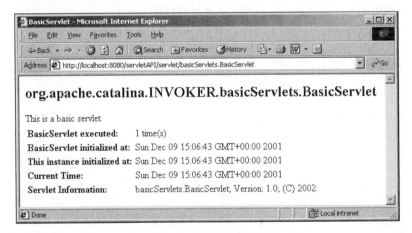

We are now going to expand our servlet horizons. We will start by considering the request-response cycle of the servlet model, and how the Servlet API wraps up the client request information and our servlet's response in the provided interfaces.

The Request-Response Cycle

Servlets are designed to receive client requests and to develop a response to return to the client. The client's request is mapped to a servlet by the container. We can specify which client requests are mapped to which servlets by configuring the web application correctly; we will come back to this issue in Chapter 4. The container also has the responsibility of processing the request into an object-oriented format that the servlet can process, which it does by wrapping the request in a `ServletRequest` object.

Request-Response Interfaces and Wrapper Classes

The `ServletRequest` interface defines the Request object that will wrap the client request, which is then passed to the servlet for processing. Similarly, the `ServletResponse` interface defines an object that is passed to the servlet in order to give the servlet access to the container's response sending mechanism.

These interfaces define the methods that are made available to the servlet for interpreting the request and returning a response. The API also makes available two convenience wrapper classes that fully wrap the functionality of their corresponding interfaces.

There are also two convenience wrapper classes included in the Servlet API to wrap the Request and Response objects (`javax.servlet.ServletRequestWrapper` and `javax.servlet.ServletResponseWrapper`). They make it easier to implement the Request and Response interfaces and extend their functionality. By default their methods call the methods of the wrapped object.

In this section we are going to take a close look at the servlet Request-Response interfaces. We will also build an example servlet, `RequestResponseServlet`, which demonstrates the use of the Request and Response objects, and returns the data to the client in HTML format.

Implementing the RequestResponseServlet

The RequestResponseServlet class extends the GenericServlet class. The purpose of the servlet is to generate a page containing two tables, one containing information about the request, the other containing information about the response from the servlet. Here's what the request table looks like:

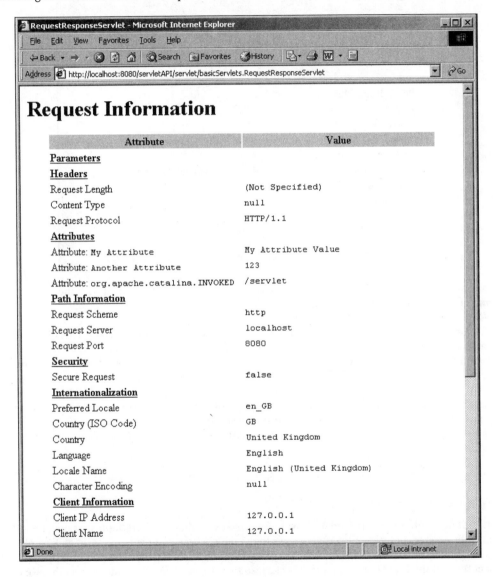

Scrolling down the page brings us to the response table:

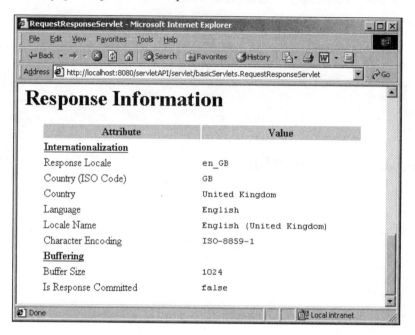

As you can see, each table simply consists of parameter-value pairs. We'll deal with the meaning of each parameter as we discuss them during the course of the chapter.

The RequestResponseServlet makes use of a simple HTMLTable utility class. This class is designed to simplify the process of creating an HTML table of data, so that we can concentrate on understanding the methods we are calling in the request and response objects. We will take a look at this utility class first, and then we'll discuss the servlet itself.

To run the example, you will need to add the two Java sourcecode files into the basicServlets package source directory. Compile the sourcecode and move the classes into the classes\basicServlets directory, and then restart Tomcat. You can then access the servlet on the following URL:

http://localhost:8080/servletAPI/servlet/basicServlet.RequestResponseServlet

The HTMLTable Utility Class

The HTMLTable utility class is used to provide a simple two column HTML table that may be dynamically created and grown by adding rows to the table. Once complete, the HTMLTable object will output a String or StringBuffer object representing the HTML table. The point of this class is to abstract some of the HTML process into this class, so that we can reuse the code, and so that we can move some of the HTML away from the servlet code. We will reuse this class in the following chapter as well.

We begin the class by creating three `StringBuffer` class variables to hold the table head code, the foot code, and a `rows` variable to store all of the added rows:

```
package basicServlets;

public class HTMLTable {
  private StringBuffer head;
  private StringBuffer rows;
  private StringBuffer foot;
```

In the `HTMLTable()` constructor method we initialize and create the table head and foot objects, and initialize the `rows` object to be ready to store row data:

```
public HTMLTable() {
   head = new StringBuffer();
   head.append("<table width=\"90%\" align=\"center\">");
   head.append("<tr><th width=\"50%\"
                        bgcolor=\"lightgrey\">Attribute</td>");
   head.append("<th width=\"50%\"
                    bgcolor=\"lightgrey\">Value</td></tr>");

   rows = new StringBuffer();

   foot = new StringBuffer();
   foot.append("</table>");
}
```

The `appendTitleRow()` method allows us to add a title to a section of the table:

```
public void appendTitleRow(String attribute) {
   rows.append("<tr><td colspan=2><b><u>").append(attribute);
   rows.append("</u></b></td></tr>");
}
```

We provide an `appendRow()` method to add rows to the table, or strictly speaking to add data to the `rows` `StringBuffer` object. We have three versions of this method overloaded, so that we can not only have two `String` parameters, but also allow the second variable to be an `int` or `boolean`. The last two overloaded methods simply convert the parameter into a `String` and forward to the first method. This allows easy maintenance or update of the HTML code, if required:

```
public void appendRow(String attribute, String value) {
   rows.append("<tr><td>").append(attribute);
   rows.append("</td><td><code>").append(value);
   rows.append("</code></td></tr>");
}

public void appendRow(String attribute, int value) {
   appendRow(attribute, new Integer(value).toString());
}

public void appendRow(String attribute, boolean value) {
   appendRow(attribute, new Boolean(value).toString());
}
```

Finally we provide a `toString()` method that overrides the `Object.toString()` method, so that printing an `HTMLTable` object will automatically call the overridden `toString()` method and output a well-formatted HTML table. We do this by appending the `rows` and `foot` to the head `StringBuffer` object. Similar to the `toString()` method, we also provide a `toStringBuffer()` method that returns the same appended HTML table in `StringBuffer` format:

```java
public String toString() {
    return head.append(rows).append(foot).toString();
}

public StringBuffer toStringBuffer() {
    return head.append(rows).append(foot);
}
}
```

The RequestResponseServlet

Our servlet extends the `GenericServlet` class and implements the `service()` method to build two tables of information about the Request and Response objects:

```java
package basicServlets;

import javax.servlet.*;
import javax.servlet.http.*;
import java.io.*;
import java.util.*;

public class RequestResponseServlet extends GenericServlet {
```

The `service()` method calls the `getRequestTable()` and `getResponseTable()` methods to build HTML tables of request and response information. These are the real content of the page and we will implement these methods later in this section, as we come to understand the `ServletRequest` and `ServletResponse` interfaces in more depth:

```java
public void service(ServletRequest request, ServletResponse response)
                             throws ServletException, IOException {
    StringBuffer requestTable = getRequestTable(request);
    StringBuffer responseTable = getResponseTable(request, response);
```

Then we display a simple HTML page with the two tables included. This completes the request processing:

```java
response.setContentType("text/html");
PrintWriter out = response.getWriter();

//HTML page
out.println("<html><head><title>RequestResponseServlet</title>");
out.println("</head><body>");
out.println("<h1>Request Information</h1>" + requestTable + "<hr>");
out.println("<h1>Response Information</h1>" + responseTable);
out.println("</body></html>");
out.close();
}
```

So, the most interesting part of the processing of the Request and Response objects takes place in the getRequestTable() and getResponseTable() methods. These methods take their corresponding ServletRequest or ServletResponse objects as parameter. They then use these objects to extract information about the request/response, and to construct an HTML table. As we discuss the methods of the ServletRequest and ServletResponse interfaces, we will develop these methods too.

The ServletRequest Interface

The ServletRequest interface wraps the client request, and provides methods that make the request information available to the servlet.

Obtaining Request Parameter Names and Values

Often the first information that we want to extract from a client request is information about the parameters given as part of the request. This usually tells the servlet what the client is requesting.

To add flexibility to the request, we don't need to know the names of the parameters that will be submitted at the development stage. Instead, we call methods that return the names of the parameters contained in the request, and methods that return the values of these parameters.

For example, we can call the getParameterNames() method to receive an Enumeration of String objects corresponding to the names of all the parameters supplied with the request. The method returns an empty Enumeration object if no parameters were supplied:

```
public java.util.Enumeration getParameterNames()
```

To find the value of a specific parameter we call the getParameter() method:

```
public String getParameter(String name)
```

This method returns null if the parameter was not included in the request. If more than one value may be returned for the parameter we should use the getParameterValues() method instead:

```
public String[] getParameterValues(String name)
```

This method returns a String array of values for the specified parameter; we can then iterate through the array to process all the values. The String array is empty if no parameters matching the name are included in the request.

We may also get a Map object, which has a mapping of all of the request parameters' names to their values, using the getParameterMap() method:

```
public java.util.Map getParameterMap()
```

The names of the parameters are the keys of the Map object, and the values of the Map object are String arrays.

Retrieving Request Parameter Values in getRequestTable()

We start our getRequestTable() method by creating the HTMLTable object that we will use to create the HTML table:

```
private StringBuffer getRequestTable(ServletRequest request) {
  HTMLTable table = new HTMLTable();
  table.appendTitleRow("Parameters");
```

After adding the title row, we use getParameterNames() to get an Enumeration of the parameter names so that we can process the parameters. We use a loop to iterate through the Enumeration:

```
Enumeration e = request.getParameterNames();
while (e.hasMoreElements()) {
  String paramName = (String)e.nextElement();
```

Once we have extracted the current parameter name, we call the getParameterValues() method on the request object with the name of the parameter we are looking for. This method returns a String array of value(s). Then we loop through the array to add each value associated with the parameter to the table:

```
String[] paramValues = request.getParameterValues(paramName);
if (paramValues != null) {
  for (int i = 0; i < paramValues.length; i++) {
    table.appendRow("Parameter: <code>" + paramName +
                    "</code>", paramValues[i]);
  }
}
}
```

Accessing Request Header Information

There are three methods that allow the servlet to access information provided in the header of the request. To get the size of the request (useful if a file or other large object is attached) we can use the getContentLength() method, which returns the length in bytes, or −1 if it is unknown:

```
public int getContentLength()
```

The getContentType() method is useful if we wish to determine the data type of the data in the request body:

```
public String getContentType()
```

It returns the MIME type of the request (if known) or null (if unknown). For example, if the client was submitting serialized Java objects to the servlet, the MIME type would probably be application/x-java-serialized-object, which is the standard MIME type for serialized Java objects.

The last method, getProtocol(), will return the name and version of the protocol that was used in making the request (for example HTTP/1.1):

```
public String getProtocol()
```

Accessing Header Information in getRequestTable()

In our example servlet, we append the title to the table and extract the content-length header from the request. If the client supplied this value, it will be some positive integer value. Otherwise, if the client did not supply it, it will be –1. In the case that it is not supplied we indicate this fact, otherwise we print out the request content size:

```
table.appendTitleRow("Headers");
int requestLength = request.getContentLength();
if (requestLength == -1) {
  table.appendRow("Request Length", "(Not Specified)");
} else {
    table.appendRow("Request Length", requestLength);
}
```

Then we find the content type and protocol used in the request:

```
table.appendRow("Content Type", request.getContentType());
table.appendRow("Request Protocol", request.getProtocol());
```

Using Attributes in the Request

Attributes are the objects (if any) associated with the request. Attributes are similar to request parameters, but instead of being set by the client, they are set by the servlet container, or they may be set by a previous servlet that used the `javax.servlet.RequestDispatcher` to forward the request and attached information (Java objects) as attributes to the request. Also, instead of just `Strings` for values, attribute values can be any Java objects.

The `getAttributeNames()` method is used to return an `Enumeration` object of the names of the attributes for this request:

```
public java.util.Enumeration getAttributeNames()
```

The following method returns the specified attribute or `null` if the attribute does not exist:

```
public Object getAttribute(String name)
```

The attribute returned is of type `Object`, so to use it as any other type of object it will have to be cast into its specific class type:

The `storeAttribute()` method is used to store the specified `Object` with the name in the `request` object. It is normally used when the request will be forwarded to another servlet (or filter) for processing:

```
public void setAttribute(String name, Object o)
```

Conversely, the `removeAttribute()` method allows us to remove the specified attribute from the request. This is normally used when the request will be forwarded to another servlet (or filter) for processing:

```
public void removeAttribute(String name)
```

Setting and Accessing Request Attributes in getRequestTable()

Since there are no attributes already set, we will first set two attributes, so that we can access them. Of course, we would not normally need to set them in the same method that we would use them in, but we will demonstrate both here:

```
    table.appendTitleRow("Attributes");
    request.setAttribute("My Attribute", "My Attribute Value");
    request.setAttribute("Another Attribute", "123");
```

The code to output the attributes is similar to that used for the request parameters. We retrieve an Enumeration of attribute names, and loop through it, printing out the attribute name and the object stored:

```
    Enumeration enum = request.getAttributeNames();
    while (enum.hasMoreElements()) {
      String attributeName = (String)enum.nextElement();
      Object attributeValue = request.getAttribute(attributeName);
      if (attributeValue != null) {
        table.appendRow("Attribute: <code>" + attributeName + "</code>",
                        attributeValue.toString());
      }
    }
```

Obtaining Request Path Information

We use path information from the request to interpret the request and gather additional information useful to processing the request. The ServletRequest interface provides a number of useful methods.

This method returns the protocol **scheme** used in making the request (for example http, https, or ftp);

public String getScheme()

For a servlet that may be configured to receive requests on more than one protocol, the scheme is important for the servlet to be able to extract additional information about the request. Different schemes may have different rules for constructing a URL, so the servlet needs to know the scheme so that the URL can be properly interpreted. Not all of the information needs to be included in the URL (for example, if not included, the port is assumed to be the default for that scheme).

An example could be a servlet that is configured to process e-mail (POP) requests and web (HTTP) requests, where in the first case it serves as a mail server, and in the second it could provide web access to the e-mail.

For further information on addressing schemes see:
http://www.w3.org/Addressing/schemes.html

The getServerName() method is used to find out the server name of the host that received this request:

public String getServerName()

This is the name by which the client addressed the server. It is possible that a web application may have more than one server name that it can be addressed by. This method will return the IP address if the server is addressed by its IP address instead of a name:

The following method returns the port number on which the server received the request:

```
public int getServerPort()
```

Various protocols have default ports that requests are made on; for instance HTTP has port 80 by default. However, servers can listen on any free valid port for requests.

Retrieving Request Path Information in getRequestTable()

We can use the methods above to access the request path information in our getRequestTable() method as follows:

```
table.appendTitleRow("Path Information");
table.appendRow("Request Scheme", request.getScheme());
table.appendRow("Request Server", request.getServerName());
table.appendRow("Request Port", request.getServerPort());
```

Checking for Secure Connections

The following method is made available to allow the servlet to determine if the request being served was made over a secure connection (for example over HTTPS):

```
public boolean isSecure()
```

For example, a servlet may check this before allowing the user to enter confidential information such as credit card or other personal/confidential data.

This method is particularly appropriate to filter or gateway servlets, that may be set up to intercept and redirect requests made to resources requiring a secure connection. Web applications transferring personal, payments, or other (moderately) sensitive data may require this.

You can find more information on security in Chapter 9.

Checking Security in getRequestTable()

In this example, we will only output whether the request was made over a secure connection, but we could, based on the result, modify the code to redirect to a secure connection, if we wanted:

```
table.appendTitleRow("Security");
table.appendRow("Secure Request", request.isSecure());
```

Using Internationalization in the Request

A few useful methods are available to developers of web applications that have international content or audience. These request methods are useful if you need servlets and filters to process and adapt request processing to different international locales and character sets.

A client may send, as part of its request, information on the preferred locales that it wishes to receive a response in. Providing a selection of locales is useful because the servlet may not support the client's first choice, but may support the second or third choice. The order of the locales supplied is the client's order of preference.

The getLocale() method will return the client's first choice of locale to be used in the request. The getLocales() method returns an Enumeration of Locale objects. By default, if no locale is specified by the client, these methods return the default locale for the server (for the getLocales() method this is a Enumeration of a single Locale object):

```
public java.util.Locale getLocale()
public java.util.Enumeration getLocales()
```

The getCharacterEncoding() method will return the name of the character encoding (null if not specified) used in the request. We may need this method to ensure that the request data is interpreted correctly, using the correct character encoding:

```
public String getCharacterEncoding()
```

The setCharacterEncoding() method can be used to override the character encoding used in the body of the request. It must be called before reading the request parameters or reading input using getReader() or getInputStream() methods. The default character encoding is ISO-8859-1 (Latin-1):

```
public void setCharacterEncoding(String env)
```

For more information on character sets see: http://www.iana.org/assignments/character-sets.

Using Internationalization in getRequestTable()

To find the locale used in the request (or the server's default if none was specified) we call the getLocale() method on the Request object:

```
table.appendTitleRow("Internationalization");
Locale locale = request.getLocale();
```

From the Locale object, we can extract information that we could use to customize our response to the client (see the Java documentation for more information about using the Locale class: http://java.sun.com/j2se/1.4/docs/api/java/util/Locale.html):

```
table.appendRow("Preferred Locale", locale.toString());
table.appendRow("Country (ISO Code)", locale.getCountry());
table.appendRow("Country", locale.getDisplayCountry());
table.appendRow("Language", locale.getDisplayLanguage());
table.appendRow("Locale Name", locale.getDisplayName());
table.appendRow("Character Encoding", request.getCharacterEncoding());
```

Reading from the Request

The Servlet API provides two I/O stream wrapper classes for the request input stream and the response output stream. The Request object allows us to read information from the request, such as included files or serialized Java objects. We can interpret the stream as binary or character data according to the method we call.

We use the getInputStream() method to get a ServletInputStream object if we need to read in a file, or serialized Java objects, or similar information from the client's request. We can use the returned object as an InputStream object, if required, which we can wrap in any valid input class (for example ObjectInputStream) to read in the data:

```
public ServletInputStream getInputStream()
```

Alternatively we can call the getReader() method to get a java.io.BufferedReader object to read the body of the request. We can read in character data using this method and wrap the returned object in a suitable input class to read the data (for example a FileReader could be used to read in a file of character data):

```
public java.io.BufferedReader getReader()
```

It is important to note that we can only call one of these methods, not both of them. If we try to call one of these methods, after already having called the other one, the method will throw an IllegalStateException to indicate that the other method was called to read the data. We can call the same method a second time, if necessary, to read more data, if the original reference to the input object is not available (such as in a method that is passed the Request object, but not the input object), however, we must ensure that the stream is not previously closed and that the end of the supplied data has not been reached.

Obtaining Client Information

The following methods return information contained in the request about the client:

```
public String getRemoteAddr()
public String getRemoteHost()
```

The getRemoteAddr() method will return the client's IP address. The server directs the response to this address. We can also access this, but while it may be useful for identifying clients in general terms, on its own it has limitations, because the IP address of a request can be that of a proxy server.

The getRemoteHost() method returns the client's fully-qualified name. Across the web we use names instead of IP addresses to access web sites normally. The mappings of IP addresses to names are stored on Domain Name Servers (DNS). For example, www.wrox.com would be the remote host that this method would return if the Wrox web server made the request. Note that this also assumes that a DNS is available to the container. If it cannot determine the fully qualified name (either no DNS is available, or the IP address was not recognized) it returns the IP address:

Retrieving Client Information in getRequestTable()

To round off the `getRequestTable()` method, we will add the client's IP address and name to the table. In this example, both methods might output the IP address (using `localhost` as the web address), although this depends on your network setup:

```
table.appendTitleRow("Client Information");
table.appendRow("Client IP Address", request.getRemoteAddr());
table.appendRow("Client Name", request.getRemoteHost());
```

We have also finished the method, so we return the table created, in a `StringBuffer` object.

```
return table.toStringBuffer();
}
```

Since we have now completed the method, let's remind ourselves of the table that it generates:

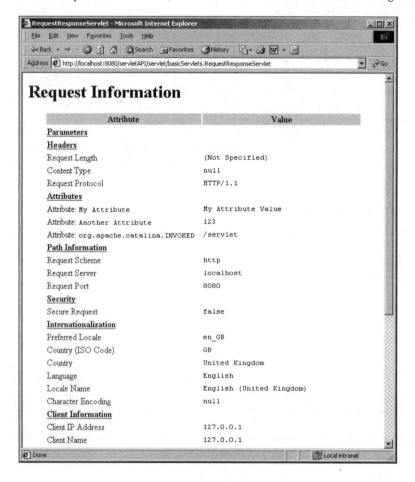

Creating a RequestDispatcher

Calling the getRequestDispatcher() method from the ServletRequest interface returns a RequestDispatcher object that wraps the resource specified in the path parameter:

```
public RequestDispatcher getRequestDispatcher(String path)
```

This allows the servlet to forward the request, or to include the requested resource's output in its own output. This method will return null if the container cannot return a dispatcher for the requested resource. The path parameter may map to another servlet, or a static resource, such as an HTML file.

The ServletResponse Interface

The ServletResponse object is used to send the servlet's response back to the client. It wraps the response (output stream, header information, data, and so on) in a single interface, allowing access to the methods that prepare and add content to the response.

Setting Content Length and MIME Types

The ServletResponse class determines two methods that can be used to set the content length and type of the response.

The setContentLength() method sets a header indicating the length of the response:

```
public void setContentLength(int len)
```

Setting this value too low will normally stop the server sending the excess data after the length specified, and most clients will stop reading the response after the specified length. Therefore, it is often better to let the server set this header (if it can buffer the full response before sending) or perhaps to leave it unset.

The second method is the setContentType() method. This is used to set the **MIME** (Multipurpose Internet Mail Extensions, RFC 2045 and 2046) type of the response. MIME types are used in many protocols other than HTTP to indicate the type of output or file following:

```
public void setContentType(String type)
```

This method should be called before any output is written to the output stream object. For example:

```
response.setContentType("text/html");
```

For standard web pages we always use "text/html", indicating text data in HTML format. If we were returning serialized Java objects we would use "application/x-java-serialized-object".

Using Internationalization in the Response

We can customize the response to the specific audience and we can also specify technical information on the locale and character set used in the response. The getLocale() and setLocale() methods allow access to and the resetting of the Locale of the response:

```
public java.util.Locale getLocale()
public void setLocale(java.util.Locale loc)
```

The setLocale() method *must* be called before a call to getWriter() as calling this method sets the character set to that appropriate for the current locale. Calling the setLocale() method after calling getWriter() has no effect, as the character set of the PrintWriter object has already been set.

The getCharacterEncoding() method returns the name of the character set used for the MIME body sent in the response. The default is ISO-8859-1 (Latin-1):

```
public String getCharacterEncoding()
```

Using Internationalization in getResponseTable()

Let's use what we have learned about the ServletResponse interface so far to begin construction of the getResponseTable() from our example RequestResponseServlet. Similar to the getRequestTable() method, getResponseTable() takes the ServletResponse object as a parameter and uses this object to extract information about the response in order to place it in an HTML table:

```
private StringBuffer getResponseTable(ServletRequest request,
                                      ServletResponse response) {
    HTMLTable table = new HTMLTable();
```

As we did from the Request object, we extract the Locale from the Response object, and then print out information about the Locale being used for the response:

```
        table.appendTitleRow("Internationalization");
        Locale locale = response.getLocale();
        table.appendRow("Response Locale", locale.toString());
        table.appendRow("Country (ISO Code)", locale.getCountry());
        table.appendRow("Country", locale.getDisplayCountry());
        table.appendRow("Language", locale.getDisplayLanguage());
        table.appendRow("Locale Name", locale.getDisplayName());
```

We can also set the Locale for the response (before the getWriter() method has been called), and in this case we are resetting it to its current value. We do this here because, with an international audience, we do not want to upset the responses for any reader. If you want to try setting the locale specifically, you can substitute the locale parameter with Locale.ENGLISH, replacing the ENGLISH constant with that relevant to your location. Check the API for the list of constants available, or construct a new Locale object for a location not specified:

```
        response.setLocale(locale);
        table.appendRow("Character Encoding", response.getCharacterEncoding());
```

Returning Data in the Response

To return data in the body of your servlet's response we need to access the output object from the Response object. We do this by calling one of the following methods:

```
public ServletOutputStream getOutputStream()
public java.io.PrintWriter getWriter()
```

We can call the getOutputStream() method that returns a ServletOutputStream object, which can be used directly or wrapped in a suitable I/O object (for example ObjectOutputStream for serialized Java objects) to output a response. Calling the getWriter() method instead returns a PrintWriter object that can be used to send text back to the client.

Only one of these methods should be called to send the response back to the client. Calling either constructs the corresponding output object, and we can't construct a second object to write to the same stream. So we need to decide what type of data we will be sending back to the client (for character data use getWriter()). If it will be a mixture of types, such as a serialized object first (to pass information about the following data) followed by other data (for example a file), use the getOutputStream() method, and wrap the OutputStream in appropriate classes for sending the data back.

Output Buffering

Buffering strategies for different servlet containers vary and are implemented in different ways. The container is not required to implement output buffering, and the choice of strategy used is up to the vendor to decide based on their implementation and their optimum performance objectives. A number of methods are available to servlets to improve or adapt the buffering strategy for their output.

The getBufferSize() method returns the size of the underlying buffer used (returns 0 if no buffering is used):

```
public int getBufferSize()
```

The setBufferSize() method allows the servlet to suggest a buffer size to the container:

```
public void setBufferSize(int size)
```

The container may chose not to implement the exact size specified by the servlet, but must implement the size to be *at least* the size specified. The setBufferSize() method *must* be called before any content is returned to the client or the method will throw a java.lang.IllegalStateException.

The isCommitted() method allows the servlet to find out if the response has begun to be sent to the client yet:

```
public boolean isCommitted()
```

The reset() method will clear any data in the buffer and the headers and status code if the response is not yet committed. If the response has been committed, it will throw an IllegalStateException:

```
public void reset()
```

Similarly, the `resetBuffer()` method will reset the data in the buffer (but not the headers or status code) and will throw the `IllegalStateException` if the response has been committed:

```
public void resetBuffer()
```

The `flushBuffer()` method will immediately flush the contents of the buffer to the client. This method will commit the response, which means that the status code and headers will be written out to the client:

```
public void flushBuffer()
```

Once a buffer is full, the container will instantly flush its contents to the client, which will commit the response.

Output Buffering in getResponseTable()

We will call a few of the buffering methods of the Response object and add the results to the table in our `getResponseTable()` method. We access the buffer size and then append it to the table:

```
table.appendTitleRow("Buffering");
int buffer = response.getBufferSize();
table.appendRow("Buffer Size", buffer);
```

We extract an attribute that may or may not be set. At this point it is not set, but in the `RequestDispatcherServlet` that we will see later this may be set. This indicates if the response it has been committed without the servlet knowing. The other servlet knows and sets that attribute as an indicator. This indicator prevents us resetting the buffer size after it has been committed:

```
String written = (String) request.getAttribute("buffer");
```

Next we increment the buffer size by one, each time this is called, but only if it has not been committed:

```
if (!response.isCommitted() && !"written".equalsIgnoreCase(written)) {
  response.setBufferSize(buffer + 1);
}
table.appendRow("Is Response Committed",
                new Boolean(response.isCommitted()).toString());
```

It is important to understand that each container request is altering the buffer size, so they have a cumulative effect. If we were to decrease the buffer size, the container may decide to keep a larger buffer size. However the container must implement at least the size we suggest (bigger if it chooses), so increasing the buffer size without careful consideration can cause the servlet to throw an exception due to the excessive memory allocated to the buffer.

> **Warning: If you increase the buffer size excessively (to the point where an exception is thrown), you will have to reset the buffer size to a sensible value (by recompiling with a new value, or restarting the server) before you can continue with this servlet.**

To see the effects of this try changing the argument to the `setBufferSize()` method to `"buffer *
2"`. Each time you execute the servlet, you are doubling the buffer size. Depending on your memory
allocation, fairly soon your servlet will throw an exception. When you do this, you have to reset the
buffer size to something sensible by recompiling (and not with `buffer + 1` but with something like
`1024`), or restarting the server.

At the end of the method, we return the table in a `StringBuffer` object:

```
        return table.toStringBuffer();
    }
}
```

Finally, let's remind you what the table produced by the `getResponseTable()` method looks like:

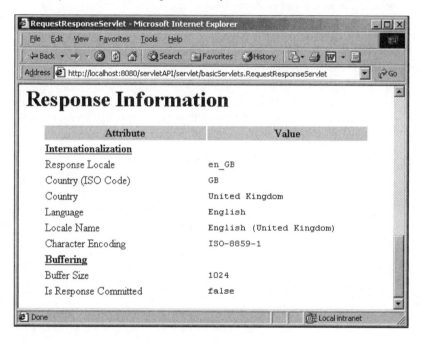

Input and Output Streams

In the previous section we noted two stream classes for reading in the request and writing back the response:

❑   `ServletInputStream`

❑   `ServletOutputStream`

These classes are abstract classes that the servlet container is responsible for implementing. The
`ServletInputStream` class extends from the abstract `java.io.InputStream` class. This is the base
class for input streams of bytes, and extending from it allows us to construct any necessary input reader
objects that take the `InputStream` class in the constructor. This allows us much greater flexibility in
terms of the data that we can read in from the client.

We can read any data that we can read from an InputStream. We can use the java.io.ObjectInputStream to read in Java serialized objects from a Java applet or application client. We could also use a java.io.BufferedInputStream to read from the input stream and buffer the input and to support the additional functionality this class provides.

Similarly the ServletOutputStream class extends from the abstract java.io.OutputStream class. This is the base class for outputting streams of bytes. This allows us to send our response data back with any I/O class that wraps the OutputStream class and enhances its functionality. Therefore, among other things, we can serialize Java objects back to the client using the java.io.ObjectOutputStream class, or use a PrintWriter to write text to the stream.

These streams provide servlets with the flexibility to support almost any type of client application, including browsers, Java applets, Java applications, and other applications. We use the streams to receive client data and to return our response back to the client. We rarely use the ServletInputStream and ServletOutputStream directly. Normally we wrap these objects in more suitable classes from the java.io package.

The ServletInputStream Class

The primary use of the ServletInputStream object is to wrap in a suitable InputStream class from the java.io package. It can be used wherever you would use an InputStream to construct an input class such as a DataInputStream for reading primitive types (and Strings), or an ObjectOutputStream for reading serialized Java objects.

For example, we could read in a number of Java objects as follows:

```
ServletInputStream input = request.getInputStream();
ObjectInputStream ois = new ObjectInputStream(input);

String someEvent = (String) ois.readObject();
Date eventDate = (Date) ois.readObject();

input.close();
```

As you can see, the three steps involved are as follows:

1. Access the request's InputStream and wrap it in an ObjectInputStream.

2. Read in the objects. If we know the objects that are being received, we can cast them into their sub-type. Alternatively we could perform a check (using the instanceof operator) before casting. Obviously if we try to cast an object invalidly we will get a run-time error.

3. Finally we close the stream.

The ServletInputStream class defines the following method, which is used to read from the input stream, a line at a time:

public readLine(byte[] b, int off, int len)

The method returns −1 if the end of the stream is reached before the line has been read.

ServletOutputStream class

Similar to the `ServletInputStream` class, the primary use by servlet programmers for this class is to wrap it in a suitable `OutputStream` class from the `java.io` package. It can be used wherever you would use an `OutputStream` to construct an output class.

For example, we could serialize a number of Java objects to a Java client, wrapping them in the `ObjectOutputStream` class as follows:

```
ServletOutputStream output = response.getOutputStream();
ObjectOutputStream oos = new ObjectOutputStream(output);

oos.writeObject("a String");
oos.writeObject(new Date());

output.close();
```

Here, the three steps involved are as follows:

1. Access the response's `OutputStream` and wrap it in an `ObjectOutputStream`

2. Write out the objects to the `ObjectOutputStream`

3. Close the stream

The `ServletOutputStream` class provides fifteen overloaded variants of the `print()` and `println()` methods.

The basic `print()` methods take the full range of primitive types (`boolean`, `char`, `double`, `float`, `int`, `long`) or a `String` object as parameters, and prints them to the stream. For example:

`public void print(boolean b)`

The following variant of the `println()` method writes a carriage return-line feed (CRLF) to the stream:

`public void println()`

The `println()` methods print the full range of primitive types (`boolean`, `char`, `double`, `float`, `int`, `long`) or a `String` object to the stream, followed by a carriage return-line feed (CRLF). For example:

`public void println(float f)`

We can also use the `java.io.PrintWriter` class for output. If we are returning character-based (text) data to the client, we would normally use a `PrintWriter` object to write to the stream. The process is similar to that shown for outputting with the `ServletOutputStream`. The main methods used are the `println()` or `print()` methods, similar to those of the `ServletOutputStream`. These are overloaded to take any primitive type or a `String` as parameter (see the Javadoc for more information at: http://java.sun.com/j2se/1.4/docs/api/java/io/PrintWriter.html). For example:

```
PrintWriter out = response.getWriter();

out.println("<html><head><title>The Page</title></head>");
out.println("<body>Some text</body></html>");

out.close();
```

Servlet-Container Communication

The servlet container is responsible for managing, creating, and destroying servlets in our web application. Therefore the container needs a way to communicate with the servlet and vice-versa.

The servlet container uses objects that implement specific interfaces to pass information into the servlet (such as initialization parameters), and to pass in information about the container or context that the servlet is being executed in.

These are implemented as interfaces because the interface defines the contract between the objects passed to the servlet and the servlet itself. However the specific implementation of the interface is the responsibility of the servlet container, and the container may incorporate other features customized to the container. The servlet is given access to the specific methods defined by the interfaces.

The ServletConfig interface is used by the servlet container to create an object that contains information that may be required to configure the servlet. It contains any servlet initialization parameters and the servlet's name (as known to the container), and has a ServletContext object. The ServletConfig object is passed to the init() method of the servlet, which then stores a reference to this object and, if required, extracts information required to initialize the servlet.

The container constructs the ServletContext interface object to hold information about the servlet and container environment (such as the server name and version, attributes, and so on). The ServletConfig object contains methods to access the ServletContext object, and vice versa.

ServletContext lifecycle events, such as changes to the ServletContext object or the ServletContext attributes, generate ServletContextEvent and ServletContextAttributeEvent objects. We can develop listener classes to listen for these events, implementing the ServletContextListener interface and the ServletContextAttributeListener interface respectively.

Implementing ContainerServlet

As we discuss the ServletConfig and ServletContext interfaces, we will implement an example ContainerServlet that will use many of the methods we will discuss.

The ContainerServlet class extends the GenericServlet class to provide a basic servlet that demonstrates the use of the ServletConfig and ServletContext objects, and returns the data to the client in HTML format. The servlet outputs a table of ServletConfig and ServletContext parameters, making use of the simple HTMLTable utility class that that we developed in the previous example (RequestResponseServlet):

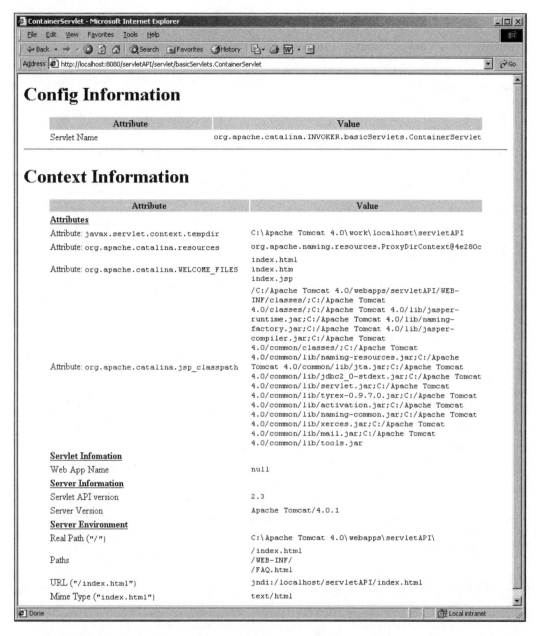

As with the previous example, if you wish to run the example yourself, you will need to place the sourcecode files in the basicServlets directory, compile them from the src directory, and then move the Java class files created to the classes\basicServlets directory.

You can access the servlet on the following URL:

http://localhost:8080/servletAPI/servlet/basicServlets.ContainerServlet

The ContainerServlet

The ContainerServlet example shows how we can retrieve information from the ServletConfig and ServletContext objects provided by the servlet container. Let's take a look at the sourcecode:

```
package basicServlets;

import javax.servlet.*;
import javax.servlet.http.*;
import java.io.*;
import java.util.*;

public class ContainerServlet extends GenericServlet {
```

The ContainerServlet class is very similar to the previous RequestResponseServlet class. We have implemented the service() method to process requests. We have two methods to build HTML tables, but in this case the tables contain information about the ServletConfig and ServletContext objects created by the servlet container:

```
public void service(ServletRequest request, ServletResponse response)
   throws ServletException, IOException {

   StringBuffer configTable = getConfigTable(getServletConfig());
   StringBuffer contextTable = getContextTable(getServletContext());

   response.setContentType("text/html");
   PrintWriter out = response.getWriter();

   //HTML page
   out.println("<html><head><title>ContainerServlet</title></head><body>");
   out.println("<h1>Config Information</h1>" + configTable + "<hr>");
   out.println("<h1>Context Information</h1>" + contextTable);
   out.println("</body></html>");
   out.close();
}
```

As we look at the methods available in the ServletConfig and ServletContext interfaces, we will build up the getConfigTable() and getContextTable() methods that give examples of how to use the interface methods.

The ServletConfig Interface

The ServletConfig interface is implemented by the GenericServlet class, so you should not be surprised to find that every method in this interface is implemented (with others) in the GenericServlet class. In fact, when you call a method on the GenericServlet class that is specified by the interface, the GenericServlet class calls the same method on the ServletConfig object passed to it (by the servlet container) in the init() method. The GenericServlet class implements this interface as a convenience, so that we do not have to directly reference the ServletConfig object every time we call the method. This means that the method calls in our example should be relatively straightforward, and analogous to some of the methods called on the BasicServlet example.

Retrieving Information from ServletConfig

We do not necessarily need to know the servlet initialization parameter names at development time (although usually we would). We can use the `getInitParameterNames()` method to return an `Enumeration` of the parameter names that we can iterate though to extract the corresponding values:

```
public java.util.Enumeration getInitParameterNames()
```

The `getInitParameter()` method is used to extract the initialization parameter values set for the servlet:

```
public String getInitParameter(String name)
```

The following method returns a reference to the `ServletContext` object:

```
public ServletContext getServletContext()
```

The following section details the methods that may be used on objects of this type. The servlet container knows each servlet by a specific name (this is normally set in the deployment descriptor file, see Chapter 4 for more information). This name can be retrieved by the `getServletName()` method (essentially the same as the `GenericServlet.getServletName()` method):

```
public String getServletName()
```

Using ServletConfig in getConfigTable()

The `getConfigTable()` method takes a reference to the `ServletConfig` object and returns an HTML table with information from the `ServletConfig` object. Strictly speaking, since this method is declared within the servlet we do not have to pass the `ServletConfig` object in as a parameter, because we could just call the `getServletConfig()` method to get a reference to it. However, this is included as a parameter because we could then refactor this method (and any additional methods) into a separate class, if required, without modification:

```java
private StringBuffer getConfigTable(ServletConfig config) {
    HTMLTable table = new HTMLTable();
```

We add the servlet name to the table, followed by the initialization parameters (if any). In this case we have not configured any for this servlet. We will explain how to add initialization parameters in Chapter 4:

```java
    table.appendRow("Servlet Name", config.getServletName());
    Enumeration e = config.getInitParameterNames();
    while (e.hasMoreElements()) {
        String paramName = (String)e.nextElement();
        String paramValue = config.getInitParameter(paramName);
        table.appendRow("Parameter: <code>" + paramName +
                        "</code>", paramValue);
    }
    return table.toStringBuffer();
}
```

Since we haven't added any initialization parameters, the Config Information table only shows the servlet name:

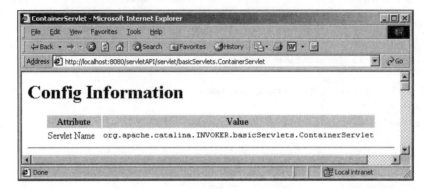

The ServletContext Interface

The `ServletContext` object contains information about the servlet and container environment. The servlet container can give the servlet additional information not already provided by this interface by adding an **attribute** object to the `ServletContext`.

Accessing ServletContext Attributes

Four methods exist to access attributes attached to the `ServletContext`. This method is used to return an `Enumeration` of the attribute names:

```
public java.util.Enumeration getAttributeNames()
```

Calling the `getAttribute()` method with a specified attribute name returns a reference to the requested attribute (or `null` if the attribute specified does not exist):

```
public Object getAttribute(String name)
```

Calling the `removeAttribute()` method will remove the specified attribute (if it exists) from the `ServletContext`:

```
public void removeAttribute(String name)
```

Calling the `setAttribute()` method with a name and `Object` stores the `Object` (as an attribute), bound to the specified name:

```
public void setAttribute(String name, Object object)
```

Using ServletContext Attributes in getContextTable()

The getContextTable() method takes a reference to the servlet's ServletContext object and returns an HTML table (in a StringBuffer object) with information from the ServletContext object. Similar to the previous method, we could access the servlet's ServletContext object using the getServletContext() method of the GenericServlet (we do not necessarily need to pass it as a parameter). However we have included it as a parameter, in case we want to reuse this method for other servlets. If we were to do so, we would abstract the method into a separate class:

```
private StringBuffer getContextTable(ServletContext context) {
   HTMLTable table = new HTMLTable();


   table.appendTitleRow("Attributes");
```

Here we will iterate through the attributes set by the servlet container. Since the attributes may be any type derived from Object, we check their type, printing the Object.toString() value if they are not String or String arrays:

```
Enumeration e = context.getAttributeNames();
while (e.hasMoreElements()) {
   String paramName = (String)e.nextElement();
   Object paramObject = context.getAttribute(paramName);
   String paramValue = "";

   if (paramObject instanceof String) {
     paramValue = (String)context.getAttribute(paramName);
   } else if (paramObject instanceof String[]) {
     String[] paramArray = (String[])context.getAttribute(paramName);
     for (int i = 0; i < paramArray.length; i++) {
       paramValue = paramValue + paramArray[i] + "<br>";
     }
   }
   else {
     paramValue = context.getAttribute(paramName).toString();
   }
   table.appendRow("Attribute: <code>" + paramName +
                   "</code>", paramValue);
}
```

Obtaining General Servlet Information

The following methods return information about the servlet and its initialization parameters. The first method returns an Enumeration of the parameter names, while the second returns the requested parameter (or null if it does not exist):

```
public java.util.Enumeration getInitParameterNames()
public String getInitParameter(String name)
```

The getServletContextName() method will return the name of this web application as known to the servlet container:

```
public String getServletContextName()
```

Retrieving General Servlet Information in getContextTable()

To extract information about the servlet we begin with the web application's name, as it is known to the servlet container. We then add any initialization parameters to the table:

```
table.appendTitleRow("Servlet Information");
table.appendRow("Web App Name", context.getServletContextName());
Enumeration enum = context.getInitParameterNames();
while (enum.hasMoreElements()) {
  String paramName = (String)enum.nextElement();
  String paramValue = context.getInitParameter(paramName);
  table.appendRow("Parameter: <code>" + paramName + "</code>",
                  paramValue);
}
```

However, since we have not configured any initialization parameters, they will not be displayed. If you wish to set up initialization parameters for this servlet, in order to test this functionality, you should refer to Chapter 4 where we discuss the subject further.

Getting Server Information

Three methods also exist to access information about the server on which the web application/servlet is running. These two methods return the major and minor versions of the Servlet API respectively:

```
public int getMajorVersion()
public int getMinorVersion()
```

The following method returns the name and version of the servlet container in which the servlet is running:

```
public String getServerInfo()
```

Getting Server Information in getContextTable()

We can access the version of the Servlet API supported as shown, and the server's information and version also. This is useful for servlets and web applications that may be deployed on different servers and need a particular version of the Servlet API, such as 2.3 or later, to function:

```
table.appendTitleRow("Server Information");
table.appendRow("Servlet API version",
        context.getMajorVersion() + "." + context.getMinorVersion());
table.appendRow("Server Version", context.getServerInfo());
```

Getting Information About the Server Environment

Additional methods exist to interact locally with the servlet environment. Calling the `getContext()` method will return a reference to the `ServletContext` object for that relative path (`null` if it does not exist):

```
public ServletContext getContext(String uripath)
```

Two methods exist to access a `RequestDispatcher` object that acts as a wrapper for a servlet or specified resource:

```
public RequestDispatcher getNamedDispatcher(String name)
public RequestDispatcher getRequestDispatcher(String path)
```

We use the first method to access a specific `RequestDispatcher` object for a specified servlet name. The second method is used to access a specific `RequestDispatcher` object for a specified resource (at the given path). This second method can take the path to a servlet or file, and can be used to include, or forward, a request to a servlet or static file.

Passing the `getRealPath()` method a virtual path returns a real file path to this resource on the current server:

```
public String getRealPath(String path)
```

This is the local file location such as `"c:\Apache Tomcat 4.0\webapps\servletAPI\index.html"` or `"/apps/tomcat/webapps/servletAPI/index.html"` that is represented by the virtual path supplied, such as `"/index.html"`.

The `getResourcePaths()` method will return a `Set`, analogous to a directory listing, of all the paths to resources within the web application, whose longest sub-path matched the parameter:

```
public java.util.Set getResourcePaths(String path)
```

The `getResource()` method returns a URL object that maps to the specified path. This must be a valid path within the current application context, such as `"/index.html"`:

```
public java.net.URL getResource(String path)
```

Calling the `getResourceAsStream()` method returns an `InputStream` object that can be used to read the specified resource. This `InputStream` object can be wrapped in a suitable input object to interpret the resource (for instance: text, serialized Java objects, a binary or other file):

```
public java.io.InputStream getResourceAsStream(String path)
```

Finally, with the `getMimeType()` method we can (attempt to) identify the MIME type of the specified file. This method returns `null` if the MIME type of this file is not recognized:

```
public String getMimeType(String file)
```

Getting Server Environment Information in getContextTable()

To complete the `getContextTable()` method, we are going to look at how we can begin to access the server environment, such as local files:

```
table.appendTitleRow("Server Environment");
table.appendRow("Real Path (<code>\"/\"<code>)",
                context.getRealPath("/"));
```

First we add the real path (file location) corresponding to a location in our application. Next we will retrieve a `Set` of resource paths for the relative location specified. Here we are looking for the listing of our root directory. We will then append the paths to a `StringBuffer` and add this row to the table:

```
Set setPaths = context.getResourcePaths("/");
Object[] arrayPaths = setPaths.toArray();
StringBuffer bufferPaths = new StringBuffer();
for (int i = 0; i < arrayPaths.length; i++) {
  bufferPaths.append((String)arrayPaths[i]).append("<br>");
}
table.appendRow("Paths", bufferPaths.toString());
```

Next we retrieve a `URL` object for the specified `index.html` page. This `URL` object could be used to retrieve the object, if required, but here we add its location to the table. If there is a problem, we output an indication that this returned a `null` URL:

```
try {
  URL url = context.getResource("/index.html");
  if (url != null) {
    table.appendRow("URL (<code>\"/index.html\"<code>)",
                    url.toString());
  } else {
    table.appendRow("URL (<code>\"/index.html\"<code>)", "null");
  }
} catch (MalformedURLException mfe) {
  table.appendRow("MalformedURLException (<code>\"/index.html\"<code>)",
                  mfe.getMessage() );
}
```

Finally we determine the MIME type for the `index.html` page. In Tomcat, this maps the extension to its MIME type, if known. It does not validate that the file exists:

```
table.appendRow("Mime Type (<code>\"index.html\"<code>)",
                context.getMimeType("index.html"));
return table.toStringBuffer();
  }
}
```

Finally, the table is then returned by the method. Here's a reminder of what it looks like in the browser:

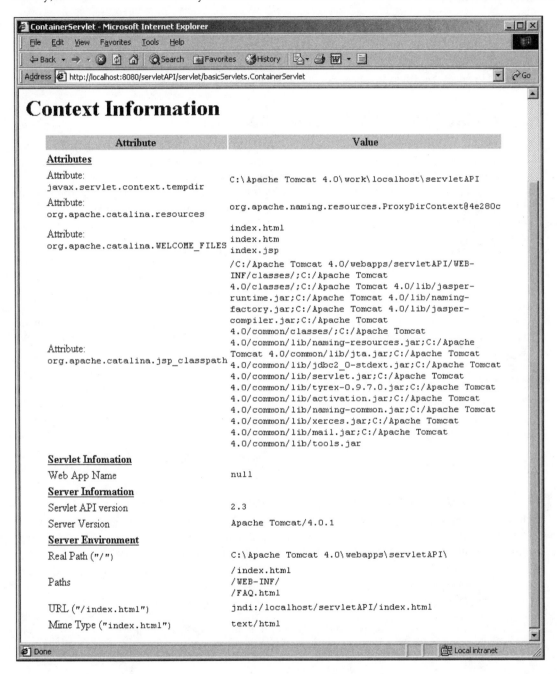

Utility Methods

A couple of log() methods (similar to those in GenericServlet) are provided to write to the web applications log file too:

```
public void log(String msg)
public void log(String message, java.lang.Throwable throwable)
```

The ServletContext Lifecycle Classes

Modifications to the ServletContext object, such as the initialisation or destruction of it by the servlet container, trigger ServletContextEvent objects. If our application needs to monitor updates to the context in which the servlet is running, we create a class that implements the ServletContextListener interface, and register it with the servlet container (in the application's web.xml deployment descriptor configuration file – Chapter 4 explains this process). A listener class method is executed when a ServletContextEvent event occurs.

Similarly, modifications to ServletContext attributes trigger ServletContextAttributeEvent objects. We can create classes that implement the ServletContextAttributeListener interface to listen for these events too.

The servlet container notifies the registered classes about the events that they are listening for. It is the container's responsibility to then call the relevant method, defined in the listener interface implemented, to process the event. If the events being listened for never occur, then the servlet container does not call the listener methods.

The ServletContextEvent Class

The ServletContextEvent object is passed to the relevant listeners for this event. This has a single method. Calling the getServletContext() method returns the ServletContext object that was modified:

```
public ServletContext getServletContext()
```

The ServletContextAttributeEvent Class

The ServletContextAttributeEvent object is generated by the servlet container when the attributes of a particular ServletContext are altered. This class has two methods. The first returns the name of the attribute changed, and the second the value of the attribute that was altered:

```
public String getName()
public Object getValue()
```

The returned Object from the getValue() method depends upon the triggering event. If the attribute was added or removed, the added or removed attribute is returned. Alternately, if the attribute was replaced, then the old value of the attribute is returned, allowing it to be saved if required.

The ServletContextListener Interface

We implement the `ServletContextListener` interface to listen for lifecycle events (initialization or destruction) of the servlet context. We implement the methods below to allow our application to react appropriately to these events:

```
public void contextInitialized(ServletContextEvent sce)
public void contextDestroyed(ServletContextEvent sce)
```

These methods are called by the servlet container, in response the initialization or the pre-shutdown of the `ServletContext`.

The ServletContextAttributeListener Interface

The `ServletContextAttributeListener` interface is implemented by classes to listen for changes to attributes in the `ServletContext` object. Three methods are provided, corresponding to the three types of action that may trigger the `ServletContextAttributeEvent`. It is the servlet container's responsibility to call these methods once the event trigger occurs:

```
public void attributeAdded(ServletContextAttributeEvent scab)
public void attributeRemoved(ServletContextAttributeEvent scab)
public void attributeReplaced(ServletContextAttributeEvent scab)
```

We implement these methods to process the addition, removal, and replacement of attributes respectively.

Additional Interfaces

Finally, the Servlet API provides two additional interfaces involving servlet threading and request dispatching.

Threading and the SingleThreadModel Interface

Normally, many different client requests may cause the `service()` method of a servlet to be executed simultaneously (or virtually simultaneously) in different threads for each request.

If the servlet class has class-level variables declared, then if the any of the threads executing update the class variable, another thread could end up with inconsistent values for the class variable through the `service()` method.

There are a number of ways around this, such as synchronizing access to the variables concerned, or moving the variables (if suitable). However synchronization or locking an object has performance implications because any other threads trying to access the synchronized resource will be blocked from execution until the synchronization lock is removed.

An alternative technique is to implement the `SingleThreadModel` interface in the servlet. This interface defines no methods, so no additional code is required. It is solely used to tag the servlet that implements this, because the servlet container treats servlets that implement this interface differently.

The container effectively guarantees that only one thread will execute concurrently in the servlet's service() method, by synchronizing access to each instance of the servlet.

The servlet may instantiate one or more instances of a servlet implementing this interface and may maintain a pool of servlet instances to process requests to this interface.

See Chapter 11 for more information on synchronization issues.

The RequestDispatcher Interface

The servlet container provides the implementation of the RequestDispatcher interface. We can use the RequestDispatcher in a servlet to forward a request to another resource (servlet, JSP, web page, and so on) once we have inspected, and possibly performed some processing on, the Request object.

There are two methods provided by the interface: forward() and include(). Using the forward() method means that you forward the request to another resource and any output in the buffer made before the method call is discarded:

```
public void forward(ServletRequest request, ServletResponse response)
```

The include() method can be used almost like a Server Side Include (SSI), where the servlet can process the request and include the resource (the servlet or HTML web page output) as part of the page:

```
public void include(ServletRequest request, ServletResponse response)
```

Now let's have an example of how we might use the RequestDispatcher interface.

Implementing RequestDispatcherServlet

This example servlet demonstrates how we can use the RequestDispatcher interface. The purpose of this servlet is to present a listbox with a list of resources (servlets and/or HTML files) available within the web application, and to return information on the requested resource beneath this. The servlet makes use of a Dispatching interface, which is used to declare constants corresponding to our previously-developed servlets. Any class that implements this interface has access to the constants as if they were declared in that class.

To use the servlet, you will need to add the sourcecode for the servlet and the interface to the \src\basicServlets directory, compile them, and move the classes to the \classes\basicServlet directory, as with previous examples. The following image shows the servlet at work, displaying the output of the BasicServlet included within the web page. The servlet can be accessed at:

http://localhost:8080/servletAPI/servlet/basicServlets.RequestDispatcherServlet

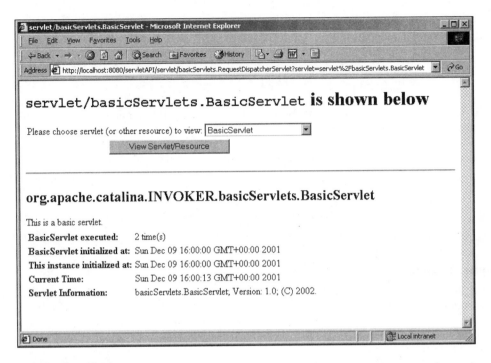

The Dispatching Interface

First we will look at the Dispatching interface. This has no methods and is simply used to declare constants that represent our previous servlets:

```
package basicServlets;

public interface Dispatching {
```

For each servlet we previously developed, we have declared two constants. The first is the mapping for the servlet resource, and the second is the name of the servlet:

```
public static final String BASIC_SERVLET =
        "servlet/basicServlets.BasicServlet";
public static final String BASIC_SERVLET_NAME = "BasicServlet";

public static final String REQUEST_RESPONSE_SERVLET =
        "servlet/basicServlets.RequestResponseServlet";
public static final String REQUEST_RESPONSE_SERVLET_NAME =
        "RequestResponseServlet";

public static final String CONTAINER_SERVLET =
        "servlet/basicServlets.ContainerServlet";
public static final String CONTAINER_SERVLET_NAME =
        "ContainerServlet";

public static final String REQUEST_DISPATCHER_SERVLET_PACKAGE =
        "basicServlets.RequestDispatcherServlet";
public static final String REQUEST_DISPATCHER_SERVLET_NAME =
        "RequestDispatcherServlet";
```

We also include the application index page, to demonstrate that our dispatcher can also use static HTML files as well as servlets:

```
public static final String INDEX_HTML = "index.html";
public static final String INDEX_HTML_NAME = "Index Page";
```

Finally we create two `String` arrays of the servlets'/resources' paths and names for use in our `RequestDispatcherServlet`:

```
public static final String[] RESOURCES =
      {BASIC_SERVLET, REQUEST_RESPONSE_SERVLET, CONTAINER_SERVLET, INDEX_HTML};

public static final String[] RESOURCES_NAMES =
      {BASIC_SERVLET_NAME, REQUEST_RESPONSE_SERVLET_NAME,
      CONTAINER_SERVLET_NAME, INDEX_HTML_NAME};
}
```

The RequestDispatcherServlet Class

Our `RequestDispatcherServlet` class implements our `Dispatching` interface in order to access the constants defined in it:

```
import java.io.IOException;
import java.io.PrintWriter;
import java.util.Enumeration;
import javax.servlet.*;
import javax.servlet.http.*;

public class RequestDispatcherServlet
                        extends GenericServlet implements Dispatching {

  private static StringBuffer form = new StringBuffer();

  public void service(ServletRequest request, ServletResponse response)
                        throws ServletException, IOException {
```

The start of the servlet code is fairly standard; we access the `PrintWriter` object and retrieve the `servlet` parameter indicating which servlet is required:

```
ServletContext servletContext = getServletContext();
ServletConfig config = getServletConfig();
PrintWriter out = response.getWriter();
String servletRequested = request.getParameter("servlet");
```

Next we access the `RequestDispatcher` object for the desired servlet. This enables us to use the `include()` method to get access to its content on our servlet page. We are using the relative path and this may include other servlets, JSP pages, and HTML files:

```
RequestDispatcher requestDispatcher =
  servletContext.getRequestDispatcher("/" + servletRequested);

response.setContentType("text/html");
out.println(getPageTitle(servletRequested));
```

We then include the requested resource in our page. This means that the output from the servlet or web page is included as part of our web page.

Before we do this, we also attach an attribute to the request. In the `RequestResponseServlet` we check at one point if the response was committed. Since we have already output from this servlet, the `response.isCommitted()` method may return an incorrect result as it is unaware of being included in this servlet's output. Therefore we attach an attribute to the request that serves as an indicator to the `RequestResponseServlet` that we have already started output, and the `response.isCommitted()` method may return an incorrect result. This is why, in the `RequestResponseServlet`, we checked for an attribute set:

```
    if (requestDispatcher != null) {
      request.setAttribute("buffer", "written");
      requestDispatcher.include(request, response);
    } else if (servletRequested == null) {
      out.println("Please chose a servlet");
    } else {
      out.println(servletRequested + " is not recognised by the server");
    }
    out.println("</body></html>");
    out.flush();
  }
```

The `init()` method initializes the form `StringBuffer` object that, because it is unchanging, need only be initialized once:

```
    public void init() throws ServletException {
      form.append(getForm());
    }
```

The `getPageTitle()` method is used to build the head of the HTML page that appears above the included resource:

```
    private StringBuffer getPageTitle(String servletRequested) {

      StringBuffer sb = new StringBuffer();
      sb.append("<html><head><title>");
      if (servletRequested == null) {
        sb.append("[no servlet requested]");
      } else {
        sb.append(servletRequested);
      }
      sb.append("</title></head><body><h1><code>");
      if (servletRequested == null) {
        sb.append("[no servlet was requested]</code>");
      } else {
        sb.append(servletRequested).append("</code> is shown below");
      }
      sb.append("</h1><p>");
      sb.append(form);
      sb.append("<hr width=100%>");
      return sb;
    }
```

The `getForm()` method sets up the HTML form. It accesses the constants from the `Dispatching` interface that contain the resources that the dispatcher object may be directed to:

```
private StringBuffer getForm() {
  StringBuffer sb = new StringBuffer();
  ServletConfig config = getServletConfig();

  sb.append("<form method=get action=\"" +
            REQUEST_DISPATCHER_SERVLET_PACKAGE + "\">");
  sb.append("<table><tr><td>Please choose servlet ");
  sb.append("(or other resource) to view:</td>");
  sb.append("<td><select name=\"servlet\">");

  for (int i = 0; i < RESOURCES.length ; i++) {
    sb.append("<option value=\"" + RESOURCES[i] + "\" >" +
            RESOURCES_NAMES[i]);
  }

  sb.append("</select></td></tr><tr><td colspan=2 align=\"center\">");
  sb.append("<input type=\"submit\" ");
  sb.append("value=\"View Servlet/Resource\"></td></tr>");
  sb.append("</table></form> ");
  return sb;
  }
}
```

Servlet Exception Classes

The servlet container normally manages exceptions that occur in servlets. Many exceptions, such as `ServletException` and `IOException` (or subclasses of these) are caught and handled by the servlet container, but it is still important to understand the exception handling process and why they may be thrown. Often if a client closes a connection prematurely, before the servlet has finished handling the request, an `IOException` will be thrown and caught by the servlet container.

Occasionally, when a server is under a heavy load, it may be unable to fulfill requests and may throw an `UnavailableException` (which is a subclass of `ServletException`). The servlet container will then return an error message to the client indicating whether this problem is permanent or temporary. Reasons for a permanent `UnavailableException` might include that the resource is configured incorrectly, while a temporary `UnavailableException` may occur if resources (for example database connections or disk space) are unavailable.

While we are unlikely to throw `ServletExceptions` directly, we may want to throw `UnavailableExceptions` when our servlet is unable to access a resource needed to complete the request. We then can indicate how long the client should wait before retrying their request.

We may also create custom exception classes extending from the standard `java.lang.Exception` or `ServletException` classes (as appropriate), which we can use in our web application.

The ServletException Class

The `ServletException` class provides the four constructors shown below to instantiate a `ServletException`:

```
public ServletException()
public ServletException(String message)
public ServletException(String message, java.lang.Throwable rootCause)
public ServletException(java.lang.Throwable rootCause)
```

It also provides a `getRootCause()` method to determine the cause of the `ServletException`:

```
public java.lang.Throwable getRootCause()
```

The UnavailableException Class

The `UnavailableException` class provides two useful constructors. The first specifies the reason, and is used for a permanently unavailable status. The second is used for a temporary problem, and takes a second parameter indicating the time (in seconds) that the servlet is expected to be unavailable:

```
public UnavailableException(String msg)
public UnavailableException(String msg, int seconds)
```

The following method returns the expected time that the resource will be unavailable. The number will be negative if there is no estimate, or if it is expected to be permanently unavailable:

```
public int getUnavailableSeconds()
```

Finally, the `isPermanent()` method indicates if the problem causing the `UnavailableException` is a permanent or temporary condition:

```
public boolean isPermanent()
```

Personal Portal Web Application

We have so far covered how to build basic servlets, extending from the `GenericServlet` class, that extract data from the `ServletRequest`, `ServletResponse`, `ServletConfig`, and `ServletContext` objects. Now is a good time to look at what is involved in building a simple web application, using servlets at the heart of it.

We are going to gain knowledge of how to build a basic web site architecture to serve a dynamic web site. We will build the bones of a web site that we could develop to act as a themed portal for clients, offering personalization and content management. Since we are only beginning to work with servlets at this point we will try to keep this pretty simple, building on what we have learned to draw the web application together.

We will implement a web application packaged as `personalPortal`. This is the building block of a web site that could be developed into a themed portal web site. We will implement a straightforward `PortalServlet` that will serve as the application gateway. All requests will enter through this servlet. The servlet will return a single web page of three panels. The top and left (menu) will be generated from the `PortalServlet` with the help of `HTMLPortal`, which is a utility class to manage the HTML preparation for the `PortalServlet`. This allows us to abstract the HTML from this servlet to keep the processing logic clear (as we did using the `HTMLTable` utility class in earlier examples).

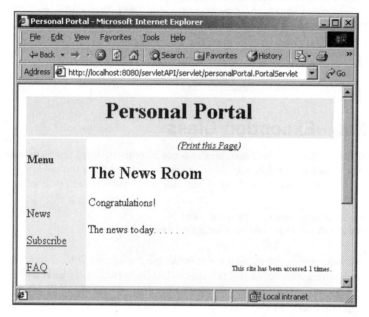

The screenshot above indicates how the initial page will look. The main right panel contains the body of the page. Our `PortalServlet` will not generate this panel. This will come from different resources in the web application, such as other servlets and HTML web pages. We will use the `RequestDispatcher` interface to include their content. While doing this we will pass an attribute to the resource receiving the request, which may pick up this attribute, if required.

Clicking on the Menu links on the left will update the page from the `PortalServlet` with updated content in the main panel, reflecting the new choice. We will also allow users to print out the page contents in a more printer-friendly format. For this we remove the right-menu panel, and display the links across the top of the page, as shown:

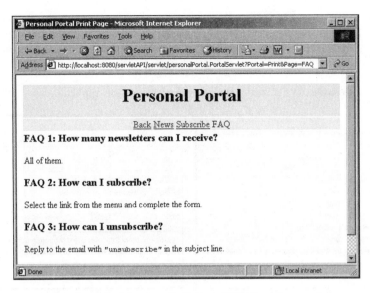

The above screenshot shows the FAQ page, which is an HTML web page (not a servlet) whose output is included by the RequestDispatcher object in the page.

Our subscription page of the PortalServlet is SubscribeServlet's contents included in the right panel. With this, the user is presented with a subscription page to add their e-mail address and select which newsletters they wish to subscribe to. They submit the form back to the PortalServlet that passes the request on to the SubscribeServlet. This then validates the user's input and, assuming the input is valid, returns to them a page indicating they have successfully signed up to the newsletters. In a real-world version of this application, the validation would be more strict (possibly using client-side JavaScript), with storage of the details to a database.

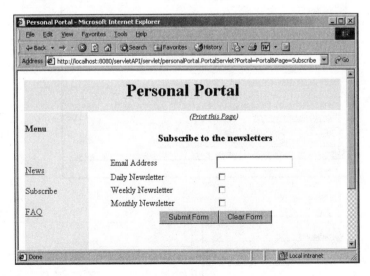

Hopefully, at this point, you will see some similarities to a standard and common web site design, where the panel on the left holds the menu items; the top-panel holds the title (and sometimes links), with a center/right panel for the body of the page. In this example, we are going to look at how we could go about building a basic implementation of this site design.

Before we look at the code, let's consider the class diagram for the application:

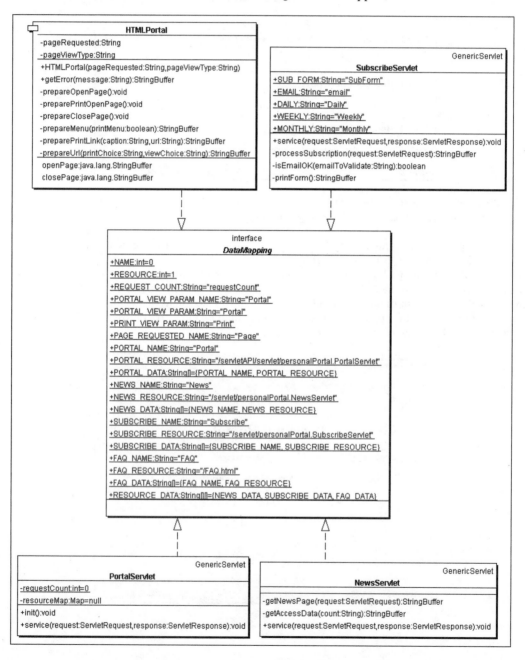

We will be developing one interface, three servlets, and an additional support class, as well as one HTML page. The DataMapping interface is designed to hold constants for use by the servlets, and defines no methods. The HTMLPortal class is a support class for PortalServlet, providing the HTML required by this servlet for the page. SubscribeServlet and NewsServlet produce content for the main panel, as does the additional FAQ.html web page.

Implementing the Personal Portal Web Application

Our next step is to create the code for the web application. Let's now walk through it.

The DataMapping Interface

Normally, when we build a web application, we place information into the initialization parameters in the web application's deployment descriptor. This stores information needed to configure the servlets and web applications. This is useful because we do not have to rebuild the application to change it, and almost anyone can make the changes. However, we will not be covering web deployment until Chapter 4, so we need to store our configuration information elsewhere for this web application.

A live application similar to this would have a database behind it, from which it might load some of these configuration values. Storing this information in a database would be a useful mechanism for accessing and updating them.

An alternative option would be to include creating a properties file to store the data. However, for simplicity's sake, we will store this data as constants in an interface with no defined methods. This means that any class (our servlets) may implement this interface and have full access to the constants, as if they were declared in the implementing class. We store these constants, and then add them to arrays so that our applications can easily iterate through them, whether they are updated or not.

```
package personalPortal;

public interface DataMapping {
```

The first items of data we store are two constants indicating the position in an array of the name and resource location. We also store some of the parameters and names made in requests:

```
public static final int NAME = 0;
public static final int RESOURCE = 1;

public static final String REQUEST_COUNT = "requestCount";
public static final String PORTAL_VIEW_PARAM_NAME = "Portal";
public static final String PORTAL_VIEW_PARAM = "Portal";
public static final String PRINT_VIEW_PARAM = "Print";
public static final String PAGE_REQUESTED_NAME = "Page";
```

The information that we hold about each page in the application is:

❑   Its name

❑   Its resource address (URI)

❑   An array to hold both of those values

```
public static final String PORTAL_NAME = "Portal";
public static final String PORTAL_RESOURCE =
    "/servletAPI/servlet/personalPortal.PortalServlet";
public static final String[] PORTAL_DATA = {PORTAL_NAME, PORTAL_RESOURCE};

public static final String NEWS_NAME = "News";
public static final String NEWS_RESOURCE =
    "/servlet/personalPortal.NewsServlet";
public static final String[] NEWS_DATA = {NEWS_NAME, NEWS_RESOURCE};

public static final String SUBSCRIBE_NAME = "Subscribe";
public static final String SUBSCRIBE_RESOURCE =
    "/servlet/personalPortal.SubscribeServlet";
public static final String[] SUBSCRIBE_DATA =
    {SUBSCRIBE_NAME, SUBSCRIBE_RESOURCE};

public static final String FAQ_NAME = "FAQ";
public static final String FAQ_RESOURCE = "/FAQ.html";
public static final String[] FAQ_DATA = {FAQ_NAME, FAQ_RESOURCE};
```

Finally, we store all of the `String` arrays with information about the different pages in a two dimensional array. We use an array instead of another structure for performance in iterating through the contents. We obviously need to keep this updated if we add additional pages to our menu:

```
public static final String[][] RESOURCE_DATA =
    {NEWS_DATA, SUBSCRIBE_DATA, FAQ_DATA};
}
```

The HTMLPortal Class

The `HTMLPortal` class is used to abstract the HTML creation from the `PortalServlet`. Creating a class to assist `PortalServlet` like this will make the logic in `PortalServlet` easier to follow and maintain.

This class implements the `DataMapping` interface, which gives it access to the `DataMapping` constants. There are two `StringBuffer` objects to hold details of the page, and two `String` objects to signify the specific page requested by the client and the type of view (normal or print view):

```
package personalPortal;

public class HTMLPortal implements DataMapping {

private StringBuffer openPage;
private StringBuffer closePage;

private String pageRequested;
private String pageViewType;
```

To construct our section of the page (the top heading and the left panel), we need to know two things:

- ❑ the page that has been requested (so we can construct our menus accordingly)
- ❑ the type of view requested (normal or print view)

```
public HTMLPortal(String pageRequested, String pageViewType) {
  this.pageRequested = pageRequested;
  this.pageViewType = pageViewType;
```

We check the type of page we are outputting, and prepare the opening and closing parts of the page:

```
if (PORTAL_VIEW_PARAM.equalsIgnoreCase(pageViewType)) {
  prepareOpenPage();
} else {
  preparePrintOpenPage();
}
prepareClosePage();
}
```

We have three public methods available to the class user:

❏ getOpenPage() – to return the opening HTML

❏ getClosePage() – to return the closing HTML

❏ getError() – to return a message in HTML

```
public StringBuffer getOpenPage() {
  return openPage;
}

public StringBuffer getClosePage() {
  return closePage;
}

public StringBuffer getError(String message) {
  StringBuffer error = new StringBuffer();
  error.append("<h2><font color=\"darkred\">");
  error.append(message);
  error.append("</font></h2>");
  return error;
}
```

Our prepareOpenPage() method builds the opening HTML data. We call the prepareMenu() and the preparePrintLink() methods to construct parts of the page:

```
private void prepareOpenPage() {
  openPage = new StringBuffer();
  openPage.append("<html><head><title>Personal Portal");
  openPage.append("</title></head><body>");
  openPage.append("<table width=\"100%\"><tr>");
  openPage.append("<td colspan=2 align=\"center\" bgcolor=\"#ffff80\">");
  openPage.append("<h1>Personal Portal</h1></td></tr><tr>");
  openPage.append("<td width=\"20%\" bgcolor=\"#ffffa0\"><br>");
  openPage.append("<b>Menu</b><br><br>");
  openPage.append(prepareMenu(false));
  openPage.append("<br><br><br><br><br><br><br><br><br>");
  openPage.append("</ul></td>");
  openPage.append("<td width=\"80%\" valign=\"top\">");
  openPage.append("<bgcolor=\"#ffffe0\">");
```

```
      openPage.append("<center><i><font size=\"-1\">(");
      openPage.append(preparePrintLink("Print this Page", pageRequested));
      openPage.append(")</font></i></center><br>");
      openPage.append("");
      openPage.append("");
}
```

Similar to the previous method, this `preparePrintOpenPage()` method prepares HTML for the page, but in this case, it is for the print version:

```
private void preparePrintOpenPage() {
   openPage = new StringBuffer();
   openPage.append("<html><head><title>Personal Portal Print Page");
   openPage.append("</title></head><body>");
   openPage.append("<table width=\"100%\"><tr>");
   openPage.append("<td align=\"center\" bgcolor=\"#ffff80\">");
   openPage.append("<h1>Personal Portal</h1></td></tr><tr>");
   openPage.append("<td align=\"center\" bgcolor=\"#ffffa0\">");
   openPage.append(prepareMenu(true));
   openPage.append("</td></tr><tr>");
   openPage.append("<td bgcolor=\"#ffffe0\">");
}
```

Next is a method used to prepare the HTML that closes the page. It adds a copyright notice to the end of the page as well:

```
private void prepareClosePage() {
   closePage = new StringBuffer();
   closePage.append("</td></tr></table>");
   closePage.append("<p align=\"right\">&copy; 2002</body></html> ");
}
```

The `prepareMenu()` method prepares an HTML menu for either the print view or the normal view of the web page:

```
private StringBuffer prepareMenu(boolean printMenu) {
   StringBuffer menu = new StringBuffer();
   StringBuffer menuBreak = new StringBuffer();
   if (printMenu) {
     menuBreak.append(" ");
     menu.append("<a href=\"javascript:history.go(-1)\">Back</a>");
   } else {
     menuBreak.append("<br><br>");
   }
```

Here we iterate through the RESOURCE_DATA two-dimensional array, to extract both the page name and the page URI for the links of the menu:

```
for (int i = 0; i < RESOURCE_DATA.length; i++) {
  menu.append(menuBreak);

  if (RESOURCE_DATA[i][NAME].equalsIgnoreCase(pageRequested)) {
    menu.append(RESOURCE_DATA[i][NAME]);
  } else {
    menu.append("<a href=\"");
    menu.append(prepareUrl(PORTAL_VIEW_PARAM, RESOURCE_DATA[i][NAME]));
    menu.append("\">");
    menu.append(RESOURCE_DATA[i][NAME]);
    menu.append("</a>");
  }
}
return menu;
}
```

The preparePrintLink() method prepares a link to a page in the print view:

```
private StringBuffer preparePrintLink(String caption, String url) {
  StringBuffer link = new StringBuffer();
  link.append("<a href=\"");
  link.append(prepareUrl(PRINT_VIEW_PARAM, url));
  link.append("\">");
  link.append(caption);
  link.append("</a>");
  return link;
}
```

While building the menu we need to construct the URLs, including the query string, to map to the linked resource. The link must include the request type and the page that was requested. This is the purpose of the prepareUrl() method:

```
private StringBuffer prepareUrl(String printChoice, String viewChoice) {
  StringBuffer url = new StringBuffer();
  url.append(PORTAL_RESOURCE);
  url.append("?").append(PORTAL_VIEW_PARAM_NAME);
  url.append("=").append(printChoice);
  url.append("&").append(PAGE_REQUESTED_NAME);
  url.append("=").append(viewChoice);
  return url;
}
}
```

The PortalServlet Class

The `PortalServlet` is essentially the application manager servlet. All requests come in through this servlet. No HTML is created directly in this class. This servlet uses the `HTMLPortal` class for HTML generation, and the right panel contents are generated by other resources (HTML or servlet). This servlet implements the `DataMapping` interface so that it can gain access to the application constants:

```
package personalPortal;

import javax.servlet.*;
import javax.servlet.http.*;
import java.io.*;
import java.util.*;

public class PortalServlet extends GenericServlet implements DataMapping {

    private static int requestCount = 0;
    private Map resourceMap = null;
```

The servlet has a static `requestCount` variable that is incremented on every page access. Normally this data would be stored to a database (or some other permanent storage facility).

In the `init()` method, we construct an object to map the resource names and locations for use later:

```
public void init() {
    resourceMap = new HashMap();
    for (int i = 0; i < RESOURCE_DATA.length; i++) {
        resourceMap.put(RESOURCE_DATA[i][NAME], RESOURCE_DATA[i][RESOURCE]);
    }
}
```

In the `service()` method, we process client requests by first determining what the client has requested. If they have passed no parameters with the request we set the default to the news page in normal view:

```
public void service(ServletRequest request, ServletResponse response)
    throws ServletException, IOException {
    requestCount++;
    ServletContext context = getServletConfig().getServletContext();

    String pageViewType = request.getParameter(PORTAL_VIEW_PARAM_NAME);
    String pageRequested = request.getParameter(PAGE_REQUESTED_NAME);

    if (pageViewType == null) {
        pageViewType = PORTAL_VIEW_PARAM;
    }
    if (pageRequested == null) {
        pageRequested = NEWS_NAME;
    }
```

Next we create our `HTMLPortal` object with this data, to build our page. We output the opening part of the page to the client:

```
HTMLPortal htmlPortal = new HTMLPortal(pageRequested, pageViewType);
String requestedResource = (String)resourceMap.get(pageRequested);

response.setContentType("text/html");
PrintWriter out = response.getWriter();
out.println(htmlPortal.getOpenPage());
```

We then retrieve a `RequestDispatcher` object for the required resource. Assuming that the `RequestDispatcher` object is valid, we set an attribute on the request (of the `count` variable) to include this data in the forwarded request, so that another servlet can retrieve this. Calling the `dispatcher.include(request, response)` method adds the output of that resource (servlet or web page) to that of this servlet:

```
RequestDispatcher dispatcher =
                    context.getRequestDispatcher(requestedResource);
if (dispatcher != null) {
  request.setAttribute(REQUEST_COUNT,
                    new Integer(requestCount).toString());
  dispatcher.include(request, response);
} else {
  out.println(htmlPortal.getError("Request Resource not found"));
}
```

Finally, we add the closing HTML to be sent to the client:

```
    out.println(htmlPortal.getClosePage());
    out.close();
  }
}
```

At this point, you could compile and run the example, but you will get a warning in the right panel that the resource was not found. This is because we have not yet created the servlets or HTML resources to include in this panel. We are now going to develop these.

SubscribeServlet Class

Our `SubscribeServlet` performs two roles. First, it generates an HTML form for the user to fill in if they want to subscribe to the newsletters. Second, it processes the submitted form from the client. In either case, this servlet's content is included in the right panel of the `PortalServlet`.

So how does the servlet know when the client is making a request for a form, or submitting a form to be processed?

```java
package personalPortal;

import javax.servlet.*;
import javax.servlet.http.*;
import java.io.*;
import java.util.*;

public class SubscribeServlet extends GenericServlet implements DataMapping {
    public static final String SUB_FORM = "SubForm";
    public static final String EMAIL = "email";
    public static final String DAILY = "Daily";
    public static final String WEEKLY = "Weekly";
    public static final String MONTHLY = "Monthly";
```

To answer this question, we have to understand that when the servlet is constructing the form, it adds a hidden parameter (SUB_FORM). By checking the request, to see if this exists, it knows whether this is a request for the default form, or to submit the form. The service() method below then delegates the request processing to a specified method depending on the type of request:

```java
public void service(ServletRequest request, ServletResponse response)
    throws ServletException, IOException {
    response.setContentType("text/html");
    PrintWriter out = response.getWriter();

    String subscribeForm = request.getParameter(SUB_FORM);

    if (subscribeForm != null) {
        out.println(processSubscription(request));
    } else {
        out.println(printForm());
    }
}
```

The processSubscription() method has to extract the specific parameters from the request for processing. In a live application, the application would perform rigorous validation of parameters, according to the business rules for the form, and would then save the submitted data to a database (or some other Enterprise Information System).

In this case we perform a basic check of the e-mail address, and if the e-mail address passes the test, we return the client a note indicating that their request is being processed. If the e-mail address fails the test, they are given a warning page:

```java
private StringBuffer processSubscription(ServletRequest request) {
    StringBuffer sub = new StringBuffer();
    String email = request.getParameter(EMAIL);
    String daily = request.getParameter(DAILY);
    String weekly = request.getParameter(WEEKLY);
    String monthly = request.getParameter(MONTHLY);
```

```
        if (!isEmailOK(email)) {
          sub.append("<h3>Error Processing Request</h3>");
          sub.append("Email entered is invalid. Please go ");
          sub.append("<a href=\"javascript:history.go(-1)\">Back</a>");
          sub.append(" to try again.");
        } else {
          sub.append("<h3>Request Processed</h3>");
          sub.append("<p>Your request is being processed. ");
          sub.append("You should receive an e-mail confirmation shortly. ");
          sub.append("<p>Thank you.");
        }
        return sub;
      }
```

Our `isEmailOK()` method performs limited e-mail address validation, checking that it is not `null` or empty, and has an @ symbol, with a period somewhere afterwards in the string:

```
      private boolean isEmailOK(String emailToValidate) {
        if (emailToValidate == null ||
            emailToValidate.trim().length() == 0) {
          return false;
        }
        int at = emailToValidate.indexOf("@");
        if (at == -1) {
          return false;
        }
        int dot = emailToValidate.indexOf(".", at);
        if (dot == -1) {
          return false;
        }
        return true;
      }
```

Our `printForm()` method is a long HTML output form. It outputs a form asking for the user's e-mail address, and newsletter selection choices. It also outputs two hidden parameters, the first to identify the page that it will return to (the subscribe page) and the second as an indicator to this servlet that the data is coming from the form, so it should process it, instead of returning it to the client:

```
      private StringBuffer printForm() {
        StringBuffer form = new StringBuffer();
        form.append("<form action=\"").append(PORTAL_RESOURCE);
        form.append("\" method=\"post\">");
        form.append("<input type=\"hidden\" name=\"");
        form.append(PORTAL_VIEW_PARAM_NAME).append("\" value=\"");
        form.append(PORTAL_VIEW_PARAM);
        form.append("\"><input type=\"hidden\" name=\"");
        form.append(PAGE_REQUESTED_NAME).append("\" value=\"");
        form.append(SUBSCRIBE_NAME);
        form.append("\"><input type=\"hidden\" name=\"");
        form.append(SUB_FORM).append("\" value=\"");
        form.append(SUB_FORM);
```

```
        form.append("\"><table align=\"center\" width=400>");
        form.append("<tr><td colspan=2><h3 align=\"center\">");
        form.append("Subscribe to the newsletters</h3></td></tr>");
        form.append("<tr><td width=\"50%\">Email Address</td>");
        form.append("<td width=\"50%\"><input type=\"text\" name=\"");
        form.append(EMAIL).append("\">");
        form.append("</td></tr><tr><td>Daily Newsletter</td>");
        form.append("<td><input type=\"checkbox\" name=\"");
        form.append(DAILY).append("\"></td></tr>");
        form.append("<tr><td>Weekly Newsletter</td>");
        form.append("<td><input type=\"checkbox\" name=\"");
        form.append(WEEKLY).append("\"></td></tr>");
        form.append("<tr><td>Monthly Newsletter</td>");
        form.append("<td><input type=\"checkbox\" name=\"");
        form.append(MONTHLY).append("\"></td></tr>");
        form.append("<tr><td colspan=2 align=center>");
        form.append("<input type=\"submit\" value=\"Submit Form\">");
        form.append("<input type=\"reset\" value=\"Clear Form\"></td></tr>");
        form.append("</table></form>");
        return form;
    }
}
```

NewsServlet Class

Our last servlet provides the news page for the web application. In a live application, we would like to create this page dynamically, based on the information in a database. We could also personalize the content for the client. However, to keep things simple, in this example we output a basic page. It also demonstrates how to extract the attribute set by the PortalServlet to indicate the number of times that the PortalServlet has been requested:

```
package personalPortal;

import javax.servlet.*;
import javax.servlet.http.*;
import java.io.*;
import java.util.*;

public class NewsServlet extends GenericServlet implements DataMapping {
```

This servlet also implements the DataMapping interface. The service() method retrieves the attribute set by the PortalServlet, prints out the news page, and then prints put the counter information:

```
public void service(ServletRequest request, ServletResponse response)
                              throws ServletException, IOException {
    response.setContentType("text/html");
    PrintWriter out = response.getWriter();

    String count = (String)request.getAttribute(REQUEST_COUNT);

    out.println(getNewsPage(request));
    if (count != null) {
        out.println(getAccessData(count));
    }
}
```

The getNewsPage() method retrieves the news page. We pass the request object as a parameter because we would probably need this if we were to adapt the method so that it personalized the content (we could extract cookie information from the client that may identify them):

```
private StringBuffer getNewsPage(ServletRequest request) {
  StringBuffer news = new StringBuffer();
  news.append("<h2>The News Room</h2>");
  news.append("<p>Congratulations!</p>");
  news.append("<p>The news today. . . . . .</p>");
  return news;
}
```

Finally we have a getAccessData() method to retrieve the HTML for the counter output:

```
private StringBuffer getAccessData(String count) {
  StringBuffer sbCount = new StringBuffer();
  sbCount.append("<br><p align=\"right\"><font size=\"-2\"");
  sbCount.append("color=\"darkred\">This site has been accessed ");
  sbCount.append(count);
  sbCount.append(" times.</font></p>");
  return sbCount;
  }
}
```

FAQ HTML Page

When we use the RequestDispatcher to include the content of a resource within a web page, we are not limited to servlet content. We can also include the content of an HTML: page. Here we demonstrate an HTML page that is included in our web application.

This is the FAQ.html file from our application:

```
<html>
  <head><title>FAQ</title></head>
<body>
  <h3>FAQ 1: How many newsletters can I receive?</h3>
    <p>All of them.</p>
  <h3>FAQ 2: How can I subscribe?</h3>
    <p>Select the link from the menu and complete the form.</p>
  <h3>FAQ 3: How can I unsubscribe?</h3>
    <p>Reply to the e-mail with <code>"unsubscribe"</code> in the
    subject line.</p>
</body>
</html>
```

We could include any HTML files in our web application in a servlet page using the RequestDispatcher class. At this point the web application is complete.

Running the Application

You should use the same directories as in the previous examples in the chapter, except that you should put your Java sourcecode files into the `personalPortal` package source directory. Place the HTML page in the root of the `servletAPI` web application directory. When you have compiled the sourcecode and moved the classes into the `classes\personalPortal` directory, restart Tomcat. You can then access the web application on the following URL:

http://localhost:8080/servletAPI/servlet/personalPortal.PortalServlet

Summary

In this chapter we introduced you to the Servlet 2.3 API, and focused upon the `javax.servlet` package.

We examined the API structure and design and then looked at the classes and interfaces of the `javax.servlet` package in detail, building some example servlets that made use of them along the way. We looked at the `Servlet` interface and the `GenericServlet` class that implements this interface, as well as the servlet lifecycle.

The request-response cycle was then covered, and we discussed the relevant `ServletRequest` and `ServletResponse` interfaces. We also reviewed their wrapper classes – the `ServletRequestWrapper` and `ServletResponseWrapper`.

We examined the design and use of the servlet input and output classes `ServletInputStream` and `ServletOutputStream`, followed by a look at servlet-container communication through the `ServletConfig` and `ServletContext` interfaces.

This was followed by a look at the `SingleThreadModel` and the `RequestDispatcher` interfaces. We concluded our look at the `javax.servlet` package by examining the two servlet exception classes `ServletException` and `UnavailableException`.

We concluded the chapter by developing a small Personal Portal application, in order to implement and demonstrate the use of the API classes, interfaces, and methods that we have learned so far. We explained how a web application like this can be run in the Catalina servlet container within the Tomcat web server.

In the next chapter we will examine HTTP servlets and the `javax.servlet.http` package in detail, and develop an example HTTP client-server (servlet) application.

3

HTTP Servlets

In the previous chapter we started to build our own servlets. Those servlets were extended directly from the superclass of all servlets, `GenericServlet`, and were not designed to handle requests made over a particular protocol.

However, in Chapter 1 we noted that the Hypertext Transfer Protocol (HTTP) is by far the most common protocol used to communicate with web applications. It should not therefore be surprising that HTTP forms the basis for most servlet communication too, and so as servlet developers we should make a special effort to understand both the protocol itself, and how to implement servlets that process requests made over it.

Therefore, in this chapter we are going to focus on HTTP and HTTP servlets. We will briefly discuss basic features of HTTP, including:

❑ Methods

❑ Headers

❑ Status Codes

❑ Authentication

Then we will move on to look at HTTP servlets. You will be introduced to the classes and interfaces of the `javax.servlet.http` package, which is used to implement HTTP servlets. We will implement a few simple HTTP servlets of our own too, and we will finish the chapter by implementing a more involved web application that demonstrates how to send and receive text files using an HTTP-based servlet and a Java client application.

Let's start simple though, and begin the chapter with a discussion of protocols used for communication between applications (including HTTP).

Application Layer Protocols

In Chapter 1 we introduced the idea of a protocol stack, where protocols are layered according to the service they provide. We saw that the **application layer** provides specific services for specific types of application. These services are protocols such as Hypertext Transmission Protocol (HTTP), File Transfer Protocol (FTP), and Simple Message Transfer Protocol (SMTP). Using such an application-layer protocol provides a level of abstraction from the transport layer that makes communication functionality in our applications easier to implement.

> **We only need concern ourselves with the application level – the other protocol layers are implemented by the underlying operating system.**

We would substitute the HTTP protocol with SMTP for e-mail applications, or FTP for file transfer applications. These run over the Transmission Control Protocol (TCP) layer. Other protocols such as file sharing (NFS) and Routing Information Protocols (RIP) use User Datagram Protocol (UDP). The Domain Name System runs over both UDP and TCP, according to the operation it is performing. The point is that once the underlying layers have provided a connection between computers we can specify additional protocols to enhance the communication at the application layer.

If we were to build a servlet-based web application we could also extend the existing generic API to provide an implementation for a particular protocol (for instance FTP), or we could write our own protocol and extend the API to use that. In either case we would add additional request methods, response codes and other information relevant to the application.

In most web server-client communication the applications use HTTP in the application layer, so it is not surprising that most servlets use an HTTP-based extension to the generic `javax.servlet` package. In this chapter, we will look more closely at the features of HTTP, and then we will discuss how we can implement servlets that handle HTTP requests and responses.

Hypertext Transfer Protocol

Two parties take part in an HTTP communication: a **client** and a **server.** The client sends an **HTTP request** and the server sends an **HTTP response**. The request can be thought of as a question by the client to the server, and the response as the server's answer to the client. Most applications act as either a client or a server, but there is no reason why an application can't be designed to act as both – for example, a web server might act as a client in order to gather information from other servers to present to its client. Web service applications are beginning to look like this in cases where they communicate over HTTP (or other protocols) with other servers for information.

Each request by a client to the server (for example, for a web page) is made with a separate connection under version 1.0 of the HTTP specification (HTTP 1.0). So, downloading a complex web page could require many requests to the server; one for each frame of the page, one for each image, one for each stylesheet, and so on. In HTTP 1.1, connections are kept open for a short time, which allows multiple requests to be made over the same connection. This reduces the overhead associated with opening separate connections.

We'll learn more about how we can manage this 'restriction' of HTTP in Chapter 5.

HTTP Methods

HTTP 1.1 provides 8 methods used to request data, and to respond to those requests. The methods are CONNECT, DELETE, GET, HEAD, OPTIONS, POST, PUT, and TRACE.

The methods we will use most often are GET and POST:

❏ GET
Clients use the GET method to request a resource from a server. By convention, the request will not change the data stored on the server. From the client's perspective, GET requests should be limited to retrieval of information only. On the server, limited side effects to the request may occur (such as logging), however the principle is that the client is not aware of these and not accountable for them.

❏ POST
Clients use the POST method to post data to the server; for example, to submit a form on an HTTP page. The response to a POST request may be nothing other than a status code that indicates the success or failure of the request.

Other useful methods include:

❏ HEAD
Clients use the HEAD method to check basic information about a resource, such as its size, or the time of its last modification. This information can then be used to decide if it is necessary to make a GET request for the full resource, or to use a cached copy.

❏ DELETE
A DELETE request asks the server to delete the specified resource from the server, which it can of course refuse to do. The ability to perform delete requests on resources of a server, if allowed, is normally restricted to authenticated users who hold an administrator role, or an equivalent role, within the application. Depending upon the configuration, the server may deny unknown users DELETE requests or request that they authenticate using HTTP access authentication before proceeding. Normally the client will receive a successful reply if the resource was removed or (more frequently) the server *intends* to remove the resource at a later point (the server may need to delay the removal for performance or other reasons).

❏ PUT
PUT requests are the converse of DELETE requests. They are used to request that the enclosed resource (a file or other resource) is stored on the requested destination on the server. The key difference between the POST and PUT request is that PUT identifies the destination of the resource, while the POST method identifies the servlet or other server resource to process the request.

You can find a complete reference for HTTP in Appendix B, which includes details of the features supported by both version 1.0 and version 1.1 of the specification.

HTTP Headers

HTTP requests contain header information that indicates information about the client and the request. It can include the request method used, information on file types accepted by the client, information on the client (for example the browser being used), client language, and the URL of the referring link to this page. Similarly, the server's response includes header information that the client can use to interpret the response. In addition to the headers already defined in HTTP, we can use our own header information in an application. Obviously, using non-standard header information means that the client applications communicating with our web application need to be able to understand this extra information as well.

There are four categories of header information that are used in HTTP communication. General and Entity headers are used in both client requests and server responses, while client requests may include Request headers and server responses may include Response headers too.

General header information may cover the date of the request/document, caching information, warnings, and other information. **Entity** headers are used to specify information about the body of the request or response. This may include the MIME type of the data being carried, its length, and other information about the entity body.

A client might include **Request** header information in order to add information about itself (what type of software/browser it is), any cookies previously sent, and the types of response (file or MIME types) that it can understand. A server might include in a **Response** header information such as setting cookies, authentication information or requests, and information about itself (the server software version).

All of this header information that is available in HTTP requests and responses is available to us as programmers. The HttpServletRequest interface exposes the client header information to the servlet, so that it can interpret and extract header information as required (if supplied).

For servlet responses, many headers are automatically set in the response by the container. The exact implementation of this is container-dependent, but we can also set or override the response headings through the HttpServletResponse interface.

Being able to set header information on both the server and client can allow web applications and client applications to add useful information to their communications simply. We will show you exactly how to do this later in the chapter.

HTTP Status Codes

In addition to being able to pass information in headers between client and server (and vice versa) the server also responds to requests and issues a status code with the response to indicate the result of the request. Often this is to indicate that the request was successful, but the status codes can also indicate not only that there was a problem, but also many different types of problems.

In case you are not aware of it, you have probably seen at least one HTTP status code during your surfing of the Internet. Frequently when we click a link on the Web to a page or resource that is broken (the page has been moved or removed without notice) you will see an error page with 404 and Not found (or a similar message). The 404 number is in fact an HTTP status code returned by the server to indicate that the file or resource that you requested was not found by the server. Depending on the configuration of the web site you might see a friendlier custom warning page instead.

The container handles the setting of status codes automatically. Normally when our servlet processes successfully and returns a response to the client, the container will automatically include the 200 code that indicates that the request was processed normally (OK). Occasionally we see on the Web (or in our web applications during development) that when an unhandled error occurs in the servlet, the server will automatically handle this by sending the response code of 500 indicating Internal Server Error.

There are five ranges of status codes that correspond to five general states. Servers can return informational, success, redirection, client error, or server error responses, depending on the result of the processing of the request.

However, we do not have to leave the setting of the status codes only to the container. The HttpServletResponse interface, as we will see later, has methods so that we can set the status code from the servlet to indicate the result of the request. This is important, as we are not always going to want to return the default code that the container may use. The HTTP status codes are provided as constants in the HttpServletResponse interface for servlets and in the J2SE java.net.HttpURLConnection class for clients needing to interpret them.

For example, if we develop an application that has areas of the site that are only availably to authenticated users (or any other relevant criteria), we can have our code return a specific error to non-authorized users such as 401 Unauthorized, 403 Forbidden, or 405 Method Not Allowed.

With custom clients we can make use of the status codes to clearly inform the client about the result of an action by simply setting the status code. The example later in the chapter makes specific use of setting status codes programmatically in the servlet, to let the Java application client know the result of their request. The client makes use of these codes to determine how to process the response and to indicate to the reason a request may have failed (or succeeded) to the user.

HTTP Authentication

HTTP offers a basic method of authentication using Base64 encoding. HTTP **Basic Access Authentication** works as follows:

1. A client makes a request for a file, servlet, or other protected resource.

2. The server replies with the Unauthorized response, including an authentication header (WWW-Authenticate).

3. The client has to respond with appropriate credentials (an encoded username and password) to gain access.

4. If the client fails authentication, the server will respond normally with "forbidden" response.

5. Browsers normally handle the authentication by presenting the user with a dialog box to enter the username and password, and custom applications will have to do the same or retrieve them from memory or storage. For servlet developers with browser clients, this is a convenient method to present authentication.

> **Base64 encoding is an extremely weak form of encoding and should not be used to exchange sensitive information over the Web. HTTPS is generally the preferred option.**

A more complex form of authentication is available called **Digest Access Authentication**, which eliminates the need to send passwords across the network. Some data from the server is used together with the password to create a secure hash, which is returned to the server. The server checks that this corresponds with the password and the data it sent to verify the client's identity. These security procedures are under constant development and improvement.

An alternative approach is to use HTTP over **Secure Sockets Layer (HTTPS)**, which uses public key cryptography. The SSL protocol sits between the TCP and HTTP layers and has become the standard for secure connections over the Internet. We can use HTTPS in conjunction with either Basic or Digest Authentication to improve security and authentication.

You can find more information about how to secure your web applications in Chapter 9.

HTTP and Servlets

The `javax.servlet` package provides generic interfaces and classes to service client requests in a protocol-independent manner. This means that all compatible requests can be made using the members of this package, but we are limited to generic servlet methods to process our request. Any protocol-specific functionality has to be incorporated into the application by the developer.

We can extend the `javax.servlet` package API to create protocol-specific servlet classes that can not only process requests, but also include any protocol-specific logic required. The `javax.servlet.http` package is just such an extension. It adds support for HTTP-specific functions including the HTTP GET or POST methods.

The `javax.servlet.http` package should be viewed in relation to the standard Servlet API. For example, the `javax.servlet.http.HttpServlet` class extends from `javax.servlet.GenericServlet`, adding a number of specific methods to process different types of HTTP requests.

116

Here's a diagram of the classes and interfaces in the `javax.servlet.http` package:

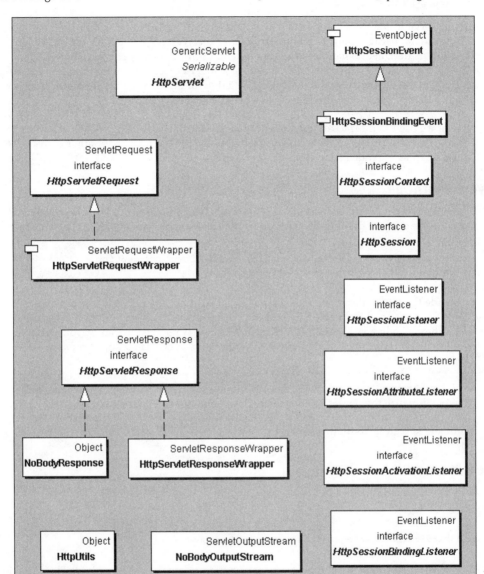

Of course, many classes and interfaces in the `javax.http.HttpServlet` package continue to make use of classes and interfaces from the `javax.servlet` package; for example the streaming and exception classes.

The HttpServlet Class

Many of the servlets that we will develop will extend from `HttpServlet`, rather than `GenericServlet`, because most communication over the Web is carried over HTTP, which `HttpServlet` is designed to handle. When we extend from `HttpServlet` we gain HTTP functionality. For example, `HttpServlet` makes use of HTTP versions of the Request and Response objects. `HttpServlet` overrides the `service()` method of `GenericServlet` and forwards requests to methods designed to process different types of HTTP requests.

Of course, if we use `HttpServlet`, then client requests must be sent using HTTP if they are to be understood. If the clients our application is expected to handle use a protocol other than HTTP we will need to use a servlet extended from `GenericServlet`.

Lifecycle Methods

`HttpServlet` inherits two important lifecycle methods from the `GenericServlet` class: `init()` and `destroy()` – we covered their use in Chapter 2. We can override one of two `init()` methods:

```
public void init(ServletConfig config) throws ServletException
public void init() throws ServletException
```

If you override the first of these you must first call `super.init(config)` to ensure that the reference to the `ServletConfig` object passed in by the servlet container is stored in the servlet instance for later use. If the second `init()` method is overridden there is no need to call `super.init(config)`; it will be called by the `init(config)` method once the `ServletConfig` object reference is stored.

> We should normally only override one version of the **init()** method, because we only need to initialize the servlet in one place. The second method is provided as a convenient alternative choice, but it does not make sense for our servlets to override both and spread the initialization logic.

Service Methods

The `HttpServlet` class defines two `service()` methods to process requests. The first of these overrides the `service()` method inherited from `GenericServlet`:

```
void service(ServletRequest req, ServletResponse res)
```

As HTTP servlet developers we should never have reason to override this method. This method simply casts the `ServletRequest` and `ServletResponse` objects into their corresponding HTTP objects (`HttpServletRequest` and `HttpServletResponse`) and forwards the request to the second `service()` method:

```
protected void service(HttpServletRequest req, HttpServletResponse resp
```

This method should also not be overridden, as it is the responsibility of this method to determine the type of the HTTP request and forward it to the appropriate method to be processed.

There are few reasons why a developer would want to override this `service()` *method. One reason might occur if the developer is working with a custom extended version of the HTTP protocol – but before doing this you should consider alternative ways of achieving your objective, because one of the biggest benefits of HTTP is its interoperability.*

Handling HTTP Requests

We saw earlier that the most common HTTP requests are GET and POST methods. We must implement methods to handle these different types of requests. The servlet container will recognize the type of HTTP request that has been made, and will pass the request to the correct servlet method. Accordingly, we do not override the `service()` methods as we did for servlets that extend GenericServlet, but rather we override the appropriate request method(s):

```
protected void doGet(HttpServletRequest req, HttpServletResponse resp)
   throws ServletException, IOException
protected void doPost(HttpServletRequest req, HttpServletResponse resp)
   throws ServletException, IOException
protected void doHead(HttpServletRequest req, HttpServletResponse resp)
   throws ServletException, IOException
protected void doPut(HttpServletRequest req, HttpServletResponse resp)
   throws ServletException, IOException
```

Not all clients or servers implement the set of HTTP (1.0 or 1.1) specifications fully. It is up to the developer to chose the appropriate way to handle the request and the appropriate method to be used in a web application. Whenever possible, this choice should be consistent with the normal use of the request type (for example, POST for posting data).

The programmer should not normally override the doHead() method because the HttpServlet implementation correctly returns the HEAD request information. The HEAD request returns the header information, but not the body of the GET request.

We must take care only to use the methods new to HTTP 1.1 when clients are known to support the latest version, such as custom Java applications or applets acting as clients. These methods are:

```
protected void doOptions(HttpServletRequest req, HttpServletResponse resp)
   throws ServletException, IOException
protected void doTrace(HttpServletRequest req, HttpServletResponse resp)
   throws ServletException, IOException
```

Clients use OPTIONS requests to determine the types of HTTP requests that the server will handle. We will rarely need to override this method, unless our application needs to 'hide' a supported request type from a client, or we implement methods additional to HTTP 1.1 (such as a later version). We may want to hide methods from client scans to prevent hacking where hidden methods perform sensitive or administrator tasks.

TRACE requests are normally used for debugging. They are designed to allow a request from a client to be sent to a server, and the server then returns the request (as received by it) in the body of the response. This is useful to identify the specific contents of the request that are being received by the server, to determine whether the client is sending the correct request, and/or to determine if the request data is being altered in any way mid-route.

The default implementation of the doTrace() method should not normally be overridden because the default implementation is the same for all servlets. The default implementation will return the header information received by the server back to the client. For applications with custom clients, requests made to the servlet can be examined (to determine if the request is being correctly made) if the request method is modified to an HTTP TRACE request and directed at the servlet.

The getLastModified() method, below, allows servlets that can easily determine the last update time of their GET request data to do so, and then include this in the doHead() and doGet() responses:

```
protected long getLastModified(HttpServletRequest req)
    throws ServletException, IOException
```

This has the effect of improving caching of output, and thereby reducing the load on the server and network.

HTTP Requests and Responses

The HttpServletRequest and HttpServletResponse interfaces extend the ServletRequest and ServletResponse interfaces respectively, in order to add methods that are specific to HTTP. We saw in Chapter 2 that the Servlet API provides two generic wrappers for ServletRequest and ServletResponse: ServletRequestWrapper and ServletResponseWrapper. These wrappers are extended further to provide convenience wrappers for the HTTP interfaces: HttpServletRequestWrapper and HttpServletResponseWrapper.

The HttpServletRequest Interface

We can use the methods defined in the HttpServletRequest interface to learn a great deal about a request.

Header Information

Objects implementing the HttpServletRequest interface contain the header information for the HTTP request. The interface defines methods that are designed to extract the information about the request.

The getMethod() method returns the name of the HTTP request method used to make the request, for example GET or POST:

```
public String getMethod()
```

The getHeaderNames() method returns a java.util.Enumeration of the names of all of the headers supplied with the request:

```
public Enumeration getHeaderNames()
```

We can use the getHeader(String) method to return the value of the header assuming that it exists:

```
public String getHeader(String name)
```

The argument to this method could be any header name, for instance one of the elements of the Enumeration returned by the previous method. For example, calling the method with the user-agent parameter would return information about the client software generating the request (such as Mozilla/4.0 (compatible; MSIE 6.0; Windows NT 5.0)).

We can also use the getHeaders() method, which returns an Enumeration of Strings that contains all the values of the header specified by the supplied name. We use the getHeaders() method where we expect more than one header value of the same name to be included in the header of the request.

public Enumeration getHeaders(String name)

However, we might not always want the value of a header to be stored in a String. If we know that the value of a header is representing a date, or an integer, we can use the getDateHeader() and getIntHeader() methods instead. The getDateHeader() method returns the value of the header specified by the supplied name as a long value that represents a Date object (which is specified by the number of milliseconds since January 1, 1970 GMT):

public long getDateHeader(String name)

If we know a header is in an int value we can use the getIntHeader() method to retrieve it from the request header:

public int getIntHeader(String name)

Putting it all together, we could use the following code snippet to find and print all the headers and corresponding values of the request:

```
Enumeration e = request.getHeaderNames();
while(e.hasMoreElements()) {
   String headerName = (String)e.nextElement();
   String headerValue = request.getHeader(headerName);
   table.appendRow("Header: <code>" + headerName + "</code>", headerValue);
}
```

The following is an example of the output produced from the code above, where the client supplied the headers shown below:

Header	Value
accept	image/gif, image/x-xbitmap, image/jpeg, image/pjpeg, application/vnd.ms-powerpoint, application/vnd.ms-excel, application/msword, */*
referer	http://localhost:8080/httpServlet/index.html
accept-language	en-ie
accept-encoding	gzip, deflate
user-agent	Mozilla/4.0 (compatible; MSIE 6.0; Windows NT 5.0)
host	localhost:8080
connection	Keep-Alive

Only the host header is really essential as many web servers house multiple web sites on one IP address, so specifying the requested web host is important.

Path Information

We can extract information about the path used in the request and the query string (for example http://localhost:8080/httpServlet/servlet/firewall.OurHttpServlet?name=Jayne&children=Luther). The `getQueryString()` method returns the query string of the request, or `null` if there was no query string associated with the request URL: For the URL given above the method would return `"name=Jayne&children=Luther"`.

```
public String getQueryString()
```

The `getContextPath()` method returns the URL context path of the request. This is the first part of the URI, starting with "/" and not ending in a "/" character. For servlets in the root or default context this returns "". In the URL example above this will return `"/httpServlet"`.

```
public String getContextPath()
```

The `getServletPath()` method will return the part of the URL that is used to call the URL (in other words our servlet or another file/resource). In the example URL above this would equate to `"/servlet/firewall.OurHttpServlet"`.

```
public String getServletPath()
```

The `getPathInfo()` method will return any additional path information sent by the client in the request URL:

```
public String getPathInfo()
```

This is any additional path information between the servlet path and the query string. In the example above this would return `null`, as there is no such additional information. We might use additional information to identify a client (for example session tracking) or to include a key or ID.

The `getPathTranslated()` method is similar to the previous `getPathInfo()` method in that it refers to the same additional path information, but in this method it translates this into a real path:

```
public String getPathTranslated()
```

The `getRequestURI()` method specifies the full URI for the request. In the example it would return `"/httpServlet/servlet/firewall.OurHttpServlet"`.

```
public String getRequestURI()
```

The `getRequestURL()` method constructs the URL that the client used to make the request and returns it. This includes the full URL except for the query parameters and would return `"http://localhost/httpServlet/servlet/firewall.OurHttpServlet"` for the example above:

```
public StringBuffer getRequestURL()
```

Let's now look at some code that calls these methods on the request object and outputs the result:

```
//Request Path Elements
out.println("<br><b>Request Context Path:</b> " + request.getContextPath());
out.println("<br><b>Request Servlet Path:</b> " + request.getServletPath());
out.println("<br><b>Request Path Info:</b> " + request.getPathInfo());
out.println("<br><b>Request Path Translated:</b> " +
            request.getPathTranslated());
out.println("<br><b>Request Request URI:</b> " + request.getRequestURI());
out.println("<br><b>Request Request URL:</b> " + request.getRequestURL());
out.println("<br><b>Query String:</b> " + request.getQueryString());
```

The result of this block of code is shown below. These are the various permutations we would get with our example URL.

Request URI: /httpServlet/servlet/firewall.OurHttpServlet
Request Context Path: /httpServlet
Request Servlet Path: /servlet/firewall.OurHttpServlet
Request Path Info: null
Request Path Translated: null
Request Request URI: /httpServlet/servlet/firewall.OurHttpServlet
Request Request URL: http://localhost/httpServlet/servlet/firewall.OurHttpServlet
Query String: name=Jayne&children=Luther&children=Mary

Authentication Information

A number of methods exist to help improve security and authentication by providing the servlet with the means to identify the user (if possible), which enables the servlet to determine what the user has access to or what actions they can perform. Authentication schemes like Basic or Digest Authentication can be used to secure the servlet.

The getAuthType() method will return the String name of the scheme being used:

```
public String getAuthType()
```

The getRemoteUser() method will determine the login name of the client making the request if the user is already authenticated to the servlet. If the user has not already been authenticated to the servlet, this method will return null:

```
public String getRemoteUser()
```

The getUserPrincipal() method is very similar to the previous method except that it returns a Principal object containing the name of the authenticated user (or null if they are not authenticated):

```
public java.security.Principal getUserPrincipal()
```

The two previous methods effectively perform similar actions, but the second returns a `Principal` object. The `Principal` object is used to represent the concept of a user entity, which could be an individual, a corporation, or a login ID. The `getUserPrincipal()` method may be used when applications use the `java.security` packages to manage access and security for the application.

The following method can be used to find out if the user who has been authenticated to the server has been designated with the specified role when using the web application:

```
public boolean isUserInRole(String role)
```

We can use this method to grant or deny access to a user, based on their role.

The HttpServletResponse Interface

The `HttpServletResponse` interface extends from the `ServletResponse` interface and is used to send the servlet's HTTP-based response back to the client. It includes additional HTTP-specific methods for setting data in the response, such as HTTP headers, sessions and cookies, and status codes.

Headers and MIME Types

The `HttpServletResponse` interface inherits two methods from the `ServletResponse` class related to setting the headers of a response.

The `setContentLength()` method sets the header indicating the length of the response. Setting this value too low will normally stop the server sending the excess data after the length specified, and most clients will stop reading the response after the specified length. Conversely, setting the size too high may leave the client hanging, waiting for more data once the response has been completed, until it times out. Therefore it is often better to let the server set this header (if it can buffer the full response before sending) or perhaps leave it unset, unless the content can be easily determined in advance.

The second method inherited from the `ServletResponse` class is the `setContentType()` method. This is used to set the **MIME** (**Multipurpose Internet Mail Extensions**, RFC 2045 and 2046) type of the response. MIME types are used in many protocols other than HTTP to indicate the type of output or file following:

```
response.setContentType("text/html");
```

Here we set the content type to `"text/html"`. For servlets sending back HTML-based web pages this is the type we always use, and is the most common type that servlets will return to the client. We change this if we are sending different data back to the client. Appendix B gives more information on MIME and common MIME types.

The most common way to set headers of a HTTP response is to use the `setHeader()` method to reset an existing header or the `addHeader()` method to add a new header to the response:

```
public void setHeader(String name, String value)
public void addHeader(String name, String value)
```

A number of other convenience header methods exist, to allow for the inclusion of data not in `String` format into headers. To set a date header we could use one of the above methods, with the date value in `String` format. However to set the date header directly we can use the `setDateHeader()` method to set or reset the specified header field. Using the `addDateHeader()` method we can add a header field with date information:

```
public void setDateHeader(String name, long date)
public void addDateHeader(String name, long date)
```

The `addIntHeader()` and `setIntHeader()` methods allows the addition/setting of `int` values in headers in a similar way:

```
public void addIntHeader(String name, int value)
public void setIntHeader(String name, int value)
```

We can check if a header has already been set using the `containsHeader()` method:

```
boolean containsHeader(String name)
```

This will return `true` if the specified header has already been set in the response object. Otherwise it will return `false`.

Redirecting Requests

To redirect a request to another resource on the server (or anywhere else), the `sendRedirect()` method may be used with the relative or absolute address as appropriate. If the server is (or may be) using URL rewriting to maintain sessions, you must call the `encodeRedirectURL()` method (on the Response object as well) with the URL that the client is being redirected to, so that the server can add the session information to the URL:

```
void sendRedirect(String location)
```

To use the `sendRedirect()` method, the response must still be buffered on the server (or not started at all), and not committed. We can check if the response has been committed yet with the `isCommitted()` method, inherited from `ServletResponse`. If we try to redirect the request after the response has been committed an `IllegalStateException` is thrown. Also, using this method effectively commits the response, so we should not write any further to the response.

Using the `sendRedirect()` method is different from using a `RequestDispatcher` object to forward (or include a response). This method is used to effectively redirect the entire request to another location for processing. Using a `RequestDispatcher` object we can either include the content of the resource that the `RequestDispatcher` object represents, or forward the request to this resource. If we forward the request using the `RequestDispatcher` object, we may have already sent some data back to the client, while the resource being forwarded to will append to the output already sent (if any). You should refer to Chapter 2 for more on the `RequestDispatcher` class and examples of its use.

Status Codes and Errors

The `HttpServletResponse` class currently has forty `static int` fields declared, corresponding to HTTP status codes that can be returned in a response to a client. The most commonly seen status code in browsers on the Internet is the `404 Not Found` error reported when a page or resource has been removed.

We can set the status code to a request using the `setStatus()` method. This is much better than just returning an error to the client and it can be much more informational, because we can specify that a resource is temporarily unavailable (`503`) or it is forbidden (`403`).

```
public void setStatus(int sc)
```

When an error occurs we can use either of the `sendError()` methods (taking a status code, or code and message):

```
public void sendError(int sc)
public void sendError(int sc, String msg)
```

These set the status code as with the `setStatus()` method, but also clear the buffer and commit the response, meaning that the servlet cannot send any further output to the client in response to this request. Most servers, depending on configuration, will present a default error page (specific to this error code or all error codes) with information for the client.

Implementing HTTP Servlets

In this section we are going to use what we have learned so far to develop some HTTP servlets, and then run them. We'll start off with a few relatively simple examples, and then at the end of the chapter we'll implement a more complex web application based upon HTTP servlets.

Implementing HttpRequestResponseServlet

Let's start by looking at two basic HTTP servlets. The first is a development of the `RequestResponseServlet` from Chapter 2. Here we will develop a similar `HttpRequestResponseServlet`, however, this class will extend from the `HttpServlet` class and will demonstrate how we can extract HTTP-specific client information such as headers, cookies, and the request path. We will also set some cookies each time we load the page, so we will see our cookies being returned to the server with each refresh. Here's what the HTTP request and response tables look like:

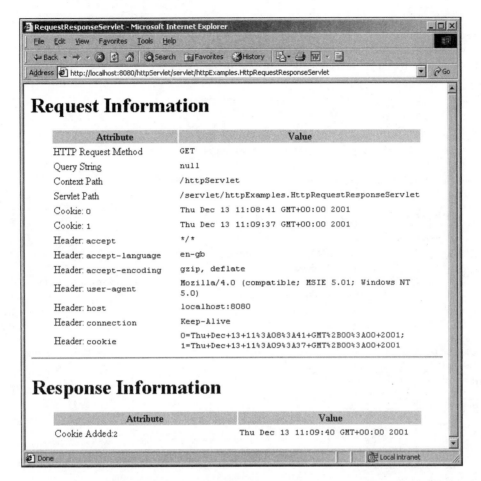

This example also uses the `HTMLTable` utility class developed in Chapter 2, that allows us to build a fully formatted HTML table of data to send to the client.

The `HttpRequestResponseServlet` is similar to that in Chapter 2, so if you are familiar with the examples there you should focus on the HTTP-specific methods available to extract client request data:

```
package httpExamples;

import javax.servlet.*;
import javax.servlet.http.*;
import java.io.IOException;
import java.io.PrintWriter;
import java.util.Enumeration;
import java.util.Date;

public class HttpRequestResponseServlet extends HttpServlet {
  private static int cookiesCreated = 0;
```

First we store a count of cookies created by the servlet, which we will use to set the names of the cookies. Then, the `doGet()` method calls the `getHttpRequestTable` and the `getHttpResponseTable` methods with their respective Request and Response objects. These extract the data and prepare an HTML table for return to the client.

```
public void doGet(HttpServletRequest request,
                  HttpServletResponse response)
                throws ServletException, IOException {
    StringBuffer httpRequestTable = getHttpRequestTable(request);
    StringBuffer httpResponseTable = getHttpResponseTable(response);
```

Then we output the HTML page, including the two HTML tables just created.

```
    response.setContentType("text/html");
    PrintWriter out = response.getWriter();
    //HTML page
    out.println("<html><head><title>RequestResponseServlet</title></head>");
    out.println("<body><h1>Request Information</h1>" + httpRequestTable);
    out.println("<hr><h1>Response Information</h1>" + httpResponseTable);
    out.println("</body></html>");
    out.close();
}
```

The `getHttpRequestTable()` method extracts data from the client Request object using HTTP-specific methods. We extract the request method used, the query string (if any) and some path information, and add them to the table:

```
private StringBuffer getHttpRequestTable(HttpServletRequest request) {
    HTMLTable table = new HTMLTable();
    table.appendRow("HTTP Request Method", request.getMethod());
    table.appendRow("Query String", request.getQueryString());
    table.appendRow("Context Path", request.getContextPath());
    table.appendRow("Servlet Path", request.getServletPath());
```

Next we extract all of the cookies associated with this request and add them to the table. If you run this example and do not see any cookies (assuming that you have cookies turned on in your browser) refresh the page and you will see cookies added to the request. This is because they are added to the Response object each time and sent back to the client:

```
    Cookie[] ourCookies = request.getCookies();
    if (ourCookies == null || ourCookies.length == 0) {
        table.appendRow("Cookies", "NONE");
    } else {
        for (int i = 0; i < ourCookies.length; i++) {
            String cookieName = ourCookies[i].getName();
            String cookieValue = ourCookies[i].getValue();
            table.appendRow("Cookie: <code>" + cookieName + "</code>",
                            cookieValue);
        }
    }
```

Next we are going to extract the header information. If you know the specific header that you are interested in you can call the `request.getHeader(String)` method with the name, and receive the value of the header (or `null` if it doesn't exist). However, we can extract an `Enumeration` of all of the request headers and use a `while` loop to iterate through and extract all of the values of the headers and then process them, or in this case, include them in our table:

```
Enumeration e = request.getHeaderNames();
while (e.hasMoreElements()) {
  String headerName = (String)e.nextElement();
  String headerValue = request.getHeader(headerName);
  table.appendRow("Header: <code>" + headerName + "</code>",
                  headerValue);
}
return table.toStringBuffer();
}
```

The `getHttpResponseTable()` method adds a `cookie` to the response sent to the client and includes the details in the table. The cookie's name is the current number of times this servlet has been called, and the current date and time, provided by the `Date` object:

```
private StringBuffer getHttpResponseTable(HttpServletResponse response) {
  HTMLTable table = new HTMLTable();
  int cookieCount = cookiesCreated++;
  String name = Integer.toString(cookieCount);
  String value = new Date(System.currentTimeMillis()).toString();
  Cookie cookie = new Cookie(name, value);
  response.addCookie(cookie);
  table.appendRow("Cookie Added:<code>" + name + "</code>", value);
  return table.toStringBuffer();
}
}
```

Compiling and Running the Example

To run the examples we need to set up the web application. Create a web application in the `webapp` directory of Tomcat called `httpServlet` that has the following subdirectories:

```
httpServlet/
          WEB-INF/
                  classes/
                          httpExamples
                  src/
                      httpExamples
```

Place the `HttpRequestResponseServlet` sourcecode, along with the `HTMLTable` sourcecode, into the `src/httpExamples` directory, and compile the code. Then move the classes to the `classes/httpExamples` directory.

Finally, to run your code, restart Tomcat and go to:

http://localhost:8080/httpServlet/servlet/httpExamples.HttpRequestResponseServlet

Implementing QuizServlet

This example presents the `QuizForm.html` form to the user and asks them to answer three questions. The `QuizServlet` retrieves the quiz parameters and calculates how well the user did. This example demonstrates using the HTTP `doGet()` and `doPost()` methods. It also shows how to extract and process parameters in order to prepare a return web page.

First, here's the `QuizForm.html` file that contains the Quiz questions:

```html
<html>
<head><title>Quiz</title></head>
<body>
  <h2>The Quiz</h2>
  <form method="post" action="servlet/httpExamples.QuizServlet">
  <table>
    <tr>
      <td><b>Name:</b></td>
      <td><input type="text" name="name" size=20></td>
    </tr>

    <tr>
      <td><b>What is the capital of Australia?</b></td>
      <td> <br>
        <input type="radio" name="australia" value="Sydney"> Sydney <br>
        <input type="radio" name="australia" value="Canberra">
                                                 Canberra<br> 
      </td>
    </tr>

    <tr>
      <td><b>What is the capital of Brazil?</b></td>
      <td> <br>
        <input type="radio" name="brazil" value="RioDeJaneiro">
                                           Rio de Janeiro<br>
        <input type="radio" name="brazil" value="Brasilia">
                                           Brasilia<br> 
      </td>
    </tr>

    <tr>
      <td><b>What is the capital of Ireland?</b></td>
      <td> <br>
        <input type="radio" name="ireland" value="Dublin"> Dublin<br>
        <input type="radio" name="ireland" value="Galway"> Galway<br> 
      </td>
    </tr>

    <tr>
      <td colspan=2 align="middle">
        <input type="submit" value="Submit Answers">
        <input type="reset" value="Reset Answers">
      </td>
    </tr>
  </table>
  </form>
</body>
</html>
```

The page asks three questions regarding capital cities:

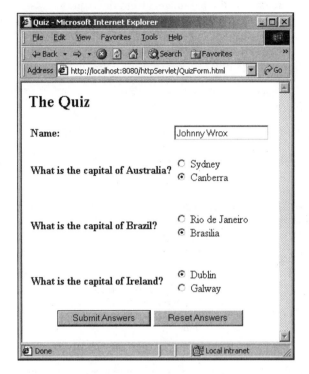

Depending on the choice made, the correct (or incorrect) parameters are sent to the servlet.

The QuizServlet opens with a number of static Strings that contain information about the questions and answers:

```
package httpExamples;

import javax.servlet.*;
import javax.servlet.http.*;
import java.io.*;
import java.util.*;

public class QuizServlet extends HttpServlet {
  private static final String AUSTRALIA = "australia";
  private static final String AUSTRALIA_CAPITAL = "Canberra";
  private static final String BRAZIL = "brazil";
  private static final String BRAZIL_CAPITAL = "Brasilia";
  private static final String IRELAND = "ireland";
  private static final String IRELAND_CAPITAL = "Dublin";
  private static final String NAME = "name";
```

The `doGet()` method processes the form submission. First it prepares a `count` variable to count the correct answers, and then it extracts the parameters from the request:

```
public void doGet(HttpServletRequest request,
                  HttpServletResponse response)
                  throws ServletException, IOException {
  int count = 0;
  String name = request.getParameter(NAME);
  String answerAustralia = request.getParameter(AUSTRALIA);
  String answerBrazil = request.getParameter(BRAZIL);
  String answerIreland = request.getParameter(IRELAND);
```

Here the `doGet()` method outputs the HTML page. If a name was supplied as a parameter, it is displayed on the page:

```
response.setContentType("text/html");
PrintWriter out = response.getWriter();
out.println("<html>");
out.println("<head><title>QuizServlet</title></head>");
out.println("<body>");

if (name != null && name.trim().length() > 0) {
  out.println("<h1>Welcome " + name + "</h1>");
} else {
  out.println("<h1>Welcome</h1>");
}
```

The `doQuestion()` method calls output and displays a response that depends on whether the question was correctly answered, and updates the count. The score is then printed out:

```
count = count + doQuestion(out, 1, answerAustralia, AUSTRALIA_CAPITAL);
count = count + doQuestion(out, 2, answerBrazil, BRAZIL_CAPITAL);
count = count + doQuestion(out, 3, answerIreland, IRELAND_CAPITAL);

out.println("<hr width=\"25%\" align=\"left\">");
out.println("You scored " + count + " out of 3");
```

After the score, we identify the browser software being used by the client from the `user-agent` header. If this has `"MSIE"` in it then this is a Microsoft browser:

```
String userAgent = request.getHeader("user-agent");
if (userAgent != null && userAgent.indexOf("MSIE") != -1) {
  out.println(" using Microsoft browser.");
} else if (userAgent != null) {
  out.println(" using Non-Microsoft browser.");
}
out.println("</body></html>");
}
```

Here is an important point. The doPost() method forwards the request to doGet() to process the request. In fact the HTTP request is a POST request as the HTML form specifies a POST request. Here we can see that processing a GET or POST request has no programmatic differences. We can process both GET and POST requests in the same way:

```
public void doPost(HttpServletRequest request,
                   HttpServletResponse response)
                   throws ServletException, IOException {
   doGet(request, response);
}
```

Finally we have an auxiliary method to process the questions:

```
private int doQuestion(PrintWriter out, int number,
                       String answer, String solution) {
   out.println("<h2>Question " + number + "</h2>");
   if (answer != null &&
       solution.equalsIgnoreCase(answer)) {
     out.println("<b>Correct</b>");
     return 1;
   } else {
     out.println("<b>Wrong:</b> The correct answer is " + solution);
     return 0;
   }
 }
}
```

Here's a typical response that the servlet will produce when the HTML form from QuizForm.html is submitted:

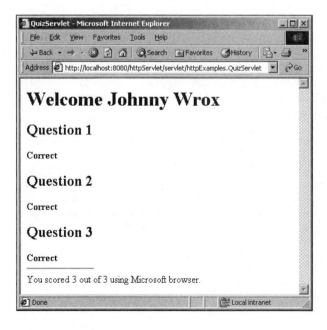

Compiling and Running the Example

Place the `QuizForm` HTML page in the top level of the `httpServlet` directory. Place all of the Java sourcecode in the `src/httpExamples` directory, compile them, and move the classes to the `classes/httpExamples` directory.

To run your code, go to http://localhost:8080/httpServlet/QuizForm.html to fill in the form. When you submit the form, the request will be passed to http://localhost:8080/httpServlet/servlet/httpExamples.QuizServlet.

Servlets and Custom Clients

Servlet applications can be designed to communicate with all types of clients, and HTTP servlet applications with clients over HTTP. To meaningfully communicate, the client and server must agree the protocol and the structure of requests and responses expected.

In this section we are going to see how a Java application can work as the client to a web application. In the application, the client is shown a protected directory by the server, and it can exchange text files with the web application. The client can view the list of files, delete files, download a copy of a file to their local machine, and upload a file to the server's protected directory.

Servlets and HTTP servlets are often seen as dynamic web page programs. In fact this is only a fraction of what they can do. This application is designed to demonstrate how we can have a servlet communicating with a Java client, sending serialized Java objects *and* files both ways between the servlet and client. We will also extensively use HTTP status codes in the web application to inform the client of the result of the request.

Using servlets for text-based communications (for example HTML, XML) is relatively straightforward, but sending objects, files, and HTML messages across a network is a little more challenging. We see in this example both sides of the communication, focusing on the servlet side. However, at the end of the day, sending messages between servlets and Java applications is really streaming data, which is very relevant in a distributed computing environment. It may appear to be wrapped in layers of complexity, but the basic principles are the same. This example should unravel many of those layers and expose the mechanisms involved in this type of application.

While this is only a demonstration application, the functionality is taken directly from real-world applications. Many trading systems send data (objects, files, and so on) containing the details of completed trades to other systems, which are stored on the server pending processing. If we were anticipating having to communicate with other non-Java systems we could develop XML-based communications, but as this is not the case here we will keep to serializing Java objects and files. By focusing on servlet application development, we should be able to see the skills used for developing in distributed applications.

Designing the Application

The Java Swing-based client application will use the techniques of HTTP tunneling to communicate with the servlet running in Tomcat. The purpose of the application is to provide the client with a view of the files within a protected folder and to allow the client to remotely manage them. There are four key functions that the client will be able to perform in conjunction with the servlet. It must be able to:

- ❑ Get a list of the files in the specified folder
- ❑ Download the files from the server's directory to a local directory
- ❑ Delete files from the server's specified directory
- ❑ Upload files from a local drive to the server's specified directory

The client will *only* be able to access and perform actions on a specified directory on the server, and on no other. This directory will be %CATALINA_HOME%/webapps/httpServlet/WEB-INF/files/. The WEB-INF directory and all of its contents are *not visible* to clients. So we have added the files directory, and ten sample text files for use. Our application only permits the transfer of a certain number of text-based files (specified in firewall.common.FileValidator).

> *You'll learn why the WEB-INF directory is kept private in Chapter 4.*

The server will allow the client application access to the contents of a specified directory, and will not provide access to other directories. All communications between the client and server will have to take place over HTTP.

> *Our application will not have strong security – we will not implement any login or other security. We will learn how to incorporate security into our web applications in Chapter 9.*

The Client Graphical User Interface

The client GUI consists of a javax.swing.JList on the top left to hold a list of files in the relevant server directory.

> *You can learn more about the Swing API in* Beginning Java 2 *(ISBN: 1-861003-66-8) published by Wrox, as well as from the online documentation at http://java.sun.com/products/jfc/.*

The JList is populated when the application loads, and after each action. Pressing the Refresh button will update the contents as well. The top right section is a javax.swing.JTextArea that will display messages to the user. The lower part of the GUI contains buttons to control the application:

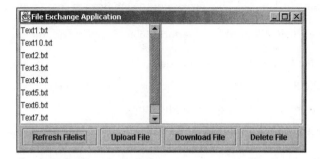

To upload a file we will present the user with a javax.swing.JFileChooser object to select a file from their system to upload to the server:

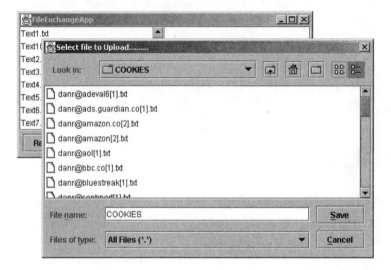

Once the upload is complete, the user will see a message indicating completion, and the file will appear in the JList:

To download a file the user must select a file and then hit the **Download File** button. To keep things simple, we download the file to the user's default directory according to the system. In my case (using Windows 2000) this is C:\Documents and Settings\Andrew.MAIN1\, however in Linux this could be usr/docs/ or similar. File deletion is similar, with the user selecting the file for deletion and then the **Delete File** button, which gives the user a message to the window once completed.

Planning the Implementation

We will use three packages in our implementation:

❑ The firewall.client package contains the classes that are used exclusively by the client. This package does not need to be deployed on the server and can safely be deleted from the server's classes. This can be significant in larger applications where client-side-only classes and ancillary files such as images can contribute to the server-side application bloat.

❑ The firewall.server package contains the servlet class and other classes used exclusively by the server. This package need not be deployed as part of the client files, and in a real-world scenario *should not* be included. It would not be included on the client side for two main reasons. Firstly, this package exclusively contains classes that are run on the server and *not* on the client. Secondly, inclusion of the server-side classes may present a security risk if they were decompiled.

❑ The firewall.common package will contain classes that are used on both the server and the client, and this package (and subpackages) must be included in both the server-side deployment and the client-side deployment. There are many types of files that may fall into this category, but two stand out. Firstly all classes that are used in communication between the client and server (the serialized objects) must be common, because both the client and server needs to access them to interpret their data. This also includes data classes (such as list objects) that may be used on both the client and server, and should be included here for consistency. In our case all of these classes are serializable and are used in client-server communication. We have an additional FileValidator helper class as well, which is not serializable. Helper classes, such as debugging classes (logging, assertions), and formatting classes should be included in the common package, if they are used, to ensure uniformity on both the client and server.

Classes Overview

The following tables briefly outline the classes and their role in the application.

The client Package

Class	Role
FileExchangeApplication	Contains the main() method for the application. Acts as 'in loco' controller.
FileExchangeView	Is the GUI of the application.
FileExchangeModel	Contains the business logic for processing user input.
FileExchangeFilter	Minor Filter class for the FileChooser.

The server Package

Class	Role
FileExchangeServlet	The server-side servlet that receives requests for processing.
RequestHandlerFactory	Identifies the incoming request type and allocates and instantiates the appropriate handler object to deal with this request.
RequestHandler	Abstract superclass handler that provides the abstract respond() method, which is implemented in all subclasses to process requests. It also provides other useful methods commonly required by subclasses.
RefreshHandler	Extends RequestHandler to process REFRESH requests.
DownloadHandler	Extends RequestHandler to process DOWNLOAD requests.
UploadHandler	Extends RequestHandler to process UPLOAD requests.
DeleteHandler	Extends RequestHandler to process DELETE requests.

The common Package

Class	Role
BaseRequest	Superclass of all of the serialized objects. Solely stores the request type for the communication.
FileName	Subclass to BaseRequest – includes the filename of the communication.
FileList	Subclass to BaseRequest – includes an array of filenames from the server directory.
FileValidator	Utility class used by both client and server to validate file extensions.

Having defined what we need from our classes, let's now see how we implement them.

Implementing the Client

The FileExchangeView class provides the GUI element, and the FileExchangeModel provides the business logic processing (which is primarily the communication with the server and sending the results to the user).

The FileExchangeApplication Class

This class incorporates the main() method for the application, and is responsible for initializing the FileExchangeView object:

```
package firewall.client;

import java.awt.*;
import java.awt.event.*;
import javax.swing.*;
import java.net.*;

public class FileExchangeApplication {

  private FileExchangeApplication () {}
```

The main() method first checks that the parameter (if any) is a correct server address so that we can access our server. By default the application uses the default server address of http://localhost:8080:

```
public static void main(String[] args) {
  URL server;
  try {
    if (args.length > 0) {
      server = new URL(args[0] +
      "/httpServlet/servlet/firewall.server.FileExchangeServlet");
    } else {
      server = new URL("http://localhost:8080/httpServlet/servlet/" +
                       "firewall.server.FileExchangeServlet");
  } catch (MalformedURLException mue) {
    System.out.println("Error in using FileExchangeApp");
    System.out.println("Usage:\n  " +
                       "java firewall.client.FileExchangeApp [ServerURL]"
                      );
    mue.printStackTrace();
    return;
  }
```

Then we initialize the FileExchangeView object:

```
  JFrame frame = new FileExchangeView(server,
                                      "File Exchange Application");
  frame.addWindowListener(new WindowAdapter() {
    public void windowClosing(WindowEvent e) {
      System.exit(0);
    }
  });
  frame.pack();
  frame.setVisible(true);
  }
}
```

The FileExchangeView Class

The `FileExchangeView` class sets up the user interface and creates the listeners needed to capture user actions, which in turn pass these on to the `FileExchangeModel` business logic object:

```java
package firewall.client;

import java.io.*;
import java.awt.*;
import java.awt.event.*;
import javax.swing.*;
import javax.swing.filechooser.*;
import java.net.*;

public class FileExchangeView extends JFrame {
```

First we prepare the URL object that stores a reference to the server's address, and initialize the `FileExchangeModel` with a reference to this `FileExchangeView` object:

```java
URL hostServlet;
FileExchangeModel model = new FileExchangeModel(this);
```

Next the GUI elements are initialized:

```java
final JTextArea messages = new JTextArea(5, 20);
final JList fileList = new JList();
final JFileChooser fc = new JFileChooser();
JButton refreshButton = new JButton("Refresh Filelist");
JButton uploadButton = new JButton("Upload File");
JButton downloadButton = new JButton("Download File");
JButton deleteButton = new JButton("Delete File");
JPanel buttonPanel = new JPanel();
JPanel displayPanel = new JPanel();
```

The constructor initializes and sets up the GUI:

```java
public FileExchangeView(URL server, String name) {
    super(name);

    this.hostServlet = server;

    //create the message window and the filelist
    messages.setMargin(new Insets(5, 5, 5, 5));
    messages.setEditable(false);
    JScrollPane messageScrollPane = new JScrollPane(messages);
    fileList.setSize(1000, 1000);
    fileList.setEnabled(true);
    fileList
        .setSelectionMode(javax.swing.ListSelectionModel.SINGLE_SELECTION);
    JScrollPane fileListScrollPane = new JScrollPane();
    fileListScrollPane.getViewport().setView(fileList);
```

Then we add the listeners to the each of the four buttons, so that we can process user actions. The listeners pass the request on to the appropriate method from the `model` object:

```
refreshButton.addActionListener(new ActionListener() {
  public void actionPerformed(ActionEvent e) {
    //call refresh method
    model.refreshRequest();
    messages.setText("");
  }
});
```

Next we add a listener to the upload button:

```
uploadButton.addActionListener(new ActionListener() {
  public void actionPerformed(ActionEvent e) {
```

After setting the file filter to our selected text-based files, we show a dialog which allows the user to select a file to send to the server:

```
fc.setDialogTitle("Select file to Upload..........");
FileExchangeFilter filter =
  new FileExchangeFilter(FileValidator.VALID_EXTENSIONS,
                                    "Text files");
fc.setFileFilter(filter);
int returnVal = fc.showSaveDialog(FileExchangeView.this);
```

Then we perform the user's selected choice:

```
if (returnVal == JFileChooser.APPROVE_OPTION) {
  File file = fc.getSelectedFile();
  messages.append("Uploading: " + file.getName() + "\n");
  model.uploadRequest(file);
} else {
  messages.append("Upload command cancelled by user.\n");
}
```

The next line of code refreshes the list of files after deletion:

```
    model.refreshRequest();
  }
});
```

Next we add listeners to the download and the delete buttons:

```
downloadButton.addActionListener(new ActionListener() {
  public void actionPerformed(ActionEvent e) {
    model.downloadRequest((String) fileList.getSelectedValue());
  }
});
deleteButton.addActionListener(new ActionListener() {
  public void actionPerformed(ActionEvent e) {
    model.deleteRequest((String) fileList.getSelectedValue());
  }
});
```

The individual objects of the GUI are then added to their respective panels, which are in turn added to this JFrame:

```
buttonPanel.add(refreshButton);
buttonPanel.add(uploadButton);
buttonPanel.add(downloadButton);
buttonPanel.add(deleteButton);
refreshButton.setNextFocusableComponent(uploadButton);
uploadButton.setNextFocusableComponent(downloadButton);
downloadButton.setNextFocusableComponent(deleteButton);
deleteButton.setNextFocusableComponent(refreshButton);
displayPanel.setLayout(new GridLayout(1, 2));
displayPanel.add(fileListScrollPane);
displayPanel.add(messageScrollPane);
Container contentPane = getContentPane();
contentPane.setLayout(new BorderLayout());
contentPane.add(buttonPanel, BorderLayout.CENTER);
contentPane.add(displayPanel, BorderLayout.NORTH);
```

Then we set up the filelist:

```
    model.refreshRequest();
  }
```

We need an accessor method for the host servlet's address.

```
public URL getHostServlet() {
  return hostServlet;
}
```

Finally, we need an `appendMessage()` method that allows the `FileExchangeModel` to update the messages for the user. We also need `refreshFileList()` method, that takes a `String` array as input parameter, to update the list of files in the `FileExchangeView`:

```
public void appendMessage(String message) {
  messages.append(message + "\n");
}

public void refreshFileList(String[] files) {
  fileList.setListData(files);
}
}
```

The FileExchangeModel Class

This class is designed to perform the application's business logic. The `FileExchangeView` essentially focuses on the GUI aspect, while the object of this class is called to process user actions according to the application's business rules:

```
package firewall.client;

import firewall.common.*;
import java.io.*;
import java.net.*;

public class FileExchangeModel {
```

First the model needs a reference to the `FileExchangeView`, so that once it has completed processing the user requests it can send the results to this object for display to the user:

```
FileExchangeView view;

public FileExchangeModel(FileExchangeView view) {
  this.view = view;
}
```

There are four major methods in this class, corresponding with the four buttons and actions a user can request from the server. Each of these methods is responsible for preparing its request to send to the server, retrieving the response, and displaying an appropriate message indicating the outcome of the request.

The `uploadRequest()` method is a request to upload a file from the client application to the server. Once the filename is validated, the process that takes place is that a `FileName` object indicating the filename and the request type is sent to the server, followed by the streamed file. Then the server returns an `HTTP` status code, indicating whether the upload was successful. Finally the method requests a refresh of the file list in the `FileExchangeView` and the user should see their file, assuming the request was processed successfully:

```
    public void uploadRequest(File uploadFile) {

   if (!FileValidator.isFileNameValid(uploadFile)) {
      view.appendMessage("Upload:Error - File selected is invalid");
      return;
   }

   URL url = view.getHostServlet();
   HttpURLConnection httpURLConnection = null;
   int status = 0;
   String message = null;
   try {
```

Here is where the application starts the process of sending a HTTP POST request to our servlet. Using the URL object we open a connection to the servlet with the getHttpURLConnection() method. Calling the sendRequest() method, we send our request object to the server:

```
   httpURLConnection = getHttpURLConnection(url);
   sendRequest(httpURLConnection,
           new FileName(BaseRequest.UPLOAD, uploadFile.getName()),
           false);
```

This application is designed to exchange text files between client and server. We could of course modify this to work with any type of file, by using different I/O classes to read and send the data.

Next the file that we have chosen must be read in and sent out to the server. We create a FileReader object to read from the selected file, and a PrintWriter object (wrapping the connection's OutputStream). Then the FileReader reads the file to the PrintWriter object, which sends it out to the server. We then close the FileReader and output objects:

```
   //now send the file to the client
   FileReader fileReader = new FileReader(uploadFile);
   OutputStream os = httpURLConnection.getOutputStream();
   PrintWriter out = new PrintWriter(os);

   char c[] = new char[4096];
   int read = 0;
   // Read until end of file and send to client
   while ((read = fileReader.read(c)) != -1) {
     out.write(c, 0, read);
   }
   // Close
   fileReader.close();
   out.close();
   os.close();
```

We must read back the server's response, so that we get the HTTP response code and message:

```
        status = httpURLConnection.getResponseCode();
        message = httpURLConnection.getResponseMessage();
    } catch (Exception e) {
        e.printStackTrace();
    }
```

Finally we inform the `FileExchangeView` of the result of the request, and refresh the file list to reflect the new file. HTTP status codes 200 to 299 indicate a successful response from the server, so if we use the constants `HttpURLConnection.HTTP_OK` (200 "OK") and `HttpURLConnection.HTTP_MULT_CHOICE` (300) as boundaries, we can check if the response is successful:

```
    //inform the client
    if (status >= HttpURLConnection.HTTP_OK ||
        status < HttpURLConnection.HTTP_MULT_CHOICE) {
      view.appendMessage("Upload:Success (" + status + ") " + message);
    } else {
      view.appendMessage("Upload:Error (" + status + ") " + message);
    }
    //refresh the file list
    refreshRequest();
}
```

The `downloadRequest()` method is a request from the client to download a file from the server. The process that takes place is that a `FileName` object, indicating the filename wanted, and the request type is sent to the server. Then the server returns the file in its response. The location that the file is saved to is determined by the location of the user's default directory. In any case the full location of the file is displayed to the user:

```
public void downloadRequest(String fileName) {

    //ensure valid file is selected
    if (!FileValidator.isFileNameValid(fileName)) {
      view.appendMessage("Download:File must be selected");
      return;
    }
```

After ensuring that a file was actually selected, the location where the file should be saved is selected via the user's default directory ("user.home"). This simply maps to the user's home directory, irrespective of the operating system being used, which is where we save files:

```
    URL url = view.getHostServlet();
    HttpURLConnection httpURLConnection = null;
    //default location to save file to
    File saveFile = new File(System.getProperty("user.home"), fileName);
    try {
```

As we did previously, we call the `getHttpURLConnection()` method to get a connection to the server, and then call our `sendRequest()` method to make the request to download the requested file:

```
httpURLConnection = getHttpURLConnection(url);
sendRequest(httpURLConnection,
            new FileName(BaseRequest.DOWNLOAD, fileName));
```

Next we check the status code for success, and update the user:

```
int status = httpURLConnection.getResponseCode();
String message = httpURLConnection.getResponseMessage();

//inform the client
if (status >= HttpURLConnection.HTTP_OK ||
    status < HttpURLConnection.HTTP_MULT_CHOICE) {
  view.appendMessage("Download:Success (" + status + ") " + message);
} else {
  view.appendMessage("Download:Error (" + status + ") " + message);
  return;
}
```

We then get an `InputStreamReader`, wrapped in a `BufferedReader` (for efficiency), to read the streamed file, while the `FileWriter` object writes the received file to our user directory. Note that, as we mentioned before, this is suitable for receiving text files only, but could be adapted for all files if required:

```
InputStreamReader isr =
    new InputStreamReader(httpURLConnection.getInputStream());
BufferedReader bfr = new BufferedReader(isr);
FileWriter fileWriter = new FileWriter(saveFile);
char c[] = new char[4096];
int read = 0;

while ((read = bfr.read(c)) != -1) {
  fileWriter.write(c, 0, read);
}
```

Finally the `FileWriter` and `InputStream` objects are closed, and a message is returned to the `FileExchangeView` to let the user know where the file was saved:

```
fileWriter.close();
isr.close();
view.appendMessage("Download:File saved to:\n" +
                   saveFile.getCanonicalPath());
} catch (Exception e) {
view.appendMessage("Download:Error downloading the file");
e.printStackTrace();
}
}
```

The refreshRequest() method (that we've already used) is a request from the client to refresh the list of files from the server. The process that takes place is that a BaseRequest object, indicating the request type, is sent to the server. Then the server returns the array of String filenames in the response, for display to the user:

```
public void refreshRequest() {
  URL url = view.getHostServlet();
  HttpURLConnection httpURLConnection = null;
  FileList files = null;
  try {
```

The first part of the request is as in the previous methods. A BaseRequest object indicating a REFRESH request is then sent to the server:

```
httpURLConnection = getHttpURLConnection(url);
sendRequest(httpURLConnection,
            new BaseRequest(BaseRequest.REFRESH));
```

The server's response status code is checked:

```
if (status >= HttpURLConnection.HTTP_OK ||
    status < HttpURLConnection.HTTP_MULT_CHOICE) {
  view.appendMessage("Refresh:Success (" + status + ") " + message);
} else {
  view.appendMessage("Refresh:Error (" + status + ") " + message);
  return;
}
```

The response from the server this time is a FileList object, which contains the array of String filenames, and the JList object on screen is refreshed with these:

```
files = (FileList) readResponse(httpURLConnection);
if (files == null) {
  view.appendMessage("Refresh:Error - directory is null");
} else {
  //refresh the filelist on the screen
  FileValidator.cleanFileList(files.getFileList());
  view.refreshFileList(files.getFileList());
}
} catch (Exception e) {
  e.printStackTrace();
  view.appendMessage("Refresh:Error refreshing the filelist");
  view.appendMessage("Using URL:" + url);
  view.appendMessage("Check the URL to the servlet including port");
}
}
```

The fourth and final important method is deleteRequest(). This is a request from the client to delete a file on the server. The process this time is that a FileName object, indicating the file to be deleted, and the request type, are sent to the server. Then the server returns a status code indicating if the file was successfully deleted. Finally, the refreshRequest() method is called to update the listing of files in the FileExchangeView:

```
public void deleteRequest(String fileName) {
  //check the file is correct and selected
  if (!FileValidator.isFileNameValid(fileName)) {
    view.appendMessage("Delete:File not selected. Please select file");
  } else {
    URL url = view.getHostServlet();
    HttpURLConnection httpURLConnection = null;
    String message = null;
    int status = 0;
    try {
```

The FileName object is sent to the server indicating the file to delete:

```
      httpURLConnection = getHttpURLConnection(url);
      sendRequest(httpURLConnection,
              new FileName(FileName.DELETE, fileName));
```

The HTTP status code is read back and the FileExchangeView is updated to reflect the success (or otherwise) of the request:

```
      status = httpURLConnection.getResponseCode();//@@
      message = httpURLConnection.getResponseMessage(); //@@
    } catch (Exception e) {
      e.printStackTrace();
    }

    //inform the application view
    if (status >= HttpURLConnection.HTTP_OK ||
        status < HttpURLConnection.HTTP_MULT_CHOICE) {
      view.appendMessage("Delete:Success (" + status + ") " + message);
    } else {
      view.appendMessage("Delete:Error (" + status + ") " + message);
      return;
    }
  }
  //refresh the file list
  refreshRequest();
}
```

Here is where the application starts the process of sending an HTTP POST request to our servlet. This method is called each time we require a connection to the server. Using the URL object we open a connection to the servlet:

```
private HttpURLConnection getHttpURLConnection(URL url)
                                           throws IOException {
    //setup connection
    HttpURLConnection httpURLConnection =
                            (HttpURLConnection) url.openConnection();
```

To use the connection for output we call the setDoOutput() method with true as input parameter, indicating we are using it for output. This triggers a POST request to be made, which means that the servlet's doPost() method will process this request. By calling the setUseCaches() method with false we are telling the connection that we do not want to use cached content if available. We also should set the Content-Type header to indicate the MIME type of the body of the request; in this case a Java serialized object (initially). Setting the Content-Type header tells the recipient of the request the type of data that we are sending. This is important, because the recipient servlet may be able to accept many types of requests and so it might need to know what type of data we are sending so that it can handle our request appropriately:

```
    httpURLConnection.setDoOutput(true);
    httpURLConnection.setUseCaches(false);
    httpURLConnection.setRequestProperty("Content-Type",
                "application/x-java-serialized-object");
    return httpURLConnection;
}
```

We have two sendRequest() methods overloaded. The first takes a connection and request object and, by default, closes the OutputStream. The second overloaded method takes an additional boolean argument to indicate if it should close the OutputStream. In any case using these methods set up the OutputStream and write the Request object out:

```
private void sendRequest(HttpURLConnection httpURLConnection,
                        BaseRequest request) throws IOException {
    sendRequest(httpURLConnection, request, true);
}
```

The application then has to get a reference to the OutputStream for the connection to be able to send data to the server, which is wrapped in an ObjectOutputStream to send our FileName request object. We then flush() the object to the server:

```
private void sendRequest(HttpURLConnection httpURLConnection,
    BaseRequest request, boolean closeStream) throws IOException {

    //send the request query object to the server
    OutputStream os = httpURLConnection.getOutputStream();
    ObjectOutputStream oos = new ObjectOutputStream(os);
    oos.writeObject(request);
    oos.flush();
    if (closeStream) {
        os.close();
    }
}
```

The `readResponse()` method allows us to read back the server's response to a request. We access the connection's `InputStream` and wrap it in an `ObjectInputStream`, so that we can read back the `serverResponse` object. Two overloaded `readResponse()` methods are provided, one of which allows the caller to determine if the `InputStream` is closed:

```java
private Object readResponse(HttpURLConnection httpURLConnection)
   throws IOException, ClassNotFoundException {
     return readResponse(httpURLConnection, true);
   }

private Object readResponse(HttpURLConnection httpURLConnection,
   boolean closeOutput) throws IOException, ClassNotFoundException {

   InputStream ins = httpURLConnection.getInputStream();
   ObjectInputStream ois = new ObjectInputStream(ins);
   Object response = ois.readObject();
   if (closeOutput) {
     ois.close();
   }
   return response;
 }
}
```

The FileExchangeFilter Class

The `FileExchangeFilter` class extends the `FileFilter` abstract class to provide the `FileChooser` with filtering ability based on our chosen criteria. We implement this class so that we can ensure that we only upload specified text/character files:

```java
package firewall.client;

import java.io.File;
import java.util.*;
import javax.swing.filechooser.*;

public class FileExchangeFilter extends FileFilter {

   private Hashtable filters = null;
   private String description = "Files";
```

The constructor takes an array (from `common.FileValidator` in our case) of `String` file extensions, and a description for them:

```java
public FileExchangeFilter(String[] extensions, String description) {
   filters = new Hashtable();
   for (int i = 0; i < extensions.length; i++) {
     filters.put(extensions[i].toLowerCase(), this);
   }
   if(description!=null) {
     this.description = description;
   }
 }
```

Users of the `FileFilter` abstract class must override two methods; `accept()` and `getDescription()`. The accept method is used to determine if a file meets the specified file extension criteria:

```java
public boolean accept(File file) {
  if(file != null) {
    if(file.isDirectory()) {
      return true;
    }
    String extension = getExtension(file);
    if(extension != null && filters.get(getExtension(file)) != null) {
      return true;
    }
  }
  return false;
}
```

Next we have a `getExtension()` helper method to return the file's extension:

```java
public String getExtension(File file) {
  if(file != null) {
    String filename = file.getName();
    int dot = filename.lastIndexOf('.');
    if(dot > 0 && dot < filename.length() - 1) {
      return filename.substring(dot + 1).toLowerCase();
    }
  }
  return null;
}
```

Finally our `getDescription()` method returns the more friendly description of the filter:

```java
public String getDescription() {
  return description;
}
}
```

Implementing the Common Classes

The classes in this project consist of serializable classes used by the client and server to send information in client requests and server responses.

The BaseRequest Class

The `BaseRequest` class is the superclass for the other classes in this package. Objects of this class contain the `requestType` field indicating which type of request is in use:

```java
package firewall.common;

import java.io.Serializable;

public class BaseRequest implements Serializable {
```

We have four constants defined for the different requests, and a `String` indicating the request type for the object of this class:

```
public static final String UPLOAD = "UPLOAD";
public static final String DOWNLOAD = "DOWNLOAD";
public static final String REFRESH = "REFRESH";
public static final String DELETE = "DELETE";
protected String requestType;
```

The constructor sets the `requestType`:

```
public BaseRequest(String requestType) {
   this.requestType = requestType;
}
```

Finally there is the accessor method for `requestType`:

```
public final String getRequestType() {
   return requestType;
}
}
```

The FileName Class

The `FileName` class extends the `BaseRequest` class to add a `String` field that holds a filename. We have get and set methods for this field:

```
package firewall.common;

import java.io.Serializable;

public class FileName extends BaseRequest implements Serializable {

   private String fileName;

   public FileName(String requestType, String fileName) {
      super(requestType);
      this.fileName = fileName;
   }

   public String getFileName() {
      return fileName;
   }

   public void setFileName(String fileName) {
      this.fileName = fileName;
   }
}
```

The FileList Class

The `FileList` class extends the `BaseRequest` class to add a field that holds a string array of filenames, with getter and setter methods for the object. The constructor doesn't yet require a request type since only one request type is used with this class, but it is a good idea to include it for flexibility, in case we extend the use of this class:

```java
package firewall.common;

import java.io.Serializable;

public class FileList extends BaseRequest implements Serializable {

  String[] fileList;

  public FileList(String requestType, String[] fileList) {
    super(requestType);
    this.fileList = fileList;
  }

  public String[] getFileList() {
    return fileList;
  }

  public void setFileList(String[] fileList) {
    this.fileList = fileList;
  }
}
```

The FileValidator Class

This class is a utility class to perform validation of filenames, and to 'clean' an array of filenames of names that do not meet the specified criteria. For a filename to be acceptable, it must have the extension of one of the `String`s in the VALID_EXTENSIONS array:

```java
package firewall.common;

public class FileValidator {
  public static final String[] VALID_EXTENSIONS =
                                 {"txt", "html", "htm", "java"};
```

The `isFileNameValid()` method validates the filename passed in, subject to it not being `null` and having a specifed extension:

```java
  public static boolean isFileNameValid(String filename) {
    if (filename == null || filename.length() == 0) {
      return false;
    }

    for (int i = 0; i < VALID_EXTENSIONS.length; i++) {
      if (filename.endsWith("." + VALID_EXTENSIONS[i])) {
        return true;
      }
    }
    return false;
  }
```

The `cleanFileList()` method takes a reference to a `String` array of filenames and 'cleans' it of any filenames that do not have an acceptable extension:

```
public static void cleanFileList(String[] files) {
  for (int i = 0; i < files.length; i++) {
    if (!isFileNameValid(files[i])) {
      files[i] = null;
    }
  }
}
```

Implementing the Web Application

The design issues facing the developer of the server side of this application are relatively easy to solve using the correct application of design patterns to the problem. The problem is that we have four request types being sent to the servlet in the current design, and possibly more in the future. Therefore we need to implement a design that will allow us to extend our application relatively easily.

The client application makes a request to the `FileExchangeServlet`. This servlet then calls the `RequestHandlerFactory` class, that implements the **Singleton** design pattern. The Singleton pattern is used to ensure that one and only one instance of a class can exist. To do this we have a static `getInstance()` method that on the first call creates the single instance, and then returns the singleton instance to the caller. The constructor is declared `private` so that only a `static` class method can create an instance (`getInstance()` in this case)). It also implements a **Factory** pattern, which means that it contains a mapping of all request types to their appropriate handlers, and can instantiate and return the correct handler object to process the request.

The handlers all extend from the abstract `RequestHandler` class, which declares the abstract `respond()` method to be overridden by all subclasses. Once the servlet has the appropriate handler object, it can call the `setHttpObjects()` method to prepare the handler and then the `respond()` method to process the request. In all cases the handler performs some task on the server directory (getting a file listing, deletion, up or download) and returns the response to the client.

This sequence of events is shown in the following diagram:

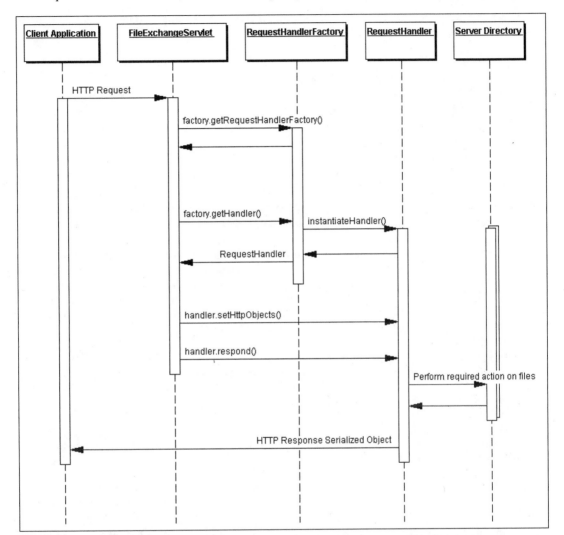

The key advantage to using the Factory pattern is that we can easily add many more request types to the RequestHandlerFactory, and simply provide another handler class that extends from RequestHandler to process each new request type. This is a relatively painless way to make the application extensible; aside from the new handler subclass, the only other class affected would be the RequestHandlerFactory, which needs a new mapping added.

The majority of the HTTP request processing is to be found in the four RequestHandler subclasses.

The FileExchangeServlet Class

This servlet handles the client requests, delegating processing to the appropriate handler through the use of the RequestHanderFactory:

```
package firewall.server;

import firewall.common.*;
import javax.servlet.http.HttpServlet;
import java.io.*;
import javax.servlet.*;
import javax.servlet.http.*;
import java.io.IOException;
import java.io.PrintWriter;
import java.util.Enumeration;

public class FileExchangeServlet extends HttpServlet {
  private RequestHandlerFactory requestHandlerFactory = null;
```

The init() method sets up the directory location for files that the servlet makes accessible to the client. Normally it would be better to do this in the initialization parameters, so that we could easily configure their location without having to recompile. Chapter 4 will describe how we do this, but for now we code it here to %CATALINA_HOME%/WEB-INF/files/, which is a location that is not normally accessible to the client (everything below the WEB-INF directory is private to the web application). It then sets the files directory in the RequestHandler for future use:

```
  public void init() throws ServletException {
    String directory = getServletContext().getRealPath("/") +
                       "WEB-INF" + File.separator + "files" +
                       File.separator ;
    RequestHandler.setStringFileBase(directory);
```

Next it initializes the RequestHandlerFactory object, by getting the servlet a reference to the singleton instance of this class:

```
    requestHandlerFactory = RequestHandlerFactory.getInstance();
  }
```

The doPost() method is a short method, but it packs a lot of processing behind the scenes by delegating the majority of the request processing to the handlers, which are created for each type of request and registered in the RequestHandlerFactory.

The method reads in the serialized object sent by the client, using the readSerializedObject() method. This object is cast into a BaseRequest object, which is the superclass for all the common communication objects. From the BaseRequest object we can determine the request type being made using the getRequestType() method of BaseRequest class. This is passed into the getHandler() method of the requestHandlerFactory, which performs all the identification and mapping of the request to the correct handler as well as instantiating the handler. The setHttpObjects() method is used to give the handler access to these objects during the processing of the request:

```
    public void doPost(HttpServletRequest request,
                       HttpServletResponse response)
                       throws ServletException, IOException {
      try {
        BaseRequest baseObject = (BaseRequest) readSerializedObject(request);
        RequestHandler handler = (RequestHandler) requestHandlerFactory
                             .getHandler(baseObject.getRequestType());
        handler.setHttpObjects(request, response);
```

Finally, the respond() method is called in the handler that processes the request:

```
        handler.respond(baseObject);
      } catch (ClassNotFoundException cnfe) {
        cnfe.printStackTrace();
      } catch (IOException ioe) {
        ioe.printStackTrace();
      }
    }
```

Currently, the doGet() method is not called because all requests from our application are POST requests, but we forward this method to the doPost() method so that we can incorporate additional request types using either HTTP request type. Our client's refresh method should probably use the GET request type for its request since it is a refresh request, and similarly the delete request could use the DELETE method, but for the sake of keeping the example straightforward we allow them to be POST requests too. From the servlet's point of view this makes no difference; it is just HTTP convention.

```
    public void doGet(HttpServletRequest request,
                      HttpServletResponse response)
                      throws ServletException, IOException {
      doGet(request, response);
    }
```

We also have the readSerializedObject() method that reads the first object from the HTTPServletRequest InputStream. However, we do not close the InputStream, which leaves it available to read further input information if some of the requests need to. In fact, the only request type that does so is the upload request, where we will also have to read in the file uploaded to the server after this serialized object:

```
    private Object readSerializedObject(HttpServletRequest httpServletRequest)
                              throws IOException, ClassNotFoundException {
      ObjectInputStream ois =
        new ObjectInputStream(httpServletRequest.getInputStream());
      Object readObject = ois.readObject();
      return readObject;
    }
  }
```

The RequestHandlerFactory Class

The `RequestHandlerFactory` is designed to manufacture `RequestHandler` subclass instances appropriate to the received request type. As mentioned previously, this class implements the singleton pattern and so only one instance of it per virtual machine can exist:

```
package firewall.server;

import firewall.common.*;
import java.util.*;

public class RequestHandlerFactory {
```

The following `Map` object stores a map of request types to `RequestHandler` subclasses:

```
    private Map requestHandlers;
```

The static `RequestHandlerFactory` singleton object is the single instance of this class. The constructor is declared `private` to prevent instantiation of this class by any other class. We populate the `Map` with the request types and associated handler classes:

```
    private static RequestHandlerFactory singleton = null;

    private RequestHandlerFactory() {
      requestHandlers = new HashMap(5);
      requestHandlers.put(BaseRequest.DELETE, DeleteHandler.class);
      requestHandlers.put(BaseRequest.REFRESH, RefreshHandler.class);
      requestHandlers.put(BaseRequest.DOWNLOAD, DownloadHandler.class);
      requestHandlers.put(BaseRequest.UPLOAD, UploadHandler.class);
    }
```

The static `getRequestHandlerFactory()` method returns the singleton instance of the class. If it is not already created it will instantiate it:

```
    public static RequestHandlerFactory getInstance() {
      if (singleton == null) {
        synchronized (RequestHandlerFactory.class) {
          if (singleton == null) {
            singleton = new RequestHandlerFactory();
          }
        }
      }
      return singleton;
    }
```

The getHandler() method receives the name of the request type as a parameter, and retrieves the appropriate handler class from the Map. It then calls the instantiateHandler() method to create an object of this class to return:

```
public RequestHandler getHandler(String name) {
  //look up the handler class in the map and create a new instance
  Class handlerClass = (Class) requestHandlers.get(name);
  RequestHandler handler = instantiateHandler(handlerClass);
  return handler;
}
```

The above call to the instantiateHandler() method will produce an instantiated object of the class provided as a parameter:

```
private RequestHandler instantiateHandler(Class handlerClass) {
  RequestHandler handler = null;
  if (handlerClass != null) {
    try {
      handler = (RequestHandler) handlerClass.newInstance();
    } catch (InstantiationException e) {
      e.printStackTrace();
    } catch (IllegalAccessException e) {
      e.printStackTrace();
    }
  }
```

In the event of problems with instantiating the class, we probably should provide a default error handler to process the request and return an error gracefully (or recover from the cause of the problem). For simplicity we return null, which the calling class can check:

```
  if (handler == null) {
    //Code here could handle instantiation problems - perhaps with
    //default handler just in case.
  }
  return handler;
  }
}
```

The RequestHandler Class

The RequestHandler class is the abstract parent class for the handler classes that process the different types of request. Extending from this class will allow a programmer to add a new request type to the web application, once they register it with the RequestHandlerFactory. The only method that must be implemented in a subclass of RequestHandler is the respond() method, which performs the bulk of the processing of the request:

```
package firewall.server;

import javax.servlet.http.*;
import firewall.common.*;
import java.io.*;

public abstract class RequestHandler {
```

To process the client's request, the handler must have access to the `HttpServletRequest` and `HttpServletResponse` objects:

```
HttpServletRequest httpServletRequest;
HttpServletResponse httpServletResponse;
```

The following `String` and `File` fields refer to the specified directory for files that is made available to the client. The `fileBase` object is instantiated by the constructor, while the `stringFileBase` object holds the default local directory, but is set with a `static` method in the servlet's `init()` method, where it can discover the files directory location:

```
static String stringFileBase = File.separator;
File fileBase;
```

The `getFileList()` method will return an array of `Strings` representing the list of files in the `fileBase` directory. The `getFile()` method will return a `File` object corresponding to the supplied filename in the `fileBase` directory:

```
protected String[] getFileList() {
  String[] list = fileBase.list();
  return list;
}

protected File getFile(String fileName) {
  return new File(fileBase, fileName);
}
```

The constructor establishes the Tomcat home directory, and determines the location of the directory made accessible to the application (that is, `%CATALINA_HOME%/webapps/httpServlet/WEB-INF/files/`):

```
public RequestHandler() {
  fileBase = new File(stringFileBase);
}
```

The `respond()` method will perform the bulk of the processing, specific to the request, and must be overridden by subclassing handlers:

```
public abstract void respond(BaseRequest baseRequest);
```

The `setHttpObjects()` method gives the handler access to the client's Request object, and allows the handler to respond using the Response object:

```
public void setHttpObjects(HttpServletRequest httpServletRequest,
                           HttpServletResponse httpServletResponse) {
  this.httpServletRequest = httpServletRequest;
  this.httpServletResponse = httpServletResponse;
}
```

The sendFile() and sendSerializedObject() methods return a file and an object to the client respectively. As noted previously, the reader and writer objects are for character based text files:

```
public void sendFile(File sendFile) throws IOException {
  FileReader fileReader = new FileReader(sendFile);
  PrintWriter out = httpServletResponse.getWriter();
  char c[] = new char[4096];
  int read = 0;

  //Read until end of file and send to client
  while ((read = fileReader.read(c)) != -1) {
    out.write(c, 0, read);
  }
  //Close
  fileReader.close();
  out.close();
}

public void sendSerializedObject(Object sendObject) throws IOException {
  OutputStream os = httpServletResponse.getOutputStream();
  ObjectOutputStream oos = new ObjectOutputStream(os);
  oos.writeObject(sendObject);
  oos.flush();
  oos.close();
}
```

We have two methods for setting HTTP status codes. SetStatusCode() simply sets the status code, while sendError() sends an error code with an accompanying message:

```
public void setStatusCode(int statusCode) {
  httpServletResponse.setStatus(statusCode);
}

public void sendError(int statusCode, String message)
  throws IOException {
  httpServletResponse.sendError(statusCode, message);
}
```

The stringFileBase object was declared static so that the directory location could be set for all instances. Hence we have provided a static setStringFileBase() method to set this:

```
public static void setStringFileBase(String fileBase) {
  stringFileBase = fileBase;
}
}
```

The RefreshHandler Class

RefreshHandler is a subclass of RequestHandler that refreshes the list of files for the client:

```
package firewall.server;

import javax.servlet.http.HttpServletRequest;
import javax.servlet.http.HttpServletResponse;
import firewall.common.*;
import java.io.*;

public class RefreshHandler extends RequestHandler {
```

The handler gets an up-to-date array of String objects representing the files in the server's directory, checks their validity, and returns it to the client (or an error if the FileList object is null):

```
public void respond(BaseRequest baseRequest) {
    FileList fileList = new FileList(BaseRequest.REFRESH, getFileList());

    try {
        if (fileList != null) {
            setStatusCode(HttpServletResponse.SC_OK);
            FileValidator.cleanFileList(fileList.getFileList());
            sendSerializedObject(fileList);
        } else {
            sendError(HttpServletResponse.SC_NOT_FOUND, "Directory not found");
        }
    } catch (IOException e) {
        e.printStackTrace();
    }
}
}
```

The DownloadHandler Class

This class retrieves and sends back to the client files that the client has requested:

```
package firewall.server;

import javax.servlet.http.HttpServletRequest;
import javax.servlet.http.HttpServletResponse;
import firewall.common.*;
import java.io.*;

public class DownloadHandler extends RequestHandler {
```

The respond() method in this class retrieves a File object for the requested file, and then uses the sendFile() method to send the file over to the client. We send an error code if the file does not exist, or if the filename supplied was invalid:

```
   public void respond(BaseRequest baseRequest) {
     String fileName = ((FileName) baseRequest).getFileName();
     try {
       if (!FileValidator.isFileNameValid(fileName)) {
         sendError(HttpServletResponse.SC_PRECONDITION_FAILED,
                   "Filename is invalid");
         return;
       }
       File fileToRead = new File(fileBase, fileName);
       if (fileToRead.exists()) {
         setStatusCode(HttpServletResponse.SC_OK);
         sendFile(fileToRead);
       } else {
         sendError(HttpServletResponse.SC_NOT_FOUND, "File not found");
       }
     } catch (IOException e) {
       e.printStackTrace();
     }
   }
}
```

The UploadHandler Class

This class processes the uploading of files to the server's `files` directory:

```
package firewall.server;

import javax.servlet.http.*;
import firewall.common.*;
import java.io.*;

public class UploadHandler extends RequestHandler {
```

Next we get the `InputStreamReader` to read in the file from the client, and use a `FileWriter` to write the file to the server. The file being sent must have a valid name. Then an HTTP status code is returned to indicate that the file was created on the server:

```
   public void respond(BaseRequest baseRequest) {
     try {
       InputStreamReader isr =
         new InputStreamReader(httpServletRequest.getInputStream());
       BufferedReader bfr = new BufferedReader(isr);
       String fileName = ((FileName) baseRequest).getFileName();

       if (!FileValidator.isFileNameValid(fileName)) {
         sendError(HttpServletResponse.SC_PRECONDITION_FAILED,
                   "Filename is invalid");
         return;
       }
```

```
        File newFile = new File(fileBase, fileName);
        FileWriter fileWriter = new FileWriter(newFile);
        char c[] = new char[4096];
        int read = 0;

        while ((read = bfr.read(c)) != -1) {
          fileWriter.write(c, 0, read);
        }

        fileWriter.close();
        isr.close();
        setStatusCode(HttpServletResponse.SC_CREATED);
    }
```

Finally, if an error occurs during IO, we send an error message to the client if possible:

```
    catch (IOException ioe) {
      try {
        sendError(HttpServletResponse.SC_INTERNAL_SERVER_ERROR,
                  "File not uploaded");
      } catch (IOException ioe2) {
        ioe2.printStackTrace();
      }
    }
  }
}
```

The DeleteHandler Class

This class processes a request from the client to delete a named file from the server's `files` directory:

```
package firewall.server;

import javax.servlet.http.HttpServletRequest;
import javax.servlet.http.HttpServletResponse;
import firewall.common.*;
import java.io.*;

public class DeleteHandler extends RequestHandler {
```

A new `File` object is created from the filename sent by the client and the `delete()` method is called to remove it. If the file is successfully deleted the response to the client indicates this; otherwise it indicates to the client that the file was not found or that the filename was invalid, using HTTP status codes:

```
      public void respond(BaseRequest baseRequest) {
        String fileName = ((FileName) baseRequest).getFileName();
        try {
          if (!FileValidator.isFileNameValid(fileName)) {
            sendError(HttpServletResponse.SC_PRECONDITION_FAILED,
                      "Filename is invalid");
            return;
          }
          File fileToDelete = new File(fileBase, fileName);
          boolean result = fileToDelete.delete();
          if (result) {
            setStatusCode(HttpServletResponse.SC_NO_CONTENT);
          } else {
            sendError(HttpServletResponse.SC_NOT_FOUND, "File not deleted");
          }
        } catch (IOException e) {
          e.printStackTrace();
        }
      }
    }
  }
```

Compiling and Running the Application

There are a number of steps that you will need to take to set up the application. If you downloaded the code from the http://www.wrox.com web site you can probably skip over a few steps, but I'll assume that you are creating the web application from the start.

First, add the following subdirectories to the httpServlet/WEB-INF/src and classes directories:

❑   firewall/client

❑   firewall/server

❑   firewall/common

Obviously these directories will contain the sourcecode for the corresponding packages described above. When you have added the sourcecode to the appropriate directories, compile the code in each directory/package from the src directory, starting with the common package. Then move the classes into their corresponding subdirectories in the classes directory.

Then create a files directory under httpServlet/WEB-INF, and add a few text files to it for exchange with the servlet-application.

Next we need to JAR up the client application. First, add a Manifest.MF text file to the classes directory with the following text:

```
Manifest-Version: 1.0
Main-class: firewall.client.FileExchangeApplication
```

Then execute the following command from the `classes` directory to create the JAR:

```
jar cvfm FileExchangeApplication.jar manifest.mf
                          firewall/common/* firewall/client/*
```

Finally, restart Tomcat, and then execute the JAR using the following command, which runs the client application:

```
java -jar FileExchangeApplication.jar "http://localhost:8080"
```

At this point you should see the File Exchange Application window pop up, and you can play with the application.

Summary

We have examined the Hypertext Transfer Protocol in some detail, including the protocol layers HTTP sits upon to function. We examined how state and connections are managed, and looked at security and authentication in the protocol. The HTTP 1.0 and now the 1.1 standard are evolving with varying levels of implementation and support.

This chapter explained how to use HTTP requests and responses with servlets, namely with `javax.servlet.http.HttpServlet`. We focused upon the HTTP 1.0-based methods such as `doGet()`, `doPost()`, and `doHead()`, and followed this by discussing the less frequently-used methods relating to HTTP 1.1 too: `doDelete()`, `doPut()`, `doOptions()`, and `doTrace()`.

The `javax.servlet.http.HttpServletRequest` interface provides access to the clients' request information, including headers, attributes, paths, authentication, sessions, cookies, and internationalization. Similarly the `javax.servlet.http.HttpServletResponse` interface allows us access to the server's response, including methods assessing headers, redirection, status codes and errors, cookies, session management, internationalization, and buffering. Finally the `HttpServletRequestWrapper` and the `HttpServletResponseWrapper` allow developers to extend the functionality of these request and response interfaces.

We concluded the chapter by developing an HTTP-based client-servlet application. This demonstrated some of the techniques involved in HTTP communications to and from a servlet. In this case we looked at a servlet processing a Java application's requests, received over HTTP. We considered the extensible design of the server classes, including the servlet, the handler classes, and the handler factory class we constructed.

In the following chapter we will discuss the deployment of web applications.

Deploying Web Applications

The previous chapters have covered the fundamental topics relating to the use of servlets in the enterprise, and those relating to the latest incarnation of the Servlet API, version 2.3. This chapter continues this look at the fundamentals by discussing servlet deployment.

With servlets, and more generally J2EE, the design and development process is very clearly isolated from the processes of application packaging and deployment. With servlets we are encouraged to develop loosely coupled components that are reusable. The components are then tied together into an application at packaging and deployment time. This allows the programmer to concentrate on what they do best during development, the process of coding business logic, leaving infrastructure issues (such as security, database connection pooling, and transactions) until the deployment stage.

As the title suggests this chapter focuses on this servlet packaging and deployment process. We will look at facilities provided by servlet-compliant web containers, which will allow us to develop flexible applications. The specific issues that we will address are:

- ❏ Web applications and their structures
- ❏ Development versus production deployment
- ❏ The web application deployment descriptor XML file
- ❏ Validating deployment descriptors
- ❏ Building web application archive files by hand
- ❏ An example of a complete web application
- ❏ Some advanced deployment issues

Let's start by defining what a web application is in the context of J2EE.

What is a Web Application?

In the early days (of servlet development at the time of the Servlet 2.0 specification), deploying your applications was nothing short of a nightmare. The files would have to be deployed in different directory structures, with completely different configuration files to write.

This can be illustrated by looking at what was required to deploy a servlet to Apache JServ (a popular, but now obsolete servlet runner) and BEA WebLogic. In JServ we had to add our servlets to what was called a servlet zone. This was achieved by adding an entry to a file called `zone.properties`, adding a mapping (in the form of a name-value pair), and then restarting the server. However in Weblogic 4.5, deploying a servlet was achieved by registering it in the `weblogic.properties` file with a line such as:

```
weblogic.httpd.register.hello = examples.servlets.HelloWorldServlet
```

> *For a detailed discussion of deploying to either of these now outdated servlet containers, you can look at the web sites of BEA, or the Apache Foundation.*

Obviously all of these differences made moving from servlet container to servlet container a very difficult and unenviable task. In some ways the benefits of using a portable technology such as Java were lost because you were all but tied in to a particular vendor for your servlet container. Java standards being what they are, something had to change. With the advent of J2EE and the Servlet 2.1 specification the concept of **web applications** was introduced. As we will see, this has removed the problems associated with deploying your applications across different vendors.

> **Put simply, a web application (often shortened to just "web app") is a collection of servlets, HTML pages, JavaServer Pages (JSP), JSP tag libraries, classes, and any other web resources that can be bundled and run on multiple web containers from multiple vendors.**

Obviously this is a very simplistic view of web applications; they are a lot more than just a bundle of web resources. For example, a web application can define many things about its behavior and configuration, such as how security is managed, how database connections are managed, and how requests are mapped to particular servlets.

The Structure of a Web Application

Armed with the knowledge of what web applications contain, and why they were introduced, we will now look at how a simple web application is structured.

The directory structure of a web application is strictly defined. This directory structure consists of two parts:

❑   Each web application has a unique context path in which all of its components reside. Within the root directory of the web application is a special subdirectory called WEB-INF that contains all private web application components that cannot be accessed by the client. This can include servlet class files, deployment descriptors, external libraries, and any other private files used by the application.

❑ All files outside of WEB-INF are considered public in that they can be accessed by name from the client. Typical examples of public resources include static HTML pages, JSP pages, and images.

To illustrate this structure, a simple web application called SimpleWebApp could have the following directory structure:

```
SimpleWebApp/
            index.html
            main.jsp
            images/
                    company.jpg
                    divider.jpg
            admin/
                    admin.jsp
            WEB-INF/
                    web.xml
                    classes/
                            servlets/
                                    LoginHandler.class
                                    ShoppingCart.class
                    lib/
                        xerces.jar
                    xalan.jar
```

It is simple to see that the public resources for the above web application are one HTML file (index.html), two JSP files (main.jsp and admin/admin.jsp), and two JPEG images (images/company.jpg and images/divider.jpg). The remaining resources, those that are under the WEB-INF directory, are not available to the client, and are resources to be used exclusively by the web container.

A resource that is termed "public" in a web application is any resource that can be directly downloaded by the client and rendered in their browser in the usual way. The resource is delivered to the client and it is the responsibility of their browser or application to make correct use of that resource.

Although JSP pages are included in the public directories of a web application, they are not sent directly to the client unmodified. When a client requests a JSP, it is compiled into a servlet, executed, and the resulting HTML is sent to the client. This might look like a lot of overhead, but it actually only happens the first time that the JSP is requested. You can learn more about JSP pages in Chapter 8.

As well as these public resources, there are many resources in a web application that should not be directly accessed or downloaded by the user. These resources include servlets, JSP pages, Java class files and any other components that contain the request processing logic behind our web application, as well as configuration files such as the deployment descriptor web.xml. Private resources are placed in the WEB-INF directory, which must be present in the top level of the web application. As you can see, the deployment descriptor is placed in the top-level of the WEB-INF directory, while any classes used by the web application are located in the classes folder, which is also placed in the top level of WEB-INF. Finally, the web application may also make use of JAR files, which should be added to the library directory (lib), again located in the top level of WEB-INF.

Using a structure such as this for your web application offers several immediate advantages. The first of these is that multiple web applications can coexist within one web container. Structuring web applications in this way allows the web container to easily understand which components belong to which web application, thus avoiding problems such as naming conflicts (for instance two different servlets could have the same name in two different web applications).

The second major advantage is that the web container knows where to look to load classes for your web application. The classpath was always a problem with web application development in the past. It was always hard to tell where classes were being loaded from. However, with this rigidly structured approach, the classloader knows that it should look in the `classes` and `lib` directories to find classes, so you do not need to explicitly add all of the JAR files used by your application to your system's classpath.

Web Application Archives

Once you have your web application in the structure detailed above, there are two options for deployment. The first, and simplest option, is to copy the whole directory structure to the web applications directory of your web container. For Tomcat this directory is the `webapps` directory (`%CATALINA_HOME%/webapps`). This method of deployment is known (for obvious reasons!) as **Exploded Directory Format**. This is by far the best way to deploy an application in a development scenario, or any scenario where a small number of files in your web application will change frequently. In order to make changes to an element in your web application, you simply copy the modified files into the appropriate point in the directory structure.

Although this format is ideal for development, it is far from an ideal way to deploy applications in a production environment, or for a situation where you wish to move your application between different web containers. Although it is possible to just copy the directory structure between servers, imagine a scenario where you have to do this via a command-line file transfer program. It would take a significant amount of effort to transfer each individual file and directory.

Fortunately for us, there is a very simple mechanism for packaging web applications so that they can easily be deployed on many different servers and containers. This format is known as the **Web Application Archive**, or **WAR** format. A WAR file is simply an archived version of the directory structure mentioned above. The WAR file is easily created using the standard Java `jar` tool, although other commercially-available archiving tools can be used (for example WinZip). The reason that a Web Application Archive does not have the standard Java archive extension (`.jar`) is to indicate that the archive has a different purpose. A WAR file represents a full structured web application and not just an archive of (possibly unrelated) Java classes.

We will see many examples of WAR file creation later in this chapter, but here's a quick example of how we could create a WAR file at the command line. First we would move to the top-level of the web app, and then we would issue the command:

```
jar -cv0f SimpleWebApp.war .
```

This would create a WAR file called `SimpleWebApp.war` that would contain the contents of the current directory. We can examine the contents of such a file using the following command:

```
jar -tvf SimpleWebApp.war
```

You can refer to the Java Development Kit documentation for additional information about other configuration options for the `jar` tool. Using WinZip is another quick and easy way to open WAR files and examine their contents.

Once we have created a WAR file, a J2EE-compliant web container (or application server) will automatically deploy the application on startup. The only caveat to this is that the application is placed in the correct directory. For Tomcat this directory is `webapps`. If you place the archive file in this directory and restart the Tomcat server, the container will automatically deploy the application. The application will be deployed with its name set as the name of the WAR file minus the `.war` extension (so for the example WAR file above, we could access the application at http://localhost:8080/SimpleWebApp/)

While WAR files are great for moving web apps between containers, they are not so appropriate to use during development. Imagine changing one file in your web application archive. In order to re-deploy the application you would have to re-archive it first. This could be fairly time-consuming for a large application, so it's usually better to use the Exploded Directory Format described above. WAR files become more appropriate the closer to a production environment you get. It is wonderfully simple to take a WAR file and deploy it to a new server for testing, for example.

It is envisaged that over time a market for WAR files will exist. As the format becomes more popular and more people develop web applications, WAR files will be available as plug-in components for web containers. These components could be downloaded from a web site, copied to the right place, and be capable of processing user requests right away, irrespective of web container.

It is worth noting at this point that although it is recommended, it is not mandatory that a web container uses the web application structure as its run-time representation. All J2EE-compliant web containers must be able to accept a web application for deployment, but what they do to that application from that point on, is undefined. For example, if we deployed the `SimpleWebApp` application to the Tomcat container, it would be automatically copied into the `%CATALINA_HOME%/work/localhost/SimpleWebApp` directory. This is where files are really taken from when requested. This facilitates the hot deployment of applications, as it is guaranteed that the files in the `webapps` directory will not be in use to service requests.

The ServletContext

In a web container, each web application is associated with a context, and all resources contained within a web application exist relative to its context. A servlet context is rooted at a known path within a web container. For example if we have a store application, it could exist under the context `/store`. Therefore if the application contained an HTML file called `home.html` if would be accessible at http://localhost:8080/store/home.html. All requests that begin with the `/store` request path, known as the **context path**, are routed to the web application associated with the servlet context.

Each context that exists in a web container has a special object called a `ServletContext` associated with it. The `ServletContext` represents the web application's view of the container that it is deployed within. Everything that the web application is allowed to know about its container can be accessed via the `ServletContext`, and it allows servlets to access resources available to them in the container. The `ServletContext` can be thought of as a sandbox for a web application. This sandbox allows us to have all of the benefits of isolating web applications that we mentioned above (no name clashes, and efficient classloading without having to set a classpath).

The ServletContext can be used to accomplish many tasks in a web application. This said, perhaps the primary use of the ServletContext is to share attributes between all of the servlets in an application, and for loading resources for use within the application. We also define application initialization parameters using the ServletContext; we will discuss this later, in the section relating to deployment descriptors.

Defining Contexts within Tomcat

In order to create a context for your completed web application in Tomcat you only have to do one thing (and you don't always have to do that).

We can examine some of the contexts that exist within a freshly installed version of Tomcat 4.0 by looking in the file %CATALINA_HOME%/conf/server.xml. If you look towards the bottom of this file you will see a line like:

```
<context path="/examples" docBase="examples" debug="0" reloadable="true">
```

This defines the context for the examples application provided with Tomcat 4.0. Later on, in the section about deploying our example application to Tomcat, we will discuss the many parameters that can be provided when defining contexts.

Lifecycle of a Web Application

At this point, it is important to know about the major events in the lifecycle of a typical web application.

In version 2.3 of the servlet specification, several application lifecycle events have been defined. This represents perhaps the most significant change to the Servlet API. These events provide a web application developer with more possibilities for interaction with the ServletContext object, as well as the HttpSession object. It is now possible for an application developer to write event listeners so that they can be notified when a certain lifecycle event occurs (example events are application creation and application destruction), or even when attributes in the ServletContext (discussed in more detail later) are modified.

We looked at event listeners in Chapter 2. For this chapter, just recall that the container is responsible for notifying a particular Java class when one of the lifecycle events occurs. The lifecycle of a web application can be broken down into two distinct parts. The first part concerns creation and destruction of the application. The events in this first part are represented by two methods:

- ❑   contextInitialized(ServletContextEvent e)
- ❑   contextDestroyed(ServletContextEvent e)

These methods are defined by the ServletContextListener interface, and should be implemented by classes that are interested in being notified when the application is initialized or destroyed. These objects register with the container at initialization time (through the deployment descriptor) and are notified by the container when the events occur. The diagram opposite illustrates the sequence of events:

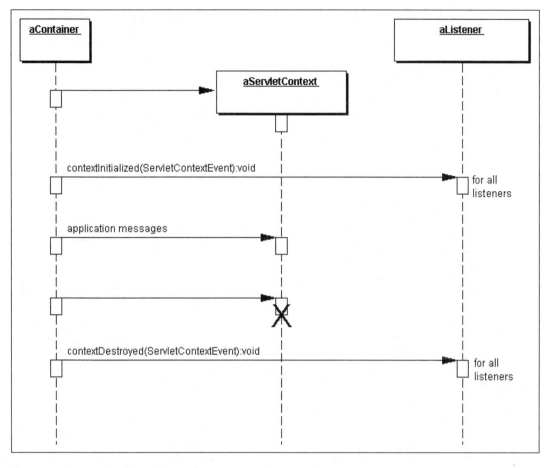

Here we can see that when the application first starts up, the contextInitialised() method is invoked on all objects that have registered themselves as ServletContextListeners. The application then goes about its business, serving requests, and providing responses until it is shut down. Once it is shut down the contextDestroyed() method is invoked on all of the objects that have registered themselves as listeners.

The events in the second part of the application's lifecycle are events that are fired when parameters are set, changed, or removed in the application (actually in the ServletContext). The three events that occur are represented by the following methods:

- ❑ attributeAdded(ServletContextAttributeEvent e)
- ❑ attributeReplaced(ServletContextAttributeEvent e)
- ❑ attributeRemoved(ServletContextAttributeEvent e)

Classes that are interested in being notified when a parameter is added, changed, or removed in the application should implement these methods, which are defined by the `ServletContextAttributeListener` interface. These objects register with the container at initialization time (through the deployment descriptor) and are notified by the container when the events occur. The diagram below illustrates the sequence of events that occur:

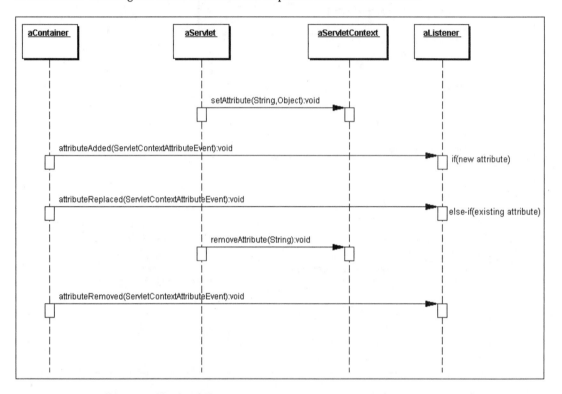

Here we can see that when a servlet adds an attribute to the `ServletContext`, the `attributeAdded()` method is invoked on all objects that have been registered as `ServletContextAttributeListeners`. When a servlet changes an existing attribute in the `ServletContext`, the `attributeReplaced()` method is invoked on all of the listeners. Finally, when a servlet removes an attribute from the context the `attributeRemoved()` method is invoked on the listeners.

The Deployment Descriptor

So far we have briefly described the deployment descriptor as a configuration file for the web application. It is perhaps the single most important item of your web application (after its content of course). In this section we are going to take a closer look at it.

In a nutshell, the deployment descriptor conveys the elements and configuration information of a web application between developers, assemblers, and deployers. All manner of information is defined in the deployment descriptor, from information about the web application itself, to information about its constituent parts, and most importantly, how those parts are assembled into a complete web application. This section will discuss the elements of the deployment descriptor that are important for most web applications. The way in which a deployment descriptor is written is often the key to how well a web application fits its purpose. It is very simple to write the components of a web application, but considering how it should be assembled is a very difficult and often neglected task.

The areas of the deployment descriptor that we are going to focus in on are:

- ❑ Servlet definitions and mappings

- ❑ Servlet context initialization parameters

- ❑ Error pages

- ❑ Welcome pages

- ❑ Simple file-based security

To illustrate the parts of the deployment descriptor, we will show a simple example descriptor file and then proceed to explain its constituent parts. First, however, you should note the following important rules about the deployment descriptor, which should be adhered to in order that the deployment descriptor is valid for web applications using the Servlets 2.3 specification:

- ❑ The deployment descriptor must reside at the top level of the WEB-INF directory of your web application

- ❑ It must be a well-formed XML file named web.xml

- ❑ This XML file must conform to Sun's web application DTD, which is defined at http://java.sun.com/dtd/web-app_2_3.dtd.

Let's now take a look at an example web.xml file.

An Example Deployment Descriptor

The example deployment descriptor is listed below. Once we have seen the relevant parts of the deployment descriptor we will then validate it against the DTD.

```
<?xml version="1.0" encoding="ISO-8859-1"?>

<!DOCTYPE web-app
    PUBLIC "-//Sun Microsystems, Inc.//DTD Web Application 2.3//EN"
    "http://java.sun.com/dtd/web-app_2_3.dtd">
<web-app>
```

At the start of the descriptor we need to declare the location of the DTD for the file, using the <!DOCTYPE> tag. This is followed by the starting tag of the <web-app> element, inside of which all the deployment information for the web app can be found. Then we encounter several elements that give information about the entire web application:

177

```
<display-name>Test Web Application</display-name>
<description>A test web application</description>
```

The `<display-name>` element allows us to specify a short name for the overall web application. This element is designed to allow the name of the web application to be displayed by tools including the GUI-based deployment utilities supplied with many of the mainstream application servers.

The `<description>` element allows us to provide a short textual description of the purpose of this web application. This is a very simple form of documentation for the overall web application.

Next we have the `<context-param>`, `<servlet>`, and `<servlet-mapping>` elements. These contain information about servlet context initialization parameters, the servlets in the application, and the mapping of the servlets to specific URLs, respectively. We'll examine these elements in more detail a little later.

```
<context-param>
  <param-name>
    adminEmail
  </param-name>
  <param-value>
    admin@wrox.com
  </param-value>
</context-param>

<servlet>
  <servlet-name>Servlet1</servlet-name>
  <servlet-class>example.Servlet1</servlet-class>
  <init-param>
    <param-name>version</param-name>
    <param-value>0.1b</param-value>
  </init-param>
</servlet>
<servlet>
  <servlet-name>Servlet2</servlet-name>
  <servlet-class>example.Servlet2</servlet-class>
</servlet>

<servlet-mapping>
  <servlet-name>Servlet1</servlet-name>
  <url-pattern>/home.html</url-pattern>
</servlet-mapping>
<servlet-mapping>
  <servlet-name>Servlet2</servlet-name>
  <url-pattern>/AnotherServlet</url-pattern>
</servlet-mapping>
```

Then we encounter `<welcome-file-list>` and `<error-page>` elements. In these elements we define the files to use as the welcome and error pages for the application. We'll talk more about these elements later too:

```
    <welcome-file-list>
      <welcome-file>
        /index.html
      </welcome-file>
    </welcome-file-list>
    <error-page>
      <exception-type>
        java.lang.ArithmeticException
      </exception-type>
      <location>
        /error.html
      </location>
    </error-page>
    <error-page>
      <error-code>
        404
      </error-code>
      <location>
        /404.html
      </location>
    </error-page>
```

The final set of elements, below, deal with security aspects for the web-application. Again, we'll be looking at these elements more closely later:

```
    <security-constraint>

      <web-resource-collection>
        <web-resource-name>SecureResource</web-resource-name>
        <url-pattern>/admin/*</url-pattern>
        <http-method>GET</http-method>
        <http-method>POST</http-method>
      </web-resource-collection>

      <auth-constraint>
        <role-name>admin</role-name>
      </auth-constraint>

    </security-constraint>

    <login-config>
      <auth-method>BASIC</auth-method>
      <realm-name>Secure Realm</realm-name>
    </login-config>

  </web-app>
```

Although the deployment descriptor above looks very daunting because of its size and use of different, perhaps unfamiliar tags, we will soon see that it is very simple.

We shall now move on and look at the parts of the example deployment descriptor that relate directly to servlet deployment.

Servlet Definitions and Mappings

Looking at the deployment descriptor we can see that it defines two servlets in the web application. We can see this by looking at the number of unique <servlet> elements. The first of our two servlets is defined below:

```
<servlet>
  <servlet-name>Servlet1</servlet-name>
  <servlet-class>example.Servlet1</servlet-class>
  <init-param>
    <param-name>version</param-name>
    <param-value>0.1b</param-value>
  </init-param>
</servlet>
```

The <servlet> element contains several child elements that give information about the declaration of the servlet. This information includes the unique name that the servlet is registered with in this web application, and the full name of the class that implements the servlet's functionality. The <servlet-name> element gives the servlet a unique name within the web application. In the case of our first servlet we can see that it is called Servlet1.

The <servlet-class> element gives the fully qualified class name of the class that implements the functionality of this servlet. In the case of our first servlet we can see that Servlet1 is implemented in the class example.Servlet1.

Looking at the <servlet> element for our first servlet we can see that it contains more than just the name and class of the servlet. It also contains an <init-param> element. This element allows us to specify initialization parameters for our servlet. These parameters can be used for many purposes, for example setting the language for an application, or defining the location of a configuration file for the application. As we can see our servlet has one parameter set. The <param-name> child element gives the name that the parameter can be accessed by, and the <param-value> gives the starting value for the parameter.

The parameter can be accessed from our first servlet using the getInitParameter() method on the ServletConfig object. So, in order to get access to the parameter defined for our first servlet we can use the following code within the servlet's class:

```
String version = getServletConfig().getInitParameter("version");
```

Note that we don't need to get the ServletConfig object explicitly, as the GenericServlet class implements the ServletConfig interface, so the method is available to us.

Servlet Mappings

Once we have defined our servlet through the `<servlet>` element, we need to map it to a particular URL pattern. This is necessary so that the web container knows which requests to send to a particular servlet.

You may think something along the lines of "Why can we not just pass all requests to the servlet with the same name as the end of the URL?" For example, http://localhost:8080/mywebapp/Servlet1, would be routed to the servlet defined with the name `Servlet1`. This would seem like a very logical approach, and is in fact the most common way of implementing the mappings between servlets and URLs. However, the approach is not very flexible. Imagine if you wanted to map more than one URL to the same servlet, which could, for example, check that a user is logged in? This is where the `<servlet-mapping>` element illustrates its power. An example of the power of this mapping is to hide the implementation of your application from the user. As far as the user is concerned, they cannot tell if your application is based on servlets, cgi-bin, or any other technology. This can minimize the risk of hacking.

In our example deployment descriptor, our first servlet is invoked every time http://localhost:8080/TestWebApp/home.html (assuming the web application is called `TestWebApp`) is encountered. The unique servlet name that we defined in the `<servlet>` element (referenced here as `<servlet-name>`) is mapped to a URL pattern, which is referenced here as `<url-pattern>`:

```
<servlet-mapping>
  <servlet-name>Servlet1</servlet-name>
  <url-pattern>home.html</url-pattern>
</servlet-mapping>
```

It is worth mentioning at this stage that servlets can be mapped to more than one URL through the use of wildcards in the `<url-pattern>` child of the `<servlet-mapping>` element. For example, the following example maps every URL encountered to the same servlet:

```
<servlet-mapping>
  <servlet-name>ValidatorServlet</servlet-name>
  <url-pattern>/*</url-pattern>
</servlet-mapping>
```

You can also have more than one `<servlet-mapping>` element per defined servlet. This allows you to map completely disparate URLs to the same target.

Servlet Context Initialization Parameters

The next section of the deployment descriptor that we are going to discuss is the section concerning application (or servlet context) initialization parameters. We have already seen how to define initialization parameters for individual servlets, now we will look at defining parameters for the whole web application.

In order to achieve this we use the `ServletContext` object. We discussed the `ServletContext` earlier in the chapter, and said that it is a servlet's view into the web application that contains it. As such, if a parameter is set in the `ServletContext`, it is accessible from all servlets in the web application.

Through the deployment descriptor we can provide the ServletContext with any number of initialization parameters. We could use such parameters to convey application information such as an administrator's e-mail address. These parameters are available to the servlets in the web application via two abstract methods of the ServletContext. These methods are:

- ❑ getInitParameter(String name)
- ❑ getInitParameterNames()

The first method returns a String containing the value of the parameter, the second returns an Enumeration containing the names of the parameters in the ServletContext.

Since these methods are abstract (like all methods on the ServletContext interface), their implementations must be provided by the web container. In our example, we define one initialization parameter for our web application. This is shown below:

```
<context-param>
  <param-name>
    adminEmail
  </param-name>
  <param-value>
    admin@wrox.com
  </param-value>
</context-param>
```

This parameter represents the e-mail address of the application's administrator. This can be pulled into any servlet in the application, so that the e-mail address used is consistent throughout the system and any modifications to it only need to be made in a single place. In order to obtain this parameter in any particular servlet we can use the following code

```
String adminEmail = getServletContext().getInitParameter("adminEmail");
```

Error Pages

In the early days of web development, if an error occurred in an application we would see the familiar HTTP Error 500, or worse still a nasty stack trace on the browser. For example if our servlet performs an operation that results in an exception, it is quite common to see the following type of output in the client browser:

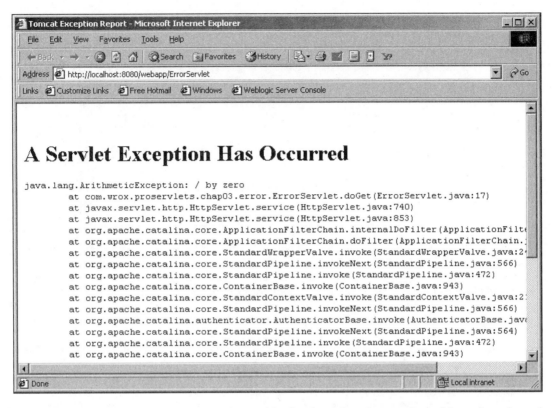

In a production system, the output of a stack trace like this does not inspire much confidence from the end user of the application! However, we can control how exceptions or errors are displayed to the user through the use of **error pages**. Error pages allow us to specify pages to be shown when particular errors occur; these errors can include Java exceptions, as well as HTTP errors (such as when a page can't be found).

Our sample deployment descriptor defines two error pages. The first error page is shown whenever the server encounters a `java.lang.ArithmeticException` (as in the above screenshot). The tags to define this are shown below:

```
<error-page>
  <exception-type>
    java.lang.ArithmeticException
  </exception-type>
  <location>
    /error.html
  </location>
</error-page>
```

As you can see, the `<error-page>` element has two children. In this case, these are `<exception-type>`, which defines the exception to catch, and `<location>`, which defines the page/resource to show on encountering the error defined.

If we were to run the same servlet that produced the screen shot above, we would see the resource error.html instead of the nasty Java stack trace that we saw above:

This is obviously a lot more user-friendly and readable, and has the added advantage that the web application developer has control over what happens when an error occurs. However, there are two sides to this coin. Hiding the error information from the user also means hiding it from the people expected to deal with the error. It would be useful, for example, to log the real error to a file, or display it in a collapsible area of the screen. This would isolate the user from a messy stack trace, but still allow the programmers to identify the root of the problem.

Our sample deployment descriptor also contains an error page definition for an HTTP error. This is defined using the tags below:

```
<error-page>
  <error-code>
    404
  </error-code>
  <location>
    /404.html
  </location>
</error-page>
```

This looks very similar to the previous example, but note the use of the <error-code> child element, instead of the <exception-type> child. This <error-code> child defines the HTTP error under which the error page defined will be shown. In this example, whenever the web container can not find a file requested in the web application, it will show the page 404.html rather than the server's default error page.

Welcome Pages

Those of you that have developed static web sites will be familiar with the concept of welcome pages. A welcome page is just a default page for a web application. Just as a web site can have a default page (typically index.html or home.html) a web application can have a page or resource that is displayed if no specific page within the application is requested.

In order to define a welcome page for a web application we use the tags below:

```
<welcome-file-list>
  <welcome-file>
    index.html
  </welcome-file>
</welcome-file-list>
```

Note that the file specified in the `<welcome-file>` element may not exist. All this element does is tells the container which files to look for if a request occurs for a directory, rather than a servlet. In this case the element instructs the container to look for the file `index.html` if no other resource is specified. You can have more than one `<welcome-file>` element, and the container will look for each resource in order, displaying the first resource found. This is useful, as you can define several common welcome file names (such as `index.html`, `home.html`, `index.htm`, `home.htm`), freeing the developers from having to name their welcome files the same across the application.

File-Based Security

So far our servlets have existed in a vacuum, where there is no hacking or distrust. Sadly this is not the case in the real world. In reality you must secure your applications from the dubious characters that exist around the Internet. If you can provide security in your applications, then you can do a whole host of things that would be unadvisable otherwise, such as accepting payments, storing credit card information, and so on.

The issue of security splits into four major areas:

❑ **Authentication** – Verification of a user interacting with a system

❑ **Authorization** – Restricting access to resources within an application

❑ **Confidentiality** – Hiding information from all but authorized parties

❑ **Integrity** – Ensuring that communications are received unmodified

In this section we will consider authentication.

HTTP Authentication

Fortunately for us, the HTTP protocol comes with a built-in authentication mechanism. This mechanism is called **Basic Authentication**. Basic authentication uses a very simple challenge/response system, based on a username and password. The web container maintains a list of usernames and passwords, and authenticates the user's details based on this information. The user's details are conveyed to the web container via a username/password box popped up by the web browser.

HTTP-based authentication is detailed in RFC 2617 available at http://www.ietf.org/rfc/rfc2617.txt.

Basic file-based authentication is very easy to configure. Let's see how to do this for the Tomcat web container.

The first step in setting up file-based basic authentication is to decide which resources in your application you wish to protect. Once you have done this you can set up your deployment descriptor.

The root of the elements defining security is the <security-constraint> element. Within this you define the resources to secure via the <web-resource-collection> element:

```
<web-resource-collection>
   <web-resource-name>SecureResource</web-resource-name>
   <url-pattern>/admin/*</url-pattern>
   <http-method>GET</http-method>
   <http-method>POST</http-method>
</web-resource-collection>
```

The collection of resources to secure is given a name via the <web-resource-name> element. The <url-pattern> element defines the URL pattern that represents the resources to secure. In the above case everything in the admin directory is secured. The <http-method> element define the HTTP methods on the secured resources to which the security applies. In this case the security is applied to both the GET and POST methods. If no <http-method> tags are present, then the security constraint applies to all HTTP methods.

Once you have described the resources to secure, you must decide which users or groups of users will be able to see the secured resources. This is done using the <auth-constraint> element:

```
<auth-constraint>
   <role-name>admin</role-name>
</auth-constraint>
```

The <role-name> element gives the role name (user or group) that is able to access this collection of resources.

Having defined the resources to secure, and the roles that are able to see the resources, we have to tell our web application that we wish to use basic authentication. This is done using the <login-config> element:

```
<login-config>
   <auth-method>BASIC</auth-method>
   <realm-name>Secure Realm</realm-name>
</login-config>
```

The <auth-method> element indicates that we wish to use basic authentication, and the <realm-name> element gives a textual name to show to the user in the pop-up login box. The setup used here would show a pop-up to the user like that shown in the following screenshot:

Defining Users in Tomcat

In order to use security, we also need to set up some users. For file-based security in Tomcat this is a very simple process. The users and groups that you wish to add can be added to the tomcat-users.xml file in the %CATALINA_HOME%/conf directory. A sample setup of this file would be:

```
<tomcat-users>
  <user name="tomcat" password="tomcat" roles="tomcat" />
  <user name="role1"  password="tomcat" roles="role1"  />
  <user name="sam"    password="dalton" roles="admin" />
</tomcat-users>
```

This defines three users, one of which has a role called admin, and as such will be able to access the resources defined above.

We'll look at securing web applications in more detail in Chapter 9.

Tag Order

A common problem when writing your deployment descriptor will be with tag order. It is important to remember that the elements in the deployment descriptor are order dependent. For example, the <servlet> elements that define servlets MUST come before the <servlet-mapping> elements that map the defined servlets to a URL pattern. Any errors with the ordering of elements will normally be picked up at deployment time, but it is possible that this will not be the case (for example, if your web container does not use a validating XML parser). In order to make sure that your deployment descriptor is correct in every way, we will discuss a small deployment descriptor validation tool in the next section.

Validating Your Deployment Descriptor

Once you have written your deployment descriptor it is important to know that you have defined the configuration of the web application correctly. You may wonder how we define 'correct' in this context. Basically a web application deployment descriptor is correct if it conforms to the published Document Type Definition (DTD) for web applications. The DTD in question is web-app_2_3.dtd. This DTD is available from the Sun web site at http://java.sun.com/dtd/web-app_2_3.dtd. This DTD is included in the /code directory for this chapter. In order to ensure that your deployment descriptor complies with this DTD, you have three options; these options are presented here in ascending order of desirability:

- ❑ Pick through the deployment descriptor and the DTD by hand, checking that you have all of the correct elements in the correct places

- ❑ Deploy your application to a web container, and see if you get any errors during deployment

- ❑ Use a validating XML parser to validate your XML deployment descriptor against the appropriate DTD

Obviously, the first option is not ideal, as it is very easy to miss items in a very large and involved deployment descriptor. If indeed you do fail to find mistakes, then you will get errors when you come to deploy your web application to a web container.

This is not actually a major problem, since most modern web containers will report the errors, and give you help in finding them. Once you have fixed any errors reported, you can re-deploy your application, and start the process again. It is possible that errors may mask the existence of other errors, so you could have to re-deploy your application quite a few times to isolate and fix all of the potential errors in your descriptor. Although this is not a huge hassle, there may be times when it is not an appropriate method for finding errors. For instance, if you are deploying a very large application, the process of preparing an application for deployment may be very time consuming (imagine trying to JAR up the contents of your company's web site).

So finally, we have the option of using a validating XML parser. Such a validating XML parser is the JAXP 1.1 Reference Implementation from Sun. This is available at http://java.sun.com/xml/download.html.

To make use of the parser to achieve our goal, we must also write a small utility program, which uses it to validate our deployment descriptor. Such a program is shown below:

```
package deployment;
import java.io.*;

import javax.xml.parsers.*;
import org.xml.sax.*;
import org.xml.sax.helpers.*;
import org.w3c.dom.*;

public class DDValidator {
  private String xmlfile;
  public DDValidator(String xmlfile) {
    this.xmlfile = xmlfile;
  }

  private boolean isValid() throws SAXException {
```

In the `isValid()` method of the `DDValidator` class, we first create a `DocumentBuilderFactory` object and configure it to validate the XML as it parses it. Then we create a `DocumentBuilder` object that satisfies the constraints specified by the `DocumentBuilderFactory`:

```
DocumentBuilderFactory dbf = DocumentBuilderFactory.newInstance();
dbf.setValidating(true);

DocumentBuilder db = null;
try {
  db = dbf.newDocumentBuilder();
```

Then we create an inner class to handle any errors encountered when parsing the document:

```
db.setErrorHandler(new DefaultHandler() {
  public void error(SAXParseException e) throws SAXException {
    throw new SAXException ("ERROR : " + e.getMessage());
  }
  public void fatalError(SAXParseException e) throws SAXException {
    throw new SAXException ("FATAL ERROR : " + e.getMessage());
  }
}
} catch (ParserConfigurationException pce) {
  System.err.println("Exception with configuration" + pce);
  System.exit(1);
}
```

Next we parse the document. Any parse errors will cause an exception to be thrown:

```
Document doc = null;
try {
  doc = db.parse(new File(this.xmlfile));
} catch (IOException ioe) {
  throw new SAXException("Document Invalid " + ioe.getMessage());
}

return true;
}
```

Finally we define the `main()` method that will use the `DDValidator` class. We get the name of the XML file as a command-line argument, and create a `DDValidator` object, passing it the name of the XML file to validate. Then we call the `isValid()` method on this object. If any errors are encountered we display an error message:

```
public static void main(String args[]) {
  if (args.length != 1) {
    System.err.println("Usage: DDValidator xml_file_to_validate");
    System.exit(0);
  }
```

```
      String xmlfile = args[0];
      DDValidator validator = new DDValidator(xmlfile);
      try {
        System.out.println(validator.isValid());
      } catch (SAXException se) {
        System.err.println(se.getMessage());
      }
    }
}
```

Let's now see how to execute this program against a valid and an invalid deployment descriptor.

Executing the Validator

In order to execute the deployment descriptor validator detailed above, you need to make sure that you have a JAXP-compatible XML parser in your CLASSPATH environmental variable. We are using Xalan, in this example, which is available from the Sun site as detailed earlier.

All we need now is a web.xml file:

```
<?xml version="1.0" encoding="ISO-8859-1"?>

<!DOCTYPE web-app
    PUBLIC "-//Sun Microsystems, Inc.//DTD Web Application 2.3//EN"
    "http://java.sun.com/dtd/web-app_2_3.dtd">

<web-app>

  <display-name>Test Web Application</display-name>
  <description>A test web application</description>

  <servlet>
    <servlet-name>Servlet1</servlet-name>
    <servlet-class>example.Servlet1</servlet-class>
    <init-param>
      <param-name>version</param-name>
      <param-value>0.1b</param-value>
    </init-param>
  </servlet>

  <error-page>
    <error-code>
      404
    </error-code>
    <location>
      /404.html
    </location>
  </error-page>

</web-app>
```

Now execute the validator, passing the path to the deployment descriptor as a command-line argument to the program. As this deployment descriptor is valid, there should be no error messages displayed:

```
C:\WINNT\System32\cmd.exe                                          _ □ ×
Microsoft Windows 2000 [Version 5.00.2195]
(C) Copyright 1985-2000 Microsoft Corp.

C:\Apache Tomcat 4.0\webapps\store\WEB-INF\classes>java deployment.DDValidator web.xml
true

C:\Apache Tomcat 4.0\webapps\store\WEB-INF\classes>_
```

Now modify the deployment descriptor so that the `<error-page>` tag comes before the `<servlet>` tag:

```xml
<?xml version="1.0" encoding="ISO-8859-1"?>

<!DOCTYPE web-app
    PUBLIC "-//Sun Microsystems, Inc.//DTD Web Application 2.3//EN"
    "http://java.sun.com/dtd/web-app_2_3.dtd">

<web-app>
  <display-name>Test Web Application</display-name>
  <description>A test web application</description>

  <error-page>
    <error-code>
      404
    </error-code>
    <location>
      /404.html
    </location>
  </error-page>

  <servlet>
    <servlet-name>Servlet1</servlet-name>
    <servlet-class>example.Servlet1</servlet-class>
    <init-param>
      <param-name>version</param-name>
      <param-value>0.1b</param-value>
    </init-param>
  </servlet>

</web-app>
```

Execute the program as before. As the XML file entered does not conform to the DTD specified, we see an error message displayed:

```
C:\WINNT\System32\cmd.exe                                          _ □ ×
Microsoft Windows 2000 [Version 5.00.2195]
(C) Copyright 1985-2000 Microsoft Corp.

C:\Apache Tomcat 4.0\webapps\store\WEB-INF\classes>java deployment.DDValidator web.xml
ERROR : Element "web-app" does not allow "servlet" here.

C:\Apache Tomcat 4.0\webapps\store\WEB-INF\classes>
```

191

This is indicating that the DTD does not allow the element `<servlet>` in the place at which we have placed it. The `<error-page>` element must come after the `<servlet>` element. As is suggested in the error message, we could set a custom error handler to report errors in validation. We will not show this here, but it would be an interesting exercise for the reader. Another interesting exercise would be to add a Swing/JFC front end to the validator. This could show the exact place that an error occurs in the descriptor.

Deploying a Sample Web Application

We are now in the position of being able to pull together all of the information in this chapter as a complete example web application.

This section will cover all of the code required to produce a sample web application. Most of the code will not be explained in great detail, as we will be focusing upon the deployment of the complete application. We will, however, discuss the servlet code in the application, and all of the code required to run the example can be found in the code download for the book.

The Store Scenario

The example used in this section is the ubiquitous web store application. We will show a simple front page, a simple shopping cart, and a simple checkout page. The pages will be output from servlets (since this is the theme of the book). The checkout page will be protected by a simple file-based security mechanism.

In the following section we will show the servlet code for the application. In the next section we will examine the deployment descriptor for the system. After we have seen all of the necessary components, we will package it up into a WAR file. The container that will be examined is Tomcat 4.0.

Servlet Code from the Store Web Application

There are three servlets from the sample application that we are going to look at:

- ❑ `MainServlet` – displays the store contents
- ❑ `CartServlet` – implements the shopping cart
- ❑ `CheckOutServlet` – handles product purchasing

Let's take a look at each of these in turn.

MainServlet

The `MainServlet` has the job of displaying the contents of our store.

```
package store;

import java.io.*;
import java.util.*;

import javax.servlet.*;
import javax.servlet.http.*;
```

```
import javax.xml.parsers.*;
import org.xml.sax.*;
import org.xml.sax.helpers.*;
import org.w3c.dom.*;

public class MainServlet extends HttpServlet {
```

The `init()` method of `MainServlet` is called once when the servlet is first constructed (either when the server starts, or when the servlet is first requested). This method reads the name of the XML file describing the products, reading this filename from a `ServletContext` initialization parameter:

```
public void init() throws ServletException {

  ServletContext context = getServletContext();
  InputStream productsFile =
    context
      .getResourceAsStream((String) context
        .getInitParameter("productsFile"));
```

It then instantiates a `DocumentBuilder` object, and uses it to parse the file:

```
DocumentBuilderFactory dbf = DocumentBuilderFactory.newInstance();
DocumentBuilder db = null;
try {
  db = dbf.newDocumentBuilder();
} catch (ParserConfigurationException pce) {
  throw new ServletException(pce.getMessage());
}

Document doc = null;
try {
  doc = db.parse(productsFile);
} catch (IOException ioe) {
  throw new ServletException(ioe.getMessage());
} catch (SAXException se) {
  throw new ServletException(se.getMessage());
}
```

Next it retrieves the products' names and values:

```
NodeList productsList = doc.getElementsByTagName("product");

HashMap products = new HashMap();
Node product;
for (int ctr = 0; ctr < productsList.getLength(); ctr++) {

  product = productsList.item(ctr);
  NamedNodeMap attribs = product.getAttributes();
  Node attrib = attribs.getNamedItem("name");
  String name = attrib.getNodeValue();
```

```
        attrib = attribs.getNamedItem("price");
        String price = attrib.getNodeValue();

        Product p = new Product(ctr, name, price);

        products.put(new Integer(ctr), p);
    }
```

The method then stores the product information in the `ServletContext`. Once this has happened, the list of products is available to all servlets in the application:

```
        context.setAttribute("products", products);
    }
```

In our servlet, the `doPost()` and `doGet()` methods should perform the same function. Therefore, as shown below, they delegate their processing to the `doGetOrPost()` method:

```
    public void doPost(HttpServletRequest req, HttpServletResponse res)
                                    throws ServletException, IOException {
      doGetOrPost(req, res);
    }

    public void doGet(HttpServletRequest req, HttpServletResponse res)
                                    throws ServletException, IOException {
      doGetOrPost(req, res);
    }
```

The following `doGetOrPost()` method implements the main functionality of our servlet, which is to display the products that we loaded earlier. The products are displayed in an HTML table, and a standard header and footer are included so that we can simply change the style of the page, without changing the code that displays products.

```
    private void doGetOrPost(HttpServletRequest req, HttpServletResponse res)
                                    throws ServletException, IOException {
      PrintWriter out = res.getWriter();
```

Here's where we include the header:

```
      RequestDispatcher dispatcher = req.getRequestDispatcher("/header.html");
      dispatcher.include(req, res);

      HashMap products =
        (HashMap) getServletContext().getAttribute("products");
```

Having retrieved the products from the `ServletContext`, we then output a table containing a list of the products and their prices. The table contains hyperlinks so that the user can click and add a product to the cart if desired:

```
      Iterator it = products.values().iterator();
      out.println("<table>");
      while (it.hasNext()) {
        out.println("<tr>");
        Product product = (Product) it.next();
        out.println("<td><a href='Cart?add=true&id=" + product.getId() + "'>"
                    + product.getName() + "</a></td><td>"
                    + product.getPrice() + "</td>");
        out.println("</tr>");
      }
      out.println("</table>");
```

Finally, we include a standard footer:

```
      dispatcher = req.getRequestDispatcher("/footer.html");
      dispatcher.include(req, res);
    }
  }
```

As you can see this servlet is fairly large. This is not surprising, as it sets up our store. The init() method handles the initialization of this servlet. In this case the initialization includes loading our store's products from an XML file. This is achieved using the line:

```
  InputStream productsFile =
    context
      .getResourceAsStream((String) context
        .getInitParameter("productsFile"));
```

This is a demonstration of how to use the ServletContext object to load resources from our application. This means that to change the products that our store stocks, we merely have to replace our XML file with another of the same form, and specify its location (relative to the root of our web app) in the deployment descriptor. The XML file used to specify products is very simple, and is shown below:

```
<products>
<product name="Fish" price="1.99"/>
<product name="Dog" price="19.99"/>
</products>
```

To add a new product, we simply add a new <product> line.

CartServlet

The cart in our store holds one of each type of product only. Obviously this is a rather forced condition, specified primarily so that we can illustrate error pages for our sample application. The code that implements our cart is another servlet and is shown below:

```
package store;

import java.io.*;
import java.util.*;
```

```
import javax.servlet.*;
import javax.servlet.http.*;

public class CartServlet extends HttpServlet {
```

As with the MainServlet, the doGet() and doPost() methods delegate to a method called doGetOrPost() to prevent duplication of code:

```
public void doPost(HttpServletRequest req, HttpServletResponse res)
                                  throws ServletException, IOException {
  doGetOrPost(req, res);
}

public void doGet(HttpServletRequest req, HttpServletResponse res)
                                  throws ServletException, IOException {
  doGetOrPost(req, res);
}
```

The doGetOrPost() method implements the main functionality of the servlet. We first check to see if we are adding to the cart, or want to display the cart:

```
private void doGetOrPost(HttpServletRequest req, HttpServletResponse res)
                                  throws ServletException, IOException {

    String adding = req.getParameter("add");

    PrintWriter out = res.getWriter();
```

Next we retrieve the cart, if it exists, from the session. If it doesn't exist we create a new cart:

```
    HttpSession session = req.getSession();
    Cart cart = (Cart) session.getAttribute("cart");

    if (cart == null) {
      cart = new Cart();
    }
```

Then if required we add to the cart using the addToCart() method, and then display its contents using displayCart() (we'll look more closely at these methods in a moment):

```
    if (adding.equalsIgnoreCase("true")) {
      addToCart(req, cart, out);
    }

    displayCart(cart, out);
}
```

In the `addToCart()` method, the item is added, and then the cart is placed into the user's HTTP session.

```
private void addToCart(HttpServletRequest req,
                       Cart cart,
                       PrintWriter out) throws ItemAlreadyAddedException {
```

We get the item to add from the request. First we retrieve the products from the servlet context:

```
HashMap products =
    (HashMap) getServletContext().getAttribute("products");
```

Then we find the product represented by the ID in the request, and add it to the cart. We then add this cart to the session and finally display a confirmation message, or an error message if something goes wrong:

```
try {
    Integer id = new Integer(Integer.parseInt(req.getParameter("id")));
    Product p = (Product) products.get(id);
    cart.addItem(p);
    req.getSession().setAttribute("cart", cart);
    out.println("<b>Succesfully added product to cart!</b><br>");
} catch (NumberFormatException nfe) {
    out.println("<b>Can't add product</b><br>");
}
}
```

As mentioned earlier, a cart can only contain one of each product. If the user tries to add more than one of the same item to the cart, an `ItemAlreadyAddedException` is thrown.

The `displayCart()` method allows us to display the contents of the cart. The contents of the cart are iterated through and displayed in an HTML table:

```
private void displayCart(Cart cart, PrintWriter out) {

    Iterator items = cart.getItems();
    out.println("<h1>Current Cart Contents:</h1>");
    out.println("<table>");
    while (items.hasNext()) {
        out.println("<tr>");
        Product p = (Product) items.next();
        out.println("<td>" + p.getName() + "</td>" + "<td>" + p.getPrice()
                    + "</td>");
        out.println("<tr>");
    }
    out.println("</table>");
}
}
```

CheckOutServlet

Obviously, a store is only useful if you can actually buy the products that you put into your cart. In our example store the CheckOutServlet handles this. Obviously, being an example, you cannot really buy the items. The checkout process in our store simply allows the user to login, and displays the contents of their cart. The code behind our CheckOutServlet is listed below.

```java
package store;

import java.io.*;

import javax.servlet.*;
import javax.servlet.http.*;

public class CheckOutServlet extends HttpServlet {

  public void doPost(HttpServletRequest req, HttpServletResponse res)
                                throws ServletException, IOException {
    doGetOrPost(req, res);
  }

  public void doGet(HttpServletRequest req, HttpServletResponse res)
                                throws ServletException, IOException {
    doGetOrPost(req, res);
  }
```

This servlet again does the bulk of its work in the doGetOrPost() method. The method simply includes the output of the CartServlet, and then presents a button for the user to click, which will take them to a confirmation page (not shown here):

```java
  private void doGetOrPost(HttpServletRequest req, HttpServletResponse res)
                                throws ServletException, IOException {
    PrintWriter out = res.getWriter();

    String userName = req.getUserPrincipal().getName();
    out.println("<h1>Hello again " + userName + "</h1>");

    RequestDispatcher dispatcher =
      req.getRequestDispatcher("/Cart?add=false");
    dispatcher.include(req, res);

    out.println("<br>Please Click Confirm to check out");
    out.println("<form action='confirmed.html'>
                <input type='submit' value='Confirm'></form>");
  }
}
```

Having seen all of the servlet code for our simple store application we will now look at the deployment descriptor required to deploy this application.

Deployment Descriptor

Now we have all of the code for our application written, it's time to deploy it. Let's walk through the deployment descriptor that we will be using to do this:

```xml
<?xml version="1.0" encoding="ISO-8859-1"?>

<!DOCTYPE web-app
    PUBLIC "-//Sun Microsystems, Inc.//DTD Web Application 2.3//EN"
    "http://java.sun.com/dtd/web-app_2_3.dtd">

<web-app>
```

The first piece of this deployment descriptor to notice is the section below, which adds an initialization value into the servlet context. This value is used in the `init()` method of the `MainServlet` to find out where to load the `products` XML file from, as we saw above:

```xml
<context-param>
    <param-name>
        productsFile
    </param-name>
    <param-value>
        products.xml
    </param-value>
</context-param>
```

Next we set up our three servlets, providing both a `<servlet>` and `<servlet-mapping>` entry for each servlet. Notice that we map the `MainServlet` servlet to the name `home.html`. This means that to access the `MainServlet`, we would use the URL http://localhost:8080/store/home.html. To the user it looks at though this is a simple HTML file, but in fact a servlet is being executed and the resulting HTML is displayed to the user.

```xml
<servlet>
    <servlet-name>HomeServlet</servlet-name>
    <servlet-class>store.MainServlet</servlet-class>
</servlet>
<servlet>
    <servlet-name>CheckOutServlet</servlet-name>
    <servlet-class>store.CheckOutServlet</servlet-class>
</servlet>
<servlet>
    <servlet-name>CartServlet</servlet-name>
    <servlet-class>store.CartServlet</servlet-class>
</servlet>

<servlet-mapping>
    <servlet-name>HomeServlet</servlet-name>
    <url-pattern>/home.html</url-pattern>
</servlet-mapping>
<servlet-mapping>
    <servlet-name>CheckOutServlet</servlet-name>
    <url-pattern>/CheckOutServlet</url-pattern>
</servlet-mapping>
<servlet-mapping>
    <servlet-name>CartServlet</servlet-name>
    <url-pattern>/Cart</url-pattern>
</servlet-mapping>
```

199

As you can see, all of the other servlets are mapped to a URI with the same name as the name of the servlet itself.

Once we have declared and mapped each of our servlets, we assign a welcome page (index.html) for the application:

```
<welcome-file-list>
  <welcome-file>index.html</welcome-file>
</welcome-file-list>
```

Next we define an error page for the application too. The section of the deployment descriptor that does this is shown below:

```
<error-page>
  <exception-type>
    store.ItemAlreadyAddedException
  </exception-type>
  <location>
    /duplicateItem.html
  </location>
</error-page>
```

This definition says that whenever the exception store.ItemAlreadyAddedException is thrown, the page duplicateItem.html will be displayed. If you recall, we have said that only one item of a specific type can be added to the user's shopping cart. If this constraint is violated, then the exception above is thrown, and the user is presented with a page telling them that they cannot add duplicate items to their cart.

The final part of the deployment descriptor defines the security policy for our application. Earlier we said that the checkout page required the user to login to the store. The following section of the deployment descriptor enforces this. If you look back over the checkout code, you will notice that we didn't need to do anything special to make logging in required. This is the power of leaving security and other system functions until deployment time. This breed of security is known as **declarative** security. The alternative, adding code to the application to perform the authentication, is known as **programmatic** security.

```
<security-constraint>

  <web-resource-collection>
    <web-resource-name>CheckOutResource</web-resource-name>
    <url-pattern>/CheckOutServlet/*</url-pattern>
    <http-method>GET</http-method>
    <http-method>POST</http-method>
  </web-resource-collection>

  <auth-constraint>
    <role-name>storeuser</role-name>
  </auth-constraint>

</security-constraint>
```

```
    <login-config>
      <auth-method>FORM</auth-method>
      <realm-name>Wrox Store Checkout</realm-name>

      <form-login-config>
        <form-login-page>
          /login.html
        </form-login-page>
        <form-error-page>
          /error.html
        </form-error-page>
      </form-login-config>
    </login-config>

  </web-app>
```

You will notice that this is set up in exactly the same way as the file-based security that we described earlier on in the chapter. The resources that we wish to secure are defined in the `<web-resource-collection>` element (in this case the `CheckOutServlet`) and the role required for access is defined in the `<auth-constraint>` section (in this case `storeuser`).

The contents of `<login-config>` have changed from our previous discussion of security. This time, we are not simply using the browser's ability to pop up a login box to get the username and password. This time we are defining a custom login page for our application. This means any request by the application for a username and password is directed to the login page. This page is very simple, and allows us to customize the user logon experience. This form-based login is configured via the `<form-login-config>` section. All that we have to do is to define a page to handle logins, and a page to redirect to on failed logins.

The form that handles logins for our application is defined by the code below:

```html
<form method="post" action="j_security_check">
  <table>
    <tr>
      <td>
        User Name:
      </td>
      <td>
        <input type="text" name="j_username">
      </td>
    </tr>
    <tr>
      <td>
        Password:
      </td>
      <td>
        <input type="password" name="j_password">
      </td>
    </tr>
    <tr>
      <td colspan=2>
        <input type="submit" value="  Login  ">
      </td>
    </tr>
  </table>
</form>
```

Notice that the form submits to a resource called j_security_check. This is the resource that all forms that handle logins must submit to. There must be a field called j_username and j_password present in order for this logon page to be processed.

Now that we have seen all of the code, as well as the deployment descriptor for our application, we need to compile the classes using javac.

Adding Users

The next step is to set up your store's users. This can be done by making entries in the %CATALINA_HOME%\conf\tomcat-users.xml file. Each user has an entry like the following:

```
<user name="sam" password="password" roles="storeuser" />
```

Our final steps are to package up the application and then deploy it.

Packaging the Application

Earlier in the chapter we discussed the concept of the Web Application Archive (WAR) file. Let's create a WAR file containing our sample application.

The first step is to make sure that the directory structure of the web application is correct, and that the files composing the application are in the correct subdirectories, as discussed earlier in the chapter. Then move to the top level of the store web app's directory structure, and issue the following command at the prompt:

```
jar -cv0f store.war .
```

This should create your store.war file. Now we need to deploy it.

Deploying the Application

We will now demonstrate how to deploy our completed and archived application to Tomcat. For very basic deployments, to do this, just copy your WAR file into the webapps directory of your Tomcat installation.

However, you may wish to keep your web application somewhere other than the top level of the webapps directory. In this case, in order to tell Tomcat where to look for the web app, we need to add a <Context> element to the %CATALINA_HOME\conf\server.xml file:

```
<Context path="/store" docBase="/store.war" reloadable="true"/>
```

This line declares a context to exist with its base URL path being /store. In other words, the application will be found at http://localhost:8080/store/. The docBase parameter tells Tomcat where to find the web app; in this case the relative path /store.war indicates that the application is located in the top level of the webapps directory. The URI you supply here could also be an absolute file path, so you could keep your web apps anywhere on your machine that you wish, although from an organizational point of view it is often best to keep web apps in the webapps folder.

If the `reloadable` parameter is set to `true` then Tomcat monitors classes in `/WEB-INF/classes/` and `/WEB-INF/lib` for changes, and automatically reloads the web application if a change is detected. This feature is very useful during application development, but it requires significant runtime overhead and is not recommended for use on deployed production applications.

There are many other parameters that can be passed. Most of these beyond the scope of this chapter, but are very useful if you wish to have more control over how your application is deployed. Details of these parameters can be found at http://jakarta.apache.org/tomcat/tomcat-4.0-doc/config/context.html.

Now restart Tomcat, and your application will be deployed. It can now be accessed at http://localhost:8080/store/. You should see the welcome page:

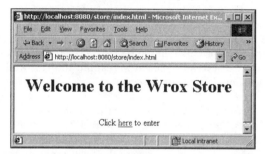

Click on here and you will see the home page for the store:

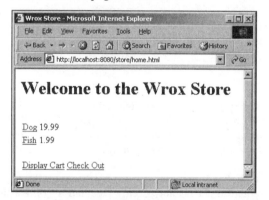

Try adding some items to your cart, and then click on Check Out. You will encounter a login page. When you have successfully logged in, you will be asked to confirm that you wish to check out. If you click on the Confirm button you will get a confirmation message:

If you make changes to the application, simply copy the new WAR file over the old one, and Tomcat will reload the application automatically.

Advanced Deployment Issues

In this section we will discuss some of the new features of the Servlet specification that relate to web applications.

JAR Dependencies

To be truly useful, a web application usually needs to have access to other libraries, both from within the J2EE framework, and from external sources. These libraries are normally contained within JAR files. For example, a web application that needs to access XML features would need to have a file such as xerces.jar available to the application.

In prior versions of the Servlet specification, you had to include all of the JAR files required by a web application in the web application archive, in the WEB-INF/lib directory of the archive. This is obviously not ideal, as it add extra weight to each web application, as well as meaning that we probably have several versions of the same JAR on each server.

In the latest version of the Servlet specification, 2.3, we are able to express dependencies on these external JAR files using the MANIFEST.MF file in the web archive's META-INF directory. Expressing dependencies in this way allows a web container to reject deployment of a web application if a dependency cannot be satisfied. This should prevent the occurrence of cryptic run-time errors when JAR files cannot be found.

Note that it is also possible to declare a dependency on a particular version of a library. It is then up to the server to find the correct package at deployment time.

Classloading

The 2.3 version of the Servlet specification introduces what appears at first sight to be a small change to the classloading mechanism for web applications. This apparently small change actually has a very big impact. In previous versions of the Servlet specification, a web application could see and use the server's implementation classes. In the latest version, this is impossible.

This may not sound like much, but it prevents situations where a collision between web application classes and server implementation classes may occur. This had become a significant problem with XML parsers, as each server had a parser to read and validate deployment descriptors, and lots of applications also used XML parsers. If the parsers implemented different standards, this could lead to an unsolvable conflict.

Summary

In this chapter we have examined many features relating to the deployment of web applications based on the Servlets 2.3 specification.

We noted that web applications can be deployed in different ways depending on whether we are deploying our application in a production or development situation. For production we can use the WAR file format, and for development we can deploy in the Exploded Directory format.

We then looked at some of the aspects of the web application that can be configured in the deployment descriptor XML file for a web application. These included:

- Servlet definitions and mappings
- Welcome pages
- Error pages
- Declarative security
- ServletContext initialization

We also discussed a strategy for validating the well-formedness and conformity of our deployment descriptors, and developed a simple validator application to inform us of errors.

To illustrate the points we had made earlier in the chapter, we then created a sample web store application, and deployed it as a WAR in Tomcat.

At the end of the chapter, we considered aspects of servlet deployment that had changed in the latest version (2.3) of the Servlet specification, including how classes are loaded and JAR dependencies within WAR files.

In the next chapter we will discuss how to track client information across requests, using sessions.

5

Session Handling

In previous chapters, we noted that HTTP is the protocol most commonly used to communicate with web applications. Unfortunately, HTTP offers no mechanism for data to be retained between requests; in other words it can't track the activities of a user across requests.

Why is this important? Well, consider the ubiquitous shopping cart application. A client using this will make several requests to the application; each request may be to add/remove a product to/from the cart, or to check out, or so on. For the application to know what the client has bought upon checking out, it is obvious that it needs to keep track of whatever the user has selected across requests. This means not only uniquely identifying the user on each request, but probably also storing data (state) across requests and associating it with the user. Associating requests with a particular user in this way is often known as maintaining a **session**, and many web applications make use of sessions.

As we often need to maintain sessions, but HTTP is stateless, there are various mechanisms that have been devised to enable us to do so. These include:

- ❑ Rewriting URLs
- ❑ Creating cookies
- ❑ Using hidden form fields

In this chapter we are going to discuss these mechanisms, and consider how they can help maintain state between requests in our web applications. We will also see how we can use a selection of interfaces and classes from the Java Servlet API to create, destroy, and manipulate Java objects that represent sessions in our servlets. We will also discuss event listener interfaces that can be used to create classes that listen out for changes to the Session object.

Over the course of the chapter, we will build a web application (based upon servlets) that allows the user to create and modify notes, so that we can demonstrate the use of these interfaces and classes too.

The Stateless Nature of HTTP

In Chapter 3 we noted that the HTTP is by far the most common protocol used to communicate with web applications.

Consider this communication process. The client sends an HTTP request to a web server. The server receives the request, applies necessary processing logic, creates a response, and sends it back to the client. This request-response process happens across a single network connection. At the end of the process the server closes the connection. In addition, any failure on the server side or any network failure could terminate the request. The client may also terminate the connection before receiving the response from the server. This means that, when the client sends another request, all the request-response cycle happens again, but a new network connection must be established.

Now, there is an optional feature in HTTP 1.1 called "keep-alive", which allows the client to use the same connection across multiple requests. However, browsers use this feature only when the server supports it, and only when the requests happen in rapid succession.

At this point, you may be asking, why do HTTP-based connections only exist for the length of a single request-response cycle? Web servers cater to a potentially large number of users. For a server, accepting a network connection means listening to incoming requests over a socket. This consumes operating system-level resources including threads and memory. In order to be able to serve a large number of users, HTTP is designed to use new connections for every request; this means that connections are not held beyond the duration of a request and a response, which minimizes the waste of system resources.

Given this stateless nature of HTTP, basic servlet programming is also stateless. Consider the `javax.servlet.Servlet` interface or the abstract `javax.servlet.http.HttpServlet` class that we use to write our own servlets. Within a service method (such as `doGet()` or `doPost()`), each servlet extracts request parameters, processes some application logic, and then generates the response. After writing the response to the HTTP request, the servlet loses its attachment to the request. For all practical purposes, you may even consider that the servlet instance does not even exist. Since an instance may or may not exist beyond a single request, we cannot store any data in the instance variables of a servlet.

From the servlet developer's point-of-view, this statelessness is a constraint. However, from the server/container's point-of-view, it is required to offer better performance and scalability by not spawning a new servlet instance for each new HTTP request. We improve web container performance because we avoid object allocation for each new request, and scalability because the container will have more resources left to serve more requests.

Why Track Client Identity and State?

The fact that HTTP is a "stateless protocol" has important consequences when we communicate with web applications via HTTP. In the introduction to this chapter, we discussed one scenario where we need to maintain state, the shopping cart application. Consider another scenario:

❑　Typical online banking can involve one or more banking transactions. Most such transactions may spawn across several pages. In order to maintain the transactions, we need a mechanism to uniquely identify the user, to track the activity of the user within the site, and to relate the transactions to the account/transaction data stored in backend systems.

In both scenarios we mentioned above there are two important activities:

❑ **Tracking the identity of a user**
As the user makes multiple requests to the same web application over a period of time, we need a mechanism that links these requests together. Effectively, this means that we need to associate each request with a client identifier, so that we can identify requests from the same user.

❑ **Maintaining user state**
Since there is often data associated with each request, we will need a way to associate the request data with the user that made the request, and a way to preserve that data across requests.

The ability to associate a request with the client that made the request is known as maintaining a **session**. However, the obvious next question to ask is: what mechanisms can we use to maintain sessions?

How do we Maintain Sessions?

In the previous section, we saw that there are many situations in which we need to keep track of state. Essentially this meant that we must preserve the identity of the client and the data associated with the client across requests. Since HTTP is a stateless protocol, just how do web applications manage to keep track of users?

In the following sections, we will discuss various mechanisms that we can use to maintain state across requests. We will consider the following approaches:

❑ URL rewriting

❑ Cookies

❑ Hidden form fields

These techniques are used to maintain sessions in not only Java-based applications, but web applications written in many other languages too. Out of these three, the most common approach is to use cookies.

The Java Servlet API provides a way of maintaining sessions via two of these techniques: cookies and URL rewriting. We will examine the session-related interfaces and classes from the API later too.

Session handling is based on a simple idea that two entities can identify each other by exchanging some token (a unique identifier that both entities recognize) with each message. For instance, if your name is "Bob", and the name "Bob" is unique as far as the server is concerned, you may send the token "Bob" with each request to the server to uniquely identify you. Of course, this token need not be your name; it can be any piece of data that uniquely identifies you. The idea behind all session handling techniques is the same: they all rely on exchanging a server-generated unique ID with each request.

Let's begin by discussing the URL rewriting approach to session tracking.

Session Tracking Using URL Rewriting

URL rewriting is based on the idea of embedding a unique ID (generated by the server) in each URL of the response from the server. That is, while generating the response to the first request, the server embeds this ID in each URL. When the client submits a request to one such URL, the browser sends this ID back to the server. The server can therefore identify the ID with all requests. Let's examine this approach with the aid of a simple servlet. This servlet does the following:

❑ Checks to see if the client sent any token with its request

❑ If no token was sent, a new one is created

❑ Provides two links back to the servlet – one including the token, and one not

Here's the sourcecode for the `TokenServlet`:

```
package sessions;

import java.io.*;
import java.util.Random;
import javax.servlet.http.*;
import javax.servlet.ServletException;

public class TokenServlet extends HttpServlet {

  protected void doGet(HttpServletRequest request, HttpServletResponse response)
      throws ServletException, IOException {
```

First we get the token from the request:

```
    String tokenID = request.getParameter("tokenID");
```

Then we prepare the response:

```
    response.setContentType("text/html");
    PrintWriter writer = response.getWriter();
    writer.println("<html><head><title>Tokens</title></head><body ");
    writer.println("style=\"font-family:verdana;font-size:10pt\">");
```

If the client did not send any token we create a new one:

```
    if(tokenID == null) {
      Random rand = new Random();
      tokenID = Long.toString(rand.nextLong());
      writer.println("<p>Welcome. A new token " +
                  tokenID + " is now established</p>");
    } else {
```

If the client sent a token then we acknowledge the client:

```
    writer.println("<p>Welcome back. Your token is " + tokenID + ".</p>");
}
```

Then we prepare the links for sending requests back:

```
String requestURLSame = request.getRequestURL().toString() +
                        "?token=" + tokenID;
String requestURLNew = request.getRequestURL().toString();
```

Finally, we write the response and close the connection:

```
writer.println("<p>Click <a href=" + requestURLSame +
               ">here</a> again to continue browsing with the " +
               "same identity.</p>");
writer.println("<p>Otherwise, click <a href=" + requestURLNew +
               ">here</a> again to start browsing with a new identity.</p>");
writer.close();
    }
}
```

Create a web application called `token`, compile the sourcecode above, and add the class to the `WEB-INF/class/sessions` directory. Then create the following simple deployment descriptor for the web application:

```
<?xml version="1.0"?>

<!DOCTYPE web-app PUBLIC "-//Sun Microsystems, Inc.//DTD Web Application 2.3//EN"
                        "http://java.sun.com/dtd/web-app_2_3.dtd">

<web-app>
  <servlet>
    <servlet-name>track</servlet-name>
    <servlet-class>sessions.TokenServlet</servlet-class>
  </servlet>

  <servlet-mapping>
    <servlet-name>track</servlet-name>
    <url-pattern>/track/*</url-pattern>
  </servlet-mapping>
</web-app>
```

Deploy the web application, restart Tomcat, and navigate to http://localhost:8080/token/track. You should see something like:

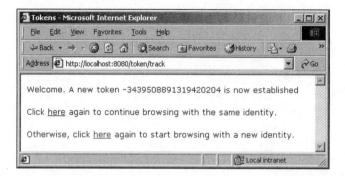

The initial request http://localhost:8080/token/track does not include the query parameter tokenID. The servlet creates a new token, and generates two links. The first link includes a query string while the second link doesn't. If you click on the first link, you will see the following page:

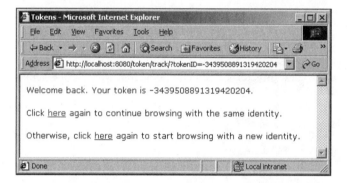

Since there is a query parameter in the request, the servlet recognizes the user from this parameter, and displays the Welcome back message. If you click instead on the second link, the browser displays a page with a different token:

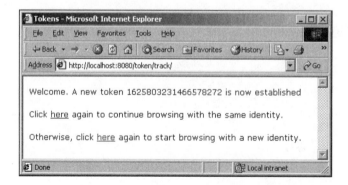

Although this technique can solve the problem of session tracking, it has two important limitations:

❑ Since the token is visible in the URL during a session, these sessions will not be very secure

❑ Since links in static pages are hard-wired, they can't be dynamically changed for every user, so we can only use this system with servlets or other dynamic pages

An alternative is to use cookies. As you will see in the following section, cookies eliminate the above limitations.

Session Tracking Using Cookies

Cookies provide a better alternative to explicit URL rewriting, because cookies are not sent as query strings but are exchanged within the bodies of HTTP requests and responses. Since there is no need to rewrite URLs, session handling via cookies does not depend on whether the content is static or dynamic.

All modern browsers can recognize and receive cookies from web servers, and then send them back along with requests. However, there is a limitation with cookies. All browsers allow users to disable this functionality, which leads to browsers not recognizing cookies. This is because cookies have a bad press – they have sometimes been used to gather information about consumers without their knowledge. Given this, it is worth simultaneously supporting an alternative technique such as URL rewriting. We shall see how we can do this with the Java Servlet API.

A cookie is a string sent via the HTTP request and HTTP response headers. A cookie has the following parameters:

Parameter	Description
Name	Name of cookie
Value	A value of the cookie
Comment	A comment explaining the purpose of the cookie
Max-Age	Maximum age of the cookie (a time in seconds after which the client should not send the cookie back to the server)
Domain	Domain to which the cookie should be sent
Path	The path to which the cookie should be sent
Secure	Specifies if the cookie should be sent securely via HTTPS
Version	Version of the cookie protocol. Version 0 means the original Netscape version of cookies. Version 1 means cookies standardized via RFC 2109.

In order to send a cookie to a client, a server creates a cookie header and attaches it to the HTTP response. The client receives the request and extracts the cookie response header. This cookie data is usually stored in a file on the client's system.

When the client makes another request, to help the client decide whether to send the cookie back to the server or not, there are two parameters: Domain and Path. The path is given relative to the domain. For instance, in the URL http://www.myserver.com/shop/top100, myserver.com is the domain, and /shop/top100 is the path. If the Path parameter is not specified, the cookie applies to any path under the specified domain. Whenever the client makes a request to any URL matching the specified path within this domain, the client sends the cookie along with the request as a header. Let's say the response from the server contains links to http://www.myserver.com, http://sales.myserver.com and http://support.myserver.com and the Path parameter has not been set. When the user clicks of any of these links, the browser sends the cookie back, since all these links are under the same myserver.com domain, and any path in this domain is appropriate.

Working with Cookies in Servlets

The Java Servlet API includes a class javax.servlet.http.Cookie that abstracts the notion of a cookie. The javax.servlet.http.HttpServletRequest and javax.servlet.http.HttpServletResponse interfaces provide methods to add cookies to HTTP responses and to retrieve cookies from HTTP requests.

The Cookie class abstracts a cookie. A Cookie instance has the following constructor, which instantiates a cookie instance with the given name and value:

```
public Cookie(String name, String value)
```

This class has many methods that make working with cookies easier. It has getter and setter methods for all of the cookie parameters, for example:

```
public String getName()
public void setName(String name)
```

You can use these methods to access or change the name of a cookie. There are similar methods to access or change other parameters (such as path, header, and so on) of a cookie.

In order to set cookies, the javax.servlet.http.HttpServletResponse interface has the following method:

```
public void addCookie(Cookie cookie)
```

We can call this method as many times as we wish in order to set multiple cookies. To extract all cookies contained in the HTTP request, the javax.servlet.HttpServletRequest interface has this method:

```
public Cookie[] getCookies()
```

Now we can rewrite our TokenServlet servlet (now called CookieServlet) to track the user using cookies instead of URL rewriting. In this case, the servlet performs the following actions:

- ❑ It checks if there is a cookie contained in the incoming request
- ❑ If there is none, it creates a cookie, and sends it along with the response
- ❑ If there is a cookie, it just displays the value of the cookie

Let's walk through the sourcecode for `CookieServlet`:

```
package sessions;

import ava.io.*;
import java.util.Random;
import javax.servlet.http.*;
import javax.servlet.http.*;
import javax.servlet.ServletException;

public class CookieServlet extends HttpServlet {

  protected void doGet(HttpServletRequest request, HttpServletResponse response)
                                      throws ServletException, IOException {
    Cookie[] cookies = request.getCookies();
    Cookie token = null;
```

The servlet first retrieves all of the cookies contained in the request object. Provided there are cookies present, the servlet then checks each cookie to see if the name of the cookie is "token":

```
    if(cookies != null) {
      for(int i = 0; i < cookies.length; i++) {
        if(cookies[i].getName().equals("token")) {
          token = cookies[i];
          break;
        }
      }
    }

    response.setContentType("text/html");
    PrintWriter writer = response.getWriter();
    writer.println("<html><head><title>Tokens</title></head><body ");
    writer.println("style=\"font-family:verdana;font-size:10pt\">");

    String reset = request.getParameter("reset");
```

If a cookie with name "token" is not found, the servlet creates a cookie called "token" and adds it to the response. The servlet creates a random number. The servlet then creates a cookie with the following parameters:

- ❑ Name: "token"
- ❑ Value: A random number (converted into a string)
- ❑ Comment: "Token to identify user"
- ❑ Max-Age: -1, indicating that the cookie should be discarded when the browser exits
- ❑ Path: "/cookie/track", so that the browser sends the cookie to only requests under http://localhost:8080/cookie/track.

Note that the following code snippet does not set `Domain`. As a matter of convention, it defaults to "localhost". If you are deploying this application on a remote machine (server) and accessing it from another machine (client), you need to set the domain name to be that of the server.

```
if(token == null || (reset != null && reset.equals("yes"))) {
  Random rand = new Random();
  long id = rand.nextLong();

  writer.println("<p>Welcome. A new token " +
                   id + " is now established</p>");

  token = new Cookie("token", Long.toString(id));
  token.setComment("Token to identify user");
  token.setMaxAge(-1);
  token.setPath("/cookie/track");
```

The servlet then adds the cookie to the Response object:

```
    response.addCookie(token);
  else {
```

In order to facilitate recreating the identity, the servlet also expects a request parameter "reset". If this parameter is sent with a value of "yes", the servlet recreates the cookie as above, so that the client gets a new token. Otherwise, the servlet does not set the cookie, and just prints a message as shown below:

```
    writer.println("Welcome back. Your token is " + token.getValue() + ".</p>");
  }

  String requestURLSame = request.getRequestURL().toString();
  String requestURLNew = request.getRequestURL() + "?reset=yes";

  writer.println("<p>Click <a href=" + requestURLSame +
                   ">here</a> again to continue browsing with the " +
                   "same identity.</p>");
  writer.println("<p>Otherwise, click <a href=" + requestURLNew +
                   ">here</a> again to start browsing with a new identity.</p>");
  writer.println("</body></html>");
  writer.close();
  }
}
```

Now create a new web application as you did for the URL rewriting example, and call it `cookie`. Compile the class above and place the class in the `cookie/WEB-INF/classes/sessions/` directory.

Create the following simple deployment descriptor for our web application:

```
<?xml version="1.0"?>

<!DOCTYPE web-app
    PUBLIC "-//Sun Microsystems, Inc.//DTD Web Application 2.3//EN"
    "http://java.sun.com/dtd/web-app_2_3.dtd">

<web-app>
  <servlet>
    <servlet-name>track</servlet-name>
    <servlet-class>CookieServlet</servlet-class>
  </servlet>
```

```
   <servlet-mapping>
     <servlet-name>track</servlet-name>
     <url-pattern>/track/*</url-pattern>
   </servlet-mapping>
 </web-app>
```

Deploy the web application, restart Tomcat, and navigate to http://localhost:8080/cookies/track. You'll see a page just like the one in the previous example:

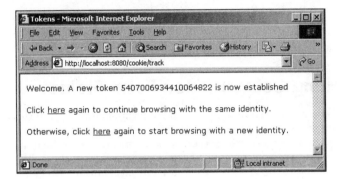

Click on the first link to get the following page:

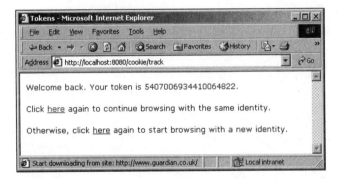

The token number is the same. The browser sent the cookie back to the server along with the request, and the server recognized it. Notice that the first link (in the second line) is the same as the one you entered in the address bar in the browser.

From the client perspective, there are two differences here from URL rewriting:

❑   The token was not included in the query string

❑   While displaying the page, the browser received a cookie from the server

If you instead click on the link on the third line, a fresh token will be created, and a new cookie will be set. In order for the server to recreate the token, you should note that there is an additional query parameter passed called "reset", with value "yes".

In order to better understand the role of the domain and path names, in the above example change the path to "/token" as shown below:

```
token.setPath("/token");
```

Recompile the servlet, and restart both Tomcat and the browser. This time, the browser does not send the cookie back when you click on the links. This is because, while the cookie is set for path "/token", the links are pointing to "/cookie". The servlet therefore cannot track the user.

Try changing the maximum age to 86400 seconds (1 day). With this setting, even if you restart the browser and Tomcat, the servlet still recognizes the cookie for one day. In this case, the browser stores the cookie locally on the disk.

Session Tracking Using Hidden Form Fields

The third alternative to session handling is via hidden form fields. HTML forms allow fields to be hidden, which means that such fields are not displayed when the form is rendered on the browser. While preparing a page with a form, the server can add one or more hidden fields within the form. When the client submits the form, the browser transfers the values in the hidden fields along with the other visible fields (if any) to the server. We can use this mechanism to track a user. The following HiddenFieldServlet illustrates this point:

```
package sessions;

import java.io.*;
import java.util.Random;
import javax.servlet.http.*;
import javax.servlet.ServletException;

public class HiddenFieldServlet extends HttpServlet {

    protected void doGet(HttpServletRequest request, HttpServletResponse response)
                                        throws ServletException, IOException {
```

First we get the token from the request:

```
String token = request.getParameter("token");
```

Then we prepare the response:

```
response.setContentType("text/html");
PrintWriter writer = response.getWriter();
writer.println("<html><head><title>Tokens</title></head><body ");
writer.println("style=\"font-family:verdana;font-size:10pt\">");
```

If the client did not sent any token we create a new one:

```
if(token == null) {
  Random rand = new Random();
  token = Long.toString(rand.nextLong());
  writer.println("<p>Welcome. A new token " +
                  token + " is now established</p>");
} else {
```

If the client sent a token we acknowledge the client:

```
  writer.println("<p>Welcome back. Your token is " + token + ".</p>");
}
```

Then we prepare a URL for the client to send requests back:

```
String requestURL = request.getRequestURL().toString();
```

We finish by writing two forms. First we write a form with the token as a hidden field:

```
writer.println("<p>");
writer.println("<form method='GET' action='" + requestURL + "'>");
writer.println("<input type='hidden' name='token' value='" + token + "'/>");
writer.println("<input type='submit' value='Click Here'/>");
writer.println("</form>");
writer.println(" to continue browsing with the same identity.</p>");
```

Then we write another form without the hidden field:

```
writer.println("<form method='GET' action='" + requestURL + "'>");
writer.println("<input type='submit' value='Click Here'/>");
writer.println("</form>");
writer.println(" to start browsing with a new identity.</p>");
writer.close();
  }
}
```

In this servlet, instead of using the usual <href> tags, we used buttons (within forms) for the user to respond to. In the first form, the only parameter is a hidden field, while the second form has no parameters at all.

Again, to run the example, you need to create a new web application as you did for the other examples, and call this one hidden. Compile the above class and place the class file in the hidden/WEB-INF/classes/sessions/ directory.

Then create the following simple deployment descriptor for the web application:

```
<?xml version="1.0"?>

<!DOCTYPE web-app PUBLIC "-//Sun Microsystems, Inc.//DTD Web Application 2.3//EN"
                        "http://java.sun.com/dtd/web-app_2_3.dtd">

<web-app>
  <servlet>
    <servlet-name>track</servlet-name>
    <servlet-class>sessions.HiddenFieldServlet</servlet-class>
  </servlet>

  <servlet-mapping>
    <servlet-name>track</servlet-name>
    <url-pattern>/track/*</url-pattern>
  </servlet-mapping>
</web-app>
```

Deploy the web application, restart Tomcat, and go to http://localhost:8080/hidden/track. You should see the following:

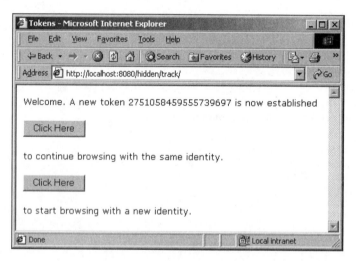

Instead of hyperlinks, the response contains two buttons. This is because the forms we created above do not have any visible fields.

Click on the first button to see a page similar to the following:

If you now click on the second button, a new token is allocated.

As you can see from our example, a significant disadvantage to this form of maintaining session is obviously that we need to create forms, which is not particularly convenient when your content has hyper links and not forms.

Session Management Using the Servlet API

In the previous section we discussed three examples, each of which demonstrates how to track user sessions programmatically, using URL rewriting, cookies, and hidden form fields respectively. Each of these techniques required some unique string to be exchanged between the client and the server, so that the server could recognize the client. However, as we can infer from these examples, there are complications with all three approaches:

❑ Creating a unique ID programmatically is not reliable, particularly in a multi-threaded environment. For instance, what prevents two users from getting the same random number? This issue gets more complicated when you consider clustered environments where the ID is required to be unique across several JVMs (we'll discuss clustering later in this chapter). We need a more robust and reliable approach for this.

❑ Programmatically retrieving an ID (either from the request parameters, or from cookies) is an additional task that each of your servlets must implement, which lowers the maintainability of the code and makes it more prone to errors.

❑ This approach requires additional coding if we need to manage state with each session.

As far as servlet programming is concerned, these additional tasks make servlet programming more complex. The Java Servlet API, however, has provisions that eliminate the need to implement these tasks. In this section, we will look at the session handling interfaces of the Java Servlet API.

The Servlet API provides the following facilities for managing sessions:

- ❑ Management of session lifecycle, including session creation and termination
- ❑ Management of session state

The Java Servlet API includes the following interfaces and classes for session management in the `javax.servlet.http` package:

Interface	Description
HttpSession	Provides an abstraction of a session
HttpSessionListener	Handles events associated with session creation and termination (lifecycle events)
HttpSessionBindingListener	Handles events associated with binding and unbinding state for sessions
HttpSessionActivationListener	Handles events associated with session activation and passivation (these processes will be explained later)
HttpSessionEvent	Encapsulates lifecycle-specific session events
HttpSessionBindingEvent	Encapsulates session binding/unbinding events

Let's begin our discussion of these interfaces by taking a closer look at the `HttpSession` interface.

The HttpSession Interface

The `HttpSession` interface provides core session-management functionality. This interface abstracts a session. The container creates a session when a client first visits a server. Conceptually an `HttpSession` object is an object that lives for the duration of a client session, and is associated with the request objects.

J2EE web containers use three mechanisms to establish sessions:

- ❑ **Cookies**
  By default, most containers rely on cookies to establish sessions.

- ❑ **URL rewriting**
  Web containers support URL rewriting to accommodate clients that do not accept or support cookies. However, in order for web applications to work correctly with URL rewriting, we need to take an extra coding step by calling the `encodeURL()` method with each URL, and using the return value in the content (instead of the original URL).

- ❑ **SSL based sessions**
  The Secure Socket Layer (SSL) protocol is used for secure HTTP (HTTPS).

This interface also acts as a placeholder for storing data associated with the current session. Using this functionality, you can place client-specific objects in the session. This interface provides `java.util.Map`-like functionality to put and get objects. The `java.util.Map` interface can store objects, with each object linked to a name (which itself can be another object). You can put an object into the map with a name, and retrieve the object using the same name. The `HttpSession` interface provides similar methods to manage state for each session. In this interface, each object (called an attribute) you add to the session should have a unique name (as a string). Servlets used during the course of a session may share these objects.

Let's now look at the methods provided by this interface. The first question is, how do we get an instance of this interface? The `HttpServletRequest` interface has the following methods to get instances of `HttpSession`:

```
public HttpSession getSession()
```

This method returns the session already associated with this request. However, if there is no session currently associated with the request, supplying `true` to the following variant creates a new Session object and returns it:

```
public HttpSession getSession(boolean create)
```

If the argument is `false`, and there is no session currently associated with this request, this method returns `null`.

The following method returns a named attribute from the session:

```
public Object getAttribute(String name)
```

The `getAttributeNames()` method returns an `Enumeration` of the names of all attributes placed into a session:

```
public java.util.Enumeration getAttributeNames()
```

The web container creates a session when a client first accesses the container. The `getCreationTime()` method returns the time (in milliseconds since midnight January 1, 1970 GMT) at which the session was created. As we shall see later, you can also recreate sessions programmatically:

```
public long getCreationTime()
```

The `getId()` method returns a unique identifier assigned to this session. This unique identifier is similar to the token we created in previous examples. Web containers use elaborate algorithms to create such identifiers so that the identifiers are unique even under concurrent requests:

```
public String getId()
```

The getLastAccessedTime() method returns the time the client last sent a request associated with this session. The time is expressed as milliseconds since midnight January 1, 1970 GMT:

```
public long getLastAccessedTime()
```

The following method returns the time the client last sent a request associated with this session. Again, the time is expressed as milliseconds since midnight January 1, 1970 GMT:

```
public int getMaxInactiveInterval()
```

The getServletContext() method, unsurprisingly, returns the ServletContext associated with the application that this session belongs to:

```
public ServletContext getServletContext()
```

The invalidate() method invalidates this session and removes any attributes bound to it:

```
public void invalidate()
```

The isNew() method returns true if the client does not yet know about this session or if the client chooses not to join the session:

```
public boolean isNew()
```

The removeAttribute() method removes the named attribute from the session:

```
public void removeAttribute(String name)
```

The following method adds the named attribute to the session. If the named attribute already exists in the session, the method replaces the old attribute value with the new value:

```
public void setAttribute(String name, Object value)
```

This method sets the maximum allowed time (in seconds) between two consecutive client requests to participate in a session. After expiry of this interval, the container invalidates the session. If a client request arrives after this interval, the request results in a new session:

```
public void setMaxInactiveInterval (int interval)
```

Let's now study the programming aspects of the session management API via a comprehensive example.

Implementing Session Management

The purpose of this example is to build a web application that allows users to create notes and store them on the server. Each note has a title and associated text, both stored in a database. This example will allow the user to:

❑ View the list of notes previously created (using the user's e-mail address to retrieve the list of notes)

❑ Create new notes

❑ Edit existing notes

❑ Change identity and create notes as a different user (identified by another e-mail address)

The following figure shows the flow of events and how we plan to implement the above functionality:

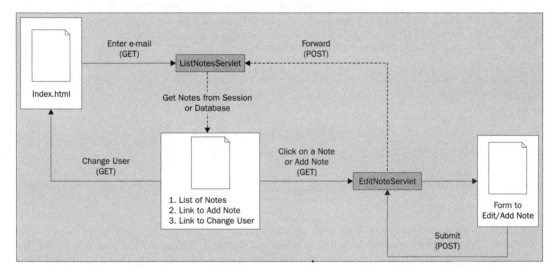

In this figure, the normal arrows indicate the actions by the user, and the dotted arrows indicate the container responses. There are three components in this application:

❑ `index.html`: This is a welcome page that collects the user's e-mail address.

❑ `ListNotesServlet`: This servlet is responsible for obtaining the list of e-mails from the session. If the session is new, this servlet gets the list of e-mails from the database. This servlet then displays a page containing the list of notes (if any, with hyperlinks), a link to add a note, and another link to change the user. The arrows from this servlet show the possible user actions.

❑ `EditNoteServlet`: This servlet performs two tasks. If the user clicks to edit a note, this servlet retrieves the note from the database and displays it in a form. If the user clicks to add a new note instead, this servlet displays an empty form. When the user submits this form, this servlet stores the note in the database, updates the list of notes in the session, and then forwards the request to the `ListNotesServlet`. The `ListNotesServlet` then displays the list of notes.

Therefore, this example relies on the session management API for the following tasks:

❑ To track a user entering notes

❑ To manage a list of notes

❑ To invalidate current sessions and create new sessions

We'll start by creating the database schema.

Database Schema

We will use the MySQL RDBMS for managing the notes persistently. This RDBMS is available to download for free from http://www.mysql.com. To use this with your web apps, you will also need to download the JDBC driver mm.mysql-2.0.8-bin.jar. The database schema is simple – each note is associated with a note_id and an email address. The actual note data consists of a note_title, note, and the last_modified time.

Use the following SQL to create the database schema:

```
CREATE DATABASE notepad;
USE notepad;

CREATE TABLE NOTES (
  note_id INT AUTO_INCREMENT PRIMARY KEY,
  email CHAR(50) NOT NULL,
  note_title CHAR(80) NOT NULL,
  note LONG VARCHAR,
  last_modified TIMESTAMP NOT NULL
);
```

This SQL creates a table called NOTES with the note_id as the primary key. We specify this column as an AUTO_INCREMENT key such that each insert will automatically increment the number. In the above SQL script, we also create two indexes on the email and note_id columns. These are the columns we use to query for NOTES' data.

You should note that this schema is not exhaustive enough for use in a general production environment. At the end of this example, we will consider possible enhancements that could make this example more robust and usable.

Welcome Page

Let us now create the welcome page (`index.html`) for the notepad web application:

```html
<html>
  <head>
    <title>NotePad</title>
    <link rel="stylesheet" type="text/css" href="style/global.css" />
  </head>
  <body>
    <h3>NotePad</h3>
    <form action="/notepad/list" method="GET">
     <p>
       Enter your email address:
       <input type="text" name="email" />
     </p>
     <p>
       <input type="submit" name="submit" value="Enter NotePad">
     </p>
    </form>
  </body>
</html>
```

This HTML displays a form for entering the e-mail address of the user. When the user enters the e-mail address, the form sends a GET request to the /notepad/list servlet.

NotePadServlet

This servlet is abstract, and does not directly handle HTTP requests. The purpose of this servlet is to provide the functionality to obtain database connections. You should note that in a production environment, we would probably want to connect to our database through JNDI, but to keep things simple, for this example we will connect to the database directly:

```java
import java.sql.*;
import javax.servlet.http.HttpServlet;

public abstract class NotePadServlet extends HttpServlet {
```

The getConnection() method returns a database connection:

```java
    protected Connection getConnection() throws NamingException, SQLException {
      Connection connection = null;
      try {
        Class.forName("org.gjt.mm.mysql.Driver").newInstance();
        connection = DriverManager.getConnection("jdbc:mysql://localhost/notepad");
      } catch(ClassNotFoundException cnfe) {
        throw new SQLException("Unable to load the driver: " + cnfe.getMessage());
      }
      return connection;
    }
}
```

ListNotesServlet

Let us now create the servlet to retrieve the notes and display them. This servlet extends from `NotePadServlet`:

```
package sessions;

import java.util.*;
import java.io.*;
import java.sql.*;
import javax.naming.NamingException;
import javax.servlet.ServletException;
import javax.servlet.http.*;

public class ListNotesServlet extends NotePadServlet {
   protected void doGet(HttpServletRequest request, HttpServletResponse response)
                                           throws ServletException, IOException {
```

This servlet retrieves the parameter `email` from the incoming request, and uses it to get a list of notes for that user. Note that the form in the welcome page contains an e-mail text field:

```
String email = request.getParameter("email");
```

The servlet then gets the current user session by calling the `getSession()` method on the Request object. When the user visits this notepad application for the first time, the container automatically creates a new session for the user. The `getSession()` method returns the same session to the servlet. When called for the first time, the session will be empty; it does not contain any attributes since we've not yet added any:

```
HttpSession session = request.getSession();
```

This servlet then checks to see if there is an attribute called `email` in the session. As you will see shortly, this web application offers functionality to change the identity of the user. Say the user revisits the `index.html` page and enters a new e-mail address to see notes stored under a different e-mail. In this case, the session would contain the old `email` attribute. The following code checks for this, and if the `email` is different from that retrieved from the request, it invalidates the current session, and obtains a new session. This step also ensures that a user with a given e-mail address cannot view the notes of another user with a different e-mail address. As we shall discuss later, we could also implement more robust security measures for this servlet:

```
String currentEmail = (String) session.getAttribute("email");
if(currentEmail != null) {
  if(!currentEmail.equals(email)) {
    session.invalidate();
    session = request.getSession();
  }
}
```

The servlet then puts the e-mail address in the session and checks if the list of notes is already available in the session. In this example, the list of notes is stored in a `java.util.Map` object. This object contains the `note_id` as the key, and the `note_title` as the value. The actual note text is retrieved from the database only on demand. This step ensures that we store only the essential information in the `HttpSession` object, for performance reasons. As we store more information in the session, the underlying JVM will have to allocate more and more memory, and as the number of concurrent users increases, it may limit the available memory for any processing. It is always a good practice to limit the number and size of attributes in the session. We should also remember to remove an attribute from the session if it is no longer required for this session:

```
session.setAttribute("email", email);
Map noteList = (Map) session.getAttribute("noteList");
Connection connection = null;
PreparedStatement statement = null;
if(noteList == null) {
```

When the user invokes this servlet for the first time, the `noteList` will be empty. The servlet then proceeds to retrieve the notes (only `note_id` and `note_title`) from the database, and fill this map, as shown below:

```
try {
  String sql =
    "SELECT note_id, note_title FROM NOTES WHERE email = ?";
  connection = getConnection();
  statement = connection.prepareStatement(sql);
  statement.setString(1, email);
  ResultSet rs = statement.executeQuery();
  noteList = new HashMap();

  while(rs.next()) {
    noteList.put(new Integer(rs.getInt(1)), rs.getString(2));
  }
} catch(SQLException sqle) {
  throw new ServletException("SQL Exception", sqle);
} finally {
  try {
    if(statement != null) {
      statement.close();
    }
  } catch(SQLException ignore) {}
  try {
    if(connection != null) {
      connection.close();
    }
  } catch(SQLException ignore) {}
}
```

This code snippet obtains a connection and executes a SQL SELECT statement using the `email`. It then initializes the `noteList` map and adds each `note_title` found into the `noteList` map using the `note_id` (converted to an `Integer` object) as the key. It then adds the `noteList` to the session under the name `noteList` as shown overleaf:

```
                session.setAttribute("noteList", noteList);
        }
```

The rest of the doGet() method prepares a response. The response includes the list of note titles. Each note is associated with a hyperlink to edit the note. The response also includes a link to add a new note, and another link to change the user. The former link takes the user to the EditNoteServlet, while the latter link takes the user back to the welcome page:

```
        response.setContentType("text/html");
        PrintWriter writer = response.getWriter();
        writer.println("<html><head>");
        writer.println("<title>NotePad</title>");
        writer.println(
          "<link rel=\"stylesheet\" type=\"text/css\" href=\"style/global.css\" />");
        writer.println("</head><body>");
        writer.println("<h3>Notes</h3>");
        if(noteList.size() == 0) {
          writer.println("<p>You do not have any notes.</p>");
        } else {
          writer.println("<p>Click on the note to edit.</p><ul>");
          Iterator iterator = noteList.keySet().iterator();
          while(iterator.hasNext()) {
            Integer noteId = (Integer) iterator.next();
            String noteTitle = (String) noteList.get(noteId);
            writer.println("<li><a href='/notepad/edit?noteId=" +
            noteId.toString() + "'>" + noteTitle + "</a></li>");
          }
          writer.println("</ul>");
        }
        writer.println("<p><a href='/notepad/edit'>Add a New Note</a></p>");
        writer.println("<p><a href='/notepad/'>Change User</a></p>");
        writer.println("</body></html>");
        writer.close();
    }
```

Finally, this servlet also implements a doPost() method. As we shall see later, this method is required for the EditNoteServlet to forward to this servlet after saving a note in the database:

```
    protected void doPost(HttpServletRequest request, HttpServletResponse response)
      throws ServletException, IOException {
      doGet(request, response);
    }
}
```

EditNoteServlet

This servlet has two parts – a doGet() method to display a form with the note title and note text (empty for new notes), and a doPost() method to store/update the note in the database. The servlet also extends from the NotePadServlet. This servlet is rather long, as it implements two core features. First, given the note_id, it retrieves a note from the database and displays it in a form, and second it stores the note into the database. Let us now study the implementation more closely:

```
package sessions;

import java.util.Map;
import java.io.*;
import java.sql.*;
import javax.naming.NamingException;
import javax.servlet.*;
import javax.servlet.http.*;


public class EditNoteServlet extends NotePadServlet {
```

The doGet() method of this servlet is responsible for retrieving a note from the database. The same method is also used to display an empty form to enter a new note:

```
protected void doGet(HttpServletRequest request, HttpServletResponse response)
   throws ServletException, IOException {
```

This method first checks whether there is a noteId in the request. If you examine the ListNotesServlet, the link to add a new note does not include a noteId in the URL, but the links to existing notes include the noteId as a query parameter. This parameter helps the EditNoteServlet to determine if the request is for a new note or for an existing note:

```
String noteId = (String) request.getParameter("noteId");
String note = "";
String title = "";
boolean isEdit = false;
Connection connection = null;
PreparedStatement statement = null;

if(noteId != null) {
  try {
```

If there is no noteId in the request, the servlet generates an HTML form. Otherwise, this servlet retrieves the note from the database:

```
String sql = "SELECT note_title, note FROM NOTES WHERE note_id = ?";
connection = getConnection();
statement = connection.prepareStatement(sql);
statement.setInt(1, Integer.parseInt(noteId));
ResultSet rs = statement.executeQuery();
rs.next();
title = rs.getString(1);
note = rs.getString(2);
isEdit = true;
} catch(SQLException sqle) {
throw new ServletException("SQL Exception", sqle);
} finally {
try {
  if(statement != null) {
    statement.close();
  }
```

```
    } catch(SQLException ignore) {}
    try {
      if(connection != null) {
        connection.close();
      }
    } catch(SQLException ignore) {}
  }
}
```

The above code retrieves the note title and the note text using the note_id. It then stores the results in the local variables title and note respectively.

The following code generates the form containing the note. In the case of a new note, the variables title and note will be empty:

```
response.setContentType("text/html");
PrintWriter writer = response.getWriter();
writer.println("<html><head>");
writer.println("<title>NotePad</title>");
writer.println(
  "<link rel=\"stylesheet\" type=\"text/css\" href=\"style/global.css\" />");
writer.println("</head><body>");
writer.println("<h3>Notes</h3>");
writer.println("<h1>Add/Edit a Note</h1>");
if(isEdit) {
  writer.println("<form action='/notepad/edit?noteId=" + noteId +
                 "' method='POST'>");
} else {
  writer.println("<form action='/notepad/edit' method='POST'>");
}
writer.println("<p>Title: <input type='text' name='title' size='40' value='" +
               title + "'></p>");
writer.println("<p><textarea name='note' cols='50' rows='15'>");
writer.println(note);
writer.println("</textarea></p>");
writer.println("<p><input type='Submit' name='submit'
               value='Save Note'></p>");
writer.println("</form></body></html>");
writer.close();
}

protected void doPost(HttpServletRequest request, HttpServletResponse response)
  throws ServletException, IOException {
```

The form makes a POST request for saving the note. When the user enters the note and clicks on the **Save** button, the doPost() method of this servlet gets invoked. The responsibility of the doPost() method is to store the note into the database. Before saving the note, this method retrieves all the necessary information from the Request and Session objects:

```
String noteId = (String) request.getParameter("noteId");
HttpSession session = request.getSession();
String email = (String) session.getAttribute("email");
Map noteList = (Map) session.getAttribute("noteList");
String title = request.getParameter("title");
String note = request.getParameter("note");
Connection connection = null;
PreparedStatement statement = null;
try {
```

This servlet uses the `noteId` parameter in the request to determine if this is a new note or an existing note. If the note is new, it inserts the note in the database:

```
if(noteId == null) {
    String sql = "INSERT INTO NOTES (email, note_title, note, last_modified)"
                 + "VALUES(?, ?, ?, ?)";
    connection = getConnection();
    statement = connection.prepareStatement(sql);
    statement.setString(1, email);
    statement.setString(2, title);
    statement.setString(3, note);
    statement.setTimestamp(4, new Timestamp(System.currentTimeMillis()));
    statement.executeUpdate();

    // Retrieve the automatically inserted NOTE_ID
    sql = "SELECT LAST_INSERT_ID()";
    statement = connection.prepareStatement(sql);
    ResultSet rs = statement.executeQuery(sql);
    int id = 0;
    while(rs.next ()) {
       id = rs.getInt(1);
    }
    noteList.put(new Integer(id), title);
} else {
```

The `note_id` is retrieved from the database after executing the `INSERT` statement. The `note_id` column is a column automatically incremented by the database whenever a new note is inserted. We therefore must retrieve the inserted value from the database.

If the note already exists, the `doPost()` method simply updates it:

```
String sql = "UPDATE NOTES SET note_title = ?, note = ?, " +
             "last_modified = ? WHERE note_id = ?";
connection = getConnection();
statement = connection.prepareStatement(sql);
statement.setString(1, title);
statement.setString(2, note);
statement.setTimestamp(3, new Timestamp(System.currentTimeMillis()));
statement.setInt(4, Integer.parseInt(noteId));
statement.executeUpdate();
```

```
      noteList.put(new Integer(noteId), title);
    }
  } catch(SQLException sqle) {
    throw new ServletException("SQL Exception", sqle);
  } finally {
    try {
      if(statement != null) {
        statement.close();
      }
    } catch(SQLException ignore) {}
    try {
      if(connection != null) {
        connection.close();
      }
    } catch(SQLException ignore) {}
  }
```

Whether we created or updated a note, this method puts the note_id and note_title in the noteList map, so that the ListNotesServlet can display the updated list of notes. After inserting/updating the note, the servlet forwards the request to the ListNotesServlet to display the updated list of notes:

```
    RequestDispatcher rd = request.getRequestDispatcher("/list?email=" + email);
    rd.forward(request, response);
  }
}
```

Since the call to the forward() method is performed via the doPost() method, the ListNotesServlet should implement the doPost() method. This is why we implemented the doPost() method in the ListNotesServlet.

This completes the coding required for this web application. The next tasks are to write a deployment descriptor, and configure Tomcat to deploy the servlets.

Deployment Descriptor

Here's the deployment descriptor for our notepad application:

```
<?xml version="1.0"?>

<!DOCTYPE web-app
    PUBLIC "-//Sun Microsystems, Inc.//DTD Web Application 2.3//EN"
    "http://java.sun.com/dtd/web-app_2_3.dtd">

<web-app>

  <servlet>
    <servlet-name>listNotes</servlet-name>
    <servlet-class>ListNotesServlet</servlet-class>
  </servlet>
```

```
<servlet>
  <servlet-name>editNote</servlet-name>
  <servlet-class>EditNoteServlet</servlet-class>
</servlet>

<servlet-mapping>
  <servlet-name>listNotes</servlet-name>
  <url-pattern>/list/*</url-pattern>
</servlet-mapping>

<servlet-mapping>
  <servlet-name>editNote</servlet-name>
  <url-pattern>/edit/*</url-pattern>
</servlet-mapping>

</web-app>
```

Compiling and Running the Example

The final step is to compile and run the example. You should create a web application called `notepad`, with following structure:

```
notepad/
        WEB-INF/
                classes/
                        sessions
                src/
                    sessions
                lib/
```

Place the welcome page in the top level of the web application, and class source files in the `src/sessions` directory. Add the `web.xml` file into the top level of the `WEB-INF` directory as usual. Next, place the `mm.mysql-2.0.8-bin.jar` file in the `lib` directory. Then compile the classes and move the class files into the `classes/sessions` directory.

Restart Tomcat, and navigate to http://localhost:8080/notepad. If you do this, you should see the welcome page:

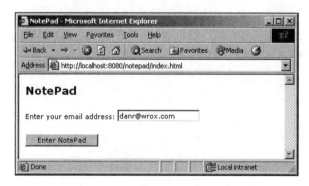

Enter an e-mail address and press the **Enter NotePad** button. This invokes the `ListNotesServlet`, retrieves notes (if any), and displays the following page:

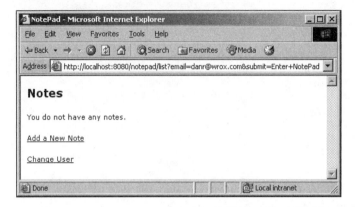

Since this is the first time the user entered this web application, there are no notes for this user, and hence the page contains only links to add a new note and to change user. Click on the **Add a New Note** link. This causes the `EditNoteServlet` to display a blank form so that we can enter a new note:

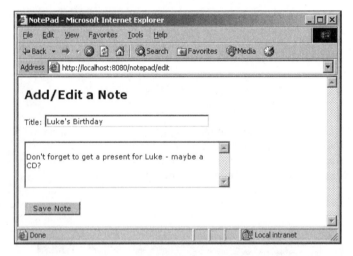

Enter any note with a title and some text, and press the **Save Note** button. This invokes the `doPost()` method of the `EditNoteServlet`, which stores the note in the database and updates the `noteList` with the new `noteId` and note `title`. This servlet then forwards the user to the `ListNotesServlet` that displays the updated note list:

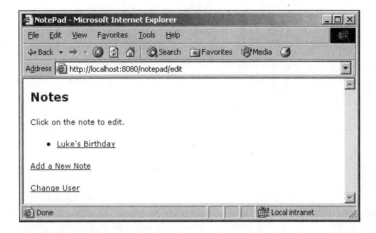

You can continue to add more notes. You may instead change your mind, and enter this application with a new e-mail address. Click on the Change User link to do so, which will then invalidate your current session, obtain a new session, and then display the index.html page to allow you enter a new e-mail address.

NotePad with URL Rewriting

To test if the above NotePad functions without cookies, let's disable cookies in our browser. Check the browser help to get directions to disable all cookies, and restart the browser. As you try entering the web site and continuing to edit a previously created note, you will encounter a NullPointerException displayed in the browser.

What causes this exception? If you look at the source of EditNoteServlet, you will find that the exception was caused due to the variable nodeList being null. The servlet obtains this variable from the session. However, since the browser does not now accept or return cookies, the web container is unable to create and maintain a session. In this case, every time a servlet calls the getSession() method on the Request object, the container returns a new HttpSession object. In our case, the ListNotesServlet creates the list of notes and puts it in the session. However, since the EditNoteServlet is getting a new Session object, there is no way for the EditNoteServlet to retrieve the list of notes.

The Java Servlet API supports URL rewriting to deal with such cases. To enable this, we need to change the two servlets as highlighted below. First, here are the changes we need to make to ListNotesServlet:

```
    ...
    } else {
      writer.println("<p>Click on the note to edit.</p><ul>");
      Iterator iterator = noteList.keySet().iterator();
      while(iterator.hasNext()) {
        Integer noteId = (Integer) iterator.next();
        String noteTitle = (String) noteList.get(noteId);
        // Rewrite the URL to the note
        String url = response.encodeURL("/notepad/edit?noteId=" +
                                 noteId.toString());
        writer.println("<li><a href='" + url + "'>" +
                   noteTitle + "</a></li>");
    }
```

```
                writer.println("</ul>");
            }
            // Also rewrite the URL for adding a new note
            String url = response.encodeURL("/notepad/edit");
            writer.println("<p><a href='" + url + "'>Add a New Note</a></p>");
            writer.println("<p><a href='/notepad/'>Change User</a></p>");
            writer.println("</body></html>");
            writer.close();
        }
        ...
    }
```

As you can see, there are two changes. In each of these changes we call the encodeURL() method on the request to "encode" the URL that is being generated. The purpose of this call is to rewrite the URL to include an ID corresponding to the session. Recall from the first example in this chapter that we programmatically rewrote URLs to include randomly generated IDs. The encodeURL() method does a similar task by including a unique ID associated with the current session in the link.

In the original servlet, the URLs it generated were of the form /notepad/edit?noteId=x where x is the note_id. After our modifications, the call to the encodeURL() method appends a token similar to the one we discussed in the first example in this chapter. This method returns a string similar to:

```
/notepad/edit;jsessionid=C61461E2A200C573A102317140948083?noteId=x
```

Note the extra parameter in this URL. The jsessionid is the token the web container uses instead of cookies. The long string following the jsessionid is a session identifier. Note that jsessionid is not an ordinary query parameter; query parameters follow the URL with a question mark, while the jsessionid is separated by a colon. This way, the container ensures that the session identifier is not confused with the query parameters.

Now make similar changes to the EditNoteServlet:

```
    ...
        response.setContentType("text/html");
        PrintWriter writer = response.getWriter();
        writer.println("<html><body>");
        writer.println("<h1>Add/Edit a Note</h1>");
        if(isEdit) {
            // Encode the URL to edit the note
            String url = response.encodeURL("/notepad/edit?noteId=" + noteId);
            writer.println("<form action='" + url + "' method='POST'>");
        } else {
            // Encode the URL to add the note
            String url = response.encodeURL("/notepad/edit");
            writer.println("<form action='" + url + "' method='POST'>");
        }
        writer.println("<p>Title: <input type='text' name='title' size='40' value='" +
                    title + "'></p>");
        writer.println("<p><textarea name='note' cols='50' rows='15'>");
        writer.println(note);
        writer.println("</textarea></p>");
        writer.println(
                    "<p><input type='Submit' name='submit' value='Save Note'></p>");
        writer.println("</form></body></html>");
        writer.close();
    }
```

```
      protected void doPost(HttpServletRequest request,
                            HttpServletResponse response)
                     throws ServletException, IOException {
...
    RequestDispatcher rd =
      request.getRequestDispatcher(response.encodeURL("/list?email=" + email));
    rd.forward(request, response);
  }
}
```

When you have made these changes, recompile your servlets, restart Tomcat, and test the application again. This time, you will find that the application functions properly, as it did when cookies were enabled.

It is always a good practice to encode all dynamically generated URLs as shown in the above servlets. Although most browsers support cookies, and most users don't disable cookies in their browsers, there are Internet-enabled devices (certain cell phones and hand-held devices) that do not recognize cookies.

As we discussed above, URL rewriting does not completely solve the problem of session handling in the absence of cookies, since you cannot encode URLs in static web pages. As you build web-enabled applications, you should always be sure to consider the impact of a lack of cookie support, and try to design the application appropriately.

Listening for Session Lifecycle Events

As the container creates sessions, and as you add, remove, or change attributes in sessions, the web container instantiates event objects so that web applications can be notified of these events. In this section, we will look at how we can make applications receive notifications upon changes to Session objects.

Except for the `HttpSessionBindingEvent`, all other events that we discuss in this section are new in version 2.3 of the Servlet specification. The following figure shows the session lifecycle with its associated event objects:

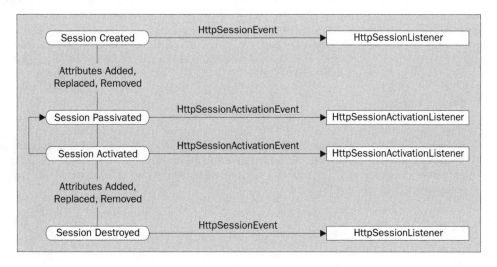

This figure shows the lifecycle of a session from creation to destruction. In-between, servlets may add, remove or replace attributes within the session. During its lifecycle a session may be passivated and activated zero or more times. In this figure, the rectangles on the right are the listeners that handle various events. In addition to the events shown above, as attributes are added/replaced/removed the container fires attribute-related events as shown below:

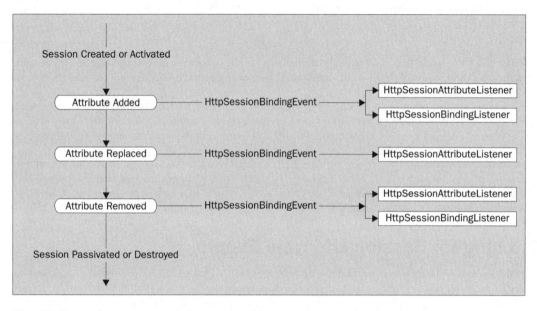

We will discuss these events and the associated listeners in more detail in this section.

Listening for Session Creation and Termination

As we discussed in the previous section, the container creates a session when the user accesses the server for the first time. The session is subsequently accessible to servlets in the application. But how long should the container keep the Session object alive? This question is important since no user is likely to use the application indefinitely. In order to conserve system resources, we need to instruct the container to terminate a session after some meaningful interval. You should consider the following while building and deploying a web application:

❑ **Session Lifetime**
Based on the nature of the application, you should identify a suitable lifetime for a session. You can specify this interval in the deployment descriptor of the web application. For instance, the following entry to the deployment descriptor of the notepad application sets the session lifetime for all users to 60 minutes. Add this element after `<servlet-mapping>` elements and before the `<resource-ref>` element. At the end of 60 minutes, the container automatically terminates the session.

```
<session-config>
  <session-timeout>60</session-timeout>
</session-config>
```

❏ **Session Inactivity**
In addition to the above, you can also instruct the container to terminate a session based on how long the session has been inactive. For instance, the user might leave the browser after using the notepad application for 30 minutes. You may want the container to wait for 15 more minutes before allowing the container to terminate the session. In order to do so, you should call the `setMaxInactiveInterval()` method on the Session object. To call this method, you should specify the interval in seconds.

The Java Servlet API includes an interface `javax.servlet.http.HttpSessionListener` that is notified when a session is created or destroyed. Let's take a closer look at it.

The HttpSessionListener Interface

This interface specifies methods to deal with session creation and session destruction.

```
public void sessionCreated(HttpSessionEvent event)
```

The container invokes the above method when a session is created. The event is specified via the `javax.servlet.http.HttpSessionEvent` class. As we shall see below, this class encapsulates the Session object.

```
public void sessionDestroyed(HttpSessionEvent event)
```

The container invokes the `sessionDestroyed()` method when a session is destroyed.

Let us now look at the `HttpSessionEvent` class. The `HttpSessionEvent` class has only one method:

```
public HttpSession getSession()
```

This method returns the Session object associated with this event.

You can implement the `HttpSessionListener` interface, and deploy your implementation, via the web application deployment descriptor:

```
<listener>
  <listener-class>YourListenerClassHere</listener-class>
</listener>
```

This element should be added before the `<servlet>` elements. When you specify a class implementing the `HttpSessionListener` interface, the container invokes the `sessionCreated()` method whenever a new session is created. The container similarly calls the `sessionDestroyed()` method whenever a session is destroyed.

What useful logic can you add into the implementation of these methods? Well, when the `sessionCreated()` method is called, your class gets access to the Session object via the `HttpSessionEvent` object passed. Since this session is newly created, it will not yet have any attributes. This precludes you from implementing any logic that relies on the state of a session. The same applies to the `sessionDestroyed()` event. This event is called after all the attributes have been removed from the session. Depending on your application, you may, however, implement any application logic that does not rely on any session data.

Note that you can specify more than one listener class by adding more `<listener>` elements to the deployment descriptor.

Listening for Session Activation and Passivation

Apart from creation and destruction, a container may generate events when two other events occur – passivation and activation. Let's see what these events are and how they may occur.

There are two ways a container may trigger these events. In a realistic production environment, you may have one or more web applications deployed on a container with several hundred (or more) users accessing the container. Of all the users, however, only a few may be actively sending requests, while the other users are temporarily not accessing the system and there is still time left before terminating such sessions. In such cases, in order to conserve memory, the container may decide to copy all of the Session objects to a persistent storage area (such as a database or a file system) and remove the sessions from memory. This is not the same as terminating the sessions. The sessions are valid, but are not there in memory. This process is called **passivation**.

The container may load the session data when the user sends a request again (before the session timeout interval and before the session inactive interval) from the persistent area. This process is called **activation**. The process of activation and passivation are not deployment-time controlled – these events happen based on container implementation and the active load on the server.

There is another way that the container uses session passivation and activation. As we will discuss shortly, you can configure a set of web containers as a cluster, with all of the container instances sharing the load between them. In this case, from time to time, the container may decide to shift the load of one session to another container instance. For this purpose, the container passivates the session on one container instance, sends the contents over the network to the other container instance, and activates the session there.

Both activation and passivation require that the attributes held in the session are serializable, otherwise the container can't passivate the session. Since your application may add non-serializable attributes (such as objects related to network/file I/O) into a session, the Java Servlet API specifies an event listener that can be notified during activation and passivation. During these events, the event listener may close the network/file resources before passivation, and may recreate the same resources during activation. The javax.servlet.http.HttpSessionActivationListener interface serves this purpose.

The HttpSessionActivationListener Interface

The HttpSessionActivationListener interface specifies methods to deal with session passivation and session activation:

```
public void sessionDidActivate(HttpSessionEvent event)
```

The container invokes the sessionDidActivate() method when a session is activated. The event is specified via the HttpSessionEvent class:

```
public void sessionWillPassivate(HttpSessionEvent event)
```

The container invokes the method above before passivating a session. You can implement this interface and deploy the implementation via the <listener> element in the deployment descriptor, as mentioned previously.

Listening for Attribute-Specific Events

The Java Servlet API includes another interface to deal with attributes. The `javax.servlet.http.HttpSessionAttributeListener` interface deals with the following events:

- ❑ Servlet adds an attribute to a session
- ❑ Servlet removes an attribute from a session
- ❑ Servlet replaces an attribute in a session with another attribute of the same name

The HttpSessionAttributeListener Interface

This interface specifies several methods.

```
public void attributeAdded(HttpSessionBindingEvent event)
```

The container calls the above method when an attribute is added to the session. This method receives an `HttpSessionBindingEvent` object; we will discuss this object in the next section.

```
public void attributeRemoved (HttpSessionBindingEvent event)
```

The container calls the `attributeRemoved()` method when an attribute is removed from the session.

```
public void attributeReplaced (HttpSessionBindingEvent event)
```

The `attributeReplaced()` method is called by the container when an attribute is replaced in the session. This happens when you call the `setAttribute()` method using the same attribute name.

All of these methods receive an instance of the `javax.servlet.http.HttpSessionBindingEvent` class. This class encapsulates the name of the attribute, the value of the attribute and the associated Session object. Let's take a closer look at the methods of this class.

The HttpSessionBindingEvent Class

This class contains the following getter methods:

```
public String getName()
public Object getValue()
```

These methods return the name and value respectively of the attribute being added, replaced, or removed:

```
public HttpSession getSession()
```

The above method returns the associated Session object.

This class has two constructors. However, you should note that the container creates instances of these objects. As before, you can deploy this class via the `<listener>` element in the deployment descriptor.

The HttpSessionBindingListener Interface

There is another approach to handling attribute-related events, via the
`javax.servlet.http.HttpSessionBindingListener` interface. Unlike the other event handling
interfaces discussed above, this interface may be implemented by the attributes themselves and an
external listener is not necessary. As an attribute is being added to a session, or removed from a session,
this container invokes methods on this interface so that the attribute being added to (known as attribute
binding) or removed from (known as attribute unbinding) the session can handle this event. Let's take a
look at the methods of the interface:

```
public void valueBound (HttpSessionBindingEvent event)
```

The container calls the `valueBound()` method when the attribute is added to the session.

```
public void  valueUnbound (HttpSessionBindingEvent event)
```

Conversely, the container calls the `valueUnbound()` method when the attribute is removed from the
session. As discussed above, any attribute may implement this interface to get notified by the container.

NotePad Revisited: Logging

Let us now modify the `NotePad` application we created earlier to illustrate how to listen for some of the
events discussed above. Our modified `NotePad` application will:

❑   Log session information when a new session is created or when an existing session is destroyed

❑   Log the e-mail of the user when the user enters and leaves the `NotePad` application

Session Logging Class

The following class provides this functionality. This class implements the `HttpSessionListener`
interface and logs data to the web container log:

```
package sessions;

import javax.servlet.http.HttpSession;
import javax.servlet.http.HttpSessionListener;
import javax.servlet.http.HttpSessionEvent;

public class SessionLogger implements HttpSessionListener {
```

The `sessionCreated()` method is called after the session is created:

```
public void sessionCreated(HttpSessionEvent event) {
  HttpSession session = event.getSession();
  session.getServletContext().log("Session with ID " + session.getId()
                                                  + " created.");
}
```

The `sessionDestroyed()` method is called after the session is destroyed:

```
public void sessionDestroyed(HttpSessionEvent event) {
  HttpSession session = event.getSession();
  session.getServletContext().log("Session with ID " + session.getId()
                                       + " destroyed.");
  }
}
```

In both methods we use the `getSession()` method to retrieve the session.

This class logs the events to the container log. Compile the above class and save the class in `notepad/WEB-INF/classes/sessions`.

User E-mail Logging Class

Let's now add a handler to handle session attribute related events. The purpose of it is to log each user e-mail address as a user enters and leaves the notepad web application. The following class provides this functionality:

```
package sessions;

import javax.servlet.ServletContext;
import javax.servlet.http.*;
```

The class implements `HttpSessionAttributeListener` to handle events associated with binding/unbinding attributes to the session:

```
public class NotePadLogger implements HttpSessionAttributeListener {
```

The `attributeAdded()` method is called when an attribute is added to the session:

```
public void attributeAdded(HttpSessionBindingEvent event){
  String name = event.getName();
  if(name.equals("email")) {
    String email = (String) event.getValue();
    log(event, "User " + email + " started.");
  }
}
```

The `attributeRemoved()` method is very similar to the previous method but is called when an attribute is deleted from the session:

```
public void attributeRemoved(HttpSessionBindingEvent event) {
  String name = event.getName();
  if(name.equals("email")) {
    String email = (String) event.getValue();
    log(event, "User " + email + " removed.");
  }
}
```

The following method is called when an attribute is replaced in the session:

```
public void attributeReplaced(HttpSessionBindingEvent event) {
  String name = event.getName();
  if(name.equals("email")) {
    String email = (String) event.getValue();
    log(event, "User " + email + " exited. ");
  }
}
```

For logging purposes we are only interested in the email attribute. Each of the above methods check if the attribute is email, and if so, log the event using the ServletContext object.

The final method in the class logs a message to the container log:

```
private void log(HttpSessionBindingEvent event, String string) {
  HttpSession session = event.getSession();
  ServletContext context = session.getServletContext();
  context.log(string);
}
}
```

Compile this class and save the class in notepad/WEB-INF/classes/sessions.

Redeploying the NotePad Application

Add the new source code to src/sessions, compile the classes, and save them in notepad/WEB-INF/classes/sessions.

In order to deploy these two classes correctly, add the following elements to web.xml as shown below:

```
<listener>
  <listener-class>sessions.SessionLogger</listener-class>
</listener>

<listener>
  <listener-class>sessions.NotePadLogger</listener-class>
</listener>
```

Add this element before all <servlet> elements.

Restart Tomcat, and use the notepad application. Then check the log file of Tomcat for event log messages. The log file will be located under the %CATALINA_HOME%/logs directory, and the file name will be of the form localhost_log.yyyy-mm-dd.txt where yyyy-mm-dd is the current date. In this file, you will find log messages of the form shown in the screenshot:

```
localhost_log.2001-12-16.txt - Notepad                         _ □ ×
File  Edit  Format  Help
2001-12-16 12:13:20 listNotes: init                                 ▲
2001-12-16 12:13:20 User samd@wrox.com exited.
2001-12-16 12:13:20 Session with ID 0644A190F903E433153893821265E584 destroyed.
2001-12-16 12:13:20 Session with ID 004601C2A525A587F3257448A680F9A4 created.
2001-12-16 12:13:21 User danr@wrox.com started.
2001-12-16 12:13:36 User danr@wrox.com exited.
2001-12-16 12:13:36 Session with ID 004601C2A525A587F3257448A680F9A4 destroyed.
2001-12-16 12:13:36 Session with ID 84A94401959666865594D6F2C9E03128 created.
2001-12-16 12:13:36 User samd@wrox.com started.                      ▼
```

As you can see, the log shows the session creation and destruction events, and the attribute addition and removal events.

Can we not use `HttpSessionListener` in place of the `HttpSessionAttributeListener` in the above example? Although the `HttpSessionListener` gets invoked when a session is created, and again when the session is destroyed, we cannot access session attributes during these calls. For instance, we add the `email` attribute *after* the session has been created. Similarly, the container deletes all of the session attributes before invoking the `HttpSessionListener`.

Advanced Session Handling

What if we considered deploying the above `NotePad` web application for public use on an Internet web site, and expected thousands of users to concurrently use this application? We would have a few issues to consider:

❑ How do we make sure that the application/server doesn't fail to respond to such heavy load?

❑ How do we make sure that a user does not lose their data if a server/OS crash occurs?

❑ How do make sure that our application code is suitable for deployment under such conditions?

There are many aspects of application design that can influence these issues, and there are a few aspects related to session handling. In this section we are going to take a look at these.

Session Handling within Clusters

Before discussing how to handle sessions for such scenarios, let us consider how such applications are often deployed. Most web servers are deployed in **clusters**. A cluster is a group of servers meant to share the incoming load of HTTP requests. In the most commonly used clustering configuration, a clustered web container is configured behind a web server such as Apache, iPlanet or IIS. Here the web server acts as a proxy for the web container cluster; all that the client sees is the web server. Note that it is also common to find more than one web server installed in a cluster. In the above configuration, the web server uses a plug-in to delegate incoming HTTP requests to a web server within the cluster. A web server plug-in is a piece of software installed on the web server that sends requests to the web container processes in the container. Note that it is also possible to configure clusters without using web servers, although such configurations are rare.

You should note that Tomcat does not support clustering, because it is only meant to be the reference implementation of the Java Servlet API.

Clustering introduces certain complexities that may affect your application:

❑ In a cluster, more than one container instance may handle the requests for a given session. This implies that the container should make the Session object available to all such instances, otherwise the user may lose the session data, or the session data may be inconsistent. This process is called **session replication**.

❑ The container may swap a session from one container instance to another instance. This process requires the container to passivate and activate the session.

These issues involve copying Session objects from one machine to another machine, which implies further complexities.

Making Session Attributes Serializable

First, since we need to copy Session objects across machines, attributes stored in a session should be serializable. If any attribute is not serializable, you should provide an implementation of the HttpSessionActivationListener interface such that the implementation may remove the non-serializable attributes from the session during passivation, and recreate them during activation.

When to Replicate Sessions

The second consideration is: what triggers session replication? Is there a chance that certain attributes do not get replicated? For example, consider the list of notes stored in the notepad web application. To modify this list, you can retrieve it from the session, and add or remove notes without the web container being aware of such modifications. Since the container does not manage session attributes, it has no way to figure out that such changes have been made. There are few questions to be considered in this case:

❑ Should the container replicate such an attribute immediately after it is set (via the setAttribute() method), or wait until the request is processed?

❑ What happens if your servlet modifies the attribute after adding it to the session?

❑ What happens if you retrieve an attribute, modify it, but don't set the attribute back in the session?

These situations arise because you can modify a session attribute via its reference. The Java Servlet specification is not clear about these situations.

Answers to the above questions depend on the specific container you are using. Most containers replicate the session attributes at the end of a request. However, to avoid replication of unchanged attributes, the container may expect you to call setAttribute() to set the attribute again. You should refer to the documentation of your web container for more information about this issue.

Minimizing the Data Stored in Sessions

There is another important consideration about sessions. Since both replication and passivation involve network traffic and possibly storage, you should always make sure that the number and the size of attributes in the session are as small as possible. Even in standalone deployments, session attributes consume memory, and the fewer attributes your applications maintain in sessions the better. In effect, you should try to build your applications as stateless as possible. For instance, when we built our NotePad application, although we could have put the note content in the session (along with the ID and the title), we did not do so because it would have increased the size of the session. Since we have the noteId in the session (via the noteList), we can retrieve any note whenever required. This helps to minimize the size of the session. Another way to avoid wasting resources is to remove attributes once they are no longer required to be in the session.

Fail-Over Considerations

In addition to these considerations, we should consider the fail-over abilities that some containers support. Fail-over allows another instance in the cluster to take over the load of an instance in the event of a system failure. However, such a fail-over is still susceptible to failures that happen while processing a request. When an instance crashes while processing a request, you may lose all the changes made to the session before the crash. In the case of mission-critical data, it is usually better to store the data immediately in a database instead of storing it in the session for long periods. Always remember – a session is a temporary area in the working memory, and it is not a data storage facility.

Summary

In this chapter, we've covered one of the most important features of the Java Servlet API. The session handling interfaces of this API allow you not only to track users across requests by establishing sessions, but also to maintain state for each session. We saw that the default mechanism used by the API to maintain sessions was to use cookies, but we noted that it is capable of using the URL rewriting mechanism instead, in the case where cookie creation was not permitted by the client.

We built a comprehensive example web application that demonstrated the use of the session handling interfaces and classes, and we saw how we could use event listener classes to notify the application when changes to the Session object occur.

We also saw that while session handling features are useful for storing information in memory, there are associated risks with doing so – particularly in production environments. These risks include loss of performance and reliability. Both of these issues can be addressed by carefully considering which attributes we should add to a session, and for how long we need to keep them in the session.

In the next chapter we will investigate the ways in which we can persist data from our servlets.

6

Servlet Persistence and Resources

As enterprise components, our servlets will often have to work with data from persistent resources. These resources could be relational databases, directory services, or XML repositories.

In this chapter we'll discuss how we can handle these resources within the servlet container. In doing so, we'll illustrate design patterns and solutions to programming issues that you can put to use in your own applications.

In particular, we will look at how to:

❑ Configure our servlets using XML descriptors and initialization parameters

❑ Bind external resources to logical names using a naming and directory service

❑ Access persistent data stores (such as a relational database) from within our servlet applications

❑ Persist the state of a servlet when the server is shutdown, including HTTP request information

We'll begin with a brief discussion of the technologies we will be working with as a detailed discussion of all the technologies we work with in this chapter would require a book of its own. The intent of this chapter is simply to illustrate the use of these technologies in a servlet scenario.

Persistent Resources

At one stage or another, when working with servlets in the enterprise, we will need to work with persistent data from an external data source. The persistent data stores most relevant to the servlet environment are databases, naming and directory services, and XML. For example:

❑ When building a web site, we might want to store the content of each web page in a relational database, such as SQL Server or Oracle

❑ Some parts of our site may be restricted to authorized users, in which case we might need to provide a means to verify user credentials against an LDAP directory service

❑ Our web site might need to access and display data from a third party, such as a weather forecast or stock information, which will probably be made accessible using XML

Databases

We can access a relational database in Java using the **JDBC** programming interface. The JDBC API consists of abstract classes and interfaces that are implemented by database vendors.

> **JDBC provides developers with a standardized way of accessing and manipulating data.**

The API is used to represent physical database connections and statements; actual database operations are expressed using **Structured Query Language (SQL)**.

More information on JDBC can be found in Beginning Java Databases *(ISBN 1-861004-37-0)* and Professional Java Data *(ISBN 1-861004-10-9) both published by Wrox Press. Sun also provides a JDBC tutorial at http://java.sun.com/products/jdbc/learning.html.*

The examples in this chapter will demonstrate of the uses of JDBC in a servlet scenario. Although all the examples will be general enough to be used with any relational database, we will demonstrate them using MySQL (available from http://www.mysql.com).

Naming and Directory Services

A **naming service** constructs a unique name (using a standard format) for any given set of data. An internet domain name, such as www.wrox.com, and an e-mail address, such as mail@wrox.com, are examples of unique names managed by a naming service.

A naming service is often used by a **directory service**, which is a special type of service used for optimizing read access to an underlying data store. A directory service is used to look up data entries by a given name or criteria, using a standard set of API calls. A telephone book is an example of a real-life directory service that we use to look up phone numbers by a person's name.

Unlike a **relational database management system (RDBMS)**, which can relate and query any number of database objects, a directory service can only work with highly specific lookup operations, which are specified by the API. For example, a naming service that stores user information can generally only be used to issue queries based on the predefined attributes of the user. For example, "give me the full name of the user with the login name *john*". If this information was stored in a relational database, we could issue any type of query (so long as it conforms to the semantics of SQL). For example, "give me the number of users whose names begin with *j* and who have less than $3000 in monthly wages".

In addition, unlike most relational databases, a directory service does not support transactions. However, the advantage of a directory service is that it is generally faster than a relational database at specific lookup operations, as it is optimized for that type of access.

Just as there are different relational database systems available, such as SQL Server and Oracle, there are many different types of directory service protocols. One of the most common is the **Lightweight Directory Access Protocol (LDAP)**. Similarly, just as JDBC provides a uniform interface to data, we can use the **Java Naming and Directory Interface (JNDI)** API to access the various types of directory service protocols.

Each J2EE-compliant application server provides a default JNDI provider implementation that can be used to look up and bind data sources and other types of objects.

> *More information about LDAP can be found in* Professional Java Data *(ISBN 1-861004-10-9), or* Implementing LDAP *(ISBN 1-861002-21-1) both published by Wrox Press.*

XML

As a language of text-based data structures **Extensible Markup Language (XML)** is ideal for storing servlet (and web application) configuration information. It is widely accepted as a standard for document storage and a number of APIs are available for parsing XML content.

Although XML is listed here alongside databases and directory services, it is merely a language for structuring data, and not a persistent data store in the sense that a relational database is. XML can be stored in virtually any type of data source, although flat text files and relational database tables are the two most common.

> *More information on XML can be found in* Beginning XML *(ISBN 1-861003-41-2) and* Professional Java XML *(ISBN 1-861004-01-X), both pubished by Wrox Press.*

Servlet Initialization and Configuration

Code can be made more maintainable if properties are not hard-coded. File names, network hosts, and database user credentials are all examples of properties that may vary without notice. Rather than hard-coding such values directly into our sourcecode, we should always maintain external configuration repositories outside the application. The ideal candidate for expressing such configuration data is XML as it provides a data structure that can be easily worked with.

It would be pointless to maintain a separate XML document for simple properties, such as a logging level or the e-mail address of a web site manager. For such easily configured properties, the servlet container allows us to set initialization parameters in the application deployment descriptor (web.xml). The deployment descriptor is convenient to use as it is automatically parsed by the servlet container, and the attributes we set are made available through common Java methods.

Initialization parameters and custom XML documents should be used in combination to achieve the best results. For example, it may be best to supply the location of XML configuration files through servlet initialization parameters, rather than hard-coding the file names in the application sourcecode. Such an approach combines the advantages of the two different configuration methods, resulting in the maximum portability and minimum maintenance of our applications.

We will look at these two approaches to custom servlet configuration in more detail. We'll understand:

❑ How a servlet can be provided with startup information through initialization parameters specified at deployment time

❑ How to develop a class that can read our XML configuration files

Initialization Parameters

It is useful to be able to supply our servlets with initialization parameters specified in the application deployment descriptor. There are two types of parameters we can set for our servlets:

❑ **Context-wide** parameters are accessible to all servlets within the application (via the associated `ServletContext` instance)

❑ **Servlet-specific** parameters apply only to a specific servlet

Context-Wide Parameters

Context-wide parameters are set using the `<context-param>` element in the application deployment descriptor. For example, here we set a parameter named `debug` with the value `false`:

```
<web-app>
    ...
    <context-param>
      <param-name>debug</param-name>
      <param-value>false</param-value>
    </context-param>
    ...
</web-app>
```

Any servlet within the application can access this parameter by using the `getInitParameter()` method of the application's `ServletContext` instance. For example, we could retrieve the value of the `debug` parameter we set above with the following code:

```
String str = getServletContext().getInitParameter("debug");
```

If a requested parameter is not set for the application, the `getInitParameter()` method will return `null`. This also applies for servlet-specific parameters.

A component in a web application can gain a list of available initialization parameters via the `getInitParameterNames()` method of `ServletContext`, which returns an `Enumeration` of parameter names. For example:

```
ServletContext ctx = getServletConfig().getServletContext();
Enumeration e = ctx.getInitParameterNames();
```

Servlet-Specific Parameters

Servlet-specific parameters are set for a specific servlet, through the `<init-param>` element contained in a `<servlet>` element in the application's deployment descriptor. For example:

```
<web-app>
  ...
  <servlet>
    <servlet-name>MyServlet</servlet-name>
    <servlet-class>mypackage.MyServlet</servlet-class>
    <init-param>
      <param-name>message</paramName>
      <param-value>You have reached my servlet!</param-value>
    </init-param>
  </servlet>
  ...
</web-app>
```

Each servlet can access its own initialization parameters through the associated `ServletConfig` instance. For example:

```
String message = getServletConfig().getInitParameter("message");
```

As with context-wide parameters, we can obtain an enumeration of available parameters, through the `getInitParameterNames()` method of each servlet's `ServletConfig`. For example:

```
Enumeration e = getServletConfig().getInitParameterNames();
```

Using Servlet Initialization Parameters

Initialization parameters can be used to provide critical setup and configuration data to our servlets, in a simple and straightforward manner. The XML deployment descriptor is automatically parsed by the servlet container, so we don't need to write our own parser program, or worry about XML structures – that has already been taken care of.

Although initialization parameters can be useful, we should not use them for all our servlet configuration. The XML syntax for declaring initialization parameters in the deployment descriptor doesn't allow us to declare anything but single parameters name-value pairs. To declare a more complex data structure, we have to write our own XML documents, using a custom structure, and parse them ourselves.

For example, suppose we need to supply the following set of properties (a set of authorized servers) to our servlets:

```
server1.myhost.com
server2.myhost.com
server3.myhost.com
```

Using initialization parameters, there would no straightforward way to declare such a collection of similar attributes, but using our own, custom XML document we could declare them as:

```
<servers>
  <server>server1.myhost.com</server>
  <server>server2.myhost.com</server>
  <server>server3.myhost.com</server>
</servers>
```

Another reason for using a custom XML file rather than initialization parameters, is that it makes it possible to modify properties at run time. The application deployment descriptor is parsed by the servlet container at initialization time, and accessible properties, such as servlet initialization parameters, are stored in memory. If we need to alter the value of an initialization parameter, we have to restart the application server for the changes to take affect. However, if we declared our own XML document to store configuration data, we would be able to monitor it for changes and reload the document as required. That way, we would be able to make changes to our application configuration without having to restart the server. In the enterprise, where computer system uptime is extremely precious, this is a powerful feature.

> The purpose of initialization parameters is to provide fundamental initialization properties, such as the logical names of application components, or the location of more generic configuration files. For more detailed data, that may be modified at run time, we should use custom XML documents.

Servlet XML Configuration

We'll implement an abstract, generic, configuration class, `Config`, that can be extended for various purposes. To actually work with the parsed contents, we'll need to define specific extensions of this class that declare public methods for retrieving parsed values. For example, to develop a class for authenticating a user against an LDAP directory we would create an extension of our base class that reads LDAP server configuration.

We will be using the **Document Object Model (DOM)** to parse the XML. Using the DOM requires the entire XML document to be read into memory and stored in a tree structure. This method can be memory-intensive but it allows us to work with a structured object hierarchy and as we will generally be working with rather small configuration files they will not take up a great deal of memory.

Implementing the Config Class

Each `Config` instance stores a reference to the root element of the document in question. Since we will be using the DOM for parsing the XML, we can iterate through the whole document from the root element reference:

```
package persistence;

import java.io.InputStream;
import javax.servlet.ServletContext;
import javax.xml.parsers.*;
import org.xml.sax.InputSource;
import org.w3c.dom.*;

public abstract class Config {

  protected Element root;
```

The `init()` method takes a reference to the application's servlet context and the path to the XML file that should be parsed as arguments. It locates the specified XML document through the `getResourceAsStream()` method of the `ServletContext` (assuming the supplied XML document path can be resolved relative to the servlet context's root directory). Once the resource stream has been resolved, the `init()` method parses the document into memory and stores a reference to the XML root element in the `root` instance variable. Nothing is done with this element in the `Config` class. It is up to the extensions of this class to handle the document appropriately:

```
protected void init(ServletContext sctx, String xmlFile)
    throws Exception {
  InputStream is = null;
  try {
    is = sctx.getResourceAsStream(xmlFile);
    DocumentBuilderFactory factory = DocumentBuilderFactory.newInstance();
    DocumentBuilder builder = factory.newDocumentBuilder();
    Document doc = builder.parse(new InputSource(is));
    root = doc.getDocumentElement();
  } finally {
    if (is != null) {
      is.close();
    }
  }
}
```

To access individual elements of the XML document, we declare a general business method that can be used by subclasses of the `Config` class. This method, `getElementText()`, takes the name and parent of the element that should be obtained as arguments. It returns the value of the element in question as a string. If the specified parent element does not contain the given child element, a value of `null` is returned:

```
protected String getElementText(Element parent, String name) {
  NodeList nodeList = parent.getElementsByTagName(name);
  if (nodeList.getLength() == 0) {
    return null;
  }
```

```
        Element element = (Element) nodeList.item(0);
        StringBuffer sb = new StringBuffer();
        for (Node child = element.getFirstChild();
             child != null;
             child = child.getNextSibling()) {
          if (child.getNodeType() == Node.TEXT_NODE) {
            sb.append(child.getNodeValue());
          }
        }
        return sb.toString().trim();
    }
```

Since we store the whole XML document as an object in memory, it is a good idea to release the document object to free up resources as soon as we have finished using it:

```
    protected void cleanup() {
      root = null;
    }
}
```

Now that we have implemented our abstract configuration class, we will be able to work with XML documents by extending Config and providing getter methods for all the relevant XML properties. We will look at examples using:

❑   DataSourceConfig – for reading JDBC data source properties

❑   LdapConfig – for reading LDAP server specification

❑   AuthenticationConfig – for reading user authentication properties

Resource Binding with JNDI

The standard way of working with an external resource in J2EE is to construct a factory object for the resource in question, and bind it to JNDI when the server is initialized. That way, it is made available to all clients through a logical bind name operation. By configuring such a factory at initialization time, we can hide the details of the underlying resource (for example, the user name and password for a relational database) and ensure that each part of our application will access the resource in a uniform manner. This also allows us to optimize access to the resource in question. For example, we could pool database connections or share a mail session between clients.

We will focus on the process of dynamically configuring and binding data source objects. A JDBC data source is a general-use connection factory, and is used to obtain a physical connection to a relational database.

Inherent JNDI Support

According to the J2EE application server specification, a J2EE-compliant servlet container must provide a default JNDI provider.

> **The default provider is used only to bind and look up entries local to the servlet container, and cannot be used for more specific protocols such as LDAP.**

The initial context set up by the default provider contains entries that are configured in the application's deployment descriptor:

Element	Description
`<env-entry>`	This element is used to add a single-value parameter, of a specified type, to the JNDI context
`<resource-ref>`	This element describes a **resource reference**, which is an object factory for persistent resources (such as a relational database)
`<resource-env-ref>`	This element is a variation of the `<resource-ref>` element that is simpler to configure for resources that do not require authentication

All entries and resources that are configured in the application's deployment descriptor will be placed by default in the `java:comp/env` portion of the JNDI namespace (although we can place our own entries in another location).

> **A namespace is a set of names in which all names are unique. JNDI namespaces can contain other sub-namespaces.**

For example, we could add the following entry to an application's deployment descriptor:

```
<env-entry>
  <env-entry-name>webmaster</env-entry-name>
  <env-entry-value>webmaster@foo.com</env-entry-value>
  <env-entry-type>java.lang.String</env-entry-type>
</env-entry>
```

Using the default provider, we could then look up this entry from the local environment context:

```
InitialContext init = new InitialContext();
Context ctx = (Context) init.lookup("java:comp/env");
String webmaster = (String) ctx.lookup("webmaster");
```

In the previous code snippet, we had to look up the `java:comp/env` portion of the JNDI namespace in order to find the entry. Another way of performing this lookup would be to add the specified bind name to the `java:/comp/env` environment context:

```
InitialContext ctx = new InitialContext();
String webmaster = (String) ctx.lookup("java:/comp/env/webmaster");
```

The difference is that we are using a relative reference to look up the specified property in the first example, while we use an absolute reference in the second example.

Although all of the pre-configured entries and resources are placed in the `java:comp/env` portion of the JNDI namespace, we can place our own entries in another location. For example:

```
Context customContext = new InitialContext();
customContext.bind("myObject", new Object());
```

This sort of environment entries can be useful, but we are more interested in seeing how standard resource factories can be configured and bound to the standard JNDI context through the `<resource-ref>` and `<resource-env-ref>` elements.

Standard Resource Binding

The J2EE 1.3 specification mandates the inclusion of two standard resource factories that can be configured through the application and server deployment descriptors: JDBC data sources and external transaction factories. These are the only resource factories guaranteed to be available on all compliant application servers. Tomcat does support other types of resource factories (such as for JavaMail) but the use of such features compromises the container-independence of web applications, as the features may not be supported on other application servers.

To configure a standard resource factory for an application, we would add a `<resource-ref>` element to the application deployment descriptor. This element contains a declaration of the application's reference to an external resource. It consists of:

❑ The reference name given to the resource factory – the object used to generate handles to your resource

❑ The type of factory – for the standard factories, this can be one of `javax.sql.DataSource` and `java.transaction.UserTransaction`

❑ The type of authentication – `Application` or `Container`

❑ A specification for the sharing of connections obtained from the resource – `Shareable` or `Unshareable`

❑ An optional description

For example, to configure a database connection factory (a `DataSource` object) for an application, we would add an entry something like this to our deployment descriptor:

```
<resource-ref>
  <res-ref-name>jdbc/ProductionDB</res-ref-name>
  <res-type>javax.sql.DataSource</res-type>
  <res-auth>Container</res-auth>
  <res-sharing-scope>Shareable</res-sharing-scope>
</resource-ref>
```

No details of the resource in question (for example, the database URL or user credentials) are given in the deployment descriptor. These attributes are specified in the server configuration descriptor and are referenced by a logical name in the deployment descriptor. That is, the value of `<res-ref-name>` must match a pre-configured entry in the server configuration.

For example, when using Tomcat, we can specify a `<Resource>` element and a matching `<ResourceParams>` element in the `server.xml` deployment descriptor. These elements are either contained within `<Context>` tags or in the `<DefaultContext>` tag. For example:

```
<Resource name="jdbc/ProductionDB" auth="Container"
          type="javax.sql.DataSource"/>
<ResourceParams name="jdbc/ProductionDB">
  <parameter>
    <name>user</name>
    <value>scott</value>
  </parameter>
  <parameter>
    <name>password</name>
    <value>tiger</value>
  </parameter>
  <parameter>
    <name>driverClassName</name>
    <value>org.gjt.mm.msql.Driver</value>
  </parameter>
  <parameter>
    <name>driverName</name>
    <value>jdbc:mysql://localhost/myDB</value>
  </parameter>
</ResourceParams>
```

> **`<Resource>` elements specify the details of a resource and `<res-ref-name>` elements specify the use of a resource.**

More information on resource configuration with Tomcat can be found at http://jakarta.apache.org/tomcat/tomcat-4.0-doc/jndi-resources-howto.html (it's also included in the documentation that comes with Tomcat).

Data Source Binding

We've already mentioned the inherent support for data source binding that is required by the J2EE 1.3 specification. The intent of this is to simplify the process of configuring and binding DataSource objects, which are standard, general-use factories that are used to obtain connections to databases for other resources to use.

The standard method of obtaining a database connection with JDBC 1.0 was to register a driver with Class.forName(). To use this method we have to specify the details of the database user and location (the username, password, database URL, and driver class) to request a connection. This means that our code becomes less portable. For example, this is how we would obtain a Connection with JDBC 1.0:

```
Class.forName("org.gjt.mm.msql.Driver");
String url = "jdbc:mysql://localhost/myDB";
String user = "scott";
String password = "tiger";
Connection conn = DriverManager.getConnection(url, user, password);
```

With JDBC 2.0, we can register a DataSource object for the application as a whole, bind it to a JNDI entity, and look it up anywhere in the application code. The benefit of this approach is that by hiding the details of the database schema, the code becomes more portable. Changes made at the database level (such as changing the database password) do not have any impact at the business level. Also, by encapsulating the nature of the data source, the application can switch easily between different connection models (for example, using cached connections or not).

However, the built-in binding method does have its drawbacks. Although we specify the driver class that should be used by the data source, we do not have control over the actual DataSource implementation that will be used. This is because DataSource is an interface, not a concrete class. For example, connection pooling can have a dramatic effect on the performance of an application. By using a connection pool for reserving and returning pooled connection objects, the overhead of separately creating and destroying connections can be (largely) avoided. If we were experiencing a lot of traffic on our web site, we might want to increase the number of available connections in the pool. However, we have no way of configuring the properties of any connection pool supported by the data source factory.

We can see an example of the problems that can arise with Tomcat. Tomcat uses the open source Tyrex data source factory as its default DataSource binding. A close look at the Tyrex implementation (available at http://tyrex.exolab.org) indicates that it neither uses a vendor-specific DataSource implementation, nor a form of connection pooling. As a result, I would strongly discourage you from using the standard data source binding methods of Tomcat in an enterprise application. Of course, this is not true of all servlet containers. For example, the WebLogic application server from BEA provides an excellent pooling implementation.

For an enterprise application, a more robust approach is required. We will implement a generic extension of our abstract Config class, and use it to dynamically configure a custom DataSource implementation whose properties are specified in an XML file.

We have not entirely abandoned the built-in data source binding method though. We'll briefly go through the steps required for using the standard resource binding approach. Then you'll have knowledge of two alternatives methods for configuring and binding JDBC `DataSource` objects to a JNDI directory:

❑ **Built-In Data Source Binding**
Using the built-in data source binding it is very simple to set up and use `DataSource` objects. We only have to configure the data source in the server's configuration file and specify a data source to use in the application's deployment descriptor.

❑ **Custom Data Source Binding**
Setting up a custom data source binding is more complex than using a built-in data source binding, but in return we have full control over the method used to obtain connections. Using vendor-specific extensions, we can even use connection pooling and caching behind the scenes to reduce the overhead associated with the connections.

Using the Built-In Data Source Binding

To use the built-in method of data source binding in an application, we add a `<resource-ref>` element to the application's deployment descriptor. The logical data source named used by this element should refer to a resource entry configured in the server's configuration descriptor.

Before we can use a specified data source, we must make sure that the driver class we specify (for example, `org.gjt.mm.mysql.Driver` for MySQL), is in the classpath of both the server and the application. We can ensure this by adding the JAR containing the driver to the server's shared library directory. If you are using Tomcat, the shared library is located at `%CATALINA_HOME%/common/lib`.

When the driver classes have been added to the classpath, and all resource entries have been properly configured, we can look up the data source. For example:

```
InitialContext init = new InitialContext();
Context ctx = (Context) init.lookup("java:/comp/env");
DataSource source = (DataSource) ctx.lookup("jdbc/ProductionDB");
Connection conn = source.getConnection();
```

We have to include the Tomcat `<Resource>` tag in the `<DefaultContext>` element (and not a `<Context>` element) of the server's `server.xml` file if we are building our application from a WAR file.

Using a Custom Data Source Binding

To provide greater flexibility in our data source configuration, we will implement a simple application that configures and binds a custom `DataSource` object when the server is initialized. This application will consist of:

❑ A `DataSourceListener` context listener that binds the actual data source when the server is started

❑ The abstract `DataSourceConfig` configuration class that extends our abstract `Config` class

❑ Optional RDBMS-specific extensions

As an example, we will illustrate how to extend the `DataSourceConfig` class for the Oracle and MySQL databases, although our methods will apply to any relational database.

Implementing the DataSourceConfig Class

So that we can dynamically configure our `DataSource` implementation, we define an extension of the abstract `Config` class (`DataSourceConfig`) that is used to read XML data source properties.

The `DataSource` interface lacks some common methods that would make it easier to construct a new `DataSource` instance dynamically (for example, by using the `Class.forName()` method) so we won't use the `DataSourceConfig` class directly. Also, although it's supposed to serve as a factory for database `Connection` objects, the `DataSource` interface defines no methods that can be used to set standard connection properties such as the user name and password of a database. This means that in order to construct a new instance we must resort to vendor-specific extensions. Accordingly, we declare the `DataSourceConfig` class as abstract, and declare extensions of that for each database vendor. We'll use the `DataSourceConfig` class to facilitate code reuse.

The XML descriptor we use for our `DataSourceConfig` class has a few standard elements:

- ❑ The root element must be a `<DataSource>` element

- ❑ The root element should contain a `<DatabaseUser>` element that specifies a user name for the database schema in question

- ❑ The root element should contain a `<DatabasePassword>` element that specifies the password for the user specified in the `<DatabaseUser>` element

- ❑ The root element should contain a `<DatabaseName>` element that specifies the name of the database

- ❑ The root element should contain a `<ServerName>` element that specifies the name of the database server

- ❑ The root element should contain a `<ServerPort>` element that specifies the port number of the database server

For example:

```xml
<?xml version="1.0" encoding="ISO-8859-1"?>

<DataSource>
  <DatabaseUser>danr</DatabaseUser>
  <DatabasePassword>wrox</DatabasePassword>
  <DatabaseName>persistence</DatabaseName>
  <ServerName>localhost</ServerName>
  <ServerPort>3306</ServerPort>
</DataSource>
```

The `DataSourceConfig` class extracts these common properties, that can then be used to connect to a database via JDBC. Extensions of `DataSourceConfig` can add their own extensions to the XML document:

```
package persistence.database;

import persistence.Config;
import javax.servlet.ServletContext;
import javax.sql.DataSource;

public abstract class DataSourceConfig extends Config {

    private static final String DATABASE_USER = "DatabaseUser";
    private static final String DATABASE_PASSWORD = "DatabasePassword";
    private static final String SERVER_NAME = "ServerName";
    private static final String DATABASE_NAME = "DatabaseName";
    private static final String SERVER_PORT = "ServerPort";

    protected DataSource ds;
    protected String databaseUser;
    protected String databasePassword;
    protected String serverName;
    protected String portNumber;
    protected String databaseName;
```

Through the `init()` method, the `DataSourceConfig` reads the common database properties:

```
    public void init(ServletContext sctx, String xmlFile) throws Exception {
        super.init(sctx, xmlFile);

        databaseUser = getElementText(root, DATABASE_USER);
        databasePassword = getElementText(root, DATABASE_PASSWORD);
        databaseName = getElementText(root, DATABASE_NAME);
        serverName = getElementText(root, SERVER_NAME);
        portNumber = getElementText(root, SERVER_PORT);
    }

    public DataSource getDataSource() {
        return ds;
    }
}
```

Implementing the Example for Oracle

To illustrate how we can use our abstract `DataSourceConfig` class, we'll implement an extension for the Oracle RDBMS. In order to use this extension for your own application, you must download the Oracle JDBC drivers and add them to `%CATALINA_HOME%/common/lib`. You can download the Oracle JDBC drivers free of charge from http://otn.oracle.com.

Using our data source application allows us to specify at deployment time what `DataSourceConfig` implementation we want to use. To use our application with a new type of relational database (for example SQL Server), we only have to write a simple extension of our `DataSourceConfig` class, which involves implementing a single method. The overhead of doing that for each type of RDBMS that we want to support is compensated by the increased control over the connection fabrication process that we gain.

We're don't have to use Oracle for this application to work. We can easily extend the
`DataSourceConfig` class to work with any RDBMS (we'll see a MySQL implementation in a moment):

```
package persistence.database.oracle;

import persistence.database.DataSourceConfig;
import javax.servlet.ServletContext;
import javax.sql.DataSource;
import oracle.jdbc.pool.OracleConnectionCacheImpl;

public class OracleConfig extends DataSourceConfig {

  private static final String MAX_CONNECTIONS = "MaxConnections";
```

For increased efficiency, our `OracleConfig` class uses the `OracleConnectionCache` implementation
provided by the Oracle JDBC extensions. This `DataSource` implementation maintains caches of
physical database connections, similar to a traditional connection pool. To illustrate the use of vendor-
specific XML properties, we let `OracleConfig` retrieve the maximum number of cached connections
from the XML file (which we would set using a custom `<MaxConnections>` element) and set the
respective property of the `OracleConnectionCacheImpl` instance accordingly:

```
public void init(ServletContext ctx, String xmlFile) throws Exception {
  super.init(ctx, xmlFile);

  //Construct the database URL
  String databaseURL = "jdbc:oracle:thin:@" + serverName + ":" +
                       portNumber + ":" + databaseName;

  ds = new OracleConnectionCacheImpl();
  ((OracleConnectionCacheImpl) ds).setURL(databaseURL);
  ((OracleConnectionCacheImpl) ds).setUser(databaseUser);
  ((OracleConnectionCacheImpl) ds).setPassword(databasePassword);

  try {
    int maxConnections = Integer.parseInt(
                                  getElementText(root, MAX_CONNECTIONS));
    ((OracleConnectionCacheImpl) ds).setMaxLimit(maxConnections);
  } catch (NumberFormatException n) {}

  cleanup();
  }
}
```

Implementing the Example for MySQL

We'll also implement an extension of `DataSourceConfig` for MySQL:

```
package persistence.database.mysql;

import persistence.database.DataSourceConfig;
import javax.servlet.ServletContext;
import javax.sql.DataSource;
import org.gjt.mm.mysql.MysqlDataSource;

public class MySQLConfig extends DataSourceConfig {
```

Just as our Oracle implementation used `OracleConnectionCache`, we will use the `MysqlDataSource` class, which is provided with the MM.MySQL JDBC driver (available from http://www.mysql.com/downloads/api-jdbc.html). This JDBC implementation doesn't support connection pooling so we don't bother with the custom `<MaxConnections>` element:

```
public void init(ServletContext sctx, String xmlFile) throws Exception {
  System.out.println("MySQL.init()");
  super.init(sctx, xmlFile);

  ds = new MysqlDataSource();
    ((MysqlDataSource) ds).setServerName(serverName);
    ((MysqlDataSource) ds).setDatabaseName(databaseName);
    ((MysqlDataSource) ds).setUser(databaseUser);
    ((MysqlDataSource) ds).setPassword(databasePassword);

  try {
    int port = Integer.parseInt(portNumber);
    ((MysqlDataSource) ds).setPort(port);
  } catch (NumberFormatException n) {}

  cleanup();
  }
}
```

Implementing a Generic Solution

Sometimes it might be useful to define a generic implementation of the `DataSourceConfig` class, that can be used when a specific `DataSourceConfig` implementation for the database in question is not available, or if the JDBC driver being used doesn't offer any specific performance enhancements. A simple way of writing such a default implementation is to use the open source PoolMan application from Code Studio (http://www.codestudio.com). This package allows you to configure a generic database connection pool, no matter what database you are working with.

Implementing the DataSourceListener

Now that we have implemented an appropriate data source configuration class, we can create the context listener that will instantiate and bind the specified DataSource object when the server starts. This class, DataSourceListener, implements the ServletContextListener interface. When the server is initialized, its contextInitialized() method is called, in which it looks up two initialization parameters:

❑ The name of the data source XML configuration file from a supplied initialization parameter (which means that we don't have to hard-code the file name in our sourcecode)

❑ The class name of the DataSourceConfig implementation it should use from a supplied initialization parameter (which the class uses to attempt to construct a new instance)

If everything goes as expected, the contextInitialized() method obtains the DataSource object and binds it to the local directory context (using a JNDI name supplied as a context-wide application parameter):

```
package persistence.database;

import javax.naming.InitialContext;
import javax.servlet.*;
import javax.servlet.http.*;

public class DataSourceListener implements ServletContextListener {

  public static String JNDI_NAME;

  private ServletContext sctx;

  public void contextInitialized(ServletContextEvent event) {

    sctx = event.getServletContext();

    try {
      Class cls = Class.forName(sctx.getInitParameter("DataSourceConfig"));
      DataSourceConfig cfig = (DataSourceConfig) cls.newInstance();
      cfig.init(sctx, sctx.getInitParameter("DataSourceConfigXML"));
      InitialContext ctx = new InitialContext();
      JNDI_NAME = sctx.getInitParameter("DataSourceConfig");
      ctx.bind(JNDI_NAME, cfig.getDataSource());
    } catch (Throwable t) {
      sctx.log("DataSourceListener", t);
    }
  }

  public void contextDestroyed(ServletContextEvent event) {
    sctx = null;
  }
}
```

Deploying the Application

To deploy the `DataSourceListener` we need to make the following additions to the application's deployment descriptor:

```xml
<context-param>
  <param-name>DataSourceConfigXML</param-name>
  <param-value>/xml/datasource-config.xml</param-value>
</context-param>

<context-param>
  <param-name>DataSourceConfig</param-name>
  <param-value>persistence.database.mysql.MySQLConfig</param-value>
</context-param>

<listener>
  <listener-class>persistence.database.DataSourceListener</listener-class>
</listener>
```

Once we have deployed the listener, we can look up and use the `DataSource` in the same way that we did for the built-in binding method:

```java
Context ctx = new InitialContext();
DataSource ds = (DataSource) ctx.lookup(DataSourceListener.JNDI_NAME);
Connection conn = ds.getConnection();
```

> **As we illustrate the use of persistent resources in your servlet applications, we'll assume that you have a valid `DataSource` that is configured and bound at server initialization time (although we won't worry about the actual method used for the binding).**

Accessing Persistent Resources

We've illustrated how to use initialization parameters, XML, and JNDI to configure properties and resource factories for servlet applications. Now we're ready to illustrate how to actually use such resource factories to work with persistent data from external data sources.

To do this, we'll develop a sample user authentication servlet application, which authenticates a supplied user name and password against information stored in an underlying data source.

The data source can be specified at deployment time, via properties in an XML configuration file. To accomplish such a level of configuration, we will make use of a common enterprise design pattern – the **Data Access Object (DAO)** pattern. This pattern specifies the separation of business logic from persistence logic, which can have many advantages.

The Data Access Object Pattern

If a business component is independent of the persistence logic, it requires no changes should the persistence logic change. This allows the business logic to be reused with different data stores.

> **The Data Access Object (DAO) pattern describes a common pattern that can be used to develop business components that are independent of the persistence logic.**

In the DAO pattern, a business object dynamically loads an instance of a specified data access object from properties specified at deployment time. The actual data access object class is either an abstract class or interface, so a specific implementation is required in order to use it.

The benefits of database independence often come at the price of performance (as we saw in our implementation of the `DataSource` interface). By using the DAO pattern, we can ensure data source independence, and still enjoy as many of the vendor-specific features and extensions.

When we use the DAO pattern we have to implement a lot of components each time we decided to support another database. In such cases, the performance advantages must be evaluated against the increased complexity in design, and development cost. You can find more information on the DAO design pattern at http://java.sun.com/blueprints/patterns/j2ee_patterns/data_access_object.

An Authentication Application Framework

To illustrate the use of the DAO pattern in an enterprise servlet scenario, we'll implement a simple servlet application that accepts a user name and password and then attempts to look up a corresponding user entry from an underlying data store. If the specified user is found, we construct an instance of a `User` class, and associate it with an array of `Group` objects, each of which represents a particular group that the user is part of. Finally, the `User` object is bound to the `HttpSession` of the requesting user, and can be used by other parts of the application to validate the user's access to various resources.

The servlet we use to authenticate the users is called `AuthenticationServlet`. Once initialized, the `AuthenticationServlet` reads a list of properties from an XML configuration file through an instance of a `AuthenticationConfig` class (which extends our abstract `Config` class). To authenticate each user, `AuthenticationServlet` makes use of an instance of the `Authenticator` interface, which defines general methods for authenticating a user.

This design follows the DAO pattern: the `AuthenticatonServlet` plays the role of the business object, and `Authenticator` serves as the abstract data access object.

Once we have set up the framework for our application, we'll illustrate two implementations of the `Authenticator` class: one using a relational database and another using an LDAP directory.

Implementing the User Class

An instance of the User class represents a particular real-life user. Each User instance stores the name of the user in question and an array of groups that user is member of:

```java
package persistence;

import java.util.Hashtable;

public class User {
  private Hashtable groups;
  private String name;

  public User(String name) {
    this.name = name;
    groups = new Hashtable();
  }

  public String getName() {
    return name;
  }

  public void addGroup(Group grp) {
    groups.put(grp.getName(), grp);
  }

  public void removeGroup(Group grp) {
    groups.remove(grp.getName());
  }

  public boolean isInGroup(Group grp) {
    return groups.containsKey(grp.getName());
  }
}
```

Implementing the Group Class

Each instance of the Group class represents a particular group of users. A group is identified only by its name (although a more detailed implementation might include other properties):

```java
package persistence;

public class Group {
  private String name;

  public Group(String name) {
    this.name = name;
  }

  public String getName() {
    return name;
  }
}
```

Implementing the Authenticator Interface

The Authenticator interface defines common methods used to authenticate a set of user credentials against a persistent data store:

```
package persistence;

import javax.servlet.ServletContext;

public interface Authenticator {

  public void init(ServletContext sctx) throws Exception;
```

The authenticate() method defined by the Authenticator interface takes a user name and password as arguments. It returns a corresponding User instance if the credentials are valid. If they are not, an AuthenticationException (a custom exception we'll define shortly), should be thrown. If an unknown error occurs, an UnknownException (another custom exception) should be thrown:

```
public User authenticate(String username, String password)
    throws AuthenticationException, UnknownException;
}
```

Implementing the Custom Exceptions

When a user supplies invalid credentials in a call to the authenticate() method of Authenticator an AuthenticationException is thrown:

```
package persistence;

public class AuthenticationException extends Exception {
  public AuthenticationException() {
    super("Invalid user name/password");
  }
}
```

If some unexpected persistence error occurs while authenticating a user, an UnknownException is thrown:

```
package persistence;

public class UnknownException extends Exception {
  public UnknownException(Exception e) {
    super("Unknown exception has occured: " + e.getMessage());
  }
}
```

Configuring the Framework

Next, we implement a class to read configuration data from an XML file. This class, AuthenticationConfig, extends our abstract Config class from earlier. It attempts to read properties from an XML file of the following structure:

```
<?xml version="1.0" encoding="ISO-8859-1"?>

<AuthenticationConfig>
  <Authenticator>[your-authentication-class]</Authenticator>
  <AuthenticationExceptionURI>
    /authentication_exception.html
  </AuthenticationExceptionURI>
  <AuthenticatedURI>/authenticated.html</AuthenticatedURI>
  <UnknownErrorURI>/error.html</UnknownErrorURI>
</AuthenticationConfig>
```

The AuthenticationConfig class is defined below. Its init() method starts by invoking the parent init() method of the Config class, and then proceeds to read properties from the XML element. Finally, it calls the cleanup() method, in order to free up some memory:

```java
package persistence.servlet;

import persistence.*;
import java.io.InputStream;
import java.util.*;
import javax.servlet.*;
import org.w3c.dom.*;
import org.xml.sax.InputSource;
import org.apache.xerces.parsers.DOMParser;

public class AuthenticationConfig extends Config {

  private static final String AUTHENTICATOR = "Authenticator";
  private static final String AUTHENTICATION_EXCPTION_URI =
                                      "AuthenticationExceptionURI";
  private static final String UNKNOWN_ERROR_URI = "UnknownErrorURI";
  private static final String AUTHENTICATED_URI = "AuthenticatedURI";

  private Authenticator auth;
  private String authenticationExceptionURI;
  private String authenticatedURI;
  private String unknownErrorURI;

  public void init(ServletContext sctx, String xmlFile) throws Exception {
    super.init(sctx, xmlFile);

    authenticationExceptionURI =
                    getElementText(root, AUTHENTICATION_EXCPTION_URI);
    authenticatedURI = getElementText(root, AUTHENTICATED_URI);
    unknownErrorURI = getElementText(root, UNKNOWN_ERROR_URI);
```

```
      String authname = getElementText(root, AUTHENTICATOR);
      auth = (Authenticator) Class.forName(authname).newInstance();
      auth.init(sctx);

      cleanup();
    }

   public Authenticator getAuthenticator() {
     return auth;
   }

   public String getAuthenticationExceptionURI() {
     return authenticationExceptionURI;
   }

   public String getAuthenticatedURI() {
     return authenticatedURI;
   }

   public String getUnknownErrorURI() {
     return unknownErrorURI;
   }
 }
```

Implementing the Authentication Servlet

Now that we have declared the foundations of our authentication application framework, we're ready to implement the actual `AuthenticationServlet`:

```
package persistence.servlet;

import persistence.*;
import java.io.IOException;
import javax.servlet.*;
import javax.servlet.http.*;

public class AuthenticationServlet extends HttpServlet {
```

The `AuthenticationServlet` declares a few public constants that it uses to identify request attributes:

```
    public static final String USER = "user";
    public static final String USER_NAME = "username";
    public static final String PASSWORD = "password";

    private Authenticator auth;
    private String authenticationExceptionURI;
    private String authenticatedURI;
    private String unknownExceptionURI;
```

When initialized, the `AuthenticationServlet` obtains an instance of the `AuthenticationConfig` class. Through public methods of this class, the servlet obtains information on the `Authenticator` implementation it should use, in addition to a list of URIs that it should use after an authentication has been attempted. A client requests an authentication (by submitting a user name and password), and if it succeeds it is redirected to a specified authenticated location. If an error occurs or the user is not authenticated, the client is redirected accordingly:

```
public void init() throws ServletException {
  try {
    ServletContext sctx = getServletContext();
    ServletConfig sc = getServletConfig();
    AuthenticationConfig cfig = new AuthenticationConfig();
    cfig.init(sctx, sc.getInitParameter("AuthenticationConfigXML"));
    auth = cfig.getAuthenticator();
    authenticationExceptionURI = cfig.getAuthenticationExceptionURI();
    authenticatedURI = cfig.getAuthenticatedURI();
    unknownExceptionURI = cfig.getUnknownErrorURI();
  } catch (Throwable t) {
    getServletContext().log("AuthenticationServlet", t);
  }
}
```

The `doPost()` method determines whether the specified request contains the user name and password, and if it does, attempts to authenticate the requesting user. The request is then redirected to the appropriate location:

```
protected void doPost(HttpServletRequest request,
                      HttpServletResponse response)
    throws ServletException, IOException {

  if (request.getParameter(USER_NAME) == null ||
      request.getParameter(PASSWORD) == null) {
    response.sendRedirect(authenticationExceptionURI);
  }

  try {
    User usr = auth.authenticate(request.getParameter(USER_NAME),
                                 request.getParameter(PASSWORD));
    request.getSession().setAttribute(USER, usr);
    response.sendRedirect(authenticatedURI);
  } catch (AuthenticationException a) {
    response.sendRedirect(authenticationExceptionURI);
  } catch (UnknownException e) {
    getServletContext().log("AuthenticationServlet", e);
    response.sendRedirect(unknownExceptionURI);
  }
}
```

Deploying the Application

To deploy the authentication servlet, we need to add the following to our application's deployment descriptor:

```
<web-app>
   ...
   <servlet>
     <servlet-name>AuthenticationServlet</servlet-name>
     <servlet-class>persistence.servlet.AuthenticationServlet</servlet-class>
     <init-param>
        <param-name>AuthenticationConfigXML</param-name>
        <param-value>/xml/authentication-config.xml</param-value>
     </init-param>
   </servlet>

   <servlet-mapping>
     <servlet-name>AuthenticationServlet</servlet-name>
     <url-pattern>/servlet/AuthenticationServlet</url-pattern>
   </servlet-mapping>
   ...
<web-app>
```

In order to actually use the application, we need a valid `Authenticator` implementation, which we'll create next.

Accessing Resources Using JDBC

In this section, we'll illustrate how to implement our `Authenticator` interface for a relational database. Using what we learned earlier, we'll be able to access the database through a `Datasource` object that is looked up from a JNDI tree, using a JNDI name obtained from a servlet initialization parameter.

Creating the Database

Before we start to implement the actual Java class, we need to set up the database tables used to store user and group information. In this example, we'll be using MySQL. The only changes you need to make if you want to run this for another type of database are at the database level (for example, modifying the SQL used to create the database tables).

Use the following SQL script to create the database and tables:

```
CREATE DATABASE persistence;
USE persistence;

CREATE TABLE users (
    user_id INTEGER PRIMARY KEY,
    user_name VARCHAR(20),
    password VARCHAR(20)
);
```

```
CREATE TABLE groups (
    group_id INTEGER PRIMARY KEY,
    group_name VARCHAR(20)
);

CREATE TABLE users_groups (
    user_id INTEGER,
    group_id INTEGER
);
```

We specify a user with a username of danr with a password of wrox for this database:

```
GRANT ALL PRIVILEGES ON persistence.* to danr IDENTIFIED BY 'wrox'
```

We'll also populate the database with some sample data:

```
INSERT INTO users VALUES (1, 'foo', 'bar');
INSERT INTO groups VALUES (10, 'Finance');
INSERT INTO groups VALUES (20, 'Research');
INSERT INTO users_groups VALUES (1, 10);
INSERT INTO users_groups VALUES (1, 20);
```

Using these values, we can log in to our application using the user name foo and a password bar.

Implementing the DatabaseAuthenticator Class

Now that we have set up the necessary database tables, it's time to implement the actual database authenticator. This class assumes that the application has already configured and bound a valid DataSource object to a JNDI logical name, as we discussed earlier. DatabaseAuthenticator stores an instance of the DataSource object it uses to obtain connections to the database:

```
package persistence.database;

import java.sql.*;
import javax.naming.InitialContext;
import javax.sql.DataSource;
import javax.servlet.ServletContext;
import persistence.*;

public class DatabaseAuthenticator implements Authenticator {

  private DataSource ds;
```

When initialized, the DatabaseAuthenticator looks up a data source object from the initial context, using the data source JNDI name specified in the application's deployment descriptor (as we have previously described).

> **In order for this component to properly work, you must set up the data source configuration we described earlier.**

277

```
public void init(ServletContext sctx) throws Exception {
  InitialContext ctx = new InitialContext();
  ds = (DataSource) ctx.lookup(sctx.getInitParameter("DataSource"));
}
```

The `authenticate()` method opens a connection to the database and attempts to look up the ID of a user with the supplied user credentials:

```
public User authenticate(String username, String password)
    throws AuthenticationException, UnknownException {
  Connection conn = null;
  PreparedStatement pstmt = null;
  ResultSet rs;
  try {
    conn = ds.getConnection();
    pstmt = conn.prepareStatement("SELECT user_id " +
                                  "FROM users " +
                                  "WHERE user_name = ? " +
                                  "AND password = ?");
    pstmt.setString(1, username);
    pstmt.setString(2, password);
    rs = pstmt.executeQuery();
```

If no matching user was found, an `AuthenticationException` is thrown:

```
if (!rs.next()) {
  throw new AuthenticationException();
}
```

Otherwise, we construct a new `User` object and select the groups this user is part of:

```
User usr = new User(username);
long userID = rs.getLong("user_id");

pstmt = conn.prepareStatement("SELECT g.group_name AS name " +
                              "FROM groups g, users_groups ug " +
                              "WHERE g.group_id = ug.group_id " +
                              "AND ug.user_id = ?");
pstmt.setLong(1, userID);
rs = pstmt.executeQuery();
while (rs.next()) {
  usr.addGroup(new Group(rs.getString("name")));
}
return usr;
} catch (SQLException e) {
```

Finally, we make sure that all database resources are properly shut down, even in the case of an exception:

```
    } finally {
      if (pstmt != null) {
        try {
          pstmt.close();
        } catch (SQLException ignored) {}
      }
      if (conn != null) {
        try {
          conn.close();
        } catch (SQLException ignored) {}
      }
    }
  }
}
```

Using the DatabaseAuthenticator

Once we have compiled DatabaseAuthenticator, we can use it by altering the value of the <Authenticator> element in authentication-config.xml:

```xml
<?xml version="1.0" encoding="ISO-8859-1"?>

<AuthenticationConfig>
  <Authenticator>persistence.database.DatabaseAuthenticator</Authenticator>
  <AuthenticationExceptionURI>
    /persistence/authentication_exception.html
  </AuthenticationExceptionURI>
  <AuthenticatedURI>/persistence/authenticated.jsp</AuthenticatedURI>
  <UnknownErrorURI>/persistence/error.html</UnknownErrorURI>
</AuthenticationConfig>
```

To run the example you should have the following web application set up:

```
persistence/
            authenticated.jsp
            authentication_exception.html
            error.html
            login.jsp
            WEB-INF/
                    web.xml
                    classes/
                            persistence/
                                        AuthenticationException.class
                                        Authenticator.class
                                        Config.class
                                        Group.class
                                        UknownException.class
                                        User.class
                                        database/
```

```
                                        DatabaseAuthenticator.class
                                        DataSourceConfig.class
                                        DataSourceListener.class
                                        mysql/
                                                MySQLConfig.class
                        servlet/
                                AuthenticationConfig.class
                                AuthenticationServlet.class
            xml/
                    authentication-config.xml
                    datasource-config.xml
```

We'll learn more about JavaServer Pages (JSP) in Chapter 8. For now, we just present them without comment. First `login.jsp`:

```
<%@ page import="persistence.servlet.AuthenticationServlet" %>

<html>
  <head>
    <title>Login Page</title>
  </head>
  <body style="font-family:verdana;font-size:10pt;">
    <h3>Login Page</h3>
    <form action="servlet/AuthenticationServlet" method="post">
      <p>
        Login name:
        <input name="<%=AuthenticationServlet.USER_NAME%>"><br>
        Password:
        <input name="<%=AuthenticationServlet.PASSWORD%>" type="password">
      </p>
      <input type="submit">
    </form>
  </body>
</html>
```

Then `authenticated.jsp`:

```
<%@ page import="persistence.*" %>
<%@ page import="persistence.servlet.*" %>

<html>
  <body style="font-family:verdana;font-size:10pt;">
    <h3>You have been authenticated</h3>
    <%
      Group grp = new Group("Finance");
      User usr = (User) session.getAttribute(AuthenticationServlet.USER);
    %>
    <p>You are
    <%if (!usr.isInGroup(grp)) {%>
      not
    <%}%>
    a memeber of group <b><%=grp.getName()%></b></p>
  </body>
</html>
```

We also have a simple HTML page, error.html, that we use to present an error message for general errors:

```html
<html>
 <head>
   <title>Error Page</title>
 </head>
 <body style="font-family:verdana;font-size:10pt;">
   <h3>An error occurred</h3>
 </body>
</html>
```

We have a more specific HTML page, authentication_error.html, to deal with incorrect usernames and passwords:

```html
<html>
 <head>
   <title>Error Page</title>
 </head>
 <body style="font-family:verdana;font-size:10pt;">
   <h3>An error occurred: Invalid username or password</h3>
 </body>
</html>
```

Deploy the application as shown, start Tomcat, and navigate to
http://localhost:8080/persistence/login.jsp. You will see the following login page:

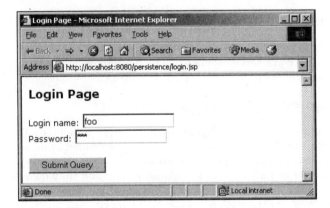

Enter a Login name of foo and a Password of bar and click on Submit Query:

If we enter an incorrect login name or password we see the following page:

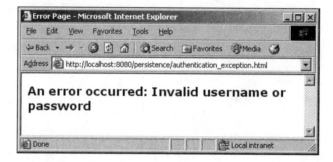

Accessing Resources Using LDAP

Another common method of storing user information is to use the LDAP directory service. We'll illustrate how to use LDAP in a servlet application, by developing an LDAP implementation of the Authenticator interface.

Installing the LDAP Service Provider

Before you can start using LDAP in your applications, you must install the LDAP service provider extension to your classpath. This extension can be freely downloaded from http://java.sun.com/products/jndi/, as a compressed archive, which contains documentation and two JAR files, provider.jar and ldap.jar. You should extract and copy them to the application server's library path (%CATALINA_HOME%/common/lib for Tomcat). Additionally, you'll need to include these JAR files in your development classpath when compiling the classes.

Implementing the LdapConfig Class

So that we can maintain the configuration for a LDAP server outside of our sourcecode, we again extend our abstract `Config` class. Our extension, `LdapConfig`, reads properties from a simple configuration file that contains the name and port of the LDAP server that we will connect to, in addition to the name of the JNDI context factory, which should be set to `com.sun.jndi.ldap.LdapCtxFactory`. For example:

```
<?xml version="1.0" encoding="ISO-8859-1"?>

<LdapConfig>
  <Server>ldap.myhost.com</Server>
  <Port>389</Port>
  <ContextFactory>com.sun.jndi.ldap.LdapCtxFactory</ContextFactory>
</LdapConfig>
```

Additionally, our class stores an LDAP-structures string that contains the search base we will use when looking up user credentials from the LDAP server. This search base takes the form:

```
dc=[root domain name],dc=[domain extension]
```

For example, if we specify `ldap.myhost.com` as an LDAP server, we would use the following as a search base:

```
dc=myhost,dc=com
```

The implementation of `LdapConfig` follows:

```java
package persistence.ldap;

import persistence.Config;
import java.io.*;
import java.util.StringTokenizer;
import javax.servlet.*;

public class LdapConfig extends Config {

  public static final String SERVER = "Server";
  public static final String PORT = "Port";
  public static final String CONTEXT_FACTORY = "ContextFactory";

  private String contextFactory;
  private String server;
  private String searchBase;
  private int port;
```

Once initialized, the LdapConfig class invokes its parent init() method. It then reads the properties and constructs the searchBase property:

```
public void init(ServletContext sctx, String xmlFile) throws Exception {
  super.init(sctx, xmlFile);

  server = getElementText(root, SERVER);
  contextFactory = getElementText(root, CONTEXT_FACTORY);
  try {
    port = Integer.parseInt(getElementText(root, PORT));
  } catch (NumberFormatException n) {
    port = 389;
  }
```

Resolve the search base:

```
  StringTokenizer tokenizer = new StringTokenizer(server, ".");
  if (tokenizer.countTokens() > 1) {
    for (int i=0; i < tokenizer.countTokens()-2; i++) {
      tokenizer.nextToken();
    }
    searchBase = "dc=" + tokenizer.nextToken() + ",dc=" +
                  tokenizer.nextToken();
  } else {
    searchBase = "dc=" + server;
  }

  cleanup();
}

public String getServer() {
  return server;
}

public String getContextFactory() {
  return contextFactory;
}

public String getSearchBase() {
  return searchBase;
}

public int getPort() {
  return port;
}
}
```

Implementing the LdapAuthenticator Class

The actual LDAP authenticator class, LdapAuthenticator, looks up the supplied user credentials in the LDAP directory specified by the server name in the configuration file. Each LdapAuthenticator instance stores a reference of the server name, the port it connects to, and a hash table of JNDI properties used each time a user makes a connection:

```
package persistence.ldap;

import persistence.*;
import java.util.Hashtable;
import javax.naming.*;
import javax.naming.ldap.*;
import javax.naming.directory.*;
import javax.servlet.ServletContext;

public class LdapAuthenticator implements Authenticator {

    private Hashtable env;
    private int port;
    private String contextFactory;
    private String server;
    private String searchBase;
```

When initialized, LdapAuthenticator constructs a new LdapConfig instance from a context-wide initialization parameter that states the location of the LDAP configuration file:

```
public void init(ServletContext sctx) throws Exception {
    LdapConfig cfig = new LdapConfig();
    cfig.init(sctx, sctx.getInitParameter("LdapConfig"));
    server = cfig.getServer();
    searchBase = cfig.getSearchBase();
    contextFactory = cfig.getContextFactory();
    port = cfig.getPort();
```

The init() method also prepares the JNDI properties table that is used when making a connection to the directory:

```
    env = new Hashtable();
    env.put(Context.INITIAL_CONTEXT_FACTORY, contextFactory);
    env.put(Context.PROVIDER_URL, "ldap://" + server + ":" + port + "/");
    env.put(Context.SECURITY_AUTHENTICATION, "simple");
}
```

The `authenticate()` method attempts to look up a user corresponding to the given user name in the underlying LDAP directory. This method follows the same basic principles as our previous JDBC implementation. If the user is not found, an `AuthenticationException` is thrown:

```
public User authenticate(String username, String password)
    throws AuthenticationException, UnknownException {
  LdapContext ctx = null;
  String login = "cn=" + username + ",cn=users," + searchBase;
  try {
    env.put(Context.SECURITY_PRINCIPAL, login);
    env.put(Context.SECURITY_CREDENTIALS, password);
    ctx = new InitialLdapContext(env, null);
  } catch (Exception e) {
    throw new AuthenticationException();
  }
```

If we manage to connect to the directory server using the supplied user credentials, then we have already authenticated the user. We then proceed to constructing a new `User` object and fetching the groups the user is part of:

```
  try {
    User usr = new User(username);
    Group grp;
    String groupname;

    String filter = "(|(uniquemember=" + login + ")(member=" +
                        login + "))";
```

Set search attributes:

```
    String[] attrIDs = {"cn"};
    SearchControls ctls = new SearchControls();
    ctls.setReturningAttributes(attrIDs);
    ctls.setSearchScope(SearchControls.SUBTREE_SCOPE);
```

Search for the groups the user is a member of:

```
    Attribute attr;
    NamingEnumeration results = ctx.search(searchBase, filter, ctls);
    NamingEnumeration ne;
    SearchResult sr;
    int i = 0;
    while (results.hasMoreElements()) {
      sr = (SearchResult) results.next();
      ne = sr.getAttributes().getAll();
      attr = ((Attribute) ne.next());
      if (ne.hasMore()) {
        groupname = (String) attr.getAll().next();
        usr.addGroup(new Group(groupname));
      }
    }
    return usr;
  } catch (Exception e) {
    throw new UnknownException(e);
```

We shut down all external resources at the end of the call:

```
    } finally {
      if (ctx != null) {
        try {
          ctx.close();
        } catch (Exception ignored) {}
      }
    }
  }
}
```

As with the `DatabaseAuthenticator`, we can use the `LdapAuthenticator` in an application by altering the value of the `<Authenticator>` element of the application's configuration file. We also need to add a single initialization parameter to the application's deployment descriptor, specifying the location of the LDAP configuration file:

```
<context-param>
  <param-name>LdapConfigXML</param-name>
  <param-value>/xml/ldap-config.xml</param-value>
</context-param>
```

Servlet Persistence

So far, we have focused entirely on how servlets *read* from persistent resources, such as relational databases and directory services. In most cases, the same rules apply when you need to *write* to a resource. For example, with JDBC the only difference between a write operation and a read operation lies in the semantics of the SQL statement in question. The actual connection and statement objects are obtained in the same manner.

However, there is one feature of the servlet specification that is of special interest in relation to the process of storing data in persistent storage – the ability to listen for session and context events such as when the servlet container is initialized or a particular session gets destroyed. This, of course, comes in addition to the ability of servlets to handle shutdown through their `destroy()` methods.

Using these features, we have the ability to persist session or servlet state in the case of a server shutdown. This can be useful in many scenarios, including when:

❑ The servlet stores a complex data object in memory that requires a lot of resources to construct (for example, an XML file matched against fields in a database). To avoid recreating this object every time the servlet container is restarted, we can have it serialized to a file at server shutdown, and read when the container goes back up.

❑ A servlet or a filter collects information on a specific session and stores it in a persistent data store, such as a relational database. Instead of performing an insert for each entry collected, we can store the entries in-memory and have them flushed to the data store when the session terminates.

> A filter is a web service component that adds functionality to the request and response processing of a web application. We'll learn more about them in Chapter 7.

In this section, we will look at two examples:

❑   How we can serialize a servlet object to a file

❑   How to perform a batch insert into a relational database when a session terminates

Persisting the Servlet State

Through the built-in methods of the Servlet API, it is straightforward to detect when the servlet container is about to shut down. We might implement a `ServletContextListener` and use its `contextDestroyed()` method to persist selected servlets or data structures. When working directly with servlets, however, it's probably easier just to extend the `destroy()` method of the `Servlet` class, as that method will be invoked before the servlet in question is terminated.

We have a number of techniques available to use to persistently store the state of a servlet. We could write each field of the servlet to a relational database table, but that would probably incur too much overhead, both when writing and reading. Better yet, we can make use of **serialization** – the conversion of an object to a byte representation. This representation can be stored in a file and used later on to restore the object.

> All Java class that implement the `java.io.Serializable` or `java.io.Externalizable` interfaces can be stored and retrieved in a serialized form.

The `Serializable` interface contains no methods that we need to implement. Simply by declaring that a given class implements `Serializable`, we can ensure that objects of that class can be written to a serialized form. If we implement `Externalizable`, the class itself is responsible for the external format of its contents (the logic of which we must implement), which is why `Externalizable` is more rarely used.

To work with serializable objects, we make use of two classes: `java.io.ObjectInputStream` and `java.io.ObjectOutputStream`. These classes are used to read and write objects in a persistent store. They contain methods for working with different data types, such as `readString()`, `writeInt()`, and `readObject()`.

A Sample Data Servlet Framework

To further illustrate the process of working with serialized objects in the servlet container, we'll demonstrate a sample servlet framework. Our servlet, when initialized, obtains the name of the file it uses to persist its state when the server shuts down. In our example, the servlet stores a hash table instance that we assume contains some mission-critical data objects that would be expensive (in terms of memory or the CPU process) to initially construct. We're not interested in the actual details of these data objects or the data source they are obtained from – our only concern is that it is better in terms of performance to store these objects in a serialized form between lifecycles of the servlet.

When our servlet is initialized, it determines whether its state has been previously stored in a serialized form in a local file. It does so by calling the private readSerialize() method, which returns true if a serialized object was successfully read. If not, the servlet proceeds to construct a new data structure from the external resource associated. It does so by calling the readResource() method.

Our servlet also contains some statements for writing to the standard output stream. The purpose of these is to illustrate the logic of the servlet and verify that it really works as expected:

```java
package persistence.servlet;

import java.io.*;
import java.util.Hashtable;
import javax.servlet.*;
import javax.servlet.http.*;

public class DataServlet extends HttpServlet implements Serializable {

    private static Hashtable data;
    private static ServletContext ctx;
    private static String filename;

    public void init() throws ServletException {
```

Determine whether the servlet has been initialized:

```java
        if (filename == null) {
          System.out.println("Initializing the data servlet...");
```

Obtain the file name of the serialized file:

```java
          filename = getServletConfig().getInitParameter("DataServletOutput");
          ctx = getServletContext();
```

Determine whether a serialized file exists:

```java
          if (!readSerialized()) {
            readResource();
          }
        }
    }
```

The first time the servlet is initialized, or when a serialized servlet state is for some reason not available, the servlet calls the private readResource() method. We assume that this method would access the data source and put a collection of objects into the hash table:

```java
    private void readResource() {
      System.out.println("Reading from resource...");
      data = new Hashtable();
      // Read data from an external data source.
    }
```

The private `writeSerialized()` method serializes the local hash table instance and writes the resulting output stream to a file to the application server's file system. The destination file is specified by the developer at deployment time, through an initialization parameter in the application's deployment descriptor:

```
private void writeSerialized() {
  System.out.print("Attempting to write object...");
  ObjectOutputStream out = null;
  try {
    out = new ObjectOutputStream(new FileOutputStream(filename));
    out.writeObject(data);
    out.flush();
    System.out.println("success!");
  } catch (Throwable t) {
    System.out.println("failed!");
    ctx.log("DataServlet", t);
  } finally {
    if (out != null) {
      try {
        out.close();
      } catch (Throwable ignored) {}
    }
  }
}
```

When the servlet is initialized, it attempts to locate and read its previous state from a serialized file in the file system, through the `readSerialized()` method. If such a file exists, and it contains a valid serialization of the hash table in question, this method returns `true`:

```
private boolean readSerialized () {
  System.out.print("Attempting to read object...");
  File f = new File(filename);
  ObjectInputStream in = null;

  try {
    if (f.exists ()) {
      in = new ObjectInputStream(new FileInputStream(f));
      data = (Hashtable) in.readObject();
      System.out.println("success!");
      return true;
    }
    System.out.println("file does not exist!");

  } catch (Throwable t) {
    System.out.println("failed!");
    ctx.log("DataServlet", t);
  } finally {
    if (in != null) {
      try {
        in .close();
      } catch (Throwable ignored) {}
    }
  }
```

Delete the file after it has been used:

```
    if (f.exists()) {
      try {
        f.delete();
      } catch (Throwable io) {
        ctx.log("DataServlet", io);
      }
    }
  }
  return false;
}
```

Finally, we implement the servlet's `destroy()` method, in which we call the `writeSerialized()` method. This will store the state of the servlet in a persistent storage, ready to be accessed the next time the servlet is initialized:

```
public void destroy() {
  System.out.println("Destroying...");
  writeSerialized();
  super.destroy();
}
}
```

Deploying the Application

To deploy our sample servlet, we need to add the following servlet declaration to the application's deployment descriptor:

```
<servlet>
  <servlet-name>DataServlet</servlet-name>
  <servlet-class>persistence.servlet.DataServlet</servlet-class>
  <init-param>
    <param-name>DataServletOutput</param-name>
    <param-value>DataServlet.ser</param-value>
  </init-param>
  <load-on-startup>1</load-on-startup>
</servlet>
```

We could easily alter the path to the file that should store the serialized form by changing the value of the <param-value> element. Files are located relative to the directory from which the server was started (probably %CATALINA_HOME%/bin).

Testing the Servlet

Once you've deployed the servlet, restart the server and monitor the output to the standard output device (that is, the command prompt from where you started the server). Once the server is started, you should observe the output:

```
Catalina
Starting service Tomcat-Standalone
Apache Tomcat/4.0.1
Initializing the data servlet...
Attempting to read object...file does not exist!
Reading from resource...
Starting service Tomcat-Apache
Apache Tomcat/4.0.1
```

Next, stop the server. When you start again, you should get different output:

```
Catalina
Starting service Tomcat-Standalone
Apache Tomcat/4.0.1
Initializing the data servlet...
Attempting to read object...success!
Starting service Tomcat-Apache
Apache Tomcat/4.0.1
```

Persisting the Session State

In the previous example, we illustrated how a servlet can persist its state by writing serialized objects to a file when the application terminates. Next, we'll focus on persisting the state of a user's session.

Session state persistence does not refer to the process of replicating session information between multiple servlet containers (which is a common procedure in clustered applications). Here, we're referring only to the task of storing session attributes in a persistent storage when the session in question is destroyed.

We will focus on the scenario in which an application gathers user information and stores attributes in each user's HttpSession object. Eventually, this information should be stored in persistent storage, such as a relational database. Before the HttpSessionListener interface was introduced to the Servlet API, we would have had to write an entry to the data store in question each time we gained new data, which would incur a great deal of I/O and networking overhead. Now by implementing an appropriate session listener, we can gather information over the course of each session, and persist the whole collection before the session terminates. That way, we will increase performance by:

❑   Reducing the number of times we prepare database statements

❑   Reduce the number of times we make round trips to the server

❑   Making use of the bulk-insert features of the JDBC drivers

This approach, however, comes with its own price. The more objects we store in a session, the greater the impact is that we have on the performance of the application server. Even though each object that we store may be small by itself, the eventual size could be unacceptably large if the application has to deal with a great many users. Fortunately, such problems can often be solved by scaling the hardware used. In a 3-tier environment, the database tier is usually running on the most powerful machines that may be expensive to upgrade. Therefore, it is usually easier to upgrade the hardware at the middle tier, or even add more machines in a cluster.

In general, if the database is the bottleneck in your application, the design approach we present in this section may help to decrease its load. However, if the database is running well, the performance gain from this approach will probably not be worth the problems it may cause in the middle tier.

To provide a concrete example of the design we've discussed, we'll implement a sample application. For this application, we will develop a filter that monitors each page request on our web site. It will store the pages requested by each user in a data object in each respective user's HttpSession object. We'll also implement a session listener that detects when sessions terminate and when new attributes are set for each session. Each time a session is destroyed, the session listener gathers the request statistics for that session, and flushes it into the database, where it can be worked with using analytical methods.

To start with, we need to set up the database in which we'll store the request information.

Creating the Database

To store requester information, we declare a specific table, requesters:

```
USE persistence;

CREATE TABLE requesters (
  requester_id INTEGER AUTO_INCREMENT PRIMARY KEY,
  remote_host VARCHAR(255) NOT NULL,
  user_agent VARCHAR(255) NOT NULL
);
```

To associate each requester with a unique ID, we automatically increment the primary key. To store the requests made by each user, we create a requests table:

```
CREATE TABLE requests (
  requester_id INTEGER,
  hitdate DATE,
  uri VARCHAR(255) NOT NULL
);
```

Implementing the Requester Class

Each instance of our Requester class represents a particular user on our web site. When a user makes their first request, a new Requester instance is created and bound to the user's HttpSession instance. For each Requester, we store:

❑　The name of the remote host

❑　The name of the user agent

❑　A list of pages this requester has requested

Each `Requester` object will hold only a little amount of data for each request being made and as the average number of requests per user is probably no more than ten, it would require a large number of concurrent users for this class to affect the overall performance of the system:

```java
package persistence.requester;

import java.util.*;
import javax.servlet.*;
import javax.servlet.http.*;

public class Requester {

  public static final String KEY = "RequesterKey";

  private String remoteHost;
  private String userAgent;
  private Vector requests;

  public Requester(HttpServletRequest request) {
    this.remoteHost = request.getRemoteHost();
    this.userAgent = request.getHeader("User-Agent");
    requests = new Vector();
  }

  public String getRemoteHost() {
    return remoteHost;
  }

  public String getUserAgent() {
    return userAgent;
  }

  public void addRequest(HttpServletRequest request) {
    requests.add(request.getRequestURI());
  }

  public Enumeration getRequests() {
    return requests.elements();
  }
}
```

Implementing the Request Filter

To register request information, we implement a filter that takes each request and determines whether it is made over HTTP. If the request is over HTTP, the filter determines whether the requester in question has already been associated with a `Requester` instance. If not, a new instance is made and bound to the session. Finally, the filter logs the request being made to the `Requester` object, via the `addRequest()` method of `Requester`:

```
package persistence.requester;

import java.io.IOException;
import javax.servlet.*;
import javax.servlet.http.*;

public class RequestFilter implements Filter {

  private String attribute = null;
  private FilterConfig filterConfig = null;

  public void destroy() {
    this.attribute = null;
    this.filterConfig = null;
  }

  public void doFilter(ServletRequest request, ServletResponse response,
                       FilterChain chain)
      throws IOException, ServletException {
    try {
      if (request instanceof HttpServletRequest) {
        System.out.println("Filtering...");
        HttpServletRequest ref = (HttpServletRequest) request;
        HttpSession session = ref.getSession();
        Requester req = (Requester) session.getAttribute(Requester.KEY);
        if (req == null) {
          req = new Requester(ref);
          session.setAttribute(Requester.KEY, req);
        }
        req.addRequest(ref);
      }
    } catch (Throwable t) {
      filterConfig.getServletContext().log("RequestFilter", t);
    }

    chain.doFilter(request, response);
  }

  public void init(FilterConfig filterConfig) throws ServletException {
    this.filterConfig = filterConfig;
  }
}
```

Implementing the Session Listener

For the purpose of handling session shutdown, we define a new session listener class that implements three interfaces:

- ❑ HttpSessionListener – so that we are notified when a session terminates.

- ❑ ServletContextListener – so that we are notified when the servlet container is initialized.

- ❑ HttpSessionAttributeListener – so that that we can keep track of sessions that have been associated with a Requester instance. Our session listener needs to be notified when sessions are associated with a Requester instance because it needs to store a local reference to each Requester. If, instead, it attempted to look up the Requester attribute in its sessionDestroyed() method (see below) an exception would be thrown as the session would already be marked for destruction (and so no attributes could be obtained from it).

Here is the implementation of SessionListener (some method bodies are empty, as although they are not required for our application they must still be implemented):

```
package persistence.requester;

import java.sql.*;
import java.util.*;
import javax.naming.InitialContext;
import javax.servlet.*;
import javax.servlet.http.*;
import javax.sql.DataSource;

public class SessionListener implements HttpSessionListener,
                                        ServletContextListener,
                                        HttpSessionAttributeListener {

    private DataSource ds;
    private ServletContext context;
    private Hashtable sessions;
```

Through its attributeAdded() method our SessionListener can determine whether the session in question has been filtered. If a Requester instance is found for that session, a reference to it is stored locally, using the session ID as a key:

```
public void attributeAdded(HttpSessionBindingEvent event) {
    if (event.getValue() instanceof Requester &&
        event.getName().equals(Requester.KEY)) {
      sessions.put(event.getSession().getId(), event.getValue());
    }
}

public void attributeRemoved(HttpSessionBindingEvent event) {}

public void attributeReplaced(HttpSessionBindingEvent event) {}
```

When the servlet context is initialized, the `SessionListener` is initialized:

```
public void contextInitialized(ServletContextEvent event) {
  context = event.getServletContext();
  sessions = new Hashtable();
}

public void contextDestroyed(ServletContextEvent event) {
  context = null;
  sessions = null;
}
```

The first time a new session is created, we get a `DataSource` from the JNDI tree. So, for this application to work, a `DataSource` must be properly configured and bound to JNDI when the server starts:

```
public void sessionCreated(HttpSessionEvent event) {
  if (ds == null) {
    ServletContext context = event.getSession().getServletContext();
    try {
      InitialContext ctx = new InitialContext();
      ds = (DataSource)ctx.lookup(context.getInitParameter("DataSource"));
    } catch (Throwable t) {
      log(t);
    }
  }
}
```

Finally, when we detect that a session is being destroyed (because it has timed out), we determine whether that session has been associated with a `Requester` instance. If not, we do not proceed any further. If a `Requester` instance is found, we open a database connection and create a new requester entry in the database. When the new entry has been created, we insert a new row for each request into the `requests` database table:

```
public void sessionDestroyed(HttpSessionEvent event) {

  Connection conn = null;
  PreparedStatement pstmt_requesters = null;
  Statement stm = null;
  PreparedStatement pstmt_requests = null;

  String sessionID = event.getSession().getId();
  Requester req = (Requester) sessions.get(sessionID);
```

To create a new requester entry, we need to make two database calls: one to insert the new row and another to select the new requester ID (that is needed for the `requests` table):

```
if (req != null) {
  try {
    System.out.println("Initialize database resources.");
    conn = ds.getConnection();

    pstmt_requesters = conn.prepareStatement("INSERT INTO requesters " +
                                             "(remote_host, user_agent)"
                                             + "VALUES (?,?)");

    pstmt_requesters.setString(1, req.getRemoteHost());
    pstmt_requesters.setString(2, req.getUserAgent());
    pstmt_requesters.execute();

    System.out.println("Get the ID of the last entry");

    stm = conn.createStatement();
    ResultSet rset = stm.executeQuery("SELECT requester_id FROM " +
                                      "requesters ORDER BY " +
                                      "requester_id DESC");
```

We need to get the value of the last ID used:

```
    rset.first();
    int lastID = rset.getInt(1);
    System.out.println("LAST ID: " + lastID);

    pstmt_requests = conn.prepareStatement("INSERT into requests (" +
                          "requester_id, hitdate, uri) " +
                          "VALUES (?,?,?)");

    for (Enumeration e = req.getRequests(); e.hasMoreElements(); ) {
        System.out.println("request...");
        pstmt_requests.setInt(1, lastID);
        pstmt_requests.setDate(2, (new java.sql.Date((
                               new java.util.Date()).getTime()))));
        pstmt_requests.setString(3, (String) e.nextElement());
        pstmt_requests.execute();
    }

  } catch (Throwable t) {
    if (conn != null) {
      try {
        conn.rollback();
      } catch (SQLException ignored) {}
    }

    log(t);
```

Make sure all resources are shut down:

```
    } finally {
      if (conn != null) {
        try {
          conn.close();
        } catch (SQLException ignored) {}
      }
      if (pstmt_requesters != null) {
        try {
          pstmt.close();
        } catch (SQLException ignored) {}
      }
      if (pstmt_requests != null) {
        try {
          cstmt.close();
        } catch (SQLException ignored) {}
      }
    }
  }
```

Remove the `requester` object:

```
    sessions.remove(sessionID);
  }
```

Finally, we declare a method for logging down exceptions that may occur.

```
    private void log(Throwable t) {
        if (context != null) {
            context.log("SessionListener", t);
        } else {
            t.printStackTrace(System.out);
        }
    }
}
```

Deploying the Application

To deploy the request filter and session listener, add the following elements to the application's deployment descriptor:

```
<filter>
  <filter-name>Request Filter</filter-name>
  <filter-class>persistence.requester.RequestFilter</filter-class>
</filter>

<filter-mapping>
  <filter-name>Request Filter</filter-name>
  <url-pattern>/*</url-pattern>
</filter-mapping>

<listener>
  <listener-class>persistence.requester.SessionListener</listener-class>
</listener>
```

To reduce the time we have to wait to see some results in the database, we can reduce the session-timeout value for our server (which is by default 30 minutes). We can change this in by setting the value of <session-timeout> to 1 minute in %CATALINA_HOME%/conf/web.xml:

```
<web-app>
  ...
  <session-config>
    <session-timeout>1</session-timeout>
  </session-config>
  ...
</web-app>
```

When you have made your changes, restart Tomcat. Then navigate to a selection of pages, before allowing the session to terminate. Then we can query our database to discover the details of the requests that were made. First we query the requesters table:

```
C:\WINNT\System32\cmd.exe - mysql                                          _ □ ×

mysql> select * from requesters;

+--------------+-------------+-----------------------------------------------------------+
| requester_id | remote_host | user_agent                                                |
+--------------+-------------+-----------------------------------------------------------+
|            1 | 127.0.0.1   | Mozilla/4.0 (compatible; MSIE 6.0; Windows NT 5.0; Q312461) |
|            2 | 127.0.0.1   | Mozilla/4.0 (compatible; MSIE 6.0; Windows NT 5.0; Q312461) |
+--------------+-------------+-----------------------------------------------------------+
2 rows in set (0.00 sec)

mysql>
```

And then we query the requests table:

```
C:\WINNT\System32\cmd.exe - mysql                                          _ □ ×

mysql> select * from requests;

+--------------+------------+-------------------------------------------------+
| requester_id | hitdate    | uri                                             |
+--------------+------------+-------------------------------------------------+
|            1 | 2001-12-13 | /persistence/servlet/AuthenticationServlet      |
|            1 | 2001-12-13 | /persistence/authenticated.jsp                  |
|            2 | 2001-12-13 | /persistence/                                   |
|            2 | 2001-12-13 | /persistence/error.html                         |
|            2 | 2001-12-13 | /persistence/login.jsp                          |
|            2 | 2001-12-13 | /persistence/servlet/AuthenticationServlet      |
|            2 | 2001-12-13 | /persistence/authentication_exception.html      |
+--------------+------------+-------------------------------------------------+
7 rows in set (0.00 sec)

mysql>
```

Summary

In this chapter, we discussed numerous aspects of resource handling and configuration for servlet applications, in relation to real-life application scenarios. We looked at:

❑   Servlet initialization parameters and how they can be used to locate XML documents and directory entities

❑   The use of XML files for servlet configuration

❑   The use of XML and initialization parameters to implement a servlet that configures and registers a database connection factory at application startup

❑   How to implement a generic servlet authentication framework that can be dynamically configured to work with different types of data stores, including LDAP and JDBC

❑   How to persist servlet and session state, using relational databases and serialized Java objects

In the next chapter we will look at a new feature of the Servlet specification that allow us to add to the request and response processing within a web application – filters.

7

Filters

The Servlet 2.3 specification introduces a new type of web application component – **filters**. Filters allow us to add functionality to our web applications that previously would have required proprietary container enhancements or other non-portable extensions to our environment. Filters sit between the client and the underlying web application, and are used to examine and modify the requests and responses that flow between them.

We can use filters to quickly prototype new concepts, or to add new functionality to our applications – without having to alter the original application.

In this chapter, we will:

❑ Discover what a filter is, and understand how they fit into the logical and physical design of our web applications

❑ Look at how filters can be configured and combined together at deployment time

Along the way, we will design and code two practical filters that can be used to log access to our applications, and to transform content for different types of clients.

What is a Filter?

Like servlets, filters are web application components that can be bundled into a web application archive. However, unlike other web application components, filters are 'chained' to the container's processing pipeline. This means that they have access to an incoming request before the servlet processor does, and they have access to the outgoing response before it is returned to the client. This access allows filters to examine and modify the contents of both requests and responses.

> **Filters are web service components that add functionality to the request and response processing of a web application.**

Due to their unique position in the request and response processing pipeline, filters can be a very useful addition to a developer's tool box. They can be used for:

❑ Prototyping new functionality for a web application

❑ Adding new functionality to legacy code

Filters are particularly useful in prototyping new concepts because their addition to the application occurs at deployment time. This means that filters can be added and removed from web applications without having to rewrite the underlying application code.

Prototyping New Functionality

Imagine a web site that wants to start charging for services it previously provided for free. To implement this we need to add billing information to certain web pages. In another attempt to increase revenue, we also want to add the site's best advertising banners to the pages that were most popular on the previous day.

This new functionality would be difficult to implement if the design of the original web application had not anticipated this scenario. However, adding this type of new functionality is made easy with filters. We could create two filters:

❑ The first filter would examine the incoming request to determine if the requested resource is one of the pages we want to charge for. On completion of the standard page processing, the filter would append its own output (which details the billing information).

❑ The second filter would maintain a list of the most frequently used pages for the previous day (probably obtained at startup from a database). The filter would examine the incoming requests to determine if the request is for one of the popular pages. If it is, the filter would generate an advertisement banner and append it to the page by modifying the output stream sent to the client.

By inserting these two filters into the web application, we can quickly prototype our proposed implementation and any changes in the implementation can be made by simply modifying the code in the two filters – we don't have to touch the underlying web application.

Adding New Functionality

Imagine an application that is used by the accounting and sales departments of a company to obtain inventory information from a database. The same servlets, JSP pages, and static web pages are used by both departments to access the database information. However, due to recent restructuring of the company, it is now necessary to hide certain information from the sales department but to continue to allow the accounting department unrestricted access. How can we do this without having to rewrite the logic contained in the servlets and JSP pages?

A filter could be used to apply a 'patch' to the legacy code. The filter would determine from the incoming request if a user is a member of the sales department. After the underlying component has completed its processing, the filter can scan the output and remove any information that should not be displayed. By inserting this single filter into the processing pipeline, we can avoid having to modify the original application.

Understanding Filters

There are two distinct ways to look at a filter:

- ❏ The logical view – the conceptual view of where filters fit within the container architecture
- ❏ The physical view – how to actually implement, package, and deploy filters

To gain a full understanding of how filters operate we need to understand both these views.

The Logical View of a Filter

A filter can examine and modify the request before it reaches the web resource that the request applies to; it can also examine and modify the response after the web resource has generated its output.

> *A web resource refers to a web application or web service component that is managed by the container – it could be a servlet, a JSP page, or even static content such as an HTML page.*

The following diagram illustrates where filters fit in a container's processing pipeline. A filter intercepts the incoming request before the servlet has access to it, and intercepts the outgoing request before it is returned to the client:

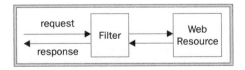

By coupling filters to specific web resources, we can effectively combine the processing performed by the filters and the processing performed by the web resource into a single unit.

Filters and Web Services

Consider a stock quotes web service, for which the underlying web resource is a servlet that provides real-time stock market quotes. This servlet accesses a cached database of recent quotes and generates XML formatted quote data.

We'll learn more about the role servlets have to play in the world of web services in Chapter 14.

Most web service clients can access this data using SOAP (Simple Object Access Protocol). However, in order to accommodate clients on wireless cell phones with no SOAP capability, we also need to send the data formatted using Wireless Markup Language (WML). To further complicate the situation, there is a group of web clients that the service must cater for that only have access to the service via web browsers. These clients need to have the data supplied formatted using HTML.

One solution to this problem would be to create three versions of the servlet, one for each type of client. However, the logic of the servlet might be fairly complicated; replicating it will waste development time and will not be conducive to effective code reuse. It is better to isolate the non-client-specific logic into a servlet and put the client-sensitive logic into a filter.

Many clients send descriptive information in a USER-AGENT header, which we can use to determine if the client is capable of supporting various features. For clients that don't generate a USER-AGENT header, we can use other properties of the request (for example, the subnet of the originating IP address) to determine if the client is accessing our application via the Web or a wireless network.

We will be practicing this technique later, when we create a transform filter that uses an XSLT stylesheet to convert XML to HTML.

Using one or more filters, we can easily process the XML generated by the servlet into SOAP, WML, or HTML as necessary. In addition, as filters can access the request before it reaches the servlet, we can identify the client type beforehand and then perform the necessary transformation after the servlet has finished its work. This will allow the SOAP clients, the cell phone clients, and the web clients to access the stock quotes from a single URL.

Filter Actions

We've seen how we can use filters to:

❑ Access request information before servlets (or other web resources) process the request

❑ Examine and modify (via a transformation) the response after servlets (or other web resources) have processed the response

We can also use filters to:

❑ Generate a response and block access to the underlying web resource – this could be used to create authorization filters

❑ Dynamically redirect clients from an old resource to a new one

❑ Expose additional functionality for the web resource to use – for example, a filter could bundle a library that encapsulates data access methods and a servlet could detect during run time if this filter is available and use the methods accordingly

The Physical View of a Filter

The physical view of a filter is the view that a web application deployer or assembler will see. It is the view that a filter developer works with when packaging the filter.

> **A filter is a Java class that we can add to a web application just as we add a servlet.**

At deployment time, we have the option of associating a filter with a particular web resource within the web application.

The Lifecycle of a Filter

A filter follows a lifecycle similar to that of a servlet. A filter has four stages: instantiate, initialize, filter, and destroy. These are analogous to the stages of a servlet: instantiate, initialize, service, and destroy. Refer to Chapter 2 to find more information about the lifecycle of servlets.

The container will supply a reference to a configuration object (`FilterConfig`) that the filter instance can use to obtain additional initialization parameters. Since the filter is a web resource, these initial parameters are set in the deployment descriptor. Like a servlet, a filter instance can throw an `UnavailableException` to indicate to the container that it is not ready to service any request.

The container then calls the `init()` method of the filter. Immediately after this call, the filter instance must be ready to handle simultaneous requests. Requests come into the filter via a `doFilter()` method, just as requests come into servlets via a `service()` method.

The container will call the filter's `destroy()` method once all outstanding `doFilter()` method calls have been returned. After the `destroy()` method call, the filter is considered inactive. All per-instance cleanup should be implemented in the `destroy()` method, as the underlying Java object may be garbage-collected shortly afterwards.

Some containers may opt to pool instances of filters for performance reasons, which means that another `init()` method call may come shortly after the `destroy()` call on the *same* instance of a filter. If you are developing filters for containers that pool filter instances you should be careful when designing your filters.

The Filter Classes and Interfaces

All filters must implement the `javax.servlet.Filter` interface, which defines three methods: `init()`, `doFilter()`, and `destroy()`.

The container calls the `init()` method to initialize the filter instance:

```
public void init(FilterConfig config) throws ServletException
```

The container passes this method a `FilterConfig` object, which contains configuration information (set using initialization parameters in the deployment descriptor).

This method is a good place to read any process and initialization parameters that may be associated with the filter as the container guarantees that this method will be called before doFilter().

The doFilter() method contains the logic of our filter – just as the service() method contains the logic of our servlets:

```
public void doFilter(ServletRequest req, ServletResponse res,
                     FilterChain chain) throws IOException, ServletException
```

Remember that a single instance of a filter can be servicing many requests simultaneously. This means that any shared (non-local) variables must be accessed via synchronized blocks.

The FilterChain argument is vital for proper filter operations. The doFilter() logic is obliged to make a call to the doFilter() method of the FilterChain object, unless it wants to block further downstream processing (that is, prevent the request from reaching the underlying web resource associated with the request). Typically, this call gives temporary control to the container before the nested call to the downstream processing is actually made.

The destroy() method will be called by the container before the container destroys the filter instance:

```
public void destroy()
```

In the doFilter() method implementation, any code that comes before the call to the doFilter() method of FilterChain is considered **pre-processing** filter logic. At this stage, the incoming request is available, but processing by the web resource has not yet occurred.

The code after the call to the doFilter() method of FilterChain makes up the **post-processing** filter logic. At this stage, the outgoing response contains the complete response from the web resource.

> **The call to the doFilter() method of FilterChain will invoke the next filter (when chaining) or the underlying web resource.**

The actual processing by any downstream filters or underlying web resources will occur *during* the call to the doFilter() method of FilterChain. From the point of view of the filter, all of the non-filter logic request processing is 'folded' into the call to the doFilter() method of FilterChain. This allows us to do something that is typically very difficult to perform in other request/response intercepting mechanisms. We can easily share variables between the pre-processing and the post-processing logic.

Configuring Filters

A web service deployer can control how the container loads and applies filters via the deployment descriptor. Just as we use <servlet> and <servlet-mapping> elements to configure servlets, we can use <filter> and <filter-mapping> elements to configure filters.

Defining Filters

A **filter definition** associates a filter name with a particular class. The association is specified using the <filter-name> and <filter-class> elements. For example, this filter instance is named Logger and the class used is filters.LoggerFilter:

```
<filter>
  <filter-name>Logger</filter-name>
  <filter-class>filters.LoggerFilter</filter-class>
</filter>
```

A filter definition can also be used to specify initialization parameters. Parameters are specified using the <init-param> element, and pairs of <param-name> and <param-value> elements. For example:

```
<filter>
  <filter-name>XSLTFilter</filter-name>
  <filter-class>filters.SmartXSLFilter</filter-class>
  <init-param>
    <param-name>xsltfile</param-name>
    <param-value>/xsl/stockquotes.xsl</param-value>
  </init-param>
</filter>
```

Each occurrence of a filter definition in the web.xml file specifies a unique instance of a filter that will be loaded by the container. If *n* filter definitions refer to the same underlying Java class, the container will create *n* distinct instances of this class.

When the web application starts up, the container creates instances of filters according to the definitions within the deployment descriptor. Instances are created and their init() methods are called according to the order that they are defined within the deployment descriptor. As a container will create a single instance of a filter per filter definition (per Java VM managed by the container), it is imperative that the filter code is thread-safe, as many requests might be processed simultaneously by the same instance.

Mapping Filters

A **filter mapping** specifies the web resource that a filter instance should be applied to. Filter mappings must be specified *after* the filter definitions. Mapping filters is very similar to how we map servlets using the <servlet-mapping> element.

Filter mappings are specified via the <filter-mapping> element. This element must have a <filter-name> element inside, in order to specify the filter that is to be mapped. The filter that is referred to must have been named in an earlier filter definition.

In addition to the <filter-name> element, a filter mapping should also contain either a <url-pattern> element or a <servlet-name> element. Using the <url-pattern> element, we can specify wild-card symbols to define the range of web resources that the filter will apply to. For example, the following Logger filter will be applied to every web resource in the web application:

```
<filter-mapping>
  <filter-name>Logger</filter-name>
  <url-pattern>/*</url-pattern>
</filter-mapping>
```

To apply the same filter to just the servlets in the application, we can use this mapping:

```
<filter-mapping>
  <filter-name>Logger</filter-name>
  <url-pattern>/servlet/*</url-pattern>
</filter-mapping>
```

In order to obtain even finer-grained control over the web resource that is associated with a filter, we can use the `<servlet-name>` element to specify a specific servlet within the application. For example, the following filter mapping specifies that the `XSLTFilter` filter will only be applied to the `XMLOutServlet` servlet. No other request will trigger this filter:

```
<filter-mapping>
  <filter-name>XSLTFilter</filter-name>
  <servlet-name>XMLOutServlet</servlet-name>
</filter-mapping>
```

Chaining Filters

It is possible to specify that multiple filters should be applied to a specific resource. For example, the following set of filter mappings will apply both the `XSLTFilter` and `AuditFilter` filters to all the resources in an application:

```
<filter-mapping>
    <filter-name>XSLTFilter</filter-name>
    <url-pattern>/*</url-pattern>
</filter-mapping>
<filter-mapping>
    <filter-name>AuditFilter</filter-name>
    <url-pattern>/*</url-pattern>
</filter-mapping>
```

Such filter chaining can be used as a 'construction set' by a web application deployer, allowing them to build versatile services. For example, an XML to HTML conversion filter, an encryption filter, and a compression filter could be chained together to produce an encrypted, compressed stream of HTML output – all from a servlet that only outputs XML.

> **The container will construct filter chains based on the order of appearance of the filter mappings within the deployment descriptor.**

The order of filters within a chain is very important for the proper operation of an application because filter chaining does not commute.

> Applying filter A and then applying filter B is not necessarily equal to applying filter B and then filter A.

Using Filters

We will briefly describe some typical uses of filters. They should provide you with ideas for how filters can be used in your own applications. These examples demonstrate how filters provide a flexible, portable, and modular method of adding functionality to our web applications:

❑ Filters can be used to implement the Adaptor architectural pattern, which can be useful when the output from one system does not match the input requirement of another system (particularly when the systems are not in our control). A filter can modify the request or response to adapt one system to another.

❑ Logging and auditing filters can be added to a set of resources within a web application to measure traffic or enforce resource quotas.

❑ Compression filters can be used to reduce the bandwidth used on expensive network connections. For example, a metropolitan radio packet network used for sending digital information to radio-equipped PDAs may be expensive. By using a compression filter on the server, along with a decompression library on the client, cost savings can be made.

❑ Encryption and decryption filters can be used to bridge a network of requests over the Internet. Encryption algorithms could be changed simply by changing the filter used. For example, a gateway filter could be added to support a hardware-based public key encryption filter. If the decryption logic is contained in a proxy, the client can access the server securely (even over an unsecured network such as the Internet), without having the decryption logic built in to it.

❑ Authentication and authorization filters can add security features to basic web services, which may have originally been written without authentication and authorization in mind. For example, we can quickly impose a fixed password to a set of web resources by adding a filter that implements the BASIC HTTP authentication protocol.

❑ Transformation filters are useful for presenting multiple views of the same content. For example, we could use a language translation filter that detects the country of origin of a client and then translates the content before sending it to the client.

A Logging Filter

The first filter that we will build is just about as simple as a filter can get – it's intended to get us acquainted with the design, coding, and deployment stages common to all filters. The filter will log access to the underlying web resource; for example:

```
2001-11-12 11:26:40  Request Orginiated from IP 32.33.23.33 (remote.access.com),
using browser (mozilla/4.0 (compatible; msie 6.0; windows nt 5.0)) and accessed
resource /filters/servlet/BasicServlet and used 40 ms
```

311

The general form of the log entry is:

```
<date and time> Request Originated from IP <xxx.xxx.xxx.xxx (xxxx.xxx.xxx.xxx)>,
using browser <browser's Agent ID> and accessed resource <URL of resource> and
used <duration> ms
```

Information will be extracted from the request, which will allow us to log the originating IP address, the date and time of request, the type of browser that makes the request, and the time spent by the underlying resource processing the request:

```java
package filters;

import java.io.*;
import javax.servlet.*;
import javax.servlet.http.*;

public final class LoggerFilter implements Filter {

  private FilterConfig filterConfig = null;
```

The `doFilter()` method is where the filter processing logic resides. A `ServletRequest` object is passed in with all the details of the incoming request. The `ServletResponse` object passed in is what the output (if any) must be written to. The filter is also obliged to call the `doFilter()` method of the `FilterChain` object passed in – this will pass the response and request (or their wrapper classes) downstream.

In our case, the `doFilter()` method performs pre-processing logic by storing the current time, and extracting the remote address, the remote hostname, the USER-AGENT header, and the URI of the request:

```java
public void doFilter(ServletRequest request, ServletResponse response,
                     FilterChain chain)
    throws IOException, ServletException {
  long startTime = System.currentTimeMillis();
  String remoteAddress = request.getRemoteAddr();
  String remoteHost = request.getRemoteHost();
  HttpServletRequest myReq = (HttpServletRequest) request;
  String reqURI = myReq.getRequestURI();
  String browserUsed = myReq.getHeader("User-Agent").toLowerCase();
```

After the pre-processing logic is completed, we must call the downstream filters (and/or resources). In this case, we simply pass the incoming Request and Response objects that were passed in to us. As our filter doesn't modify the Request or Response objects, there's no need to create wrappers for them:

```java
chain.doFilter(request, response);
```

After the downstream `doFilter()` call, we are ready to perform the post-processing logic. In this case, we simply write a log entry, reflecting the processed request. We could not have written this entry in the pre-processing logic as we needed to calculate the time the resource spent processing the request:

```java
filterConfig.getServletContext().log(
    "Request Originated from IP " + remoteAddress + "(" + remoteHost +
    "), using browser (" + browserUsed + ") and accessed resource " +
    reqURI + " and used " + (System.currentTimeMillis() - startTime) +
    " ms"
);
}
```

In the destroy() method we release the FilterConfig reference:

```
public void destroy() {
  this.filterConfig = null;
}
```

In the init() method the container passes in a FilterConfig object, which we store for later use:

```
public void init(FilterConfig filterConfig) {
  this.filterConfig = filterConfig;
  }
}
```

Now, let's turn our attention to the web resource we will apply our filter to. We'll create a simple servlet named XMLOutServlet, which will simply return the following XML when invoked:

```
<?xml version="1.0" ?>
<quote.set>
  <stock.quote><stock>IBM</stock><price>100.20</price></stock.quote>
  <stock.quote><stock>SUNW</stock><price>28.20</price></stock.quote>
</quote.set>
```

This XML contains data for two stock quotes. In a production application of course, XMLOutServlet would obtain its data via a live data feed, a JDBC data source, or other web services. However, so long as it outputs XML, the filtering logic will remain the same.

The code for the servlet is straightforward:

```
package filters;

import java.io.*;
import javax.servlet.*;
import javax.servlet.http.*;

public class XMLOutServlet extends HttpServlet {

  public void doGet(HttpServletRequest request,
                    HttpServletResponse response)
      throws ServletException, IOException {
    PrintWriter out = response.getWriter();
    out.println("<?xml version=\"1.0\" ?>");
    out.println("<quote.set>");
    out.println("<stock.quote><stock>IBM</stock>" +
                "<price>100.20</price></stock.quote>");
    out.println("<stock.quote><stock>SUNW</stock>" +
                "<price>28.20</price></stock.quote>");
    out.println("</quote.set>");
  }
}
```

Deploying the Filter

The deployment descriptor, web.xml, must contain the filter definition and mapping information before the filter can be used:

```xml
<?xml version="1.0" encoding="ISO-8859-1"?>
<!DOCTYPE web-app PUBLIC
            "-//Sun Microsystems, Inc.//DTD Web Application 2.3//EN"
            "http://java.sun.com/dtd/web-app_2_3.dtd">
<web-app>
```

The name of the filter is set to Logger:

```xml
<filter>
  <filter-name>Logger</filter-name>
  <filter-class>filters.LoggerFilter</filter-class>
</filter>
```

The filter is mapped to all the resources served within this application context:

```xml
<filter-mapping>
  <filter-name>Logger</filter-name>
  <url-pattern>/*</url-pattern>
</filter-mapping>
<servlet>
  <servlet-name>XMLOutServlet</servlet-name>
  <servlet-class>filters.XMLOutServlet</servlet-class>
</servlet>
</web-app>
```

Compile all of the classes. Then we need to create the WAR containing the required files. You should have the following file and directory structure:

```
WEB-INF/
        web.xml
        classes/filters/
                        XMLOutServlet
                        LoggerFilter
```

Create the WAR using the following command:

```
jar cvf filters.war WEB-INF/*
```

Deploy the web application by moving filters.war to Tomcat's webapps folder, and restart the server.

Using the Filter

Before you access XMLOutServlet, check out the logs directory of Tomcat. You should find a log file with a name that follows the following scheme:

> *<hostname>*_log_*yyyy-mm-dd*.txt

Where *<hostname>* is the local host name, and *yyyy-mm-dd* is the date of the log. This is the file that our logging filter will write to. Navigate to http://localhost:8080/filters/servlet/XMLOutServlet. The result you see will depend on whether your browser understands XML. I used Internet Explorer 6, which does:

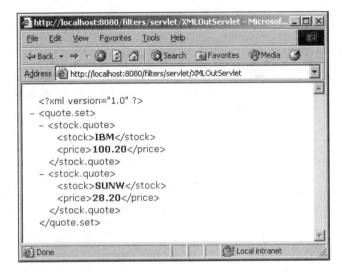

Examine the end of the log file; you will find that it contains the output from our logging filter. It will be similar to this:

A XSLT Transformation Filter

Our second example filter will be more complex than the first, although we will be applying this filter to the same XMLOutServlet servlet. This filter will first check the browser type of the client and then:

❑ If the client's browser is Internet Explorer, the XML output is passed directly back to the browser.

❑ If the browser is any other type, we will assume that it cannot display XML properly. So, we will use an XSLT stylesheet to transform the XML into HTML, and then pass the HTML back to the client.

Detecting the Browser Type

We will use the USER-AGENT header, which contains information on the browser version and vendor, and the operating system of the client to detect the browser type. Internet Explorer 6 on Windows 2000 sends the following USER-AGENT header:

```
mozilla/4.0 (compatible; msie 6.0; windows nt 5.0)
```

Unlike Internet Explorer, the USER-AGENT headers of other browsers do not contain the msie string. We'll use this fact to detect if the browser is Internet Explorer. For example, the USER-AGENT header for Netscape 6.1 on Windows 98 is:

```
mozilla/5.0 (windows; u; win98; en-us; rv:0.9.2) gecko/20010726 netscape6/6.1
```

Converting XML to HTML

The XSLT stylesheet used to transform the content is named stockquotes.xsl, and is stored in an xsl directory in the root directory of the web application. It will transform the output from our XMLOutServlet servlet into an HTML page:

```xml
<?xml version="1.0"?>
<xsl:stylesheet xmlns:xsl=
    "http://www.w3.org/1999/XSL/Transform" version="1.0">
  <xsl:template match="/">
    <html>
      <head>
        <title>Wrox Stock Quote Page</title>
      </head>
      <body>
        <h1>Wrox Quote Service</h1>
        <table border="1">
          <tr>
            <td width="100">
              <b>Symbol</b>
            </td>
            <td width="100">
              <b>Price</b>
            </td>
          </tr>
          <xsl:for-each select="quote.set/stock.quote">
            <tr>
              <td><xsl:value-of select="stock"/></td>
              <td><xsl:value-of select="price"/></td>
            </tr>
          </xsl:for-each>
        </table>
      </body>
    </html>
  </xsl:template>
</xsl:stylesheet>
```

You can learn more about how to use XML and XSLT in Professional Java XML *(ISBN 1-861004-01-X) and* Java XML Programmer's Reference *(ISBN 1-861005-20-2) both published by Wrox Press.*

Content Substitution Filters

In many filters, such as our earlier logging example, the Request and Response objects that we pass down are the same that are passed into the doFilter() method. Filters that replace content do *not* pass the same Request and Response objects downstream. Instead, they pass a wrapper Request object that can intercept calls by downstream components in order to provide access to a modified version of the request data.

In filters that modify or transform the response, we also pass a wrapper Response object that will capture the response from the next downstream component in a memory buffer. After the chained call returns, this buffer can be examined, and the transformed or replaced output written to the actual response. Our XSLT transform filter will do exactly this.

Implementing the Filter

This XSLT filter requires an XSLT parser. The JAXP library used by Tomcat will access the Xalan parser by default so you should download the latest version of xalan.jar from http://xml.apache.org/xalan-j/index.html and place it in %CATALINA_HOME%\common\lib\.

Before we can implement our filter, we need to create a wrapper class for a buffer:

```
package filters;

import java.io.*;
import javax.servlet.http.*;

public class OutputCapturer extends HttpServletResponseWrapper {
  private CharArrayWriter buffer;
```

The buffer allows us to easily convert between the output capture buffer and a string – allowing us to work with the captured output. This is the buffer that the filter will use to capture the output of the web resource (or downstream filter). In our case, it will be the output of XMLOutServlet:

```
public OutputCapturer(HttpServletResponse resp) {
    super(resp);
    buffer = new CharArrayWriter();
}
```

Downstream filters and resources will actually write their output into the buffer via a call to getWriter(). This is how the output is effectively 'captured':

```
public PrintWriter getWriter() {
    return new PrintWriter(buffer);
}
```

The toString() method provides an easy way to access the buffer containing the captured output:

```
public String toString() {
    return buffer.toString();
  }
}
```

317

The filter class is named `SmartXSLFilter` and has three instance variables:

- ❑ `filterConfig` – stores the context and instance information passed in from the container
- ❑ `xsltFactory` – stores the JAXP XSLT transformation factory class used in this filter instance
- ❑ `xsltTemplates` – stores the pre-loaded XSLT transformation template used in this filter instance

The filter's `init()` method will initialize these instance variables with the appropriate references and the `destroy()` method will release them:

```
package filters;

import java.io.*;
import javax.servlet.*;
import javax.servlet.http.*;
import javax.xml.transform.*;
import javax.xml.transform.stream.*;

public final class SmartXSLFilter implements Filter {
  private FilterConfig filterConfig = null;
  private TransformerFactory xsltFactory = null;
  private Templates xsltTemplates = null;
```

In the `init()` method we use JAXP to create a XSLT template for transformations. The XSLT template is based on an XSLT stylesheet source file, which is specified by a initialization parameter in the deployment descriptor. The `getInitParameter()` method of the `FilterConfig` object can be used to retrieve these initialization parameter values:

```
public void init(FilterConfig filterConfig) {
  this.filterConfig = filterConfig;
  this.xsltFactory = TransformerFactory.newInstance();
  String xsltfile = filterConfig.getInitParameter("xsltfile");
```

The template object allows the transformation to occur efficiently. By creating a template based on the XSLT source, we will not need to re-read and re-process the template for each incoming request:

```
try {
  this.xsltTemplates = xsltFactory.newTemplates(new StreamSource(
    this.filterConfig.getServletContext().getRealPath(xsltfile)));
} catch (Exception ex) {
  this.filterConfig.getServletContext()
    .log("SmartXSLFilter - cannot create template - init failed - " +
      ex.toString());
  }
 }
}
```

The `doFilter()` method contains the core logic of the filter. The first section contains the pre-processing logic, in which we decode the USER-AGENT header of the request, and determine if the request is from an Internet Explorer browser:

```
public void doFilter(ServletRequest request,
                     ServletResponse response,
                     FilterChain chain)
                     throws IOException, ServletException {

String browserUsed =
  ((HttpServletRequest) request).getHeader("User-Agent").toLowerCase();
boolean isMSIE = (browserUsed.indexOf("msie") >= 0);
```

The exact way we call downstream filters will depend on whether we are dealing with Internet Explorer or not. If it is not Internet Explorer, we will need to transform the output from XML to HTML. This is done by creating an instance of the OutputCapturer wrapper class, and then handing it downstream:

```
if (!isMSIE) {
   PrintWriter realOutput = response.getWriter();
   OutputCapturer myCapture =
                   new OutputCapturer((HttpServletResponse) response);
   chain.doFilter (request, myCapture);
```

After the chained call, myCapture now contains the output of XMLOutServlet. We will now transform this XML into HTML using the XSLT template that we obtained during initialization:

```
try {
   Source xfrmSrc =
             new StreamSource(new StringReader(myCapture.toString()));
   Transformer tpXfrmer = xsltTemplates.newTransformer();
   CharArrayWriter finalOut = new CharArrayWriter();
   StreamResult xfrmResult = new StreamResult(finalOut);
   tpXfrmer.transform(xfrmSrc, xfrmResult);
```

The transformed output is stored in finalOut, and we use this to write the actual response:

```
   response.setContentLength(finalOut.toString().length());
   realOutput.write(finalOut.toString());
   filterConfig.getServletContext().log(
                     "SmartXSLFilter activated - completed transform");
} catch (Exception ex) {
   filterConfig.getServletContext().log(
     "SmartXSLFilter - XSLT transformation failed - " + ex.toString());
}
```

If the request is from Internet Explorer, we simply pass the incoming request and response. The output from XMLOutServlet is not touched at all, and the browser can be used to view the resulting XML data:

```
} else {
   chain.doFilter(request, response);
}
}
```

The destroy() method sets the instance variables to null, which will release the associated objects and enable a container to reuse this filter instance (if the functionality is implemented) – avoiding the overhead of destroying and creating a new instance:

```
public void destroy() {
  this.filterConfig = null;
  this.xsltFactory = null;
  this.xsltTemplates = null;
}
}
```

Deploying the Filter

To configure the filter we need to add the filter definition and mapping information to web.xml:

```
<?xml version="1.0" encoding="ISO-8859-1"?>
<!DOCTYPE web-app
  PUBLIC "-//Sun Microsystems, Inc.//DTD Web Application 2.3//EN"
  "http://java.sun.com/dtd/web-app_2_3.dtd">
<web-app>
  <filter>
    <filter-name>XSLTFilter</filter-name>
    <filter-class>
      filters.SmartXSLFilter
    </filter-class>
```

An initialization parameter named xsltfile is given a value of /xsl/stockquotes.xsl (which is the path to the XSLT stylesheet that the filter uses):

```
    <init-param>
      <param-name>xsltfile</param-name>
      <param-value>/xsl/stockquotes.xsl</param-value>
    </init-param>
  </filter>
```

The filter mapping we make in this case is done via a <servlet-name> element, which will associate a specific servlet (XMLOutServlet) with the filter. The filter will only be activated when this servlet is accessed:

```
  <filter-mapping>
    <filter-name>XSLTFilter</filter-name>
    <servlet-name>XMLOutServlet</servlet-name>
  </filter-mapping>
  <servlet>
    <servlet-name>XMLOutServlet</servlet-name>
    <servlet-class>filters.XMLOutServlet</servlet-class>
  </servlet>
</web-app>
```

Compile all of the classes, making sure you include `jaxp.jar` and `xalan.jar` in your classpath. Then we need to create the WAR. You should have the following file and directory structure:

```
WEB-INF/
        web.xml
        classes/filters/
                        XMLOutServlet
                        SmartXSLFilter
                        OutputCapturer
xsl/
    stockquotes.xsl
```

Then, create the WAR with the following command:

```
jar cvf filters.war WEB-INF/* xsl/*
```

Deploy the web application by copying `filters.war` to Tomcat's `webapps` folder, and restarting the server.

Using the Filter

Use Internet Explorer to navigate to http://localhost:8080/filters/XMLOutServlet to access the servlet (and our filter). Our filter will have detected the browser, and passed the XML output straight through, so we'll see the same output as we did during our logging example.

Now, try accessing the same URL using another type of browser (I used Netscape 6.2). Our `SmartXSLFilter` will detect the non-IE browser, and perform the XML to HTML conversion before sending back the response. The output will look similar to this:

Chaining Filters

The `Logger` and `XSLTFilter` filters can be chained together by including both in `web.xml`:

```xml
<?xml version="1.0" encoding="ISO-8859-1"?>
<!DOCTYPE web-app
  PUBLIC "-//Sun Microsystems, Inc.//DTD Web Application 2.3//EN"
  "http://java.sun.com/dtd/web-app_2_3.dtd">
<web-app>

  <filter>
    <filter-name>Logger</filter-name>
    <filter-class>filters.LoggerFilter</filter-class>
  </filter>

  <filter>
    <filter-name>XSLTFilter</filter-name>
    <filter-class>filters.SmartXSLFilter</filter-class>
    <init-param>
      <param-name>xsltfile</param-name>
      <param-value>/xsl/stockquotes.xsl</param-value>
    </init-param>
  </filter>

  <filter-mapping>
      <filter-name>Logger</filter-name>
      <url-pattern>/*</url-pattern>
  </filter-mapping>

  <filter-mapping>
    <filter-name>XSLTFilter</filter-name>
    <servlet-name>XMLOutServlet</servlet-name>
  </filter-mapping>

  <servlet>
    <servlet-name>XMLOutServlet</servlet-name>
    <servlet-class>filters.XMLOutServlet</servlet-class>
  </servlet>
</web-app>
```

Restart Tomcat, and try accessing `XMLOutServlet` using both Internet Explorer and Netscape once more. The `XSLTFilter` will work as before. Now check out the log file in the `logs` directory of Tomcat and you will see that each and every access to `XMLOutServlet` is logged by the `Logger` filter. The two filters have been chained together.

The log entry from the `Logger` filter always precedes the entry from the `XSLTFilter`, which indicates that the `Logger` filter is always upstream. This behavior is defined in the Servlet 2.3 specification: all filters with `<filter-mapping>` elements that use `<url-pattern>` elements are chained (in the order that they appear in the `web.xml` file) before the `<filter-mapping>` elements that use `<servlet-name>` elements (again in the order that they appear in the `web.xml` file).

Designing Filters

To round off the chapter, I'll mention a few guidelines that you should keep in mind when you're developing filters:

❑ Filters should be designed to be easily configurable at deployment time. Often, a filter can be reused through the careful planning and use of initialization parameters.

❑ Filtering logic, unlike that of servlets, should not depend on session state information that is maintained between requests because a single filter instance may be servicing many different requests at the same time.

❑ When mapping filters, always use the most restrictive mapping possible – use <servlet-name> instead of <url-pattern> if possible. The overhead of filter operations can be significantly increased if the filter is consistently applied to web resources that don't need it.

Summary

We saw in this chapter how filters can be used to add functionality such as auditing, logging, authentication, transformation, compression, and encryption to our applications at *deployment* time. Such functionality can be easily added and removed as business requirements change.

Filters can be used without having to touch existing code. Filter definitions and filter mapping within the deployment descriptor are used to indicate to the container how filters should be chained together and which web resource the filters should apply to. Multiple instances of the same underlying filter can even be configured within the deployment descriptor together with different initialization parameters. The container manages the lifetime of a filter, and will create and destroy instances of the filter as specified in the deployment descriptor.

To complete the chapter, we built two filters: a simple logging filter, and a transformation filter. The transformation filter allowed the same underlying service logic to service a variety of different clients Finally, we saw how these two filters could be chained together in order to combine their functionality.

In the next chapter we're going to look at how we can harness the power of servlets with the flexibility and ease of use of a markup language – by using JavaServer Pages

8

JavaServer Pages

Although servlets are powerful web components, they are not the ideal technology available to us to build presentation elements. This is because:

❑ Amending the look and feel of the system involves recompiling the servlet classes

❑ The presence of HTML within the servlets tightly couples the presentation and the content, which blurs the roles of presenting and providing content

❑ Lots of HTML code within the servlet classes make them difficult to maintain

JavaServer Pages (JSP) addresses these concerns. JSP pages are text files similar to HTML files but have extra tags that allow us to:

❑ Interact with dynamic content

❑ Include content from other web application resources

❑ Forward the response to other web application resources

❑ Perform custom processing on the server when the page is served by the web container

In this chapter we will look at:

- ❑ How JSP pages are processed by the web container
- ❑ JSP declarations, scriptlets, and expressions
- ❑ JSP directives
- ❑ JSP standard actions
- ❑ JSP custom actions

We'll round off the chapter by looking at an example in which we'll construct an application that demonstrates how we can use servlets and JSP pages in tandem.

JSP Fundamentals

JSP pages are converted to servlets by the **JSP container** in a process that is transparent to the developer. We'll author a simple JSP page that prints out the current date to demonstrate how this works:

```
<html>
  <head>
    <title>Date</title>
  </head>
  <body>
    <h3>
      The date is
      <% out.println((new java.util.Date()).toString()); %>
    </h3>
  </body>
</html>
```

Notice how easy it is to combine HTML and Java code in a JSP page. It would be a lot easier to alter the way the page is presented than it would be if the same page were written as a servlet. Save this JSP page as %CATALINA_HOME%/webapps/jsp/date.jsp, start Tomcat, and navigate to http://localhost:8080/date.jsp:

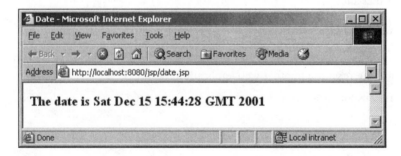

Quite a lot of things happen behind the scenes when a JSP page is deployed in a web container and is first served to a client request. Deploying and serving a JSP page involves two distinct phases:

- ❑ **Translation phase** – In this phase the JSP page is transformed into a Java servlet and then compiled. This phase occurs only once for each JSP page and must be executed before the JSP page is served. The generated servlet class is known as a **JSP page implementation class**. The translation phase results in a delay when a JSP page is requested for the first time. To avoid this delay, JSP pages can be precompiled before they are deployed using tools that perform the translation phase when the server starts up.

- ❑ **Execution phase** – This phase (also known as the **request processing phase**), is executed each time the JSP page is served by the web container. Requests for the JSP page result in the execution of the JSP page implementation class.

The actual form of the sourcecode for the JSP page implementation class depends on the web container. Normally, the class implements `javax.servlet.jsp.HttpJspPage` or `javax.servlet.jsp.JspPage`, both of which extend `javax.servlet.Servlet`. The following code (tidied up a bit) is the source for the page implementation class of `date.jsp` as generated by Tomcat 4, which stores these files in `%CATALINA_HOME%/webapps/work`.

The class extends `HttpJspBase`, which is a class provided by Tomcat that implements the `HttpJspPage` interface.

```
package org.apache.jsp;

import javax.servlet.*;
import javax.servlet.http.*;
import javax.servlet.jsp.*;
import org.apache.jasper.runtime.*;

public class date$jsp extends HttpJspBase {

public class MyFirstJSP$jsp extends HttpJspBase {

  static {}

  public date$jsp() {}

  private static boolean _jspx_inited = false;
```

When a request comes for the JSP page, the container creates an instance of the page and calls the `jspInit()` method on the page implementation object. It's worth noting that it is up to the container's implementation whether a new instance of the page is used each time, or if a single instance is serviced by multiple threads (which is the most common scenario):

```
public final void _jspx_init()
  throws org.apache.jasper.runtime.JspException {}
```

The generated class overrides the _JSP pageservice() method. This method is called each time the JSP is accessed by a client browser. All the Java code and template text we have in our JSP pages normally go into this method. It is executed each time the JSP page is served by the web container:

```java
public void _JSP pageservice(HttpServletRequest request,
                        HttpServletResponse  response)
    throws java.io.IOException, ServletException {

  JspFactory _jspxFactory = null;
  PageContext pageContext = null;
  HttpSession session = null;
  ServletContext application = null;
  ServletConfig config = null;
  JspWriter out = null;
  Object page = this;
  String  _value = null;
  try {
    if (_jspx_inited == false) {
      synchronized (this) {
        if (_jspx_inited == false) {
          _jspx_init();
          _jspx_inited = true;
        }
      }
    }
  _jspxFactory = JspFactory.getDefaultFactory();
  response.setContentType("text/html;charset=ISO-8859-1");
  pageContext = _jspxFactory.getPageContext(this, request, response,
                                      "", true, 8192, true);
```

Here we initialize the implicit variables (which we cover shortly):

```java
application = pageContext.getServletContext();
config = pageContext.getServletConfig();
session = pageContext.getSession();
out = pageContext.getOut();
```

Write the template text stored in the text file to the output stream:

```java
// HTML // begin [file="/date.jsp";from=(0,0);to=(7,6)]
out.write("<html>\r\n<head>\r\n<title>Date</title>\r\n" +
        "</head>\r\n<body>\r\n<h3>\r\n" +
        "The date is\r\n");
// end
// begin [file="/date.jsp";from=(7,8);to=(7,57)]
out.println((new java.util.Date()).toString());
// end
// HTML // begin [file="/date.jsp";from=(7,59);to=(10,7)]
out.write("\r\n    </h3>\r\n  </body>\r\n</html>");
// end
```

```
    } catch (Throwable t) {
      if (out != null && out.getBufferSize() != 0) {
        out.clearBuffer();
      }
      if (pageContext != null) {
        pageContext.handlePageException(t);
      }
    } finally {
      if (_jspxFactory != null) {
        _jspxFactory.releasePageContext(pageContext);
      }
    }
  }
}
```

Now that we've covered the basic objectives and working principles of JSP pages, we'll take a closer look at the various features of JSP that enable the building of powerful enterprise-class presentation components.

JSP Scripting Elements

There are three kinds of scripting element in JSP:

❑   Declarations

❑   Scriptlets

❑   Expressions

Declarations

Declarations are used to define methods and instance variables. They do not produce any output that is sent back to the client. Declarations in JSP pages are embedded between <%! and %> delimiters, for example:

```
<%!
  public void jspDestroy() {
    System.out.println("JSP destroyed");
  }

  public void jspInit() {
    System.out.println("JSP loaded");
  }

  int myVariable = 123;
%>
```

The two methods and the variable will be made available to the page implementation class and we can access these functions and variables within the JSP page.

Scriptlets

Scriptlets are used to embed Java code within JSP pages. The contents of scriptlets go within the _JSP pageservice() method. The lines of code embedded in JSP pages should comply with the syntactical and semantic constructs of Java. Scriptlets are embedded between <% and %> delimiters, for example:

```
<%
  int x = 10;
  int y = 20;
  int z = 10 * 20;
%>
```

Expressions

Expressions in JSP pages are used to write dynamic content back to the browser and are embedded in <%= and %> delimiters. If the output of the expression is a Java primitive, the value of the primitive is printed back to the browser. If the output is a Java object, the result of calling the toString() method on the object is written back to the browser.

For example this would print the string Fred Flintstone to the client:

```
<%="Fred" + "Flintstone" %>
```

This expression would print the string 10 to the client:

```
<%= Math.sqrt(100) %>
```

JSP Implicit Objects

In the service methods of servlets we have references to many server-side objects that represent the incoming request, response, and session. JSP provides a set of **implicit objects** that can be used to access such objects. These objects are actually defined in the _JSP pageservice() method of the page implementation class and initialized with appropriate references.

JSP defines four scopes for the objects that can be used by the JSP authors:

Scope	Description
page	Objects can be accessed only within the JSP page in which they are referenced.
request	Objects can be accessed within all the pages that serve the current request. These include pages that are forwarded to, and included in, the original JSP page to which the request was routed.
session	Objects can only be accessed within the JSP pages accessed within the session for which the objects are defined.
application	Application scope objects can be accessed by all JSP pages in a given context.

The following table lists the implicit objects that can be used in scriptlets:

Implicit Object	Type	Scope	Description
request	Protocol-dependent sub-type of `javax.servlet.ServletRequest`	request	A reference to the current request
response	Protocol-dependent sub-type of `javax.servlet.ServletResponse`	page	The response to the request
pageContext	`javax.servlet.jsp.PageContext`	page	Provides a common point to access the request, response, session, and application, associated with the page being served
session	`javax.servlet.http.HttpSession`	session	The session associated with the current request
application	`javax.servlet.ServletContext`	application	The servlet context to which the page belongs
out	`javax.servlet.jsp.JspWriter`	page	The object that writes to the response output stream
config	`javax.servlet.ServletConfig`	page	The servlet configuration for the current page
Page	`java.lang.Object`	page	An instance of the page implementation class that is serving the request (synonymous with the `this` keyword if Java is used as the scripting language)
exception	`java.lang.Throwable`	page	Available with JSP pages that act as error pages for other JSP pages

The following JSP page illustrates the use of implicit objects in JSP pages. Save this as `%CATALINA_HOME%/webapps/jsp/Implicit.jsp`:

```html
<html>
  <head>
    <title>Implicit Objects</title>
  </head>
  <body style="font-family:verdana;font-size:10pt">
    <p>
      Using Request parameters...<br>
```

We print the request parameter `name`:

```html
      Using Request parameters...<br>
      Name: <%= request.getParameter("name") %>
    </p>
```

We print a sentence using the `out` implicit variable:

```html
    <p>
      <% out.println("This is printed using the out implicit variable"); %>
    </p>
```

We store and retrieve an object of type `String` using the `session` implicit variable:

```html
    <p>
      Storing a string to the session...<br>
      <% session.setAttribute("name", "Meeraj"); %>
      Retrieving the string from session...<br>
      <b>Name:</b> <%= session.getAttribute("name") %>
    </p>
```

Store and retrieve an object of type `String` in the servlet context using the `application` implicit variable:

```html
    <p>
      Storing a string to the application...<br>
      <% application.setAttribute("name", "Meeraj"); %>
      Retrieving the string from application...<br>
      <b>Name:</b> <%= application.getAttribute("name") %>
    </p>
```

Finally, store and retrieve an object of type `String` in the page context using the `pageContext` implicit variable:

```html
    <p>
      Storing a string to the page context...<br>
      <% pageContext.setAttribute("name", "Meeraj"); %>
      Retrieving the string from page context...</br>
      <b>Name:</b> <%= pageContext.getAttribute("name") %>
    </p>
  </body>
</html>
```

Access this JSP page at http://localhost:8080/jsp/Implicit.jsp?name=Meeraj and you will see:

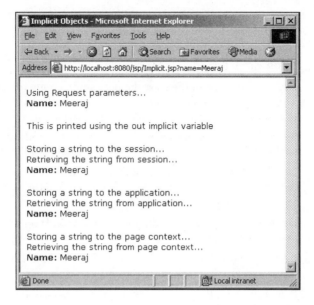

Directives

Directives are messages sent by the JSP author to the JSP container to aid the container in the process of page translation. These directives are used by the JSP container to import tag libraries, import required classes, set output buffering options, and include content from external files. The JSP specification defines three directives:

- ❑ page – provides general information about the page, such as the scripting language that is used, content type, or buffer size

- ❑ include – used to include the contents of external files

- ❑ taglib – used to import custom actions defined in tag libraries

The page Directive

The page directive sets a number of page dependent properties that can be used during the translation phase by the container. A JSP page can contain any number of page directives. However only the import attribute should appear more than once.

The following table shows the different attributes associated with the page directive:

Attribute	Description
language	Defines the server-side scripting language used in the JSP. The only language that is currently supported is Java.
extends	Defines the name of the class the page implementation class should extend. This attribute is generally not used by page authors. It is left to the container to decide the ancestor of the page implementation class.
import	Allows us to import packages and classes to be used within scriptlets. The packages and classes are defined as a comma-separated list.
session	Defines whether the page should participate in a session. The session implicit variable is available for scripting only if the value of this attribute is set to true. The default value is true.
buffer	Defines the buffer size for the JSP in kilobytes. If set to none, the output of the JSP is not buffered.
autoFlush	If set to true the buffer will be flushed when the maximum limit is reached. Otherwise an IllegalStateException is thrown.
isThreadSafe	If set to false, the page implementation class will implement the SingleThreadModel interface. The default value is true.
info	The value of this attribute is returned by the getServletInfo() method of the page implementation class.
errorPage	Defines the relative URI of the web resource to which the response should be forwarded if an exception is thrown in the JSP page.
contentType	Defines the MIME type for the output response. The default value is text/html.
isErrorPage	Should be set to true for JSP pages that are defined as error pages.
pageEncoding	Defines the character encoding for the page.

The following snippet shows an example of the page directive:

```
<%@ page language="java" buffer="10Kb" autoFlush="true"
        errorPage="/error.jsp" import="java.util.*,javax.sql.RowSet" %>
```

This directive defines the following properties for the JSP page:

❑ The scripting language is set as Java

❑ The buffer size is set to 10 kilo bytes

❑ The container will flush the contents if it exceeds the specified size

❑ The error page is defined as error.jsp

❑ The JSP page may use classes and interfaces from the java.util package and the interface javax.sql.RowSet within its scriptlets

The include Directive

The include directive is used to insert template text and JSP code during the translation phase. The contents of the included file specified by the directive is included in the including JSP page. For example:

```
<%@ include file="included.jsp" %>
```

The included file is searched relative to the location of the current JSP unless it is preceded with a forward slash.

JSP Actions

JSP actions are processed during the request processing phase (as opposed to directives, which are processed during the translation phase). The JSP specification defines a few standard actions that must be supported by all compliant web containers. JSP also provides a powerful framework for developing custom actions, which are included in a JSP page using the taglib directive.

The jsp:include Action

The JSP specification defines the include action for including static and dynamic resources in a JSP page. With the include directive the contents of the included resource is substituted into the JSP page at *translation* phase but with the include action the response of the included resource is added to the current response output stream during the *request processing* phase.

The include action is the same as including resources using the RequestDispatcher interface. In fact, this is how the page implementation class achieves this functionality.

The following code shows how we can use the include action:

```
<jsp:include page="includedPage.jsp"/>
```

This action will include the output of processing includedPage.jsp within the output of the JSP page during the request processing phase.

There are some important points to note regarding the include action and directive:

❑   Changing the content of the included resource used in the include action is automatically reflected the next time the including JSP is accessed. The JSP 1.2 specification doesn't specify whether containers should detect changes made to resources included using the include directive.

❑   The include directive is normally used for including both dynamic and static resources, the include action is used for including only dynamic resources.

The jsp:forward Action

The JSP specification defines the `forward` action to be used for forwarding the response to other web application resources. The `forward` action is the same as forwarding to resources using the `RequestDispatcher` interface.

The following code shows how to use the forward action:

```
<jsp:forward page="Forwarded.html"/>
```

This action will forward the request to `Forwarded.html`.

We can only forward to a resource if content is not committed to the response output stream from the current JSP page. If content is already committed, an `IllegalStateException` will be thrown. To avoid this we can set a high buffer size for the forwarding JSP page.

The jsp:param Action

The JSP `param` action can be used in conjunction with the `include` and `forward` actions to pass additional request parameters to the included or forwarded resource. The `param` tag needs to be embedded in the body of the `include` or `forward` tag.

The following code shows how we can use the `param` action:

```
<jsp:forward page="Param2.jsp">
    <jsp:param name="name" value="Meeraj"/>
</jsp:forward>
```

In addition to the request parameters already available, the forwarded resource will have an extra request parameter named `name`, with a value of `Meeraj`.

A JSP Loan Calculator

We'll develop a simple JSP-based loan calculator that will use most of the concepts we have covered so far. The loan calculator will provide a simple interface in which we can enter an amount, an interest rate, a loan period, and the type of interest (simple or compound). The application will then calculate and display the total amount to be paid back over the loan period.

All the JSP pages will share a common header and footer. The header will display a welcome message and the footer will display the current time. To illustrate the use of the `include` action and directive we'll store the contents of the header and footer in two files. We'll include the header using the `include` directive and the footer using the `include` action.

The request is sent to a JSP page when the form is submitted. Depending on the type of the interest selected by the user this JSP page will use the `forward` action to forward the request to JSP pages that are responsible for handling the request appropriately. We will create separate JSP pages to calculate the loan amount for simple and compound interest rates.

The two JSP pages used for calculating interest will use a combination of scriptlets, expressions, and declarations to calculate and display the interest. They will also use the `errorPage` attribute of the `page` directive to handle errors if invalid data is supplied.

Implementing the Loan Calculator

`header.html` is shared by all pages. The JSP pages use the `include` directive to include the contents of this file:

```
<h1>Loan Calculator</h1>
```

`footer.jsp` is also shared by all pages. The JSP pages use the `include` action to include the response of the resource, which is the current date:

```
<%= new java.util.Date() %>
```

`index.jsp` displays the form for entering the information:

```
<html>
  <head>
    <title>Include</title>
  </head>
  <body style="font-family:verdana;font-size:10pt;">
```

We include the header file using the `include` directive:

```
<%@ include file="header.html" %>
```

The we display the form for entering the information. The request is sent to `controller.jsp` when the form is submitted:

```
<form action="controller.jsp">
  <table border="0" style="font-family:verdana;font-size:10pt;">
    <tr>
      <td>Amount:</td>
      <td><input type="text" name="amount" /></td>
    </tr>
    <tr>
      <td>Interest in %:</td>
      <td><input type="text" name="interest"/></td>
    </tr>
    <tr>
      <td>Compound:</td>
      <td><input type="radio" name="type" value="C" checked/></td>
    </tr>
    <tr>
      <td>Simple:</td>
      <td><input type="radio" name="type" value="S" /></td>
    </tr>
    <tr>
      <td>Period:</td>
      <td><input type="text" name="period"/></td>
    </tr>
  </table>
  <input type="submit" value="Calculate"/>
</form>
```

We include the footer using the `include` action:

```
   <jsp:include page="footer.jsp"/>
  </body>
</html>
```

`controller.jsp` processes the request when the form is submitted from `index.jsp`:

```
<%
  String type = request.getParameter("type");
  if(type.equals("S")) {
%>
```

We forward the request to `simple.jsp` if the value of the `type` request parameter is `S`:

```
<jsp:forward page="/simple.jsp"/>
<%
  } else {
%>
```

We forward the request to `compound.jsp` if the value of the `type` request parameter is not `S`:

```
<jsp:forward page="/compound.jsp"/>
<%
  }
%>
```

`compound.jsp` uses scriptlets, declarations, and expressions to calculate and display the principal using compound interest. If any of the values entered by the user are less than zero an exception is thrown, and the request is forwarded to an error page defined using the `page` directive:

```
<%@ page errorPage="error.jsp" %>
```

We use the JSP declaration element to define a function for calculating compound interest:

```
<%!
  public double calculate(double amount, double interest, int period) {
```

Throw an exception if a negative value is entered for the amount:

```
  if(amount <= 0) {
    throw new IllegalArgumentException(
                       "Amount should be greater than 0: " + amount);
  }
```

Throw an exception if a negative value is entered for the interest rate:

```
if(interest <= 0) {
  throw new IllegalArgumentException(
                      "Interest should be greater than 0: " + interest);
}
```

Throw an exception if a negative value is entered for the loan period:

```
if(period <= 0) {
  throw new IllegalArgumentException(
                      "Period should be greater than 0: " + period);
}
```

Return the principal using compound interest:

```
    return amount*Math.pow(1 + interest/100, period);
  }
%>
```

Next, include the header file:

```
<html>
  <head>
    <title>Include</title>
  </head>
  <body style="font-family:verdana;font-size:10pt;">
    <%@ include file="header.html" %>
```

Use JSP scriptlets to extract the request parameters:

```
<%
  double amount = Double.parseDouble(request.getParameter("amount"));
  double interest = Double.parseDouble(
                        request.getParameter("interest"));
  int period = Integer.parseInt(request.getParameter("period"));
%>
<b>Pincipal using compound interest:</b>
```

Use a JSP expression to display the principal:

```
<%= calculate(amount, interest, period) %>
<br/><br/>
```

Finally, include the footer:

```
<jsp:include page="footer.jsp"/>
  </body>
</html>
```

`simple.jsp` uses scriptlets, declarations, and expressions to calculate and display the principal using simple interest. Again, if any of the values entered by the user are less than zero an exception is thrown and the request is forwarded to an error JSP defined using the `page` directive:

```
<%@ page errorPage="error.jsp" %>
<%!
  public double calculate(double amount, double interest, int period) {
    if(amount <= 0) {
      throw new IllegalArgumentException(
                          "Amount should be greater than 0: " + amount);
    }
    if(interest <= 0) {
      throw new IllegalArgumentException(
                          "Interest should be greater than 0: " + interest);
    }
    if(period <= 0) {
      throw new IllegalArgumentException(
                          "Period should be greater than 0: " + period);
    }
    return amount*(1 + period*interest/100);
  }
%>
<html>
  <head>
    <title>Compound</title>
  </head>
  <body style="font-family:verdana;font-size:10pt;">
    <%@ include file="header.html" %>
    <%
      double amount = Double.parseDouble(request.getParameter("amount"));
      double interest = Double.parseDouble(
                                request.getParameter("interest"));
      int period = Integer.parseInt(request.getParameter("period"));
    %>
    <b>Pincipal using simple interest:</b>
    <%= calculate(amount, interest, period) %>
    <br/><br/>
    <jsp:include page="footer.jsp"/>
  </body>
</html>
```

`error.jsp` displays the error message, if an exception is thrown from the JSP pages that calculate the interest. First we define the JSP as an error page using the `isErrorPage` attribute of the `page` directive:

```
<%@ page isErrorPage="true" %>
<html>
  <head>
    <title>Simple</title>
  </head>
  <body style="font-family:verdana;font-size:10pt;">
    <%@ include file="header.html" %>
```

We use the `exception` implicit object to display the error message:

```
<p style="color=#FF0000"><b><%= exception.getMessage() %></b></p>
```

Include the footer:

```
    <jsp:include page="footer.jsp"/>
  </body>
</html>
```

Using the Loan Calculator

You should have the following web application set up:

```
%CATALINA_HOME%/
                webapps/
                        jsp/
                            compound.jsp
                            controller.jsp
                            error.jsp
                            footer.jsp
                            header.html
                            index.jsp
                            simple.jsp
                        WEB-INF/
                                classes/
```

Deploy the web application and restart Tomcat. Then navigate to http://localhost:8080/jsp/index.jsp:

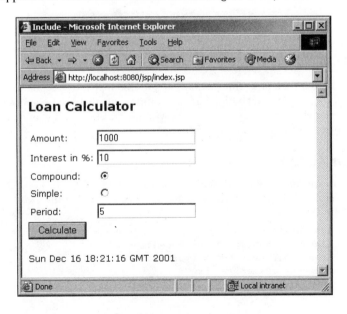

Enter some valid values in the form and click Calculate. If you select Compound the compound.jsp JSP page will be used to calculate the principal:

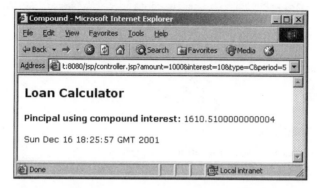

If instead we enter a value less than zero for the amount, we will see the error JSP page that we defined:

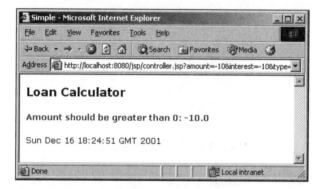

Using JavaBeans with JSP Pages

The JSP specification defines a powerful standard action that helps to separate presentation and content by allowing page authors to interact with JavaBean components that are stored as page, request, session, and application attributes. The useBean tag along with the getProperty and setProperty tags allows JSP pages to interact with JavaBean components.

The jsp:useBean Action

The useBean action creates or finds a Java object in a specified scope. The object is also made available in the current JSP page as a scripting variable. The syntax for the useBean action is:

```
<jsp:useBean id="name" scope="page | request | session | application"
             class="className" type="typeName" |
             bean="beanName" type="typeName" |
             type="typeName" />
```

At least one of the type and class attributes must be present, and we can't specify values for both the class and bean name. The useBean JSP tag works according to the following sequence:

❑ First, the container tries to find an object by the specified name in the specified scope.

❑ If an object is found, a scripting variable is introduced with the name specified by the id attribute and type specified by the type attribute. If the type attribute is not specified the value of the class attribute is used. The variable's value is initialized to the reference to the object that is found. The body of the tag is then ignored.

❑ If the object is not found and both class and beanName are not present, an InstantiationException is thrown.

❑ If the class defines a non-abstract class with public no-argument constructor an object of that class is instantiated and stored in the specified scope using the specified ID. A scripting variable is introduced with the name specified by the id attribute and type specified by the class attribute. If the value of the class attribute specifies an interface, a non-public class or a class without a public no-argument constructor, an InstantiationException is thrown. The body of the useBean tag is then executed.

❑ If the beanName attribute is used then the java.beans.Bean.instantiate() method is called, passing the value of the attribute beanName. A scripting variable is introduced with the name specified by the id attribute and type specified by the type attribute. The body useBean of the tag is then executed.

The body of the useBean tag is normally used for initializing the Java object that has just been created. For example:

```
<jsp:useBean id="myName" class="java.lang.String" scope="request">
  <% myName = "Meeraj"; %>
</jsp:useBean>
```

This creates a new string and stores it as a request attribute with the name myName. A scripting variable is also made available in the request scope via the same name and is initialized to the value Meeraj.

The jsp:getProperty Action

The getProperty action can be used in conjunction with the useBean action to get the value of the properties of the bean defined by the useBean action. For example:

```
<jsp:getProperty name="myBean" property="firstName"/>
```

The name attribute refers to the id attribute specified in the useBean action. The property attribute refers to the name of the bean property. In this case the bean class should have a method called getFirstName() that returns a Java primitive or object.

The jsp:setProperty Action

The setProperty action can be used in conjunction with the useBean action to set the properties of a bean. We can even get the container to populate the bean properties from the request parameters without specifying the property names. In such cases the container will match the bean property names with the request parameter names. The syntax for the setProperty action is shown overleaf:

```
<jsp:setProperty name="beanName"
                 property="*"  |
                 property="propertyName" |
                 property="propertyName" param="paramName" |
                 property="propertyName" value="value" />
```

To set the value of the name property of myBean to Meeraj we would use:

```
<jsp:setProperty name="myBean" property="name" value="Meeraj"/>
```

To set the value of the name1 property of myBean to the value of the request parameter name2 we would use:

```
<jsp:setProperty name="myBean" property="name1" param="name2"/>
```

To set the value of the name property of myBean to the value of the request parameter by the same name we would use:

```
<jsp:setProperty name="myBean" property="name1"/>
```

Finally, to set all the properties of myBean with matching request parameters from the request parameter values we would use:

```
<jsp:setProperty name="myBean" property="*"/>
```

The jsp:plugin Action

The plugin action enables the JSP container to render appropriate HTML to initiate the download of the Java plugin and the execution of the specified applet or bean, depending on the browser type. The plugin standard action allows us to embed applets and beans in a browser-neutral manner as the container takes care of the user agent-specific issues. For example:

```
<jsp:plugin type="applet" code="MyApplet.class" codebase="/">
   <jsp:params>
      <jsp:param name="myParam" value="123"/>
   </jsp:params>
   <jsp:fallback><b>Unable to load applet</b></jsp:fallback>
</jsp:plugin>
```

The params and param tags are used to define applet parameters. The fallback tag can be used to define any HTML markup that needs to be rendered upon failure to start the plugin.

Tag Libraries

Tag libraries are used to define custom actions on top of the standard actions defined by the JSP specification. Custom actions allow us to insert our own tags inside the JSP pages to instigate custom processing on the server when the page is served. Custom actions are defined in a tag library descriptor.

These custom tags can be used in JSP pages by importing them using the `taglib` directive. Custom action names are associated with tag handler classes in the tag library descriptor. These classes provide standard callbacks to the container by implementing one of the following interfaces:

- `javax.servlet.jsp.tagext.Tag`
- `javax.servlet.jsp.tagext.IterationTag`
- `javax.servlet.jsp.tagext.BodyTag`

These interfaces define various methods that are called by the container on the tag handler instance when the tag is parsed. These methods represent various events like the start of the tag, start of the body, and end of the tag. By returning various enumerated constants from these methods, tag class authors can get the container to perform the following tasks:

- Skip the body
- Evaluate the body again
- Skip or evaluate the rest of the page

Using Servlets and JSP Together

In this section we'll build an application that demonstrates servlets and JSP pages working in tandem. The application is a simple database application that maintains the items stored in an inventory database. The functionality provided by the application to the end user is illustrated in the following use case diagram:

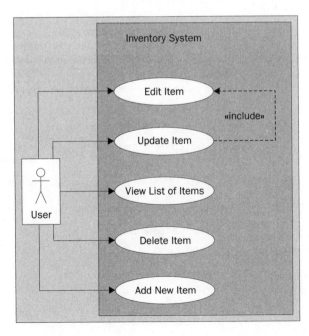

Creating the Database

The database uses a single `item` table. The database I used for this example was MySQL. However, the example can be easily altered to use any JDBC-compliant database. Create a database called `inventory` and a table called `item` (along with some sample data) using the following SQL script:

```
CREATE DATABASE inventory;
USE inventory;

CREATE TABLE item (
   id INTEGER NOT NULL PRIMARY KEY AUTO_INCREMENT,
   name VARCHAR(30) NOT NULL,
   description VARCHAR(30) NOT NULL,
   price DOUBLE NOT NULL,
   stock INTEGER NOT NULL);

INSERT INTO item (name, description, price, stock)
   VALUES ('Straw Hat', 'The best in town', 78.99, 9012);
INSERT INTO item (name, description, price, stock)
   VALUES ('Polo Shirt', 'The latest fashion', 49.99, 99);
```

System Architecture

For the purposes of this example, we won't be delving into the details of J2EE web application architecture and design patterns; such discussions are reserved for Chapter 12. It's sufficient to say that we will be using servlets as **request processing components** and JSP pages as **presentation components** (this is a flavor of the very popular Model 2 architecture).

All the use cases that involve data access will be sent to specific servlets. These servlets will look up a data source, the database connections will then be used to perform the various database operations, and then the request will be forwarded to the JSP page that renders the next view using the request dispatcher. If the JSP page requires data from the database, the servlet will store the data as a request attribute that can be retrieved by the JSP using the `useBean` action. All this is illustrated in the following diagram:

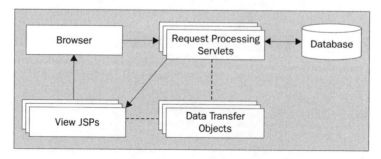

Choosing a Data Transfer Object

Traditionally, custom Java classes that comply with the JavaBeans design pattern have been used to transfer data from the request processing tier to the presentation tier. These objects are populated by request delegate classes from SQL result sets and are stored as request attributes. These components are later extracted and rendered by the view JSP pages. In the View Dispatcher pattern the actual data retrieval is performed at the time of processing the view JSP pages.

However, in this case, the tabular data stream present in the SQL result set is transformed into a hierarchy of objects. The rendering JSP pages will then use custom tags or scriptlets to transform the data into an HTML table. This means that we are performing redundant data transformation and, depending on the size of the system, we may end up with a plethora of custom JavaBean components.

Ideally the JSP pages should loop through the result set and render the data. However, this is not good practice because iterating through the result set requires the underlying database connection to be open as we would be accessing the database resources directly. This has got lots of implications for performance, scalability, error handling, extensibility, and resource cleanup. The `javax.sql.RowSet` interface from the JDBC optional extensions comes to our rescue. This interface adds support to the JDBC API for the JavaBeans component model.

Sun provides an implementation of this interface called `CachedRowSet` that can function in a disconnected mode from the connection that is used to populate it. The interface provides methods for setting the JNDI name of the data source used to acquire connections, and for setting the SQL command string. When the `execute()` method on the interface is called, it uses the specified connection and SQL command to populate the internal data structure with the resulting data. The `CachedRowSet` implementation closes the connection after retrieving the data. This can then be used in the JSP pages in the same way as the result set for iterating through and retrieving the data.

Accordingly, we will use `CachedRowSet` in our example.

Listing Items

The following occurs when we want to list the items:

1. The browser sends the request to an instance of `ListServlet`

2. The servlet executes the SQL and populates the resulting row set as a request attribute

3. The request is forwarded to `List.jsp`

4. The JSP iterates through the row set and renders the data

The following servlet processes the request to list the items:

```
package jsp;

import javax.servlet.*;
import javax.servlet.http.*;
import javax.sql.*;
import sun.jdbc.rowset.CachedRowSet;
```

```
public class ListServlet extends HttpServlet {

  public void init(ServletConfig config) throws ServletException {
    super.init(config);
  }

  public void doPost(HttpServletRequest req, HttpServletResponse res)
      throws ServletException {
    doGet(req, res);
  }

  public void doGet(HttpServletRequest req, HttpServletResponse res)
      throws ServletException {
    try {
```

Create a new cached row set:

```
RowSet rs = new CachedRowSet();
```

Set the JNDI name of the data source. Note that you need to configure this in your web container. Accomplishing this using Tomcat is explained in the section on deploying the application:

```
rs.setDataSourceName("java:comp/env/jdbc/inventoryDB");
```

Set the SQL command for getting the list of items:

```
rs.setCommand("SELECT * FROM item");
```

Execute the SQL, which will close the underlying connection:

```
rs.execute();
```

Store the row set as a request attribute:

```
req.setAttribute("rs", rs);
```

Forward the request to `List.jsp`:

```
getServletContext().getRequestDispatcher("/List.jsp").
    forward(req, res);
  } catch(Exception ex) {
    throw new ServletException(ex);
  }
 }
}
```

`List.jsp` renders the list of items as an HTML table and provides links for editing and deleting individual items and adding new items:

```
<%@page contentType="text/html"%>
```

Now we define the row set as a bean:

```
<jsp:useBean id="rs" scope="request" type="javax.sql.RowSet" />

<html>
  <head>
    <title>Inventory - List</title>
  </head>
  <body style="font-family:verdana;font-size:10pt;">
    <table cellpadding="5" style="font-family:verdana;font-size:10pt;">
      <tr>
        <th>Name</th>
        <th>Description</th>
        <th>Price</th>
        <th>Stock</th>
        <th></th>
        <th></th>
      </tr>
```

Next, we must iterate through the row set (we could write a custom tag to avoid the use of scriptlets):

```
<%
    while(rs.next()) {
%>
```

Render the various item attributes:

```
<tr>
  <td><%= rs.getString(2) %></td>
  <td><%= rs.getString(3) %></td>
  <td><%= rs.getString(4) %></td>
  <td><%= rs.getString(5) %></td>
  <td>
```

Render the link to delete an item:

```
    <a href="Delete?id=<%= rs.getString(1) %>">
      Delete
    </a>
  </td>
  <td>
```

Render the link to edit an item:

```
    <a href="Edit?id=<%= rs.getString(1) %>">
      Edit
    </a>
  </td>
</tr>
<%
  }
%>
</table>
```

Render the link to add a new item:

```
      <a href="New.html">New Item</a>
    </body>
  </html>
```

Deleting Items

The following occurs when we delete an item:

1. The browser sends the request to an instance of `DeleteServlet`

2. The servlet looks up the data source and gets the connection

3. The servlet then executes the SQL to delete the selected item

4. The request is then forwarded to the URI that is mapped to `ListServlet` to display a new list of items

The following servlet processes the deletion:

```
package jsp;

import javax.servlet.*;
import javax.servlet.http.*;
import javax.sql.DataSource;
import javax.naming.InitialContext;
import java.sql.*;

public class DeleteServlet extends HttpServlet {

  public void init(ServletConfig config) throws ServletException {
    super.init(config);
  }

  public void doPost(HttpServletRequest req, HttpServletResponse res)
      throws ServletException {
    doGet(req, res);
  }

  public void doGet(HttpServletRequest req, HttpServletResponse res)
      throws ServletException {

    Connection con = null;

    try {
```

Create the JNDI initial context:

```
        InitialContext ctx = new InitialContext();
```

Look up the data source:

```
DataSource ds =
            (DataSource) ctx.lookup("java:comp/env/jdbc/inventory");
```

Get a connection:

```
con = ds.getConnection();
```

Create the prepared statement to issue the delete SQL statement:

```
PreparedStatement stmt =
            con.prepareStatement("DELETE FROM item WHERE id = ?");
```

Set the selected item id as an SQL input parameter:

```
stmt.setInt(1, Integer.parseInt(req.getParameter("id")));
```

Execute the SQL:

```
stmt.executeUpdate();
stmt.close();
```

Forward the request to the URI that is mapped to ListServlet to display a new list of items:

```
        getServletContext().getRequestDispatcher("/List").
        forward(req, res);

    } catch(Exception ex) {
        throw new ServletException(ex);
    } finally {
      try {
        if(con != null) con.close();
      } catch(Exception ex) {
        throw new ServletException(ex);
      }
    }
  }
}
```

Editing Items

An item can be edited by clicking on the edit link against the item. The following occurs when an item is edited:

1. The browser sends the request an instance of `EditServlet`

2. The servlet executes the SQL to get the details of the selected item and populates the resulting row set as a request attribute

3. The request is then forwarded to `Edit.jsp`

4. The JSP page extracts the data and renders it as an HTML form

The following servlet processes the edit:

```
package jsp;

import javax.servlet.*;
import javax.servlet.http.*;
import javax.sql.*;
import sun.jdbc.rowset.CachedRowSet;

public class EditServlet extends HttpServlet {

  public void init(ServletConfig config) throws ServletException {
    super.init(config);
  }

  public void doPost(HttpServletRequest req, HttpServletResponse res)
      throws ServletException {
    doGet(req, res);
  }

  public void doGet(HttpServletRequest req, HttpServletResponse res)
      throws ServletException {

    try {
```

Create a cached row set:

```
        RowSet rs = new CachedRowSet();
```

Set the data source:

```
        rs.setDataSourceName("java:comp/env/jdbc/inventory");
```

Set the SQL command:

```
        rs.setCommand("SELECT * FROM item WHERE id = ?");
```

Set the selected item `id` as the SQL input parameter:

```
rs.setInt(1, Integer.parseInt(req.getParameter("id")));
```

Populate the row set and store it as a request attribute:

```
rs.execute();
req.setAttribute("rs", rs);
```

Forward the request to `Edit.jsp`:

```
getServletContext().getRequestDispatcher("/Edit.jsp").
forward(req, res);

    } catch(Exception ex) {
        throw new ServletException(ex);
    }
  }
}
```

`Edit.jsp` is used to edit an item:

```
<%@page contentType="text/html"%>
```

Define the row set as a bean:

```
<jsp:useBean id="rs" scope="request" type="javax.sql.RowSet" />

<html>
  <head>
    <title>Inventory - Edit</title>
  </head>
  <body style="font-family:verdana;font-size:10pt;">
```

Move the cursor to the first record in the row set:

```
<%
  if(rs.next()) {
%>
<form action="Update">
```

Render the ID as a hidden parameter:

```
<input name="id" type="hidden" value="<%= rs.getString(1) %>"/>
<table cellpadding="5" style="font-family:verdana;font-size:10pt;">
  <tr>
    <td><b>Name:</b></td>
    <td>
```

Render the name:

```
            <input name="name" type="text"
            value="<%= rs.getString(2) %>"/>
        </td>
      </tr>
      <tr>
       <td><b>Description:</b></td>
       <td>
```

Render the description:

```
            <input name="description" type="text"
            value="<%= rs.getString(3) %>"/>
        </td>
      </tr>
      <tr>
       <td><b>Price:</b></td>
       <td>
```

Render the price:

```
            <input name="price" type="text"
            value="<%= rs.getString(4) %>"/>
        </td>
      </tr>
      <tr>
       <td><b>Stock:</b></td>
       <td>
```

Render the number of items in the stock:

```
            <input name="stock" type="text"
            value="<%= rs.getString(5) %>"/>
        </td>
      </tr>
      <tr>
       <td></td>
       <td>
         <input type="submit" value="Update"/>
        </td>
      </tr>

    </table>
    <%
       }
    %>

  </body>
</html>
```

Updating Items

The following occurs when we update an item:

1. The browser sends the request an instance of UpdateServlet.

2. The servlet looks up the data source and gets the connection.

3. The servlet executes the SQL to update the selected item. (The modified details of the items are extracted from the request parameter list.)

4. The request is then forwarded to the URI that is mapped to ListServlet to display a new list of items.

The following servlet is used to update items:

```java
package jsp;

import javax.servlet.*;
import javax.servlet.http.*;
import javax.sql.DataSource;
import javax.naming.InitialContext;
import java.sql.*;

public class UpdateServlet extends HttpServlet {

  public void init(ServletConfig config) throws ServletException {
      super.init(config);
  }

  public void doPost(HttpServletRequest req, HttpServletResponse res)
      throws ServletException {
    doGet(req, res);
  }

  public void doGet(HttpServletRequest req, HttpServletResponse res)
      throws ServletException {

    Connection con = null;

    try {
```

Look up the data source and get the connection:

```java
      InitialContext ctx = new InitialContext();
      DataSource ds =
      (DataSource)ctx.lookup("java:comp/env/jdbc/inventoryDB");

      con = ds.getConnection();
```

Create the prepared statement for updating the item:

```
PreparedStatement stmt = con.prepareStatement("UPDATE item " +
                                              "SET name = ?, " +
                                              "description = ?, " +
                                              "price = ?, " +
                                              "stock = ? " +
                                              "WHERE id = ?");
```

Set the modified item details as SQL in parameters:

```
stmt.setString(1, req.getParameter("name"));
stmt.setString(2, req.getParameter("description"));
stmt.setDouble(3, Double.parseDouble(req.getParameter("price")));
stmt.setInt(4, Integer.parseInt(req.getParameter("stock")));
stmt.setInt(5, Integer.parseInt(req.getParameter("id")));
```

Issue the update:

```
stmt.executeUpdate();
stmt.close();
```

Forward the request to the URI that is mapped to `ListServlet` to display a new list of items:

```
      getServletContext().getRequestDispatcher("/List").
      forward(req, res);

    } catch(Exception ex) {
      throw new ServletException(ex);
    } finally {
      try {
        if(con != null) {
          con.close();
        }
      } catch(Exception ex) {
        throw new ServletException(ex);
      }
    }
  }
}
```

Adding New Items

Adding new items involves two separate tasks:

❑   Clicking on the link to add a new item in the screen that displays the list of items. This will send the request to the HTML page `New.html`, which will display a form for adding the new item.

❑   Updating this form will create a new item record in the database with the details entered by the user.

We use the following page to enter the information for a new item:

```html
<html>
  <head>
    <title>Inventory - Add New Item</title>
  </head>
  <body style="font-family:verdana;font-size:10pt;">

    <form action="Create">
      <table cellpadding="5" style="font-family:verdana;font-size:10pt;">
        <tr>
          <td><b>Name:</b></td>
```

Input field for entering the name:

```html
        <td><input name="name" type="text"/></td>
      </tr>
      <tr>
        <td><b>Description:</b></td>
```

Input field for entering the description:

```html
        <td><input name="description" type="text"/></td>
      </tr>
      <tr>
        <td><b>Price:</b></td>
```

Input field for entering the price:

```html
        <td><input name="price" type="text"/></td>
      </tr>
      <tr>
        <td><b>Stock:</b></td>
```

Input field for entering the stock:

```html
        <td><input name="stock" type="text"/></td>
      </tr>
      <tr>
        <td></td>
        <td><input type="submit" value="Create"/></td>
      </tr>
    </table>
  </body>
</html>
```

The sequence of events in submitting the above form is:

1. The browser sends the request an instance of `CreateServlet`.

2. The servlet looks up the data source and gets the connection.

3. Then it executes the SQL to create the new item. (The details of the new item are extracted from the request parameter list.)

4. The request is then forwarded to the URI that is mapped to `ListServlet` to display a new list of items.

The following servlet is used to create a new item:

```java
package jsp;

import javax.servlet.*;
import javax.servlet.http.*;
import javax.sql.DataSource;
import javax.naming.InitialContext;
import java.sql.*;

public class CreateServlet extends HttpServlet {

  public void init(ServletConfig config) throws ServletException {
    super.init(config);
  }

  public void doPost(HttpServletRequest req, HttpServletResponse res)
      throws ServletException {
    doGet(req, res);
  }

  public void doGet(HttpServletRequest req, HttpServletResponse res)
      throws ServletException {

    Connection con = null;

    try {
```

Look up the data source and get the connection:

```java
        InitialContext ctx = new InitialContext();
        DataSource ds =
        (DataSource)ctx.lookup("java:comp/env/jdbc/inventoryDB");

        con = ds.getConnection();
```

Create the prepared statement by specifying the insert SQL statement:

```
PreparedStatement stmt = con.prepareStatement(
                            "INSERT INTO item " +
                            "(name, description, price," +
                            " stock) VALUES (?, ?, ?, ?)");
```

Set the details of the new items as SQL in parameters:

```
stmt.setString(1, req.getParameter("name"));
stmt.setString(2, req.getParameter("description"));
stmt.setDouble(3, Double.parseDouble(req.getParameter("price")));
stmt.setInt(4, Integer.parseInt(req.getParameter("stock")));
```

Execute the insert SQL:

```
stmt.executeUpdate();
stmt.close();
```

Forward the request to the URI that is mapped to `ListServlet` for displaying the new list of items:

```
getServletContext().getRequestDispatcher("/List").
forward(req, res);

} catch(Exception ex) {
throw new ServletException(ex);
} finally {
try {
   if(con != null) con.close();
} catch(Exception ex) {
   throw new ServletException(ex);
}
}
}
}
```

Deploying and Running the Application

This is the deployment descriptor for the application. It defines the servlets and URI mappings:

```
<?xml version="1.0" encoding="ISO-8859-1"?>

<!DOCTYPE web-app
  PUBLIC "-//Sun Microsystems, Inc.//DTD Web Application 2.3//EN"
         "http://java.sun.com/dtd/web-app_2_3.dtd">

<web-app>

 <servlet>
  <servlet-name>List</servlet-name>
  <servlet-class>jsp.ListServlet</servlet-class>
 </servlet>
```

```
<servlet>
 <servlet-name>Edit</servlet-name>
 <servlet-class>jsp.EditServlet</servlet-class>
</servlet>

<servlet>
 <servlet-name>Delete</servlet-name>
 <servlet-class>jsp.DeleteServlet</servlet-class>
</servlet>

<servlet>
 <servlet-name>Update</servlet-name>
 <servlet-class>jsp.UpdateServlet</servlet-class>
</servlet>

<servlet>
 <servlet-name>Create</servlet-name>
 <servlet-class>jsp.CreateServlet</servlet-class>
</servlet>

<servlet-mapping>
 <servlet-name>List</servlet-name>
 <url-pattern>/List</url-pattern>
</servlet-mapping>

<servlet-mapping>
 <servlet-name>Edit</servlet-name>
 <url-pattern>/Edit</url-pattern>
</servlet-mapping>

<servlet-mapping>
 <servlet-name>Delete</servlet-name>
 <url-pattern>/Delete</url-pattern>
</servlet-mapping>

<servlet-mapping>
 <servlet-name>Update</servlet-name>
 <url-pattern>/Update</url-pattern>
</servlet-mapping>

<servlet-mapping>
 <servlet-name>Create</servlet-name>
 <url-pattern>/Create</url-pattern>
</servlet-mapping>

</web-app>
```

To deploy and run the application, perform the following steps:

1. Start your database (I used MySQL).

2. Create the `inventory` database using the supplied SQL script.

3. Download the row set implementation from
http://developer.java.sun.com/developer/earlyAccess/crs/.

4. Compile the servlet classes. Remember to include the JDBC extension API (`jdbc2_0-ext.jar`) and the row set implementation (`rowset.jar`) in your classpath.

5. Create the following web application:

```
webapps/
        inventory/
                     Edit.jsp
                     List.jsp
                     New.html
                     WEB-INF/
                                  web.xml
                                  classes/
                                          jsp/
                                              ListServlet.class
                                              EditServlet.class
                                              DeleteServlet.class
                                              CreateServlet.class
                                              UpdateServlet.class
                                  /lib/
                                         rowset.jar
```

6. Make sure that you have the MM.MySQL driver in your classpath.

7. Add the following context to the Tomcat configuration file:

```xml
<Context path="/inventory" docBase="inventory">

  <Resource name="jdbc/inventoryDB" auth="Container"
    type="javax.sql.DataSource"/>
  <ResourceParams name="jdbc/inventoryDB">
    <parameter>
      <name>driverClassName</name>
      <value>org.gjt.mm.mysql.Driver</value>
    </parameter>
    <parameter>
      <name>driverName</name>
      <value>jdbc:mysql://localhost:3306/inventory</value>
    </parameter>
  </ResourceParams>

</Context>
```

Now we can start Tomcat and run the application. Navigate to http://localhost:8080/inventory/List:

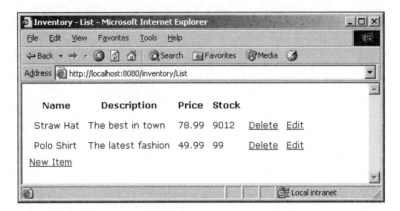

Then if we click on New Item we can add an item to the inventory:

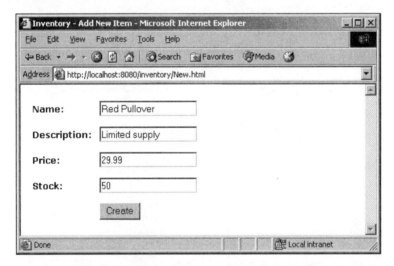

Then we can delete our supply of polo shirts by clicking the Delete link next to the item:

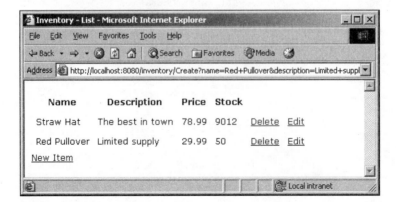

Summary

In this chapter we had a brief introduction and overview of JSP pages. We looked at the main features of JSP, including:

- ❑ The advantages of using JSP pages over servlets for presentation
- ❑ How JSP pages can be used to write both dynamic and static data back to the browser
- ❑ The use of JSP scriptlets and declarations for performing computations within JSP pages
- ❑ The use of JSP directives to convey messages to the JSP container, to assist it in the process of generating the page implementation servlet
- ❑ JSP actions such as `include`, `forward`, and `param`
- ❑ The use of JavaBeans with JSP pages

We concluded the chapter with an application that showed how JSP pages and servlets can be used together, each performing the roles they are best suited to.

We've taken a *very* quick look at JSP in this chapter. You can find out more about what JSP has to offer, and how it can be used in your web applications in *Professional JSP 2nd Edition* (ISBN: 1-861004-95-8) published by Wrox Press.

In the next chapter we'll turn our attention to studying the issues surrounding the security of our servlets as well as container authentication.

Security and Container Authentication

The execution of third-party servlets is increasingly common. Consider an Application Service Provider (ASP) that hosts many web applications on virtual hosts supported by a single servlet container instance. It is vital that the actions of one web application doesn't bring down the entire server. The ability to restrict certain actions is vital to the well-being of a server and the web applications running on it.

The Servlet 2.3 specification is very particular as to which type of security support compliant containers should provide. In this chapter, we'll examine the various components of servlet security, including:

❑   How we can use server-side policy files

❑   How we can configure Tomcat to use Secure Socket Layer (SSL)

❑   How SSL relates to public key encryption, digital signature, and transitive trust

❑   Tomcat 4 Realms, which provide a platform-independent way of performing authentication and role mapping

❑   Container-managed security

❑   BASIC, FORM-based, DIGEST, and CLIENT-CERT authentication

❑   Tomcat's single sign-on mechanism that eliminates multiple authentication requests

The Java 2 Security Model on the Server

The Java 2 security model provides a fine-grained, policy-based mechanism with which we can control programmatic access to system resources. The level of protection is set by modifying a **policy file** for individual Java Virtual Machines (JVMs).

> **Once security is enabled, resources cannot be accessed unless access is explicitly granted in a policy file.**

Policy files can be used to:

❑ Only allow connections to the host from which the code was originally loaded

❑ Prevent access to the local file system

❑ Prevent access to JVM and OS properties

A policy file contains **grant statements**, which grant permission for a specific type of access by a specific principal:

❑ A **security principal** is associated with a body of code

❑ A **permission** encapsulates the action of accessing a protected system resource

The following table describes some of the most frequently used permissions in typical policy files.

Permission	Description
`java.lang.RuntimePermission`	Controls the runtime execution of vital system calls, such as `exitVM()`, `setSecurityManager()`, and `createClassLoader()`
`java.util.PropertyPermission`	Controls access (both read and write) to system properties
`java.io.FilePermission`	Controls access (read, write, delete, and execution) to files and directories
`java.net.SocketPermission`	Controls access (connect, listen, accept, and resolve) to network sockets
`java.security.AllPermission`	Enables access to *all* protected resources

You can find a complete list of security permissions in the online documentation at http://java.sun.com/security/.

Server-side Policy Files

When we start Tomcat using the default `startup` script, it is started without security enabled, which is equivalent to a grant of `java.security.AllPermission`. Tomcat comes with a default policy file that is used when we start Tomcat with security enabled. This policy file is named `catalina.policy` and is stored in the `%CATALINA_HOME%\conf` directory.

Let's examine some interesting parts of this policy file, starting with the system code permissions:

```
grant codeBase "file:${java.home}/lib/-" {
        permission java.security.AllPermission;
};
```

The Java compiler needs to be called from within Catalina (the servlet container used by Tomcat) and this policy will enable it to access everything (as we trust the Java compiler to consist of benevolent code). The same permission is granted to system extensions:

```
grant codeBase "file:${java.home}/jre/lib/ext/-" {
        permission java.security.AllPermission;
};
```

Although the Catalina server code is not system library it is granted all permissions to facilitate its operation:

```
grant codeBase "file:${catalina.home}/bin/bootstrap.jar" {
        permission java.security.AllPermission;
};
```

The code in the `common` library will also be granted all permissions, which means that we should be careful about what we place into this directory:

```
grant codeBase "file:${catalina.home}/common/-" {
        permission java.security.AllPermission;
};
```

The policy file goes on to grant permissions to the container's core code, the JSP page compiler, the shared web application libraries, and the shared web application classes.

Using Server-Side Policy Files

We're now ready to try out a malicious servlet to see how a server-side policy file can protect us from its mischief. Consider the following servlet:

```
import javax.servlet.*;
import javax.servlet.http.*;

public class MaliciousServlet extends HttpServlet {
```

```
    public void doGet(HttpServletRequest request,
                      HttpServletResponse response)
       throws IOException, ServletException {
     System.exit(1);
   }
 }
```

The `System.exit(1)` system call is designed to stop the execution of the JVM that is hosting the servlet container. This represents the type of mistake that could be made by an inexperienced developer working on a shared servlet hosting environment.

Start Tomcat *without* security enabled and access our servlet by navigating to
http://localhost:8080/policytest/servlet/MaliciousServlet. Tomcat will shutdown because with security not enabled, any servlet can shut down the JVM that Tomcat is running on.

Next, we'll start Tomcat *with* security enabled, which by default will grant the permissions specified in `catalina.policy`. This policy file does not grant `java.lang.RuntimePermission` for `exitVM()` to any web application, which means that web applications will not be able to successfully call the `exit()` method.

Use the following command to start Tomcat in security enabled mode:

```
catalina start -security
```

Now, when we navigate to http://localhost:8080/policytest/servlet/MaliciousServlet we'll see something like:

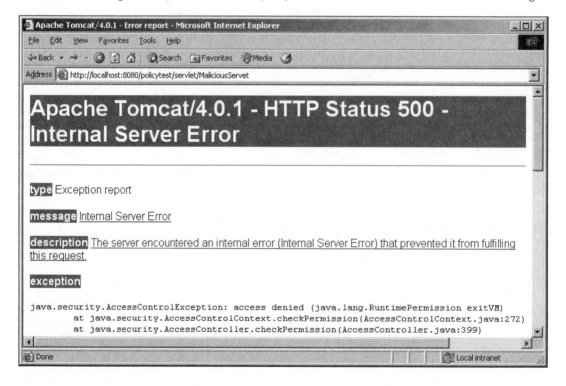

The servlet has committed an access violation, but in this case the server is spared a complete crash.

Let's create another servlet that accesses a known URL, and passes its content to the client. This means that it will require permission to access a specific host and socket:

```
import java.net.*;
import java.io.*;
import javax.servlet.*;
import javax.servlet.http.*;

public class NetAccessServlet extends HttpServlet {

    public void doGet(HttpServletRequest request,
                      HttpServletResponse response)
        throws IOException, ServletException {
      PrintWriter out = response.getWriter();
      String tpString = null;
```

The servlet creates a connection to http://localhost:8080/ and then creates a `BufferedReader` from the content of the URL connection. Once the connection is opened, it simply sends everything to the servlet's response:

```
      try {
        URL myConn = new URL("http://localhost:8080/");
        BufferedReader myReader =
          new BufferedReader((new InputStreamReader(myConn.openStream())));
        while ((tpString = myReader.readLine()) != null) {
          out.println(tpString);
        }
      } catch (Exception ex) {
        ex.printStackTrace(out);
      }
    }
}
```

Start Tomcat *without* security and navigate to http://localhost:8080/policytest/servlet/NetAccessServlet. You should be redirected to the Tomcat home page, (although without the images as they are located at a different URL).

Shut down Tomcat, restart it *with* security, and navigate again to http://localhost:8080/policytest/servlet/NetAccessServlet. Once more, we will see an access exception, which means that by default, servlets are not allowed to directly access any network resource. In order to enable the specific network access required by our `NetAccessServlet`, we must add the following entry into `catalina.policy`:

```
grant codeBase "file:${catalina.home}/webapps/policytest/WEB-
INF/classes/NetAccessServlet.class" {
  permission java.net.SocketPermission "localhost:8080", "connect";
};
```

This entry grants `NetAccessServlet` (but no other class) the privilege of connecting to `localhost` at port `8080`. Make the addition to `catalina.policy`, restart Tomcat 4 with security, and navigate to http://localhost:8080/policytest/servlet/passthru. This time, you will see Tomcat's home page.

Secure Socket Layer

Commercial web sites make extensive use of **Secure Socket Layer (SSL)**, which has emerged as the standard security mechanism on the Web. It provides a secure connection between the client and the server.

> *SSL is an international standard, in the form of an IETF RFC called Transport Layer Security (TLS) 1.0 – accessible at http://www.ietf.org/rfc/rfc2246.txt.*

You're probably familiar with the way SSL works on your browser – look for the "secure indicator" (typically a small padlock) when you visit a secure site. Once we have made a successful SSL connection we can be sure that:

❑ We have reached a legitimate web site

❑ The data sent between our browser and the server will be encrypted

The SSL Operation Model

In order to understand how to configure SSL for servlet containers we need to understand how SSL works, and how it relates to public key encryption. An SSL connection provides three guarantees:

❑ The authenticity of the server

❑ The privacy of data transferred via encryption

❑ The integrity of the data when it is transferred (the data must not be modified during transfer between client and server)

The third guarantee provides protection against a "man-in-the-middle" security attack, in which the message is intercepted between the client and the server. SSL provides this authentication, privacy, and integrity using a combination of **public key encryption** and **shared secret encryption**.

Data Encryption Fundamentals

Encryption is the act of transforming a message (via some mathematical algorithm) into an unintelligible form. Typically the encryption transformation is performed using a sequence of numeric values or a **key**, which is also used in the decryption process. Possession of the key enables the recipient to decode the message. This sort of encryption is frequently referred to as **shared secret encryption** as each party shares a common key.

SSL uses this simple form of encryption to encode the stream of data between the client and the server. Anyone who learns the shared key will be able to access the transmitted data, but both the client and the server need to know the key. Consequently, SSL depends on a considerably stronger form of encryption during its handshaking phase (prior to the creation of the shared secret session), in order to establish a secured session between a client and a server – **public key encryption**.

Public Key Encryption

Unlike shared secret encryption, public key encryption uses two keys that differ in value. The keys are generated using a mathematical algorithm in which anything encrypted with one of the keys can only be decrypted with the other. Such keys are known as **asymmetric keys**. What makes public key encryption so strong is that having one of the keys in the key pair will not allow you to work out the other (at least not without trying different sequences for a very long time).

Having generated two keys with such a special property, we can then designate one of them as a **public key**, and the other one as a **private key**. The private key is *never* shared with anyone else. Compromising the private key will leave your data unsecured. The public key on the other hand, can be widely circulated, so that any client who wishes to communicate with the server can use it.

During an encrypted communications session between the server and the client:

❑ The server can encrypt all the data going to the client using its private key

❑ The client can then use the public key to decrypt the data

Going the other way:

❑ The client can use the server's public key to encrypt the data

❑ The server can use its private key to decrypt it

Since the public key is the only key in the world that can decrypt data encrypted by the server's private key the client can be assured that it is indeed talking to the server (as only the server possesses the private key).

This all sounds elegant and straightforward, but unfortunately there is a problem. Public key encryption requires tremendous processing power to encrypt and decrypt the data. For this reason SSL uses the faster and simpler shared secret encryption for encrypting its data stream. Public key encryption is used only to exchange the key that is to be used for shared secret encryption.

Phases of SSL Communication

SSL utilizes public key encryption during its handshaking process (when a client wants to establish a secured session with a server). After that, SSL enters into a communication session in which shared secret encryption is used to encrypt the data.

The following occurs during the SSL handshaking phase:

❑ The server is authenticated

❑ The client and server agree on a set of encryption algorithms to use

❑ Optionally, the client can also be authenticated (although this is not done in the usual client to web server connection)

❑ The client and server negotiate a shared secret key, which is used to encrypt the data during the second communications phase of the protocol

> **The key negotiated between the client and the server is only valid for a single session.**

In the next few sections we'll take a closer look at how the first step of the handshaking phase – server authentication – is accomplished in SSL.

Digital Signatures, Certificates, and Trust

Public key encryption requires the wide distribution of the public key. This is more difficult than it first appears. Imagine the hundreds of sites that you may visit through an SSL connection. If we were to use public key encryption directly, we would need to have possession of a site's public key before we could establish a session with that site. Storing and managing so many public keys would become a problem; particularly when a site changes its key pair.

One solution would be to have the server send its public key immediately upon connection, but this would mean that we have a server handing a client its own public key, and the client will be using this public key to assert the server's identity, opening up a large security loophole.

While we may not trust a server handing out a public key that it claims as its own, we can collectively trust groups such as VeriSign (http://www.verisign.com) or Thawte (http://www.thawte.com/). These are **Certification Authorities (CA)**, and they provide a mechanism by which we can validate a server's public key as it is handed to us.

This mechanism makes use of transitive trust. First, we must assume that we have obtained the public key of the CA, obtained through some highly secured means (built right into modern browsers). Now we only need to have faith in the CA's public key because they will in turn vouch for the authenticity of a server's public key. This is done through a **digital certificate (cert)**.

A cert is an *unencrypted* message that contains a server's public key as well as other information such as domain name, IP, name of issuing CA, and expiration date, together with a digital signature that is obtained from a CA. The CA will take the server's information and authenticate it via some external means (for example, human intervention), and will then vouch for the authenticity of that information by signing it with its own private key. This signing is done using a **digital signature**.

A digital signature is appended at the end of a message, and is used to ensure the integrity of the message during transmission. In this case, the message plus the signature forms the certificate. A digital signature is computed by putting the content of the message through the one-way hash algorithm (MD5) that produces a **message digest**. MD5 is a frequently used algorithm, details of which can be found at http://www.ietf.org/rfc/rfc1321.txt. The digest is then encrypted using the private key of the CA and appended to the message.

When it receives a certificate supplied by the server, a client can ascertain the validity of the information on the certificate by performing the same one-way hash on the content; decrypting the signature using the CA's well-known public key; and finally comparing the two hash values. In this way, the authenticity of the server is established through the transitive trust relationship between the client, CA, and the server:

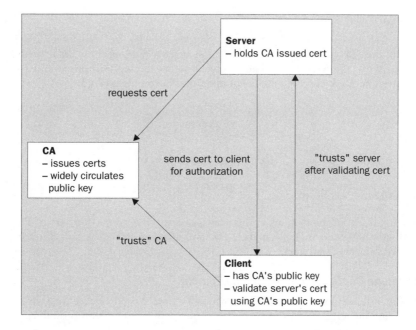

One of the most frequently used formats for certificates is based on the X.509 format, described at http://www.ietf.org/rfc/rfc2459.txt. Tomcat's SSL implementation supports the use of this standard format.

SSL Server Authentication

During SSL server authentication, a client checks the identity of the server to make sure that it is contacting the genuine server. After the connection of a client via unencrypted sockets, the server sends a cert to the client. The client then performs a series of checks to authenticate the server, including:

- ❏ Verifying that the certificate hasn't expired
- ❏ Verifying that the CA issuing the certificate is to be trusted
- ❏ Verifying the domain name against the one on the certificate
- ❏ Validating the CA's digital signature on the certificate (by decrypting the signature with the CA's public key and comparing it against the message digest), in order to ensure that the certificate is issued by the CA and the information has not been tampered with

After server authentication is performed, the client and server will check the set of cryptographic algorithms available to them and negotiate a **cipher suite** that represents the algorithms that are available to both of them. Finally, a key is generated (using one of the shared secret encryption algorithms from the cipher suite) and shared between the client and server for the communication phase of the protocol.

Possible SSL-Enabled Container Configurations

There are at least two ways that one can set up an SSL-enabled web site based on Tomcat 4 (and most other servlet containers/application servers): using a web server front end and using a standalone configuration.

Using a Web Server Front End

When we use a web server front end, we use a connector between the web server and Tomcat. The establishment of the SSL connection, and encryption and decryption of the data stream, all occur between the client and the web server. The connection between the web server and Tomcat 4 is via a physically secured network and the data is not encrypted when transferred:

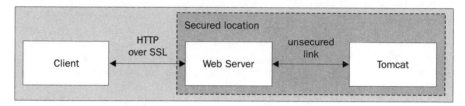

The exact configuration of the systems in this scenario is specific to the web server. The documentation of all the leading web servers such as Apache, IIS, and iPlanet provides details of setting up an SSL server, so we won't cover them here.

Using the Standalone Configuration of Apache Tomcat

We can also use a standalone configuration in which Tomcat is used as both the web server (for serving static content), and the application server. In this case, the SSL connection is established between a client's browser and Tomcat 4 directly:

Enabling SSL on Tomcat 4

Instead of re-implementing the complex SSL layer, Tomcat makes use of the **Java Secure Socket Extension (JSSE)** standard extension that is available from http://java.sun.com/products/jsse/ (JSSE comes as an integral part of J2SE 1.4). JSSE provides a pure Java implementation of SSL, implemented as a set of custom socket factory classes that enable any non-SSL application to easily use SSL by simply specifying one of the factory classes when creating a socket.

Installing JSSE

JSSE consists of a set of JAR files: `jsse.jar`, `jcert.jar`, and `jnet.jar`. While Tomcat 4 can use an environment variable named JSSE_HOME for locating these extensions, the most reliable way is to install JSSE as a standard extension by copying these JAR files to the `%JAVA_HOME%\jre\lib\ext` directory or to make them available to Tomcat by copying them to the `%CATALINA_HOME%\common\lib`.

Creating a Server-Side Keystore

JSSE obtains public key and cert information from a **keystore**. The keystore used by JSSE is in a proprietary format called **Java Key Store (JKS)**. Users can create a keystore, generate public key pairs, and create certificates using a tool that is part of the standard JDK: `keytool`, which has several options:

Option	Description
`-genkey`	Generates a public and private key pair, and creates a self-signed cert
`-export`	Exports a cert in binary or text format
`-alias`	Specifies a text alias that can be use to retrieve the keys after creation
`-list`	Lists the content of the store
`-keyalg`	Specifies a key generation algorithm (RSA is usually used)
`-keystore`	Specifies the path to the keystore
`-storepass`	Specifies the password for the keystore
`-validity`	Lists the number of days that the cert will be valid for

Self-signed certificates represent a cert vouching for our authenticity, whose signing CA is ourselves. While not useful in production environments, they are useful for testing as obtaining custom certs can be expensive.

To create a keystore that we can use on Tomcat, we can use the following command:

```
keytool -genkey -alias wrox -keystore .\keystore -keyalg RSA -validity 365
```

When we execute this command, `keytool` will prompt for some additional information. Answer them according to the following screenshot (blank entries indicate that we do not need to enter any value and can simply press the return key):

```
C:\WINNT\System32\cmd.exe
C:\ProJavaServlets\Ch09>keytool -genkey -alias wrox -keystore .\keystore -keyalg
 RSA -validity 365
Enter keystore password:  abc123
What is your first and last name?
  [Unknown]:  localhost
What is the name of your organizational unit?
  [Unknown]:  IT
What is the name of your organization?
  [Unknown]:  Wrox Press
What is the name of your City or Locality?
  [Unknown]:
What is the name of your State or Province?
  [Unknown]:
What is the two-letter country code for this unit?
  [Unknown]:  UK
Is <CN=localhost, OU=IT, O=Wrox Press, L=Unknown, ST=Unknown, C=UK> correct?
  [no]:  y

Enter key password for <wrox>
        (RETURN if same as keystore password):

C:\ProJavaServlets\Ch09>
```

The fields for the cert are standard X.509 required fields. As we are creating a cert for our server, it is important to use the server's name when prompted – in our case `localhost`. We also need to be careful to set the same password for the keystore and for the cert entry (here we set it to `abc123`). This is because Tomcat only allows us to specify a single password for both.

There may be a significant delay during the generation of the public key pair and the creation a self-signed cert, after which there will be a file named `keystore` in your working directory. We can see the content of the keystore by running this command:

```
keytool -keystore .\keystore -list
```

You will be prompted for the keystore password. The tool will then list the content of the keystore (in this case it only contains the self-signed cert we just created).

We need to move this keystore to a location where Tomcat can locate it. Create a `keystore` directory underneath `%CATALINA_HOME%` and copy the keystore file to it.

Exporting a CA Certificate for a Client Browser

Next, we need to get our browser to recognize us as a CA. This can be done by exporting our cert and then importing it into the browser we are using. The command to export a cert using `keytool` is:

```
keytool -export -keystore .\keystore -alias wrox -rfc -file wrox.cer
```

The tool will prompt for our password, and then generate a key file in RFC 1421, Base64-encoded format (which is easily transportable). The key file is stored as `wrox.key` in our working directory and will look something like this:

```
-----BEGIN CERTIFICATE-----
MIICQDCCAakCBDwLYykwDQYJKoZIhvcNAQEEBQAwZzELMAkGA1UEBhMCVUsxEDAOBgNVBAgTB1Vu
a25vd24xEDAOBgNVBAcTB1Vua25vd24xEzARBgNVBAoTCldyb3ggUHJlc3MxCzAJBgNVBAsTAklU
MRIwEAYDVQQDEwlsb2NhbGhvc3QwHhcNMDExMjAzMTEzNDAxWhcNMDIxMjAzMTEzNDAxWjBnMQsw
CQYDVQQGEwJVUSzEQMA4GA1UECBMHVW5rbm93bjEQMA4GA1UEBxMHVW5rbm93bjETMBEGA1UEChMK
V3JveCBQcmVzczELMAkGA1UECxMCSVQxEjAQBgNVBAMTCWxvY2FsaG9zdDCBnzANBgkqhkiG9w0B
AQEFAAOBjQAwgYkCgYEA59pRG46XWhV7syzNeZqPv00NDSHYRO9zK0xWnxe3SNHUSNRhrVbRJ89y
E5jWmjXz4fZtE1W9DADN6NBgQVyYmbcu68hqeqmzsM4bGxYVMRNCkIFtkawgYBD9CKSgKdDGvean
nugTSiHBF6xRfkUy4wUbLo0ECZ4utZQHFYcYCTMCAwEAATANBgkqhkiG9w0BAQQFAAOBgQAuQ66L
EXaCrNTI8jyw9TcOZsKS3+LWJNOnAnitURfSkejgzmOYkLYdwCagvU3eLPPe7BCOndqiYZQmuSod
o8C+wBaCyLYcg3BqBuOs/RLxUooNA5EpU5W2rhJotW9vkiEGPhRCjZGuM+jvAc3zIsVJCQFqrqK0
aaphYb5gre8t7g==
-----END CERTIFICATE-----
```

We will import this as a CA to Internet Explorer (to import to other browsers you should consult their documentation). Select Internet Options under the Tools menu. Click on the Content tab and you should see something similar to the following:

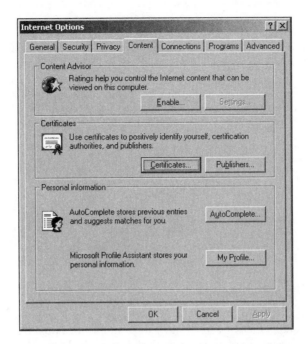

Click the Certificates... button, and then the Trusted Root Certification Authorities tab. You should see a list of already installed CAs:

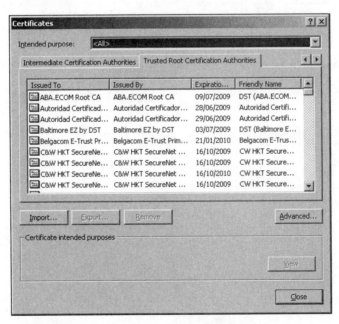

Click the Import... button, and walk through the wizard, importing our wrox.cer file. The wizard will recognize the certificate format and install it into the Root Certificate Store.

Adding an SSL Connector to Tomcat 4

Finally, we can configure Tomcat to take advantage of the server-side SSL setup. This can be done by editing `server.xml`:

```
<Connector className="org.apache.catalina.connector.http.HttpConnector"
           port="8443" minProcessors="5" maxProcessors="75"
           enableLookups="true" acceptCount="10" debug="0"
           scheme="https" secure="true">
   <Factory className="org.apache.catalina.net.SSLServerSocketFactory"
            keystoreFile="keystore/keystore" keystorePass="abc123"
            clientAuth="false" protocol="TLS"/>
</Connector>
```

Within the `<Service name="Tomcat-Standalone">` element, you should find an entry already in place. All we need to do is to uncomment it and add the `keystoreFile` and `keystorePass` attributes. The `<Factory>` element instructs Tomcat on where to access the public key and certs required for the SSL session (as implemented by the JSSE socket factory classes).

Trying Out SSL Enabled Tomcat

Remember that the JSSE JAR files will need to be available to Tomcat for this to work. Using the browser that you have added the CA cert to, navigate to https://localhost:8443/. You should now get the SSL-enabled Tomcat home page (note the padlock icon in the lower right-hand corner):

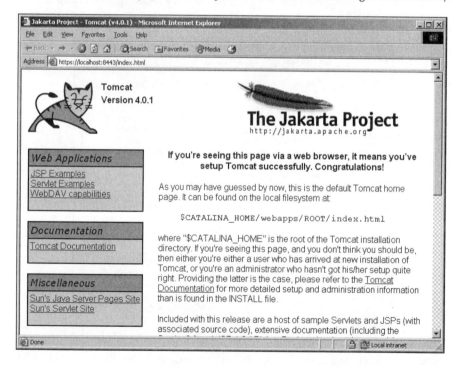

> **Non-SSL access is still available via port 8080. The portion of an application that does not need a secure connection should avoid using SSL access as it is considerably more processor-intensive that non-SSL access.**

It's worth taking a moment to examine what's happening here. The browser authenticates the server by:

- Receiving a certificate from Tomcat (`localhost`)
- Validating the certificate against a trusted CA
- Checking the hostname used to access the resource (`localhost`)
- Checking the expiration date of the certificate (a year from now)

All of the above checks must be successful before a shared secret key is generated and used for communication. If we try to access https://localhost:8443/index.html using a browser that hasn't had our certificate installed, we'll see a warning. For example, the following dialog is presented by Netscape 6.2:

Servlet 2.3 Security

The Servlet 2.3 specification, consistent with J2EE philosophy, prescribes a model that separates the developers from the deployers of a web application:

- It is the responsibility of the developers to anticipate how the application will be used after deployment, and to make it flexible enough to adapt to different environments
- A deployer is responsible for deploying the web application to the actual environment within which it will run

Developers will not know ahead of time the specific users that may be using the application but there are many situations in which access to web resources must be partitioned depending on the users involved. For example, if Jane and Jill are peers in the same department, they should not be able to access each other's salary information Accordingly, developers need to be able to build security into the web applications without referring to the actual users who may use the application. The deployer understands the relationships in the deployment environment and so should decide who can access what.

We need to be able to map names to the final users and security principals. These mappable textual names are called **roles**. For example:

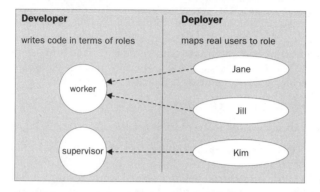

> **Roles serve as an indirect mapping to users and security principals in the deployed environment.**

Roles isolate developers from changes in the physical deployment. For example, a web application developer need only write code that will prevent one worker from accessing another's salary record. The fact that Jane and Jill both map to the role of a worker is not of concern to the developer. The decision to map Jane and Jill to worker is the responsibility of the deployer. We can envision a real life scenario in which Jane gets a promotion and therefore requires a supervisor role. In this case, Jane will be able to access the salary information of Jill because the web application developer has written the code to allow a supervisor role to access the information belonging to a worker.

Access Security and J2EE Business Logic

The fact that a supervisor can access worker's salary records is a business rule. The Servlet 2.3 specification provides mechanisms that make it possible (and easy) to code such business security logic without the need to implement a security infrastructure of our own. The combination of all the business security rules that are implemented in a web application is referred to as the web application's security model.

The Servlet 2.3 specification describes two ways that containers can help in implementing an application's security model. The indirect mapping offered by roles is essential in enabling both:

❑ **Declarative security** – refers to security constraints that can be configured at deployment time by the deployer. This includes, but is not limited to, mapping roles to users/principals, configuring authentication for certain resources, and restricting access to other resources. The deployment descriptor file of the web application is where all of these actions are defined.

❑ **Programmatic security** – refers to interfaces and methods that a web application developer can use to enforce business security requirements during the coding of the business logic within a web application. Since changes in these rules would require re-writing and re-compiling the code, they should be used only when absolutely necessary. However, there are certain situations when implementation via declarative security may be insufficient. For example, if it is absolutely necessary that a worker cannot access the salary information of another worker (even if they are promoted to supervisor) we need to code this within the application.

Security with Tomcat 4

The Servlet 2.3 specification is careful to avoid platform-specific features. This presents an interesting challenge for Tomcat, a product that is expected to run well across a variety of OS and systems. While the Servlet 2.3 specification describes features in generic terms, the designers of Tomcat 4 must actually ensure that the features work on different platforms.

The Tomcat solution is illustrated in the following figure:

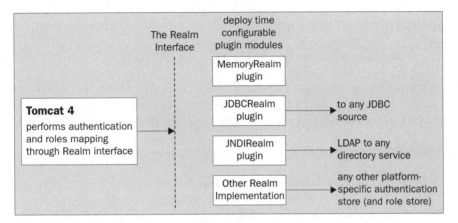

Users to roles mappings are maintained through **realms**. In programmatic terms, a realm is nothing more than a programming interface. By specifying this interface, and not dictating the means by which this mapping is done, Tomcat can be adapted for new platforms. New means of authentication and roles mapping tracking can be accommodated via the creation of a new realm component, or access can be provided through standard data access interfaces such as JDBC.

> By factoring out the means of authenticating a user, and retrieving the role mapping to a user, Tomcat is able to participate in server-managed security without being tied down to any specific operating system and/or platform implementation.

Realms

The programming interface that Tomcat requires every implementation of a realm to support is called `org.apache.catalina.Realm`. This interface defines the following methods:

```
public void addPropertyChangeListener()
```

This adds a listener to monitor property changes in the realm.

```
public Principal authenticate(String username, String credentials)
public Principal authenticate(String username, byte[] credentials)
public Principal authenticate(String username, String digest, String nonce,
                    String nc, String cnonce, String realm,
                    String md5a2,)
public Principal authenticate(java.security.cert.X509Certificate[] certs)
```

These methods are used to authenticate users and principals using simple credentials, password, RFC 2096, or chains of X.509 certs.

```
public Container getContainer()
```

This method returns the container that the realm is operating under.

```
public String getInfo()
```

This method returns implementation-specific information, including a version number.

```
public boolean hasRole(Principal principal, String role)
```

We can use this method to determine if a principal has a certain role within this realm.

```
public void removePropertyChangeListener(PropertyChangeListener listener)
```

This method is used to remove a previously registered listener for the realm.

```
public void setContainer(Container container)
```

This method sets the container associated with this realm.

The operational model of realms is quite straightforward. On the first access by a user of any declaratively protected resource, the applicable realm's `authenticate()` method is called. The user's password and roles are then cached by Tomcat for the duration of the session. This means that any database changes will not be visible until the next time `authenticate()` is called.

While Tomcat provides a means to access realm information for authentication and role query, it does not provide any way of creating and maintaining the information store.

Realm Implementations

By default an in-memory realm based on an XML file will be used. This base realm is *only* loaded at Tomcat startup. The static nature of this in-memory realm means that it is only really useful for testing purposes.

Tomcat provides an implementation of a **JDBCRealm** for use in production systems. A JDBCRealm will access any JDBC source to obtain user-to-roles mapping information. User authentication and role information can be stored in any information store that provides JDBC access.

Since much of the enterprise-based user and access information is accessible via directory services, Tomcat also provides an implementation of a **JNDIRealm** that can interface to any LDAP-accessible directory service.

Realms Association

In an application-hosting environment, we might want to have various levels of administrative users. Some owners may be granted control over certain web applications, others over a complete virtual server. A system-level user may want to have system-wide access to some resources, across all virtual hosts, and across all the web applications running within the same engine instance. Realms in Tomcat 4 can be configured to fulfill all of these requirements.

A realm can be defined and associated within the server configuration file (server.xml) with a <Context>, <Host>, or <Engine> element:

❑   When a realm is defined as a sub-element of a <Context> element, it means that the group of users and roles managed by the realm is applicable only within the web application that the <Context> element defines.

❑   When a realm is defined as a sub-element of a <Host> element, it means that the group of users and roles managed by the realm is applicable across the web applications running under the same virtual host.

❑   When a realm is defined as a sub-element of a <Engine> element, it means that the group of users and roles managed by this realm is across all the applications running across all the virtual hosts running on the same Tomcat instance. This can be used to provide system-administrator-level access to all the applications on a particular Tomcat instance.

Inner scope always overrides outer scope. So, if a JDBCRealm is defined in the <Engine> scope, but subsequently a MemoryRealm is defined in the <Context> scope, users' authentication will be done against the MemoryRealm (and not the global JDBCRealm) for the application associated with the specific <Context>.

Container-Managed Security

Now that we have the authentication database and roles mapping, we need to put protection on some resources. The Servlet 2.3 specification defines two new elements in the deployment descriptor to support this declarative security mechanism. They are <security-constraint> and <login-config>:

❑   The <security-constraint> element specifies what web resources need to be protected, the type of authentication required, and what roles should have access to the resource. This is declarative security in action, also known as **container-managed security**. There can be as many <security-constraint> entries in a web.xml file as there are different sets of resources to protect.

❑   The <login-config> element specifies the style of authentication required by the application.

Under container-managed security, a J2EE application builder can specify security constraint and role mapping purely using GUI tools and have the container implement the actual access control. The GUI configuration process is the declarative means by which the application deployed can give instructions to the container on how to manage security. While GUI based security administration tools exist for many commercial products, servlet containers are not required to implement them in any standard manner. The Servlet 2.3 specification is the first revision to formalize this as a requirement for every compliant container.

Let's take a look at the sub-elements of a `<security-constraint>` element:

Sub-element	Description
`<display-name>`	This is the name for the constraint, typically used by a GUI tool to refer back to this specific constraint.
`<web-resource-collection>`	This specifies a group of resources to protect within a web application. We can use one or more `<url-pattern>` elements to specify the set(s) of resources. An `<http-method>` element can also be used to specify the specific HTTP method to constrain (GET or POST, and so on).
`<auth-constraint>`	This contains `<role-name>` elements, each of which specifies the role that is allowed to access this constrained set of resources.
`<user-data-constraint>`	This specifies the transport guarantee (via a `<transport-guarantee>` element) that must be met when access to the resources is attempted. The transport guarantee can be NONE, INTEGRAL, or CONFIDENTIAL. If INTEGRAL or CONFIDENTIAL is applied the access must usually be made through an SSL connection; otherwise the request is refused.

The `<login-config>` element specifies the authentication method to be used within an application when the container attempts to authenticate a user. Let's take a look at the sub-elements of `<login-config>`.

Sub-element	Description
`<auth-method>`	The value of this can be one of BASIC, DIGEST, FORM, and CLIENT-CERT.
`<realm-name>`	This is *not* a Tomcat realm. It is simply a text string that is used when a BASIC authentication dialog is displayed.
`<form-login-config>`	If the FORM authentication method is specified, this provides more information on the web page and the error page that will be used during the custom form authentication process.

Methods of Authentication

Since resources in a web application are accessed via HTTP, authentication methods are restricted to those supported by HTTP. The set of authentication methods supported by Tomcat 4 (as defined in the Servlet 2.3 specification) includes:

- ❑ BASIC authentication
- ❑ FORM-based authentication
- ❑ DIGEST authentication
- ❑ CLIENT-CERT authentication

BASIC Authentication

BASIC Authentication is the most popular form of HTTP authentication around. You've probably experienced BASIC authentication many times: when you reach a web destination, the web browser pops up a dialog box prompting you to enter user name and password. The user name is passed in clear text, and the password is transferred in very easily decoded Base64 encoding. This method of authentication is the least secure, but the most widely supported, of the four.

FORM-Based Authentication

FORM-based authentication uses a custom form supplied by the web application deployer to perform the actual authentication. Once the user has completed the user and password information in the custom form, the information is sent back to the server for processing. If the authentication fails an error page is displayed to the user. As a standard POST is used to send password information back to the server this is a very weak form of authentication; although the additional protection methods described in the BASIC authentication section may be used in conjunction with this type of authentication.

DIGEST Authentication

In DIGEST authentication, the password is transmitted in an encrypted digest form, using a one-way hash algorithm such as MD5. At the server end, a pre-hashed digest of the password is stored and this is compared to the one received. Since the actual password is never transmitted directly, this form of authentication is significantly more secure than BASIC authentication. This form of authentication is not in widespread use, although it is supported in the latest version of most web browsers.

CLIENT-CERT Authentication

Even though BASIC and FORM-based authentication are not intrinsically strong methods of authentication, they can be made strong by deploying them over a secured transport such as SSL. We can use X.509 client-side certificates to perform client authentication. The server can authenticate a cert passed by the client by:

- ❑ Verifying that the certificate comes from a trusted CA
- ❑ Using the CA's public key to validate that the cert has not been tampered with
- ❑ Checking the cert's expiry date
- ❑ Checking the client information on the cert (in order to authenticate the client)

The latest versions of Internet Explorer and Netscape both support this feature.

Using Declarative Security

We've covered enough theory and background regarding the operation model of Tomcat 4's declarative container-managed security – it's time to put our knowledge to work with some examples.

Using a MemoryRealm

Our first example will make use of a MemoryRealm. We'll do the following:

- ❏ Protect the NetAccessServlet that we worked with earlier in a new web application called wroxrealms

- ❏ Set up a MemoryRealm to supply a username, password, and role to the Tomcat container

- ❏ Set up the declarative security by adding a <security-constraint> and <login-config> entry to the deployment descriptor

- ❏ Test declarative security by accessing the protected NetAccessServlet

We'll define a MemoryRealm, based on the worker and supervisor scenario that we introduced earlier. The MemoryRealm implementation will take user authentication data and role information from an XML file (wroxUsers.xml) when Tomcat starts up. Tomcat requires that the document element of this file be <tomcat-users>:

```
<tomcat-users>
  <user name="jane" password="abc123" roles="worker" />
  <user name="jill" password="cde456" roles="worker"  />
  <user name="kim"  password="efg789" roles="worker,supervisor" />
</tomcat-users>
```

Next, we must configure a MemoryRealm to associate with our wroxrealms web application. We need to create a <Context> for our wroxrealms application and associate a MemoryRealm with it. Here's what needs to be added to server.xml:

```
<Context path="/wroxrealms" docBase="wroxrealms" debug="0"
         reloadable = "true">
  <Realm className="org.apache.catalina.realm.MemoryRealm"
         pathname="webapps/wroxrealms/WEB-INF/wroxUsers.xml" />
</Context>
```

We use the pathname attribute of the realm element to point directly to the XML file that contains the user, password, and role information. The attributes supported by the realm element depend on the type of realm used.

We need to configure container-managed security in the deployment descriptor:

```
<?xml version="1.0" encoding="ISO-8859-1"?>

<!DOCTYPE web-app
    PUBLIC "-//Sun Microsystems, Inc.//DTD Web Application 2.3//EN"
    "http://java.sun.com/dtd/web-app_2_3.dtd">

<web-app>

  <servlet>
    <servlet-name>passthru</servlet-name>
    <servlet-class>NetAccessServlet</servlet-class>
  </servlet>
```

Access is restricted to the role of supervisor only:

```
<security-constraint>
  <web-resource-collection>
    <web-resource-name>Access Through Servlet Name</web-resource-name>
    <url-pattern>/servlet/passthru</url-pattern>
  </web-resource-collection>
  <auth-constraint>
    <role-name>supervisor</role-name>
  </auth-constraint>
</security-constraint>
```

Using the `<login-config>` entry, we have associated the BASIC method of authentication with this web application:

```
<login-config>
  <auth-method>BASIC</auth-method>
  <realm-name>Wrox Supervisors Only</realm-name>
</login-config>

</web-app>
```

Start Tomcat 4 and navigate to http://localhost:8080/wroxrealms/servlet/passthru. We will then be prompted with the familiar login dialog:

The realm that we have specified in the `<login-config>` shows up as a simple string label in this dialog. This has nothing to do with the realm that we use in Tomcat, it's just an unfortunate coincidence in terminology.

Enter a user name of "jane" and a password of "abc123". When we do this, Tomcat will perform authentication by calling the `authenticate()` method of the associated realm (`org.apache.catalina.realm.MemoryRealm` in our case). It will also call the `userInRole()` method of the realm to determine if the user belongs to a role that is needed to access this resource. The authentication succeeds, but Jane is not allowed to access the protected resource because she does not map to the role of supervisor.

Now, let's try to access the servlet via an unprotected backdoor. Navigate to
http://localhost:8080/wroxrealms/servlet/NetAccessServlet. Jane can now access the protected servlet.
Our protection specified in the deployment descriptor has a loophole since a servlet can be accessed
directly with its class name. In the <url-pattern> specified in the <security-constraint>
element, we should have been more thorough (by using "/*", or specifying "/servlet/*").

Many browsers will cache the username and password once authentication succeeds, so you should
restart the browser before attempting authentication with another user name. Navigate to
http://localhost:8080/wroxrealms/servlet/passthru and use the user name "kim" and password
"efg789". This time, you will notice that authentication succeeds and you will be able to access
NetAccessServlet.

Using Digested Passwords

Let's modify the example to use digested passwords, which is supported by the MemoryRealm that we
use. Shutdown Tomcat, and make the following amendments to server.xml:

```
<Context path="/wroxrealms" docBase="wroxrealms" debug="0"
         reloadable="true">
  <Realm className="org.apache.catalina.realm.MemoryRealm"
         pathname="webapps/wroxrealms/WEB-INF/wroxUsersDigested.xml"
         digest="MD5" />
</Context>
```

wroxUsersDigested.xml has replaced the clear text passwords with their MD5 hashed equivalents:

```
<tomcat-users>
  <user name="jane" password="e99a18c428cb38d5f260853678922e03"
        roles="worker" />
  <user name="jill" password="b7e64172f775d1df1348da7e925be164"
        roles="worker"  />
  <user name="kim" password="236ef0ed108857aecd3d328485e402da"
        roles="worker,supervisor" />
</tomcat-users>
```

The MemoryRealm implementation in Tomcat acts also as a standalone password hashing utility. We
can use the following command to obtain the hash string for "abc123":

```
java -classpath %CATALINA_HOME%\server\lib\catalina.jar
org.apache.catalina.realm.RealmBase -a MD5 abc123
```

The other two passwords for users kim and jill are hashed in the same way. Start Tomcat and
navigate to http://localhost:8080/wroxrealms/servlet/passthru. Using the identity of "kim" and then
"jane" the behavior stays exactly the same. BASIC authentication is still used as specified by the
<login-config> associated with the web application. However, the wroxUsers.xml file now
contains the digested passwords that are difficult to decode.

Using Form-Based Authentication

It is possible to supply our own customized web pages to authenticate the user, instead of using the default dialog box supplied by the browser. First, we must modify the `<login-config>` element in the deployment descriptor. Instead of using the BASIC authentication method, we now use the FORM method. We specify `<form-login-page>` and `<form-error-page>` elements that will define our login and error pages. These paths are specified relative to the root of the web application:

```
<login-config>
   <auth-method>FORM</auth-method>
   <realm-name>Wrox Supervisors Only</realm-name>
   <form-login-config>
      <form-login-page>/formlogin/login.htm</form-login-page>
      <form-error-page>/formlogin/error.htm</form-error-page>
   </form-login-config>
</login-config>
```

We need to create additional web pages to authenticate the user. First, we create `login.htm`:

```html
<html>
  <head>
    <title>Customized Page for Authentication</title>
    <style>
      body, table, td {background-color:#FFFFFF; color:#000000;
                       font-family:verdana; font-size:10pt;}
      input {font-family:verdana; font-size:10pt;}
    </style>
  </head>
  <body>
    <h3>Wrox Login</h3>
    <form method="post" action="j_security_check">
      <table>
        <tr>
         <td>User Name:</td>
         <td><input type="text" name="j_username"></td>
        </tr>
        <tr>
          <td>Password:</td>
          <td><input type="password" name="j_password"></td>
        </tr>
      </table>
      <p><input type="submit" value="Authenticate"></p>
    </form>
  </body>
</html>
```

> The action associated with the POST for the form must be **j_security_check** in order for the authentication to be handled properly. The username must be contained in a field called **j_username**, and the password in **j_password**.

The error page (`error.htm`) will be used to indicate a login error:

```html
<html>
  <head>
    <title>Error Page for Authentication</title>
    <style>
      body {background-color:#FF3333; color:#FFFFFF;
            font-family:verdana; font-size:10pt;}
    </style>
  </head>
  <body>
    <h3>Wrox Security</h3>
    <p><b>Sorry, your login request has been denied.</b></p>
  </body>
</html>
```

Start Tomcat 4 and navigate to http://localhost:8080/wroxrealms/servlet/passthru in order to access the protected servlet. Instead of the rather mundane authentication dialog box, you should now see our custom form:

If you enter the user name "jane", and password "bbbccc" our error page will be displayed:

Let's attempt login again. Enter the user name "kim" and password "efg789" in login.htm. As expected, we are allowed to access the protected URL.

Finally, let's try again using "jane" and the correct password "abc123" – remember to restart your browser first, to flush the cached credentials. When you try it this time, you will (perhaps surprisingly) see this page:

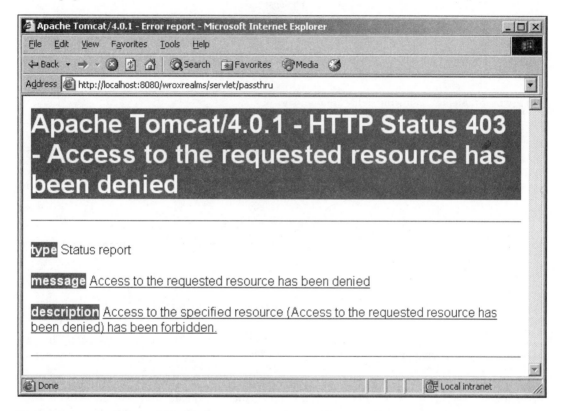

This is the correct behavior because:

❑ The authentication is successful, and user "jane" is authenticated – therefore there is no login error, so the error page is not displayed

❑ The user "jane", does not map to the supervisor role required to access the resource and so is denied access

Using a JDBCRealm

A JDBCRealm accesses user login information and role mapping information through a JDBC source, instead of the simple XML file as in MemoryRealm. The utility of a JDBCRealm is not restricted to only relational database management systems, it can be used to access information from any storage facility that exposes a JDBC-compatible interface.

In order for a JDBC source to work with a JDBCRealm, the database storing the mapping information must have specific table layout:

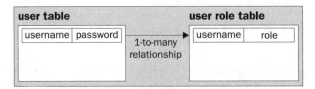

The actual name of the table and fields in the JDBC source are not specified by the Realm implementation, but can be assigned at deployment time based on the attributes of the <Realm> element.

In the **user table**, the following fields are mandatory:

Required Field	Description
username	The name of the user for authentication
password	Contains the password associated with the user

The **user role table** consists of the following mandatory fields:

Required Field	Description
username	The name of the user for authentication
role	One of the roles that the user is mapped to

In the user role table, there must be one row for each role that a user is associated with. The tables used can in fact contain other fields, however, the JDBCRealm implementation will only make use of the required fields noted above.

As with the MemoryRealm, or any other realm implementation, the definition for the realm is associated with either a <Context>, <Host>, or <Engine> and appears in the server.xml file. For JDBCRealm, the following attributes of the <Realm> element are important:

Attribute Name	Description
classname	Must be for org.apache.catalina.realm.JDBCRealm Tomcat 4's JDBCRealm implementation
driverName	The Java class name of the JDBC driver, used in typical JDBC programming
connectionName	The name of the JDBC connection to access
connectionPassword	The password used when making the JDBC connection
connectionURL	The database URL used to locating the JDBC source

Attribute Name	Description
userTable	The name of the table that contains the two required fields of a user table
userRoleTable	The name of the table that contains the two required fields of a user role table
userNameCol	The name of the field, in both the userTable and the userRoleTable, which contains the username information (both fields must have the same name across the two tables)
userCredCol	The name of the field in the userTable that contains the password of the user
roleNameCol	The name of the field in the userRoleTable that contains a role associated with the user

We'll use MySQL and the MM.MySQL JDBC driver in our example, although the example could be easily adapted for any other database and JDBC driver. Use the following SQL script to create the database and tables, and supply sample data:

```
CREATE DATABASE realmDB;
USE realmDB;

CREATE TABLE deptusers (
  wroxusername VARCHAR(15) NOT NULL PRIMARY KEY,
  password     VARCHAR(15) NOT NULL
);

CREATE TABLE deptroles (
  wroxusername VARCHAR(15) NOT NULL,
  wroxrole     VARCHAR(15) NOT NULL,
  PRIMARY KEY (wroxusername, wroxrole)
);

INSERT INTO deptusers VALUES ('jane', 'abc123');
INSERT INTO deptusers VALUES ('jill', 'cde456');
INSERT INTO deptusers VALUES ('kim',  'efg789');
INSERT INTO deptroles VALUES ('jane', 'worker');
INSERT INTO deptroles VALUES ('jill', 'worker');
INSERT INTO deptroles VALUES ('kim',  'worker');
INSERT INTO deptusers VALUES ('kim',  'supervisor');
```

Now, we have everything to fill out the attributes of the JDBCRealm:

Attribute	Our Value
className	org.apache.catalina.realm.JDBCRealm
driverName	org.gjt.mm.mysql.Driver

Table continued on following page

Attribute	Our Value
connectionURL	jdbc:mysql://localhost/realmDB
userTable	deptusers
userRoleTable	deptroles
userNameCol	wroxusername
userCredCol	password
roleNameCol	wroxrole

We should replace our previously associated `MemoryRealm` for the `wroxrealms` web application with this new `JDBCRealm`. Here is the `<Realm>` element that we must add:

```
<Context path="/wroxrealms" docBase="wroxrealms" debug="0"
         reloadable="true">
  <Realm className="org.apache.catalina.realm.JDBCRealm"
         driverName="org.gjt.mm.mysql.Driver"
         connectionURL="jdbc:mysql://localhost/realmDB"
         userTable="deptusers" userRoleTable="deptroles"
         userNameCol="wroxusername" userCredCol="password"
         roleNameCol="wroxrole" />
</Context>
```

Make sure you have the MySQL running, start Tomcat, and navigate to http://localhost:8080/wroxrealms/servlet/passthru. The custom form-based login will be displayed, so enter in "jill" for the user and "cde456" for the password. Access to the servlet will be denied.

Restart your browser to clear the credentials cached, and try entering "kim" and "efg789" for the user and password respectively. Kim is allowed to access the protected servlet because she has a role of supervisor, this time authenticated through the newly configured `JDBCRealm`.

Imagine the scenario in which the user "jill" has been promoted to a supervisor. We simply need to use MySQL to add a single row to the `deptroles` table within the database:

```
INSERT INTO deptroles VALUES ('jill', 'supervisor');
```

Restart your browser, and try authenticating with "jill" and "cde456" as the user and password once more. Immediately upon promotion, the user "jill" can now access the protected resource – without having even to restart Tomcat.

> The ability to reflect dynamic change in the authentication data and role mapping is a pre-requisite for any production environment – and Tomcat's **JDBCRealm** implementation satisfies this requirement.

Multiple Authentication Requests

Now we'll illustrate a potential problem that users may encounter. We'll deploy two trivial web applications, wroxapp1 and wroxapp2 on the same virtual host (each will have its own context of course). Each application contains a servlet that provides a link to the other web application. The only difference between the servlets is their name. One is called TrivialServlet1 and the other TrivialServlet2. We show TrivialServlet1 here:

```
import javax.servlet.*;
import javax.servlet.http.*;
import java.io.*;

public class TrivialServlet1 extends HttpServlet {

  public void doGet(HttpServletRequest request,
                    HttpServletResponse response)
      throws IOException, ServletException{
    PrintWriter out = response.getWriter();
    out.println("<html><head><style>");
    out.println("body {background-color:#FFFFFF;color:#000000;" +
                "font-family:verdana;font-size:10pt;}");
    out.println("</style></head>");
    out.println("<body>");
    out.println("Thank you for visiting Service <br><h1>#1</h1><p>");
    out.println("Please visit our " +
                "<ahref=\"http://localhost:8080/wroxapp2/servlet/trivial\">"
                + other service</a>.");
    out.println("</body></html>");
  }
}
```

We have to associate the JDBCRealm with the <Host> entry instead of individual <Context> entries. Here is the configuration for wroxapp1 and wroxapp2 that needs to be added to server.xml:

```
<Realm className="org.apache.catalina.realm.JDBCRealm"
       driverName="org.gjt.mm.mysql.Driver"
       connectionURL="jdbc:mysql://localhost/realmDB"
       userTable="deptusers" userRoleTable="deptroles"
       userNameCol="wroxusername" userCredCol="password"
       roleNameCol="wroxrole" />

<Context path="/wroxapp1" docBase="wroxapp1" debug="0" reloadable = "true">
</Context>
<Context path="/wroxapp2" docBase="wroxapp2" debug="0" reloadable = "true">
</Context>
```

So, wroxapp1 and wroxapp2 share quite a few things in common: the same virtual host, the same authentication realm, and a very similar servlet class. However, there is one key difference, the deployer of wroxapp1 has opted to configure the BASIC method of authentication, whereas the deployer of wroxapp2 has chosen to configure the FORM method of authentication. The deployment descriptor for wroxapp1 is:

```
<?xml version="1.0" encoding="ISO-8859-1"?>

<!DOCTYPE web-app
    PUBLIC "-//Sun Microsystems, Inc.//DTD Web Application 2.3//EN"
    "http://java.sun.com/dtd/web-app_2_3.dtd">

<web-app>

  <servlet>
    <servlet-name>trivial</servlet-name>
    <servlet-class>TrivialServlet1</servlet-class>
  </servlet>

  <security-constraint>
    <web-resource-collection>
      <web-resource-name>Protected Servlet</web-resource-name>
      <url-pattern>/servlet/trivial</url-pattern>
    </web-resource-collection>
    <auth-constraint>
       <role-name>supervisor</role-name>
       <role-name>worker</role-name>
    </auth-constraint>
  </security-constraint>

  <login-config>
    <auth-method>BASIC</auth-method>
    <realm-name>All Wrox Users</realm-name>
  </login-config>
</web-app>
```

While the `web.xml` deployment descriptor for `wroxapp2` is:

```
<?xml version="1.0" encoding="ISO-8859-1"?>

<!DOCTYPE web-app
    PUBLIC "-//Sun Microsystems, Inc.//DTD Web Application 2.3//EN"
    "http://java.sun.com/dtd/web-app_2_3.dtd">

<web-app>

   <servlet>
    <servlet-name>trivial</servlet-name>
    <servlet-class>TrivialServlet2</servlet-class>
  </servlet>

  <security-constraint>
    <web-resource-collection>
      <web-resource-name>Protected Servlet</web-resource-name>
      <url-pattern>/servlet/trivial</url-pattern>
    </web-resource-collection>
    <auth-constraint>
       <role-name>Supervisor</role-name>
       <role-name>Worker</role-name>
    </auth-constraint>
  </security-constraint>
</security-constraint>
```

```
<login-config>
  <auth-method>FORM</auth-method>
    <realm-name>All Wrox Users</realm-name>
    <form-login-config>
     <form-login-page>/formlogin/login.htm</form-login-page>
     <form-error-page>/formlogin/error.htm</form-error-page>
    </form-login-config>
</login-config>
</web-app>
```

Deploy the web applications and navigate to http://localhost:8080/wroxapp1/servlet/trivial. You should be prompted to enter a user name and password with a browser dialog. Enter any one of "jane", "jill", or "kim". You'll see the output of the protected TrivialServlet1:

This servlet invites us to visit another service hosted on the same virtual host. We can try it by following the link:

We are asked to authenticate ourselves again, this time via the custom FORM method of authentication, until we finally reach the requested service:

Imagine a virtual host with associated services such as travel, stock quotes, news, and so on. This requirement to authenticate each time a service is accessed even though the authentication is done against the same realm would be tedious. Fortunately, we can use an elegant solution to avoid this problem – **single sign-on**.

Single Sign-on

Single sign-on allows a single user authentication to work across all the web applications within a single virtual host, so long as they are all authenticating against the same realm. This is a very useful feature that avoids unnecessary calls to authentication.

> **The mechanism used to achieve single sign-on is Tomcat 4-specific, and not part of the Servlet 2.3 specification requirements.**

Single sign-on is accomplished using a **valve**. A valve is the system-level equivalent of a filter. A valve is inserted into the request processing pipeline, and given an opportunity to modify a request if necessary. The valve caches authentication information and role mappings across web applications within the same virtual host, and automatically uses the cached information for web applications that require authentication.

This authentication and role information caching is done during the very first authentication against a web application. Therefore, if we accesses wroxapp1 first, we will encounter a BASIC authentication dialog box. If, on the other hand, we tried to access wroxapp2 first, then we would encounter the custom FORM-based authentication. Regardless of the method of authentication, we will not have to re-authenticate when we access the other service.

Let's install the Tomcat single sign-on valve and see it in action. To do so, simply add the following <Valve> element to server.xml:

```
<Host name="localhost" debug="0" appBase="webapps" unpackWARs="true">
<Valve classname="org.apache.Catalina.authenticator.SingleSignOn"
       debug="0"/>
```

Restart Tomcat and navigate to http://localhost:8080/wroxapp1/servlet/trivial. Authenticate with one of the Wrox user credentials through the BASIC authentication box. You should now see the output of TrivialServlet1. Click on the link to TrivialServlet2. You'll no longer be required to authenticate against this totally separate web application.

> **The single sign-on valve uses HTTP cookies, so the client must have cookies enabled for it to work properly.**

Programmatic Security

Every aspect of the application security model that can be implemented via declarative security should be, as declarative security allows the deployer to change or alter policy according to the deployment situation. In some cases, however, programmatic security must be used. To use programmatic security, we will need to become familiar with three specific methods of the HttpServletRequest interface.

```
public java.lang.String getRemoteUser()
```

If the user has been authenticated, this method returns the name of the user, otherwise it returns null.

```
public boolean isUserInRole(java.lang.String role)
```

If the user has been authenticated, this method can be called to determine if a specific role has been mapped to the user.

```
public java.security.Principal getUserPrincipal()
```

This method returns a java.security.Principal object associated with the authenticated user. If no object is associated with the user it returns null.

As an example we'll create another servlet under the wroxapp1 application:

```java
import javax.servlet.*;
import javax.servlet.http.*;
import java.io.*;

public class SupersOnly extends HttpServlet {
  public void doGet(HttpServletRequest request,
                    HttpServletResponse response)
     throws IOException, ServletException {
    PrintWriter out = response.getWriter();
```

We call `getRemoteUser()` to obtain the authenticated username. We only print the welcome message if the user has been authenticated, and indeed has a role of supervisor:

```
String user = request.getRemoteUser();
out.println("<html><head><style>");
out.println("body {background-color:#FFFFFF;color:#000000;" +
            "font-family:verdana;font-size:10pt;}");
out.println("</style></head>");
if (user != null) {
  if (request.isUserInRole("supervisor")) {
    out.println("<body><h3>Welcome, " + user +
                ", you are a supervisor!</h3>");
  } else {
    out.println("<body><h3>Sorry, " + user +
                ", but only supervisors can see the message.</h3>");
  }
  out.println("</body>");
}
out.println("</html>");
}
}
```

Before trying this servlet, we need to make a servlet definition and a security constraint modification to the deployment descriptor of our application:

```
<?xml version="1.0" encoding="ISO-8859-1"?>

<!DOCTYPE web-app
    PUBLIC "-//Sun Microsystems, Inc.//DTD Web Application 2.3//EN"
    "http://java.sun.com/dtd/web-app_2_3.dtd">

<web-app>

  <servlet>
    <servlet-name>trivial</servlet-name>
    <servlet-class>TrivialServlet1</servlet-class>
  </servlet>

  <servlet>
    <servlet-name>supercheck</servlet-name>
    <servlet-class>SupersOnly</servlet-class>
  </servlet>

  <security-constraint>
    <web-resource-collection>
      <web-resource-name>Protected Servlet</web-resource-name>
      <url-pattern>/servlet/*</url-pattern>
    </web-resource-collection>
    <auth-constraint>
      <role-name>supervisor</role-name>
      <role-name>worker</role-name>
    </auth-constraint>
  </security-constraint>

  <login-config>
    <auth-method>BASIC</auth-method>
    <realm-name>Wrox Supervisors Only</realm-name>
  </login-config>
</web-app>
```

Restart Tomcat and navigate to http://localhost:8080/wroxapp1/servlet/supercheck. Login with "kim" and "efg789". You should see the following screen:

Restart your browser, and try again. This time, authenticate with "jane" and "abc123". Since jane is not a supervisor, we get the following message:

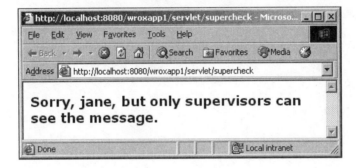

Summary

In this chapter, we saw how we can use server-side policy files to protect against badly-written or malevolent code. Such policy files are especially important when third-party code is hosted on a server.

We covered SSL, and the technologies that make it possible, including shared secret encryption and public key encryption. We saw how easy it is to configure SSL both on the server and the client side – we configured Tomcat to use SSL and created a certificate and imported it into Internet Explorer.

We also explored both declarative and programmatic security. Tomcat 4 provides a highly customizable declarative security implementation, and includes support for container-managed security. Through the use of realms, Tomcat fulfills its authentication and security requirements without becoming platform-dependent. Single sign-on with Tomcat demonstrated how we can make a system significantly more user-friendly by avoiding several tedious authentications when a service spans web applications.

Although as much security as possible should be declarative in nature, there are time when we need to define security programmatically. So, we took a quick look at programmatic security to see how it can be used to implement an application's security model.

In the next chapter we're going to turn our attention to how we can effectively debug servlets.

10

Servlet Debugging Techniques

In this chapter we'll look at how to get hold of information that tells us what's going on inside the servlet container at run time. We'll cover three different techniques: using filters, using event listeners, and finally using the **Java Platform Debugger Architecture (JPDA)**, which although not part of the Servlet API is useful and interesting nonetheless.

Specifically, we'll cover:

- ❑ Some of the problems associated with servlet development that make debugging important
- ❑ Using servlet filters and event listeners as non-invasive plug-in components to debug any web application
- ❑ The Java Platform Debugger Architecture
- ❑ Visualizing our debugger results
- ❑ Using the J2SE 1.4 Logging API to create a flexible debugging architecture
- ❑ The prospect of a novel run-time reverse-engineering tool for UML

We won't go over old ground in this chapter so the coverage of filters and event listeners will be kept relevant to the task at hand.

Servlet Debugging Issues

When using web applications we can expect to see the same types of bugs as we see in standalone Java applications as well as problems that arise from the subtleties of the servlet model and the nature of web application programming. For example:

❑ A single servlet instance may support multiple concurrent users in multiple threads. This has major synchronization implications if we're relying on the values we've stored in instance variables (as we'll see in the Chapter 11).

❑ The servlet container is an active partner to our web applications. It manages the lifecycle of servlets, it handles incoming requests, and it tracks session-specific user data. When debugging web applications it is just as important to know what the container is doing as it is to know what our own classes are doing.

❑ In a multi-user system, performance bottlenecks may occur due to multiple concurrent requests for common resources. So it is important to understand the interplay between the competing requests.

To help with this final point our definition of debugging includes **profiling** (the determination of the flow of control and use of resources) and **performance monitoring** (the measurement of the time taken for requests to complete). In fact, many of the techniques we'll learn in this chapter will be applicable to our investigation of performance and scalability in Chapter 13.

Debugging Techniques

A common debugging technique is the strategic insertion of `System.out.println()` statements at key points in code. It's certainly mine. The problem is that it's an **invasive** technique; it requires the modification of the sourcecode. Modifying the sourcecode might be acceptable at development time, but what if we want to investigate the inner workings of an deployed application, or one for which the sourcecode is not available?

What we need is a **non-invasive** mechanism that can be easily added and removed with no adverse effects on the classes being scrutinized. All of the techniques described in this chapter are non-invasive:

❑ Filters can trap servlet invocations as they occur, which allows us to record the sequence in which requests are processed

❑ Event listeners provide an insight into how the container handles sessions and context variables

❑ The Java Platform Debugger Architecture (JPDA) provides the basis for a comprehensive debugging tool that rivals those that are commercially available

Debugging Tools

An Integrated Development Environment (IDE) such as VisualAge or JBuilder will incorporate a debugger and these days there's a good chance it will also offer distributed debugging facilities for web applications. There are some good third-party debugging and profiling tools too. However, there are downsides to using some of the commercial debugging tools:

❑   They may be proprietary, which means that we can only debug servlets that are running in the servlet engine of the IDE itself, or in the vendor's application server

❑   They can be difficult to configure

❑   They can be expensive

❑   The information provided by those tools, though comprehensive, might not be quite what we require

In this chapter we'll focus on how to apply some simple techniques that are platform- and vendor-independent. These techniques will allow us to capture just the information we need (and for free).

I'm not against using tools, and I understand the "buy, don't build" philosophy. But you'll be able to make a more informed decision about what tools will suit you once you know what the do-it-yourself approach has to offer.

There is a non-proprietary, free, debugging tool called JDB. Although now superseded by JPDA, there is still a JDB tool provided as an example JPDA client with the JDK. You'll learn a lot by taking a look at the sourcecode for the new JDB in file `%JAVA_HOME%\demo\jpda\examples.jar` (the class to examine is `com/sun/tools/example/debug/tty/TTY.java`).

Event-Driven Debugging

Automated debugging is an event-driven process. When certain events occur in the target program, the debugger application must be alerted so that it may take appropriate action. The kinds of events we'll be interested in are:

❑   Method calls, particularly those that result in servlet invocations

❑   Updates to values stored in variables, particularly session and context attributes

❑   The creation and destruction of objects, particularly session and context instances

The appropriate action by the debugging application may be passive (simply reporting what happened) or active (perhaps halting the program and affecting its future course).

Filters and event listeners are by their very nature passive. The JPDA approach we will take will also be passive but it's worth pointing out that with JPDA it is possible to take a more active role by taking control of the target virtual machine. It's not a good idea to halt or take control of the servlet container, as it may be running other web applications.

Debugging with Filters

Filters give us the ability to intercept, in a non-intrusive way, servlet invocations as they happen. This means that we can configure the container to ensure that all inbound requests to one or more servlets are channelled through our filter, and all output responses are returned via our filter. We can add and remove filters without having to modify the servlets themselves.

If your debugging requirements are limited to discovering the usage pattern for servlet invocations from multiple remote clients (perhaps to investigate a scalability or performance problem) a filter offers a simple but effective approach.

Implementing the Debugging Filter

We'll implement just one filter, DebugFilter. As a generic invocation trapper it can be used with any web application:

```
package debugging;

import java.io.*;
import javax.servlet.*;
import javax.servlet.http.*;
import java.util.*;

public class DebugFilter implements Filter {

  private FilterConfig filterConfig = null;

  public void init(FilterConfig config) {
    this.filterConfig = config;
  }

  public void destroy() {}

  public void setFilterConfig(FilterConfig filterConfig) {
    this.filterConfig = filterConfig;
  }

  public FilterConfig getFilterConfig() {
    return this.filterConfig;
  }
```

This is where our filter starts to get interesting. All incoming requests must pass through our filter's doFilter() method before arriving at one of the target servlet's own service() methods (either doGet() or doPost()). This method does the following:

- ❑   It extracts information from the ServletRequest referenced by the request variable
- ❑   It constructs an output message that incorporates tags of the form
  <invocation><sender>localhost</sender>...</invocation>
- ❑   It sends the message to the server log file

```
public void doFilter(ServletRequest request, ServletResponse response,
                     FilterChain chain)
    throws IOException, ServletException {
```

We only proceed if we have a `FilterConfig` object to get the `ServletContext` from:

```
if (filterConfig != null) {
```

The tagged output will be stored here:

```
StringBuffer messageBuffer = new StringBuffer();
```

We record the sender of the request:

```
messageBuffer.append("<invocation>");
messageBuffer.append("<sender>");
messageBuffer.append(request.getRemoteHost());
messageBuffer.append("</sender>");
```

We record the message (that is, the posted parameters):

```
messageBuffer.append("<message>");
Enumeration parameterNames = request.getParameterNames();
boolean firstTime = true;
while (parameterNames.hasMoreElements()) {
  String thisName = (String) parameterNames.nextElement();
  String[] parameterValues = request.getParameterValues(thisName);
  String thisValue = parameterValues[0];

  if (firstTime) {
    messageBuffer.append("?");
  } else {
    messageBuffer.append("&");
  }
  messageBuffer.append(thisName + "=" + thisValue);
  firstTime = false;
}
messageBuffer.append("</message>");
```

We record the URL that the message was sent to:

```
if (request instanceof HttpServletRequest) {
  messageBuffer.append("<receiver>");
  messageBuffer.append(((HttpServletRequest)request).getRequestURI());
  messageBuffer.append("</receiver>");
}
```

We time the servlet invocation and record it:

```
long startTime = System.currentTimeMillis();
chain.doFilter(request,response);
long endTime = System.currentTimeMillis();
long duration = endTime - startTime;
messageBuffer.append("<duration>" + duration + "</duration>");
messageBuffer.append("</invocation>");
```

Finally, we write the result to the server log:

```
filterConfig.getServletContext().log(messageBuffer.toString());
      }
    }
  }
```

We're writing an entry to the log file *after* the request has completed, which allows us to capture timing information. Later we'll investigate a side-effect of this approach.

For simplicity we're using the server log file to store our results. We could write the results into a dedicated text file, or to a database, or even send them to a remote monitoring process using RMI, CORBA, or raw sockets. We could also channel the output through the J2SE 1.4 Logging API (as we'll discuss later).

Using the Debugging Filter

As a test, we can apply our filter to the example servlets that come with Tomcat. First compile and copy DebugFilter into %CATALINA_HOME%/webapps/examples/WEB-INF/classes/debugging. Then add the following entry to the web.xml file in %CATALINA_HOME%/webapps/examples/WEB-INF (after the existing <filter> entries):

```
<filter>
  <filter-name>DebugFilter</filter-name>
  <filter-class>debugging.DebugFilter</filter-class>
</filter>
```

Add this element after the existing <filter-mapping> elements:

```
<filter-mapping>
  <filter-name>DebugFilter</filter-name>
  <url-pattern>/*</url-pattern>
</filter-mapping>
```

Restart Tomcat and access one of the example servlets. I accessed the SessionExample servlet at http://localhost:8080/examples/servlet/SessionExample.

The tagged output from the Debugging Filter can be found in the examples log file in the `%CATALINA_HOME%/logs` directory. I saw the following entry:

```
<invocation>
  <sender>127.0.0.1</sender>
  <message></message>
  <receiver>/examples/servlet/SessionExample</receiver>
  <duration>140</duration>
</invocation>
...
<invocation>
  <sender>127.0.0.1</sender>
  <message></message>
  <receiver>/examples/images/code.gif</receiver>
  <duration>10</duration>
</invocation>
...
<invocation>
  <sender>127.0.0.1</sender>
  <message></message>
  <receiver>/examples/images/return.gif</receiver>
  <duration>10</duration>
</invocation>
```

We now have the ability to record the sequence in which invocations of this servlet are made from various remote clients (the <sender> element) with various parameter lists (the <message> element). So we can determine a typical multi-user usage pattern for our web application and capture some performance data (the <duration> element).

Debugging with Event Listeners

The event listener mechanism allows us to trap certain container events such as the creation and destruction of contexts and sessions as well as the modification of session and context attributes. This is important information that will allow us to debug problems associated with session tracking and the use of data held in the session or the context.

Implementing the Debugging Listener

We have a single event listener to implement, which will implement four interfaces:

- ❑ `ServletContextListener` – through which we're notified of context creation and destruction

- ❑ `HttpSessionListener` – through which we're notified of session creation and destruction

- ❑ `ServletContextAttributeListener` – through which we're notified when context attributes are added, modified, and removed

- ❑ `HttpSessionAttributeListener` – through which we're notified when session attributes are added, modified, and removed

```
package debugging;

import java.io.*;
import javax.servlet.*;
import javax.servlet.http.*;

public class DebugListener implements ServletContextListener, HttpSessionListener,
                                      ServletContextAttributeListener,
                                      HttpSessionAttributeListener {

    private ServletContext servletContext = null;
```

We implement two utility methods that are used to write information to the log. By using these methods we can easily change the way in which we output our debugging information – we might, for example, want to write to a file other than the servlet log:

```
    private void logContext(String message) {
      if (servletContext != null) {
        StringBuffer messageBuffer = new StringBuffer();
        messageBuffer.append("<invocation><sender>");
        messageBuffer.append(servletContext.getServerInfo());
        messageBuffer.append("</sender><message>" + message +
                             "</message><receiver>");
        String contextName = servletContext.getServletContextName();
        if (contextName == null) {
          contextName=servletContext.toString();
        }
        messageBuffer.append("CONTEXT: " + contextName);
        messageBuffer.append("</receiver></invocation>");
        servletContext.log(messageBuffer.toString());
      }
    }

    private void logSession(String message, HttpSessionEvent event) {
      if (servletContext != null) {
        StringBuffer messageBuffer = new StringBuffer();
        messageBuffer.append("<invocation><sender>");
        messageBuffer.append(servletContext.getServerInfo());
        messageBuffer.append("</sender><message>" + message +
                             "</message><receiver>");
        messageBuffer.append("SESSION: " + event.getSession().getId());
        messageBuffer.append("</receiver></invocation>");
        servletContext.log(messageBuffer.toString());
      }
    }
```

We need a set of methods to record the context initialization and destruction, the session creation and destruction, and the modification of attribute values:

```
    public void contextInitialized(ServletContextEvent event) {
      servletContext = event.getServletContext();
      logContext("init()");
    }
```

```java
public void contextDestroyed(ServletContextEvent event) {
  logContext("destroy");
  servletContext = null;
}

public void attributeAdded(ServletContextAttributeEvent event) {
  logContext("setAttribute(" + event.getName() + "," +
             event.getValue().toString() + ")");
}

public void attributeReplaced(ServletContextAttributeEvent event) {
  logContext("setAttribute(" + event.getName() + "," +
             event.getValue().toString() + ")");
}

public void attributeRemoved(ServletContextAttributeEvent event) {
  logContext("removeAttribute(" + event.getName() + ")");
}

public void sessionCreated(HttpSessionEvent event) {
  logSession("create", event);
}

public void sessionDestroyed(HttpSessionEvent event) {
  logSession("destroy", event);
}

public void attributeAdded(HttpSessionBindingEvent event) {
  logSession("setAttribute(" + event.getName() + "," +
             event.getValue().toString() + ")", event);
}

public void attributeReplaced(HttpSessionBindingEvent event) {
  logSession("setAttribute(" + event.getName() + "," +
             event.getValue().toString() + ")", event);
}

public void attributeRemoved(HttpSessionBindingEvent event) {
  logSession("removeAttribute(" + event.getName() + ")", event);
}
```

Using the Debugging Listener

As with the Debugging Filter, we'll test the Debugging Listener by applying it to the example servlets that come with Tomcat. Compile and copy DebugListener into %CATALINA_HOME%/webapps/examples/WEB-INF/classes/debugging. Then add the following entry to the web.xml file in %CATALINA_HOME%/webapps/examples/WEB-INF:

```xml
<listener>
  <listener-class>debugging.DebugListener</listener-class>
</listener>
```

Restart Tomcat and again try an example servlet. I accessed the `SessionExample` servlet at http://localhost:8080/examples/servlet/SessionExample and saw the following entry in the server's log file:

```
<invocation>
  <sender>127.0.0.1</sender>
  <message></message>
  <receiver>/examples/images/code.gif</receiver>
  <duration>10</duration>
</invocation>
...
<invocation>
  <sender>127.0.0.1</sender>
  <message></message>
  <receiver>/examples/images/return.gif</receiver>
  <duration>0</duration>
</invocation>
...
<invocation>
  <sender>127.0.0.1</sender>
  <message></message>
  <receiver>/examples/servlet/SessionExample</receiver>
  <duration>201</duration>
</invocation>
```

This technique is complementary to the one we created using filters. Using both methods we can now trace:

❑ The creation of a servlet context (using an event listener)

❑ Each servlet invocation with its request parameters (using a filter)

❑ Whether a request triggered creation of a new session (using an event listener)

❑ Whether any session or context attributes were modified by the servlet (using an event listener)

❑ The destruction of the session and the context (using an event listener)

For many debugging tasks, that's all that's required.

Debugging with the JPDA

Let's turn our attention to the Java Platform Debugger Architecture (JPDA). The JPDA offers an alternative method that we can use to capture debugging information. We need the JPDA to write a debugger that's not limited to web applications and that can debug remotely across a network.

> **The Java Platform Debugger Architecture provides a standard set of protocols and APIs at three levels that facilitate the construction of (remote) debugging and profiling tools.**

The JPDA consists of three parts:

❏ The **Java Virtual Machine Debug Interface (JVMDI)** – the entry point to the target Java Virtual Machine (JVM)

❏ The **Java Debug Wire Protocol (JDWP)** – an inter-process communication protocol

❏ The **Java Debug Interface (JDI)** – the front-end API

Any application that we want to debug must be running in a JVM that supports the JVMDI (such a JVM has been available since J2SE version 1.3 on all platforms).

Interesting events such as method invocations and variable modifications are propagated, via the JDWP, from the JVMDI to any front-end debugger that is listening. The JDI hides the details of the JVMDI and JDWP behind a set of Java interfaces that simplify the task of writing a debugger front end.

We could actually use the JDWP to write a debugger in a language other than Java; and as a wire protocol it supports remote debugging across a network.

The following diagram shows how the various parts of the JPDA fit together:

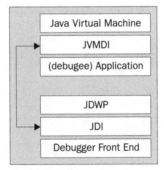

Implementing the JPDA Debugger

We'll implement a front end to the JPDA that we can attach to any application. The JVM that the application is running within does not have to be the same JVM as the debugger is running on. The JVMs could even be running on different networks or operating systems.

We'll implement a single class, JPDADebugger, which will listen for method entry events from the remote JVM. JPDADebugger will perform a similar function to DebugFilter, but is not limited to only trapping the service methods of a servlet.

This is the implementation of `JPDADebugger`. To compile this class we need to include `%JAVA_HOME%/lib/tools.jar` in the classpath:

```
package debugging;

import com.sun.jdi.*;
import com.sun.jdi.event.*;
import com.sun.jdi.connect.*;
import com.sun.jdi.request.*;
import java.util.*;

public class JPDADebugger {
   private static int SOCKET_ATTACH = 1;
   private VirtualMachine vm = null;
   private boolean running;
```

Our entry point for this class will be the `main()` method, which takes two command-line arguments. The first allows the location of the target VM to be specified:

```
-attach targetMachine:targetPort
```

The second allows us to specify the subset of classes that we want to watch, so that we're not overwhelmed by method entry events:

```
-include apackage.*:apackage.apackage.*
```

The `main()` method parses these command-line arguments, creates an instance of `JPDADebugger`, and sets it running with the supplied arguments:

```
public static void main(String args[]) {
   String attachAddress = null;
   Vector includeClasses = new Vector();
   for (int i = 0; i < args.length; i++) {
     String thisArg = args[i];
     if (thisArg.equals("-attach")) {
       attachAddress = args[++i];
     } else if (thisArg.equals("-include")) {
       String incString = args[++i];
       StringTokenizer st = new StringTokenizer(incString,":",false);
       while (st.hasMoreTokens()) {
         String thisOne = st.nextToken();
         System.out.println("including " + thisOne);
         includeClasses.addElement(thisOne);
       }
     }
   }
   JPDADebugger thisDebugger = new JPDADebugger();
   try {
     thisDebugger.execute(attachAddress, includeClasses);
   } catch (Exception ex) {
     ex.printStackTrace();
   }
}
```

Next we create an `execute()` method, in which we we attach to the remote VM and go into a loop while we wait for debug events:

```
public void execute(String attachAddress, Vector includeClasses) {
  if (includeClasses == null) {
    includeClasses = new Vector();
  }
```

Our connection to the remote virtual machine will be defined by four values. Here we initialize them to default values that will be overwritten by the values supplied on the command line:

```
String connectorName = null;
int connectType = -1;
String connectHost = null;
String connectPort = null;
```

The JPDA supports various techniques for connecting to an application running in a target VM, so the following `if` statement could be extended with `else` clauses that correspond to the different connection techniques. For example, the user could provide the name of the main class of an application to be debugged (and launched automatically) rather than the network address of an already-running virtual machine. If our class did support various connection methods we'd want to know which one had succeeded, which is why the `connectType` variable is set to the constant `SOCKET_ATTACH`:

```
if (attachAddress != null) {
  connectorName = "com.sun.jdi.SocketAttach";
  connectType = SOCKET_ATTACH;
  int index = attachAddress.indexOf(":");
  connectHost = attachAddress.substring(0,index);
  connectPort = attachAddress.substring(index + 1);
} else {
  throw new Exception ("ERROR: No attach address specified");
}
```

Our target application will be the servlet container, which will most likely be running on a remote machine, possibly on a different operating system, and with no possibility of us launching it on demand. This leaves the socket attaching connector as the only suitable connector:

```
Connector connector = null;
List connectors = Bootstrap.virtualMachineManager().allConnectors();
Iterator iter = connectors.iterator();
while (iter.hasNext()) {
  Connector thisConnector = (Connector)iter.next();
  if (thisConnector.name().equals(connectorName))
    connector = thisConnector;
}
```

If we didn't find a connector we throw an exception:

```
if (connector == null) {
  throw new Exception("ERROR: No connector with name " + connectorName);
}
```

Set the host and port arguments of the connector:

```
Map arguments = connector.defaultArguments();
Connector.Argument hostname = (Connector.Argument)arguments.get("hostname");
Connector.Argument port = (Connector.Argument)arguments.get("port");
hostname.setValue(connectHost);
port.setValue(connectPort);
```

Cast the connector to an `AttachingConnector` and try to attach to the remote VM:

```
AttachingConnector attacher = (AttachingConnector) connector;
vm = null;
try {
  vm = attacher.attach(arguments);
} catch (Exception e) {
  e.printStackTrace();
  throw new Exception ("ERROR: " + e + "@ attempting socket attach.");
}
```

Throw an exception if we can't get hold of the remote VM:

```
if (vm == null) {
  throw new Exception("ERROR: No VM process connected.");
}
```

Now that we've connected to the remote JVM we can register our interest in certain method invocations. We get the JVM's `EventRequestManager` and add a `MethodEntryRequest` with a filter for each included class. We'll be trapping events relating to a subset of the classes that compose the target application. Not only does this aid our comprehension of the results, but it also helps not to overload the target JVM:

```
EventRequestManager em = v m.eventRequestManager();
for (Enumeration e = includeClasses.elements(); e.hasMoreElements(); ) {
  MethodEntryRequest meR = em.createMethodEntryRequest();
  String pattern = (String) e.nextElement();
  meR.addClassFilter(pattern);
  meR.enable();
}
```

We get hold of the JVM event queue. The target JVM places events corresponding with our method entry requests onto a queue as they occur. We repeatedly poll this queue in order to obtain sets of events that we've not yet processed:

```
EventQueue eventQ = vm.eventQueue();
running = true;

while (running) {
  EventSet eventSet = null;
  try {
    eventSet = eventQ.remove();
  } catch (Exception e) {
    System.err.println("ERROR: Interrupted Event Loop");
    e.printStackTrace();
  }
```

We step through the events and process each one. For each set of events that we pop from the queue, we call our processMethodEntryEvent() method to log them:

```
EventIterator eventIterator = eventSet.eventIterator();
while (eventIterator.hasNext()) {
  Event event = eventIterator.nextEvent();
  if (event instanceof MethodEntryEvent) {
    processMethodEntryEvent((MethodEntryEvent)event);
  }
}
```

Finally, we tell the target JVM to resume. Not only do we listen in to the remote JVM, but we can also control it. So, once we've processed each set of events, we restart the suspended JVM:

```
    vm.resume();
  }
}
```

For each event that we receive, the processMethodEntryEvent() method is invoked. For each MethodEntryEvent, we discover and record the name of the method that was called, the thread on which it occurred, and the names of the caller and called objects:

```
private void processMethodEntryEvent(MethodEntryEvent event) {
  String methodString = event.method().toString();
  ThreadReference thread = event.thread();
```

Get hold of the stack frames for this thread:

```
List stackList = null;
try { stackList = thread.frames(); }
catch (Exception e) { return; }
```

Initialize the caller and callee information:

```
String calleeID = "?";
String calleeClass = "?";
String callerID = "?";
String callerClass = "?";
```

To discover the sender and receiver of the message, the caller and called objects, we'll be looking on the thread's stack frame. The topmost item will be the object that received the message, and the next item will be the object that sent the message:

```
int level = 0;
for (Iterator it = stackList.iterator(); it.hasNext();) {
  StackFrame stackFrame = (StackFrame) it.next();
  ObjectReference thisObject = stackFrame.thisObject();
```

417

```
    if (thisObject == null) {
      continue;
    }
    if (level == 0)
      calleeID = String.valueOf(thisObject.uniqueID());
      String classString = thisObject.referenceType().toString();
      StringTokenizer st = new StringTokenizer(classString," ");
      calleeClass = st.nextToken();
      calleeClass = st.nextToken();
    } else if (level == 1) {
      callerID=String.valueOf(thisObject.uniqueID());
      String classString = thisObject.referenceType().toString();
      StringTokenizer st = new StringTokenizer(classString," ");
      callerClass = st.nextToken();
      callerClass = st.nextToken();
    }

    level++;
    if (level > 1) {
      break;
    }
  }
}
```

To be consitent with the output from our filter and the event listener we print the result with tags:

```
System.out.println("<invocation><sender>" + callerID + ":" + callerClass +
                   "</sender><message>" + methodString +
                   "</message><receiver>" +
                   calleeID + ":" + calleeClass + "</receiver><thread>" +
                   thread.name() + "</thread></invocation>");
  }
```

That completes JPDADebugger, which we can now use to trace the progress of any Java application. However, before we can run our debugger we need to give it something to attach to.

Running the Server in Debug Mode

We'll be using JPDADebugger to inspect the servlet container as it runs. Before we can do this we need to make the container available to our debugger by running the server in debug mode.

Whatever servlet container you're using, there will be a file that starts the server via a Java command. For Tomcat, you should make the following addition to the catalina script in the %CATALINA_HOME%\bin directory:

```
%_STARTJAVA%
-Xdebug -Xnoagent -Xrunjdwp:transport=dt_socket,server=y,address=8124,suspend=n
%CATALINA_OPTS% -Dcatalina.home="%CATALINA_HOME%"
org.apache.catalina.startup.Bootstrap %2 %3 %4 %5 %6 %7 %8 %9 start
```

If you're using a different servlet container, you'll need to make a similar change to the command that sets it running. So that you know what you're doing, here's an explanation of the options we use with Tomcat:

❑ `-Xdebug` and `-Xnoagent`
Tells the JVM to run in debug mode but not to use the debugging agent for the legacy Java debugger, `jdb`

❑ `-Xrunjdwp:transport=dt_socket,server=y,address=8124,suspend=n`
Tells the JVM to listen for socket connections on port 8124 (which was chosen at random), to act as a server for events, and not to suspend its execution before a connection is made

You can now start Tomcat using the `catalina` script:

```
catalina start
```

With the target server running, we can run our JPDA debugger.

Using the JPDA Debugger

Remember to include `%JAVA_HOME%/lib/tools.jar` in your classpath. Then run the debugger with the following command:

```
java debugging.JPDADebugger -attach localhost:8124 -include
SessionExample:javax.servlet.http.* > debug.txt
```

Recall the command-line arguments processed by the `main()` method:

❑ The first instructs our debugger to attach to the appropriate port on the relevant machine. We set this port number when we modified the `catalina` script.

❑ The second tells the debugger to listen in on events relating to certain classes, in this case the `SessionExample` servlet and all classes in the `javax.servlet.http.*` package. If you want to include all classes in the debug trace, you can specify `'*'` on the command line. (The quotes are needed to prevent the command interpreter from replacing the `*` symbol before passing it as a parameter to the Java program.)

The output is redirected to a text file (`debug.txt`) because as we're running our debugger outside the servlet container, we have no server log file to write to. If you want to see the events in real-time simply remove the file redirection from the command line and watch the console output.

Output from the JPDA Debugger

Once we've started Tomcat in debug mode, and started the debugger, we can test it by running one of the example servlets. Once again, I accessed http://localhost:8080/examples/servlet/SessionExample and saw the following output from the debugger:

```
<invocation>
    <sender>10:org.apache.catalina.connector.http.HttpProcessor</sender>
    <message>
        javax.servlet.http.Cookie.<init>(java.lang.String, java.lang.String)
    </message>
    <receiver>7:javax.servlet.http.Cookie</receiver>
    <thread>HttpProcessor[8080][4]
    </thread>
</invocation>
<invocation>
    <sender>7:javax.servlet.http.Cookie</sender>
    <message>javax.servlet.http.Cookie.isToken(java.lang.String)</message>
    <receiver>7:javax.servlet.http.Cookie</receiver>
    <thread>HttpProcessor[8080][4]</thread>
</invocation>
<invocation>
    <sender>10:org.apache.catalina.connector.http.HttpProcessor</sender>
    <message>javax.servlet.http.Cookie.getName()</message>
    <receiver>7:javax.servlet.http.Cookie</receiver>
    <thread>HttpProcessor[8080][4]</thread>
</invocation>
<invocation>
    <sender>10:org.apache.catalina.connector.http.HttpProcessor</sender>
    <message>javax.servlet.http.Cookie.getValue()</message>
    <receiver>7:javax.servlet.http.Cookie</receiver>
    <thread>HttpProcessor[8080][4]</thread>
</invocation>
<invocation>
    <sender>30:org.apache.catalina.core.ApplicationFilterChain</sender>
    <message>
        javax.servlet.http.HttpServlet.service(javax.servlet.ServletRequest,
        javax.servlet.ServletResponse)
    </message>
    <receiver>26:SessionExample</receiver>
    <thread>HttpProcessor[8080][4]</thread>
</invocation>
```

This output contains a lot of useful information but it's not too pleasant to look at. We'll do something about that now.

Visualizing the Debug Trace

We placed the output from all three techniques within tags. This allows the results to be easily interpreted by other applications. By preceding the logged results with an appropriate XML DTD we could use the Java API for XML Processing (JAXP) as a basis for additional programs that analyze the results (for example by counting up the number of calls to each method) or that present the results in a more readable form.

I've created a trace viewer that takes the file produced by the JPDA Debugger, or an equivalent file that you create by picking out blocks of `DebugListener` and `EventListener` entries from the Tomcat server log file.

The sourcecode for this class won't teach you about debugging, so we won't show it here. It is, however, included in the code download available from http://www.wrox.com/.

To use the `TraceViewer` you'll need a file that contains tagged output from the JPDA Debugger, or built from entries taken from the server log file. If the output is in a file called `debug.txt`, you can view it by running this command:

```
java debugging.TraceViewer debug.txt
```

Sample Debug Trace Visualizations

We'll look at two sample visualizations of the debugging output. We'll do this not only to illustrate how the output may be presented in a more aesthetically pleasing way but also to highlight one of the subtleties of our debugging code.

We'll run the `SessionExample` servlet simultaneously in two browser windows, to demonstrate a multi-user scenario. In one window we set the attribute `name` to value `bill` and in the other window we set it to value `ben`:

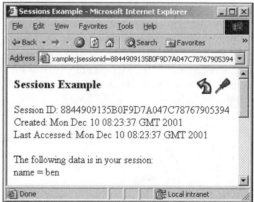

In this sample visualization I've combined events from the Debugging Filter and the Debugging Listener, with both sets of events taken from the server log file:

```
SENDER: Apache Tomcat/4.0.1
  MESSAGE: setAttribute(name,bill)
  RECEIVER: SESSION: 3342D16261A961C30231E25050F59897
  THREAD:
  DURATION:

SENDER: 127.0.0.1
  MESSAGE: ?datavalue=bill&dataname=name
  RECEIVER: /examples/servlet/SessionExample
  THREAD:
  DURATION: 10ms

SENDER: Apache Tomcat/4.0.1
  MESSAGE: setAttribute(name,ben)
  RECEIVER: SESSION: B1C2095069E1C3C440E6A44872F39076
  THREAD:
  DURATION:

SENDER: 127.0.0.1
  MESSAGE: ?datavalue=ben&dataname=name
  RECEIVER: /examples/servlet/SessionExample
  THREAD:
  DURATION: 10ms
```

This is easier to follow than the tagged text, and it shows something very important. According to this trace, the attributes have been set before the servlets that set them have actually been invoked. The container is not psychic, and it's not broken either. The problem can be found back in the doFilter() method of the DebugFilter class, which included these lines of code:

```
long startTime = System.currentTimeMillis();
chain.doFilter(request, response);
long endTime = System.currentTimeMillis();
long duration = endTime - startTime;
messageBuffer.append("<duration>" + duration + "</duration>");
messageBuffer.append("</invocation>");
filterConfig.getServletContext().log(messageBuffer.toString());
```

In order to record the duration of each servlet invocation, we didn't add the invocation to the server log file until it completed, during which time some attribute modifications occurred and were trapped by the event listener. So to see messages in the correct order we would need to move the final line of code to precede the call to chain.doFilter(), although this would result in the loss of the duration information.

Here is the JPDA Debugger view of the same scenario:

```
SENDER: 44:SessionExample
  MESSAGE: javax.servlet.http.HttpServlet.service(javax.servlet.http.HttpServletRequest, javax.servlet.http.HttpServletResponse)
  RECEIVER: 44:SessionExample
  THREAD: HttpProcessor[8080][2]
  DURATION:

SENDER: 44:SessionExample
  MESSAGE: SessionExample.doPost(javax.servlet.http.HttpServletRequest, javax.servlet.http.HttpServletResponse)
  RECEIVER: 44:SessionExample
  THREAD: HttpProcessor[8080][2]
  DURATION:

SENDER: 120:org.apache.catalina.connector.http.HttpResponseImpl
  MESSAGE: javax.servlet.http.HttpUtils.getRequestURL(javax.servlet.http.HttpServletRequest)
  RECEIVER: 120:org.apache.catalina.connector.http.HttpResponseImpl
  THREAD: HttpProcessor[8080][1]
  DURATION:

SENDER: 44:SessionExample
  MESSAGE: SessionExample.doGet(javax.servlet.http.HttpServletRequest, javax.servlet.http.HttpServletResponse)
  RECEIVER: 44:SessionExample
  THREAD: HttpProcessor[8080][2]
  DURATION:
```

This sample visualization illustrates two very important things about the JPDA Debugger:

❑ It can be used to discover the inner workings of the servlet container down to the deepest level, limited only by the class packages that are specified when it is run.

❑ It can record the thread on which each event occurred (in the form of `HttpProcessor[8080][1]`). This shows that multiple concurrent clients (in this case two) are serviced by separate threads (more about that in the next chapter).

Both of those features are only available by using the JPDA.

Choosing a Debugging Technique

The three techniques we've looked at are not mutually exclusive. It's perfectly possible to combine output from all three methods in a single output file or, with a bit of ingenuity, pass it through to a real-time debugger front end of a centralized logging service (perhaps an Enterprise JavaBean). Combining all three will give the most comprehensive picture of what's going on inside your servlets and the container.

The filter and the event listener are particularly cohesive because they are so similar in operation and in deployment. So we'll put them together and contrast that combination with the JPDA approach.

You might think that the JPDA is the obvious choice because:

❑ We can watch *any* combination of classes that compose your web application, plus those of the supporting container

❑ We can run the debugger front end on a remote machine

❑ It's not limited to servlet debugging

423

However, the run-time overhead and the relative complexity of the API mean that:

❑ The servlet container runs much slower in debug mode, so it's not ideal for tracking problems in a live system, particularly performance problems

❑ A JPDA debugger front end is much more difficult to write than a filter and event listener combination

❑ The sheer level of information produced as output can make it difficult to pick out the important details

Also, if you work in a corporate environment that restricts your control over the server, you'll have to convince someone else to start it up in debug mode.

The main limitations of a filter and event listener combination are:

❑ The range of events that you can trap is quite limited

❑ It is limited to debugging servlet applications

❑ We have to modify the deployment descriptor for each application that we wish to debug, although (crucially) not the code of the servlets themselves

Of course, the limited information available via this approach may be exactly the kind of information you want for servlet debugging. You might simply want to know:

❑ Which servlets are invoked, in what order, from which remote clients, and with what request parameters

❑ When sessions and contexts are created and destroyed, and how the attributes are managed so as to maintain isolation between multiple client requests

Also, there is very little impact on performance, which makes this approach suitable for performance measurement.

The information provided by the filter and listener combination is much more meaningful in a web context. Messages are sent from IP addresses to servlet URLs or to numbered sessions, and the messages provide the parameter and attribute values, not just the method signatures. Getting that kind of meaningful information out of the JPDA would not be so easy.

> **Filters and event listeners are my preferred approach for debugging web applications. They're easy to write, easy to deploy, have a low performance overhead, and provide meaningful (if somewhat limited) information. A well-written filter or listener class is a handy component that can be inserted into any web application.**

Logging Enhancements in J2SE 1.4

In this chapter we've used the Tomcat server log file as a central holding area for debug messages from the filter and the event listener. That was simple to do but it was not without its problems:

- ❑ The messages that we're interested in may be interspersed with other log file entries that we need to strip out prior to visualization

- ❑ Our JPDA Debugger had no comprehension of the server log file so we had to direct its output to a standalone file

For the full picture of what's happening in our servlets and container it would be best for all debugging messages to be channeled through to a common file or a real-time analyzer.

We haven't used any of the new features available in J2SE version 1.4 so far, but if you are using that version, or will be soon, then there's some good news. Its Logging API allow you to send debug messages to a `Logger` object, which publishes those messages (`LogRecord` objects) with the help of a `Handler` object. The various styles of publication, such as writing to a file or sending to a remote monitoring process, are handled by the various types of `Handler`:

- ❑ `StreamHandler` – A simple handler for writing formatted records to an `OutputStream`

- ❑ `ConsoleHandler` – A simple handler for writing formatted records to `System.err`

- ❑ `FileHandler` – A handler that writes formatted log records either to a single file, or to a set of rotating log files

- ❑ `SocketHandler` – A handler that writes formatted log records to remote TCP ports

- ❑ `MemoryHandler` – A handler that buffers log records in memory

Coupling the Debugging Components with J2SE 1.4

The logging feature does nothing to help us capture the debugging information in the first place. It won't tell us which servlets have been called, in what order, or by which remote clients. It won't tell us when sessions are created and destroyed, and how the session attributes are modified. It won't tell us what interactions have occurred between low-level container objects. So it won't replace the debugging mechanisms we developed earlier.

What it will do is provide a standard coupling mechanism for debugging components. The following diagram shows how the components we've developed could be connected via the Logging API:

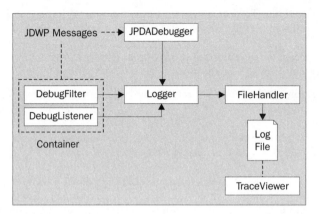

When debugging web applications I think it's better to review the object interactions in the form of a trace, after the event, than it is to step through the events one-by-one as your would with a standalone single-user program. However, if you want to step through the events then the following configuration would be more appropriate:

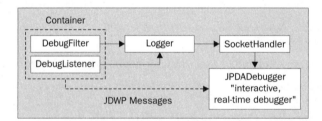

Formatting the Debugging Output with J2SE 1.4

We wrote our debugging output with embedded tags in order to make the results suitable for further processing. As a consequence, the logged output was not very readable until we looked at it using the `TraceViewer` class.

The Logging API can help us out there because it supports the idea of Formatters that render the debugging output in various ways. You can write your own Formatters or take advantage of the two that are supplied by default:

❑ `SimpleFormatter` – Writes brief, readable summaries of log records

❑ `XMLFormatter` – Writes detailed XML-structured information

The following listing shows some typical output using `XMLFormatter` (which is similar to what we produced):

```
<?xml version="1.0" encoding="UTF-8" standalone="no"?>
<!DOCTYPE log SYSTEM "logger.dtd">
<log>
<record>
  <date>2000-08-23 19:21:05</date>
  <millis>967083665789</millis>
  <sequence>1256</sequence>
  <logger>kgh.test.fred</logger>
  <level>INFO</level>
  <class>kgh.test.XMLTest</class>
  <method>writeLog</method>
  <thread>10</thread>
  <message>Hello world!</message>
</record>
</log>
```

We'll round off the chapter with an idea for enhancing the software that we've developed so far.

Runtime Reverse Engineering with UML

You're probably used to reverse-engineering Java code into a UML model. Just feed in some Java source files and you're rewarded with a class diagram that shows the static relationships between the classes in your application.

What about other UML diagrams, such as sequence diagrams, that describe the dynamic behavior of an application? We can draw them up-front to show how we expect the application to behave, but it would be useful if we could reverse-engineer them as well, in order to find out if the actual behavior of the system matched the original design.

Well, we've actually developed a rudimentary **runtime reverse-engineering tool** that allows you to do just that. Look back at the sample visualizations produced by `TraceViewer`. We have all the information we need to render a proper UML sequence diagram: a sender object, a message, and a receiver object. With a little more ingenuity we could even come up with something like this:

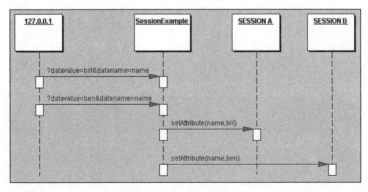

We wouldn't even have to write our own visualization tool; we could simply output the debugging messages in an XML format that could be loaded into a UML tool such as Rational Rose or TogetherJ.

Summary

We started this chapter by listing some of the problems associated with servlet development that make servlet debugging different from traditional debugging. We don't want our application to be adversely affected by simply observing it, which established that non-invasive techniques were the preferred approach to debugging web applications.

We demonstrated the usefulness of filters and event listeners by developing some simple non-invasive debugging components that could be added to any web application. These components were used to capture information about how a web application operates. As an alternative, we looked at the Java Platform Debugger Architecture (which is not part of the Servlets API). We saw how the JPDA offers greater debugging possibilities but at the cost of additional complexity and performance degradation.

For each of the techniques we produced debugging output in a consistent tagged format that lent itself to visualization and further processing. The `TraceViewer` class provided a simple example of this.

After comparing the three approaches, with filters and events listener coming out (just about) on top, we discussed how they could be brought together into a flexible debugging architecture based on the J2SE 1.4 Logging API.

Finally we looked briefly at the idea of a novel run-time reverse-engineering tool, based entirely on what we covered in this chapter.

In the next chapter we'll look at some real-life servlet problems involving class loading and synchronization that can be investigated using the techniques we've learned.

11

Class Loading and Synchronization

We've learned a lot about the power of servlets and how we can use them in web applications, but when we were testing all of these things, we did so on a single computer, with no more than a few users accessing the web application at a time. This is not the situation we would find our web applications and servlets dealing with in a production environment – then they would be expected to deal with thousands of simultaneous connections. There are many considerations we must make for a production system that can be easily overlooked when we are developing and testing applications in an environment that we control.

In an environment that we don't control, changes might be made to the system that adversely affect our application. We might have to share a server with a number of other web applications. How can we be sure that changes made to these applications won't affect our own? What happens if the developer of another web application decides to use a different XML parser from ours. Can we continue to use our own parser?

In this chapter, we'll look at these considerations. We'll try to understand the root cause of the problems, and we'll learn how to stop them from occurring in our own applications. Specifically, we'll look at:

❑ How the server (in particular Tomcat) loads classes, where it looks for classes to load, and the order it looks for classes in different locations

❑ The implications of using multi-threaded rather than single-threaded servlets, the conflicts that can occur, as well as the benefits it can bring

As we work our way through the chapter we'll use the debugging components and debug trace viewer we created in Chapter 10 to show what is really happening inside the container in each scenario.

Class Loading

Java applications, including web applications, are built from a collection of classes at *run* time, not at *development* time. The programs are built from classes loaded into memory by **classloaders**. This means that we can factor-out classes that are common to many applications and deploy them in a central location, to be found and loaded into those applications only when they are needed. This means:

- ❑ Applications can be much smaller
- ❑ We can change generic (non application-specific) behavior globally, without the need to recompile and redeploy individual applications

We'll concentrate on the second of these. We'll investigate how the Java Virtual Machine (JVM) looks for classes at run time; the locations that it looks in; and the order that it looks in different locations. Once we understand this, we'll be able to ensure that our applications work the way we intend them to.

Here are some typical statements that will result in a class being loaded. In the first case we would probably assume the StringBuffer class to be a standard Java runtime class, to be loaded from the runtime library rt.jar:

```
StringBuffer sb = new StringBuffer("This will load into memory");
```

In this case we would probably assume class Bank to be specific to our application, contained in the application's JAR file:

```
Bank theBank = new Bank ("BigBank");
```

In this case we probably would expect the JDBC driver class to be used by many applications and hence deployed in a common location:

```
Class.forName("org.gjt.mm.msql.Driver");
```

The JVM makes no such assumptions and there's nothing in these statements to indicate that the classes should be loaded from specific locations. The decision on where to look for classes is the responsibility of the classloader, or rather, the chain of classloaders.

> **Classloaders exist in a chain. Each classloader has its own special way of finding classes at a specific location (for example in the application's JAR file, in a library JAR file, from a URL, or in the standard Java runtime library).**

If the current classloader can find and load the required class, it will. If it can't it will ask its parent, which might ask its parent, and so on up the chain until the class is found and loaded, or the end of the chain is reached.

What does this mean for web applications? Firstly it means that we must deploy our application-specific classes and application-independent classes in one of the locations that the servlet container's chain of classloaders will look for them – otherwise the classes will not be found at all.

Secondly, it means that we need to take special care if classes with the same name, but different implementations, are deployed in more than one place. The behavior of our application will depend on which version of the class is actually loaded.

Thirdly, it means that we need to understand the scope of a class (in particular, the scope of its static variables) according to the location from which it is loaded. The logic of an application may be adversely affected by simply deploying a class in the wrong place.

Class Loading in the Servlet Container

We have a choice of how we package and deploy the classes that compose our web applications. We could put everything in a single WAR. Alternatively, we could decide that some classes or groups of classes are reusable between applications, so it makes more sense to create a separate JAR that can be deployed alongside any web application that requires it. We could even have some classes (such as JDBC drivers or XML parsers) that we want to make available to all applications. Then, when we want to upgrade the classes they only need to be replaced once.

Exactly where to deploy classes is an often-misunderstood topic that even experienced developers run into trouble with. There are three important considerations to make:

❑ **Accessibility**
Can an application and the container find the required classes?

❑ **Reusability**
Should we deploy the same set of classes separately for each application that uses them?

❑ **Separation**
What conflicts might occur when several applications use the static values of common classes?

Deployment Organization

There are five locations where we could conceivably deploy classes within Tomcat:

❑ The `%CATALINA_HOME%/common/lib` directory

❑ The `%CATALINA_HOME%/lib` directory

❑ The `%CATALINA_HOME%/server/lib` directory

❑ The `WEB-INF/classes` directory of a web application

❑ The `WEB-INF/lib` directory of a web application

In general, application-independent classes should be packaged in a JAR and placed in the `/lib` or `/common/lib` directory of Tomcat. Application classes should be placed (within their package structure) in the `WEB-INF/classes` directory of the application context, or in a JAR within the `WEB-INF/lib` directory.

It would be useful if the container could discover the dependencies of a deployed web application so it could ensure that those dependencies are satisfied prior to attempting to run the application. The Servlet 2.3 specification suggests a mechanism for this based on specifying dependencies to common JARs in the `MANIFEST.MF` file of a WAR. However, at the time of writing, Tomcat does not yet support this feature.

Locating Classes and Other Resources

To investigate the problems associated with class loading it would be useful to have a simple way of finding out the location from which the servlet container will load any given class; and in the case of a class deployed in multiple locations, to tell us which version of the class will take precedence.

The following servlet will allow us to do just that. It could be deployed as part of any web application to aid in debugging:

```
package classloading;

import java.net.*;
import java.io.*;
import javax.servlet.*;
import javax.servlet.http.*;

public class ResourceLocatorServlet extends HttpServlet {
```

The doGet() method takes a resource name (which in most cases will be the name of a class) as a parameter:

```
public void doGet (HttpServletRequest req, HttpServletResponse res)
  throws ServletException, IOException {
```

We try to find the resource using the current classloader:

```
String resource = req.getParameter("resource");
URL resourceURL = null;
String resourceURLString = null;
```

The next clause is key. It asks the servlet to get hold of the resource (the supplied class name) using its classloader (or another classloader in the chain). We receive a URL that indicates where the given class would be loaded from if it were to be instantiated within our application:

```
if (resource != null) {
  resourceURL = this.getClass().getResource(resource);      }
if (resourceURL != null) {
  resourceURLString = resourceURL.toString();
}

PrintWriter writer = res.getWriter();
```

We're using the getResource() method of Class; javax.servlet.ServletContext also has a getResource() method that does not use classloaders.

Finally, we communicate to the user the location of the requested resource:

```
    writer.println("<html><head></head>");
    writer.println("<body style=\"font-family:verdana;font-size:8pt\">");
    writer.println("<h3>Resource Locator</h3>");
    writer.println("<p>" + resource + "</p><p>Found at:</p>");
    writer.println(resourceURLString);
    writer.println("</body></html>");
    writer.close();
  }
}
```

> *We can also use the* `getResource()` *method to get hold of other resources, such as image or sound files from within a JAR. If you've ever written an application that loads graphics or sounds from files and you wonder why it no longer works when you package everything in a JAR file, try using* `getResource()` *to get hold of those files.*

We'll deploy `ResourceLocatorServlet` in a web application called `ClassLoading`. Then we can use the servlet to find any given class. For example, we can find the location of `javax.servlet.http.HttpServlet` by navigating to http://localhost:8080/ClassLoading/servlet/classloading.ResourceLocatorServlet?resource=/javax/servlet/http/HttpServlet.class (notice how we must replace the package separator periods with forward slashes):

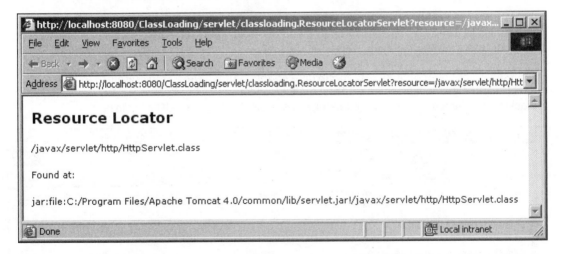

The resulting information is very useful. It tells us the preferred location from which the class will be loaded (if the same class is deployed in more than one place).

Class Loading Precedence in Tomcat 4

We're going to use ResourceLocator to discover the class loading precedence in Tomcat 4. We want to discover what version of a class will be loaded if that class can be found in more than one location. That is, in what order do the different classloaders used by Tomcat check the different locations?

We going to need a target class for the container to locate and load (TargetClass is probably the simplest class in the book):

```
package classloading;

public class TargetClass {
}
```

We'll put TargetClass and a JAR (targetclass.jar) containing TargetClass into the following directories of Tomcat:

```
webapps/ClassLoading/WEB-INF/classes/classloading/TargetClass.class
webapps/ClassLoading/WEB-INF/lib/targetclass.jar
server/lib/targetclass.jar
common/lib/targetclass.jar
lib/targetclass.jar
```

To test the class loading precedence we'll run through a series of steps using ResourceLocatorServlet. Each time we find out from where the class would be loaded, we'll delete the class from that location before repeating the process.

Run ResourceLocatorServlet, specifying TargetClass.class as the resource to look for by navigating to http://localhost:8080/ClassLoading/servlet/classloading.ResourceLocatorServlet?resource=/classloading/TargetClass.class:

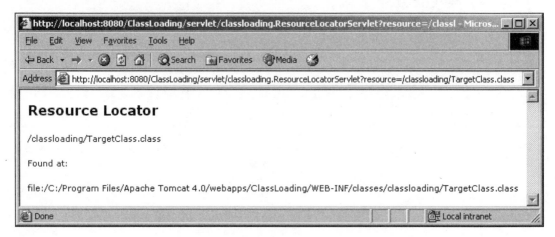

The result tells us that the preferred location for loading classes is from the WEB-INF/classes directory of the web application. This is consistent with the Servlet 2.3 specification, which states:

> **"The web application classloader must load classes from the WEB-INF/classes directory first, ..."**

Delete TargetClass from WEB-INF/classes and enter the same URL again. You'll find that now the location corresponds with the library JAR provided in the WEB-INF/lib directory of our application.

> *Tomcat keeps a copy of web applications in %CATALINA_HOME%/work. You may need to delete the contents of this folder and restart Tomcat for the example to behave as expected.*

This too is consistent with the Servlet 2.3 specification, which states:

> **"The web application classloader must load classes from the WEB-INF/classes directory first, and then from library JARs in the WEB-INF/lib directory."**

Delete targetclass.jar from WEB-INF/lib. TargetClass is no longer deployed anywhere within the application context. Locate the class once more. This time it will be found in the application-independent Tomcat directory, %CATALINA_HOME%/lib. Delete the JAR from this location and relocate the class. This time it will be found in %CATALINA_HOME%/common/lib. When the JAR is removed from this location the result of ResourceLocatorServlet will be:

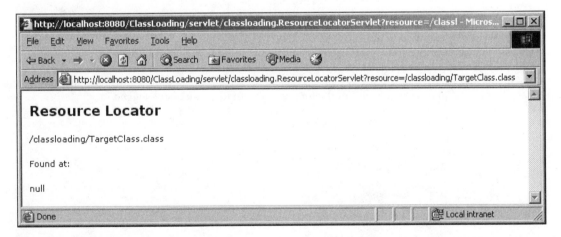

This means that %CATALINA_HOME%/server/lib is never searched. It is accessed only by Tomcat.

We've established the class loading order of precedence for Tomcat as:

❑ Classes deployed in the WEB-INF/classes directory of a web application

❑ Classes in application-specific archives (in WEB-INF/lib)

❑ Classes deployed in Tomcat's /lib directory

❑ Classes deployed in Tomcat's /common/lib directory

> **The order of precedence we've established is for Tomcat 4. If you're using a different servlet container the precedence could be different. It's well worth running through these steps in your deployment environment to determine the exact order.**

These results mean that if we try to modify our web application by creating a new version of a class, we will only see the change if we deploy the new version in the location of highest precedence. For example, if we deploy a new version of a class in an application archive, we must remove any previous version of the class from the WEB-INF/classes directory.

The Effect of Class Loading on Application Logic

Our choice of where to deploy classes can have a subtle but often significant effect on the logic of an application. If we deploy classes in the wrong place, or if we fail to understand the class loading precedence, our application may not behave in the way that we expect. Let's look at an example.

A User-Tracking Application

Consider the following simple class, which can be used to track the users that are logged in to the system. Each time the user logs in we'll use the static login() method as a factory method to instantiate and return a new User instance. As each instance is created the constructor increments the static users variable to keep count of the total number of users that have logged in:

```
package classloading;

public class User {
  public static int users = 0;

  public static User login() {
    return new User();
  }

  public User() {
    users++;
  }

  public static int getUsers() {
    return users;
  }
}
```

Users will log in by invoking `LoginServlet`:

```
package classloading;

import java.io.*;
import javax.servlet.*;
import javax.servlet.http.*;

public class LoginServlet extends HttpServlet {

  public void doGet (HttpServletRequest req, HttpServletResponse res)
      throws ServletException, IOException {
    User thisUser=new User();
    PrintWriter writer = res.getWriter();
    writer.println("<html><head></head>");
    writer.println("<body style=\"font-family:verdana;font-size:8pt\">");
    writer.println("<b>"+ User.getUsers() + "</b> users now logged in.");
    writer.println("</body></html>");
    writer.close();
  }
}
```

We're not worried about security in this example, so no user name and password are requested. The servlet reports back the total number of users on the system by calling the static method `getUsers()` of `User`.

Deploying the Application

We'll deploy this application in two separate contexts, `TestContext1` and `TestContext2`:

```
%CATALINA_HOME%/webapps/TestContext1/WEB-INF/classes/User.class
%CATALINA_HOME%/webapps/TestContext1/WEB-INF/classes/LoginServlet.class
%CATALINA_HOME%/webapps/TestContext2/WEB-INF/classes/User.class
%CATALINA_HOME%/webapps/TestContext2/WEB-INF/classes/LoginServlet.class
```

After running `LoginServlet` from both contexts in that configuration we'll remove the `User` class from those deployed locations and put it instead into Tomcat's `lib` directory, in its own JAR. The second configuration will look like this:

```
%CATALINA_HOME%/webapps/TestContext1/WEB-INF/classes/LoginServlet.class
%CATALINA_HOME%/webapps/TestContext2/WEB-INF/classes/LoginServlet.class
%CATALINA_HOME%/lib/user.jar
```

Testing the User Tracking Application

In the first configuration we invoke `LoginServlet` from the first context until we have logged in five users:

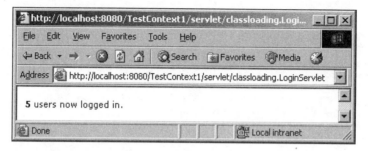

Then we invoke `LoginServlet` in the second context just once, so that there is a single user logged in:

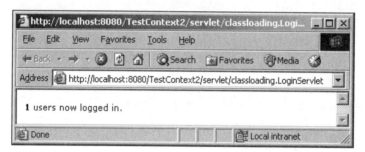

In this configuration each application is maintaining its own count of users, because in each case the User class has been loaded from the web context of the application. Two contexts means two separate occurrences of the User class, and two separate occurrences of the static users variable.

> **Static variables of a class deployed in the WEB-INF/classes or WEB-INF/lib directories will be consistent within the application context.**

In the second configuration we see quite different behavior. Again we run up five users in the first context, but then our first attempt in the second context yields this result:

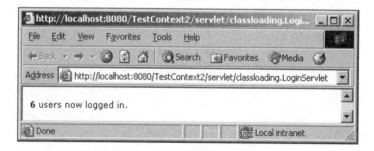

In this configuration a single count of users is maintained across all application contexts, because in each case the User class has been loaded from the same location.

> Static variables of a class deployed outside of the `WEB-INF/classes` or `WEB-INF/lib` directories may be shared across application contexts.

The implication is clear. What the programmer intends at development time can be affected by the decisions made at deployment time, so take care when deciding where classes should be deployed. Do we want the class, and the values it holds, to be loaded from a common location and shared between applications? Or do we want each application to load its own private version of the class, that is not visible to other applications?

Servlet Loading and Reloading

We've looked at how the application classloaders of the container load the 'ordinary' classes that compose a web application. But what of the servlet classes themselves? Although a servlet is a class like any other, we need to take extra care if the container supports servlet reloading.

For convenience during development some servers allow the redeployment of servlets on-the-fly, sometimes even by simply dropping them into a directory. The new versions are automatically reloaded by the server. However, previous generations of servlet containers have handled servlet reloading by creating a new classloader to load the servlet, distinct from the classloaders used to load other servlets or classes. So once again, we can't rely on values held in static variables.

To solve this problem, the Servlets 2.3 specification states:

> "Although a Container Provider implementation of a class reloading scheme for ease of use is not required, any such implementation must ensure that all servlets, and the classes they use, are loaded in the scope of a single class loader."

One further issue to consider for servlets is not *where* they get loaded from, but *when* they get loaded into memory. We can:

❑ Load servlets into memory when the application server starts up, which will increase the start-up time and use more memory.

❑ Load servlets into memory at their first invocation. In this case servlets that are never invoked will never occupy memory and the server as a whole will start up quicker, but the first request to each servlet will be delayed.

This is a deployment issue that has no effect on how we code the servlets, but the impact on the performance of a web application could be significant.

Threading and Synchronization

Web applications are not single-user systems. Any servlet that we write may need to cope with concurrent requests from remote clients. We'd like those requests to be handled with no side effects resulting from multiple users trying to do the same thing at the same time. In this section we'll look at some of the issues involved in this, particularly how to use:

❑   Threading to improve scalability and throughput

❑   Synchronization to ensure data integrity

We'll investigate the effects of container threading on application logic. While multi-threading can have a very positive impact on the performance and scalability of an application, it contains traps for the unwary. Even if we play it safe with single-threaded servlets, we might still need to rethink the way we use instance and class variables to propagate state information between method invocations.

We won't be creating and managing any threads of our own, rather we'll be letting the container use its own threading model with just an instruction from us as to whether our servlets should be single-threaded or multi-threaded. All you really need to understand about threads is that they allow a single piece of code to be executed many times, concurrently, within a single process. A method on a single instance may be executed in parallel on separate threads, with each thread maintaining its own progress through the method.

A Banking Application

We'll implement a very simple web-based banking service, first as a single-threaded servlet and then as a multi-threaded servlet. It will allow money transfers between bank accounts, and the results of each invocation will show the latest balance in each account and a list of transactions.

This will be a multi-user application, with many online users wanting to perform transactions at the same time. As a banking application, those users will want the integrity of the data to be maintained. I certainly would.

Using a Single-Threaded Servlet

We'll start with a single-threaded version of the servlet as the simplest case. We'll ensure that our servlet really is single-threaded by implementing the `javax.servlet.SingleThreadModel` interface.

> Implementing the `javax.servlet.SingleThreadModel` interface guarantees that no two threads will execute concurrently in the servlet's `service()` method.

```
package synchronization;

import java.io.*;
import java.util.*;
import javax.servlet.*;
import javax.servlet.http.*;

public class SingleThreadBankServlet extends HttpServlet
    implements SingleThreadModel {
```

We have two instance variables. One to hold the balances of the accounts at the bank and one to hold the list of user transactions:

```
private Hashtable accounts;
private Vector userTransactions;
```

When the servlet is initialized we'll reset the state of the member variables by calling the resetValues() method:

```
public void init() throws ServletException {
  resetValues();
}
```

In the doGet() method we'll find out what the user wants to do by looking at the request parameters. We're also calling an in() method on a separate class called InOut (which will be explained shortly). As we've implemented the SingleThreadModel interface, only one request thread can run this service method at any one time:

```
public void doGet (HttpServletRequest req, HttpServletResponse res)
    throws ServletException, IOException {
  InOut.in();
  String reset = req.getParameter("reset");
  String fromAccount = req.getParameter("from");
  String toAccount = req.getParameter("to");
  String amount = req.getParameter("amount");
  PrintWriter writer = res.getWriter();
  writer.println("<html><head></head>");
  writer.println("<body style=\"font-family:verdana;font-size:8pt\">");
```

If the user supplies a reset parameter, we reset the state of the member variables (this is for convenience during testing):

```
if (reset != null) {
  resetValues();
}
```

If the user specifies fromAccount, toAccount, and amount parameters, we perform a money transfer by calling the transfer() method:

```
if ((fromAccount != null) && (toAccount != null) && (amount != null)) {
  transfer(fromAccount, toAccount, amount);
}
```

In every case we show the latest account balances and the list of user transactions via the showData() method:

```
showData(writer);
```

443

Finally we make a call to the out() method of the InOut class:

```
    writer.println("</body></html>");
    writer.close();
    InOut.out();
}
```

The resetValues() method simply initializes the member variables to a known state:

```
public void resetValues() throws ServletException {
    userTransactions = new Vector();
    accounts = new Hashtable();
    accounts.put("000001", "1000");
    accounts.put("000002", "1000");
}
```

The showData() method produces output for the latest account balances and the history of user transactions (in reverse order with the latest transaction in bold):

```
private void showData(PrintWriter writer) {
    writer.println("<b>Account Balances</b><br><br>");
    for (Enumeration keys = accounts.keys(); keys.hasMoreElements();) {
        String thisKey = (String) keys.nextElement();
        String thisBalance = (String) accounts.get(thisKey);
        writer.println("Account " + thisKey + " has balance " +
                        thisBalance + "<br>");
    }
    writer.println("<br><b>User Transactions</b><br><br>");
    int i = userTransactions.size() - 1;
    if (i >= 0) {
        writer.println("<b>" + userTransactions.elementAt(i) + "</b><br>");
    }
    while (--i >= 0) {
        writer.println("" + userTransactions.elementAt(i) + "<br>");
    }
}
```

The transfer() method simply reads the values from the toAccount and fromAccount request parameters, calculates new account balances based on the transfer amount, and then writes the new balances back into the accounts hashtable. We've done that in a rather convoluted way because we want to increase the chance of a conflict, but just to make sure we also include a five second delay:

```
private void transfer(String fromAccount, String toAccount, String amount) {
    int fromAccountBalance =
                    new Integer((String)accounts.get(fromAccount)).intValue();
    int newFromAccountBalance =
                    fromAccountBalance - (new Integer(amount).intValue());
    int toAccountBalance =
                    new Integer((String)accounts.get(toAccount)).intValue();
    int newToAccountBalance = toAccountBalance + (new Integer(amount).intValue());
```

```
    try {
      Thread.sleep(5000);
    } catch (java.lang.InterruptedException ex) {}

    accounts.put(fromAccount, "" + newFromAccountBalance);
    accounts.put(toAccount, "" + newToAccountBalance);

    String transaction = "Transfer of " + amount + " from account " +
                         fromAccount + " to account " + toAccount;
    userTransactions.add(transaction);
  }
}
```

In this single-threaded servlet we're not expecting a conflict at all, but we'll be taking exactly the same code forward to a multi-threaded scenario to show the difference in behavior.

Finally, you're probably wondering about the `InOut` class that we called at the beginning and end of the `doGet()` method. It provides something for our debugger (from Chapter 10) to latch onto as we conduct our tests:

```
package synchronization;

public class InOut {
  public static void in() {}
  public static void out() {}
}
```

Deploying the Application

We'll deploy this application in a context called `Synchronization`:

```
Synchronization/
              WEB-INF/
                    classes/
                          SingleThreadBankServlet.class
                          InOut.class
```

If you want to reproduce the debug trace we show in this section you'll need to run Tomcat in debug mode (as described in Chapter 10).

Using Single-Threaded Servlets

Launch two browser windows, and navigate in each to
http://localhost:8080/Synchronization/servlet/synchronization.SingleThreadBankServlet?reset=true.
Each browser window will show this:

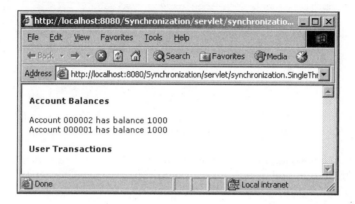

Now we can make use of the JPDA Debugger we created in Chapter 10 to record what really happens
in the code. Start the debugger with this command:

```
java debugger.JPDADebugger -attach localhost:8124 -include synchronization.InOut >
singlethread.txt
```

We're including our `InOut` class as the `-include` parameter so the debugger will record all entries to
the servlet's `doGet()` method (`InOut.in()`) and all exits (`InOut.out()`).

Now transfer 500 from account 000001 to account 000002 in both browsers by navigating to
http://localhost:8080/Synchronization/servlet/synchronization.SingleThreadBankServlet?from=00000
1&to=000002&amount=500. In the first window we see this:

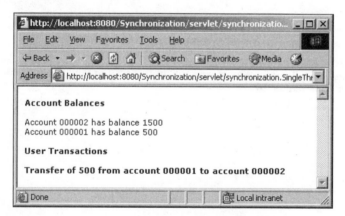

In the second window we see this:

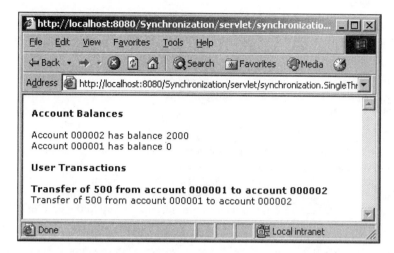

That result is just what we would expect. To clarify the sequence of events we can look at the debug trace using the debug trace viewer from Chapter 10:

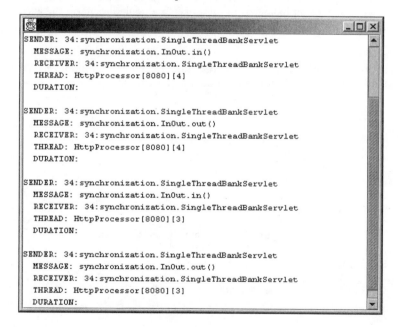

Notice that execution went into the servlet doGet() method, and back out again, on thread HttpProcessor[8080][4] before going in and out of the same doGet() method of the same servlet on thread HttpProcessor[8080][3]. The two threads are executed in strict order. The threads are only allowed into the service method of the servlet one-at-a-time.

Servlet Pooling

Although Tomcat 4 queues requests to servlets that implement `SingleThreadModel`, some other servlet containers (such as WebLogic) improve throughput by starting up additional servlet instances in response to multiple client requests.

> **Implementing `SingleThreadModel` flags up to certain servlet containers that a servlet may be pooled.**

To reduce the cost of starting up new instances of servlets each time, and to limit the total number of instances, servers use a **servlet pool**. At startup, a number of servlets of each type are created in the pool. As each client request comes in, one of the unused servlet instances from the pool is allocated to handle the request. On completion that instance is returned to the pool for reuse. This way, even servlets that implement `SingleThreadModel` can service concurrent requests (up to the limit of the pool size).

This has implications for instance variables. Developers often use an instance variable in servlets to record information (such as hit counts) across all users of the servlet, on the assumption that there will only ever be one servlet instance handling multiple requests on separate threads. The same situation exists in our `SingleThreadBankServlet` example, where we assume that the `accounts` hashtable holds a common view of account balances for all users. In a pooled scenario the account balances that we see would depend on which servlet instance handled our request.

> **If servlets that implement `SingleThreadModel` are pooled we cannot rely on a single set of instance variables to be common to all users of the servlet.**

If you're using Tomcat 4 you might decide to relax because it does not support servlet pooling, but your servlet could well behave quite differently when deployed in a different container.

Multi-Threaded Servlets

The problem with using `SingleThreadModel` is that all requests to the servlet are fed through a single servlet instance, and so must be queued if that instance is busy servicing another request. This is not desirable in an web application that must simultaneously support many users.

> **Throughput can be significantly improved by allowing our servlets to process multiple concurrent requests on separate threads.**

To make our sample servlet multi-threaded we simply remove the `implements SingleThreadModel` statement from our code and rename our servlet to `BankServlet`:

```
public class BankServlet extends HttpServlet
```

That's the only change we'll need to make before running through our tests again.

Using Multi-Threaded Servlets

Let's look at what happens when we step through the same sequence of events as before, this time with the multi-threaded servlet. The end result in the first window looks like this:

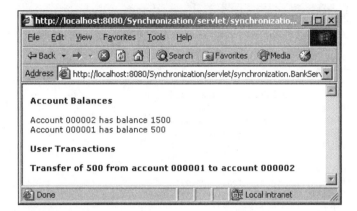

In the second window the result looks like this:

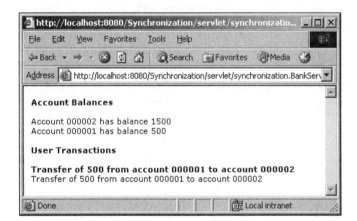

Clearly there is a problem. We've transferred a total of 1000 from account 000001 to account 000002 yet the final balances do not reflect this. To clarify why this problem has occurred we should look at the debug trace:

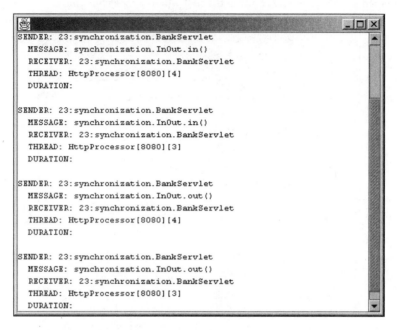

We can see that the two threads are intertwined as they progress through the servlet doGet() method. This means that we've read the old account balances in the second thread before writing the new account balances in the first thread. This is a classic **race condition**.

> **In multi-threaded servlets the use of instance variables may be inconsistent and unpredictable.**

We introduced an artificial delay in the code to ensure that this would happen, but this is the type of problem that could easily occur in a multi-user environment.

Explicit Synchronization

The use of instance variables can cause problems whether we're multi-threaded or single-threaded-with-pooling, but for two different reasons:

❑ For single-threaded servlets the problem is that pooled servlets will maintain separate sets of instance variables, unless we take the performance hit of not using a servlet pool

❑ For multi-threaded servlets the problem is that race conditions may result in unpredictable values in instance variables

It's best to avoid the use of instance variables in servlets whenever possible, but clearly they were used in the first place for a good reason – to propagate information between servlet invocations.

If you decide that you really can't do without instance variables, one possible solution to the second problem is to use a multi-threaded servlet with the critical sections of code explicitly synchronized to make them **thread-safe**. In our example the critical code is within the transfer() method so we can synchronize it by changing the method definition to this:

```
private synchronized void transfer(String fromAccount, String toAccount,
                                    String amount)
```

You might be tempted to synchronize the servlet's service methods, doGet() and doPost(). However, the Servlet 2.3 specification advises against this approach because it offers the disadvantage of the SingleThreadModel (all servlet requests are serialized) without providing the benefit that some servers may employ a pooling mechanism to improve throughput.

If we run through our tests with the synchronized method, the end result (in the browser windows) is the same as for the single-threaded servlet. However, the debug trace shows that the servlet requests themselves have not been serialized. We get a debug trace similar to that of the non-synchronized multi-threaded servlet:

This approach would work if we're meticulous in explicitly synchronizing all methods that may compete for instance variables. In addition, the throughput will be higher than a SingleThreadModel (fully synchronized) servlet if we keep the synchronized parts of our code as small as possible.

Servlet using Session and Context Attributes

Say that we want to be able to record a list of transactions performed by a particular end user during a particular session. We don't want to do it via an instance variable because instance variables are per servlet, not per client, so for a multi-threaded servlet there would only ever be one list of transactions regardless of the number of end users. For a single-threaded servlet (with pooling) we have no way of knowing how many instances the server will create to handle the load.

Let's say we would also like to be able to record the latest account balances. Again, we don't want to do this via an instance variable that is specific to an individual servlet instance, or in a static class variable whose exact scope will be determined by the class loading mechanism.

There is a way to handle these two situations:

❑   **Session attributes** – these support the propagation of information relating to a particular end user's sequence of events, and are isolated from information relating to other end users

❑   **Context attributes** – these support the propagation of information between a group of components deployed within the same web context, even in a distributed scenario

We'll concentrate on the implications of concurrent access to context and session attributes for our banking servlet – you can learn more about sessions in general in Chapter 5. We'll use a version of BankServlet called SyncSessionBankServlet that is adapted to store the accounts balances as a context attribute and the list of user transactions as a session attribute:

```
package synchronization;

import java.io.*;
import javax.servlet.*;
import javax.servlet.http.*;
import java.util.*;
```

```
public class SyncSessionBankServlet extends HttpServlet {
    private ServletContext servletContext = null;
```

The transfer() method has changed to take in the current HTTP request as a parameter. This is so that we can get hold of the current user session:

```
private void transfer(String fromAccount, String toAccount, String amount,
    HttpServletRequest req) {
```

We get the accounts hashtable from the application's servlet context and read the old account balances as before. The accounts hashtable gets into the context via a modified version of the resetValues():

```
Hashtable accounts = (Hashtable) servletContext.getAttribute("accounts");
if (accounts == null) {
    return;
}
```

```
int fromAccountBalance =
                  new Integer((String)accounts.get(fromAccount)).intValue();
int newFromAccountBalance =
                  fromAccountBalance - (new Integer(amount).intValue());
int toAccountBalance =
                  new Integer((String)accounts.get(toAccount)).intValue();
int newToAccountBalance = toAccountBalance + (new Integer(amount).intValue());
```

We retain the delay of five seconds so that we can test the race condition later:

```
try {
  Thread.sleep(5000);
} catch (java.lang.InterruptedException ex) {}
```

We put the new account balances back into the context:

```
accounts.put(fromAccount, "" + newFromAccountBalance);
accounts.put(toAccount, "" + newToAccountBalance);
servletContext.setAttribute("accounts", accounts);
```

We get hold of the user session and extract the list of transactions for this user, or start a new list if no transactions have been performed:

```
HttpSession session = req.getSession(true);
Vector userTransactions = (Vector) session.getAttribute("transactions");
if (userTransactions == null) {
  userTransactions = new Vector();
}
```

Finally, we add the current transaction and put the list back as a session attribute:

```
String transaction = "Transfer of " + amount + " from account " +
                  fromAccount + " to account " + toAccount;
userTransactions.add(transaction);
session.setAttribute("transactions", userTransactions);
}
```

The logic is exactly the same as for our earlier servlets except that we're now using context and session attributes (for account balances and user transactions respectively) rather than instance variables.

We also re-write of the showData() method to take attribute values from the context and the session:

```
private void showData(PrintWriter writer, HttpServletRequest req) {
  Hashtable accounts = (Hashtable) servletContext.getAttribute("accounts");
  if (accounts==null) {
    return;
  }
```

```
      writer.println("<b>Account Balances</b><br><br>");
      for (Enumeration keys = accounts.keys(); keys.hasMoreElements();) {
        String thisKey = (String) keys.nextElement();
        String thisBalance = (String) accounts.get(thisKey);
        writer.println("Account " + thisKey + " has balance " +
                       thisBalance + "<br>");
      }
```

```
      HttpSession session = req.getSession(true);
      Vector userTransactions = (Vector) session.getAttribute("transactions");
      if (userTransactions == null) {
        return;
      }
```

```
      writer.println("<br><b>User Transactions</b><br><br>");
      int i = userTransactions.size() - 1;
      if (i >= 0) {
        writer.println("<b>" + userTransactions.elementAt(i) + "</b><br>");
      }
      while (--i >= 0) {
        writer.println("" + userTransactions.elementAt(i) + "<br>");
      }
    }
```

We also have modified versions of the init() and resetValues() methods:

```
    public void init(ServletConfig config) throws ServletException {
      super.init(config);
      this.servletContext = config.getServletContext();
      resetValues(null);
    }
```

```
    public void init() throws ServletException {}
```

```
    public void resetValues(HttpServletRequest req) throws ServletException {
      Hashtable accounts = (Hashtable) servletContext.getAttribute("accounts");
      if (accounts == null) {
        accounts = new Hashtable();
      }
```

```
      accounts.put("000001", "1000");
      accounts.put("000002", "1000");
```

```
      servletContext.setAttribute("accounts",accounts);
      if (req == null) {
        return;
      }
      HttpSession session = req.getSession(true);
      Vector userTransactions = new Vector();
      session.setAttribute("transactions", userTransactions);
    }
  }
```

Using Servlets with Session and Context Attributes

To show the behavior we invoke the servlet, and reset it in two separate browser windows, by accessing http://localhost:8080/Synchronization/servlet/synchronization.SessionBankServlet?reset=true. In the first window we then access http://localhost:8080/Synchronization/servlet/synchronization.SessionBankServlet?from=000001&to=000002&amount=500 twice. The end result is a transfer of 1000 from account 000001 to account 000002:

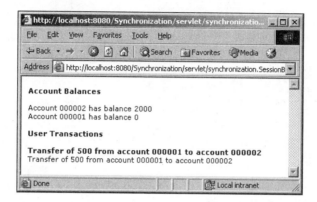

In the second browser window we invoke the same servlet by accessing http://localhost:8080/Synchronization/servlet/synchronization.SessionBankServlet?from=000002&to=000001&amount=500. There are two things to note here. The account balances show (correctly) that we've transferred 500 back from account 000002 to account 000001. Also, the transaction list contains only one entry – the one we made in this window (on behalf of this user) and not the complete list of transactions made in all windows (by all users):

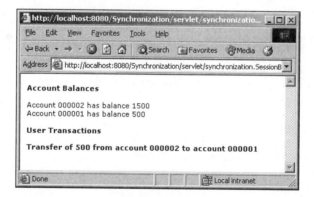

We've succeeded in recording a list of transactions on a per-user basis by using the application's servlet context. No matter how many servlet instances are created (if we used SingleThreadModel and the container supported pooling, or if the servlet was part of a distributed application) these account balances will still be held in common.

To further understand what has happened in the container, we'll look at debug trace produced by the DebugListener from Chapter 10. If you want to record this kind of information you'll need to set up the Debugging Filter and Event Listener for this web application as set out in Chapter 10. You'll also need to make the following addition to web.xml:

```
<web-app>
   ...
   <filter>
     <filter-name>DebugFilter</filter-name>
     <filter-class>debugging.DebugFilter</filter-class>
   </filter>

   <filter-mapping>
     <filter-name>DebugFilter</filter-name>
     <url-pattern>/*</url-pattern>
   </filter-mapping>

   <listener>
     <listener-class>debugging.DebugListener</listener-class>
   </listener>
   ...
</web-app>
```

Inside the Container

Here is the debug trace for the sequence of interactions that we've just run through. The first block of three entries tells us that the account balances in context org.apahce.catalina.core.ApplicationContext@8238f4 have been set to 1500 and 500 as a result of a transfer recorded on session D466...765, which resulted from the request ?to=000002&from=000001&amount=500 on servlet SessionBankServlet:

```
SENDER: Apache Tomcat/4.0.1
  MESSAGE: setAttribute(accounts,{000002=1500, 000001=500})
  RECEIVER: CONTEXT: org.apache.catalina.core.ApplicationContext@2af0b3
  THREAD:
  DURATION:

SENDER: Apache Tomcat/4.0.1
  MESSAGE: setAttribute(transactions,[Transfer of 500 from account 000001 to account 000002])
  RECEIVER: SESSION: D46622F8A362B3B8A1B3548521F34765
  THREAD:
  DURATION:

SENDER: 127.0.0.1
  MESSAGE: ?amount=500&to=000002&from=000001
  RECEIVER: /Synchronization/servlet/synchronization.SessionBankServlet
  THREAD:
  DURATION: 5007ms
```

The second block of three entries tells us that the account balances in the same context have been set to 2000 and 0 as a result of a transfer transaction recorded on the same session, which resulted from the request ?to=000002&from=000001&amount=500 on the same servlet:

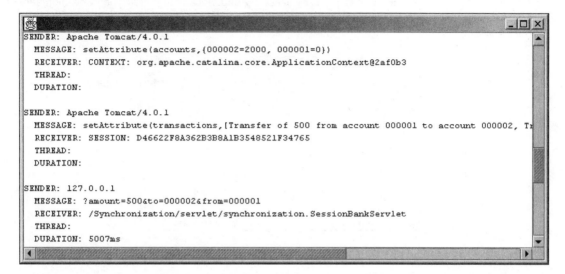

```
SENDER: Apache Tomcat/4.0.1
  MESSAGE: setAttribute(accounts,{000002=2000, 000001=0})
  RECEIVER: CONTEXT: org.apache.catalina.core.ApplicationContext@2af0b3
  THREAD:
  DURATION:

SENDER: Apache Tomcat/4.0.1
  MESSAGE: setAttribute(transactions,[Transfer of 500 from account 000001 to account 000002, Tr
  RECEIVER: SESSION: D46622F8A362B3B8A1B3548521F34765
  THREAD:
  DURATION:

SENDER: 127.0.0.1
  MESSAGE: ?amount=500&to=000002&from=000001
  RECEIVER: /Synchronization/servlet/synchronization.SessionBankServlet
  THREAD:
  DURATION: 5007ms
```

The final block of three entries tells us that the account balances in the same context have been set to 1500 and 500 as a result of a transfer transaction recorded on a *different* session D00...371, which resulted from the request ?to=000001&from=000002&amount=500 on the same servlet:

```
SENDER: Apache Tomcat/4.0.1
  MESSAGE: setAttribute(accounts,{000002=1500, 000001=500})
  RECEIVER: CONTEXT: org.apache.catalina.core.ApplicationContext@2af0b3
  THREAD:
  DURATION:

SENDER: Apache Tomcat/4.0.1
  MESSAGE: create
  RECEIVER: SESSION: D003E521A9E9B273F705A434A2C54371
  THREAD:
  DURATION:

SENDER: Apache Tomcat/4.0.1
  MESSAGE: setAttribute(transactions,[Transfer of 500 from account 000002 to account 000001])
  RECEIVER: SESSION: D003E521A9E9B273F705A434A2C54371
  THREAD:
  DURATION:

SENDER: 127.0.0.1
  MESSAGE: ?amount=500&to=000001&from=000002
  RECEIVER: /Synchronization/servlet/synchronization.SessionBankServlet
  THREAD:
  DURATION: 5028ms
```

Testing the Race Condition

So far so good, but we were careful to invoke the servlets from the two windows in series. Let's look at what happens if we issue concurrent requests by accessing http://localhost:8080/Synchronization/servlet/synchronization.SessionBankServlet?from=000001&to=000002&amount=500 simultaneously in the two browser windows. In the first browser window we see:

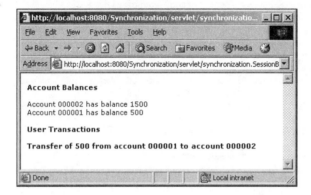

And in the second browser window we see:

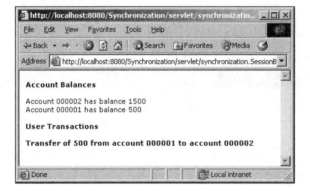

This is exactly the same race condition as the one we encountered when using instance variables. Although the context and session both provide convenient data stores with predictable scope, access to the values in those data stores must still be synchronized by implementing `SingleThreadModel`. In our case we must explicitly synchronize the `transfer()` method once more:

```
private synchronized void transfer(String fromAccount, String toAccount,
                                   String amount)
```

> **Multiple servlets executing request threads may have active access to a single session or context object at the same time, so the developer has the responsibility to synchronize access to these resources as appropriate.**

Summary

We started this chapter by looking at how Java programs, including web applications, are built at run time from classes loaded into memory by **classloaders**. We saw how classloaders look for classes in locations in a predictable order. The order of precedence determines whether separate web applications each see their own versions of those classes, or whether the classes they use are shared. To help in our investigation we created a servlet, ResourceLocatorServlet, that we used to determine the location from which any given class (or any other resource) will be loaded within Tomcat.

We saw how the container's default model for servlets (multi-threading) can be overridden by implementing the SingleThreadModel interface. Although this guarantees that requests to a particular servlet are serialized it can result in some unwanted side effects. Tomcat actually discourages the use of the SingleThreadModel by not supporting servlet pooling. This means that for maximum concurrency, the default multi-threaded model for servlets must be used.

Finally, we saw how multi-threaded servlets can suffer from race conditions that require the developer to explicitly synchronize access to shared resources such as the instance and class variables, and even context and session attributes in order to make the code thread-safe.

In the next chapter we're going to look at the importance of good design within web applications.

12

Designing Web Applications and Servlet Patterns

In previous chapters we've seen that servlets are great at handling requests and responses, but they're not so good for generating content for end users. We also wouldn't use JSP pages to process business logic, although they do handle content generation very effectively. To make the most of servlets, or any other components within a web application, we need to understand when and where we should use them – what tasks do they perform best?

In this chapter we're going to look at the design of web applications, focusing particularly on when and where we should use servlets within the application.

We'll begin by discussing the most commonly used web application architectures:

❑   Model 1

❑   Model 2

We'll look at important factors such as the maintainability, reusability, and extensibility of each. We'll introduce **design patterns**, which we can use to recognize and solve common design problems. Then we'll demonstrate how these patterns can be applied to a web application.

In order to put all of these concepts into context we'll create an example application – an online discussion forum, to which we'll apply our designs and patterns. In order to compare and contrast good and bad design, we'll build two versions of this example: the first using Model 1 architecture, and the second using Model 2.

However, let's start simple, by considering why good application design is important.

Why is Good Application Design Important?

The design of applications is an important aspect of the project lifecycle, but one that is often neglected. When we design an application we should aim to enhance the following features:

- ❑ **Maintainability**
- ❑ **Reusability**
- ❑ **Extensibility**

Let's now take a closer look at each of these aspects of design.

Maintainability

Maintainability describes the amount of effort required to keep an application running correctly. Obviously, in a commercial sense, more maintenance means more time and more money spent. In reality the maintainability of an application is difficult to quantify, but there are techniques that we can use to increase the maintainability of a system.

So what aspects of the application need to be maintained? First of all there is the sourcecode itself. An undocumented, unstructured, and badly-formatted body of sourcecode will be harder to maintain than documented code with a clearly defined structure. If we make code easy to follow and understand, debugging and code modification usually become faster and easier too. As an example, trying to maintain a very large method that performs a lot of processing will be much more complex than trying to maintain a collection of shorter methods that achieve the same result.

The structure of the application also plays an important part. Designing a meaningful, logically partitioned application will greatly increase the maintainability of the application. In a typical application there might be several distinct parts; for example the user interface, classes that perform business processing, and classes that represent business entities. Introducing structure and making a distinction between these types of classes will increase the maintainability because it will be more apparent to developers how the pieces of the application fit together. Although creating neatly formatted sourcecode is undoubtedly important, knowing how to quickly find the piece of functionality that needs to be fixed is just as important.

Reusability

One of the goals of OO design and implementation is to strive for reusable components. Reusability is enhanced when a class has a low reliance on other objects, or **low coupling,** and provides a specialized set of tasks, or **high cohesion**.

Some degree of reusability is achievable without design, but thinking about the structure beforehand will help to ensure that the classes that we create are reusable across the application. Stepping back to look at the big picture will help in identifying those places in the system where functionality can be reused later if we wish to modify or enhance the application.

Extensibility

Changes in the business require changes in software. The extensibility of our software determines how much it can be extended and enhanced after it has been put into production use.

Ideally, we would like to add functionality to an application without altering the original code – much as we extend existing Java classes.

A good design will attempt to take extensibility into account. Of course it's impossible to foresee every eventual circumstance, such as a drastic change in the business, or other major changes in functional requirements. We can often enhance extensibility by logically partitioning the application into smaller parts, reducing the impact of changes on other parts of the system.

J2EE Web Application Design

Servlets are just one component that can be used in building a web application. We can also use JSP pages, JSP tag libraries, JavaBeans, and even business components such as Enterprise JavaBeans (EJBs) if we need or wish to. Each of these components has its strengths and weaknesses, so each is suited to a different role. Identifying the roles needed within the application and finding the components most suitable for these roles is the first step in understanding the design of our applications.

Two of the most commonly used web application architectures are known as **Model 1** and **Model 2**. In the next few sections we will discuss each of these, in order to understand where our different components will fit into them. Model 1 architecture is the simpler of the two, so let's consider this first.

Introducing Model 1 Architecture

A web application based on the Model 1 architecture is composed of a number of pages with which the user interacts. These pages generally utilize a **model**, which represents the business logic for the application. For example (and as shown in the diagram below), the pages could be implemented using JSP pages, with the model being one or more JavaBeans. In this situation, these beans would be used to represent information found in the application and might also contain a small amount of business logic:

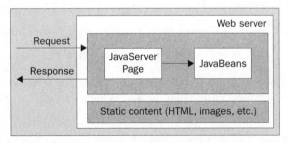

In fact, the pages in Model 1 architecture are usually implemented using JSP pages (or sometimes servlets), so Model 1 architecture is known as **page-centric**.

The client directly accesses the pages served up by the web container through the web server, and these pages are used to service the entire request and send the response back. Any links to other parts of the web application are given as direct links to other pages.

Although each individual page could contain complex logic, this type of web application is very easy to assemble and is therefore very useful where there are a small number of pages, or where the structure of the application is very simple. However, problems with maintainability, extensibility, and security can arise if we attempt to use a page-centric architecture with larger or more complex web applications.

Maintainability Problems

If we consider a typical Model 1 web application, the structure of the application will be embodied within the pages. The pages will include diverse functionality, such as:

❑ Complex business logic

❑ Links to other parts of the web application

❑ The names of pages to which forms should be submitted

The fact that the pages often contain business logic often provides the biggest potential problem regarding the maintainability of a Model 1 architecture. It is usual to find blocks of Java code, known as **scriptlets**, in the page. This not only makes the code within the page more difficult to understand, but if we wanted to reuse the scriptlet code we would have to copy and paste it. If we wanted to incorporate the functionality into lots of pages this would be a time consuming (and error-prone) process.

Additionally, modifying the structure of our web application in any way would mean that we would need to search through the entire site to remove and/or change the names of the pages; again, a time-consuming and costly process.

Extensibility Problems

The extensibility of our web applications is also limited, as it is hard to modify or extend the functionality provided by the application since the pages contain such diverse functionality and are relatively tightly-coupled together. Changing some functionality could ripple horribly through the system causing more bugs and unexpected results.

Security Problems

Security is also a major problem for Model 1 architectures. For example, a web-based discussion forum might be divided into two distinct sections:

❑ Public area – for reading discussion threads and locating general information

❑ Restricted area – for creating threads and posting responses

If we used Model 1 architecture to implement the forum, each page in the restricted area would have to perform its own security checks to ensure that the user is logged in and that the user is permitted to see the contents of the page.

To circumvent this problem, we could place the authorization and authentication code into reusable components such as JavaBeans or custom JSP tags, or at the simplest level another JSP that is included in a page wherever necessary. However, we still need to include the authentication and authorization code in each secure page using some approach. This invites trouble: for example developers may accidentally forget to include this security code in pages they create for the site.

A simpler approach to security would be to provide a central access point for all users of the site; this central point would contain the authentication and authorization code, so we only need to include it once in our application. We will see how we can adopt this approach using Model 2 architecture in the next section.

Introducing Model 2 Architecture

The Model 2 architecture overcomes many of the problems of the Model 1 architecture. Model 2 is based upon the **Model-View-Controller (MVC)** architecture. In a Model 1 web application, the pages are accessed directly, in a Model 2 architecture all access is routed through a **controller** component (typically implemented by a servlet). This architecture is shown below:

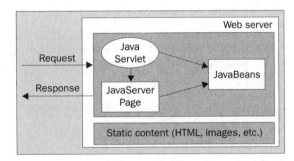

We can use the same controller for the entire site, or multiple controllers that are each responsible for sections of the site. For both, the principle of the design is the same: requests from clients are routed to a central controller, which decides how the request should be serviced. Later on we'll see how a controller can delegate this task but for now we'll assume that the controller processes the request.

When it processes the request, the controller may make some modifications to the underlying model (often JavaBeans). Once the request has been serviced, the controller delegates the task of sending back the response to a view component (often implemented by JSP pages). The view component generally contains a minimal amount of code and is focused on the task of presenting information to the end user. Both the controller and the view components can access and modify model components.

Benefits of Model 2 Architecture

So how does using Model 2 architecture improve the design of our web application over using Model 1?

Enhancing Maintainability

As the controller component in our architecture is responsible for determining which page in our web application we should see next, the structure of the web application is defined in a single place. This increases the maintainability of the application, particularly if we go further, separating out the structural definition from the controller to make the structure externally configurable. Additionally, the processing and business logic associated with servicing requests is easy to find as it is not embedded and scattered throughout the pages of the system (unlike in the Model 1 architecture).

Promoting Extensibility

The logic that processes each type of request in Model 2 is now much more centralized. This centralization, in conjunction with splitting the view components from the logic that services the request, means that the system is now much easier to extend than in Model 1 architecture. By introducing more componentization we make extensions easier to write and the chances of a ripple effect throughout the application much less likely.

For example, to extend the application by adding new pages, all that we need to do is add new view components and make appropriate modifications to the controller component – either directly or through external configuration files.

Ensuring Security

When we discussed the security aspects of Model 1 earlier, we noted that routing all requests through a single point of entry is a simple way to handle web application security. In Model 2, we can use this technique, because all security processing can be moved to the controller(s), reducing the burden on developers and the risk of accidental security breaches.

Using Other J2EE Components in Model 2 Architecture

For many applications we use technologies other than JSP pages, servlets, and JavaBeans. We may want to introduce an EJB layer containing session and entity beans, where we place complex business processing or represent persistent business data:

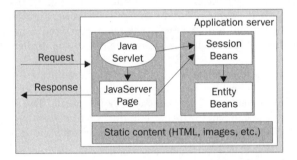

While the basic architecture remains unchanged, introducing these additional components does, however, raise some questions:

❑ How should the functionality of our application be split between the components?

❑ What effect does introducing these components have on performance and scalability?

We will examine these issues more closely in the next two sections.

Using Entity Beans

Entity beans are used to represent data that is stored in some type of persistent data store such as a relational database. In smaller applications, we'd probably have the web components (our Servlets and JSPs) using JDBC to communicate with the database instead (possibly with JavaBeans representing the data).

Introducing entity beans means that they become the model on which our web application operates. For both Model 1 and Model 2 the components that handle the presentation of data on a web page (in other words the JSPs and servlets in the web container) will access and modify business data residing in the EJB tier.

From an architectural and design perspective, this separation of the components in our web application is certainly beneficial. Splitting these out makes for a more maintainable system since functionality has been logically partitioned across the application. When the entities in the business layer change, we instantly know which part of the application needs to change to reflect this. In addition, we might also end up with some components that we can reuse in future projects.

There are disadvantages to using entity beans though. From an implementation perspective, entity beans are remote components that are able to execute on a separate machine from the code that calls them. Introducing remote components means introducing additional network overhead in terms of the remote method calls that are required to access and modify the data residing within the EJBs. As always, you should weigh up the advantages and disadvantages in the context of the application(s) that will make use of entity beans before you decide to use them.

Using Session Beans

Traditionally, business logic has been embedded into client applications, whether they are desktop-based or web-based. Session beans can instead encapsulate this logic in a robust and reusable manner. However, session beans, like entity beans, are intended to be remote components and so the same network overheads may be incurred when using the functionality contained within session beans.

With these issues in mind, let's look at roles and responsibilities in a Model 2 architecture.

Component Roles in Model 2 Architecture

Let's consider the role of the controller in the Model 2 architecture example. It should:

- ❏ Act as a single point of entry for requests
- ❏ Process the requests, accessing and modifying the underlying model
- ❏ Delegate the task of presenting information to a specific view component

The controller can process requests in a number of ways. It can process requests itself which means that the controller encapsulates business logic. However, this is probably not an effective solution, as the controller would rapidly become bloated.

A more efficient system might be to delegate processing tasks to other components such as JavaBeans or session EJBs, or even standard Java classes. If this strategy is selected, how do we determine where specific functionality is to be situated, including that associated with servicing the request, validating any data, and of course, security? When we design our application, we need to answer these questions, deciding on the roles and responsibilities of components. This is often a tricky task, but fortunately many of the common problems encountered during the design process have been tackled before, and the solutions to these problems are well-documented in the form of **design patterns**.

Documenting Design Principals

Industry-recognized standards and guidelines help those involved with a project to communicate in a consistent and effective way. For example, we can use the Unified Modeling Language (UML) to represent the design of an application.

In the same way that coding conventions are important when writing sourcecode, the use of a standard means of documenting designs is also important, especially when reviews and walkthroughs are undertaken. Such documentation allows the developer to question the business and its methods by providing a platform that can be understood by non-technical personnel.

Using Design Patterns

Design patterns capture reusable solutions to common design problems, and provide a common language with which to describe them. In *"Design Patterns, Elements of Reusable Object-Orientated Software"* (Addison Wesley, ISBN 0-201633-61-2) twenty four common design problems are described and considered. Many other patterns in software development have been documented, including some directly related to J2EE development.

J2EE Patterns

The J2EE patterns catalog documents a number of patterns that provide solutions to frequently encountered problems in the design and implementation of J2EE applications. This includes issues such as decreasing the number of fine-grained method calls across the network by using value objects, encapsulating business logic and workflow into session beans through a session façade, and accessing large amounts of read-only data through data access objects. The catalog also contains patterns that are relevant when designing the presentation tier of J2EE applications.

> *Detailed information on all of the patterns contained within the J2EE patterns catalog can be found at* http://developer.java.sun.com/developer/technicalArticles/J2EE/patterns/.

Why Use Patterns?

Without patterns it is still possible to build fairly complex systems that achieve the desired end goal. However, the problem with this approach is that more often than not, the way that problems are tackled and subsequently solved within the application may not be consistent. This inconsistency decreases the maintainability of the application.

Although using patterns does tend to increase the initial complexity of the implemented solution, patterns are an important tool for helping us structure our applications in a proven and consistent manner. Each component has a predefined purpose and a predefined way in which to interact with the others involved in the system. This is good from a maintainability perspective because it is easier to get to grips with a system based upon familiar, common structures than one that isn't.

In addition to this, some of the patterns are optimized for high performance and scalability. Another important benefit of using patterns is that they also provide developers with a standard way of communicating design ideas.

Creating a Web-Based Discussion Forum

In this section, we'll implement a small web application to illustrate the concepts of good and bad design we've been discussing. We'll create a discussion forum, as seen on many web sites. Before we can start designing our forum we need to define its features. This is an important stage in the development process, and it's important to fully state the requirements of our application:

- ❑ The discussion forum contains a number of topics

- ❑ Each topic may contain zero or more responses

- ❑ A user can view the list of topics, and also view all the responses made to a topic

- ❑ A user can post a response to a topic, but to ensure that responses are not anonymous, the user must be logged in

- ❑ We'll allow the users to delete their own responses too

This is a fairly simple set of requirements, so building the application shouldn't be too difficult. However, before we start implementing the functionality, we need to understand the underlying domain on which the application will operate.

Entities Within the Business Domain

An important aspect of object-orientated (OO) analysis and design is to identify the entities that are present in the application's domain. For our discussion forum we have three entities:

- ❑ **Topic** – represents a topic on the discussion forum

- ❑ **Response** – a response to a topic on a discussion forum, of which there may be zero or more

- ❑ **User** – the author of a topic or response

Our next step is to model the entities and the relationships between them using UML. This allows us to represent the domain clearly and concisely, so that we can communicate it effectively to both developers and non-developers within the team.

> You can learn more about UML in "UML Distilled ", 2nd edition (Addison Wesley, ISBN 0-201657-83-X), or "Instant UML " (Wrox Press, ISBN 1-861000-87-1).

The Class Model for the Discussion Forum

From our model of the domain and through a process of steps beyond the scope of this book, we eventually arrive at a design for the classes in our system that will represent the entities within our business domain. This could be a simple process such as picking out the nouns in a requirements specification, or by looking at the entities present in a UML analysis model of the business.

The classes required for our application map almost exactly onto the entities discovered in the business domain, and this is often the case in real-world projects. Here is the class diagram:

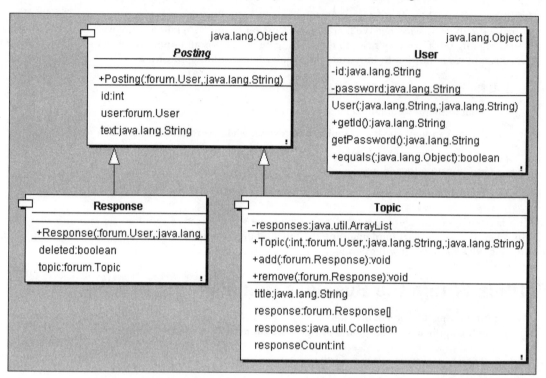

As you can see, we have `Topic`, `Response` and `User` classes that map to our entities, and we also have a `Posting`. This is an abstraction of both `Topic` and `Response` and represents the commonality between them. In this case, both topics and responses have some text (the message) and a user associated with them.

The User Class

The `User` class in this example is just a wrapper for a user `id` and a `password`. In the future, however, we might want to modify it to contain further information, so a reference to the `User` object is stored in the `Posting` rather than just the username. The complete `User` class is as follows:

```
package forum;

public class User {

  private String id;
  private String password;

  User(String id, String password) {
    this.id = id;
    this.password = password;
  }
```

```
    public String getId() {
      return this.id;
    }

    String getPassword() {
      return this.password;
    }

    public boolean equals(Object o) {
      if (o instanceof User) {
        User u = (User)o;
        return getId().equals(u.getId());
      } else {
        return false;
      }
    }
  }
}
```

The Posting Class

A `Posting` object is an abstraction of both a topic and a response. Here's the class:

```
package forum;

public abstract class Posting {

  protected int id;
  protected String text;
  protected User user;

  public Posting(User user, String text) {
    this.user = user;
    this.text = text;
  }

  public int getId() {
    return this.id;
  }

  public void setId(int id) {
    this.id = id;
  }

  public User getUser() {
    return this.user;
  }

  public String getText() {
    return this.text;
  }
}
```

As mentioned, topics and responses have an `id`, some `text` (the message) and an associated `User`. In a similar way to the `User` class, `Posting` is again a wrapper around this basic information.

471

The Topic Class

The Topic class is a little more than a simple wrapper this time. It extends Posting and therefore inherits all of the basic information illustrated previously. In addition to this, Topic introduces a title and a collection of responses that have been made.

Topic also introduces some functionality – the ability to add a response, remove a response, get a response(s), and finally get a count of the number of responses that have been added so far.

> **Many users would use a real-world discussion forum concurrently. For this reason, we would need to ensure that data is not corrupted by synchronizing access to the data. However, for simplicity's sake, this example does not include such synchronization code.**

```java
package forum;

import java.util.*;

public class Topic extends Posting {

  private String title;
  private ArrayList responses = new ArrayList();

  public Topic(int id, User user, String title, String text) {
    super(user, text);

    this.id = id;
    this.title = title;
  }

  public String getTitle() {
    return this.title;
  }

  public void add(Response response) {
    responses.add(response);

    response.setId(responses.size() - 1);
    response.setTopic(this);
  }

  public void remove(Response response) {
    response.setDeleted(true);
  }

  public Response getResponse(int id) {
    return (Response)responses.get(id);
  }

  public Collection getResponses() {
    return responses;
  }
```

The `getResponseCount()` method gets the number of (non-deleted) responses that have been made to this topic:

```
public int getResponseCount() {
  int count = 0;
  Response response;

  Iterator it = responses.iterator();
  while (it.hasNext()) {
    response = (Response)it.next();
```

We don't include those responses that have been deleted:

```
    if (!response.isDeleted()) {
      count++;
    }
  }
  return count;
}
}
```

The Response Class

Finally we have the `Response` class. Again this extends `Posting`, this time adding a reference to the parent `Topic` and a flag to indicate whether the response has been deleted:

```
package forum;

public class Response extends Posting {

  private Topic topic;

  private boolean deleted = false;

  public Response(User user, String text) {
    super(user, text);
  }

  public boolean isDeleted() {
    return this.deleted;
  }

  public void setDeleted(boolean b) {
    this.deleted = b;
  }

  public void setTopic(Topic topic) {
    this.topic = topic;
  }

  public Topic getTopic() {
    return this.topic;
  }
}
```

Building the Forum Using Model 1 Architecture

As our discussion forum is only simple, we'll just go straight ahead and build it using a Model 1 page-centric architecture.

The presentation and logic of our application will be constructed from a number of JSP pages. We've already designed the underlying representation of our domain model so all we have to do now is build the user interface. With this in mind, we'll develop JSP pages that make use of our `Topic`, `Response`, and `User` classes.

Although we are building an application based upon the Model 1 architecture, we could in fact use servlets to make use of the classes that we have just defined. However, because the majority of the code associated with building these pages is presentational, using JSP pages makes this easier. The same results could be achieved with servlets, but in this case the code would become complex and cluttered with statements simply printing the HTML back to the client.

Viewing the Topics

The first page that we need to build is the home page (`index.jsp`), which shows a list of the topics that are currently in our system. Here's what the page looks like in the browser:

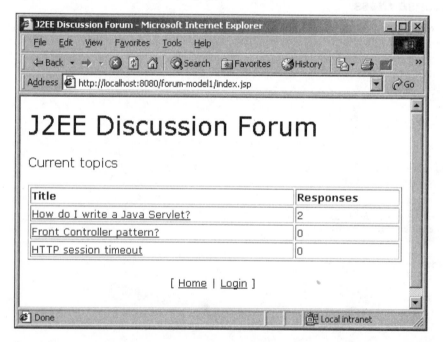

We've created links for each topic title so that the user can navigate to another page showing the responses that have been made so far. In terms of how this has been implemented, the table of topics is generated by some Java code embedded inside a JSP scriptlet. Our JSP page looks up the topics that are currently known by the system and then iterates over them. We make use of a class called `Topics`, which represents the set of sample data for this example. In a real system the topics would probably be stored in a database.

> You should note that, for simplicity, surrounding HTML tags (such as `<head>` and `<body>`), Java import statements, and so on, have been omitted in the code below.

Here's the relevant code from `index.jsp`:

```
<h2>Current topics</h2>

<p>
<table width="100%" border="1">

  <tr>
    <td><b>Title</b></td>
    <td><b>Responses</b></td>
  </tr>

  <%
    Collection topics = Topics.getTopics ();
    Iterator it = topics.iterator();
    Topic topic;
    int id;

    while (it.hasNext()) {
      topic = (Topic)it.next();
      id = topic.getId();
  %>

    <tr>
      <td>
```

In order to generate the appropriate hyperlink that will take the user to the responses page, we've just hard-coded the name of the page, passing the `id` of the topic as a parameter:

```
        <a href="view-topic.jsp?id=<%= id %>"><%= topic.getTitle() %></a>
      </td>
      <td>
        <%= topic.getResponseCount() %>
      </td>
    </tr>
  <%
    }
  %>

</table>
</p>
```

The Login Page

In order to keep anonymous responses off our discussion forum we will require users to log in. If we assume that the users are already set up on the system, then they simply need to log in with their username and password. For our forum there are two users set up – Sam and Simon, both with a password of password. Here's what the page looks like:

As you can see, we have a simple HTML form containing two text fields – one for the user ID (called id) and one for the password (called password): Once a user types in their information and clicks the Submit button, we need to process it and determine whether they are a valid user. To do this, we specify the name of another JSP in the action attribute of the form tag. So that the user's password doesn't get displayed in the address bar at the top of the browser, we've opted to use the POST method, again defined within the opening form tag of login.jsp:

```
<h2>Login</h2>

<form action="process-login.jsp" method="post">
User id : <input type="text" name="id">
<br>
Password : <input type="password" name="password">
<br>
<br>
<input type="submit" value="Submit">
</form>
```

Processing the Login

Next is the page that processes the login details, `process-login.jsp`. We've decided that the user should be forwarded back to the home page once they successfully log in. Therefore, this JSP page doesn't actually contain any visual element. Once more we use a class to represent sample data that would usually be stored in a database, in this case `Users`. Here's the relevant code from the JSP page:

```
<%@ page import="forum.*" %>

<%
  String id = request.getParameter("id");
  String password = request.getParameter("password");
  if (Users.exists (id, password)) {
    session.setAttribute("user", Users.getUser(id));
    pageContext.forward("index.jsp");
  } else {
    pageContext.forward("login.jsp");
  }
%>
```

We get the values of the user ID and password that were sent as a result of the user submitting the form and use them to determine whether a user exists on the system. If this is the case, we look up the appropriate `User` instance, place this in the HTTP session under the name `user`, and redirect them to the home page:

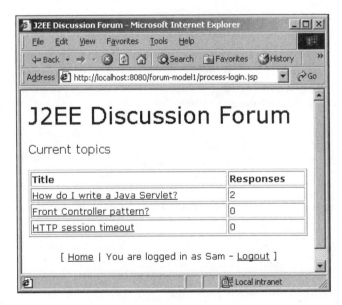

If a user doesn't exist with the specified user ID and password, we'll (perhaps unhelpfully) simply return them to the login page.

Viewing the Responses

Next we want the page to display the responses to a particular topic, reached by clicking on a linked topic title on the home page:

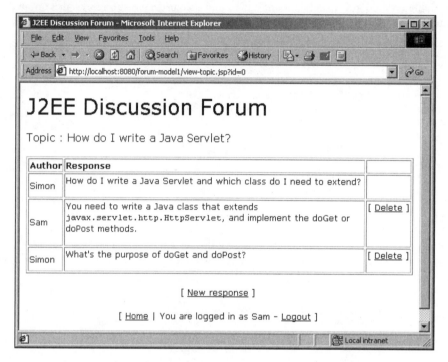

Again, this was built as a JSP page, `view-topic.jsp`. It takes the `id` parameter passed as part of the query string and uses it to look up the appropriate `Topic`:

```
<%
   String id = request.getParameter ("id");
   Topic topic = Topics.getTopic(Integer.parseInt (id));
%>
```

Once it has these parameters, it can get a list of all of the responses to the selected topic and again generate an HTML table:

```
<h2>Topic : <%= topic.getTitle() %></h2>

<p>
<table width="100%" border="1">

<tr>
  <td><b>Author</b></td>
  <td><b>Response</b></td>
  <td> </td>
</tr>
```

```
<tr>
  <td><%= topic.getUser().getId() %></td>
  <td><%= topic.getText() %><br><br></td>
  <td> </td>
</tr>

<%
  Iterator it = topic.getResponses().iterator();
  Response res;
```

Here it builds up the table one row at a time, only displaying those responses that have not been deleted:

```
while (it.hasNext()) {
  res = (Response)it.next();

  if (!res.isDeleted()) {
%>
    <tr>
```

The first row of data in the table contains the message associated with the original topic, with the remainder representing each response in the order in which it was added. As we're going to offer the ability to delete responses, we have an appropriate link for this that is generated in the last column. This is just a dynamically generated hyperlink that appends the following information to the query string:

❑   topic – the ID of the current topic

❑   response – the ID of the response to be deleted

```
        <td><%= res.getUser().getId() %></td>
        <td><%= res.getText() %><br><br></td>
        <td valign="top" align="center">
          [ <a href="delete-response.jsp?
              topic=<%= topic.getId() %>&response=<%= res.getId() %>">
            Delete</a> ]
        </td>
      </tr>
  <%
    }
  }
  %>

</table>
</p>
```

Finally, we have a link that will allow users to add new responses:

```
<p>
<center>
[ <a href="new-response.jsp?id=<%= topic.getId() %>">New response</a> ]
</center>
</p>
```

Adding a New Response

Adding a new response to an existing topic is a straightforward process, captured by a small HTML form containing a text area in which to write the response. Here's what it looks like:

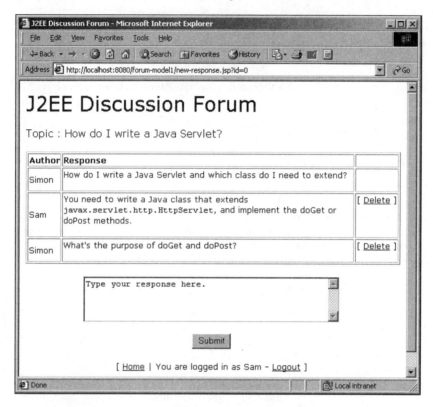

And here is the relevant HTML in the JSP page, new-response.jsp:

```
// ... same as view-topic.jsp ...

<p>
<center>
<form action="process-new-response.jsp" method="post">
<textarea name="text" rows="4" cols="48">Type your response here.</textarea>
<input type="hidden" name="id" value="<%= id %>">
<br>
<br>
<input type="submit" value="Submit">
</form>
</center>
</p>
```

Here we have a text area called text representing the body of the response, and a hidden field representing the id of the topic to which the new response should be added.

Processing a New Response

When the Submit button is clicked on the new-response.jsp page, we need to extract the information from the request and use it to add a new response to the appropriate topic. This can be performed as follows (this code is from process-new-response.jsp in the code download):

```
<%@ page import="forum.*" %>

<%
  String text = request.getParameter("text");
  int id = Integer.parseInt(request.getParameter("id"));

  User user = (User)session.getAttribute("user");

  Topic topic = Topics.getTopic(id);
  topic.add(new Response(user, text));

  pageContext.forward("view-topic.jsp?id=" + id);
%>
```

We extract the text and the topic ID from the HTTP request, while the user information can be found in the HTTP Session object because that's where we placed it when the user logged in. Using all of this information we can find the appropriate Topic instance and add a new Response. Once complete we can forward the user to the responses page once again so that they can see their new response.

Deleting an Existing Response

Finally we must build the functionality to delete a response. Once again, this is provided by a JSP (delete-response.jsp) as follows:

```
<%@ page import="forum.*" %>

<%
  int topicId = Integer.parseInt(request.getParameter("topic"));
  int responseId = Integer.parseInt(request.getParameter("response"));

  User user = (User)session.getAttribute("user");

  Topic topic = Topics.getTopic(topicId);
  Response res = topic.getResponse(responseId);
```

We must check to see if the user is the author of the response. We won't allow deletion if this is not the case:

```
  if (res.getUser().equals(user)) {
    topic.remove(res);
  }

  pageContext.forward("view-topic.jsp?id=" + topicId);
%>
```

This is again fairly straightforward. Whatever happens, we simply forward back to the view-topic.jsp page where the current state of the topic will be seen.

A Closer Look at the Page Flow for the Application

With our development complete, we can begin to test our web application. The page flow is as shown below:

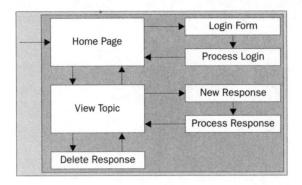

As with most web sites, all pages link back to the home page. For clarity these links have not been included on the diagram. Also not included on the diagram are the constraints to indicate that a user must be logged in to be able to post a new response, or delete a response, and so on.

As it stands, the application works, but there are a few problems that you may have spotted already.

Authentication

Although we have a login link on the front page, the current structure of the web site means that people can look at the topics without logging in. In fact, any user could bypass the login page completely, meaning that they would also be able to add new responses anonymously. For example, a user could open their browser and jump straight to the following page: http://localhost:8080/forum-model1/new-response.jsp?id=0.

One solution would be to require users to login before they can view the list of topics in the forum. However, this might reduce the likelihood of them visiting our site in the future. A better alternative would be to ask the user to login the first time that they wanted to perform some action on the site such as adding or deleting a response – that way they can still view all the valuable information quickly and easily.

This is easy enough and can be achieved by adding the following scriptlet to the top of those restricted pages:

```
<%
  if (session.getAttribute("user") == null) {
    pageContext.forward("login.jsp");
  }
%>
```

In this scriptlet we check whether a `User` instance has been set in the user's session. If one does exist, we can assume that the user has already logged in and the page will be rendered as usual. If a `User` instance doesn't exist (under the name of `user`), we can forward the user to the login page.

This code fragment could be copied and pasted into each JSP that needs to be secure. This style of reuse is a step in the right direction but is hardly the most efficient. After all, if we needed to make some changes then we've certainly got our work cut trying to find each and every place that it's used.

Of course we could place this functionality into a reusable software component such as a JavaBean or a custom tag, or at a simpler level, another JSP that gets included wherever necessary. This is a further step in the right direction but still requires that we make use of the functionality everywhere that we need it. We've already noted earlier in the chapter that centralizing user access would make securing our application an easier task.

Authorization

In the same way as we have done for authentication, authorization code could be duplicated throughout the system. An example of this is the code that checks whether the current user can delete the selected response. If we forgot to make use of this functionality somewhere then data could become available to or corrupted by inappropriate users. While it is probably not much of a problem in a small discussion forum, e-commerce sites generally have confidential information available (such as user's credit card numbers and home addresses). This information should certainly not be accessed by anybody except its rightful owner.

Extending the Application

We might want to extend our application so that we log a user's progress through the system, and track which pages in the system are being used more than others. This is especially useful for e-commerce type solutions where customers often leave if a web site is deemed too slow.

If we wanted to create a log that tracked the users throughout the site, whereabouts would this functionality be placed? Also, how easily could it be turned off when we've finished analyzing the data? In this example application, there is no single place – no central point – where such logging could be located. Instead, it would have to be placed into each page, either explicitly, by calling some included code, or by using a reusable component such as a JavaBean or custom tag. The decision to include a logging facility is therefore one that should be made at design time, before the coding commences.

Refactoring Applications

The problems we've seen in our discussion forum highlight the types of problems that often tend to appear in applications. Fortunately all is not lost, even if the application contains such problems: we can attempt to refactor the application. **Refactoring** basically means changing from one form to another, and although not strictly "design", it does promote some of the same thought processes. When we refactor a piece of software, it generally means that we change the internal structure in some way without damaging the functionality that it provides.

Refactoring is something that we probably all do already without realizing. Some of the reasons why we might want to refactor a particular piece of software might include to tidy it up, to fix bugs, or to simply extend it. The downside to all of this is that refactoring can be a very time-consuming process.

If we had taken a step back before we plowed straight into coding our discussion forum, we could have foreseen that we needed authentication on many pages and designed a flexible, standard way of performing this task. As it stands, we've had to copy the same piece of code into several different pages in our application, therefore reducing the maintainability and increasing the likelihood that somebody might breach our system.

We highlighted many of these issues when we discussed the Model 1 architecture near the start of the chapter. Lack of extensibility is one of the key downsides to web applications built upon the Model 1 architecture – there is no centralized place for business logic and it is generally embedded into the view components such as JSPs. This makes extensibility difficult to achieve, which in turn makes it hard to keep up with the ever-changing requirements of businesses in the internet world. This isn't to say that applications built using a Model 1 architecture don't have their place – small sites, prototypes, and proofs of concepts are well-suited to this. It's just that most large-scale web sites need a more maintainable and extensible solution.

With this in mind (and instead of refactoring the entire system), let's look at how we can use Model 2 architecture and a handful of J2EE patterns to design and build a more maintainable, extensible, and secure version of our discussion forum.

Building the Forum Using Model 2 Architecture

Model 2 architecture accepts requests through a controller component where it can service the request itself or delegate this task to some other component. The task of rendering the response is then dispatched to the appropriate view component. There are of course various ways in which this can be implemented. We're going to look at four of these design patterns:

❑ Front Controller

❑ Intercepting Filter

❑ View Helper

❑ Service to Worker

Using the Front Controller Pattern

Our current discussion forum has many views. System services (for example, data retrieval) and business logic are intermingled within the views, leading to a decrease in maintainability and a reduction in reusability. JSP pages are often developed by two types of people: web designers (who handle the look and feel of the site) and J2EE developers (who take care of the business logic). Placing too much Java code into the page usually makes it more difficult for web designers to modify the look and feel as they battle with Java code that they might not understand. For example, the logic that retrieves a `Topic` instance from the "database" based upon a topic ID, or the business rule that says only the author of a response can delete that response.

The other feature of our current implementation is that all of the links to other pages are hard-coded within the pages themselves. Should we need to change the flow of the system in any way, we'll have to resort to modifying a number of JSP pages.

Ideally we would like to place all of this logic in a single location to help us ensure that this type of functionality is consistent, maintainable, and extensible in the future. The **Front Controller** pattern can help us to achieve these goals. Here's how it fits into the Model 2 (programming-centric) architecture:

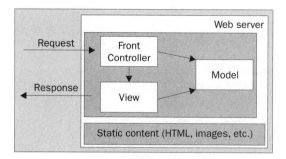

This is exactly the same as the Model 2 architecture diagram that we saw towards the start of the chapter where a controller component is the entry point for web requests. The controller performs some processing of the request and may make changes to the underlying model. The task of rendering the response is then dispatched to a view component.

A front controller is also a good place in which to centralize services such as error handling and logging. Centralizing system services and the flow between pages has many benefits as it moves business logic and other system-level service code out of JSP scriptlets, back into reusable components, therefore promoting reusability of functionality across different types of requests, as we'll be seeing shortly.

There are various strategies by which a front controller can be implemented, with the typical strategy focusing on the use of a servlet. There are several reasons why this role is better implemented using a servlet than a JSP. As we've noted before, outputting content back to the client is not an ideal use for a servlet because it involves writing lots of print statements – effectively tying together the content and the logic. JSP pages, on the other hand, are much better suited to delivering content, because they are written as content containing small bits of logic wherever necessary. As a controller component doesn't actually deliver any content itself, implementing it as a JSP results in a page containing no content – just the logic required to process the requests. For this reason, a servlet is the preferred strategy.

Of course centralizing all of this functionality can lead to a large, bloated controller component that has responsibilities for the entire web application. There are a number of ways in which this problem can be solved, one of which is to have several front controllers, each responsible for particular area of the site. For example, an e-commerce site might have one controller responsible for servicing all requests related to products and another to service all payment requests. Another solution is to use the **Command and Controller** implementation strategy we will discuss shortly.

Implementing the Front Controller Pattern

For the moment, here is an example skeleton implementation of the Front Controller pattern.

```
package forum;

import java.io.IOException;

import javax.servlet.*;
import javax.servlet.http.*;

public class FrontController extends HttpServlet {
```

```
    protected void processRequest(HttpServletRequest req,
                              HttpServletResponse res)
                          throws ServletException, IOException {
  RequestDispatcher dispatcher =
    getServletContext().getRequestDispatcher("name of view component");
  dispatcher.forward(req, res);
}

protected void doGet(HttpServletRequest req, HttpServletResponse res)
    throws ServletException, IOException {

  processRequest(req, res);
}

protected void doPost(HttpServletRequest req, HttpServletResponse res)
    throws ServletException, IOException {

  processRequest(req, res);
}
}
```

In this case, the front controller is simply an extension of `HttpServlet` with default implementations of the `doGet()` and `doPost()` methods that delegate processing of the request to another method called `processRequest()`. This is done to ensure that no matter how the request is made, the front controller will service it.

We've left out the majority of the body of the `processRequest()` method, but essentially a front controller will perform some processing that is associated with a request, and then dispatch to a view component to render the response. The view components are typically JSP pages. Once the controller has completed performing its business logic, it can dispatch to a JSP page through the `RequestDispatcher`.

At this point, you may have a question. If the controller is to be responsible for handling all requests, how does it know what the request is and therefore how to handle it?

The Command and Controller Strategy

In the Command and Controller strategy the logic to handle each specific request is moved out into a separate component. This architecture is illustrated below:

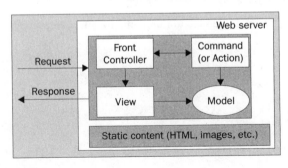

Each of these extra components represents a specific command (or **action**), and the component encapsulates the logic to perform that action.

The front controller delegates the handling of requests to the appropriate command component, which may modify the state of the underlying model. Once the command component has completed its work, the controller again dispatches the task of rendering the response to the appropriate view component. But how does the controller know which command component to use? We'll tackle this issue in a moment.

Action Classes

The first thing we need to do to implement the Command and Controller strategy is to define the interface between the controller and action components. We can do this either by creating an interface or an abstract class. For the purposes of our example, we'll define an abstract class that all actions in our web application must extend (this means that we have a single place in which to add common functionality for all actions in the future):

```
package forum;

import javax.servlet.http.*;

public abstract class Action {
```

Subclasses will implement their specific business and processing logic in the `process()` method. To ensure that the action classes have access to the same environment and information as servlets, the `process()` method takes a reference to the HTTP Request and Response objects in the same way that the `processRequest()` method in the `FrontController` class did. Once the processing has been completed, the action can return a string to identify the view component to which the controller should dispatch next:

```
    public abstract String process(HttpServletRequest request,
        HttpServletResponse response);
    }
```

Defining the interface between the controller and the action components helps to decouple them from each other, which means that we can change the controller or the actions without affecting the other.

The next stage is to put together the logic that will figure out what the request is and delegate the processing to the appropriate action component.

Communicating the Type of Request

There are a number of ways that the type of request can be communicated to the controller servlet, most of which are focused around passing parameters to the servlet over HTTP (in a similar way to how we pass the topic id to the `view-topic.jsp` page). The problem with sending additional parameters to indicate the type of request is that the URLs need to be written carefully – after all, it is easy to misspell parameter names and get the query string syntax wrong.

Another mechanism would be to use a string that represented the type of request that we wanted to perform and pass this to the servlet as additional path information. We already know how mappings can be defined between a servlet and a URI via the `web.xml` file. An example of this is shown overleaf, which defines a mapping between our `FrontController` Servlet and the URI `/controller/*`:

```
<?xml version="1.0" encoding="ISO-8859-1"?>

<!DOCTYPE web-app
    PUBLIC "-//Sun Microsystems, Inc.//DTD Web Application 2.3//EN"
    "http://java.sun.com/dtd/web-app_2_3.dtd">

<web-app>
```

```
  <servlet>
    <servlet-name>FrontController</servlet-name>
    <servlet-class>forum.FrontController</servlet-class>
  </servlet>

  <servlet-mapping>
    <servlet-name>FrontController</servlet-name>
    <url-pattern>/controller/*</url-pattern>
  </servlet-mapping>
```

```
</web-app>
```

Now we can make calls to the controller by appending controller/ViewTopic?id=0 to our URL. Here, ViewTopic is the additional path information (also known as **path info**) and represents the type of request we are making. The query string can be used as usual, with id=0 providing the parameters for our specific request to view a topic. This is much cleaner than adding additional parameters to indicate the type of request. Instead, this information is now part of the URL that we use. With this side of the request figured out, how does the controller know what do, and where does this logic reside?

What we need to do here is to map the string that we obtain from the additional path info onto a specific action instance. Once again there are many strategies for this, with the most flexible being externalizing this mapping, through an XML file for example. Other examples here include hard-coding the mapping inside the controller, or perhaps using a properties file.

For simplicity, in our example we'll build a separate component in which this mapping will be encapsulated. In a production application, hard-coding such configuration information means that changes require the appropriate Java class to be modified, recompiled, and redeployed. In other words, it decreases the maintainability. However, hard coding this information into a separate component will suffice for our simple example and we'll call this class our ActionHelper. The mapping information is stored in a HashMap. Here's the code listing for this class:

```java
package forum;

import java.util.HashMap;

public class ActionHelper {

  private static HashMap actions = new HashMap();

  static {
    actions.put("ViewTopic", "forum.ViewTopicAction");
    actions.put("Login", "forum.LoginAction");
    actions.put("Logout", "forum.LogoutAction");
    actions.put("NewResponse", "forum.NewResponseAction");
    actions.put("ProcessNewResponse", "forum.ProcessNewResponseAction");
    actions.put("DeleteResponse", "forum.DeleteResponseAction");
  }
```

The `ActionHelper` class effectively maintains a mapping between request names (or types) and the fully qualified class names of the classes that can process the requests. Given the name of a request, the static `getAction()` method returns an instance of an `Action` class that can be used for processing:

```
public static Action getAction(String name) {
  Action action = null;

  try {
    Class c = Class.forName((String)actions.get(name));
    action = (Action)c.newInstance();
  } catch (Exception e) {
    e.printStackTrace();
  }

  return action;
}
}
```

The next step is to plug all of this into the `processRequest()` method of our `FrontController` as this will be the single entry point for all requests in our web application:

```
package forum;

import java.io.IOException;

import javax.servlet.*;
import javax.servlet.http.*;

public class FrontController extends HttpServlet {

  protected void processRequest(HttpServletRequest req,
                                HttpServletResponse res)
                   throws ServletException, IOException {
```

Here we find which action should be used:

```
String actionName = req.getPathInfo().substring(1);
```

Now we use the helper class to locate the action:

```
Action action = ActionHelper.getAction(actionName);
```

The next step is to process the action, so that we can find out which view to show the user next:

```
String nextView = action.process(req, res);
```

Finally we redirect to the appropriate view:

```
    RequestDispatcher dispatcher =
        getServletContext().getRequestDispatcher(nextView);
    dispatcher.forward(req, res);
}
```

```
    protected void doGet(HttpServletRequest req, HttpServletResponse res)
        throws ServletException, IOException {

    processRequest(req, res);
    }

    protected void doPost(HttpServletRequest req, HttpServletResponse res)
        throws ServletException, IOException {

    processRequest(req, res);
    }
}
```

With the code to look up actions and process requests encapsulated elsewhere, our controller servlet is fairly minimal. In fact all of the components that we have implemented as part of the Command and Controller strategy have been fairly lightweight. This is good from both a maintainability and reusability perspective as small components are generally easier to maintain (and bug fix) and are also more likely to be reusable elsewhere. The framework that we've built is also extensible because new request handlers (actions) can easily be built and added to the system.

The Apache Struts Framework

The implementation of the Front Controller pattern presented here is fairly simple and straightforward but there are many improvements that can be made. One such example is externalizing the mapping between action names and the `Action` classes that are going to service the request. Although such work isn't particularly complex, it is still time consuming nonetheless. For this reason, there are number of third-party frameworks available for developers to use as a starting point for their web applications. Once such example is **Struts** from the Jakarta Project (http://jakarta.apache.org).

Struts is an open source framework providing an implementation of not only a front controller, but a complete implementation (or **framework**) of the Model 2 architecture. The key components are similar to those presented here, including for example, a controller servlet (called `ActionServlet`), `Action` classes in which to place functionality for processing a request and `ActionBean` classes in which to encapsulate data coming in from a request. In addition to this, Struts also contains a comprehensive collection of JSP tag libraries for the easy assembly of HTML-based forms and JSP pages in general.

One of the most important features of Struts is that pretty much everything about it is externally configured through the `struts-config.xml` file. This includes the mappings between action names and `Action` classes (called `ActionMappings`) and also a concept called `ActionForwards`.

For the simple example presented here, the `Action` classes return a string representing the URI of the JSP that should be displayed next. In Struts, however, the `Action` classes return a symbolic name (wrapped up in an `ActionForward` instance) representing which view component should be displayed next. As an example, consider a login form containing a username and password. On submission of the form, the login is either successful or not. In this case, the `Action` class could return symbolic names such as `success` or `failure`. These symbolic names are then configured in the `struts-config.xml` file and it's here that the physical URI to the appropriate JSP is specified. This is a very powerful feature and is yet another way in which the flow and structure of the web application can be taken out of the code to increase maintainability. After all, if the structure of the site changes, only the configuration file needs to change.

> *A full explanation of Struts is beyond the scope of this book, but a more detailed study of this framework can be found in the following Wrox titles:* Professional JSP, 2nd Edition *(ISBN 1-861004-95-8) and* Professional JSP Site Design *(ISBN 1-861005-51-2).*

Now let's get back on track. With the design and framework of a Model 2-based discussion forum in place, let's take a look at how the forum can be implemented once again in Model 2 architecture.

Viewing the Responses

Previously, to view the responses to a topic we made a direct request to the `view-topic.jsp` page, passing the `id` of the specific topic. At the top of this page was a JSP scriptlet that found this parameter and used it to look up the appropriate `Topic` instance for use further down the page when building up the table of responses. One of the benefits of the Command and Controller strategy is that we can move this sort of code out of the JSP and back into a reusable component. With this in mind, we can implement the action to view a topic:

```
package forum;

import javax.servlet.http.*;

public class ViewTopicAction extends Action {

  public String process(HttpServletRequest request,
      HttpServletResponse response) {
```

In the `process()` method, we first get the `id` parameter and use it to look up the appropriate `Topic` instance:

```
    String id = request.getParameter("id");
    Topic topic = Topics.getTopic(Integer.parseInt(id));
```

Now that we have the topic, we place it in the request ready for use on the view:

```
    request.setAttribute("topic", topic);
    return "/view-topic.jsp";
  }
}
```

We've literally just moved the code into an `Action` subclass. Once the `Topic` instance has been located, we then need to make this available to the page in order that it can build the table of responses. To do this we use the HTTP Request object as a temporary storage area for this object:

```
request.setAttribute("topic", topic);
```

Using the HTTP Request (or even the Session) is a useful and frequently used mechanism for passing information between the various components within web applications. This works between two servlets, two JSP pages, or a mixture of the two.

On completion of this action, the controller will dispatch control to the `view-topic.jsp` page on which we can use the standard `<jsp:useBean/>` action to locate the object again. The remainder of the page remains unchanged:

```
<jsp:useBean id="topic" class="forum.Topic" scope="request"/>

<p>
<h2>Topic : <%= topic.getTitle() %></h2>
</p>
```

Following this we just build the table of responses as before.

The final step in using this is to ensure that we change all direct links to the `view-topic` JSP into links to the controller, not forgetting to include the name of the action that we wish to perform.

```
/controller/ViewTopic?id=0
```

Although this particular action is fairly small, it does illustrate the point that we raised earlier about enhanced maintainability and reusability. We can now make use of this action elsewhere in our application rather than coding a scriptlet on a JSP. This means that should we wish to modify this behavior, we'll know where to find it and the modifications will be reflected elsewhere in our application automatically.

Processing the Login

In a similar way, we can encapsulate the logic associated with processing the user's login into an `Action` class, `LoginAction`:

```java
package forum;

import javax.servlet.http.*;

public class LoginAction extends Action {

    public String process(HttpServletRequest request,
        HttpServletResponse response) {
```

```
        String id = request.getParameter("id");
        String password = request.getParameter("password");
        String view;
        if (Users.exists(id, password)) {
          request.getSession().setAttribute("user", Users.getUser(id));
          view = "/index.jsp";
        } else {
          view = "/login.jsp";
        }

        return view;
    }

}
```

As you can see, we've literally moved the code from the process-login.jsp page. This page didn't actually contain any presentation at all in the page-centric implementation and this is another good reason for moving the code into a small reusable component. It's not only easier to find this code to maintain it in the future, but JSP pages are really suited to rendering responses rather than being containers for lots of Java code.

To ensure that our action gets called, we again need to change any references to the process-login.jsp page, including the action attribute of HTML form tags:

```
<form action="controller/Login" method="post">
```

Adding a New Response

We've already seen how the view-topic.jsp page has changed: the short scriptlet at the top of the page has been removed. The new-response.jsp page is effectively the same, with an additional HTML form underneath the table of responses. For this reason and rather than recoding the logic to look up the appropriate topic, we can extend the ViewTopicAction class helping to ensure that the functionality is consistent.

```
package forum;

import javax.servlet.http.*;

public class NewResponseAction extends ViewTopicAction {

    public String process(HttpServletRequest request,
        HttpServletResponse response) {

      super.process(request, response);

      return "/new-response.jsp";
    }
}
```

Although a simple example, this shows how the action components can be reused across different types of requests. Here, we are using the same functionality but dispatching to a different view.

Processing a New Response

The logic to add a new response from the HTML form can also be placed within an `Action` class as illustrated next.

```
package forum;

import javax.servlet.http.*;

public class ProcessNewResponseAction extends Action {

  public String process(HttpServletRequest request,
      HttpServletResponse response) {

    String text = request.getParameter("text");
    int id = Integer.parseInt(request.getParameter("id"));

    User user = (User)request.getSession().getAttribute("user");

    Topic topic = Topics.getTopic(id);
    topic.add(new Response(user, text));

    return "/controller/ViewTopic?id=" + id;
  }
}
```

Instead of dispatching to a JSP, we've asked that the request be forwarded onto the `ViewTopic` action. This is a useful way of chaining actions together and again shows the ability to reuse them across different types of requests.

Deleting an Existing Response

The final action that we have in our web application is the ability to delete an existing response. Once again we can move the business logic associated with this into an `Action` component:

```
package forum;

import javax.servlet.http.*;

public class DeleteResponseAction extends Action {

  public String process(HttpServletRequest request,
      HttpServletResponse response) {

    int topicId = Integer.parseInt(request.getParameter("topic"));
    int responseId = Integer.parseInt(request.getParameter("response"));

    User user = (User)request.getSession().getAttribute("user");

    Topic topic = Topics.getTopic(topicId);
    Response res = topic.getResponse(responseId);
```

Only the original author of a response can delete it, and for this reason the `DeleteResponseAction` contains the appropriate logic to make this check. However, what it (or the other actions) doesn't check is whether the user is actually logged on. We'll deal with this issue in the next section.

```
    if (res.getUser().equals(user)) {
      // yes, so delete it
      topic.remove(res);
    }

    return "/controller/ViewTopic?id=" + topicId;
  }
}
```

Using the Intercepting Filter Pattern

Checking that the user is logged on is another common piece of functionality that would be an ideal candidate to encapsulate into a reusable component. We could of course wrap this verification up into a small component and call it from the appropriate actions. However, what we really want is for unauthenticated requests to be redirected to the login page. Let's look at how the **Intercepting Filter** pattern can help.

A Closer Look at User Verification in the Discussion Forum

One of the features that our discussion board doesn't support is anonymous response to topics. To ensure that this doesn't happen, our current implementation uses a small snippet of code at the top of those pages that require a user to be logged in:

```
<%
  if (session.getAttribute("user") == null) {
    // no, so redirect them to the login page
  }
%>
```

We've seen this already, and all it does is check that the user is logged in before allowing them to see the page that they requested. If the user isn't logged in yet, we simply forward them on to the login page.

The problem with this approach is that this code is scattered throughout the views (pages) in our application. This means that we might not be entirely sure which views contain the code. Subsequently, some pages that should have this code may not, and if we need to update the verification code we need to modify every page that contains it.

One way around this problem is to use intercepting filters. Intercepting filters are a useful way of performing pre-processing on requests before they are handled by the components in our web application. If we extend the architecture yet further, we can insert an intercepting filter to pre-process the requests:

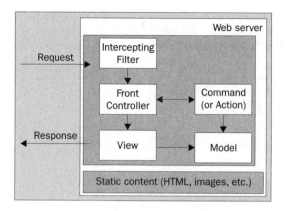

The types of tasks that we might want an intercepting filter to perform could be:

❑   Checking the client type so that the appropriate type of site can be served up

❑   Checking whether the user has a valid session

❑   Checking that the user is logged in

In our discussion forum we can use an intercepting filter to ensure that any requests to specific pages are authenticated. Having identified that an intercepting filter is a useful component to have in our web application, how do we go about building one?

Implementing an Intercepting Filter

In a previous chapter we introduced **filters**, a new feature of the Servlet 2.3 specification. Using the same techniques as we described in that chapter, we can build a simple filter, and define a handful of mappings specifying those URLs on which we wish it to operate.

First of all, let's start with the filter class itself. We'll call it `AuthenticationFilter`:

```
package forum;

import java.io.IOException;

import javax.servlet.*;
import javax.servlet.http.*;

public class AuthenticationFilter implements Filter {

  private FilterConfig filterConfig;

  public void init(FilterConfig filterConfig) throws ServletException {
    this.filterConfig = filterConfig;
  }

  public void doFilter(ServletRequest req, ServletResponse res,
                  FilterChain chain) throws IOException, ServletException {

    HttpServletRequest request = (HttpServletRequest)req;
    HttpServletResponse response = (HttpServletResponse)res;
```

In the doFilter() method, we check to see if the current user logged in. If not, we redirect them to the login page:

```java
    if (request.getSession().getAttribute("user") == null) {
      RequestDispatcher dispatcher =
        filterConfig.getServletContext().getRequestDispatcher("/login.jsp");
      dispatcher.forward(request, response);
    } else {
      chain.doFilter(request, response);
    }
  }

  public void destroy() {
  }
}
```

What is important here is that the functionality associated with this filter is almost identical to the scriptlet of code that we used in our Model 1 version of the discussion forum. All it does is check that the user is logged in and redirect them to the login.jsp page if this is not the case. One of the goals of OO is to encapsulate reusable functionality and that's exactly what we've done here. We've moved this logic out of the views and back towards the front of the request handling process.

With the filter built, we now need to plug it into our web application. As we've seen before, this is achieved through the web application deployment descriptor – the web.xml file:

```xml
<?xml version="1.0" encoding="ISO-8859-1"?>

<!DOCTYPE web-app
    PUBLIC "-//Sun Microsystems, Inc.//DTD Web Application 2.3//EN"
    "http://java.sun.com/j2ee/dtds/web-app_2_3.dtd">

<web-app>
```

```xml
  <filter>
    <filter-name>AuthenticationFilter</filter-name>
    <filter-class>forum.AuthenticationFilter</filter-class>
  </filter>

  <filter-mapping>
    <filter-name>AuthenticationFilter</filter-name>
    <url-pattern>/controller/NewResponse</url-pattern>
  </filter-mapping>

  <filter-mapping>
    <filter-name>AuthenticationFilter</filter-name>
    <url-pattern>/controller/ProcessNewResponse</url-pattern>
  </filter-mapping>

  <filter-mapping>
    <filter-name>AuthenticationFilter</filter-name>
    <url-pattern>/controller/DeleteResponse</url-pattern>
  </filter-mapping>
```

```
<servlet>
  <servlet-name>FrontController</servlet-name>
  <servlet-class>forum.FrontController</servlet-class>
</servlet>

<servlet-mapping>
  <servlet-name>FrontController</servlet-name>
  <url-pattern>/controller/*</url-pattern>
</servlet-mapping>

</web-app>
```

We've already defined that all URLs starting /controller/ are directed to our FrontController servlet. Alongside this we define a filter called AuthenticationFilter and tell our web application to use the AuthenticationFilter class from the forum package. Once this has been set up, we can specify the set of URLs that trigger the filter. In our application, we need to pre-process all requests coming in for the following actions:

❑ NewResponse

❑ ProcessNewResponse

❑ DeleteResponse

This is a very powerful and flexible mechanism, because we can easily reconfigure our filter should the security requirements of our application change.

The patterns that we have just discussed cover much of our example application. Although this book is about servlets, a chapter about web application design wouldn't be complete without a quick look at a few more patterns:

❑ View Helper

❑ Service to Worker

Using the View Helper Pattern

The View Helper pattern is a way of taking logic embedded in the view (for example scriptlets inside a JSP) and wrapping it up as reusable functionality for use in other view components.

Advantages of the View Helper Pattern

Although we've tried to move much of the functionality away from the view components and back towards the front of the request handling cycle, there still remains some functionality in the views. A good example would be the JSP scriptlets inside the view-topic.jsp page that determine whether a particular response has been deleted and should be hidden.

The purpose of the view component is to present information back to the user. All of the business processing associated with the request should have been performed by this stage, leaving the view component to perform any logic specifically related to presenting the information. While we can include business logic in a JSP page via scriptlets, we have already noted that this is not a wise approach because the code in the scriptlet is not in a very reusable form.

To solve this problem, this type of functionality can be moved into helper components and subsequently reused across the web application. On an implementation level, these helpers could be built as either of the following:

❑ JavaBeans – for use in servlet/JSP views

❑ Custom tags – for use in JSP views

In fact we've already seen an example of the View Helper pattern in the `view-topic.jsp` page. The `ViewTopicAction` looks up the appropriate `Topic` instance and places it into the HTTP Request object, ready for the JSP to find it. To recap, here's the code for the `process()` method in the `ViewTopicAction`:

```java
public String process(HttpServletRequest request,
                      HttpServletResponse response) {

   String id = request.getParameter("id");
   Topic topic = Topics.getTopic(Integer.parseInt(id));
   request.setAttribute("topic", topic);
   return "/view-topic.jsp";
}
```

To make use of the information that this action places into the HTTP request, we might have implemented this lookup in `view-topic.jsp` using a simple JSP scriptlet as follows:

```jsp
<%
  Topic topic = (Topic)request.getAttribute("topic");
%>
```

Instead, however, we decided to use the `<jsp:useBean/>` action in `view-topic.jsp`:

```jsp
<jsp:useBean id="topic" class="forum.Topic" scope="request"/>
```

This is just one such example, and it just happens that in this situation the helper is already written for us. What is important is that we are removing as much logic as possible from the view components in our web application, and placing it inside reusable components.

Another example includes the JSP scriptlet that is used to iterate over a collection of Response objects in the `view-topic.jsp` page:

```jsp
<%
   Iterator it = topic.getResponses().iterator();
   Response res;

   while (it.hasNext()) {
      res = (Response)it.next();
      if (!res.isDeleted()) {
%>
```

```
<tr>
  <td><%= res.getUser().getId() %></td>
  <td><%= res.getText() %><br><br></td>
  <td valign="top" align="center">
    [ <a href="controller/DeleteResponse?
      topic=<%= topic.getId() %>&response=<%= res.getId() %>">
      Delete</a> ]
  </td>
</tr>
<%
      }
    }
%>
```

In this example there is much more Java code and therefore much more that can go wrong. Ideally we would like to be able to reuse this type of functionality on other pages that build up the content by iterating over a collection of Java objects. In this situation, a JSP custom tag could be used as a view helper as follows:

```
<forum:iterate id="res"
               className="forum.Response"
               collection="<%= topic.getResponses() %>">
  <%
    if (!res.isDeleted()) {
  %>
    <tr>
      <td><%= res.getUser().getId() %></td>
      <td><%= res.getText() %><br><br></td>
      <td valign="top" align="center">
        [ <a href="controller/DeleteResponse?
          topic=<%= topic.getId() %>&response=<%= res.getId() %>">
          Delete</a> ]
      </td>
    </tr>
  <%
      }
  %>
</forum:iterate>
```

Here, the Java code responsible for performing the iteration has been moved inside a custom tag, moving it away from the page and resulting in a much cleaner JSP containing much less Java code than before. In doing this, we have created a reusable view helper that can be used on other pages in the web application.

Although the discussion of how such a custom tag might be implemented is beyond the scope of this chapter, the full sourcecode for it is provided with the downloadable sourcecode for the book.

The type of functionality that this pattern is applicable to includes:

❑ Retrieval of data (for example getting data from the model to display)

❑ Logic related to presentation of data but not to formatting (for instance determining whether a particular piece of data should be displayed)

❑ General presentation layer-related logic (such as iterating over a collection of data items)

Using the Service to Worker Pattern

The final pattern we will consider is **Service to Worker**, which can be described as a "macro pattern". It's really just a combination of a front controller pattern, along with views and their helpers.

This pattern describes the architecture of our discussion forum, where we've wrapped up a large amount of the processing and presentation logic into reusable components. In other words, we're delegating the task off to worker components as illustrated in the following diagram:

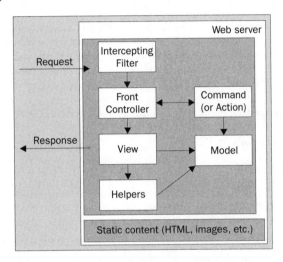

As with our discussion forum, the controller delegates processing to the actions, which in turn perform processing associated with servicing the request. These actions may modify the underlying model. The controller then dispatches the request to the next view component, which will in turn use the underlying model and helper components (such as JavaBeans and/or custom tags) to build and render the response.

Each of the patterns that we've looked at focuses on one particular area of development:

❑ Front Controller – a centralized place for logic associated with servicing requests; here views are responsible only for the presentation of information to the user

❑ Intercepting Filter – a centralized place for intercepting requests, for example to allow or disallow them

❑ View Helper – wraps up reusable functionality used by the views and moves unnecessary logic away from them

Although each of these does address a particular problem, using them in isolation means that only that particular problem will be solved. In the case of our discussion forum, using the Front Controller in isolation may still mean that the view components contain unnecessary Java code embedded inside the JSP pages. On the other hand, using View Helpers in isolation means that the pages will contain unnecessary business logic required to process the request.

The Service to Worker pattern is a combination of all of these patterns and ensures that each of the problem areas is addressed. This means that the logic associated with processing a request is centralized, while the logic associated with presenting information is also centralized, and reusable.

As we can now see from our discussion forum, we not only have a more structured system, but one that is easily maintainable. If we encounter a bug, it shouldn't take us long to track it down. We also have a system that is extensible. The addition of new functionality simply entails adding new actions into our request-handling framework. There is now much more scope for reusability of the components within our application and this again improves the maintainability.

Summary

Application design is an important facet of software development and is often neglected because of the ever-decreasing timescales of Internet development and time-to-market. Including time in the development process to perform design will ultimately save time in the long term. While it is very easy to put together a web application representing the business needs of a company, the lack of good design will result in an application that is expensive to maintain and extend.

We've covered two common architectures for building web applications in this chapter:

❑   Model 1 – page-centric

❑   Model 2 – programming-centric

During our discussion of these two architectures, we looked at the typical implementation strategies along with some of their characteristics, including:

❑   Maintainability – how easy it is to keep the application running smoothly

❑   Extensibility – the ease with which we can add new functionality to the system

❑   Security

We then introduced some of the other J2EE components into the picture and this lead us to a discussion about how to partition functionality within the web application.

Following this we looked more closely at application design. We considered how designs are documented, introducing the concept of a design pattern, and the J2EE patterns catalog.

We then moved on to look at how a simple discussion forum application could be built using a Model 1 architecture. This was approached without any design consideration and subsequently we found some problems with authentication and duplication of business logic – both of which were intermingled within the view components – which adversely affect maintainability, extensibility, and reusability.

Following on from this, we took a step back and looked at designing the application using a Model 2 architecture which makes use of a handful of J2EE patterns:

❑ Front Controller

❑ Intercepting Filter

❑ View Helper

❑ Service to Worker

We explored the purpose of these patterns and looked at how they are useful when we design our discussion forum to maximize maintainability, extensibility, and reusability. During this we looked at some of the implementation strategies for these patterns and presented a new implementation for our example application.

In the next chapter we will look at how we can optimize and scale web applications effectively.

13
Performance and Scalability

Performance and scalability are two important issues that you will need to consider when building enterprise-class commercial web applications. For web applications:

❑ **Performance** is a measure of the time elapsed between sending a request to a server and receiving a response

❑ **Scalability** is a measure of the number of concurrent users and sessions a system can support without an unacceptable deterioration in the performance of the application

Why are these issues important? The simple answer is that the speed at which web applications respond to user requests is an important factor in the commercial success of those applications. Most clients are not prepared to submit a form or a click a link and wait for an unreasonable amount of time for the response. The reality is that they may move to a different web site. Therefore it is important that your applications should provide split-second responses, and that performance shouldn't deteriorate when the user load on your applications increases.

In this chapter, we will cover the various factors involved in building high-performance and highly-scalable J2EE web applications. We'll begin by discussing good coding practice for writing servlets (although many of the tips we recommend apply equally when we create any Java class). Then we'll look at how we can design applications to improve their performance and scalability, by making correct use of:

❑ Handling business logic

❑ Data access

❑ Caching data

❑ Session management

❑ Asynchronous communication

❑ Deployment strategies to improve performance, such as load balancing and clustering

After we have considered these issues we'll examine some tools that we can use to **stress test** and analyze performance and scalability. We'll finish by building a custom performance monitor using filters.

Good Coding Practice

Programmers who write poor code can wreck the performance and scalability of even the best-designed system. In this section, we will cover good practices that will help you to write efficient servlet code (although the following tips are equally relevant to any Java code).

Using Classes

In this first section we'll consider how we should approach coding classes.

Use Shallow Inheritance Hierarchies

Deep inheritance hierarchies impose extra burden on the VM (virtual machine) for executing all of the superclass constructors. To avoid this use shallow inheritance hierarchies. One of the basic lessons of object-oriented programming is that object composition is preferred to class inheritance.

Use Classes from the Collections Framework Instead of Vectors

The classes from the collections framework like ArrayList, HashMap, and so on are faster than the Vector class. This is because all of the methods on the Vector class are synchronized to make them thread-safe whereas the classes belonging to the collections framework are not thread-safe.

Use Reflection Sparingly

Using reflection extensively in your code can degrade the performance of your system. However, JDK 1.4 offers considerable performance improvement when using reflection.

Avoid SingleThreadModel

Avoid making your servlets implement the SingleThreadModel interface. It is always better to write thread-safe code.

Use Stateful Session Beans Sparingly

Stateless session beans are always more efficient than their stateful counterparts. Use stateful session beans only if you want the state to be maintained between public method calls.

Using Variables and Operators

This section contains some guidance for how you should approach the use of variables and operators in your code.

Local Variables are Faster to Access

Local variables are faster to access than instance variables, because they are stored in the stack instead of the heap.

Avoid Declaring Variables Inside Loops

It is always faster to declare variables outside a loop even if they are used only inside the loops, because we then we don't instantiate an object with each new loop. For example:

```
for(int j = 0; j < 10; j++) {
  MyObject myObject = new MyObject(j);
  myObject.someMethod();
}
```

The above code may be rewritten as shown below to improve performance.

```
MyObject myObject;
for(int j = 0; j < 10; j++) {
  myObject = new MyObject(j);
  myObject.someMethod();
}
```

Use the final Modifier for Immutable Instance Variables

Defining instance or class variables that are only used for storing constant values can improve performance.

Use char Arrays

Character arrays are faster than strings and string buffers.

Use StringBuffer Instead of the + Operator

String objects in Java are immutable. This means that whenever you invoke a method on a String variable that amends its contents, the original contents of the String is left unaltered and a new string that contains the result of invoking the method on the original content is created. If your servlet performs content generation and involves quite a lot of string concatenation it is better to use a StringBuffer rather than the + operator. For example:

```
String myString = "";
for(int i = 0; i < 1000; i++) {
  myString += "test";
}
System.out.println(myString);
```

507

The above code snippet will perform lot better if written as shown below:

```
StringBuffer myString = new StringBuffer();
for(int i = 0; i < 1000; i++) {
  myString.append("test");
}
System.out.println(myString);
```

Compound Operators are Faster

Compound operators generate less byte code and are hence faster than normal operators.

```
int j = 10;
j = j + 20;
```

The above code may be rewritten as:

```
int j = 10;
j += 20;
```

Using Methods

In this section we'll discuss a few hints for good coding practice related to method design.

Use Monitor Locks Sparingly

Only lock (synchronize) the required bits of code, to avoid lock contention that negatively impacts upon performance in a multi-threaded environment. For instance:

```
public synchronized void myMethod() {
  //Thread safe code;
  //Thread unsafe code;
}
```

The above method may be rewritten as:

```
public void myMethod() {
  //Thread safe code;
  synchronized(this) {
    //Thread unsafe code;
  }
}
```

Method Inlining

Declaring a method as `final`, `static`, or `public` will help the Java compiler optimize the code during compilation without worrying about late binding.

Use arraycopy() for Copying Arrays

Using the `arrayCopy()` method defined in the `java.lang.System` class is much faster than looping through the source array and copying the items. This is because this method is defined natively.

Use notify()

Use the `notify()` method instead of `notifyAll()` for notifying the threads waiting on monitor locks, as it is faster.

Use charAt()

The `charAt()` function is faster than the `startsWith()` method in the `String` class, if you are comparing only one character. In other words, the following code:

```
System.out.println("Meeraj".startsWith("M"));
```

is slower than:

```
System.out.println("Meeraj".charAt(0) == 'M');
```

Using Databases

The way that you enable data access within your application often has a major effect on your application's performance. We will discuss this in more depth later in the chapter. First, here are some coding tips related to database access.

Select Only Required Columns

When you select columns from a database table using JDBC, select only those columns you need. This will restrict the amount of data transferred between the data server and your application, improving performance.

Use Appropriate Getter Methods on ResultSets

When retrieving data from `ResultSet` objects, use the appropriate version of the get method corresponding to the expected type of the column, instead of using generic `getObject()` and `getString()` calls. This will avoid overheads associated with unnecessary type conversions.

Use JDBC PreparedStatements

`PreparedStatements` are considerably faster than normal statements in JDBC, if the driver supports pre-compilation of `PreparedStatements`.

Other Miscellaneous Coding Tips

Here are some other useful rules-of-thumb for when you are coding.

Optimize During Compilation

Optimize your code during compilation using the `-O` option. However, you should note that this may hinder byte code debugging and increase class size.

Use Short Transactions

Make your transactions as short as possible. This will release locks on objects more quickly, thereby reducing lock contention.

Tune Heap Size

Use the -Xmx and -Xms options with the JVM to set the maximum and initial amount of heap as required.

Use Asynchronous Logging

Use asynchronous logging to improve performance. This means sending a log message to an in-memory buffer like a JMS destination, which is later written to the disk by a different thread.

Use the transient Modifier

To speed up serialization, declare the fields that need not be serialized, using the transient modifier.

Use Externalization

Use externalization to create faster custom serialization algorithms.

Use Non-blocking I/O

JDK 1.4 provides options for non-blocking I/O that can improve scalability and performance.

Streams are Faster

Streams that deal with eight bit data are faster than readers and writers that use Unicode format. Use readers and writers only if you need internationalization.

Cloning is Faster

Cloning is a very effective way of creating a huge number of similar objects, rather than using the new operator.

Architectural Considerations

The architecture that a web application uses greatly influences the resulting performance and scalability. The following figure depicts the most commonly-used architectural model for J2EE web applications (as we saw in Chapter 1):

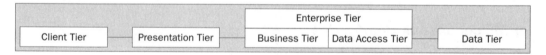

Communication between tiers will slow down the generation of a response, so it might appear sensible to reduce the number of tiers – effectively moving all the application processing into the presentation tier. However, in-memory session management, business logic, and data access will utilize the VM heap and CPU resources on the machine that hosts the presentation tier. When a lot of client threads start executing in the VM that hosts the presentation tier, there will be resource contention, which will result in degradation of performance – our application will not scale well.

It is important to partition the application across multiple tiers and to implement the different pieces of application logic in the most appropriate tier. It is also important to keep the presentation tier as thin as possible and to perform basic validation checks in the presentation tier.

In this section we are going to consider several architectural issues that impact upon the performance of applications:

- ❑ Handling business logic
- ❑ Accessing data
- ❑ Caching data
- ❑ Session management
- ❑ Using asynchronous communication
- ❑ Load balancing and clustering

Handling Business Logic

All enterprise-class web applications apply business logic during request processing. For a simplistic example, in an online banking system, if a user requests a transfer of funds between two accounts, the system may need to perform the following business rule checks:

- ❑ Check the validity of the debiting account
- ❑ Check the validity of crediting account
- ❑ Check the availability of funds in the debiting account

Well architected enterprise applications always centralize business rule validations in a specific tier of the application. The choice of where the business rules are validated greatly impacts on the performance and scalability of the system. In this section, we will look at the various options for performing business rule validations and compare their advantages and disadvantages.

Requests from clients' browsers are normally received by request processing servlets or request delegate objects chosen by a controller servlet (depending on the architecture you use for your web tier). These elements that process the requests will normally have access to the request data, like request parameters and request attributes.

The snippet below shows a basic way to perform business rule validation within the request processing servlet. The excerpt is from the doPost() method of a request processing servlet:

```
InitialContext ctx = new InitialContext();

Object ref = ctx.lookup("java:comp/env/UserTransaction");
UserTransaction trans =
  (UserTransaction)PortableRemoteObject.narrow(ref, UserTransaction.class);

trans.begin();

DataSource ds = ctx.lookup("java:comp/env/jdbc/myDB");
Connection con = ds.getConnection();

String creditAccountID = request.getParameter(""CREDIT_ID");
//Use JDBC to check the validity of the credit account
```

```
String debitAccountID = request.getParameter(""DEBIT_ID");
//Use JDBC to check the validity of the debit account

double amount = Double.parseDouble(request.getParameter("AMOUNT");

//Use JDBC to check the balance in the debit account

//Use JDBC to credit the credit account
//Use JDBC to debit the debit account

trans.commit();
```

The above snippet performs the following tasks:

1. Looks up a user transaction provided by the J2EE web container

2. Starts a transaction

3. Looks up the datasource object and gets a connection

4. Validates the debit and credit account

5. Verifies the balance in the debit account

6. Debits the debit account

7. Credits the credit account

8. Commits the transaction

Even though the code looks fine, we are cluttering the presentation component (the request processing servlet) with both business and data access logic. This not only impacts on the performance and scalability of the system, but also degrades the extensibility and maintainability of the system.

Using Task Delegation

Well designed applications always delegate specific tasks to specific entities with in the system. For example, these systems will have:

❑ Business objects handling business logic

❑ Data access objects that handle data access logic

❑ Domain objects that model the system

In the above example, we can have a domain object called Account that will provide methods to get and set the account ID, account balance, and so on. There can be an AccountDAO to handle the data access logic and an AccountBO that handles the business logic. The presentation component will only interact directly with the business object for performing a business operation. As a result if we decide to partition the application to improve performance, we can move all the business, data access, and domain objects to the enterprise tier and make the business object a remote object. The presentation component will look up the business object and delegate the task of business processing to the business component as shown in the following sequence diagram:

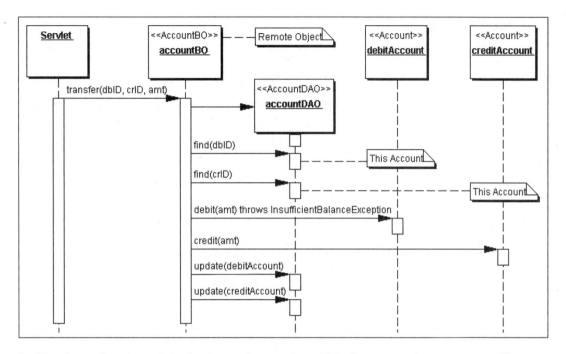

In this scheme there is a minimal amount of processing within the presentation component. The business object may provide the functionality for demarcating transactions and the data access object for the task of establishing database connections. Therefore it will be easier to decentralize business processing by partitioning the application to multiple tiers and making the business object available as a remote object. This may be accomplished either by using vanilla Java RMI or making the business object a session EJB. The advantage in making it a session EJB is that all the system-level tasks like transaction management may be declaratively delegated to the EJB container. However, a comprehensive coverage of session EJBs is beyond the scope of this book and chapter. For more information, you should refer to *Professional EJB* (Wrox, ISBN 1-861005-08-3) and *Professional Java Server Programming J2EE, 1.3 Edition* (Wrox, ISBN 1-861005-37-7).

Accessing Data

Data access is one of the most important performance hotspots in most enterprise J2EE web applications. This predominantly because in many cases the enterprise's data is managed by processes running outside the VM hosting the web applications, such as relational database management systems. Optimizing the design of your data access layer can significantly improve performance and scalability.

Many of the measures you can use for improving data access involve shifting the data access logic to the enterprise tier, and using coarse-grained entity beans and session beans that act as data access objects. However, a comprehensive coverage of EJBs is beyond the scope of this chapter and the book. Hence in this section we will be concentrating more on improving data access performance within the presentation tier.

Data Access Objects

If you decide to perform data access within the web tier it is always better to design for data access later within your web tier, rather than using direct JDBC calls within your servlets. This will not only improve maintainability of the system, but it will also make it easier to refactor the system when you decide to perform data access within the enterprise tier. A standard pattern for implementing data access objects is to define one for every domain object within your system. The data access object will take care of all the logic related to persisting the instance of the domain object in the backend storage. This will include calls for:

- ❑ Creating a new instance
- ❑ Updating an existing instance
- ❑ Deleting an existing instance
- ❑ Finding an instance by primary key
- ❑ Finding an instance or collection of instances for a given predicate

If you have a domain object called Customer, the skeleton for a data access object CustomerDAO may look like the following:

```
public class CustomerDAO {

  public void create(Customer val) {
    //JDBC call for creating the instance
  }

  public void update(Customer val) {
    //JDBC call for updating the instance
  }

  public void delete(Customer val) {
    //JDBC call for deleting the instance
  }

  public Customer findByPrimaryKey(Object key) {
    //JDBC call for finding the instance by primary key
  }

  public Collection findByLastName(String name) {
    //JDBC call for finding all the instances by last name
  }

}
```

Pooling JDBC Connections

In the pattern shown above, all of the methods will need to get a reference to a JDBC connection to the underlying resource manager used for persisting the data. However, physically opening and closing connections each time a method is accessed can involve heavy resource usage and significantly degrade performance and scalability. To avoid this, it is better to keep a pool of open connections, getting a connection from the pool when required, and returning the connection after use. To implement a connection pool, you have three different options:

❑ Write your own connection pool using the JDBC core API

❑ Using a third-party pooling API

❑ Rely on the container implementation of the JDBC optional extension interfaces such as `DataSource`, `ConnectionPoolDataSource`, and `PooledConnection`

Your Own Connection Pool

In this section we will write a small connection pool based on JDBC core API. The class will provide methods for getting a connection from the pool, releasing the connection, initializing the pool, and so on.

The pool is initialized by specifying the JDBC URL, driver class name, number of connections, request timeout, and security credentials. The initialization method creates the specified number of open connections and maintains them in a stack. When a client thread requests a connection, a connection is popped from the stack, and when a client thread releases a connection the connection is pushed onto the stack. If the stack is empty, the client thread releases the monitor lock and waits for the specified period of timeout. When a connection is released the client thread notifies all the current threads waiting on the monitor lock. The listing below shows the code for our connection pool:

```
package pool;

import java.util.Stack;

import java.sql.Connection;
import java.sql.SQLException;
import java.sql.DriverManager;

public final class ConnectionPool {
```

First we create the `Stack` object that stores the pooled connections, and the timeout value:

```
private Stack pool;
private long timeout;
```

Then we create a single instance of the pool. The singleton pattern ensures that only one instance of the pool is available for the given VM and classloader. You may also configure the pool and make it available in a JNDI namespace as an alternative:

```
private static ConnectionPool mySelf;
```

We have a private constructor to avoid public instantiation:

```
private ConnectionPool() {}
```

Next we define the singleton accessor method:

```
public static ConnectionPool getInstance() {
  if(mySelf == null) {
    mySelf = new ConnectionPool();
  }
  return mySelf;
}
```

The `initialize()` method, below, initializes the pool:

```
public synchronized void initialize(String url, String driver,
                                    int numCons, long timeout)
                                    throws SQLException {
```

The method throws an exception if the pool is already initialized:

```
if(pool != null) {
  throw new SQLException("Pool already initialized");
}

try {
```

We set the timeout and load the driver class:

```
this.timeout = timeout;
Class.forName(driver);
```

Then we instantiate the stack instance and initialize the connections:

```
pool = new Stack();

for(int i = 0; i < numCons; i++) {
  pool.push(DriverManager.getConnection(url));
}

} catch (ClassNotFoundException ex) {
  throw new SQLException("Driver not found.");
}
}
```

The `getConnection()` method obtains connections from the pool:

```
public synchronized Connection getConnection() throws SQLException {
```

The method throws an exception if the pool is not initialized:

```
if(pool == null) {
    throw new SQLException("Pool not initialized");
}
```

If the pool is empty, we relinquish the monitor lock and wait for the specified timeout in a `while` loop. If the connection is still not available, we throw an exception:

```
while(pool.empty()) {
    try {
        wait(timeout);
    } catch (InterruptedException ex) {
        throw new SQLException("Connection not available");
    }
}
```

Then we return the connection:

```
    return (Connection)pool.pop();
}
```

The `releaseConnection()` method releases the connection to the pool:

```
public synchronized void releaseConnection(Connection con)
                                        throws SQLException {
```

As with the previous method, we throw an exception if the pool is not initialized:

```
if(pool == null) {
    throw new SQLException("Pool not initialized");
}
```

If it is, we push the connection to the stack and notify all of the threads waiting on the monitor lock:

```
    pool.push(con);
    notifyAll();
}
```

This last method closes all of the connections in the pool:

```
public void destroyPool() throws SQLException {
```

Throw an exception if the pool is not initialized:

```
if(pool == null) {
    throw new SQLException("Pool not initialized");
}
```

Close the connection and dereference the `Stack` object:

```
        while(!pool.empty()) ((Connection)pool.pop()).close();
        pool = null;
    }
}
```

Using JDBC Optional Extension

A more elegant way of using pooled connections is to use the JDBC optional extension API. The JDBC optional extension specifies interfaces that may be used for pooling JDBC connections. The main interfaces are:

- ❑ `javax.sql.DataSource`
  This provides a factory-based approach for obtaining database connections.

- ❑ `javax.sql.PooledConnection`
  This interface encapsulates physical connections to the database

- ❑ `javax.sql.ConnectionPoolDataSource`
  This extends the `DataSource` interface and manages pooled connections

These interfaces are normally implemented by the container provider. Instances of the `DataSource` or `ConnectionPoolDataSource` interfaces may be configured within the container and made available to client programs using standard JNDI lookup. The J2EE 1.3 specification mandates that the web container should provide `DataSource` implementations that may be configured in a JNDI namespace.

The connections that are obtained from `DataSource` objects are intended to be returned to the pool when the `close()` method is called, rather than being physically closed. The snippet below shows the use of `DataSource` objects for getting JDBC connections:

```
//Create JNDI initial context
InitialContext ctx = new InitialContext();
//Lookup the datasource object
DataSource ds = ctx.lookup("java:comp/env/jdbc/myDB");

//Get the connection
Connection con = ds.getConnection();
//Perform JDBC operations

//Release the connection
con.close();
```

Optimizing Record Retrieval

In the snippet for `CustomerDAO` we saw a method called `findByLastName()` that returns a collection. Assume we are displaying a list of Customer objects nested with other domain objects like customer rating, address, and so on, and the data is coming from multiple database tables. In the JDBC call we will issue a SQL command that joins all the relevant tables. Now the question is: what do we return back to the request processing servlet that will render the data in a HTML table? In an ideal object-orientated world we would have a Customer domain object composed of domain objects representing rating, address etc. We would create the required domain objects from the JDBC result set, compose the collection and return it to the request processing servlet.

In effect, the more complex your query, the more complex your tree of objects. Hence we have created a tree of objects from the relational tabular stream of data present in JDBC ResultSet. However, in the request processing servlet, we will again transform this tree of objects into tabular form to display as an HTML table.

We can therefore significantly improve the performance if we return the data in tabular form back to the servlet. However, we can't return the JDBC ResultSet back to the web tier, because in most of the JDBC driver implementations, as soon as you close the connection associated with the result set, the result set is also closed making it useless. This is where the RowSet interface defined in JDBC optional extension API comes into our rescue. The RowSet interface adds support to the JDBC API for the JavaBeans component model, and Sun provides an excellent implementation of this interface called CachedRowSet that can be downloaded from the Javasoft web site. This implementation can work in a disconnected mode from the JDBC connection because it enables us to cache the data extracted from the database, and it therefore makes an excellent DTO (Data Transfer Object).

The snippet below demonstrates how the finder method can work with a CachedRowSet:

```
import javax.sql.DataSource;
import javax.sql.RowSet;
```

We need to import the RowSet implementation:

```
import sun.jdbc.rowset.CachedRowSet;

public Class CustomerDAO {

  public RowSet findByLastName(String name) {

    try {
```

In the findByLastName() method, we start by creating a new CachedRowSet:

```
        RowSet rs = new CachedRowSet();
```

Then we set the JNDI name of the datasource that will provide the database connection:

```
        rs.setDataSourceName("java:comp/env/jdbc/inventoryDB");
```

Next we define the SQL query used to retrieve the data:

```
        String sql = ("SELECT a.Name, b.rating, c.address " +
          "FROM customer a, rating b, address d " +
          "WHERE a.id = b.id " +
          "AND a.id = c.id " +
          "AND a.lastName = ?";
```

We then use this to set the SQL command for the RowSet, and we also set the input parameter:

```
        rs.setCommand(sql);
        rs.setString(1, name);
```

The execute() method will execute the SQL, fill the RowSet, and close/release the connection.

```
    rs.execute();
```

The final step is to return the RowSet to the servlet:

```
        return rs;
    } catch (Exception ex) {
      //Handle exception
    }
  }
}
```

The servlet may simply iterate through the returned RowSet and print the data stored in it as shown below:

```
RowSet rs = new CustomerDAO().findByLastName("Flintstone");
while(rs.next()) {
  out.println("rs.getString(1));
  out.println("rs.getString(2));
  out.println("rs.getString(3));
}
```

As it is relatively simple to use, CachedRowSet is ideal for caching database data in smaller web applications where using EJBs for this purpose would be over the top.

Caching Data

Caching data that is frequently accessed and shared by the users of the application helps to achieve high levels of scalability and performance in web applications that support a large number of concurrent users.

There are different types of objects and resources we would like to cache, such as domain objects that are shared between users, expensive resources, and data retrieved from external systems running outside the process space of the web container VM.

There are different strategies we can take towards caching, each suitable for different objects. Most caching strategies either use a LRU (Least Recently Used) or a MRU (Most Recently Used) replacement algorithm. In LRU, when the cache is full and a new object needs to be placed in the cache, the least recently used object in the cache is replaced. In the MRU mechanism, the new object is added to the top of the cache (which contains the most recently-used objects), but the object at the other end (the least recently-used end) of the cache is removed. Commercial frameworks may also use complex caching algorithms based on access patterns.

There are various caching applications and APIs available. PoolMan from http://www.codestudio.com/ is one of the popular frameworks used for SQL data caching. Many of the commercial Object-Relational mapping tools like TopLink and CocoBase also provide a caching layer. However, these commercial frameworks are often quite expensive, so you may consider developing your own.

We are going to develop a caching framework following a simple LRU replacement algorithm that is easy to develop and use. The strategy you choose depends very much on your caching requirements. For example, if your application tends to access the same objects in quick succession it is better to go for the LRU algorithm as the most recently accessed object may be required again in the near future. However, if your application tends not to access an object that is quite recently accessed, it is better to go for an MRU strategy.

Developing a Simple Caching Framework

We're going to develop a simple caching mechanism based on the Least Recently Used (LRU) algorithm. In a cache that implements LRU replacement algorithm, the least recently used object is replaced from the cache when the cache is full. Our caching service must be able to:

- Manage multiple caches that cache different types of objects. For example you may need a cache for Customer objects and a different one for Product objects.

- Provide a global point of access for the caching service within the application. This will provide a singleton instance of the cache manager that can be accessed from anywhere within the application.

- Provide access to each of the objects that are stored in the cache via a unique identifier.

- Set a size limit for the cache, restricting the number of objects that may be stored in the cache.

- Allow the addition of new objects to the cache, replacing the least recently used object when the cache is full.

- Expire cached objects after predefined intervals, to avoid "dirty" data (how we define "dirty" data depends on our application requirements).

From the requirements we specified, we identify three basic interfaces that make up the caching framework. These interfaces define the methods that need to be implemented by the objects that are cached, the objects that serve as caches, and the objects that manage a collection of caches. We're also going to provide simple implementations for the cache and cache manager objects.

Defining the Caching Interfaces

The ICacheable interface defines the methods that need to be implemented by the objects that are cached. It contains methods to:

- Get the object's unique identifier
- Get and set the time the cached object was last accessed
- Set the expiry time for the cached object

Here's the interface:

```
package cache;

public interface ICacheable {
  public Object getIdentifier();
  public long getLastAccessedTime();
  public void setLastAccessedTime(long time);
  public long getExpiryTime();
}
```

The `ICache` interface defines the methods that need to be implemented by objects that function as caches. It defines methods to:

- Get and set the name of the cache
- Get and set the size of the cache
- Get a cacheable object via its unique identifier
- Expire all objects with an expiry time less than the current time
- Add a new cacheable object

Here's the `ICache` interface:

```
package cache;

public interface ICache {
  public String getName();
  public void setName(String name);
  public int getSize();
  public void setSize(int size);
  public ICacheable getCacheable(Object identifier);
  public void expire();
  public void addCacheable(ICacheable cacheable);
}
```

The `ICacheManager` interface defines the methods that need to be implemented by the objects that manage a collection of caches. It defines two methods to:

- Get a cache by its name
- Add a new cache

The `ICacheManager` interface is defined below:

```
package cache;

public interface ICacheManager {
  public ICache getCache(String cacheName);
  public void addCache(ICache cache);
}
```

Implementing the Interfaces

Our next task is to provide simple implementations for the interfaces we defined. We'll begin with the cache manager interface.

The Cache Manager

In most cases an application requires a single cache manager instance that can be accessed globally by client classes. This is because the cache may be initialized at one point in the application but used at a different point. Accordingly, this class is implemented using the singleton pattern.

> Using a singleton pattern ensures that there is only one instance of a class instantiated for a given VM and classloader. Please note that in a clustered environment you may typically end up with a cache manager per VM. In such cases it is better to implement the cache manager and caches as remote objects, and leave the task of replicating the state to the container and the cluster management software.

Here's the implementation of the `ICacheManager` interface, `CacheManagerImpl`:

```
package cache;

import java.util.*;

public final class CacheManagerImpl implements ICacheManager {
```

This is the singleton instance:

```
    private static CacheManagerImpl mySelf;
```

This hash map stores the collection of managed caches:

```
    private HashMap cacheMap = new HashMap();
```

The constructor starts a low-priority thread that goes through all the managed caches and expires the cached objects that are due for expiry:

```
    private CacheManagerImpl() {
      Thread th = new Thread(new Runnable() {
        public void run() {
          try {
            Thread.sleep(60*1000);
          } catch(InterruptedException ex) {
            throw new RuntimeException(ex.getMessage());
          }
          expire();
        }
      };
      th.setPriority(th.MIN_PRIORITY);
      th.start();
    }
```

We will define the `expire()` method a little later. Next we define a method to provide access to the singleton instance:

```
public static ICacheManager getInstance() {
  if(mySelf == null) {
    synchronized(ICacheManager.class) {
      if(mySelf == null) {
        mySelf = new CacheManagerImpl();
      }
    }
  }
  return mySelf;
}
```

Next, we implement the two methods defined in the `ICacheManager` interface. The first gets a cache from the collection of managed caches via its name:

```
public ICache getCache(String cacheName) {
  synchronized(this) {
    return (ICache)cacheMap.get(cacheName);
  }
}
```

The second adds a cache to the collection of managed caches:

```
public void addCache(ICache cache) {
  synchronized(this) {
    cacheMap.put(cache.getName(), cache);
  }
}
```

In the constructor we made use of an `expire()` method that we define here. This private method is called from the low-priority thread in order to expire cached objects. It goes through all the managed caches and expires the cached objects that are due for expiry:

```
private void expire() {
  synchronized(this) {
    Iterator it = cacheMap.values().iterator();
    while(it.hasNext()) {
      ((ICache)it.next()).expire();
    }
  }
}
```

The Cache

Next, we implement the `ICache` interface in the `SimpleCacheImpl` class:

```
package cache;

import java.util.*;

public class SimpleCacheImpl implements ICache {
```

We define private fields to hold the name of the cache, its maximum size (which we set to 100), its current size, and a collection to stored the cached objects in:

```
private String name = "";
private int size = 100;
private int currentSize = 0;
private HashMap objectMap;

public SimpleCacheImpl() {
   objectMap = new HashMap();
}
```

We implement methods to get and set the name of the cache, and to get and set the size of the cache:

```
public String getName() {
   return name;
}

public void setName(String name) {
   this.name = name;
}

public int getSize() {
   return size;
}

public void setSize(int size) {
   this.size = size;
}
```

We implement the method to get a cached object corresponding to the specified identifier too. This method sets the last accessed time of the cached object to the current time:

```
public ICacheable getCacheable(Object identifier) {
   synchronized(this) {
     ICacheable cacheable = (ICacheable)objectMap.get(identifier);
     if(cacheable != null) {
       cacheable.setLastAccessedTime(System.currentTimeMillis());
     }
     return cacheable;
   }
}
```

The `expire()` method removes all the cached objects that are due for expiry. The current size of the cache is also updated accordingly. An expiry date of zero is understood to mean that the cached object will never expire:

```
public void expire() {
  synchronized(this) {
    Iterator it = objectMap.keySet().iterator();
    while(it.hasNext()) {
      ICacheable current = (ICacheable)objectMap.get(it.next());
      if(current.getExpiryTime() <= System.currentTimeMillis()
        && current.getExpiryTime() != 0) {
        currentSize--;
        objectMap.remove(current.getIdentifier());
      }
    }
  }
}
```

The `addCacheable()` method adds a new object to the cache. If the cache is full, the least recently used object is removed from the cache.

```
public void addCacheable(ICacheable cacheable) {
  synchronized(this) {
```

If the object is already present in the cache, we return:

```
    if(objectMap.containsKey(cacheable.getIdentifier())) {
      return;
    }
```

If the current size is equal to the maximum size, we iterate through the cache to find the least recently used object:

```
    if(currentSize == size) {
      Iterator it = objectMap.keySet().iterator();
      long time = System.currentTimeMillis();
      ICacheable lastAccessed = null;
      while(it.hasNext()) {
        ICacheable current = (ICacheable)objectMap.get(it.next());
        if(current.getLastAccessedTime() < time) {
          time = current.getLastAccessedTime();
          lastAccessed = current;
        }
      }
```

Then we remove the least recently used object and decrement the current size:

```
        if(lastAccessed != null) {
          currentSize--;
          objectMap.remove(lastAccessed.getIdentifier());
        }
      }
      cacheable.setLastAccessedTime(System.currentTimeMillis());
      objectMap.put(cacheable.getIdentifier(), cacheable);
      currentSize++;
    }
  }
}
```

Using the Caching Framework

To use the caching framework, the objects that are cached should implement the ICacheable interface. Please note that if you want to cache third-party objects you can wrap the third-party objects in a wrapper object that implements this interface. Then you can either use the cache and cache manager implementations provided by the framework, or write your own implementations.

We'll define an Employee object that we want to cache:

```
package cache;

public class Employee implements ICacheable {

  private String id;
  private String name;
  private long lastAccessedTime;
  private long expiryTime;
```

The constructor initializes the id and name, and the expiry time is set to zero:

```
  public Employee(String id, String name) {
    this.id = id;
    this.name = name;
    this.expiryTime = 0;
  }

  public Object getIdentifier() {
    return id;
  }

  public String getName() {
    return name;
  }

  public long getLastAccessedTime() {
    return lastAccessedTime;
  }
```

```
    public void setLastAccessedTime(long time) {
      lastAccessedTime = time;
    }

    public long getExpiryTime() {
      return expiryTime;
    }
  }
```

The example below demonstrates how the caching framework may be used within a servlet. The servlet initializes the cache in the init() method, and after that the doGet() method uses the singleton accessor to get a reference to the cache manager and extract the cached objects. Please note that the cache manager may be initialized in the init() method and later accessed from anywhere in the web application:

```
package cache;

import javax.servlet.ServletConfig;
import javax.servlet.ServletException;

import javax.servlet.http.HttpServlet;
import javax.servlet.http.HttpServletRequest;
import javax.servlet.http.HttpServletResponse;

import java.io.IOException;
import java.io.PrintWriter;

public class CacheServlet extends HttpServlet {

  public void init(ServletConfig config) throws ServletException {
    super.init(config);
```

At the start of the init() method of the servlet, we initialize the cache manager and create a new cache:

```
    ICacheManager manager = CacheManagerImpl.getInstance();
    System.out.println("");
    System.out.println("Cache manager retrieved");
    ICache cache = new SimpleCacheImpl();
    cache.setName("employeeCache");
    cache.setSize(10);
    System.out.println("Cache created");
```

Then we add this cache to the cache manager, and finally add a cached object to the cache:

```
    manager.addCache(cache);
    System.out.println("Cache added");
    cache.addCacheable(new Employee("123", "Meeraj"));
    System.out.println("Object added to cache");
  }

  public void doGet(HttpServletRequest request,
                    HttpServletResponse response)
                    throws ServletException, IOException {
```

The doGet() method gets a reference to the cache manager singleton, retrieves the cache by name, and then accesses the cached object from the cache by specifying the identifier:

```
ICacheManager manager = CacheManagerImpl.getInstance();
System.out.println("");
System.out.println("Cache manager retrieved");
ICache cache = manager.getCache("employeeCache");
Employee emp = (Employee)cache.getCacheable("123");
if(emp == null) {
  //return the employee from the database and add it to the cache
}
System.out.println("Employee "+emp.getName()+" retrieved from cache");
  }
}
```

Running the Caching Application

To run the application you will need a web app. Place the classes above in a folder called cache in the WEB-INF directory of the web application and compile them. Also add the following servlet declaration and servlet mapping to the web.xml file of the web app:

```
...
<servlet>
  <servlet-name>CacheServlet</servlet-name>
  <servlet-class>cache.CacheServlet</servlet-class>
</servlet>

<servlet-mapping>
  <servlet-name>CacheServlet</servlet-name>
  <url-pattern>/CacheServlet</url-pattern>
</servlet-mapping>
...
```

Now start up Tomcat, and access the CacheServlet via http://localhost:8080/cache/CacheServlet (you should replace cache with the name of your web app). You should see the following output at the command console:

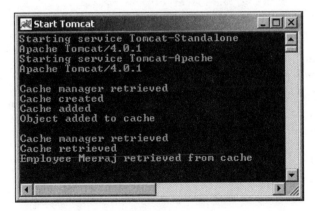

As you can see, the init() method of the servlet is accessed first, where the cache manager is retrieved, the cache is created and added, and an Employee object is added to the cache. Then the doGet() method is accessed on request; in this method the cache is retrieved and the Employee object corresponding to the id 123 (Meeraj) is retrieved. If you accessing the servlet again, the doGet() method will get called again, so the same Employee object will be retrieved from the cache again.

Session Management

The HTTP protocol that is most commonly used in J2EE web applications is a stateless protocol – in other words one that doesn't preserve state across multiple requests from the same web client to the J2EE web application. HTTP sessions provided by the J2EE Servlet API provide an excellent way of linking multiple requests from a single web client as parts of a conversation. HTTP sessions also provide a great way of storing client-specific data on the server, thereby avoiding the tedious task of transferring huge amounts of data back and forth during requests and responses. In this section we will have a look at the various options for storing session data to improve performance and scalability.

The default way of handling HTTP sessions in J2EE web applications is to use the HTTPSession interface provided by the Servlet API. This interface provides methods for storing and retrieving user data into the session.

Once a session is established, the session data is stored on the server and only a string that identifies the session is sent back and forth, between the client and server during the subsequent requests and responses. The Servlet specification states that this string should be sent as a cookie or a rewritten URL and should be called jsessionid. However, the process by which the session ID is transmitted should be transparent to the application developer. The HTTPServletRequest interface provides methods for getting a reference to the session associated with the current request and establishing a new session. A session becomes invalid when it times out or when it is programmatically invalidated at the server. The snippet below demonstrates the basic way of handling sessions via the doGet() method, as we saw in Chapter 5:

```
public void doGet (HttpServletRequest req,
                   HttpServletResponse res)
                   throws ServletException, IOException {
    HttpSession sess = req.getSession();
    sess.setAttribute("myName", "Meeraj");
    String myName = (String)sess.getAttribute("myName");
    sess.removeAttribute("myName");
}
```

Web containers normally store the HTTP sessions as in-memory objects in the VM heap that runs the web container. This will provide very good performance as the session data is held very close to the client tier. However, when the load on the application increases, this may pose serious problems with resource contention and have a negative impact on the scalability of the system. This problem can be resolved either by clustering the web application across multiple servers, or delegating the session management logic to a different tier in a partitioned J2EE application.

Now we will have a look at the other viable options for storing session data.

Storing Sessions in Backend Databases

In this solution the actual session data is stored in a database table as a BLOB. The session IDs of the sessions that are stored in the database table act as the primary key for the table. This ID is sent back forth, between the client and the server. When a session is requested, the session ID from the current request is used to retrieve the session data that is stored as a BLOB from the database table. However, if your chosen application server implements this strategy by appropriately implementing the HTTPSession and HTTPServletRequest interfaces, the actual session data management mechanism will be transparent to the application developers. They only need to know about the contracts defined by the relevant interfaces.

This solution can significantly reduce the amount of resources used within the VM heap that hosts the web container, significantly improving scalability. Another advantage is that the session data is persisted and the sessions may be maintained across shutdowns and startups of your web server. However, this approach incurs a performance cost to the system since it involves frequent database access. Also, if the application server doesn't implement this approach, you will end up writing the code that implements your database-based session management scheme.

Storing Sessions in Stateful Session Beans

In this case, we use the session management facilities to only a limited extent. We store the real session data within the enterprise tier using stateful session beans. This is illustrated in the diagram below:

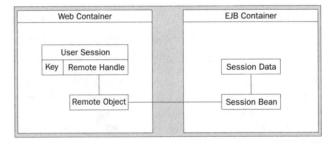

In this case, the first time a session is established, a stateful session EJB that mimics the functionality of an HTTP session object is created, and the EJB remote handle stored in the real HTTP session object is associated with the request. Each time the session is accessed, the remote handle is used to obtain a reference to the EJB remote object. The EJB remote interface will expose methods for adding, retrieving, and removing session data. However, in this case the session data is stored in the EJB container.

In this approach we distribute the session management functionality between the web and the EJB tiers. Even though this approach requires more initial programming and doesn't provide the same performance as the first approach, this scheme does increase scalability.

However, most of the web containers won't provide an implementation for handling sessions using EJBs, so you will end up writing the implementation on your own. A possible way of doing this is to write your own implementations for the HTTPSession and HTTPServletRequest interfaces that use EJBs for session management. Then use a servlet filter to create your own implementations of the Session and Request objects that wrap the original container implementations. Your implementations will delegate most of the methods defined by the interfaces to the container implementations. However, the methods for handling sessions will be implemented differently, to use stateful session EJBs instead. When you forward the request and response within the filter class, you will pass your objects instead of the container object.

Comparing Schemes for Storing Session Data

The table below compares the various approaches for maintaining HTTP sessions.

Scheme	Ease of Use	Performance	Scalability	Development Time
In-Memory	High	High	Low	Low
Vendor BLOB	High	Moderate	High	Low
Custom BLOB	Moderate	Moderate	High	High
Session EJB	High	Moderate	High	Very High

Using Asynchronous Communication

Some user requests initiate processes in a web application that take a relatively long time to complete. In this case, it is not a good idea to make the request thread wait for the processing to finish before a response is sent back to the browser. Traditionally the way J2EE web applications dealt with such scenarios was to spawn a new thread from the request thread, delegating the responsibility of processing the request, and then immediately returning an information message back to the server. However, there are two main disadvantages to this approach:

❑   Most of the mainstream application server vendors put restrictions on spawning new threads

❑   More importantly, spawning a lot of threads within the web container can lead to heavy resource usage and so poor performance and scalability

Since JMS (Java Message Service) became a mandatory API with J2EE 1.3, and with the advent of MDBs (message-driven beans), a plethora of avenues for **asynchronous** processing in J2EE applications have been opened. In asynchronous communication, the message recipient doesn't need to receive or respond to the message immediately after it is sent, and the sender doesn't need to receive a reply from the sender immediately either.

MDBs are EJB components that get activated by JMS messages. They provide all of the features that are provided by other types of EJBs, such as declarative transaction, security management, and so on. Let's now take a closer look at JMS-enabled asynchronous messaging, so that we can understand how this form of communication can improve the scalability of our applications.

An Overview of the JMS Architecture

The **Java Message Service (JMS)** specifies a standard set of interfaces for enabling Java applications to exchange enterprise messages asynchronously in an efficient and vendor-neutral manner. The JMS interfaces and classes belong to the package `javax.jms` and are available with Java 2 Platform, Enterprise Edition. In this section we're going to take a look at the architecture of this service.

JMS Providers and Clients

The software vendors who provide the messaging products implement the interfaces defined in the JMS specification. These software vendors are called **JMS providers** in JMS terminology. Java applications that use JMS for exchanging enterprise messages are called **JMS clients**. JMS clients that don't use any vendor-specific features, only standard JMS interfaces for implementing their messaging solutions, are portable across different JMS providers. Clients normally connect to a central messaging hub supplied by the JMS provider, and exchange messages through this messaging hub instead of connecting to each other directly. In addition, clients use the services provided by the JMS provider for sending and receiving enterprise messages.

JMS Messages

The JMS specification defines different kinds of messages that can be exchanged by JMS clients. JMS messages can be plain text messages or an entire serialized web of Java objects. The JMS specification defines messages containing:

- Plain text
- Serialized Java objects
- An uninterpreted stream of bytes
- A stream of Java primitives and strings
- A map of Java primitives and strings

Additionally JMS providers may provide their own message extensions. For instance, providers may provide messages that extend plain text messages that can support XML.

Administered Objects

Administered objects are pre-configured objects stored in a namespace by JMS administrators for the use of JMS clients. An administrator is the person responsible for ensuring the proper day-to-day functioning of the JMS system. Administered objects form the basis for writing portable JMS applications. They are normally available for standard JNDI (Java Naming and Directory Interface) lookup, even though the JMS specification doesn't make this a requirement. Administered objects can be stored outside the JMS provider, in the namespace of any naming and directory service provider. JMS defines two kinds of administered objects:

- One for obtaining connections with the JMS provider
- One for specifying the destinations to which JMS clients send messages, and the sources from which they receive messages

These objects include factory objects for creating connections as well as message destinations. **Connection factories** are used for creating **connections** that can represent an open TCP/IP socket to the provider. All configuration information required for creating the connection is stored in the administered object by the JMS administrators. Connections also act as factories for creating JMS sessions. Connections are explained in further detail in the coming sections.

Sessions are single-threaded contexts for sending and receiving messages, and are used as factories for creating different kind of JMS messages. They are also used for creating objects that send and receive messages. These objects are called **message producers** and **message consumers** respectively.

533

Message consumers and producers are associated with specific message destinations/sources. A consumer can receive messages only from the message source it is associated with and a producer can send messages only to the message destination it is associated with. JMS supports both synchronous and asynchronous message delivery to message consumers.

The diagram below depicts the high-level architecture of a JMS system as explained above.

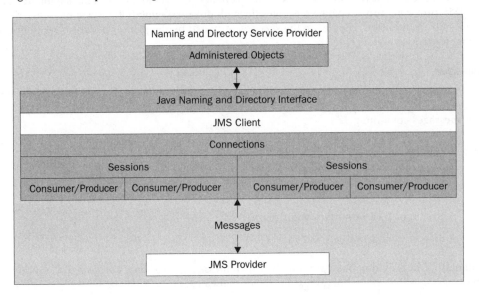

The JMS specification defines interfaces for all the JMS entities explained above like connections, sessions, connection factories, destinations, and so on. Portable JMS clients need to be aware of only these interfaces and should not be using any of the provider-specific implementation classes in their application code.

Messaging Models

JMS specification supports two messaging models:

❑ **Point-to-Point (PTP)**
The PTP messaging model is based upon **message queues**. JMS clients send messages to and receive messages from specific message queues provided by the JMS provider. In the PTP messaging model, only one client can retrieve a message from the message queue. Once a JMS client has retrieved a message from a message queue, the message is no longer available for any other JMS client accessing the message queue. A message is addressed to a specific message queue and it remains in the queue until a client removes it. Message queues are generally configured and stored in a JNDI namespace and are available for clients by standard JNDI lookup. In the PTP model message producers are called **queue senders** and message consumers are called **queue receivers**.

❏ **Publish/Subscribe (Pub/Sub)**
   This model enables messages to be addressed to more than one client. In the Pub/Sub model, message producers are called **topic publishers** and message consumers are called **topic subscribers**. Publishers send messages to **topics** to which multiple clients can subscribe. Topics are generally configured and stored in a JNDI namespace and are available for clients by standard JNDI lookup. A topic can have multiple publishers as well.

In both messaging models clients can act as both message producers and message consumers.

Message-Driven EJBs

Message-driven beans (MDB) provide an elegant way of registering components that are activated by asynchronous JMS messages delivered to specific JMS destinations. These EJBs implement `javax.ejb.MessageDrivenBean` and `javax.jms.MessageListener` interfaces. The `MessageListener` interface defines the `onMessage(Message msg)` method that is called by the container when a message is delivered to a JMS destination monitored by the bean.

The destination type, transaction contexts, security details, and so on, are defined in the deployment descriptor of the bean.

Improving Scalability Through Asynchronous Messaging

In the case of requests that take a long time to process, when it receives a request, a request-processing servlet can send a JMS message to a JMS destination, wrapping the request data. The thread that runs the servlet can immediately return, providing an informational message. The MDB listening on the JMS destination can retrieve the message and perform the required processing. This is illustrated in the diagram shown below:

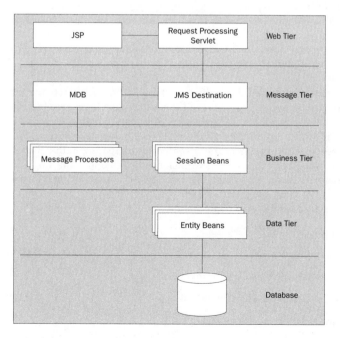

Load Balancing and Clustering

In most cases scalability is adversely affected by a huge number of client threads contending for a limited amount of resources on the machine that hosts the web container. Clustering is an effective solution to this problem, which allows us to construct highly available and scalable web applications. Clusters let the load on the web application be shared across multiple VMs running on different machines participating in the cluster. A cluster may be basically defined as a group of web containers hosted by different physical machines that run a web application as a single entity in a transparent manner. Machines that participate in the cluster may transparently share J2EE resources like JSPs, servlets, HTTP sessions, JNDI namespaces, EJB components, and so on.

The main elements that are involved in a clustered architecture are the following:

❑ Load balancers – these are the common entry points to the cluster and routers to the web containers participating in the cluster

❑ J2EE web containers

❑ Gateway routers – these are exit points from the internal network

❑ Multi-layer switches –these elements make sure the individual machines in the cluster receive only information specific to that machine

Types of Clusters

There are two different schemes adopted by web container vendors for implementing clustering. The first solution defines the machines participating in the cluster totally independently of each other. The machines participating in the cluster are integrated using a dispatcher element, which receives the client requests and sends a response with a redirect header directing the client to access a particular machine in the cluster.

The second solution uses a tightly coupled group of machines that are aware of each other and the resources running within them.

The clusters are basically classified depending on the type of sharing scheme they use for resources. In the first scheme, the participating machines in the cluster have their own file systems and have their own running copies of the application. This makes application upgrades very difficult for large clusters as the latest versions must be applied to all the machines participating in the cluster. The second scheme uses a shared storage space from where the machines participating in the cluster may acquire the latest running copy of the web applications. A drawback of this scheme is the single point of failure in the cluster. The main factors that need to be considered when you choosing a cluster implementation are:

❑ Failover services for the web components

❑ Failover services for HTTP sessions

❑ Software maintenance

❑ Replication schemes for web components

❑ Replication schemes for HTTP sessions

❑ Single point of failure in the cluster

Distributed Sessions and Clusters

The web applications that run on clustered servers should be marked as distributable in the web deployment descriptor, and all of the objects that are stored in the HTTP sessions should be tagged as serializable by implementing the `java.io.Serializable` interface. Most of the cluster schemes promote server affinity, which in turn enables sticky sessions. This means that once a client connection is attached to a server in the cluster, the subsequent requests from that client are directed to the same server by the load balancer, and the primary HTTP sessions for those requests are maintained on the server to which the requests are attached.

However, the main purpose of session failover is that when a request is redirected to a different server on failure of the server to which the client is attached, the session data should be persisted. Commercial web containers provide different schemes for the replication of session data. This ranges from JDBC-based session stores to in-memory session stores (with session data replicated after each request or depending on the events fired on session attribute listeners). The scheme used for session replication mainly impacts upon the cluster performance.

Content Type and Scalability

The choice of the type of software used on the machines that participate in the cluster greatly depends on the type of content that is served. If your application serves a lot of static content, you can serve it directly using a web server without depending upon a J2EE web container. In this case you can improve the scalability of your application by adding more web servers in the cluster, because the bulk of the client requests will be for static content. However, if your application serves more dynamic content, you can improve the scalability of the system by adding more web containers to the cluster.

Analysis Tools

In this section we will provide a brief overview of the tools available for stress testing the performance and scalability of web applications, as well as analyzing and profiling performance and scalability-related issues of J2EE web applications. We will cover both leading commercial and freeware tools.

Stress Testing Tools

The tools we will cover in this section that can be used for stress testing performance and scalability. We will look at:

❑ Microsoft Web Application Stress, which is a commercial tool available from http://webtool.rte.microsoft.com/

❑ Apache JMeter, which is freeware available from http://www.apache.org/jmeter

Most of these tools provide a browser-like user interface for accessing your web applications and recording the various HTTP GET and POST requests. After the user actions are recorded, you can use the tool for stress testing the application. The tool will send the recorded GET and POST requests with a simulated load by spawning multiple threads from the client.

Microsoft Web Application Stress

Microsoft Web Application Stress simulates multiple browsers requesting pages from a web application. The tool is easy to use and provides a variety of features for testing the performance and scalability of web applications.

The main features of the tool include:

- ❑ We can test scripts which may be run using any number of client machines, controlled by one centralized client

- ❑ The tool takes care of synchronizing the clients on allocating simulated client threads, gathering and recording test data

- ❑ It supports the creation of multiple users for stress testing authenticated and personalized web sites

- ❑ It supports HTTP sessions and cookies

- ❑ It provides bandwidth throttling, to simulate modem throughput and increasing numbers of concurrent users

- ❑ It provides a tool to import, store, and edit complex request parameter name-value pair collections

- ❑ It supports DNS names, so you can use the IP address of a specific server or use the DNS name to have the tool round-robin among the servers in your cluster

- ❑ It can define groups of request pages to organize the request sequence and hit percentage

- ❑ It supports changeable delay between requests to test race conditions

- ❑ It provides a user-friendly graphical user interface

- ❑ It supports customizable request headers and form encoded data

Apache JMeter

Apache JMeter is a generic test tool developed as desktop Java application designed to load test functional behavior and measure performance. It can be used to test the performance of both static and dynamic content. It can simulate a heavy load on the web container for testing scalability under varying load. Please note that JMeter is not only designed for web applications but can be used for other kinds of applications as well.

The main features of JMeter include:

- ❑ It can load and performance test HTTP and FTP servers, and arbitrary databases

- ❑ It is completely written in Java and hence is highly portable

- ❑ It provides an excellent user interface

- ❑ It supports concurrent sampling by many threads and simultaneous sampling of different functions by separate thread groups

- ❑ It provides faster operation and precise timings

- ❑ It supports caching and offline analysis/replaying of test results

JMeter is also highly extensible, it supports:

❑ Pluggable Samplers allowing unlimited testing capabilities

❑ Choice of several load statistics with pluggable timers

❑ Data analysis and visualization plug-ins allowing great extensibility as well as personalization

Using JMeter

JMeter may be started by running the `jmeter.bat` file present in the `/bin` directory of the JMeter installation.

The user interface is divided into two sections. The left-panel contains a tree that represents the test configuration. A test may consist of one or more subtests. The display on the right panel is controlled by the element that is selected on the tree in the left panel.

The test configuration tree initially contains the **TestPlan** and **WorkBench** elements. The TestPlan element contains the elements that make up a test. The WorkBench may be used to store test elements while you are running a test.

A TestPlan may contain one or more **ThreadGroups**. ThreadGroups may be added to the TestPlan by right-clicking on the TestPlan in the tree.

The following elements may be added to a ThreadGroup:

❑ A **Timer** element defines the time interval between requests sent by JMeter. You can have constant timers, ramped timers, and so on. A Timer can be added to a ThreadGroup using the right mouse button.

❑ A **Listener** receives information about the response when the test is run. JMeter provides different types of listeners that plot the data graphically, provide an XML representation of the response data, and so on. You can click on a Listener when a test is run, to access real-time information about the test. A Listener can be added to a ThreadGroup using the right mouse button.

❑ **Controllers** are used for performing various kinds of tests. JMeter provides both logic controllers and generative Controllers. Generative Controllers may be used for testing web applications. A Controller can be added to a ThreadGroup using the right mouse button.

❑ **Config** elements are used for defining configuration information for the different test protocols like JDBC connection pools, SQL queries, web applications, and so on. A Config element can be added to a ThreadGroup using the right mouse button too.

A ThreadGroup also defines the number of threads available for testing.

Now we will have a quick look at using JMeter for running web applications. First start JMeter by running the batch file. This will display the window shown below:

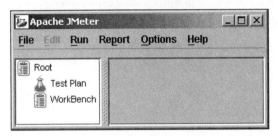

Right-click on the TestPlan element to Add a new ThreadGroup, and then define the number of client threads as five:

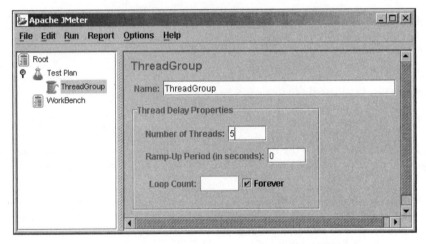

Add a new Generative Controller for Web (application) Testing by right-clicking on the ThreadGroup.

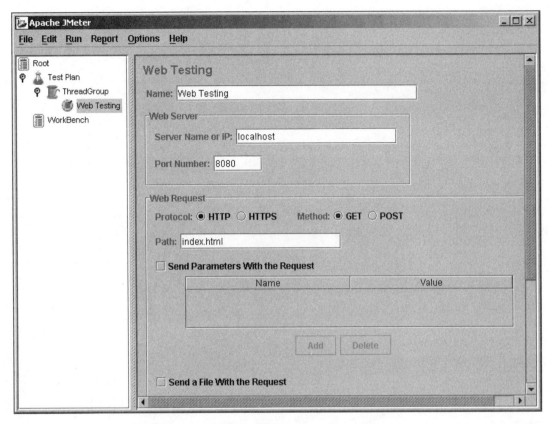

Then define the host address, port number, and URL path of the web application you are testing as shown above. I have added the index page on Tomcat root running locally on my machine at port 8080. You may also define the HTTP method, request parameters, and so on.

Right-click on ThreadGroup and Add a Listener, a Spline Visualizer, to provide real-time feed back of the test. Then start the test from the main Run menu and select the Spline Visualizer element in the tree. You should see something like this:

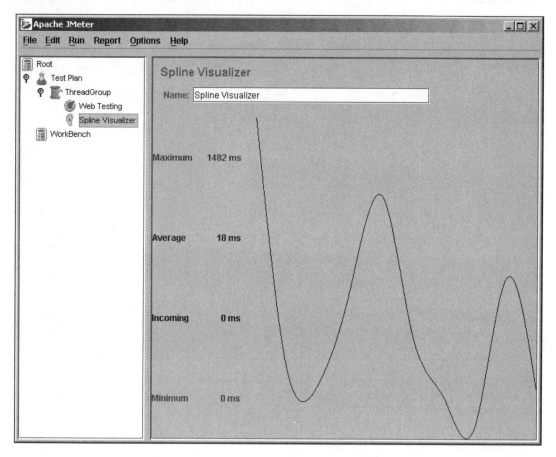

Here, the curve represents the history of the test; in other words it shows graphically how the response changed over time. Relevant statistics such as maximum and minimum response times are displayed too.

Profiling Tools

In this section we will briefly discuss the commercial tools available for profiling and analyzing performance-related issues with J2EE web applications.

Profiling provides detailed information about your application, such as the most frequently accessed methods, the most instantiated objects, stack traces, and so on. This will help you significantly when you need to identify the performance bottlenecks within your applications.

The tools we are going to cover include the suite of products that compose:

❑ JProbe available at http://www.jprobe.com

❑ Optimizeit available at http://www.vmgear.com

We will also provide a brief overview of the `hprof` option that can be used with the JVM.

The general features of a profiling tool are:

❑ Report generation – depicting object instantiation, method access, stack dumps, and so on

❑ Thread monitoring

❑ Monitoring VM heap utilization

❑ Monitoring CPU cycle utilization

JProbe ServerSide Suite

The JProbe ServerSide Suite from Sitraka Software (formerly KL Group) provides performance profiling, memory debugging, code coverage, and thread analysis capabilities in an integrated suite, focusing on server-side Java. JProbe provides efficient sourcecode profiling. The JProbe suite of products provides an intuitive user interface for everything from memory usage to calling relationships. The suite comprises:

❑ Profiler (with fully integrated JProbe Memory Debugger) – to eliminate performance bottlenecks, and memory leaks in your Java code

❑ Threadalyzer – to detect deadlocks, stalls, and race conditions

❑ Coverage – to locate and quantify untested Java code

JProbe ServerSide Suite provides servlet and server-side application-tuning capabilities, as well as comprehensive and convenient integration with popular web applications.

Optimizeit

Optimizeit ServerSide Suite from VM Gear provides a similar set of tools to those provided by JProbe:

❑ Profiler – provides useful information on issues such as CPU utilization, and memory leaks

❑ Thread debugger – provides comprehensive real-time information on running threads, monitor locks, and so on

❑ Code Coverage – provides a real-time matrix describing the number of times each line of code within the application is executed

JDK hprof

If you don't want to spend a huge amount of money on commercial profiling tools, the JDK comes with an option for profiling your applications. The `hprof` option provided with the JVM can provide you with a wealth of information about object allocation, CPU cycle contention, stack traces, thread information, and so on. In this section we will provide a brief overview of using JDK `hprof`.

The hprof option can be used for profiling Java applications when the JVM is invoked as shown below:

```
java -Xrunhprof[:help]|[<option>=<value>, ...] MyClass
```

Here MyClass is the class to be profiled. To use hprof to analyze your servlets, you will need to modify your web container startup script to invoke the JVM with the hprof option. For example, in Tomcat you may modify the catalina.bat file to add the hprof option. The table below describes the hprof options available:

Option	Description
heap	This is used for profiling the VM heap. The possible values are dump, sites, and all with the default value being all.
cpu	This is for profiling CPU usage. The possible values are samples, times and old. By default this option is not enabled. With sampling, the JVM regularly pauses execution and checks to see which method call is active. With enough samples (and a decent sampling rate), you can pinpoint where your code spends its time.
monitor	This enables profiling monitor lock contention. The possible values are y and n, with the default value being n.
format	This option defines the output format. A value of a indicates ASCII and b indicates binary. The default value is a.
file	This option identifies the file to which the output is written.
net	This option can be used to define an IP address and port if the output is to be sent over a remote socket.
depth	This can be used to define the stack depth and the default value is 4.
cutoff	This can be used to define the output cutoff size and the default value is 0.0001.
lineno	If this option is set to y, the stack trace will show the line number. The default value is n.
thread	If set to y shows the thread in stack traces. The default value is n.
doe	A value of y dumps the output on VM exit. The default value is y.

A Custom Performance Monitoring Tool

We will conclude the chapter by developing a simple yet effective J2EE performance monitoring tool for web applications. The advantage of developing such a tool in-house is that most of the commercially-available performance monitoring tools and stress testers are pretty expensive.

We will use the servlet filter API for this purpose. We will write a filter through which all of the requests are passed. The filter will record the request path and the response time for all the requests. To avoid the filter affecting the performance of the system, we will just dump the performance data into an application-scope bean when the request passes through the filter. We will then provide a servlet that will extract this data, and compute and display the following information:

- ❑ Request path
- ❑ Total number of hits
- ❑ Total response time
- ❑ Minimum response time
- ❑ Maximum response time
- ❑ Average response time

Monitor Framework Classes

The UML diagram below depicts the relationships between the classes that compose the monitor framework:

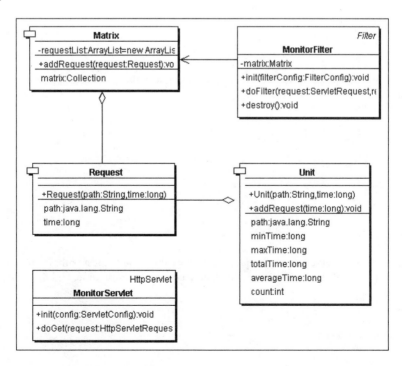

- ❑ The `Request` class represents the request path and response time each time a request is executed

- ❑ The `Matrix` class functions as an accumulation of Request objects

- ❑ The `Unit` class represents data relevant to unique request paths, such as total time it was accessed, average response time, minimum and maximum response time, and so on

- ❑ The `MonitorFilter` class acts as our filter

- ❑ The `MonitorServlet` class extracts the performance data and displays it back to the client browser

The Request Class

The sourcecode for the `Request` class is shown below.

```
package monitor;

public class Request {
```

First we define the string that represents the request path, and the response time for the request:

```
    private String path;
    private long time;
```

Then we define the constructor:

```
    public Request(String path, long time) {
      this.path = path;
      this.time = time;
    }
```

Finally, the `getPath()` method fetches the request path, and the `getTime()` method fetches the response time:

```
    public String getPath() {
      return path;
    }
    public long getTime() {
      return time;
    }
  }
```

The Unit Class

This class functions as an aggregation of requests that share the same request path. It provides methods for accessing the path, the minimum, maximum, total, and average response time, and the total number of hits.

```
package monitor;

public class Unit {
```

The following variable holds the request path:

```
private String path;
```

We define variables to hold the minimum, maximum, and total response time for the requests:

```
private long minTime;
private long maxTime;
private long totalTime;
```

A variable to hold the total number of hits for the request path:

```
private int count;
```

An instance of this class is instantiated every time a request having the particular request path is accessed for the first time:

```
public Unit(String path, long time) {
  this.path = path;
  minTime = time;
  maxTime = time;
  totalTime = time;
  count = 1;
}
```

Here are the getter methods:

```
public String getPath() {
  return path;
}

public long getMinTime() {
  return minTime;
}

public long getMaxTime() {
  return maxTime;
}

public long getTotalTime() {
  return totalTime;
}

public long getAverageTime() {
  return totalTime/count;
}

public int getCount() {
  return count;
}
```

Every time the filter receives a request corresponding to a particular request path, the minimum response time, maximum response time, total response time, and the total number of hits are updated:

```
public void addRequest(long time) {
    if(time < this.minTime) this.minTime = time;
    if(time > this.maxTime) this.maxTime = time;
    totalTime += time;
    count++;
  }
}
```

The Matrix Class

The `Matrix` class maintains a collection of Request objects, and also provides a method to compute and return a collection of `Unit` objects from the available collection of Request objects.

```
package monitor;

import java.util.ArrayList;
import java.util.Collection;
import java.util.HashMap;
import java.util.Iterator;

public class Matrix {
```

This class stores a collection of Request objects:

```
private ArrayList requestList = new ArrayList();
```

The `addRequest()` method adds a new request to the collection:

```
public void addRequest(Request request) {
    requestList.add(request);
  }
```

The `getMatrix()` method computes and returns a collection of `Unit` objects from the collection of Request objects.

```
public Collection getMatrix() {
    ArrayList clone;
    HashMap unitMap = new HashMap();
```

First we clone a list of Request objects from the existing list:

```
synchronized(this) {
    clone = (ArrayList)requestList.clone();
  }
```

Then we iterate through the list, and compute the list of `Unit` objects corresponding to unique request paths:

```
    Iterator it = clone.iterator();
    while(it.hasNext()) {
      Request request = (Request)it.next();
      if(!unitMap.containsKey(request.getPath())) {
        unitMap.put(request.getPath(),
        new Unit(request.getPath(), request.getTime()));
      }else {
        Unit unit = (Unit)unitMap.get(request.getPath());
        unit.addRequest(request.getTime());
      }
    }
    return unitMap.values();
  }
}
```

The MonitorFilter Class

This class acts as our filter.

```
package monitor;

import javax.servlet.Filter;
import javax.servlet.FilterConfig;
import javax.servlet.ServletRequest;
import javax.servlet.ServletResponse;
import javax.servlet.FilterChain;
import javax.servlet.ServletException;
import javax.servlet.ServletContext;

import javax.servlet.http.HttpServletRequest;
import javax.servlet.http.HttpServletResponse;

import java.io.IOException;

public class MonitorFilter implements Filter {

    private Matrix matrix;
```

We create a `Matrix` object, and store it as an application-scope bean in the filter initialization method:

```
    public void init(FilterConfig filterConfig) {
      matrix = new Matrix();
      filterConfig.getServletContext().setAttribute("MATRIX", matrix);
    }

    public void doFilter(ServletRequest request,
                         ServletResponse response,
                         FilterChain chain)
                         throws IOException, ServletException {
```

In the doFilter() method, we start by getting the request start time:

```
long time = System.currentTimeMillis();
```

Then we get the request path and process the request, and derive how long this process took:

```
String path = ((HttpServletRequest)request).getServletPath();
chain.doFilter(request, response);
time = System.currentTimeMillis() - time;
```

Finally we create and add the Request object, once the request is processed, by storing the request path and total elapsed time:

```
    matrix.addRequest(new Request(path, time));
  }

  public void destroy() {
    matrix = null;
  }
}
```

The MonitorServlet Class

The MonitorServlet computes and displays the performance data:

```
package monitor;

import javax.servlet.*;
import javax.servlet.http.*;
import java.io.*;
import java.util.Iterator;

public class MonitorServlet extends HttpServlet {

  public void init(ServletConfig config) throws ServletException {
    super.init(config);
  }

  public void doGet(HttpServletRequest request,
                    HttpServletResponse response)
                    throws ServletException, IOException {
```

In the doGet() method, we retrieve the Matrix object stored as an application scope bean:

```
Matrix matrix = (Matrix)getServletContext().getAttribute("MATRIX");
```

Then we get an Iterator for the collection of Unit objects:

```
Iterator it = matrix.getMatrix().iterator();
```

Next we display the performance data as an HTML table. You may very well display this data using JSPs and custom tags:

```
        StringBuffer sb = new StringBuffer();
        sb.append("<html><head><title></title></head><body><table border=1>");
        sb.append("<tr>");
        sb.append("<th>Request Path</th>");
        sb.append("<th>Number of Hits</th>");
        sb.append("<th>Total Response Time</th>");
        sb.append("<th>Min Response Time</th>");
        sb.append("<th>Max Response Time</th>");
        sb.append("<th>Average Response Time</th>");
        sb.append("</tr>");

        while(it.hasNext()) {
          Unit unit = (Unit)it.next();
          sb.append("<tr>");
          sb.append("<th>" + unit.getPath() + "</th>");
          sb.append("<th>" + unit.getCount() + "</th>");
          sb.append("<th>" + unit.getTotalTime() + "</th>");
          sb.append("<th>" + unit.getMinTime() + "</th>");
          sb.append("<th>" + unit.getMaxTime() + "</th>");
          sb.append("<th>" + unit.getAverageTime() + "</th>");
          sb.append("</tr>");
        }

        sb.append("<html><head><title></title></head><body><table>");

        PrintWriter writer = response.getWriter();
        writer.println(sb.toString());
        writer.flush();
        writer.close();
    }
}
```

Using the Monitor

To use the monitor in your application, you need to compile all the above classes and add them to the `/WEB-INF/classes/monitor` directory of the web application. You will also have to add the filter and servlet entries to your deployment descriptor as shown below:

```
    . . .
      <filter>
        <filter-name>monitor</filter-name>
        <filter-class>monitor.MonitorFilter</filter-class>
      </filter>

      <filter-mapping>
        <filter-name>monitor</filter-name>
        <url-pattern>/*</url-pattern>
      </filter-mapping>
```

```
<servlet>
  <servlet-name>monitor</servlet-name>
  <servlet-class>monitor.MonitorServlet</servlet-class>
</servlet>

<servlet-mapping>
  <servlet-name>monitor</servlet-name>
  <url-pattern>/monitor</url-pattern>
</servlet-mapping>
```
. . .

The screenshot below displays the output of the monitor servlet used with a test application.

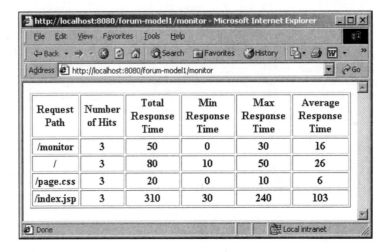

Summary

In this chapter we have covered various issues related to analyzing, improving, and monitoring J2EE web application performance and scalability. The topics we covered include:

❑ The impact of architectural decisions on web application performance and scalability

❑ Design issues for improving performance and scalability, such as session management, data access, handling business logic, and using message-based interfaces

❑ Coding tips for improving performance

❑ Load balancing and clustering

❑ Using various commercial and freeware tools for performance and scalability monitoring and profiling

❑ Creating in-house monitor applications for analyzing web application performance

In the next chapter we will be examining the role of servlets in web services.

14

Web Services and Servlet Agents

Most of this book has focused on how we can use servlets as web server components that provide services to clients. For example, a servlet might be responsible for the presentation of information to a client, perhaps by generating HTML that is rendered by a browser. We've also seen how servlets can act as clients to data sources that contain information that the servlet needs to build its response.

In this chapter we're going to look at how servlets can act as clients to **web services**. Then we'll look at how we can use such servlets to act as agents on our behalf. For example, a **servlet agent** could execute a web service on a regular basis in order to update an internal table of exchange rates.

In particular, we'll look at how we can:

❑   Generate and consume the messages used by web services

❑   Create and deploy web services using Apache SOAP

❑   Invoke web services and retrieve information from them

❑   Create servlet agents that can collect, cache, and aggregate information from web services

To do justice to web services and their associated technologies would require a book of its own. We're going to stick to looking at how web services are tools to be used by servlets. A more general discussion of how to create and use web services can be found in *Professional Java Web Services* (ISBN: 1-861003-75-7) published by Wrox Press.

Web Services

Organizations often need to share and exchange computing resources. For example:

❑   A portfolio management application would need to periodically check the prices of the stocks and bonds

❑   An automated store restocking system would need to be able to place orders with manufacturers and wholesalers

❑   A doctor would need to be able to exchange patient information with insurance companies and other physicians

In the past, the problems of implementing these connections have been solved on a case-by-case basis. Some solutions used technologies such as CORBA and COM, others provided custom file or record exchange schemes, some even required manual re-entry of the information.

In each of these cases, we are essentially trying to solve the same problem: how to share resources, functionality, and information between different computing systems. Web services represent a new approach to addressing this challenge.

> **A web service is an application component that is accessible via standard web protocols.**

Web services expose components for remote execution using the technology and infrastructure of the Web. A **remote procedure call (RPC)** is executed by passing arguments through some type of connection (such as an HTTP connection) to a function, which then executes using those arguments and returns its results back to the requesting agent.

> **Servlets provide a natural mechanism for delivery of web services because they are designed to process requests and responses over the Web.**

Web services are easy for most programmers to understand and implement, and it is easy for a company to integrate existing computing resources through web services because they are built using the same web and application servers that companies are already using. There's no need to go out and purchase new or expensive tools to use or to create web services.

In addition, web services are interoperable. They can be implemented using any number of languages on any platform, and can use different technologies behind the scenes. A web service written as a servlet for the J2EE platform using RMI and JDBC could call another web service on the .NET platform that is implemented in C#. Consequently, web services present low barriers to entry and as a web service request travels over the same infrastructure as if it were a web browser-generated HTTP request it will not be hindered by firewalls.

Crucially, web services have broad industry support. The world's largest software companies, including Microsoft, IBM, and Sun Microsystems have worked together to establish standards for web services to ensure their interoperability.

How Web Services Work

Web services work as follows:

❏ A client (also known as the user agent) invokes a web service by generating an HTTP request – just as a browser requests a web page. The HTTP request identifies the component that will be invoked and provides the parameters or arguments needed to run the component – just as we request a CGI program or servlet.

❏ The server converts the arguments as required and sends the request to the appropriate component, which performs its calculations (retrieving information from other systems and databases as needed) and returns its results.

❏ The results are then formatted so as to be compatible with the HTTP response that will be interpreted by the client.

❏ The HTTP response is then returned to the requesting client.

This is illustrated in the following diagram:

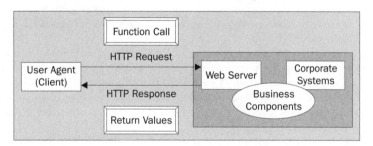

In order for this to work, both the client and the server must agree on:

❏ How a specific component is accessed or selected from other available components

❏ How arguments are passed in

❏ How results are returned

❏ How errors are handled

For most web services developed today, this is done using the **Simple Object Access Protocol (SOAP)**.

Simple Object Access Protocol

The Simple Object Access Protocol (SOAP) is an XML-based protocol that allows the exchange of information in a decentralized, distributed environment. SOAP consists of three parts:

❏ An **envelope** that provides a framework for describing what is in a SOAP message and how it is to be processed

❏ A set of **encoding rules** that define how parameters and return values are encoded

❏ A convention for implementing remote procedure calls (RPC)

SOAP is a one-way messaging system. This means that when SOAP is used in a request-response pattern, *separate* messages are sent in each direction. SOAP also provides the ability for messages to be broadcast to a large number of target systems or for messages to be forwarded to multiple systems, with each system processing part of the SOAP message.

SOAP is rapidly becoming a major industry standard. It offers independence from the underlying implementation technology and can be implemented in many languages, on many platforms using different component technologies.

> *More information on SOAP can be found in* Professional Java SOAP *(ISBN: 1-861006-10-1) published by Wrox Press.*

Using Web Services

Let's look at a typical problem that can be solved using web services. Consider a company that offers online financial information, including the latest currency exchange rates. This exchange rate information is used by customers within a travel voucher processing system. Such a system has a single use case: to get the exchange rate between one country's currency and US dollars.

The client system initiates the action by generating an HTTP request and providing the standard two-letter country code. The server system will respond with a single floating-point number that represents the exchange rate between the requested country's currency and US dollars (this number will be expressed in currency units per dollar). The initial implementation must support the Canadian Dollar, the Japanese Yen, the British Pound, the Euro, and the Mexican Peso. It should return a value of 1.0 for the US Dollar.

Although it is simple, this example models a number of real-world business situations and it could be generalized to address a number of similar challenges. For example, instead of exchange rates, the service could return stock quotes based on a ticker symbol, or it could return a product price based on stock number.

The following code implements a class that meets the requirements of our system:

```java
import java.util.Hashtable;

public class ExchangeRate {

  private Hashtable rate_table;

  public ExchangeRate() {
    rate_table = new Hashtable(6);
    rate_table.put("CA", new Double(1.562600));   //Canada
    rate_table.put("EU", new Double(1.090394));   //Euro
    rate_table.put("JP", new Double(120.435000)); //Japan
    rate_table.put("MX", new Double(9.589000));   //Mexico
    rate_table.put("UK", new Double(0.676133));   //United Kingdom
    rate_table.put("US", new Double(1.000000));   //United States
  }
```

The getExchangeRate() method is the method that we will expose as a web service. This method looks up the country code and returns the exchange rate. If the country requested is not found the component returns a zero value. In a real system, we would probably look up the exchange result from a database, or even another web service:

```
public double getExchangeRate(String country_code) {
    Object obj = rate_table.get(country_code);
    double rval = 0;
    if (obj != null) {
        rval = ((Double)obj).doubleValue();
    }
    return rval;
}
}
```

The SOAP Request

Our interest is in using SOAP over HTTP. SOAP has always been expected to work within an HTTP framework and although SOAP can be used as a one-way protocol, it easily accommodates HTTP. We'll examine an example of a SOAP HTTP request for our Exchange Rate service. We won't have to generate these SOAP requests ourselves, that will be done by tools that you'll be introduced to shortly. Note that a SOAPAction attribute has been added to the HTTP request headers:

```
POST /soap/servlet/rpcrouter HTTP/1.0
Host: localhost
Content-Type: text/xml; charset=utf-8
Content-Length: 464
SOAPAction: ""
```

The envelope contains the body and the optional header. The attributes of the envelope are used to identify namespaces (xsi and xsd in this case). The envelope must have an attribute that associates it with the http://schemas.xmlsoap.org/soap/envelope/ namespace. An optional encoding style can also be included:

```
<?xml version='1.0' encoding='UTF-8'?>
<SOAP-ENV:Envelope
    xmlns:SOAP-ENV="http://schemas.xmlsoap.org/soap/envelope/"
    xmlns:xsi="http://www.w3.org/1999/XMLSchema-instance"
    xmlns:xsd="http://www.w3.org/1999/XMLSchema">
```

The SOAP body contains the information needed to execute our RPC. The first element in the body provides the information about how to handle the request. This element is associated with, or bound to, an implementation on the server. In our case it will be associated with the getExchangeRate() method. The xmlns attribute establishes a namespace for our service and the encodingStyle attribute determines how the arguments will be represented (or marshaled):

```
<SOAP-ENV:Body>
  <ns1:getExchangeRate
    xmlns:ns1="SoapExchangeRate"
    SOAP-ENV:encodingStyle="http://schemas.xmlsoap.org/soap/encoding/">
```

A server must parse and extract the parameters by their names. The parameter name forms an element, the contents of which is the value of the argument. The type of the argument is determined by the attributes and is based on schema data types that are referenced in the envelope:

```
        <country xsi:type="xsd:string">JP</country>
      </ns1:getExchangeRate>
    </SOAP-ENV:Body>
  </SOAP-ENV:Envelope>
```

Apart from the SOAPAction header, this is an ordinary HTTP request. The actual SOAP message is contained the body of the request. The SOAPAction header provides the intent of the message – it allows servers and firewalls to determine how to handle, filter, or route the SOAP request appropriately. This header can have a value of an empty pair of quotes (as shown above), or could be followed by a URI. The empty quotes mean that the URI information is carried in the HTTP request URI.

The SOAP Response

The response header is a normal HTTP response header. Apache SOAP (which we will use shortly) adds a cookie, which can be used to support complex systems in which state needs to be maintained between RPCs. However, this is an optional feature that is not supported by all servers and clients:

```
HTTP/1.1 200 OK
Content-Type: text/xml; charset=utf-8
Content-Length: 485
Date: Wed, 14 Dec 2001 19:33:27 GMT
Server: Apache Tomcat/4.0 (HTTP/1.1 Connector)
Set-Cookie: JSESSIONID=6186631705A6F044B5E057B361A50893;Path=/soap
```

The SOAP response is a SOAP message that follows the same rules as we laid out for the SOAP request. Of course, the values and elements within this document reflect the new message being sent:

```
<?xml version='1.0' encoding='UTF-8'?>
<SOAP-ENV:Envelope
    xmlns:SOAP-ENV="http://schemas.xmlsoap.org/soap/envelope/"
    xmlns:xsi="http://www.w3.org/1999/XMLSchema-instance"
    xmlns:xsd="http://www.w3.org/1999/XMLSchema">
  <SOAP-ENV:Body>
    <ns1:getExchangeRateResponse
      xmlns:ns1="SoapExchangeRate"
      SOAP-ENV:encodingStyle="http://schemas.xmlsoap.org/soap/encoding/">
      <return xsi:type="xsd:double">120.435</return>
    </ns1:getExchangeRateResponse>
  </SOAP-ENV:Body>
</SOAP-ENV:Envelope>
```

The Error Response

If an error occurs during the processing of the SOAP request, the server must issue an HTTP 500 Internal Server Error response, which must also include a message with a SOAP fault element that indicates the SOAP processing error. A `<SOAP-ENV:Fault>` element, included in the body of the response, details the fault that occurred. The error that resulted in this error response was generated by passing three arguments to our server instead of the one or two arguments supported by `ExchangeRate`:

```
HTTP/1.1 500 Internal Server Error
Content-Type: text/xml; charset=utf-8
Content-Length: 578
Date: Wed, 14 Dec 2001 20:22:48 GMT
Server: Apache Tomcat/4.0 (HTTP/1.1 Connector)
Set-Cookie: JSESSIONID=A9C7A201A43594C4A9237205E46184E5;Path=/soap

<?xml version='1.0' encoding='UTF-8'?>
<SOAP-ENV:Envelope
    xmlns:SOAP-ENV="http://schemas.xmlsoap.org/soap/envelope/"
    xmlns:xsi="http://www.w3.org/1999/XMLSchema-instance"
    xmlns:xsd="http://www.w3.org/1999/XMLSchema">
  <SOAP-ENV:Body>
    <SOAP-ENV:Fault>
      <faultcode>SOAP-ENV:Server</faultcode>
      <faultstring>
        Exception while handling service request:
        ExchangeRate.getExchangeRate(java.lang.String,java.lang.String,
        java.lang.String) -- no signature match
      </faultstring>
      <faultactor>/soap/servlet/rpcrouter</faultactor>
    </SOAP-ENV:Fault>
  </SOAP-ENV:Body>
</SOAP-ENV:Envelope>
```

The client can use the fault code to help it deal with the fault. There are a few standard codes that have already been defined:

Fault Code	Reason for Fault
VersionMismatch	The processing party found an invalid namespace for the SOAP Envelope.
MustUnderstand	An immediate child element of the SOAP Header, that was either not understood or not obeyed by the processing party, contained a SOAP `mustUnderstand` attribute with a value of 1.
Client	The message was incorrectly formed or did not contain the appropriate information in order to succeed. For example, the message could lack the proper authentication or payment information. The message will not succeed without change.
Server	The message could not be processed for reasons not directly attributable to the contents of the message itself, but rather to the processing of the message. For example, processing could include communicating with an upstream processor that didn't respond. The message may succeed at a later point in time.

The fault string is intended to be understood by end users and the fault actor should identify what part of the system caused the fault. In this case, our message identified the Apache `rcprouter` servlet. A `<detail>` element can be used to allow the service to provide detailed error information. For example, if we handled invalid country names as an error we could include detailed information in this section.

Apache SOAP

The Apache project provides two different Java SOAP servers – **Apache SOAP** and **Axis**. We will use both of them in this chapter but we'll begin with the older (and for the time being, more stable) Apache SOAP.

First, download Apache SOAP from http://xml.apache.org/soap/. The Apache SOAP download includes a web archive named `soap.war`. Copy this file into `%CATALINA_HOME%/webapps`. Then expand the archive (making sure that you preserve the directory structure). This will create a `soap` directory. For Apache SOAP to run correctly the web application needs access to the following JAR files:

❑   `mail.jar` – available from http://java.sun.com/products/javamail/

❑   `activation.jar` – available from http://java.sun.com/products/beans/glasgow/jaf.html

❑   `xerces.jar` – available from http://xml.apache.org

We can either place these JAR files in `%CATALINA_HOME%/webapps/soap/WEB-INF/lib` or we can place them in the server classpath by copying them to `%CATALINA_HOME%/common/lib`.

Now we're ready to go. We can test our installation by starting Tomcat and navigating to http://localhost:8080/soap/servlet/rpcrouter. If Apache SOAP is working correctly we will see this message:

With Apache SOAP installed, we're ready to deploy our web service.

Deploying Web Services

We have a choice of two methods to use to deploy web services (such as our Exchange Rate service) to the server. In both cases, we need to tell the server what methods of which class we want to expose as web services. In our case we want to expose the `getExchangeRate()` method of `ExchangeRate`.

First we'll deploy the service using a deployment descriptor. Save the following as `SoapDeploy.xml`:

```
<isd:service
  xmlns:isd="http://xml.apache.org/xml-soap/deployment"
  id="urn:SoapExchangeRate" >
```

The `<service>` element assigns a name to the service (set in the `id` attribute). This is the name our clients will use to reference the service. We use `SoapExchangeRate`.

A `<provider>` element tells the server what is to be exposed as a service. Apache SOAP can expose services written in languages other than Java, so we use the type attribute to tell it we want to expose a Java class. The `scope` attribute indicates the lifetime of the object. There are three supported lifetimes:

- ❏ `Request` – the object will be removed after this request has completed
- ❏ `Session` – the object will last for the current lifetime of the HTTP session
- ❏ `Application` – the object will last until the servlet servicing the requests is terminated

We will use `Request`. The `methods` attribute provides the name of the method(s) we want to expose, in our case `getExchangeRate()`:

```
<isd:provider
  type="java"
  scope="Request"
  methods="getExchangeRate">
```

The next element identifies the Java class that implements the method:

```
    <isd:java class="ExchangeRate" />
  </isd:provider>
  <isd:faultListener>
    org.apache.soap.server.DOMFaultListener
  </isd:faultListener>
</isd:service>
```

The next step is to copy the `ExchangeRate.class` file into the `%CATLALINA_HOME%/webapps/soap/WEB-INF/classes` directory and to restart Tomcat. Then, to deploy the service we run the following command:

```
java org.apache.soap.server.ServiceManagerClient
http://localhost:8080/soap/servlet/rpcrouter deploy SoapDeploy.xml
```

The classpath of our command prompt (not the server) must include `soap.jar`, `xerces.jar`, `mail.jar`, and `activation.jar`. The following command will list all the deployed services:

```
java org.apache.soap.server.ServiceManagerClient
http://localhost:8080/soap/servlet/rpcrouter list
```

We can use this command to check that our service has been successfully deployed:

It is also possible to deploy a service by using a browser-based service manager. This can be accessed at http://localhost:8080/soap/admin/index.html:

Selecting the Deploy option offers a form that prompts for the same information that we have entered in the deployment descriptor. While this web interface may seem to be easier to use, it quickly gets tiresome if you need to re-deploy the service several times. However, the web interface does provide a convenient means of listing and removing deployed services:

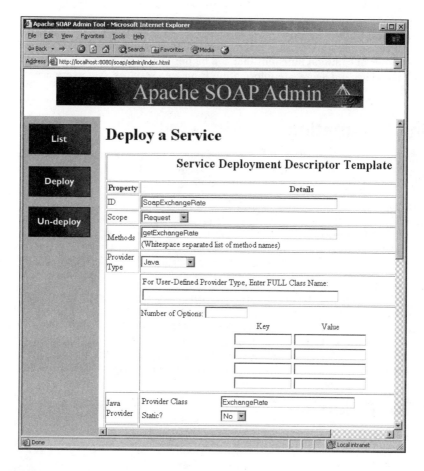

Apache Axis

Axis is the next generation SOAP server being developed by the Apache project. Although it is in the very early stages of availability Axis already has some significant strengths, foremost of which is the ease of deployment of a Java class as web service.

For the next (very quick) exercise you will need Axis installed in %CATLALINA_HOME%/webapps/axis. Axis can be downloaded from http://xml.apache.org/axix/ and is installed easily by following the installation instructions included with the download.

To deploy our web service we only need to rename ExchangeRate.java as ExchangeRate.jws and copy it to the %CATLAINA_HOME%/webapps/axis directory. That's all there is to it. Once the axis web application is running clients can access our Axis-based service at http://localhost:8080/axis/ExchangeRate.jws.

Now that we've seen how we can create and deploy web services, we're ready to create some agents that can interact with them.

Servlet Agents

There are a number of common functions that can be performed by a servlet agent. We'll look at how they can collect, cache, and aggregate information from web services. Not every agent will do all of these things, but every agent will do at least one.

Collecting Information

The web service we've created allows us to look up the exchange rate between two currencies. We'll implement a client for this web service that will act as an agent and will retrieve information from our service. The servlet then presents the data to the requesting browser:

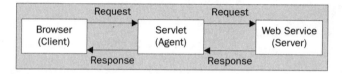

The **client** is the consumer of the information. The client can be any web browser or other program that generates an HTTP request. It could even be another agent. The **agent** acts as the middleman. In our case, the agent is a servlet that is both a client and a server. From the point of view of the browser, the agent acts as a server but from the point of view of the web service, the agent acts as a client. The **server** is where the agent goes to find what it needs to satisfy the client. The agent may go to a single server or to many servers to complete its task. The server is the fundamental provider of information.

Using a SOAP Service

The sourcecode for our agent is:

```
import java.io.*;
import java.net.*;
import java.util.*;
import javax.servlet.*;
import javax.servlet.http.*;
import org.apache.soap.*;
import org.apache.soap.rpc.*;

public class SoapClientServlet extends HttpServlet {
```

The `doPost()` method starts building an HTML document as a response and calls the `getExchangeRate()` method:

```java
public void doPost (HttpServletRequest request,
                    HttpServletResponse response)
   throws ServletException, IOException {
   PrintWriter out = response.getWriter();
   out.println("<html>");
   out.println("<head>");
   out.println("</head>");
   out.println("<body>");
   out.println("Exchange rate for Japan is: " +
            getExchangeRate("JP") + " Yen/Dollar");
     out.println("</body>");
   out.println("</html>");
   out.close();
 }
```

The `getExchangeRate()` method is where all of the interesting code appears. First, we get a connection to the service. The URL uses port 8088 to support the `TcpTunnelGui` program, which will allow us to monitor the requests to, and responses from, our web service:

```java
private String getExchangeRate(String country) {
   String rateString;

   try {
     URL url = new URL( "http://localhost:8088/soap/servlet/rpcrouter" );
     String encodingStyleURI = Constants.NS_URI_SOAP_ENC;
     URLConnection connection = url.openConnection();
```

Then we create a instance of a SOAP `Call` object. The target URI must be set to the same value that was used for the `id` attribute of the service when it was deployed. We also need to tell it which method we want to execute:

```java
     Call call = new Call();
     call.setTargetObjectURI("urn:SoapExchangeRate");
     call.setMethodName("getExchangeRate");
```

Then we can add the arguments we want to pass to this method. We only have one argument but `setParams()` still requires a `Vector`:

```java
     Vector params = new Vector();
     call.setEncodingStyleURI(encodingStyleURI);
     params.addElement(new Parameter("country", String.class,
                                 country, null));
     call.setParams (params);
```

Now that the call has been built, we invoke the service. The `invoke()` method returns a `Response` object that can be used to get the result or examine any fault that has occurred. The result is extracted by retrieving the response as a `Parameter`:

```
      if (resp.generatedFault()) {
        Fault fault = resp.getFault();
        rateString = fault.getFaultString();
      } else {
        Parameter result = resp.getReturnValue ();
        rateString = ((Double)result.getValue()).toString();
      }
    } catch(Exception e) {
      rateString = e.getMessage();
    }
    return rateString;
  }

  public void doGet (HttpServletRequest request,
                     HttpServletResponse response)
      throws ServletException, IOException {
    doPost( request, response );
  }
}
```

The `TcpTunnelGui` program, which is provided with the Apache SOAP distribution, is a Java-based proxy program that will allow us to monitor TCP traffic. It can be invoked with the following command:

```
java -cp soap.jar org.apache.soap.util.net.TcpTunnelGui 8088 localhost 8080
```

The arguments for `TcpTunnelGui` are:

❑   The capture port (8088)

❑   The target machine (localhost)

❑   The target port (8080)

`TcpTunnelGui` is a good way to see what is happening within the protocol. All the examples in this chapter have all been written to use `TcpTunnelGui` on port 8088.

We're ready now to test our servlet agent. You should have a web application with the following files and directories:

```
webservices/
            WEB-INF/
                    classes/
                            SoapClientServlet
                    lib/
                        soap.jar
```

Once this web application has been deployed, we can invoke our agent by navigating to
http://localhost:8080/webservices/servlet/SoapClientServlet:

The output from `TcpTunnelGui` shows the SOAP messages that were sent to and from our web service:

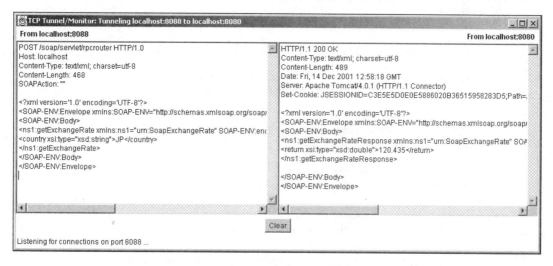

It's very easy to alter our agent so that it uses a different web service. To allow the agent to access the web service deployed on Axis we just need to change the URL and target URI used in the `getExchangeRate()` method:

```
    private String getExchangeRate(String country) {
    ...
        URL url = new URL( "http://localhost:8088/axis/ExchangeRate.jws" );
    ...
        call.setTargetObjectURI("ExchangeRate ");
    ...
    }
```

With another couple of quick changes we could use our agent to access an Exchange Rate service available from http://www.xmethods.com/:

```java
import java.io.*;
import java.net.*;
import java.util.*;
import javax.servlet.*;
import javax.servlet.http.*;
import org.apache.soap.*;
import org.apache.soap.rpc.*;

public class XMethodsClientServlet extends HttpServlet {

  private String getExchangeRate(String country) {
    String rateString;

    try{
      URL url = new URL("http://services.xmethods.net:9090/soap");

      String encodingStyleURI = Constants.NS_URI_SOAP_ENC;
      URLConnection connection = url.openConnection();

      Call call = new Call();
      call.setTargetObjectURI("urn:xmethods-CurrencyExchange");
      call.setMethodName("getRate");

      Vector params = new Vector();
      call.setEncodingStyleURI(encodingStyleURI);
```

This web service requires both country codes. To gain the same functionality we have in our ExchangeRate class we hard-code the first country as the US:

```java
      params.addElement(new Parameter("country1", String.class,
                                      "us", null));
      params.addElement(new Parameter("country2", String.class,
                                      country, null));
      call.setParams(params);

      Response resp = call.invoke(url, "");

      ...

    return rateString;
  }

  public void doPost (HttpServletRequest request,
                      HttpServletResponse response)
      throws ServletException, IOException {
    PrintWriter out = response.getWriter();
    out.println("<html>");
    out.println("<head>");
    out.println("</head>");
    out.println("<body>");
```

We also need to change the country code from "JP" to "japan" to fit the requirements of the XMethods web service:

```
out.println("Exchange rate for Japan is: "+
            getExchangeRate("japan")+" Yen/Dollar");

    out.println("</body>");
    out.println("</html>");
    out.close();
}
```

Caching Information

An agent typically accesses services across the Internet. The performance associated with pulling information across the Internet varies from location to location and with the time of day. It may take 10 seconds or longer each time an agent goes to the Internet to get a specific piece of information but less than a second to get the same information from a local data store. If that same piece of information is requested 100 times, the total time the agent spends retrieving data from the Internet is 1000 seconds. However, if the agent caches the data the first time it retrieves the data, the agent will only spend 10 seconds for the first retrieval and then 1 second for each of the others.

An agent should cache its data when:

❑   There is a high probability that the data it retrieves will be used again.

❑   The data will not have aged before it is needed again. If the data changes rapidly then the data in the cache could be invalid.

❑   There is a large difference between the time it takes to retrieve the data from its source location and the time it takes to get the data from the cache.

❑   The data cannot be generated as quickly as it can be retrieved from the cache.

We also need to manage how much data is cached at any one time. The cost of the cache storage must not be out of proportion to the performance savings that the cache represents. For example, we might have an agent that finds and returns MP3 files. We might discover that 20 or so MP3 files are the most requested at any point in time. Maybe as much as 80% of the traffic to your agent is for those 20 files. Caching just those 20 files represents a storage tradeoff. We could cache everything that is asked for, but eventually we would have to start removing things from our cache because we would physically run out of storage space. What is sought is a tradeoff between how much data is stored in the cache versus how frequently the data is used.

Next, we'll implement a simple cache for our Exchange Rate agent.

An Example Caching Agent

The sourcecode for `CacheServlet` follows:

```
import java.io.*;
import java.net.*;
import java.util.*;
import javax.servlet.*;
import javax.servlet.http.*;


public class CacheServlet extends HttpServlet {
```

The `doPost()` method calls a static member component from the `ExchangeRateCache` class. The country is passed either as a parameter or from a form:

```
public void doPost (HttpServletRequest request,
                       HttpServletResponse response)
    throws ServletException, IOException {
  PrintWriter out = response.getWriter();
  out.println("<html>");
  out.println("<head>");
  out.println("</head>");
  out.println("<body>");

  out.println("Exchange rate for Japan is: " +
            ExchangeRateCache.getExchangeRate("JP") + " Yen/Dollar");

  out.println("</body>");
  out.println("</html>");
  out.close();
  }
}
```

The sourcecode for the `ExchangeRateCache` class is shown next:

```
import java.io.*;
import java.net.*;
import java.util.*;
import org.apache.soap.*;
import org.apache.soap.rpc.*;

public class ExchangeRateCache {
```

The hashtable `rate_table` serves as the cache for previously retrieved exchange rates:

```
private static Hashtable rate_table = new Hashtable(6);
```

When we just need to get values from the cache, there is no need to synchronize access since the table is not being modified. This method first checks the cache and if the rate is found it immediately returns it. If not, it then invokes the synchronized method `callExchangeRateService()`:

```
public static String getExchangeRate(String country) {
    String rateString = (String)rate_table.get(country);
    if(rateString != null) {
        return rateString + " (old)";
    } else {
        return callExchangeRateService(country);
    }
}
```

The `callExchangeRateService()` method also checks the cache first. The reason for this is that the previous caller might have put the value into the cache while the current caller was waiting for synchronization. There is no need to make two costly network calls if the value was already cached by the first caller. The rest of the method was implemented in `SoapClientServlet`:

```
public static synchronized String callExchangeRateService(String country)
{
    String rateString = (String)rate_table.get(country);
    if(rateString != null) {
        return rateString + " (got)";
    }

    try {
        URL url = new URL("http://localhost:8088/soap/servlet/rpcrouter");
        String encodingStyleURI = Constants.NS_URI_SOAP_ENC;
        URLConnection connection = url.openConnection();
        // Build the call.
        Call call = new Call ();
        call.setTargetObjectURI("urn:SoapExchangeRate");
        call.setMethodName("getExchangeRate");
        Vector params = new Vector ();
        call.setEncodingStyleURI(encodingStyleURI);
        params.addElement(new Parameter("country", String.class,
                                        country, null));
        call.setParams(params);
        Response resp = call.invoke (url, "");
        if (resp.generatedFault()) {
            Fault fault = resp.getFault();
            rateString = fault.getFaultString ();
        } else {
            Parameter result = resp.getReturnValue ();
            rateString = ((Double)result.getValue()).toString();
            rate_table.put( country, rateString );
            return rateString + " (new)";
        }
    } catch(Exception e) {
        rateString = e.getMessage();
    }
    return rateString;
}
}
```

This is provided as a simple example of caching. In this case the cache is only cleared when the servlet container is reset. A more robust caching application would need to make provision for aging and expire cached values and would provide methods to invalidate cache entries or the entire cache. We could also pre-fill cache entries. For example if we knew that certain countries were always going to be hit, we could initialize those entries in the `rate_table` in the servlets `init()` method.

Once the servlet has been compiled and deployed, it can be accessed at http://localhost:8080/webservices/servlet/CacheServlet. The initial response will be:

Later responses will show that the data was retrieved from the cache:

If you have `TcpTunnelGui` running you will observe that the first time a request is made a SOAP service request is also made. For subsequent requests the SOAP service request is never made because the value is already in the cache.

Aggregation and Conglomeration

If I wanted to purchase a book I could visit several web sites and purchase the book from the store that gave me the best price. Better yet, I could create a program that visits many web sites for me. This program would get the price for the book that I am planning to buy from each web site. I can then look at and compare all of these prices and determine where to go to purchase my book.

Consider another example in which I'm interested in monitoring the performance of the companies in my stock portfolio. There are of course, sites that provide a wealth of information about publicly traded companies. I can get the stock ticker price, the opening and closing prices, the company's financials, and lists of news items from several different sites. This time, instead of visiting several different site to make sure that I have the information that I need, I could create a site that combines that information into one convenient site.

In each case we could use a servlet agent to visit a number of other sites to retrieve information. The agent could then combine the information in a way that it more valuable to us. This gathering and combining of information is known as **aggregation** and **conglomeration**:

- ❑ Aggregation is the combination of *similar* types of information collected from different sources. An example of aggregation is comparison shopping by collecting the prices of similar items from several different vendors.

- ❑ Conglomeration is the combination of *different* types of information. A portal showing news headlines and stock prices is an example of conglomeration.

Next we'll look at how we can create an aggregating servlet agent.

Aggregation Example

This aggregating agent builds and displays a table comparing exchange rates:

```
import java.io.*;
import java.net.*;
import java.util.*;
import javax.servlet.*;
import javax.servlet.http.*;

public class AggregateServlet extends HttpServlet {
```

The doPost() method calls buildTable(), which builds the table for the response:

```
public void doPost (HttpServletRequest request,
                    HttpServletResponse response)
    throws ServletException, IOException  {
  PrintWriter out = response.getWriter();
  out.println("<html>");
  out.println("<head>");
  out.println("</head>");
  out.println("<body>");
  buildTable(out);
  out.println("</body>");
  out.close();
}
```

The buildTable() method does most of the work by calling buildRow() and buildCell():

```
private void buildTable(PrintWriter out) {
  out.println("<table border=\"1\">");
  out.print("<tr><td>  </td>");
  out.println("<th>CA</th><th>EU</th><th>JP</th>" +
              "<th>MX</th><th>UK</th><th>US</th></tr>");
  buildRow(out, "CA");
  buildRow(out, "EU");
  buildRow(out, "JP");
  buildRow(out, "MX");
  buildRow(out, "UK");
  buildRow(out, "US");
  out.println("</table>");
}
```

The `buildRow()` method handles the building of each row of the table by calling `buildCell()` for each column:

```
private void buildRow(PrintWriter out, String country) {
  out.println("<tr>");
  out.print("<th>"+country+"</th>");
  buildCell(out, "CA", country);
  buildCell(out, "EU", country);
  buildCell(out, "JP", country);
  buildCell(out, "MX", country);
  buildCell(out, "UK", country);
  buildCell(out, "US", country);
  out.println("</tr>");
}
```

The `buildCell()` method gets the exchange rate for a particular cell based on the countries for the row and column and calls a static method in a helper class (similar to the caching example):

```
private void buildCell(PrintWriter out, String country1,
                       String country2) {
  out.print("<td>");
  out.print(RateHelper.getExchangeRate(country1, country2));
  out.println("</td>");
}
```

The `RateHelper` class is based on the `ExchangeRateCache` class. To improve performance `RateHelper` caches the rates in order to minimize the number of remote calls made:

```
import java.io.*;
import java.net.*;
import java.util.*;
import org.apache.soap.*;
import org.apache.soap.rpc.*;

public class RateHelper {

  private static Hashtable rate_table = new Hashtable(6);
```

We have provided two versions of the `getExchangeRate()` method. One version takes a single argument and returns the rate per US dollar. It first looks in the cache and if the rate is not found calls the `callExchangeRateService()` method to fill the cache:

```
public static double getRate(String country) {
  Double rate = (Double)rate_table.get(country);
  if(rate == null) {
    try {
      rate = callExchangeRateService(country);
    } catch(Exception e) {
      e.printStackTrace();
      rate = new Double(0.0);
    }
  }
  return rate.doubleValue();
}
```

The second implementation uses the first to calculate the rate between any two supported currencies by first converting to dollars:

```
public static double getRate(String country1, String country2) {
  double rval;
  double currency1_per_usdollar = getRate(country1);
  double currency2_per_usdollar = getRate(country2);

  if(currency2_per_usdollar > 0.0) {
    rval = currency1_per_usdollar/currency2_per_usdollar;
  } else {
    rval = 0.0;
  }
  return rval;
}
```

This is the method that will actually be called by our aggregating client:

```
public static String getExchangeRate(String country1, String country2) {
  double rate = getRate(country1, country2);
  return Double.toString(rate);
}
```

Finally, we have modified the callExchangeRateService() method so that it now returns a double. It also stores doubles into the cache instead of strings and passes exceptions through by re-throwing them:

```
public static synchronized Double callExchangeRateService(String country)
    throws Exception {
  Double rate = (Double)rate_table.get(country);
  if(rate != null) {
    return rate;
  }

  try {
    URL url = new URL( "http://localhost:8088/soap/servlet/rpcrouter" );
    String encodingStyleURI = Constants.NS_URI_SOAP_ENC;
    URLConnection connection = url.openConnection();
    Call call = new Call ();
    call.setTargetObjectURI ("urn:SoapExchangeRate");
    call.setMethodName ("getExchangeRate");
    Vector params = new Vector ();
    call.setEncodingStyleURI(encodingStyleURI);
    params.addElement(new Parameter("country", String.class,
                                    country, null));
    call.setParams (params);
    Response resp = call.invoke (url, "");
    if (resp.generatedFault ()) {
      Fault fault = resp.getFault ();
      String faultString = fault.getFaultString ();
      System.out.println( faultString );
    } else {
      Parameter result = resp.getReturnValue ();
```

```
            rate = (Double)result.getValue();
            rate_table.put(country, rate);
            return rate;
        }
    } catch(Exception e) {
        throw(e);
    }
    return rate;
    }
}
```

Navigate to http://localhost:8080/webservices/servlet/AggregateServlet to run this servlet:

Of course, our servlet could have got this information from a number of different web services and used the different exchange rates to form a comparison service.

Sampling Applications

A sampling application is one that samples several sites for similar information. It is a special case of an aggregation. For example, a shopping bot that samples book prices for the same title at several sites is a sampling application. An aggregation agent would show the prices for all the sites at once. A sampling agent might just show the top three. A sampling agent may have a list of 100 stores to sample, but may only sample 25 of them at any time. The decision on which stores to sample might be based on previous history, or might be made randomly.

Design Considerations

There are a number of issues to consider when designing an agent that performs aggregation or conglomeration:

❑ Is the information cacheable?

❑ Does all information have to be refreshed each time?

❑ Can the information be collected in advance?

❑ Is the order that the information is retrieved important?

❑ Can the information be retrieved in a reasonable amount of time?

It is very likely that for some agents, some information will be cacheable and some will not be. Or that some of the information caches will need to be refreshed at a different rate from others. For example, if you are trying to match 15-minute stock quotes with daily news items, the stock quotes have a cache aging cycle of no more than 15 minutes. The news items may only need to be refreshed once or twice a day.

Collecting information in advance prevents delays for those first requestors. In this case, it makes sense to have a separate daemon or process that runs externally to the application server and refreshes the data cache.

Dependencies may exist between data items. For example, if the agent is to give the monthly lease price of a vehicle, it must get lease rates and vehicle prices. Often lease rates are based on the value of what is being leased. This means the prices must be available to provide the lease quoting services before the lease rates can be determined.

The amount of time it takes an agent to build its response is important. If it takes too long, the information may no longer be valid or useful. Dependencies between services and non-cacheable items can create long assembly times and when possible these should be worked around or avoided.

Parallel vs. Sequential Processing

An agent that is performing aggregation and conglomeration typically needs to perform several tasks that could be performed independently of each other. If the queries to the remote systems are independent of each other then these queries can be done in parallel, by allocating each query to a separate thread. As each thread spends most of the time waiting for a response, this improves performance even on a single-CPU system.

Present and Future Challenges

We've seen how we can use servlets to implement both web services and web service agents or clients. Web services are rapidly becoming the preferred means of web-based data exchange between businesses. Web service and agent development is such a broad topic that it is difficult to provide much detail in a book focused on servlet development. However, it is necessary for us to understand how web services will operate so that we can develop effective servlet agents.

Web Services Description Language

CORBA, RMI, and Microsoft COM are all examples of distributed component technologies. Each one of these technologies provides an Interface Definition Language (IDL), used to automatically generate stubs needed to create client programs and skeletons needed to create servers. These stubs and skeletons handle exchange of parameters and return values across the network. **Web Services Description Language (WSDL)** provides this capability for web services.

A WSDL document provides all of the information needed to interact with a web service. A WSDL file is an XML file that can be read and interpreted manually by a developer who needs to implement a web service or an agent. It can also be used to automatically generate proxy classes or stubs to access a web service automatically.

Apache Axis already includes the capability to automatically create client proxies and server skeletons based on a WSDL file. Axis can also be used to automatically create a WSDL file for a service deployed in the Axis server. Since these tools are so readily available, we don't need to worry about manually creating WSDL files.

So we have a standard way of describing a web service. The next problem is how do we find the web services we want to use?

Universal Description, Discovery, and Integration

Universal Discovery, Description, and Integration (UDDI) can be thought of as a phone book for web services (although UDDI can be used for more than just web services). With UDDI, we can have the massive telephone directories such as those that the telephone companies use, or local ones just for a company or organization.

A UDDI directory entry can contain things like personal contact names, addresses, and telephone numbers as well as information like URL's and service names. It also provides a mechanism for exposing WSDL files that describe web services.

UDDI provides three types of directory:

❑   The first is similar to the **white pages** type of phonebook. It lists entries alphabetically according to the organization or entry name.

❑   The next is like the **yellow pages** or business directory. It classifies entries according taxonomy of businesses and entry types.

❑   Finally, we have **green pages**. It lists technology like URLs and WSDL files.

The Web Services Stack

The following figure illustrates the web-services stack. It shows how the web-service technologies work together to support the distributed computing model:

UDDI is used first to find the WSDL of a web-service, which describes the service and provides the interface definition (a contract to which the client and server will adhere). The SOAP layer provides the common messaging system and supports the standardized marshaling or serialization of parameters and return values. XML is the common language that everyone uses to communicate. Finally, HTTP is the carrier that moves it all around. These five layers represent the current direction of distributed computing.

Transactions and Web Services

As web services become widely implemented they will provide the major framework for integration between companies in the future. As this occurs web services agents will be involved in ever more complex interactions between multiple service supported by different companies. The example services we have examined in this chapter only gather information from services to present to the user. Web service agents and web services can also be used collect information from the user and distribute this information to many services. Web service agents could be used to make travel arrangements or to purchase office supplies from the lowest priced supplier. These scenarios require a web service agent to deal with complex transactions.

In this section, we'll provide a brief overview of how transactions are normally handled. We'll then look at some of the topics that are being researched to deal with the unique problems of dealing with transactions in complex, servlet agent environments.

A **transaction** is a series of actions or operations that transform a system from one consistent state to another consistent state. For example, if I wanted to move $50 from my savings to my checking account, I would subtract $50 from one account and add $50 to the other. In this case, it takes two operations in order to complete the transaction. If only one of the operations was performed, the system would no longer be in a stable state. It would either have $50 too much (my preference certainly) or might have lost $50. This sort of problem is not new to distributed computing, but it is new to web services and web agents.

Transactions were originally created with databases in mind. As distributed computing grew in importance, the concepts were extended to deal with distributed computing environment. Yet, the basic definition of a series of operation that transforms a system from one consistent state to another consistent state remains. Every transaction must be **A**tomic, **C**onsistent, **I**solated, and **D**urable – **ACID**.

ACID

Atomicity is also known as the "all or nothing" property. All component parts of a transaction must occur none should occur. This means a transaction is a single unit of operation.

Consistency means that the system moves from one stable state to the next stable state. Each state, the beginning and end states, must be stable. This means that if I started with $200 in my combined accounts and I shift money between my accounts, then I should still have two hundred dollars when I am done. The money may be distributed between the accounts differently but the total will remain the same.

Isolation of transactions means that one transaction does not have an effect on another transaction while the transaction is occurring. Transactions cannot expose their intermediate results. They must be completed (by committing or rolling back) before other transactions have access to the results. Each transaction will always see a consistent system state. This is necessary because otherwise if two concurrent transactions were to access the same data item it would be impossible to ensure a consistent state at the end of either transaction.

Durability ensures that once a transaction has completed, it is permanent. If the system is not changed by another transaction, the system will remain in its current state. Durability also implies a certain amount of persistence to the state of the system.

XAML and XLANG

Transactions and the computing theories surrounding them were created in the context of databases. In most of these cases, transactions can be completed in seconds or minutes. Web services and web service agents may deal with large numbers of other services, with each one taking significant lengths of time. The normal transaction model does not work as well in this situation. This is true for two reasons:

❑ Web services transactions are spread across diverse systems with different transaction management tools

❑ Web service transactions may span great lengths of time (even days) and tie up resources while waiting for a commit

Technologies that address these issues will play a significant role in the development of web service agents and web services in the future. **XAML** and **XLANG** are two technologies that are now trying to rise to meet these challenges.

XAML (http://www.xaml.org/index.html) is a standard being developed by a group of companies to help bring transactions to the world of web services. XAML is supposed to expose transaction manager services as web services. The basic idea is to allow complex web services to be built using transaction managers to ensure that each piece of the transaction either occurs or is rolled back.

Another standard (being developed and supported by Microsoft) is XLANG (http://www.gotdotnet.com/team/xml_wsspecs/xlang-c/default.htm). XLANG is not a transaction management standard but a part of it does cover the concept of Long Running Transactions (LTR). These transactions might take days or weeks to accomplish instead of seconds or minutes. The concept for handling these transactions involves a corrective action. In our bank account example, we have a LTR if the $50 was removed from my checking account and a check was sent by postal mail to my savings account. If something fails, like there was not enough money in the account, the check will bounce. A corrective action would be applied to make sure the $50 check is taken from my savings account.

Another common scenario is what happens when a less important part of a transaction fails. For example, we may elect to have an online purchase insured when shipped. The transaction now involves three parties, the shipper, the insurer and you the customer. If for some reason the insurance carrier was unwilling to insure the package the transaction would normally fail. But the package may be inexpensive and not important to you if it is lost. In this case there is an alternative action that can allow the rest of the transaction to move forward. The alternatives are to either ship without insurance, or find another insurer. If one of these is acceptable, the transaction continues.

Transaction management in web services and agent environments is still a very new technology and there are few available toolkits to even allow experimentation at this time. Yet transaction management will be an important technology for the future of web services. IBM, Microsoft, and Hewlett Packard seem to be leading the technology discussions around web services and transactions at this time. This will be an interesting area to watch in the future.

Summary

This chapter has focused on the delivery of web-services by using Java servlet-based technologies and consumption of web services through servlet agents. In this chapter, we created a demonstration web-service that returns exchange rates between currencies using SOAP. The web service was deployed using Apache SOAP and Apache Axis servers running on Tomcat.

We went on to create servlet agents that could access this web service and manipulate its results. Our agents demonstrated how they could collect, cache, and aggregate information from web services.

Finally, we examined the emerging web services infrastructure, providing discovery through UDDI, publication through WSDL, and transaction management services appropriate for web service transactions.

Installing Tomcat 4.0

In this appendix we'll discuss the basics of how to install and configure Tomcat 4.0, the latest version of the open source JSP and Servlet Reference Implementation.

Installing Tomcat 4.0

While there are many servlet and JSP engines available (as of this writing, Sun's "Industry Momentum" page at http://java.sun.com/products/jsp/industry.html lists nearly 40), we have chosen to focus our attention on Tomcat 4.0. Tomcat is produced by the Apache Software Foundation's Jakarta project, and is freely available at http://jakarta.apache.org/tomcat/.

As Tomcat is primarily used by programmers, its open source development model is of particular benefit as it brings the developers and users close together. If you find a bug, you can fix it and submit a patch. If you need a new feature, you can write it yourself, or suggest it to the development team.

Tomcat is also the reference implementation of the JSP and Servlet specifications, version 4.0 supporting the latest Servlet 2.3 and JSP 1.2 versions. Many of the principal developers are employed by Sun Microsystems, who are investing considerable manpower into ensuring that Tomcat 4.0 provides a high-quality, robust web container with excellent performance.

A Word on Naming

The naming of Tomcat 4.0 components can be a little confusing, with the names **Tomcat**, **Catalina**, and **Jasper** all flying around. So, to avoid any problems with terminology:

❑   **Catalina** is a servlet container – that is, an environment within which Java servlets can be hosted.

❑   **Jasper** is the JSP component of Tomcat – in fact, it's just a servlet that understands how to process requests for JSP pages.

❑   **Tomcat** comprises Catalina, plus Jasper, plus various extra bits and pieces including batch files for starting and stopping the server, some example web applications, and mod_webapp.

❑   **mod_webapp** is the component that will allow you to connect Tomcat to the Apache web server. Catalina includes a web server of its own, but you may also wish to connect it to an external web server to take advantage of Apache's extra speed when serving static content, or to allow you to run JSP or servlet-based applications alongside applications using other server-side technologies such as PHP. As of this writing mod_webapp is in beta testing, but expect it to become stable soon. In time, connectors for other major web servers should also appear.

Basic Tomcat Installation

These steps describe installing Tomcat 4.0 on a Windows 2000 system, but the steps are pretty generic; the main differences between platforms will be the way in which environment variables are set:

❑   You will need to install the Java 2 Platform, Standard Edition software development kit, if you have not already done so. JDK 1.3 can be downloaded from http://java.sun.com/j2se/1.3/.

❑   Download a suitable Tomcat 4.0 binary distribution from (for example, jakarta-tomcat-4.0.1.zip from http://jakarta.apache.org/builds/jakarta-tomcat-4.0/release/v4.0.1/bin/) and unzip it into a suitable directory.

❑   On Windows 2000 you have the alternative of downloading a Windows installer, jakarta-tomcat-4.0.1.exe, and simply double-clicking its icon. Note that installing Tomcat 4 as a Windows service is as easy as ticking a box.

❑   Create CATALINA_HOME and JAVA_HOME environment variables pointing to the directories where you installed the Tomcat and Java 2 SDK files. Typical values are C:\jakarta-tomcat-4.0.1 for CATALINA_HOME and C:\jdk1.3 for JAVA_HOME.

Under Windows 2000, environment variables are set using the **System** control panel. On the **Advanced** tab, click on the **Environment Variables...** button. In the resulting dialog box, add CATALINA_HOME and JAVA_HOME as system variables:

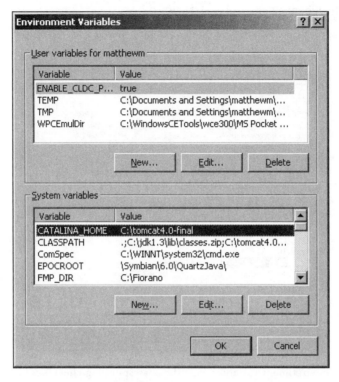

These environment variables allow Tomcat to locate both its own files (using CATALINA_HOME), and the Java 2 SDK components it needs, notably the Java compiler, (using JAVA_HOME).

If you are using Windows 98, environment variables are set by editing the C:\autoexec.bat file. Add the following lines:

```
set CATALINA_HOME=C:\jakarta-tomcat-4.0.1
set JAVA_HOME=C:\jdk1.3
```

Under Windows 98 you will also need to increase the environment space available, by right-clicking on your DOS prompt window, selecting **Properties**, going to the **Memory** tab, and setting the initial environment to 4096 bytes.

Editing the autoexec.bat file doesn't work the same on Windows Me as it does on Windows 95/98. First, you need to start Microsoft System Information. You can use either of the following methods:

❑ Click Start | Programs | Accessories | System Tools | System Information

❑ Click Start | Run, and type msinfo32.exe in the **Open** box, and then click **OK**

To create a new entry:

❑ Select **Tools** | **System Configuration Utility**

❑ Click the **Environment** tab, and click **New**

❑ Enter the appropriate information in the **Variable Name** and **Variable Value** boxes, and then click **OK**

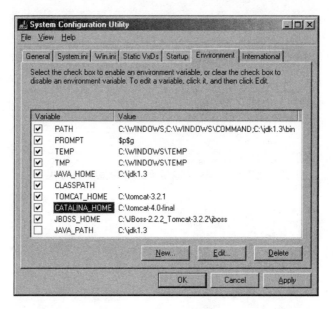

To activate the new environment variable select the corresponding checkbox for this entry, and restart your computer.

Running Tomcat

Start Tomcat by running the `startup.bat` batch file (`startup.sh` on Unix-type systems), which can be found in the `<CATALINA_HOME>\bin\` directory (in other words, the `bin` directory inside the directory where Tomcat is installed). Alternatively, Windows users can run Tomcat from the **Start** menu. Choose **Start** | **Programs** | **Apache Tomcat 4** | **Start Tomcat**.

Tomcat will start up and print some status messages:

If you have installed Tomcat 4.0 as a service on Windows 2000, it is controlled instead by the Services utility within Administrative Tools.

We now have Tomcat 4.0 up and running, using its internal web server (on port 8080). Point your web browser at http://localhost:8080/. You should see the default Tomcat home page:

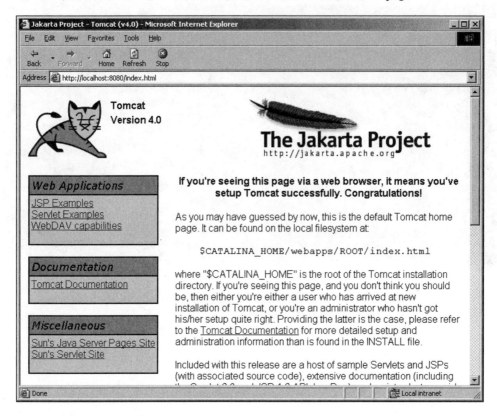

Spend some time exploring the examples and documentation provided with Tomcat.

To shut down Tomcat, run the shutdown.bat batch file (shutdown.sh on Unix-type systems), again from the <CATALINA_HOME>\bin\ directory. Again, Windows users can accomplish the same task from the Start menu. Choose Start | Programs | Apache Tomcat 4 | Stop Tomcat.

The Tomcat 4.0 Directory Structure

Looking inside our Tomcat installation directory we find a few text files, and various directories:

❑ bin
  Contains Windows batch files and Unix shell scripts for starting and stopping Tomcat, and for other purposes, together with the bootstrap.jar JAR file needed for the first stage of starting Tomcat.

❑ classes
  Not created by default, but if it exists any .class files it contains will be visible to all web applications.

❏ common

Contains Java code needed by all parts of Tomcat: JAR files in the `common\lib\` directory, and `.class` files in `common\classes\`. Notable among the JAR files is `servlet.jar`, which contains the classes defined by the Servlet 2.3 and JSP 1.2 specifications. You will need to have `servlet.jar` listed in your `CLASSPATH` environment variable when compiling classes (for example, servlets) that use these APIs.

❏ conf

Contains Tomcat's configuration files, notably `server.xml` (dealt with in the *Tomcat 4.0 Configuration* section below) and the server-wide `web.xml`.

> Note that settings in the server-wide **web.xml** file apply to the whole server, but that this behavior is not mandated by the Servlet specification. Applications making use of it will not be portable to other servlet containers.

❏ lib

Populated with various JAR files required by web applications, including parts of the JSP engine. You can add your own JAR files here and they will be visible to all web applications.

❏ logs

Contains Tomcat's log files. Logging is configured in `server.xml`.

❏ server

Contains the files composing Catalina, and other required libraries: JAR files in `server\lib\`, and `.class` files in `server\classes\`.

❏ src

Contains the sourcecode for Tomcat, along with the documentation (interspersed with the sourcecode).

❏ webapps

The location where Tomcat looks for web applications to deploy. Any WAR file placed here, or any expanded web application directory structure stored within the directory, will automatically be deployed when Tomcat starts up.

The URL path under which the application is deployed will correspond to the name of the WAR file or directory; for example, if you place a `myapplication.war` file or a `myapplication` directory within `webapps`, Tomcat will automatically deploy it as http://localhost:8080/myapplication/.

The automatic deployment settings may not suit your application, in which case you may prefer to store the application outside the `webapps\` directory and configure it as desired using `server.xml`.

❏ work

Used by Tomcat to store temporary files, notably the `.java` source files and compiled `.class` files created when processing JSP pages.

Tomcat 4.0 Configuration

The Tomcat documentation has improved vastly compared to early versions and should be your first stop if you need to configure Tomcat in any way. However, there are a few steps that are sufficiently common that we cover them here.

Deploying a Web Application

There are two ways to tell Tomcat to deploy a web application:

❑ As mentioned above, you can deploy an application simply by placing a WAR file or an expanded web application directory structure in the webapps directory.

❑ However, the default settings may not be suitable for your application, in which case it will be necessary to edit <CATALINA_HOME>\conf\server.xml and add a <Context> element for your application.

The default server.xml file is well commented, and you should read these comments to familiarize yourself with the contents of this file. Various additional elements, not shown or described here but included in the default server.xml, provide for logging and other similar functionality, and define authentication realms. The default server.xml also includes commented-out sections illustrating how to set up a secure (HTTPS) connector, and to set up database-driven authentication realms. It also includes elements that work together with the mod_webapp Apache module.

The outline structure of server.xml is as follows:

```
<Server>
  <Service>
    <Connector/>
    <Engine>
      <Host>
        <Context/>
      </Host>
    </Engine>
  </Service>
</Server>
```

At the top level is a <Server> element, representing the entire Java Virtual Machine:

```
<Server port="8005" shutdown="SHUTDOWN" debug="0">
```

The <Server> element may contain one or more <Service> elements. A <Service> element represents a collection of one or more <Connector> elements that share a single 'container' (and therefore the web applications visible within that container). Normally, that container is an <Engine> element:

```
<Service name="Tomcat-Standalone">
```

A <Connector> represents an endpoint by which requests are received and responses are returned, passing them on to the associated <Container> (normally an <Engine>) for processing. This <Connector> element creates a non-secure HTTP/1.1 connector, listening on port 8080:

```
<Connector className="org.apache.catalina.connector.http.HttpConnector"
           port="8080" minProcessors="5" maxProcessors="75"
           acceptCount="10" debug="0"/>
```

An <Engine> element represents the Catalina object that processes every request, passing them on to the appropriate <Host>:

```
<Engine name="Standalone" defaultHost="localhost" debug="0">
```

The <Host> element is used to define the default virtual host:

```
<Host name="localhost" debug="0" appBase="webapps">
```

A <Context> element is used to define an individual web application:

```
<Context path="/examples" docBase="examples" debug="0"
         reloadable="true">
</Context>
```

The attributes of the <Context> element are:

❑ path
Determines the URL prefix where the application will be deployed. In the example above, the application will be found at http://localhost:8080/examples/.

❑ docBase
Specifies the whereabouts of the WAR file or expanded web application directory structure for the application. Since a relative file path is specified here, Tomcat will look in its webapps directory (this was configured in the <Host> element, above) but an absolute file path can also be used.

❑ debug
Specifies the level of debugging information that will be produced for this application.

❑ reloadable
Intimates whether the container should check for changes to files that would require it to reload the application. When deploying your application in a production environment, setting its value to false will improve performance, as Tomcat will not have to perform these checks.

```
      </Host>
     </Engine>
   </Service>
   <!-- Snip details of service for the mod_webapp connector -->
 </Server>
```

The Manager Application

Tomcat 4.0's default configuration includes a web application that allows web applications to be deployed, undeployed, and reloaded while Tomcat is running. This application is installed by default as the `manager` web application, and contains four commands:

- ❑ http://localhost:8080/manager/list
  List all web applications currently deployed in this virtual host.

- ❑ http://localhost:8080/manager/deploy?path=/myapp&war=mywar
  Deploy the web application specified by the `war` request parameter, at the context path given by the `path` parameter.

- ❑ http://localhost:8080/manager/reload?path=/myapp
  Reload all the Java classes in the specified web application. This works even if automatic class reloading is disabled.

- ❑ http://localhost:8080/manager/undeploy?path=/myapp
  Shut down and undeploy the specified web application.

When specifying a web application to the `deploy` command, the value of the `war` request path must have one of these forms:

- ❑ file:/absolute/directory/path
  The absolute path to the directory containing the unpacked web application

- ❑ jar:file:/absolute/path/to/mywar.war!/
  A URL specifying the absolute path to the WAR file

- ❑ jar:http://host:port/path/to/mywar.war!/
  A URL specifying the location of the HTTP-accessible WAR file

Before you can use the manager application you need to set up a user in `tomcat-users.xml` with the role `manager`:

```
<tomcat-users>
   <user name="tomcat" password="tomcat" roles="tomcat" />
   <user name="role1"  password="tomcat" roles="role1"  />
   <user name="both"   password="tomcat" roles="tomcat,role1" />
   <user name="admin"  password="adminpassword" roles="manager" />
</tomcat-users>
```

With this addition, the manager application works just fine:

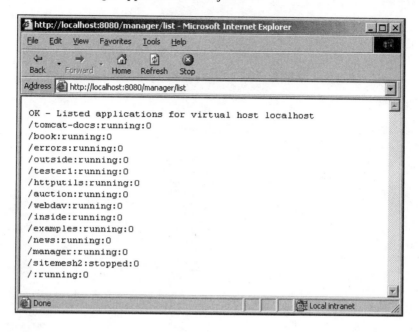

Getting Help

If you need help with Tomcat 4.0, and this appendix and the documentation just haven't helped, your first port of call should be the Tomcat web site, http://jakarta.apache.org/tomcat/. There are two mailing lists dedicated to Tomcat issues:

❑ tomcat-user
This is where you can ask questions on configuring and using Tomcat. The Tomcat developers should be on hand to help out as necessary.

❑ tomcat-dev
This is where the developers themselves lurk. If you decide to get stuck in with contributing to improving Tomcat itself, this is where the action is.

B

HTTP Reference

The **Hypertext Transfer Protocol (HTTP)** is the main protocol underlying web-based communication. Understanding HTTP is important for Java servlet and web application developers since much if not most web-based communication runs over HTTP. HTTP is also extensible, and we can, if required by our web application, extend the protocol for our programs.

HTTP is commonly associated with browser-to-server communications, but this is only a fraction of its possibilities. We can use HTTP to communicate between applications or applets and our web applications. Using HTTP we can serialise Java objects, raw text, XML data, binary files, and any other data or files. Often company firewalls block almost all communication except that running over the HTTP protocol for security reasons. We can use HTTP tunneling, which is communication over HTTP to access across a firewall so we can send data between clients and servers.

This appendix will look at the structure and contents of HTTP transactions. We look at client requests and server responses and the various methods available for the requests. We will examine the HTTP headers available and the wide range of responses that the server may return to the client.

We will also include a reference of HTTP status codes and a reference of MIME types available.

HTTP Versions

The initial version of HTTP seen on the web was HTTP/0.9, which contained only the most basic functionality for retrieving mainly static resources from a web server. This evolved into the HTTP/1.0 specifications that were issued as "Informational" only. The reasons for this were because of perceived scale and performance issues. However in real terms, implementation of the HTTP/1.0 (unofficial) standard was varied and there were almost as many versions as there were HTTP/1.0 products.

With the introduction of the HTTP/1.1 standard, the implementation of HTTP became somewhat more standardised (perhaps because it is a wider, more comprehensive protocol definition), but it still varies to some extent from vendor to vendor. Coupled with this is still the fact that there are many HTTP clients and servers in use still supporting a variant of HTTP/1.0.

The HTTP standards are backwards compatible so any remaining clients supporting the initial HTTP/0.9 standard will continue to work, albeit with limited functionality.

HTTP Transactions

The main characteristic in HTTP communications is that there are two parties to an **HTTP transaction:**

- ❑ There is the client (called User-Agent in HTTP specifications) that has the responsibility for sending the request to instigate the communication, called a **request**.

- ❑ Then there is the server that waits for a client request and then processes the client request and returns a relevant **response** to the client.

In Internet terms, the client is commonly seen as a web browser, using mostly HTML and image files, communicating with a web server. However in reality the client possibilities are much wider than the browser. A client is simply the party that initiates the request to the server that processes it and returns a response. The client may in fact be another server, acting as client, requesting a resource of the server. In fact, proxy servers fulfil this role, where a client (possibly a browser) makes a request to the proxy server (in this case acting as server), which in turn acts as a client to the server holding the requested resource indicated by the URI.

Proxy servers are often used in companies with firewalls to monitor and direct HTTP traffic through the proxy to the outside Internet. The diagram below outlines this relationship where there are two sets of HTTP transactions, with the proxy server acting as both server on one side and client on the other side:

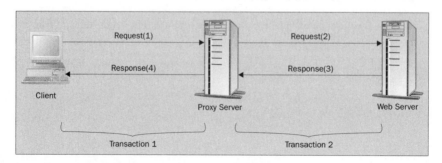

The above shows how, in HTTP Transaction 1, the client makes an HTTP request (1) to the proxy server, and waits for the proxy server's response (4). While the client waits on the first transaction, the proxy server starts a separate (related) transaction with the web server and makes a request (2) to it and receives a response (3) which the proxy server in turn returns to the client of the first transaction.

In HTTP/1.0, client connections were closed after each request. In HTTP/1.1 client connections were allowed to be persistent to allow a client to maintain a connection with the server. For example this allows a client to request a web page and subsequently request images for that page without having to make separate connections for each image, thus saving the overhead cost of creating each connection. In a Java application, similarly this could allow the client to follow up the initial request with subsequent requests, possibly based on the initial response over the same connection.

HTTP is designed as a **stateless** protocol (no state is maintained by the server between client requests). However, there are two main methods that servers use to maintain state. The first is URL rewriting (where additional information is included in the URL) and the second is cookies. Cookies allow the server to send small pieces of information to the client for retrieval from the client on subsequent requests. These are not part of the core HTTP specification document but are included as part of the wider specifications in separate documents specifying their uses.

The HTTP requests and responses contain text-based communication in the headers with possibly text (or binary files) in the message body.

A sample HTTP client request for the default index page of a web site may look as follows:

```
GET / HTTP/1.1
Accept: image/gif, image/x-xbitmap, image/jpeg, image/pjpeg, */*
Accept-Language: en-ie
Accept-Encoding: gzip, deflate
User-Agent: Mozilla/4.0 (compatible; MSIE 6.0; Windows NT 5.0)
Host: localhost
Connection: Keep-Alive
```

To briefly explain the client request above, the first line indicates that the request is a GET request for the root directory ("/") using HTTP/1.1 version of the protocol. The second line indicates the types of data it will accept from the server (images or anything "*/*"). Line three specifies the language is English (Irish version). The fourth line (Accept-Encoding) indicates the encoding or compression the client uses. The fifth line (User-Agent) indicates the details of the client making the request. The penultimate line indicates the specific host requested, while the last line indicates that the connection should be kept open by the server for further requests. This will be explained in more detail in the following section.

The server may respond with:

```
HTTP/1.1 200 OK
Date: Tue, 01 Jan 2002 09:50:17 GMT
Content-Type: text/html
Server: Tomcat 4
Content-Location: http://localhost/index.html
Last-Modified: Fri, 28 Sep 2001 23:18:50 GMT

<html>
<head>< title >The Page</title></head>
<body><h1>The page body</h1></body>
</html>
```

The server's response will be examined in more detail later on, but we will have a brief look at the example response given above. The first line indicates the version of HTTP being used with the 200 OK indicating the request was processed without problems. Line two indicates the date of the response, while the third line indicates the type of the body of the response returned, in this case an HTML text file. The Server header on line four indicates the HTTP server and version, while line five details the location of the resource being returned in the response. Finally in the header fields, the Last-Modified header field indicates the date the document was last changed.

A blank line follows indicating that the header data is completed and the body of the response, if there is one, will begin; in this case a simple HTML page.

In the following subsections we will look at the detail of the HTTP client request and the server's response. We will look at the methods available and headers that can be used in requests/responses.

The HTTP Client Request

The HTTP client is responsible for initiating the communication with the server. To do this it sends a formatted request and waits for a response from the server. The format of the request is as follows:

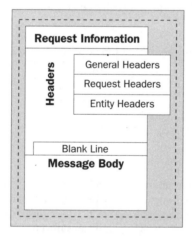

At a minimum the request will include the method **request information**, which is in the following format:

    Method URI HTTPVersion

This tells us the method being used to make the request, the URI of the requested resource, and the version of HTTP, such as:

    GET /index.html HTTP/1.1

Technically, the **Header** information is optional but many servers, methods, and resources will require some data in various header fields. For HTTP/1.1, at a minimum, the Host header is required as servers may share the same IP address among different web applications on different host URIs so this is the only way they can identify the actual resource requested.

600

General header information is used in both requests and responses and includes information such as the date, connection, or caching information. For example:

```
Date: Tue, 01 Jan 2002 09:50:17 GMT
Connection: Keep-Alive
```

Request header information is obviously used only in the request, and is used to specify relevant information about the client for the server such as the data it prefers to receive, any conditions to the request, or the maximum number of times the request can be forwarded. For example:

```
Accept: image/gif, image/x-xbitmap, image/jpeg, image/pjpeg, */*
Accept-Language: en-ie
Accept-Encoding: gzip, deflate
User-Agent: Mozilla/4.0 (compatible; MSIE 6.0; Windows NT 5.0)
Host: localhost
If-Modified-Since: Tue, 01 Jan 2002 09:50:17 GMT
```

The **Entity** header information is used to specify information about the body (entity) of the request being sent, such as the type of the data, the length etc. In Java applications it could specify the type of the data (such as serialized Java objects) being sent. For example:

```
Content-Type: application/x-java-serialized-object
Content-Length: 158
```

The **blank line** always follows the request header to indicate the end of the header information, and possibly the start of the body of the request (if included).

The **Body** of the request may contain POST method parameters, files PUT on the server, other files, Java data etc.

HTTP Request Methods

The initial HTTP/0.9 version only supported the GET method for retrieval of resources. As the "informational" specifications evolved into HTTP/1.0, a number of additional request methods were added with varying support. With the advent of HTTP/1.1 two methods (LINK and UNLINK) were dropped and three methods were added. We will examine each of these methods in the following subsections.

All of the request methods, except where noted in the relevant subsection, are supported methods of `javax.servlet.http.HttpServlet`, and are available to Java programmers.

HTTP/1.0 Request Methods

HTTP/1.0 added HEAD and POST methods to the GET method already in use. It also added the PUT, DELETE, LINK, and UNLINK methods, but the support from servers and clients for these methods was more patchy.

GET Method

The GET method, introduced in HTTP/0.9 was the original request method designed to retrieve information, described as an entity, referenced by the request URI. This is, by convention, only a retrieval method and should not change the information or resources on the server.

We can also use conditional GET requests if one or more conditional If- headers are used. If the range header field is used it may be a partial GET, allowing large documents or data to be more efficiently retrieved in one or more pieces.

Both the conditional GETs and the partial GETs are designed to improve efficiency by reducing the unnecessary network traffic to a minimum.

HEAD Method

The HEAD method (since HTTP/1.0) is essentially the GET request without the return of the message body. The point of the HEAD request is to allow the client to access the header information, without receiving the resource information associated with the request. The header information is identical to that of the GET request, just no entity body is attached after the blank line.

POST Method

This method is designed to allow the client to send a block of data to the server in the message body of the request. This method may result in a new resource URI being created, for example in the case of a post to a notice board, or may involve the sending of data from a form to the server and/or database for processing.

Essentially in Java terms, programmers can treat the GET and POST methods similarly in certain situations, in that similar form parameters may be submitted though each request method, although the POST request is suited also for other data such as files, XML requests, serialized objects etc.

It is also ideal for HTTP tunneling as we can send Java objects, files and other data in a request to the server.

PUT Method

The PUT request is used to store the body of the request at the requested URI. The body may be a file, or other resource such as HTML or XML data, or even a servlet or JSP, and is in effect similar to the File Transfer Protocol (FTP) in relation to transferring files.

The key difference between the POST method and the PUT method is that the PUT method requests that the body of the request is stored at the specified URI, while the POST method requests that the URI specified handles the request, and often will not create a new resource.

DELETE Method

The DELETE method is the converse method to the PUT request. This method allows the client to request that the given resource at the specified URI is deleted, or at least removed to an inaccessible location.

The client is not guaranteed success, even once the response indicating the operation was completed is returned. The server should only return a status code indicating success if, and only if it intends to delete (or already has deleted) the resource at the time of the response.

LINK and UNLINK Methods

The LINK method establishes one or more Link relationships between the existing resource identified by the URI and other existing resources. The UNLINK method removes one or more LINK relationships from the existing resource identified by the URI.

> The LINK and UNLINK methods are only mentioned here because they are mentioned in the HTTP/1.0 document, however they are rarely, if ever, used, and should be avoided.
>
> They have been dropped completely from the HTTP/1.1 specifications and are not supported request methods in Java servlets (`javax.servlet.http.HttpServlet`). Of course this class and/or the Servlets API could be extended to support these methods, but this is not advisable.

HTTP/1.1 Additional Request Methods

The HTTP/1.1 specifications define three additional, new methods. One is not implemented yet, while the other two may be more useful to client-side developers.

> Remember here that when we talk about client-side and client applications this also applies to proxy servers or other servers (in other words Java web applications are included) that need to access external HTTP resources acting as a client in these HTTP conversations.

OPTIONS Method

The OPTIONS method is most useful to the client-side developer as it allows the client to determine the options or methods available from a given resource URI on a server. If the request URI is an asterisk, the OPTIONS method applies to the server in general instead of a specific URI resource.

For Java programmers the `doOptions()` method in `HttpServlet` need not be overridden, as it will automatically detect the available methods in normal operation. The only reasons for overriding this method are if the servlet has reason to hide a specific method available, or if the servlet extends or implements additional methods beyond those already available.

This HTTP request method could be useful in client applications accessing new or dynamic resources, or if the client is trying to access resources that may not support all of the current HTTP methods.

TRACE Method

The TRACE method should simply return the header information received by the server, back to the client in the body of the response. This is used to allow the client to see exactly what the server received and its primary use is for debugging. This method never includes a body or entity header fields in the request and the response is of the Content-Type `message/http` with the request in the body.

For Java programmers the `doTrace()` method in `HttpServlet` implements this HTTP method and should not be overridden on the server side. The Java client side may use this request for debugging purposes.

CONNECT Method

This CONNECT method is not yet implemented, and is reserved by HTTP/1.1 for use with a proxy server that can dynamically switch to being a tunnel.

This method is not implemented in `javax.servlet.http.HttpServlet` and is not available to the Java programmer yet.

HTTP Server Response

The structure of the servers response is similar to the client request with two main differences – the response information line and the response headers:

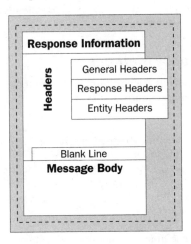

The **Response information** includes the HTTP version of the response, the status code indicating the result of the request and the message associated with the status code:

HTTPVersion StatusCode Message

This line indicates the request was processed successfully:

```
HTTP/1.1 200 OK
```

while the following is an example of where the requested resource was not located:

```
HTTP/1.1 404 Not Found
```

General headers are used by both request and response and the following is an example of them from a response:

```
Date: Fri, 28 Sep 2001 09:43:29 GMT
Cache-Control: private
Via: 1.1 ni-cache (NetCache NetApp/5.1R2)
```

Response headers are specific to the server response and are used to include server-specific information such as cookie setting, or authentications:

```
Set-Cookie: ASPSESSIONIDQQRTPFWW=MMHTTSHHHYSSWFFYBVWCCRHR; path=/
Location: http://www.harbourne.com
Server: Microsoft-IIS/4.0
```

Similar to requests, **Entity** headers in responses indicate information about the body of the request:

```
Content-Length: 0
Content-Type: text/html
Last-Modified: Fri, 02 Jan 2002 09:43:29 GMT
```

HTTP Headers

As we outlined before, there are four types of HTTP headers. General headers and Entity headers are used in both the request and response, while Request and Response headers may only be used on the relevant side of the communication.

The subsections below detail the headers from HTTP/1.0 and HTTP/1.1, and include the additional standard headers for authentication and cookie management.

For each header, the column **Since** indicates when the header was introduced. As shown, some existed only for HTTP/1.0 and were not included in the HTTP/1.1 specifications:

❑ **1.1**: since HTTP/1.1

❑ **1.0**: since HTTP/1.0 (core)

❑ **1.0***: since HTTP/1.0 (appendix)

❑ **1.0 only**: only HTTP/1.0

❑ *****: Defined in associated specifications (Security and Cookies)

❑ **Note:** No headers were defined for HTTP/0.9

General Headers

Header	Since	Use
Cache-Control	1.1	This is used to specify under what conditions a cached response should be returned (by a client), or for a server, under what conditions the response may be cached (if at all).
		Frequently used with no-cache, no-store, max-age etc.
Connection	1.1	Introduced in version 1.1 to allow connections to remain open to server for more than one request rather than having to reconnect for every resource required from a server. Options are close and keep-alive for persistent connections.

Table continued on following page

Header	Since	Use
Date	1.0	The date/time that the request was served. Three date formats exist but the format "Tue, 01 Jan 2002 09:50:17 GMT" is preferred.
Pragma	1.0	Retained for backward compatibility with HTTP/1.0. Used in caching with no-cache for documents that should not be cached.
Trailer	1.1	This may be used when chunked transfer encoding is used for the message body.
Transfer-Encoding	1.1	Used with chunked to indicate that the message is encoded.
Upgrade	1.1	This may be used to indicate that communication should upgrade the protocol used for communication to a higher level or preferable system (such as HTTPS).
URI	1.0* only	Used only in HTTP/1.0. Indicates some or all of the URIs by which the requested URI may be identified with.
Via	1.1	This header is useful in debugging problems, usually in association with the TRACE method, as each proxy adds its protocol and host details to the request.
Warning	1.1	This is used to include additional information that may not be included in the response status code.

Request Headers

Header	Since	Use
Accept	1.0*	This is used to indicate the media type or types (separated by commas) that are accepted by the client. Standard ones include "text/html", "application/x-java-serialized-object", etc.
Accept-Charset	1.0*	Indicates the charset(s) that the client is willing to accept.
Accept-Encoding	1.0*	Used to specify the types of encoding that the client understands, such as x-gzip, to reduce network traffic for large amounts of data.
Accept-Language	1.0*	This indicates the language(s) that the client prefers to receive. Useful in internationalization, possibly with Filters in Java servlets.
Authorization	1.0	This contains the client's encoded username and password to the selected resource, usually as a result of the server sending the WWW-Authenticate header.

Header	Since	Use
Cookie	*	Contains cookie information, previously sent by the server to the client.
Cookie2	*	This is used to indicate the version of the state management specifications that the client supports.
Expect	1.1	This is used to indicate specific client expectation, which, if not fulfilled by the server will result in the server returning the 417 status code.
From	1.0	May be used to indicate the e-mail address of the client. This is rarely used due to privacy concerns and Spam e-mail.
Host	1.1	Used to indicate the specific URL being communicated with. This required in version 1.1 as multiple web hosts may share the same IP address.
If-Match	1.1	Conditional request, only to return a body if the ETag header matches one supplied.
If-Modified-Since	1.0	Conditional request, if the server has a later copy of the resource, otherwise the client/proxy will use a cached version.
If-None-Match	1.1	The reverse to If-Match, returning the entity if the ETag does not match one of those supplied.
If-Range	1.1	Used to retrieve part of the data when part of it is already cached.
If-Unmodified-Since	1.1	Obviously the reverse of the If-Modified-Since header indicating the server should not return the entity if it has been modified since the time specified.
Max-Forwards	1.1	This will limit the number of proxy servers or gateway servers that can forward the request. This may be specifically useful in debugging, in association with the TRACE method.
Proxy-Authorization	1.1	Used by the client to identify itself to the proxy server.
Range	1.1	Specifies the byte range of the resource data to return. Useful for large files or data where the download was interrupted.
Referer	1.0	Used to indicate the document or resource that referred the client (by a link) to the resource.
TE	1.1	Indicates the list of transfer encodings that the client will accept.
User-Agent	1.0	Identifies the client program making the request (such as browser or application).

Response Headers

Header	Since	Use
Accept-Ranges	1.1	Indicates if the server will accept Range requests, and if so, the units that the requests are made in (for example none, or bytes).
Age	1.1	This field is used to indicate the age of the document/data being returned, in seconds.
Authentication-Info	*	Used in authentication to indicate the client has been successfully authenticated.
ETag	1.1	Entity Tag associated with the specific resource requested and may be used for caching and conditional requests.
Location	1.0	This specifies the new location for the resource (either created or moved).
Proxy-Authenticate	1.1	This is used for authentication to the proxy, and is used when the client must authenticate with the proxy. The client may resubmit the request with its authentication details.
Retry-After	1.0*	This header indicates that the client may retry its request after the specified date/time or time interval (specified in seconds).
Server	1.0	This is used to identify the server software (including version) used to process the request.
Set-Cookie	*	This is used to send data to the client in a cookie to be returned to the server in subsequent requests, until the specified interval has elapsed (specified time or date or until the browser shuts down).
Set-Cookie2	*	Slightly modified version of Set-Cookie, but essentially performs the same service with cookies.
Vary	1.1	This header is used to indicate to the client that the requested resource has multiple potential sources, based on the information supplied by the client in the headers returned in the Vary header.
WWW-Authenticate	1.0	This is used to indicate to the client that it must authenticate itself to the server before accessing the requested resource.

Entity Headers

Header	Since	Use
Allow	1.0	This is normally used by the server to indicate that the request method used was not supported (or allowed) and the included request methods are permitted.
Content-Encoding	1.0	This specifies the encoding algorithm used for the body of the request or response. Servers should only use encoding that is supported by the client in the Accept-Encoding header.
Content-Language	1.1	This header specifies the language that the body is in, or aimed at. Can be used in conjunction with the client's Accept-Language header by the server.
Content-Length	1.0	This specifies the length of the body of the entity in bytes.
Content-Location	1.1	Specifies the location that the content body was sourced from.
Content-MD5	1.1	This is used to ensure that the receiver received the entity body without modification or alteration. This is done by running the Message Digest 5 algorithm over the data to produce this header value.
Content-Range	1.1	This is normally used by the server to indicate the range of the data being returned to the client. This allows the client to resume receiving a large response (for example a large file) from the server.
Content-Type	1.0	This header field specifies the media type of the entity body.
Expires	1.0	This is used to indicate the date/time after which the data becomes invalid and needs to be refreshed from the server.
Last-Modified	1.0	This is used to indicate the time of the last change or modification to the entity.
Link	1.0* only	This is used to indicate relationships between the entity and another resource or resources. (Dropped for HTTP/1.1)
MIME-Version	1.0* only	This is used to indicate the MIME type of the entity body. (Dropped for HTTP/1.1)
Title	1.0* only	Used to indicate the title of the entity. (Dropped for HTTP/1.1)

MIME Types

HTTP clients let the server know the data types that they are able to handle by using the `Accept` header with the types listed. The server responds by telling the client the type returned in the body by using the `Content-Type` header field. Clients will also use the `Content-Type` header field for request methods such as POST and PUT where files may be uploaded to the server.

Media types, or MIME types are made up of a small number of types (such as text, application, video etc.) and a much larger number of subtypes relating to specific uses or data/file types. **MIME** stands for **Multipurpose Internet Mail Extensions**, which were originally developed for e-mail messages, however HTTP uses these for sending files and data as a standard.

Standard HTML files use the `text` type with the `html` subtype – given as `text/html`. The tables below give the MIME types for many of the types available.

Application files

type/subtype	File extension
application/dsptype	tsp
application/futuresplash	spl
application/mac-binhex40	hqx
application/mspowerpoint	ppt, ppz, pps, pot
application/msword	doc
application/octet-stream	bin, exe
application/oda	oda
application/pdf	pdf
application/pgp-encrypted	
application/pgp-keys	
application/pgp-signature	
application/postscript	ai, eps, ps
application/rtf	rtf
application/vnd.framemaker	
application/vnd.lotus-1-2-3	wks, wk1
application/vnd.lotus-approach	
application/vnd.lotus-freelance	
application/vnd.lotus-organizer	
application/vnd.lotus-screencam	scr
application/vnd.lotus-wordpro	

type/subtype	File extension
application/vnd.mif	
application/vnd.ms-artgalry	
application/vnd.ms-excel	xls
application/vnd.ms-powerpoint	ppt
application/vnd.ms-project	prj
application/vnd.ms-tnef	
application/vnd.ms-works	wks
application/vnd.xara	xar
application/vocaltec-media-desc	vmd
application/vocaltec-media-file	vmf
application/wordperfect5.1	
application/wpc	wpc
application/x-asap	asp
application/x-cdlink	vcd
application/x-chat	chat
application/x-csh	csh
application/x-director	dcr
application/x-director	dir
application/x-director	dxr
application/x-dvi	dvi
application/x-envoy	evy
application/x-hdf	hdf
application/x-java-archive	jar, war, ear
application/x-javascript	js
application/x-java-serialized-object	
application/x-java-vm	class
application/x-latex	latex
application/x-mif	mif
application/xml	xml
application/xml-dtd	dtd
application/xml-external-parsed-entity	xml

Table continued on following page

type/subtype	File extension
application/x-netcdf	nc, cdf
application/x-sh	sh
application/x-shockwave-flash	swf
application/x-sprite	sprite, spr
application/x-streaming-audio	key
application/x-tar	tar
application/x-tcl	tcl
application/x-tex	tex
application/x-texinfo	texinfo, texi
application/x-troff	t, tr, roff
application/x-troff-man	man
application/x-troff-me	me
application/x-troff-ms	ms
application/x-wais-source	src
application/zip	zip

Audio files

type/subtype	File extension
audio/basic	au, snd
audio/mpeg	mpg, mpeg
audio/tone	
audio/vnd.lucent.voice	
audio/vnd.nortel.vbk	
audio/voxware	vox
audio/x-aiff	aif, aiff, aifc
audio/x-midi	mid, midi
audio/x-mod	mod
audio/x-pn-realaudio	ram, rm, ra, rv
audio/x-pn-realaudio-plugin	rpm
audio/x-s3m	s3m
audio/x-wav	wav

Image files

type/subtype	File extension
image/cgm	cgm
image/cis-cod	cod
image/fif	fif
image/g3fax	
image/gif	gif
image/ief	ief
image/jpeg	jpeg, jpg, jpe
image/png	
image/tiff	tiff, tif
image/vasa	mcf
image/vnd.wap.wbmp	
image/x-cmu-raster	ras
image/x-portable-anymap	pnm
image/x-portable-bitmap	pbm
image/x-portable-graymap	pgm
image/x-portable-pixmap	ppm
image/x-rgb	rgb
image/x-xbitmap	xbm
image/x-xpixmap	xpm
image/x-xwindowdump	xwd

Messages

type/subtype	File extension
message/delivery-status	
message/disposition-notification	
message/external-body	
message/http	
message/news	
message/partial	
message/rfc822	
message/s-http	

Text files

type/subtype	File extension
text/calendar	
text/css	css
text/directory	
text/enriched	
text/html	html, htm
text/plain	txt, c, ec
text/richtext	rtx
text/rtf	rtf
text/sgml	sgml
text/tab-separated-values	tsv
text/uri-list	
text/vnd.curl	curl
text/vnd.wap.wml	wml
text/vnd.wap.wmlscript	wml
text/xml	xml
text/x-setext	etx
text/x-speech	talk, spc

Video/VRML/Model files

type/subtype	File extension
model/vrml	vrml
video/mpeg	mpeg, mpg, mpe
video/quicktime	qt, mov
video/vnd.vivo	vivo, viv
video/x-msvideo	avi
video/x-sgi-movie	movie
x-world/x-vrml	wrl

Status Codes

HTTP status codes are used by the HTTP server in the response to indicate the result of the request. The most commonly used codes are 200 OK meaning that the request was successful and the requested file or resource is enclosed in the body of the response, and 404 Not Found meaning that the requested resource could not be found. However, there are many more codes available to indicate other conditions, such as the requested resource has been moved (permanently or temporarily), client or server errors, and other details. These are not only used by web servers for static resources, but are also used for dynamic resources including servlets and JSPs.

The javax.servlet.http.HttpServletResponse class supports all HTTP/1.1 (and HTTP/1.0) status codes and web applications should make appropriate use of the status codes. For web applications with browsers as clients, the browser will be able to interpret the response status code correctly and display the resource or take the required action (for example a redirect). To ensure compatibility with HTTP/1.0 clients, if required, programmers should only use those status codes marked with "*", which indicates a status code that exists in HTTP/1.0 and on.

When working with Java client applications correct use of status codes can simplify the treatment of the returned data (if any), and convey information. Hence Java clients are recommended to check the status code during receiving the server's response.

The following table outlines the ranges of codes available and their general meanings.

Status Code Range	Meaning	Description
1xx	Informational	These codes are informational, indicating that the server has received the HTTP request and the client can continue the request.
		As no 1xx codes were defined by HTTP/1.0, these should only be used with HTTP/1.1 clients, or under experimental or custom conditions.
2xx	Success	2xx status codes indicate that the request was successfully received, understood, and accepted by the server. Information/data may or may not be returned to the client depending on the specific code.
3xx	Redirection	These response codes indicate that further action is required to complete the request. Only GET or HEAD requests may allow the client to automatically redirect on receiving this response. Other requests methods require user input according to the specifications.
		Those clients automatically redirecting should limit the number of redirects (to prevent infinite or excessive loops). HTTP/1.1 does not specify a specific maximum number, but in HTTP/1.0 redirects are limited to five at a maximum.

Status Code Range	Meaning	Description
4xx	Client Error	The 4xx series of status codes indicates that the client appears to have made an error, such as making a request for a resource that does not exist or is forbidden to the client, or used bad syntax/badly formed request etc.
		The server normally should include an entity containing an explanation of the error also indicating if the error situation is temporary or permanent (except for HEAD requests). Normally the client should display the entity to the user, which will explain the error. For web pages and HTML/browser requests the entity will be an HTML error page, however for Java applications, this may be a standard serialized error object explaining the problem.
5xx	Server Error	5xx status codes indicate that a server-side error occurred while processing the request. Most often these are as a result of a programmer's error or in the case of high server load where the server has not enough resources to fulfill the request etc.
		As for 4xx client errors, the server should included an entity in the response that explains the error situation and indicates whether this situation is temporary (for example server overload) or permanent. Again HEAD requests do not require the entity body. As before, for HTML/browser web requests this will normally include an HTML page explaining the error, and for Java client applications may include a serialized Java error object or other entity depending on the communication (for example XML).

The following tables covers all the HTTP/1.1 status codes and meanings and gives an explanation for each code. It also indicates the constant used in `javax.servlet.http.HttpServletResponse` for this code. Codes indicated with "*" were also included in the HTTP/1.0 specifications and can be safely used with all HTTP/1.0 and HTTP/1.1 clients.

Range: 1xx – Informational

Status Code	Message	HttpServletResponse Constant	Explanation
100	Continue	SC_CONTINUE	This indicates that the initial part of the request was successfully (so far) received by the server and the client should continue by sending the remainder of the request, if any more exists. The client may ignore this message if it has completed the request. In any case, after the request has been completed, the server must send a final response. For Java web applications with Java clients this is useful for sending a request in a number of parts, which may help speed up the request processing.
101	Switching Protocols	SC_SWITCHING_PROTOCOLS	This indicates that the server has understood the request and will process it. The server returns an Upgrade message header field indicating the preferred protocol. The server will automatically upgrade to the new protocol after the empty line ending this response. Different protocols should only be used when they improve the communication such as improving security or taking advantage of additional features in the new protocol.

Range: 2xx – Success

Status Code	Message	`HttpServletResponse` Constant	Explanation
200*	OK	SC_OK	This indicates that the request has succeeded normally. Depending on the request method used additional information will be returned to the client.
			A GET request returns the requested resource. A HEAD request will return the entity header fields without any message body. The POST method will return the entity containing or describing the result of the action. The TRACE method will return the request message as received by the server.
201*	Created	SC_CREATED	This indicates that the server has successfully created the resource requested by the client on the server. This is not returned until after the resource is created (202 Accepted should be used if resource is not yet created).
			The URI location(s) of the new resource are returned to the client.
202*	Accepted	SC_ACCEPTED	This indicates that the request has been accepted but not completed yet. The request will be processed at a later point and may or may not be successful at this point. Whether it is successful or unsuccessful at the later point is not known by the client (unless there is a mechanism to check this).
			This may be used, for example when data is stored on the server or database temporarily and only updated at specific intervals, such as trades to be settled etc.
			Normally the response should include an indication of the current status of the request and when it will be processed, or other relevant information.

Status Code	Message	HttpServletResponse Constant	Explanation
203	Non-Authoritative Information	SC_NON_AUTHORITATIVE_ INFORMATION	This code is equivalent to the 200 OK response, however this indicates that the information contained within the response did not originate from the server, but from a local or other copy. In web terms this could be used by a proxy server serving cached content which cannot be verified due network problems etc.
204*	No Content	SC_NO_CONTENT	This response is similar to the 200 OK response in that the request was successful, but in this case there is no content or no new content to return. There will be no message body to this request.
205	Reset Content	SC_RESET_CONTENT	Similar to the previous code, the request was processed and the client should reset the view that caused the request to be made. Examples of this include HTML or Java application/applet forms that should be reset after the data in the request has been processed.
206	Partial Content	SC_PARTIAL_CONTENT	The request generating this must have included a Range header field, and maybe an If-Range field, and this response code indicates that the data returned is the part specified by the Range requested.

Range: 3xx – Redirection

Status Code	Message	HttpServletResponse Constant	Explanation
300*	Multiple Choices	SC_MULTIPLE_CHOICES	This code indicates that more than one location or representation is available for the request. The response should indicate the preferred (if any) option and include a list of choices.
			For example, this could be used for servers serving browser clients and other clients (such as XML) and may include the location of the HTML representation of the information as default (for browsers that will automatically choose the default), with other choices such as XML available for other types of clients.
301*	Moved Permanently	SC_MOVED_PERMANENTLY	This indicates that the requested resource has been moved permanently to a new location given in the header field (and clients should update the location).
			GET or HEAD requests may automatically redirect, however, other request methods should not automatically redirect, at least until user agreement.
302*	Found	SC_MOVED_TEMPORARILY	This indicates that the resource requested by the client has been moved temporarily and clients should return to the current URI to access the resource.
			As with 301, the client may automatically redirect GET or HEAD requests, but other methods require user intervention.
			HTTP/1.0 defined the message as Moved Temporarily while HTTP/1.1 defines it as Found. This is why the constant name for this code is substantially different from the message.

Status Code	Message	`HttpServletResponse` Constant	Explanation
303	See Other	SC_SEE_OTHER	This indicates that the requested resource exists under a different URI and this allows for the conversion of a POST request into a GET request on the new resource.
			In case clients may use HTTP/1.0, code 302 may be a better alternative in some cases.
304*	Not Modified	SC_NOT_MODIFIED	When a client makes a conditional GET request and the resource requested has not been modified, the server will return this status code indicating that the client has the latest version of the resource.
			This can be useful where clients have to request and update large amounts of data, and the server can check if the data has been changed recently. This can be used when the client-side data is up-to-date.
305	Use Proxy	SC_USE_PROXY	This indicates that the requested resource must be accessed using the proxy indicated in the Location header field.
307	Temporary Redirect	SC_TEMPORARY_DIRECT	This indicates that the resource requested by the client temporarily resides under a different URI (given in the Location field) and clients should return to the current URI to access the resource.
			The client may automatically redirect GET or HEAD requests, but other methods require user intervention.

Range: 4xx - Client Error

Status Code	Message	HttpServletResponse Constant	Explanation
400*	Bad Request	SC_BAD_REQUEST	This code when sent from the server indicates that the client's request was incorrectly formed (syntactically incorrect) and the server cannot process the request. The client should not repeat the request as-is without making modifications.
401*	Unauthorized	SC_UNAUTHORIZED	This indicates that the client has requested a resource that requires user authentication that has not been supplied, or has failed authorization.
			The response includes the WWW-Authenticate header field to which the client may reply with a suitable Authorization header field.
			In web browsers this normally means that the user will be presented with a dialog box into which they can enter their username and password for authentication. In Java applications or applets the client should also provide a login box for the username and password or use a previously supplied username and password to authenticate the client to the server.
402	Payment Required	SC_PAYMENT_REQUIRED	This code has been reserved for future use in connection with payment information, but has not yet been implemented or standardized.

Status Code	Message	HttpServletResponse Constant	Explanation
403*	Forbidden	SC_FORBIDDEN	The server has understood the client's request, but has refused the client access to the requested resource.
			For requests other than HEAD requests the server may give a reason in the body. This is not an authentication problem and authentication information will not change the result.
			This may be used in web applications where certain resources are protected, possibly by security stronger than HTTP types of security (own application algorithms etc.), and where access is required though a specific gateway or where access is restricted to clients within certain limits (for example only within company networks or geographical domains).
404*	Not Found	SC_NOT_FOUND	This is commonly used on web servers that cannot locate a resource at the requested URI. It means that the server does not know, or indicate, why the resource is unavailable. Where a server knows that the resource is permanently unavailable (with no forwarding location), it should return 410 Gone.
			This is commonly seen on the Internet when web resources have been changed or updated and old links remain pointing to an old location for the removed or relocated resource.

Table continued on following page

Status Code	Message	HttpServletResponse Constant	Explanation
405	Method Not Allowed	SC_METHOD_NOT_ALLOWED	A server response returning this code is indicating that the request method of the client is not permitted for this resource. The server must include an `Allow` header to indicate acceptable request methods for this resource, in case the client may retry or reform the request using a different method.
406	Not Acceptable	SC_NOT_ACCEPTABLE	This code can be returned where the MIME type specified by the `Content-Type` header is not acceptable to the options specified by the client. Except for HEAD requests the server should include a list of options from which the user can chose. It is not always preferable to send this message, and sometimes it may be better to return the response (in spite of the types indicated as accepted) with all content as per normal and let the client/user decide how to handle it (for example save it for future use). This is essentially a programmer's decision based on the type of data involved.
407	Proxy Authentication Required	SC_PROXY_ AUTHENTICATION_ REQUIRED	The server returns this code when the client must authenticate with the proxy. The client may repeat the same request with a suitable `Proxy-Authorization` field to authenticate. This is similar to `401 Unauthorized`, however in this case the client is authenticating with the proxy.

Status Code	Message	HttpServletResponse Constant	Explanation
408	Request Time-out	SC_REQUEST_TIMEOUT	This is returned when the client fails to send its request within the timeout period of the server. The client can repeat the request later, if required.
			This is normally used for multi-part requests from the client.
409	Conflict	SC_CONFLICT	The server will return this code when the request cannot be completed due to a conflict in the current state of the resource. This status code should only be returned when the client may be able to resolve the conflict, and if possible the response should contain information that will help the client resolve the problem.
			The specifications envisage that these conflicts are most likely to occur in response to a PUT request in cases such as versioning conflicts. In Java terms this could occur when code or web applications are uploaded with inconsistent or incompatible versions or requiring specific versions of libraries (such as XML parsers) not available on the server. In this case the server should return information about the library (or other) conflict.
410	Gone	SC_GONE	The 410 Gone status code is used to indicate when a resource has been removed permanently with no URI to forward the request to. Links to this resource should be removed.
			Often the 404 Not Found code is used in place of this code, as it is not always practical to mark or configure every removed resource to have a 410 Gone status code returned in every case.

Table continued on following page

Status Code	Message	HttpServletResponse Constant	Explanation
411	Length Required	SC_LENGTH_REQUIRED	This code is returned in the server's response when it requires the client to define the Content-Length header. The client could repeat the request adding in the Content-Length header.
412	Precondition Failed	SC_PRECONDITION_FAILED	If one of the client's request header field preconditions (If headers) fails, the server will return this code in the response.
413	Request Entity Too Large	SC_REQUEST_ENTITY_TOO_LARGE	When the server receives a request entity larger than it is configured or able to process it may return this response code. In these cases, the Content-Length header (possibly with the 411 Length Required code) is normally used to perform the check, although a byte count of the request length may be used. The server may close the connection after reading the Content-Length and returning the code (or after the limit of bytes is reached). If this occurs as a result of a temporary situation (such as high server load) the server can include a Retry-After header to indicate that the client could try again after the specified time.
414	Request-URI Too Large	SC_REQUEST_URI_TOO_LONG	This indicates that the URI used to make the request is too long, possibly as a result of a POST request being inappropriately converted into a GET request, or simply too much path or parameter information being supplied in the request. Many servers limit the length of the URI that may be processed in a request and will return this code when that limit is exceeded.

Status Code	Message	HttpServletResponse Constant	Explanation
415	Unsupported Media Type	SC_UNSUPPORTED_ MEDIA_TYPE	A server will return this error code when the body of the request is in a format that the resource requested by the client is unable to handle.
			This could be part of a PUT request or other request such a as POST request where the data supplied is in an incorrect, or unsupported format for the resource.
			For example a servlet may be configured to handle data only in XML format and so is not configured to handle binary files, or serialized Java objects.
416	Requested range not satisfiable	SC_REQUESTED_ RANGE_NOT_SATISFIABLE	The Range header of the request condition is not satisfiable by the response resource, as it does not overlap with the range of the potential response.
417	Expectation Failed	SC_EXPECTATION_FAILED	Clients may include an Expect header in the request, which if the server is unable to satisfy it, will result in the server returning this code.

Range: 5xx - Server Error

Status Code	Message	HttpServletResponse Constant	Explanation
500*	Internal Server Error	SC_INTERNAL_ SERVER_ERROR	This indicates that an unexpected error has occurred within the server or resource processing the request and it is unable to carry out the request.
			This often occurs as a result of an error (such as a programmer's error) in the resource (for example servlet) code or of the resource not being able to process an unexpected value for a request parameter. It may also occur when the request cannot be processed because another resource required by the requested resource is not available.
			In Java terms this can mean that there is a processing error in a servlet as a result of programmer error, incorrect request parameters (normally the servlet should handle this gracefully and return a more appropriate error) or when a database, or other resource required by the servlet is unavailable. Again the code should normally handle this eventuality gracefully, but if an uncaught exception is thrown to the web container, this status code will be returned.
501*	Not Implemented	SC_NOT_IMPLEMENTED	The server will return the 501 Not Implemented status code if the request requires functionality not supported by the server. This could appear when the request method is not supported or recognized by the server.
			HTTP/1.0 servers would throw this error code if a request type that was introduced in HTTP/1.1 (such as OPTIONS or TRACE) was made to them.

Status Code	Message	HttpServletResponse Constant	Explanation
502*	Bad Gateway	SC_BAD_GATEWAY	This indicates that the HTTP server, while it was acting as a proxy or gateway server, received an invalid response from an upstream server.
503*	Service Unavailable	SC_SERVICE_ UNAVAILABLE	When a server is overloaded it may return this code to indicate that it cannot handle the request due to the server load. It may indicate, with a Retry-After header, when the client should retry the request, otherwise the client should react as if it was a 500 Internal Server Error.
			However a server that is overloaded may refuse connection or may be unable to handle the connection due to the overload.
504	Gateway Time-out	SC_GATEWAY_TIMEOUT	This indicates that the HTTP server, while it was acting as a proxy or gateway server, did not receive a response from an upstream server within the server's timeout period.
			The upstream server may be any server or auxiliary server requested or needed to serve the request (for example HTTP, FTP, DNS etc.).
505	HTTP Version not supported	SC_HTTP_VERSION_NOT_ SUPPORTED	The server does not support the version of HTTP that the request is made in. The server's response should comprise an entity including a list of other protocols supported by that server, and if possible, describe why the HTTP version is not supported.

Further Information

For further information on HTTP and the HTTP specifications see:

- ❑ http://www.w3.org/Protocols is a good general starting point for the HTTP specifications and related specifications and documents

- ❑ http://www.w3.org/Protocols/#Specs for information on the various specifications that relate to HTTP

- ❑ RFC 2616: Hypertext Transfer Protocol – HTTP/1.1: http://www.w3.org/Protocols/rfc2616/rfc2616.html

- ❑ HTTP/1.0 – Informational RFC 1945: http://www.w3.org/Protocols/rfc1945/rfc1945

For information on the HTTP Basic and Digest Authentication see:

- ❑ RFC 2617: HTTP Authentication: Basic and Digest Access Authentication: http://www.ietf.org/rfc/rfc2617.txt

For information on the State Management (and Cookies):

- ❑ HTTP State Management Mechanism – Proposed Standard RFC 2109: http://www.w3.org/Protocols/rfc2109/rfc2109

For information on MIME:

- ❑ RFC1521: MIME Part One: Mechanisms for Specifying and Describing the Format of Internet Message Bodies ftp://ftp.isi.edu/in-notes/rfc1521.txt or ftp://ftp.isi.edu/in-notes/rfc1521.pdf

- ❑ Or for information about the list and details of MIME types registered ftp://ftp.isi.edu/in-notes/iana/assignments/media-types/

Servlet 2.3 API Reference

This appendix describes the Java classes and interfaces defined in the Servlet 2.3 specification. These are contained in two packages:

- ❑ `javax.servlet` contains classes and interfaces related to servlet programming
- ❑ `javax.servlet.http` contains classes and interfaces related specifically to servlets using the HTTP protocol

In many cases, the actual objects passed will be instances of container-specific implementations of interfaces specified here, or concrete subclasses of abstract classes specified here.

javax.servlet

The `javax.servlet` package provides interfaces and classes that support servlet programming in the broadest, non-protocol-specific, sense. It includes the `Servlet` interface, which all servlets must ultimately implement.

javax.servlet Interfaces

Filter

```
public interface Filter
```

A `Filter` component can intercept a request to a resource to perform filtering tasks. The `Filter` interface has three methods:

```
public void setFilterConfig(FilterConfig filterConfig)
```

setFilterConfig() is called when the filter is instantiated, and is passed a `FilterConfig` object containing configuration information about the filter's environment.

```
public FilterConfig getFilterConfig()
```

getFilterConfig() returns the `FilterConfig` object for this filter.

```
public void doFilter(ServletRequest request,
                     ServletResponse response,
                     FilterChain chain)
         throws java.io.IOException, ServletException
```

doFilter() is called each time a request is received for a resource for which this filter is registered. An implementation would typically examine the Request object, then either invoke the next object in the `FilterChain` by calling chain.doFilter() (optionally wrapping the Request and Response objects) or generate the response itself.

FilterChain

```
public interface FilterChain
```

A `FilterChain` represents the series of filters to be invoked during a request to a resource. The `FilterChain` interface has one method:

```
public void doFilter(ServletRequest request,
                     ServletResponse response)
         throws java.io.IOException, ServletException
```

doFilter() either invokes the next filter in the chain, or (if this is the last filter in the chain) invokes the filtered resource itself.

FilterConfig

```
public interface FilterConfig
```

A `FilterConfig` object is used by the servlet container to pass configuration information to a filter while it is being initialized. The `FilterConfig` interface has four methods:

```
public String getFilterName()
```

`getFilterName()` returns the name of the filter, as declared in `web.xml`.

```
public ServletContext getServletContext()
```

`getServletContext()` returns the `ServletContext` in which this filter is running.

```
public String getInitParameter(String name)
```

`getInitParameter()` returns a `String` containing the named initialization parameter, or `null` if there is no such parameter.

```
public java.util.Enumeration getInitParameterNames()
```

`getInitParameterNames()` returns an `Enumeration` containing the names of the initialization parameters.

RequestDispatcher

```
public interface RequestDispatcher
```

A `RequestDispatcher` is an object that sends requests to the appropriate resource (servlet, HTML file, etc.) within the server. The servlet creates the `RequestDispatcher` object, which is used as a wrapper around a particular resource. A `RequestDispatcher` object was intended to wrap servlets, but can be used to wrap any type of resource on a server. The `RequestDispatcher` interface has two methods:

```
public void forward(ServletRequest request,
                    ServletResponse response)
        throws ServletException, java.io.IOException
```

`foward()` forwards a client request to another resource (servlet, HTML file, etc.). This method allows a servlet to serve as a "request processor", performing some preliminary work before sending the request to the resource that will ultimately respond to it. The `forward()` method can be used if the servlet has not already opened a `PrintWriter` or `ServletOutputStream` back to the client machine. If an output stream has been created, use the `include()` method instead. The request and response must be either the same objects that were passed to this Servlet's `service()` method, or `ServletRequestWrapper` or `ServletResponseWrapper` subclass instances that wrap them.

```
public void include(ServletRequest request,
                    ServletResponse response)
     throws ServletException, java.io.IOException
```

include() allows a resource to be included in the response to a client request. This method is used to include some content to the response after the response has been initiated by opening a PrintWriter or ServletOutputStream back to the client machine. The request and response must be either the same objects that were passed to this servlet's service() method, or ServletRequestWrapper or ServletResponseWrapper subclass instances that wrap them.

Servlet

```
public interface Servlet
```

Every servlet must implement the Servlet interface. It declares the methods that govern the lifecycle of the servlet as well as methods to access initialization parameters and information about the servlet. The Servlet interface has five methods:

```
public void init(ServletConfig config)
     throws ServletException
```

init() is called when the servlet is put into service. The ServletConfig object is used to provide the Servlet with initialization parameters.

```
public ServletConfig getServletConfig()
```

getServletConfig() returns the ServletConfig object associated with the servlet. A ServletConfig object contains parameters that are used to initialize the servlet.

```
public void service(ServletRequest req,
                    ServletResponse res)
     throws ServletException, java.io.IOException
```

service() is called to respond to a request from a client machine. The code representing what the servlet is supposed to do is placed in this method, which is only called after the init() method has completed successfully.

```
public String getServletInfo()
```

getServletInfo() returns a String containing useful information about the servlet. By default, this method returns an empty String, but it can be overridden to provide more useful information.

```
public void destroy()
```

destroy() is called when the servlet is being taken out of service, allowing the servlet to release any resources associated with it.

ServletConfig

```
public interface ServletConfig
```

A ServletConfig object is used to pass initialization parameters (name-value pairs) to a servlet during its initialization. The ServletConfig interface declares four methods, which can access the parameters, as well as returning the name of the servlet and its associated ServletContext object. A ServletContext object contains information about the server on which the servlet resides.

```
public String getServletName()
```

getServletName() returns the name of the servlet. If the servlet is unnamed, the method will return the servlet's class name.

```
public ServletContext getServletContext()
```

getServletContext() returns the ServletContext object associated with the invoking servlet. A ServletContext object contains information about the environment in which the servlet is running.

```
public String getInitParameter(String name)
```

getInitParameter() returns the value of the specified initialization parameter, or null if the parameter does not exist.

```
public java.util.Enumeration getInitParameterNames()
```

getInitParameterNames() returns an Enumeration of String objects containing the names of all of the Servlet's initialization parameters.

ServletContext

```
public interface ServletContext
```

The ServletContext interface declares 23 methods that a servlet uses to communicate with its host server, of which four are deprecated. The methods declared in this interface allow a servlet to obtain information about the server on which it is running.

```
public ServletContext getContext(String uripath)
```

getContext() returns the ServletContext object for the resource at the specified path on the server. The path argument is an absolute URL beginning with "/".

```
public int getMajorVersion()
```

getMajorVersion() returns the major version of the Java Servlet API that the server supports. For servers supporting version 2.3 of the Servlet specification, this method will return 2.

```
public int getMinorVersion()
```

getMinorVersion() returns the minor version of the Java Servlet API that the server supports. For servers supporting version 2.3 of the Servlet specification, this method will return 3.

```
public String getMimeType(String file)
```

getMimeType() returns the MIME type of the specified file or null if the MIME type cannot be ascertained. Typical return values will be "text/plain", "text/html", or "image/jpg".

```
public java.util.Set getResourcePaths()
```

getResourcePaths() returns all the paths to resources held in the web application as Strings beginning with a "/".

```
public java.net.URL getResource(String path)
        throws java.net.MalformedURLException
```

getResource() returns a URL object that is mapped to the specified path, or null if there is no resource mapped to the path. The path must begin with "/" and is interpreted relative to the current context root.

```
public java.io.InputStream getResourceAsStream(String path)
```

getResourceAsStream() returns the resource at the specified path as an InputStream object.

```
public RequestDispatcher getRequestDispatcher(String path)
```

getRequestDispatcher() returns a RequestDispatcher object that acts as a wrapper around the resource located at the specified path. The path must begin with "/", and is interpreted relative to the current context root.

```
public RequestDispatcher getNamedDispatcher(String name)
```

getNamedDispatcher() returns a RequestDispatcher object that will be wrapped around the named servlet.

```
public void log(String msg)
public void log(String message,
                Throwable throwable)
```

log() is used to write a message to the servlet engine's log file. The second version writes both an explanatory message and a stack trace for the specified Throwable exception to the log file.

```
public String getRealPath(String path)
```

getRealPath() returns a String object containing the real path, in a form appropriate to the platform on which the servlet is running, corresponding to the given virtual path. An example of a virtual path might be "/blah.html".

```
public String getServerInfo()
```

getServerInfo() returns a String object containing information on the server on which the Servlet is running. At a minimum, the String will contain the servlet container name and version number.

```
public String getInitParameter(String name)
```

getInitParameter() returns a String object containing the value of the specified initialization parameter, or null if the parameter does not exist.

```
public java.util.Enumeration getInitParameterNames()
```

getInitParameterNames() returns a Enumeration containing the initialization parameters associated with the invoking ServletContext object.

```
public Object getAttribute(String name)
```

getAttribute() returns the value of the specified attribute name. The return value is an Object or sub-class if the attribute is available to the invoking ServletContext object, or null if the attribute is not available.

```
public java.util.Enumeration getAttributeNames()
```

getAttributeNames() returns an Enumeration containing the attribute names available to the invoking ServletContext object.

```
public void setAttribute(String name,
                         Object object)
```

setAttribute() binds a value to a specified attribute name.

```
public void removeAttribute(String name)
```

removeAttribute() makes the specified attribute unavailable to the invoking ServletContext object. Subsequent calls to the getAttribute() method for this attribute will return null.

```
public String getServletContextName()
```

getServletContextName() returns the name of the web application, as specified in the <display-name> element in web.xml.

```
public Servlet getServlet(String name)
        throws ServletException
public java.util.Enumeration getServlets()
public java.util.Enumeration getServletNames()
public void log(Exception exception,
                String msg)
```

These methods are deprecated.

ServletContextAttributesListener

```
public interface ServletContextAttributesListener
   extends java.util.EventListener
```

An object implementing ServletContextAttributesListener can be registered to receive notification when attributes are added to, removed from, or replaced in the ServletContext. This interface declares three methods:

```
public void attributeAdded(ServletContextAttributeEvent scab)
```

attributeAdded() is called when an attribute is added to the ServletContext. It is passed a ServletContextAttributeEvent containing information about the event.

```
public void attributeRemoved(ServletContextAttributeEvent scab)
```

attributeRemoved() is called when an attribute is removed from the ServletContext. It is passed a ServletContextAttributeEvent containing information about the event.

```
public void attributeReplaced(ServletContextAttributeEvent scab)
```

attributeReplaced() is called when a ServletContext attribute is replaced. It is passed a ServletContextAttributeEvent containing information about the event.

ServletContextListener

```
public interface ServletContextListener
   extends java.util.EventListener
```

An object implementing ServletContextListener can be registered to receive notification when the ServletContext is initialized or destroyed. This interface declares two methods.

```
public void contextInitialized(ServletContextEvent sce)
```

contextInitialized() is called when the ServletContext is initialized. It is passed a ServletContextEvent containing information about the event.

```
public void contextDestroyed(ServletContextEvent sce)
```

contextDestroyed() is called when the ServletContext is destroyed. It is passed a ServletContextEvent containing information about the event.

ServletRequest

```
public interface ServletRequest
```

The ServletRequest interface contains 25 methods that are used to provide client request information to a servlet, of which one is deprecated. This information can include parameter name-value pairs, attributes, and an input stream. A ServletRequest object is passed to the service() method defined in the Servlet interface, as well as the forward() and include() methods from the RequestDispatcher interface.

```
public Object getAttribute(String name)
```

getAttribute() returns the value of the specified request attribute name. The return value is an Object or sub-class if the attribute is available to the invoking ServletRequest object, or null if the attribute is not available.

```
public java.util.Enumeration getAttributeNames()
```

getAttributeNames() returns an Enumeration containing the attribute names available to the invoking ServletRequest object.

```
public String getCharacterEncoding()
```

getCharacterEncoding() returns a String object containing the character encoding used in the body of the request, or null if there is no encoding.

```
public void setCharacterEncoding(String env)
        throws java.io.UnsupportedEncodingException
```

setCharacterEncoding() overrides the character encoding used in the body of this request.

```
public int getContentLength()
```

getContentLength() returns the length of the body of the request in bytes, or –1 if the length is not known.

```
public String getContentType()
```

getContentType() returns a String object containing the MIME type ("text/plain", "text/html", "image/gif", etc.) of the body of the request, or null if the type is not known.

```
public ServletInputStream getInputStream()
        throws java.io.IOException
```

getInputStream() returns a ServletInputStream object that can be used to read the body of the request as binary data.

```
public String getParameter(String name)
```

getParameter() returns a String object containing the value of the specified parameter, or null if the parameter does not exist.

```
public java.util.Enumeration getParameterNames()
```

getParameterNames() returns a Enumeration containing the parameters contained within the invoking ServletRequest object.

```
public String[] getParameterValues(String name)
```

getParamterValues() is used when a parameter may have more than one value associated with it. The method returns a String array containing the values of the specified parameter, or null if the parameter does not exist.

```
public java.util.Map getParameterMap()
```

getParameterMap() returns a Map containing the request parameters.

```
public String getProtocol()
```

getProtocol() returns the name and version of the protocol used by the request. A typical return String would be "HTTP/1.1".

```
public String getScheme()
```

getScheme() returns the scheme ("http", "https", "ftp", etc.) used to make the request.

```
public String getServerName()
```

getServerName() returns a String object containing the name of the server that received the request.

```
public int getServerPort()
```

getServerPort() returns the port number that received the request.

```
public java.io.BufferedReader getReader()
        throws java.io.IOException
```

getReader() returns a BufferedReader object that can be used to read the body of the request as character data.

```
public String getRemoteAddr()
```

getRemoteAddr() returns a String object containing the IP address of the client machine that made the request.

```
public String getRemoteHost()
```

getRemoteHost() returns a String object containing the name of the client machine or the IP address if the name cannot be determined.

```
public void setAttribute(String name,
                         Object o)
```

setAttribute() binds a value to a specified attribute name. Note that attributes will be re-set after the request is handled.

```
public void removeAttribute(String name)
```

removeAttribute() makes the specified attribute unavailable to the invoking ServletRequest object. Subsequent calls to the getAttribute() method for this attribute will return null.

```
public java.util.Locale getLocale()
```

getLocale() returns the preferred locale of the client that made the request.

```
public java.util.Enumeration getLocales()
```

getLocales() returns an Enumeration containing, in descending order of preference, the locales that are acceptable to the client machine.

```
public boolean isSecure()
```

isSecure() returns true if the request was made using a secure channel, for example HTTPS.

```
public RequestDispatcher getRequestDispatcher(String path)
```

getRequestDispatcher() returns a RequestDispatcher object that acts as a wrapper around the resource located at the specified path. The path must begin with "/" and can be a relative path.

```
public String getRealPath(String path)
```

This method is deprecated – use ServletContext.getRealPath() instead.

ServletResponse

```
public interface ServletResponse
```

The ServletResponse interface declares 13 methods that are used to assist the servlet in sending a response to the client machine.

```
public String getCharacterEncoding()
```

getCharacterEncoding() returns a String object containing the character encoding used in the body of the response. The default is "ISO-8859-1", which corresponds to Latin-1.

```
public ServletOutputStream getOutputStream()
        throws java.io.IOException
```

getOutputStream() returns a ServletOutputStream object that can be used to write the response as binary data.

```
public java.io.PrintWriter getWriter()
        throws java.io.IOException
```

getWriter() returns a PrintWriter object that can be used to write the response as character data.

```
public void setContentLength(int len)
```

setContentLength() sets the length of the response body.

```
public void setContentType(String type)
```

setContentType() sets the content type of the response sent to the server. The String argument specifies a MIME type and may also include the type of character encoding, for example "text/plain; charset=ISO-8859-1".

```
public void setBufferSize(int size)
```

setBufferSize() requests a buffer size to be used for the response. The actual buffer size will be at least this large.

```
public int getBufferSize()
```

getBufferSize() returns the buffer size used for the response, or 0 if no buffering is used.

```
public void flushBuffer()
        throws java.io.IOException
```

flushBuffer() causes any content stored in the buffer to be written to the client. Calling this method will also commit the response, meaning that the status code and headers will be written.

```
public void resetBuffer()
```

resetBuffer() clears the content of the response buffer without clearing the headers or status code. It will throw an IllegalStateException if the response has been committed.

```
public boolean isCommitted()
```

`isCommitted()` returns `true` if the response has been committed, meaning that the status code and headers have been written.

```
public void reset()
```

`reset()` clears the status code and headers, and any data that exists in the buffer. If the response has already been committed, calling this method will cause an exception to be thrown.

```
public void setLocale(java.util.Locale loc)
```

`setLocale()` specifies the locale that will be used for the response.

```
public java.util.Locale getLocale()
```

`getLocale()` returns the locale that has been assigned to the response. By default, this will be the default locale for the server.

SingleThreadModel

```
public interface SingleThreadModel
```

The `SingleThreadModel` interface declares no methods. A servlet that implements this interface will allow only one request at a time to access its `service()` method. The server will achieve this by either synchronizing access to a single instance of the servlet, or by assigning a separate instance of the servlet for each request.

javax.servlet Classes

GenericServlet

```
public abstract class GenericServlet
    extends Object
        implements Servlet, ServletConfig, java.io.Serializable
```

The `GenericServlet` class defines a generic, protocol-independent servlet. It provides implementations of the methods declared in the `Servlet` and `ServletConfig` interfaces. Since `GenericServlet` is an abstract class, a `GenericServlet` object is never created. To create a generic servlet, a class must be written that extends the `GenericServlet` class and overrides the `service()` method.

```
public GenericServlet()
```

This constructor does nothing. The `init()` methods are used for servlet initialization.

```
public void destroy()
```

destroy() unloads the servlet from the server's memory and releases any resources associated with it.

```
public String getInitParameter(String name)
```

getInitParameter() returns the value of the specified initialization parameter from the ServletConfig object associated with the invoking GenericServlet object.

```
public java.util.Enumeration getInitParameterNames()
```

getInitParameterNames() returns an Enumeration of String objects containing the names of all of the Servlet's initialization parameters.

```
public ServletConfig getServletConfig()
```

getServletConfig() returns the ServletConfig object associated with the invoking GenericServlet sub-class object. A ServletConfig object contains parameters that are used to initialize the Servlet.

```
public ServletContext getServletContext()
```

getServletContext() returns the ServletContext object associated with the invoking GenericServlet sub-class object. A ServletContext object contains information about the environment in which the servlet is running.

```
public String getServletInfo()
```

getServletInfo() returns a String containing useful information about the servlet. By default, this method returns an empty String. It can be overridden to provide more useful information.

```
public void init(ServletConfig config)
        throws ServletException
public void init()
        throws ServletException
```

init() is called when the servlet is loaded into the address space of the server. If a ServletConfig object is specified, it can be used to provide the servlet with initialization parameters. The no-argument version is provided as a convenience, for sub-classes to override.

```
public void log(String msg)
public void log(String message,
                Throwable t)
```

log() is used to write a message to the servlet's log file. The second version writes an explanatory message and a stack trace for the specified Throwable exception to the log file.

```
public abstract void service(ServletRequest req,
                             ServletResponse res)
        throws ServletException, java.io.IOException
```

`service()` is called to respond to a request from a client machine. The code representing what the servlet is supposed to do is placed in this method. As this method is declared abstract, a concrete implementation must be provided by a concrete (non-abstract) sub-class of `GenericServlet`.

```
public String getServletName()
```

`getServletName()` returns the name of the invoking `GenericServlet` object.

ServletContextAttributeEvent

```
public class ServletContextAttributeEvent
    extends ServletContextEvent
```

A `ServletContextAttributeEvent` is the event object used when an attribute is added to, removed from, or replaced in the `ServletContext`.

```
public ServletContextAttributeEvent(ServletContext source,
                                    String name,
                                    Object value)
```

The constructor simply requires references to the `ServletContext` in which the event took place, and the name and value of the attribute.

```
public String getName()
```

`getName()` returns the name of the new/removed/replaced attribute.

```
public Object getValue()
```

`getValue()` returns the name of the new/removed/replaced attribute.

ServletContextEvent

```
public class ServletContextEvent
    extends java.util.EventObject
```

A `ServletContextEvent` is the event object used when a `ServletContext` is created or destroyed.

```
public ServletContextEvent(ServletContext source)
```

The constructor takes a reference to the `ServletContext` in question.

```
public ServletContext getServletContext()
```

`getServletContext()` returns `ServletContext` in which the event took place.

ServletInputStream

```
public abstract class ServletInputStream
   extends java.io.InputStream
```

The ServletInputStream class is used to read binary data from a client request when the HTTP POST and PUT methods are used. It provides a single method in addition to those in InputStream, which reads the data one line at a time.

```
protected ServletInputStream()
```

This constructor does nothing. Because ServletInputStream is an abstract class, a ServletInputStream object is never created directly.

```
public int readLine(byte[] b,
                    int off,
                    int len)
         throws java.io.IOException
```

readLine() reads data one line at a time and stores it in a byte array (b). The read operation starts at the specified offset (off) and continues until the specified number of bytes is read (len), or a newline character is reached. The newline character is stored in the byte array as well. The method returns −1 if the end-of-file is reached before the specified number of bytes is read.

ServletOutputStream

```
public abstract class ServletOutputStream
   extends java.io.OutputStream
```

The ServletOutputStream class is used to write binary data to a client machine. It provides overloaded versions of the print() and println() methods that can handle primitive and String datatypes.

```
protected ServletOutputStream()
```

This constructor does nothing. Since ServletOutputStream is an abstract class, a ServletOutputStream object is never created directly.

```
public void print(String s)
        throws java.io.IOException
public void print(boolean b)
        throws java.io.IOException
public void print(char c)
        throws java.io.IOException
public void print(int i)
        throws java.io.IOException
public void print(long l)
        throws java.io.IOException
public void print(float f)
        throws java.io.IOException
public void print(double d)
        throws java.io.IOException
```

print() prints the specified primitive datatype or String to the client, without a carriage return/line feed at the end.

```
public void println(String s)
        throws java.io.IOException
public void println(boolean b)
        throws java.io.IOException
public void println(char c)
        throws java.io.IOException
public void println(int i)
        throws java.io.IOException
public void println(long l)
        throws java.io.IOException
public void println(float f)
        throws java.io.IOException
public void println(double d)
        throws java.io.IOException
```

print() prints the specified primitive datatype or String to the client, followed by a carriage return/line feed.

```
public void println()
        throws java.io.IOException
```

The no-argument version of println() simply writes a carriage return/line feed to the client.

ServletRequestWrapper

```
public class ServletRequestWrapper
  extends Object
    implements ServletRequest
```

ServletRequestWrapper provides an implementation of ServletRequest that can be subclassed when it is desired to adapt in some way the request to a Servlet. By default, its methods call the same methods on the wrapped Request object.

```
public ServletRequestWrapper(ServletRequest request)
```

The constructor creates a ServletRequestWrapper around the specified ServletRequest object.

```
public ServletRequest getRequest()
```

getRequest() returns the wrapped ServletRequest.

```
public void setRequest(ServletRequest request)
```

setRequest() sets the ServletRequest to be wrapped.

```
public Object getAttribute(String name)
public java.util.Enumeration getAttributeNames()
public String getCharacterEncoding()
public void setCharacterEncoding(String enc)
        throws java.io.UnsupportedEncodingException
public int getContentLength()
public String getContentType()
public ServletInputStream getInputStream()
        throws java.io.IOException
public String getParameter(String name)
public java.util.Map getParameterMap()
public java.util.Enumeration getParameterNames()
public String[] getParameterValues(String name)
public String getProtocol()
public String getScheme()
public String getServerName()
public int getServerPort()
public java.io.BufferedReader getReader()
        throws java.io.IOException
public String getRemoteAddr()
public String getRemoteHost()
public void setAttribute(String name,
                         Object o)
public void removeAttribute(String name)
public java.util.Locale getLocale()
public java.util.Enumeration getLocales()
public boolean isSecure()
public RequestDispatcher getRequestDispatcher(String path)
public String getRealPath(String path)
```

These methods, unless overridden in a subclass, call the equivalent method on the wrapped ServletRequest.

ServletResponseWrapper

```
public class ServletResponseWrapper
   extends Object
     implements ServletResponse
```

ServletResponseWrapper provides an implementation of ServletResponse that can be subclassed when it is desired to adapt in some way the response from a servlet. By default, its methods call the same methods on the wrapped Response object.

```
public ServletResponseWrapper(ServletResponse response)
```

The constructor creates a ServletResponseWrapper around the specified ServletResponse object.

```
public ServletResponse getResponse()
```

getResponse() returns the wrapped `ServletResponse`.

```
public void setResponse(ServletResponse response)
```

setResponse() sets the `ServletResponse` to be wrapped.

```
public String getCharacterEncoding()
public ServletOutputStream getOutputStream()
        throws java.io.IOException
public java.io.PrintWriter getWriter()
        throws java.io.IOException
public void setContentLength(int len)
public void setContentType(String type)
public void setBufferSize(int size)
public int getBufferSize()
public void flushBuffer()
        throws java.io.IOException
public boolean isCommitted()
public void reset()
public void resetBuffer()
public void setLocale(java.util.Locale loc)
public java.util.Locale getLocale()
```

These methods, unless overridden in a subclass, call the equivalent method on the wrapped `ServletRequest`.

javax.servlet Exceptions

ServletException

```
public class ServletException
   extends Exception
```

`ServletException` is a general exception thrown by Servlets in difficulty.

```
public ServletException()
public ServletException(String message)
public ServletException(String message,
                        Throwable rootCause)
public ServletException(Throwable rootCause)
```

The constructors allow a `String` message and/or a `Throwable` representing the root cause of the problem to be encapsulated.

```
public Throwable getRootCause()
```

getRootCause() returns the `Throwable` that was the root cause of this exception.

UnavailableException

```
public class UnavailableException
extends ServletException
```

UnavailableException is thrown by a servlet to indicate that it is unavailable, either permanently or temporarily.

```
public UnavailableException(String msg)
```

This constructor indicates that the Servlet is permanently unavailable. The String parameter is a message describing the problem.

```
public UnavailableException(String msg,
                           int seconds)
```

This constructor indicates that the servlet is temporarily unavailable. It must be passed a String describing the problem, and an estimate in seconds of how long the servlet will be unavailable. (Zero or a negative number indicate that it is impossible to estimate.)

```
public boolean isPermanent()
```

isPermanent() returns true if the servlet is permanently unavailable.

```
public int getUnavailableSeconds()
```

getUnavailableSeconds() returns the estimated number of seconds that the servlet will be unavailable.

```
public UnavailableException(Servlet Servlet,
                            String msg)
public UnavailableException(int seconds,
                            Servlet Servlet,
                            String msg)
public Servlet getServlet()
```

These constructors and methods are deprecated.

javax.servlet.http

The javax.servlet.http package provides classes and interfaces that are used to create HTTP protocol-specific servlets. The abstract class HttpServlet is a base class for user-defined HTTP servlets and provides methods to process HTTP DELETE, GET, OPTIONS, POST, PUT, and TRACE requests. The Cookie class allows objects containing state information to be placed on a client machine and accessed by a servlet. The package also enables session tracking through the HttpSession interface.

javax.servlet.http Interfaces

HttpServletRequest

```
public interface HttpServletRequest
   extends ServletRequest
```

The HttpServletRequest interface extends ServletRequest to provide methods that can be used to obtain information about a request to an HttpServlet.

```
public static final String BASIC_AUTH
public static final String FORM_AUTH
public static final String CLIENT_CERT_AUTH
public static final String DIGEST_AUTH
```

These String constants are used to identify the different types of authentication that may have been used to protect the servlet. They have the values "BASIC", "FORM", "CLIENT_CERT", and "DIGEST" respectively.

```
public String getAuthType()
```

getAuthType() returns the name of the authentication scheme used in the request, or null if no authentication scheme was used.

```
public Cookie[] getCookies()
```

getCookies() returns an array containing any Cookie objects sent with the request, or null if no cookies were sent.

```
public long getDateHeader(String name)
```

getDateHeader() returns a long value that converts the date specified in the named header to the number of milliseconds since January 1, 1970 GMT. This method is used with a header that contains a date, and returns -1 if the request does not contain the specified header.

```
public String getHeader(String name)
```

getHeader() returns the value of the specified header expressed as a String object, or null if the request does not contain the specified header.

```
public java.util.Enumeration getHeaders(String name)
```

getHeaders() returns an Enumeration containing all of the values associated with the specified header name. The method returns an empty enumeration if the request does not contain the specified header.

```
public java.util.Enumeration getHeaderNames()
```

653

getHeaderNames() returns an Enumeration containing all of the header names used by the request.

```
public int getIntHeader(String name)
```

getIntHeader() returns the value of the specified header as an int. It returns -1 if the request does not contain the specified header, and throws a NumberFormatException if the header value cannot be converted to an int.

```
public String getMethod()
```

getMethod() returns the name of the HTTP method used to make the request. Typical return values are "GET", "POST", or "PUT".

```
public String getPathInfo()
```

getPathInfo() returns any additional path information contained in the request URL. This extra information will be after the servlet path and before the query string. It returns null if there is no additional path information.

```
public String getPathTranslated()
```

getPathTranslated() returns the same information as the getPathInfo() method, but translated into a real path.

```
public String getContextPath()
```

getContextPath() returns the part of the request URI that indicates the context path of the request. The context path is the first part of the URI and always begins with the "/" character. For servlets running in the root context, this method returns an empty String.

```
public String getQueryString()
```

getQueryString() returns the query string that was contained in the request URL, or null if there was no query string.

```
public String getRemoteUser()
```

getRemoteUser() returns the login of the user making the request, or null if the user has not been authenticated.

```
public boolean isUserInRole(String role)
```

isUserInRole() returns true if the authenticated user has the specified logical role, or false if the user is not authenticated.

```
public java.security.Principal getUserPrincipal()
```

getUserPrincipal() returns a Principal object representing the authenticated user, or null if the user is not authenticated.

```
public String getRequestedSessionId()
```

getRequestedSessionId() returns the session ID that was specified by the client, or null if the request did not specify an ID.

```
public String getRequestURI()
```

getRequestURI() returns a sub-section of the request URL, from the protocol name to the query string.

```
public StringBuffer getRequestURL()
```

getRequestURL() reconstructs the URL used to make the request including the protocol, server name, port number, and path, but excluding the query string.

```
public String getServletPath()
```

getServletPath() returns the part of the request URL that was used to call the servlet, without any additional information or the query string.

```
public HttpSession getSession(boolean create)
public HttpSession getSession()
```

getSession() returns the HttpSession object associated with the request. By default, if the request does not currently have a session calling this method will create one. Setting the boolean parameter create to false overrides this.

```
public boolean isRequestedSessionIdValid()
```

isRequestedSessionIdValid() returns true if the session ID requested by the client is still valid.

```
public boolean isRequestedSessionIdFromCookie()
```

isRequestedSessionIdFromCookie() returns true if the session ID came in from a cookie.

```
public boolean isRequestedSessionIdFromURL()
```

isRequestedSessionIdFromURL() returns true if the session ID came in as part of the request URL.

```
public boolean isRequestedSessionIdFromUrl()
```

This method is deprecated.

HttpServletResponse

```
public interface HttpServletResponse
  extends ServletResponse
```

The HttpServletResponse interface extends the functionality of the ServletResponse interface by providing methods to access HTTP-specific features such as HTTP headers and cookies.

```
public static final int SC_CONTINUE
public static final int SC_SWITCHING_PROTOCOLS
public static final int SC_OK
public static final int SC_CREATED
public static final int SC_ACCEPTED
public static final int SC_NON_AUTHORITATIVE_INFORMATION
public static final int SC_NO_CONTENT
public static final int SC_RESET_CONTENT
public static final int SC_PARTIAL_CONTENT
public static final int SC_MULTIPLE_CHOICES
public static final int SC_MOVED_PERMANENTLY
public static final int SC_MOVED_TEMPORARILY
public static final int SC_SEE_OTHER
public static final int SC_NOT_MODIFIED
public static final int SC_USE_PROXY
public static final int SC_BAD_REQUEST
public static final int SC_UNAUTHORIZED
public static final int SC_PAYMENT_REQUIRED
public static final int SC_FORBIDDEN
public static final int SC_NOT_FOUND
public static final int SC_METHOD_NOT_ALLOWED
public static final int SC_NOT_ACCEPTABLE
public static final int SC_PROXY_AUTHENTICATION_REQUIRED
public static final int SC_REQUEST_TIMEOUT
public static final int SC_CONFLICT
public static final int SC_GONE
public static final int SC_LENGTH_REQUIRED
public static final int SC_PRECONDITION_FAILED
public static final int SC_REQUEST_ENTITY_TOO_LARGE
public static final int SC_REQUEST_URI_TOO_LONG
public static final int SC_UNSUPPORTED_MEDIA_TYPE
public static final int SC_REQUESTED_RANGE_NOT_SATISFIABLE
public static final int SC_EXPECTATION_FAILED
public static final int SC_INTERNAL_SERVER_ERROR
public static final int SC_NOT_IMPLEMENTED
public static final int SC_BAD_GATEWAY
public static final int SC_SERVICE_UNAVAILABLE
public static final int SC_GATEWAY_TIMEOUT
public static final int SC_HTTP_VERSION_NOT_SUPPORTED
```

These constants represent the status codes defined in the HTTP specification (see Appendix B for further details).

```
public void addCookie(Cookie cookie)
```

`addCookie()` adds the specified cookie to the response (more than one cookie can be added).

```
public boolean containsHeader(String name)
```

`containsHeader()` returns `true` if the response header includes the specified header name. This method can be used before calling one of the `set()` methods to determine if the value has already been set.

```
public String encodeURL(String url)
```

`encodeURL()` encodes the specified URL by including the session ID or returns it unchanged if encoding is not needed. All URLs generated by a servlet should be processed through this method to ensure compatibility with browsers that do not support cookies.

```
public String encodeRedirectURL(String url)
```

`encodeRedirectURL()` encodes the specified URL or returns it unchanged if encoding is not required. This method is used to process a URL before sending it to the `sendRedirect()` method.

```
public void sendError(int sc,
                      String msg)
        throws java.io.IOException
public void sendError(int sc)
        throws java.io.IOException
```

`sendError()` sends an error response back to the client machine using the specified error status code. A descriptive message can also be provided. This method must be called before the response is committed (in other words, before the status code and headers have been written).

```
public void sendRedirect(String location)
        throws java.io.IOException
```

`sendRedirect()` redirects the client machine to the specified URL. This method must be called before the response is committed (in other words, before the status code and headers have been written).

```
public void setDateHeader(String name,
                          long date)
```

`setDateHeader()` sets the time value of a response header for the specified header name. The time is the number of milliseconds since January 1, 1970 GMT. If the time value for the specified header has been previously set, the value passed to this method will override it.

```
public void addDateHeader(String name,
                          long date)
```

`addDateHeader()` adds a response header containing the specified header name and the number of milliseconds since January 1, 1970 GMT. This method can be used to assign multiple values to a given header name.

```
public void setHeader(String name,
                      String value)
```

setHeader() sets a response header with the specified name and value. If the value for the specified header has been previously set, the value passed to this method will override it.

```
public void addHeader(String name,
                      String value)
```

addHeader() adds a response header with the specified name and value. This method can be used to assign multiple values to a given header name.

```
public void setIntHeader(String name,
                         int value)
```

setIntHeader() sets a response header with the specified name and int value. If the int value for the specified header has been previously set, the value passed to this method will override it.

```
public void addIntHeader(String name,
                         int value)
```

addIntHeader() adds a response header with the specified name and int value. This method can be used to assign multiple values to a given header name.

```
public void setStatus(int sc)
```

setStatus() sets the return status code for the response. The status code should be one of SC_ACCEPTED, SC_OK, SC_CONTINUE, SC_PARTIAL_CONTENT, SC_CREATED, SC_SWITCHING_PROTOCOLS, or SC_NO_CONTENT.

```
public String encodeUrl(String url)
public String encodeRedirectUrl(String url)
public void setStatus(int sc,
                      String sm)
```

These methods are deprecated.

HttpSession

```
public interface HttpSession
```

The HttpSession interface provides methods that define a session between a client and server, despite the stateless nature of the HTTP protocol. The session lasts for a specified time period and can encompass more than one connection or page request from the user. The methods declared by this interface allow access to information about the session and enable the binding of objects to sessions. The bound object can contain the state information that each request should be able to access.

```
public long getCreationTime()
```

getCreationTime() returns the time when the session was created in milliseconds since midnight Jan 1, 1970 GMT.

    public String **getId**()

getId() returns a String object containing a unique identifier for this session.

    public long **getLastAccessedTime**()

getLastAccessedTime() returns the last time a client request associated with the session was sent. The return value is the number of milliseconds since midnight Jan 1, 1970 GMT.

    public void **setMaxInactiveInterval**(int *interval*)

setMaxInactiveInterval() specifies the number of seconds the server will wait between client requests before the session is invalidated. If a negative value is passed to this method, the session will never time out.

    public int **getMaxInactiveInterval**()

getMaxInactiveInterval() returns the number of seconds the server will wait between client requests before the session is invalidated. A negative return value indicates the session will never time out.

    public Object **getAttribute**(String *name*)

getAttribute() returns the Object bound to the specified name in this session, or null if it doesn't exist.

    public java.util.Enumeration **getAttributeNames**()

getAttributeNames() returns an Enumeration of String objects containing the names of all the objects bound to this session.

    public void **setAttribute**(String *name*,
                             Object *value*)

setAttribute() binds an Object to the specified attribute name, in this session. If the attribute name already exists, the Object passed to this method will replace the previous Object.

    public void **removeAttribute**(String *name*)

removeAttribute() removes the Object bound to the specified name from this session.

    public void **invalidate**()

invalidate() invalidates the session and unbinds any objects bound to it.

```
public boolean isNew()
```

isNew() returns true if the server has created a session that has not yet been accessed by a client.

```
public HttpSessionContext getSessionContext()
public Object getValue(String name)
public String[] getValueNames()
public void putValue(String name,
                          Object value)
public void removeValue(String name)
```

These methods have been deprecated.

HttpSessionActivationListener

```
public interface HttpSessionActivationListener
```

Objects implementing the HttpSessionActivationListener interface will be informed when the session they are bound to is going to be passivated and activated, for example when a session is going to be persisted or migrated to another Virtual Machine.

```
public void sessionWillPassivate(HttpSessionEvent se)
```

sessionWillPassivate() is called when the session is about to be passivated.

```
public void sessionDidActivate(HttpSessionEvent se)
```

sessionDidActivate() is called when the session has just been activated.

HttpSessionAttributeListener

```
public interface HttpSessionAttributeListener
   extends java.util.EventListener
```

An object implementing HttpSessionAttributeListener can be registered to receive notification when attributes are added to, removed from, or replaced in the HttpSession.

```
public void attributeAdded(HttpSessionBindingEvent se)
```

attributeAdded() is called when an attribute is added to the HttpSession. It is passed an HttpSessionBindingEvent containing information about the event.

```
public void attributeRemoved(HttpSessionBindingEvent se)
```

attributeRemoved() is called when an attribute is removed from the HttpSession. It is passed an HttpSessionBindingEvent containing information about the event.

```
public void attributeReplaced(HttpSessionBindingEvent se)
```

attributeReplaced() is called when an `HttpSession` attribute is replaced. It is passed an `HttpSessionBindingEvent` containing information about the event.

HttpSessionBindingListener

```
public interface HttpSessionBindingListener
    extends java.util.EventListener
```

The methods declared in the `HttpSessionBindingListener` interface are called when an object is bound to or unbound from a session.

```
public void valueBound(HttpSessionBindingEvent event)
```

valueBound() is called when an object is being bound to a session.

```
public void valueUnbound(HttpSessionBindingEvent event)
```

valueUnbound() is called when an object is being unbound from a session.

HttpSessionContext

```
public interface HttpSessionContext
```

This interface is deprecated.

```
public HttpSession getSession(String sessionId)
public java.util.Enumeration getIds()
```

These methods are deprecated.

HttpSessionListener

```
public interface HttpSessionListener
```

An object implementing `HttpSessionListener` can be registered to receive notification when an `HttpSession` is created or destroyed.

```
public void sessionCreated(HttpSessionEvent se)
```

sessionCreated() is called when a session is created. It is passed an `HttpSessionEvent` containing information about the event.

```
public void sessionDestroyed(HttpSessionEvent se)
```

sessionDestroyed() is called when a session is destroyed. It is passed an `HttpSessionEvent` containing information about the event.

javax.servlet.http Classes

Cookie

```
public class Cookie
    extends Object
        implements Cloneable
```

A Cookie is an object that resides on a client machine and contains state information; each cookie has a name, a single value, and some other optional information. Cookies can be used to identify a particular user and provide information such as name, address, account number, etc. They are sent by a server to a web browser, saved on the client machine, and can later be sent back to the server.

The optional information that can be attached to a cookie includes an expiration date, path and domain qualifiers, a version number, and a comment. The expiration date specifies when the cookie will be deleted from the client machine. If no date is given, the cookie is deleted when the session ends.

A Servlet sends cookies to a browser using the addCookie() method defined in the HttpServletResponse interface, which adds fields to the HTTP response header. The browser returns cookies to the servlet by adding fields to the HTTP request header, and the cookies can be retrieved from a request by invoking the getCookies() method defined in the HttpServletRequest interface.

```
public Cookie(String name,
              String value)
```

Creates a Cookie object with a specified name and value. The name must consist only of alphanumeric characters. Once the name is set by the constructor, it cannot be changed.

```
public void setComment(String purpose)
```

setComment() changes or sets the comment associated with the Cookie object. A Cookie can contain a comment that is normally used to describe the purpose of the Cookie.

```
public String getComment()
```

getComment() returns the comment associated with the Cookie object, or null if there is no comment.

```
public void setDomain(String pattern)
```

setDomain() sets the domain name within which the Cookie will be visible.

```
public String getDomain()
```

getDomain() returns the domain name set for the Cookie object.

```
public void setMaxAge(int expiry)
```

setMaxAge() sets the length of time in seconds that the Cookie will persist on the user's machine. A negative value means the Cookie will not be stored on the user's machine and will be deleted when the browser terminates. A value of zero means the Cookie will be deleted immediately.

```
public int getMaxAge()
```

getMaxAge() returns the length of time in seconds that the Cookie will persist on the user's machine. A return value of –1 indicates that the cookie will persist until the browser shuts down.

```
public void setPath(String uri)
```

setPath() specifies the path on the server where the browser will return the Cookie object. The Cookie will also be visible to all sub-directories of the specified path.

```
public String getPath()
```

getPath() returns the path on the server where the browser will return the Cookie object.

```
public void setSecure(boolean flag)
```

setSecure() specifies whether the browser should send the Cookie object using a secure protocol. The default is false, meaning the Cookie will be sent using any protocol.

```
public boolean getSecure()
```

getSecure() returns true if the browser will send the Cookie object using a secure protocol.

```
public String getName()
```

getName() returns the name of the Cookie object.

```
public void setValue(String newValue)
```

setValue() changes the value of the Cookie object.

```
public String getValue()
```

getValue() returns a String containing the value of the Cookie object.

```
public void setVersion(int v)
```

setVersion() sets the version number of the protocol with which the Cookie complies: 0 for the original Netscape specification, or 1 for cookies compliant with RFC 2109.

```
public int getVersion()
```

getVersion() returns 0 if the invoking Cookie object complies with the original Netscape specification, or 1 if it complies with RFC 2109.

```
public Object clone()
```

clone() overrides the clone() method from the Object class to return a copy of the Cookie object.

HttpServlet

```
public abstract class HttpServlet
  extends GenericServlet
    implements java.io.Serializable
```

The HttpServlet class extends GenericServlet to provide functionality tailored to the HTTP protocol. It provides methods for handling HTTP DELETE, GET, OPTIONS, POST, PUT, and TRACE requests. Like the GenericServlet class, the HttpServlet class provides a service() method, but unlike the GenericServlet class the service() method is rarely overridden since the default implementation of service() dispatches the request to the appropriate handler method.

A concrete sub-class of HttpServlet must override at least one of the methods defined in the HttpServlet or GenericServlet classes. The doDelete(), doGet(), doPost(), and doPut() methods are the ones most commonly overridden.

```
public HttpServlet()
```

This constructor does nothing. As HttpServlet is an abstract class, an HttpServlet object is never created directly.

```
protected void doGet(HttpServletRequest req,
                     HttpServletResponse resp)
        throws ServletException, java.io.IOException
```

doGet() is called by the server via the service() method to handle an HTTP GET request. A GET request allows a client to send form data to a server. With the GET request, the form data is attached to the end of the URL sent by the browser to the server as a query string. The amount of form data that can be sent is limited to the maximum length of the URL.

```
protected void doHead(HttpServletRequest req,
                      HttpServletResponse resp)
        throws ServletException, java.io.IOException
```

doHead() is called by the server via the service() method to handle an HTTP HEAD request. A HEAD request allows a client to retrieve only the response headers, rather than the body.

```
protected void doPost(HttpServletRequest req,
                      HttpServletResponse resp)
        throws ServletException, java.io.IOException
```

doPost() is called by the server via the service() method to handle an HTTP POST request. A POST request allows a client to send form data to a server. With the POST request, the form data is sent to the server separately instead of being appended to the URL. This allows a large amount of form data to be sent.

```
protected void doPut(HttpServletRequest req,
                     HttpServletResponse resp)
        throws ServletException, java.io.IOException
```

doPut() is called by the server via the service() method to handle an HTTP PUT request. A PUT request allows a client to place a file on the server and is conceptually similar to sending the file to the server via FTP.

```
protected void doDelete(HttpServletRequest req,
                        HttpServletResponse resp)
        throws ServletException, java.io.IOException
```

doDelete() is called by the server via the service() method to handle an HTTP DELETE request. A DELETE request allows a client to remove a document or web page from a server.

```
protected void doOptions(HttpServletRequest req,
                         HttpServletResponse resp)
        throws ServletException, java.io.IOException
```

doOptions() is called by the server via the service() method to handle an HTTP OPTIONS request. An OPTIONS request determines which HTTP methods the server supports and sends the information back to the client by way of a header.

```
protected void doTrace(HttpServletRequest req,
                       HttpServletResponse resp)
        throws ServletException, java.io.IOException
```

doTrace() is called by the server via the service() method to handle an HTTP TRACE request. A TRACE request returns the headers sent with the TRACE request back to the client. This can be useful for debugging purposes. This method is rarely overridden.

```
protected long getLastModified(HttpServletRequest req)
```

getLastModified() returns the time the requested resource was last modified. The return value is the time in milliseconds since midnight Jan 1, 1970.

```
protected void service(HttpServletRequest req,
                       HttpServletResponse resp)
        throws ServletException, java.io.IOException
public void service(ServletRequest req,
                    ServletResponse res)
        throws ServletException, java.io.IOException
```

The service() methods receive HTTP requests and send them to the appropriate do() method. They are generally not overridden.

HttpServletRequestWrapper

```
public class HttpServletRequestWrapper
   extends ServletRequestWrapper
      implements HttpServletRequest
```

HttpServletRequestWrapper provides an implementation of HttpServletRequest that can be subclassed when it is desired to adapt in some way the request to a servlet. By default, its methods call the same methods on the wrapped Request object.

```
public HttpServletRequestWrapper(HttpServletRequest request)
```

The constructor creates an HttpServletRequestWrapper around the specified HttpServletRequest object.

```
public String getAuthType()
public Cookie[] getCookies()
public long getDateHeader(String name)
public String getHeader(String name)
public java.util.Enumeration getHeaders(String name)
public java.util.Enumeration getHeaderNames()
public int getIntHeader(String name)
public String getMethod()
public String getPathInfo()
public String getPathTranslated()
public String getContextPath()
public String getQueryString()
public String getRemoteUser()
public boolean isUserInRole(String role)
public java.security.Principal getUserPrincipal()
public String getRequestedSessionId()
public String getRequestURI()
public StringBuffer getRequestURL()
public String getServletPath()
public HttpSession getSession(boolean create)
public HttpSession getSession()
public boolean isRequestedSessionIdValid()
public boolean isRequestedSessionIdFromCookie()
public boolean isRequestedSessionIdFromURL()
public boolean isRequestedSessionIdFromUrl()
```

These methods, unless overridden in a subclass, call the equivalent method on the wrapped HttpServletRequest.

HttpServletResponseWrapper

```
public class HttpServletResponseWrapper
   extends ServletResponseWrapper
      implements HttpServletResponse
```

HttpServletResponseWrapper provides an implementation of HttpServletResponse that can be subclassed when it is desired to adapt in some way the response from to a Servlet. By default, its methods call the same methods on the wrapped Response object.

```
public HttpServletResponseWrapper(HttpServletResponse response)
```

The constructor creates an HttpServletResponseWrapper around the specified HttpServletResponse object.

```
public void addCookie(Cookie cookie)
public boolean containsHeader(String name)
public String encodeURL(String url)
public String encodeRedirectURL(String url)
public String encodeUrl(String url)
public String encodeRedirectUrl(String url)
public void sendError(int sc,
                      String msg)
        throws java.io.IOException
public void sendError(int sc)
        throws java.io.IOException
public void sendRedirect(String location)
        throws java.io.IOException
public void setDateHeader(String name,
                          long date)
public void addDateHeader(String name,
                          long date)
public void setHeader(String name,
                      String value)
public void addHeader(String name,
                      String value)
public void setIntHeader(String name,
                         int value)
public void addIntHeader(String name,
                         int value)
public void setStatus(int sc)
public void setStatus(int sc,
                      String sm)
```

These methods, unless overridden in a subclass, call the equivalent method on the wrapped HttpServletResponse.

HttpSessionBindingEvent

```
public class HttpSessionBindingEvent
   extends HttpSessionEvent
```

An HttpSessionBindingEvent represents an object being added to, removed from, or replaced in an HttpSession.

```
public HttpSessionBindingEvent(HttpSession session,
                               String name)
public HttpSessionBindingEvent(HttpSession session,
                               String name,
                               Object value)
```

Creates an `HttpSessionBindingEvent` object. The `session` and `name` are the parameters to which the `HttpSessionBindingEvent` object is bound or unbound.

```
public HttpSession getSession()
```

`getSession()` returns the session associated with the object that is bound or unbound.

```
public String getName()
```

`getName()` returns the name associated with the object that is bound or unbound.

```
public Object getValue()
```

`getValue()` returns the value of the attribute being added, removed, or replaced. (If the attribute was replaced, `getValue()` returns the attribute's old value.)

HttpSessionEvent

```
public class HttpSessionEvent
    extends java.util.EventObject
```

`HttpSessionEvent` represents an event for changes to a session.

```
public HttpSessionEvent(HttpSession source)
```

The constructor must be passed a reference to the `HttpSession` to which the event relates.

```
public HttpSession getSession()
```

`getSession()` returns the session attached to this event.

HttpUtils

```
public class HttpUtils
    extends Object
```

This class has been deprecated.

```
public HttpUtils()
public static java.util.Hashtable parseQueryString(String s)
public static java.util.Hashtable parsePostData(int len,
                                                ServletInputStream in)
public static StringBuffer getRequestURL(HttpServletRequest req)
```

The constructor and methods have been deprecated.

Index

A Guide to the Index

The index is arranged hierarchically, in alphabetical order, with symbols preceding the letter A. Most second-level entries and many third-level entries also occur as first-level entries. This is to ensure that users will find the information they require however they choose to search for it.

The ~ character is used to reduce the need to duplicate almost identical entries (e.g. getBufferSize()/set~() methods means getBufferSize()/setBufferSize() methods).

The use of XYZ indicates that numerous options exist. The page locators apply to all options (e.g. Content-XYZ headers includes Content-Encoding header, Content-Language header, etc.).

G

O

P

S

X

Programmer to Programmer™

Wrox writes books for you. Any suggestions, or ideas about how you want information given in your ideal book will be studied by our team. Your comments are always valued at Wrox.

Free phone in USA 800-USE-WROX
Fax (312) 893 8001

UK Tel.: (0121) 687 4100   Fax: (0121) 687 4101

Professional Java Servlets 2.3 – Registration Card

Name _____

Address _____

_____

_____

_____

City _____ State/Region _____

Country _____ Postcode/Zip _____

E-Mail _____

Occupation _____

How did you hear about this book?

☐ Book review (name) _____

☐ Advertisement (name) _____

☐ Recommendation _____

☐ Catalog _____

☐ Other _____

Where did you buy this book?

☐ Bookstore (name) _____ City_____

☐ Computer store (name) _____

☐ Mail order_____

☐ Other _____

What influenced you in the purchase of this book?

☐ Cover Design ☐ Contents ☐ Other (please specify):

_____

How did you rate the overall content of this book?

☐ Excellent ☐ Good ☐ Average ☐ Poor

What did you find most useful about this book? _____

_____

What did you find least useful about this book? _____

_____

_____

Please add any additional comments. _____

_____

_____

What other subjects will you buy a computer book on soon?

_____

What is the best computer book you have used this year?

_____

wrox

Programmer to Programmer™

Note: If you post the bounce back card below in the UK, please send it to:

Wrox Press Limited, Arden House, 1102 Warwick Road,
Acocks Green, Birmingham B27 6HB. UK.

Computer Book Publishers